YOUR GUIDE
TO
CANADIAN
LAW

YOUR GUIDE
TO
CANADIAN
LAW

Answers to the Most Frequently
Asked Questions

ANTREE DEMAKOS, LL.B.

IAN D. LEVINE, D.M.A.

MICHAEL G. CRAWFORD, LL.B.

JAMES C. MIDDLEMISS, LL.B.

Fitzhenry & Whiteside

Your Guide to Canadian Law

Fitzhenry and Whiteside Limited
195 Allstate Parkway
Markham, Ontario L3R 4T8

In the United States:
311 Washington Street,
Brighton, Massachusetts 02135

www.fitzhenry.ca godwit@fitzhenry.ca

Fitzhenry & Whiteside acknowledges with thanks the Canada Council for the Arts, and the Ontario Arts Council for their support of our publishing program. We acknowledge the financial support of the Government of Canada through the Book Publishing Industry Development Program (BPIDP) for our publishing activities.

Library and Archives Canada Cataloguing in Publication
Your guide to Canadian law: Answers to the most frequently
asked questions / Antree Demakos ... [et al.]
Includes index.
ISBN 1-55041-835-1
1. Law—Canada—Miscellanea. 2. Law—Canada—Popular works.
I. Demakos, Antree
KE447.Y686 2006   349.71   C2005-903961-2
KF387.Y68 2006

United States Cataloguing-in-Publication Data
Demakos, Antree.
Your guide to Canadian law: Answers to the most frequently asked questions / Antree Demakos;
Ian D. Levine; Michael G. Crawford; James C. Middlemiss.
[480] p.: cm.
Includes index.
ISBN: 1-55041-835-1 (pbk.)
1. Law—Canada—Miscellanea. 2. Law—Canada—Popular works. I. Levine, Ian D.
II. Crawford, Michael G. III. Middlemiss, James C. IV. Title.
349.71 dc22   KE387.D463 2006

Design: Darrell McCalla
Printed and bound in Canada

1 3 5 7 9 10 8 6 4 2

CONTENTS

Section Four: TAKING CARE OF BUSINESS

INTRODUCTION

A Legal Guide for Canadians

ALL CANADIANS HAVE THE RIGHT to understand the laws that affect us every day. Complicated legal terms and the enormous volume of laws have always made it extremely difficult for people to get the information they need. Canadians need simple, straightforward legal information and answers.

In 1993, I decided to remedy this problem and began working on Legal Line. My goal was to bring basic understanding of the law to the public by providing answers to common legal questions through the Legal Line telephone, fax-on-demand and internet systems. By understanding your rights and obligations, you become empowered to make informed decisions, and any fear you may have about the law diminishes.

I sought and received a tremendous amount of help from friends and colleagues. At the onset, this project was fortunate to have the assistance of Larry Banack, Civil Litigation Specialist, Bencher of the Law Society of Upper Canada, Chair, Board of Trustees of the Law Foundation of Ontario and a great humanitarian. Larry devoted many hours to discussing the details of Legal Line. His expertise, objectivism and common sense gave me the direction I needed to proceed with the work.

From there, I was privileged to share several pancake breakfasts with Justice Marvin Zuker. After presiding over both Family Law and Small Claims Courts, Justice Zuker possesses a real connection to the community and has a clear view of the legal issues facing us all. His sense of humour and practical approach to complicated issues helped me turn "legalese" into understandable English, while maintaining the meaning of the laws.

It became clear that the major areas of law had to be broken down into individual topics which could be easily understood by all. With the help of my friend and colleague, Steven Bromberg, volumes of law were neatly sorted into over 1,000 bite-sized topics.

The final important step in the creation of Legal Line was a meeting with the then Treasurer of the Law Society of Upper Canada, Harvey Strosberg. Amongst the sweet smell of his cigar and numerous suspender adjustments, Harvey asked the difficult questions. He confirmed important aspects of the work that had been decided, and brought to light the challenges that had yet to be dealt with.

While I undertook the task of translating the law for public use, my resourceful husband, Ian Levine, diligently undertook every other major job that needed doing. Owing to the fact that Ian runs "parallel brains", he was able to accomplish twice as much in half the time. While acting as Information Technology Director, Ian (accurately referred to by the *Toronto Star* as the "whiz") also managed to enlist the assistance of over 300 busy lawyers, each of whom is an expert in his or her area of law.

Many months of writing and reviewing followed. The responsibility of overseeing this massive project fell to our Project Manager, Angela Mallon. Under Angela's austere supervision it all came together and Legal Line was ready to be delivered to the public.

Awareness and distribution of this legal information to the public was made possible by the assistance of the Canadian Broadcasting Corporation, Ministry of the Attorney General, Ministry of Labour, Ministry of Public Safety, Human Resources and Skills Development Canada, the Supreme Court of Canada and numerous other government departments.

As good fortune would have it, two of the most capable lawyers (who are also journalists) took an interest in Legal Line. Michael Crawford and Jim Middlemiss offered to compile the information contained in Legal Line and help create the ultimate legal reference book. Now, with the work and flourish of Michael and Jim, *Your Guide to Canadian Law* is available for every school, office and home in the country.

Antree C. Demakos, B.A., LL.B.
Founder, Legal Line
Executive Director, Legal Information Canada
Director, The Law Guild of Upper Canada

ACKNOWLEDGEMENTS

A heartfelt thanks to the many lawyers, other professionals
and organizations for their valuable contributions.

LAWYERS

Cyril J. Abbass

Larry Banack

Leonard Banks

Nicholas Best

Stephen Bird

Lesli Bisgould

David Brady

Richard Braiden

Kevin Brown

Randall J. Bundus

Margaret Capes

Zenny Chung

Detective Sergeant
  George H. Cowley

Leslie J. Dorrett

Peter Dotsikas

Daniel R. Dowdall

Randall K. Echlin

Mark K. Evans

Alec Farquhar

Norm Fera

Delee Fromm

Cynthia Fromstein

Fay Fuerst

Alan Gahtan

Rocco Galati

Marshall Garnick

Linda J. Godel

The Honourable
  Judge M.D. Godfrey

Allan Goodman

Marvin Gorodonski

William K. Greenaway

Norman Groot

Isak Grushka

Simon Gulden

Bruce Haines, Q.C.

Malcolm Heins

Judith Holzman

Ian Hull

H. John Kalina

Kathleen Kelly

Laura Kerr

Stanley J. Kershman

Marion F. Korn

Vern Krishna, Q.C.

John M.H. Lamont

Jonathan Lapid

Shirley Levitan

Howard Levitt

Audrey Loeb

Henry Lowi

Morag MacGougan

J. Fraser Mann

Donna Martin Sidey

The Honourable Mr. Justice
Edward J. McGrath

Sean McKenna

Neil Milton

Joseph Monaco

John Morrissey

Kenneth Movat

Andrew M. Pinto

Leslie Pringle

Paul Quance

Debra M. Ram

Peter Rizakos

Leonard Rodness

Clayton C. Ruby

Neil Sacks

Sil Salvaterra

Stewart D. Saxe

Vince Scaramuzza

Donna Shier

Alistair Simpson

Steven Skurka

Barry Spiegel

John G. Starzynski

Harvey Strosberg, Q.C.

Anita Szigeti

Gordon Thompson

Wendy J. Thompson

Stephen Traviss

Judith Wahl

Michael O. Watson

Danny Webber

Thane Woodside

Carolyn C. Worthington

Nicholas Xynnis

John Yiokaris

Janice Younker

The Honourable
  Mr. Justice Marvin A. Zuker

Other Professionals

Christopher J. Barry, C.J. Barry & Associates

Charles Black, Canadian Life and Health Insurance

Jodi Carrera, Ontario Reports

Diana Clarke, Ministry of Labour

Gail Cohen, *Law Times*

Sheila Cuthbertson, Ontario Civilian Commission

Joseph Dykas, IT specialist

John Ferguson, Environmental Commissioner of Ontario

Dolly Konzelmann, The Law Society of Upper Canada

John Potter, A&A Investigations and Paralegal Services

Justice Donovon Robinson

Robert Rogers, Allstate Insurance Company of Canada

Ellen Roseman, *The Toronto Star*

Heather Rosenthal, The Law Society of Upper Canada

Mile Stojanovski, Toronto Public Library

Elisha Wagman, Pro Bono Law Ontario

Gemma Zecchini, The Law Society of Upper Canada

Government and Organizations

AT&T

Apple Canada Inc.

BDO Dunwoody Chartered Accountants

BMO Nesbitt Burns

BAR-eX

Block Parent

Bell Canada

CIBC

Caldwell Bankers

Child Find Ontario

City of Toronto

Clarica

Deloitte & Touche

Government of Canada

IBM

Integra Care

International Academy of Mediation

Human Resources Development Canada

Legal Aid Ontario

Marsh Canada Insurance

Merrill Lynch

Ontario Bar Assistance Program

Ontario Securities Commission

Osgoode Hall Law School

Quicklaw

Royal LePage

Royal & Sun Alliance

The Law Foundation

The Law Society of Upper Canada

The Salvation Army

United Way

University of Toronto, Faculty of Law

Section One

GETTING JUSTICE

Canada's Justice System

Canada's justice system is made up of two branches — the legislative arms of our various levels of governments and the courts. Thanks to Canada's Constitution, our courts are independent of the government, which means politicians and bureaucrats cannot influence or dictate how the courts administer and enforce the law. In turn, courts can only interpret the laws that governments create and cannot make their own laws. Ideally, our courts and governments check and balance the excesses of each other and, we all see justice done in the end (we hope).

Canada is a parliamentary democracy based on the British form of government. There are three levels of government: federal, provincial, and municipal. Each level has its own law-making powers and jurisdiction — often, to the exclusion of any other level of government. Towns and cities, for example, don't have the authority to create new criminal laws and the federal and provincial governments typically don't get involved in creating local by-laws on how many pets you can own or whether a specific street goes one-way only.

As the theory goes, the federal Parliament and provincial legislatures make the laws and the courts interpret and enforce them. Increasingly, however, the line between our government's law-making abilities and the courts' responsibility to merely interpret the laws is blurring. Whether laws have been poorly written or so-called "judicial activism" is at work, our courts sometimes end up making new laws by virtue of the way legislation is interpreted.

The power and authority of Canada's governments is derived from the Constitution, which draws from British Constitutional tradition and includes, among others, *The Constitution Act, 1867* and the *Canadian Charter of Rights and Freedoms.*

The Constitution Act created two primary levels of government in Canada — federal and provincial. The third level, municipalities, are "children" of the provinces. In other words, your local town, city, or municipality can only create laws in certain areas allowed by the province.

The *Charter of Rights and Freedoms* sets out the "rules of the game" for government lawmakers and imposes limits on government activity relating to our fundamental rights and liberties. These include the right to liberty, equality, freedom of religion, freedom of expression, freedom to associate with a group, and to be presumed innocent until proven guilty in a court of law.

Contrary to popular thought, these *Charter* rights only protect someone from the actions of government or a government agent, and not from private citizens or businesses. For example, courts use the *Charter* to strike down laws or government actions that unjustifiably restrict our freedom of expression or that allow police unchecked powers to search or seize our property. If a business or fellow citizen is infringing one of your fundamental rights, chances are the *Charter* will not be used to give you a remedy. Other laws will likely apply, such as your province's human rights law or the *Criminal Code.*

In creating laws, the federal government particularly must also be mindful of the fact that the *Québec Act of 1774* created two systems of law — the "civil law" in Québec and the common law in all other provinces. The common law system of justice, similar to that found in the United States, relies on the historical record of court interpretations of laws (called "precedents"). The civil law system of justice in Québec also uses court decisions to interpret the intentions and allowable authority of law-makers, but also relies on a written Civil Code that sets out standards of acceptable behaviour or conduct in private legal relationships.

As you can tell, the boundaries of various levels of government and the courts are not always clear, sometimes making the justice system complex and frustrating for citizens.

1. What is the federal government's role in the justice system?

Parliament is comprised of three parts — the House of Commons, the Senate, and Her Majesty. Members of Parliament, commonly called MPs, are elected representatives from over 300 "ridings" or regions across Canada who sit in the House of Commons, which is located in Ottawa.

The party that controls the most seats in the House of Commons forms the ruling government of the day. The Official Opposition is the party that holds the second highest number of seats.

The so-called Upper House of Parliament is made up of 105 Senators appointed by the Governor General on the advice of the Prime Minister.

The Parliament of Canada writes (or "drafts," as they say), debates, and eventually approves or "enacts" all new federal laws and amendments. Before becoming an enforceable law, a proposed "Act of Parliament" is called a "Bill."

The House of Commons is the only Constitutionally authorized body to introduce legislation concerned with the raising or spending of funds. For example, the House makes and approves laws concerning matters such as:

- Immigration
- Canada Pension Plan
- Employment Insurance benefits
- Old Age Security

Other areas of law that Parliament is solely responsible for include criminal law, Aboriginal issues, income taxes, and regulations affecting industries that are national or international.

Once a new law or amendments to existing laws are voted on and approved by the House of Commons, the proposed legislation must then be debated and voted upon by the Senate. Senators, in theory, provide a check against the potential excesses of the ruling party. If the Senate approves a law or its changes, the legislation is usually "enacted" or "proclaimed" to be in force in the weeks or months to follow by the British Queen's representative — the Governor General.

2. What is a provincial government's role in the justice system?

Each province or territory has its own government, which is responsible for passing laws that fall within provincial jurisdiction. Some of the areas of law provinces are responsible for include family law, health law, labour standards, education, social services, and housing.

Similar to the federal Parliament, voters in provinces elect members from their ridings to sit in the provincial legislature. These elected officials are Members of the Legislative Assembly (known as MLAs) or Members of Provincial Parliament (MPPs). The government is the party that controls the most seats in the legislature and the opposition is the party that holds the second highest number of seats.

3. What is a municipal government's role in the justice system?

Municipal governments are given their legislative authority by the provincial government. Municipalities are responsible for property taxes, property standards, zoning, business licences, and local by-laws. Municipalities are often divided into wards and voters will elect councillors or aldermen who represent them at city or town council. Municipal voters also elect an overall leader, such as a mayor or reeve. Municipal governments make laws concerning areas such as:

- Smoking in public places
- Zoning
- Parking by-laws
- Property taxes

4. If I have a problem with the justice system or laws, can an elected representative help me?

If you feel you have been treated unfairly under the law or if your concern requires government action, you can write to your riding's MP, MLA, MPP, or city councillor. These people are elected officials whose job it is to represent your interests along with those of other citizens in your riding. In deciding which elected representative can best help you, it is important to know the level of government your representative works with and whether your issue is within that government's responsibility. Your MP, MLA, MPP, or councillor may be able to help you if you are having a problem with something like employment insurance or workers' compensation.

Your elected representative cannot influence the courts or any tribunals administering the law. For example, if you are charged with a criminal offence or another citizen is suing you, your elected representative can likely do little to help.

■ Where to write

If you are writing to your MP, MLA or your MPP about a personal problem, write to the local office. If you are writing about a law, or something to do with the government, write to the House of Commons or your provincial legislature.

Write to your MP or a federal cabinet minister in Ottawa at: The House of Commons, Parliament Buildings, Ottawa, Canada, K1A 0A6. If you are writing to the Prime Minister, send to: Office of the Prime Minister, Langevin Block, 80 Wellington Street, 2nd Floor, Ottawa, Canada, K1A 0A2. You do not have to put a stamp on your letter to an MP or the Prime Minister.

Provincial politicians have both a local constituent office and an office in the legislature. To find the local office of your provincial politician, look in the blue pages of your telephone book under "M" in the government section. Municipal politicians are best contacted at your local city hall.

■ What you should say in your letter

When you are writing to a federal or provincial politician, begin with the words "The Honourable" followed by his or her name and then MP, MPP, or MLA, whichever is applicable. When writing your letter, you should include the following information:

- Your name and address
- What you are writing about
- How you feel
- What you want done
- A date by which you want to hear about what they are going to do

It is also a good idea to send copies of your letter to the opposition party and other ministers. Call Elections Canada to find out who your MP is. To find out who your provincial politician is, contact your provincial elections offices. To find out if your problem or concern is federal or provincial, call your local library or local Conservative, NDP, or Liberal party office.

5. What is the role of the courts in the justice system?

As noted above, the government makes the laws and the courts interpret and enforce them. Generally, there are two main bodies of law administered by Canada's courts. "Civil law" is concerned with the private rights and remedies regarding individuals, organizations, governments, and businesses, such as settling disputes over obligations in contracts.

"Criminal law" punishes behaviour that not only harms the well-being of individual citizens, but also behaviour that is an offence against society as a whole. Theft, assault, and murder are obvious examples of crimes that deserve punishment and society's condemnation.

How do the courts know what law is to be applied to each civil or criminal case? Canada's courts look to many sources of information to interpret our laws. First, for example, courts consider what our government lawmakers have to say about an issue in "statutes" or "Acts" (that is, the legislation). From the *Criminal Code* to the *Sales of Goods Act*, there are literally thousands of statutes written and enforced by federal and provincial governments. Along with each statute, there may also be "regulations" that explain the administrative workings of each statute. And, in our municipalities, there are also many thousands of "by-laws" to guide the courts and law enforcement authorities.

Courts will also pay close attention to the country's founding documents or Constitution. For example, the *Canadian Charter of Rights and Freedoms* contains a list of basic or fundamental rights that we, as Canadians, value and protect, such as freedom of expression and the right to be protected from unreasonable search and seizure by police.

The documents and unwritten traditions or customs that form our Constitution date from early English history to Confederation (1867) to the present. The Constitution is sometimes referred to as the "Supreme Law of the Land" because it forms the basis upon which the courts determine the individual powers, and limits, of the federal and provincial legislatures.

Next, Canadian courts will look to previous cases decided by other judges. These cases, or "case precedents," are referred to as the "common law" and can stretch back hundreds of years. In many respects, common law is simply common sense. In some instances, Canadian courts will even consider the court decisions of other countries, particularly those in the United Kingdom and the United States, if our courts have not dealt with the issue at hand.

The courts give precedents great authority and judges are often obliged to follow the same line of thinking and decision-making of previous judges, particularly when higher level courts in the same jurisdiction (such as a provincial appeal court or the Supreme Court of Canada; see question 6 below) have spoken on the issue.

All provinces, except Québec, use common law or "case precedents" to help decide disputes in civil courts. In Québec there is a European-based "civil law" system (don't get confused by the use of "civil" again).

A precedent is authoritative in Québec's civil courts only because of the soundness of its reasoning, rather than the fact other judges have followed it. Québec courts are not bound to follow the previous decisions of other judges but decide cases according to the legal principles set out in a lengthy text known as the Civil Code. The Code contains basic statements or principles that were created in an attempt to address every possible legal problem. In practice, though, Québec courts generally also follow precedents.

6. What is Canada's court structure?

Sometimes, your daily newspaper will have bold headlines about a controversial court decision that you may find completely illogical or simply wrong. An understanding of Canada's court structure will help you determine whether you need to hit the streets in protest or simply wait for the decision to be overturned on appeal.

Canada's court system is like a pyramid. At the top sits the Supreme Court of Canada which is the ultimate court of appeal and has the final word on the interpretation of the law of the country. Disputes involving important national or legal issues make it to this level, and this court can choose which cases it wants to hear. The Supreme Court of Canada can declare all or part of a law invalid or require all other courts in the land to follow a specific line of decision-making when dealing with similar matters. Only an Act of Parliament or legislature can change the effect of the top court's interpretation.

At the next level down is the Court of Appeal in each province. Like the Supreme Court of Canada, provincial appeal courts can refuse to hear unimportant or frivolous cases. Provincial court of appeal decisions are binding on all lower courts in their respective provinces. Other courts will seriously note decisions of their appeal colleagues from other provinces, but there is no requirement to follow the decisions of another province's appeal court.

Below each province's appeal courts are trial courts, where most civil and criminal matters are decided after hearing all the evidence, testimony, and legal arguments of a case. In most provinces or jurisdictions, there are specialized courts dealing with minor criminal offences, family law disputes, youth crime, and small civil actions.

7. What role do judges play in the justice system?

Either a provincial or federal government appoints judges. Unlike the United States, judges in Canada are never elected. They are the masters of the courtroom and their role is to interpret and apply the law. They are there to keep order in the court and rule on the evidence presented to them. They hear motions, oversee jury trials, or sit in judgment of cases without juries. They can also sit as a panel or group to hear appeals of lower court cases.

■ Judicial powers

Judges can uphold laws or strike them down as unconstitutional. They are responsible for setting the rules governing the court and the matters before them. Their jurisdiction to hear a case depends on the matter at issue.

■ Provincially appointed judges

Provincial court judges are limited to hearing provincial and summary conviction offences and have jurisdiction over certain matters of family law. Generally, provincially appointed judges do not hear cases involving litigation between private parties.

■ Federally appointed judges

Federally appointed judges tend to hear cases where more is at stake in terms of crime and hear matters involving indictments. They are also responsible for civil litigation of commercial disputes and private litigation over things like libel, negligence, administrative law involving federal institutions, and contractual disputes.

8. What is a Justice of the Peace?

A justice of the peace (JP) is the judicial officer with whom the public usually has the first and often only contact. They have province-wide jurisdiction and preside over more than 90 percent of cases involving provincial offences, including complex environmental and industrial safety cases.

■ Powers

Justices of the peace have a broad range of power. They rule on municipal by-law infractions and hear cases about minor traffic and parking infractions. They can also receive private information from members of the public who wish to lay charges against another person. They issue summons and arrest warrants for those accused to appear before the court to defend themselves or give evidence. They preside at bail hearings and can set the terms of the release of an accused. A justice of the peace can order a mental health assessment and issue child apprehension warrants.

Pop Quiz! Test Your Understanding

1. The federal government is responsible for passing laws on:
   a) Immigration, Canada Pension Plan, employment insurance benefits
   b) Family benefits, workers' compensation, municipal governments
   c) Zoning, parking by-laws, property taxes

2. Provincial governments conduct business in:
   a) The House of Commons
   b) A legislature
   c) Town hall
   d) Council chambers

3. A Member of Parliament represents a:
   a) Provincial riding
   b) Municipality
   c) Federal riding

4. Which of the following are rights in the Canadian *Charter of Rights and Freedoms?*
   a) Right to liberty
   b) Freedom of religion
   c) Freedom of expression
   d) Freedom to associate with a group
   e) All the above
   f) None of the above

Answers

1. a   2. b   3. c   4. e

Government Web Sites	
Federal Government	www.canada.gc.ca
Alberta	www.gov.ab.ca
British Columbia	www.gov.bc.ca
Manitoba	www.gov.mb.ca
New Brunswick	www.gnb.ca
Newfoundland & Labrador	www.gov.nf.ca
Northwest Territories	www.gov.nt.ca
Nova Scotia	www.gov.ns.ca
Nunavut	www.gov.nu.ca
Ontario	www.gov.on.ca
Prince Edward Island	www.gov.pe.ca
Québec	www.gov.qc.ca
Saskatchewan	www.gov.sk.ca
Yukon	www.gov.yk.ca

Lawyer & Clients

One of the great ironies of the legal profession is that while lawyers as a group may be held in low regard by some members of the public and are the target of many (often funny) jokes, surveys frequently reveal that most of us have great respect and appreciation for the lawyers we actually get to know.

That said, people are often uncomfortable dealing with lawyers. Some lawyers, like some doctors and auto mechanics, can make you feel uneducated, naive, and overly emotional. They know the mysterious intricacies of the law and legal system — something many people have only a fleeting encounter with during their lifetimes.

Facing a major challenge or opportunity in your life can be stressful, and many of us look anxiously to lawyers for help and expertise. Even the most sophisticated and experienced business people may surrender themselves over to a lawyer, questioning nothing and dutifully paying the bills.

Truth be told, a working relationship with a lawyer is no different than any other business relationship. As the bill-paying client, it is up to you to take charge of the relationship you have with your lawyer and ensure that you get value for your money. You must ask questions, learn enough about your legal issue to be a smart consumer, and, most important, understand what your lawyer can and cannot do for you.

1. When do I need a lawyer?

Lawyers play an important role at many points in our lives, when buying a home to getting a divorce to running a business. Most of us know to get a lawyer's help when we are directly confronted by a legal issue, such as a lawsuit or a police arrest. Some, however, may not realize lawyers can also offer valuable advice when planning or readying for major events in our personal and business affairs — advice that can save you time and money later.

A lawyer can help even if you have a short question to ask or a small task to do. You do not have to hire a lawyer for a minimum number of hours or an extended period. You do not have to wait until you actually have a problem to contact a lawyer. In fact, it is better to seek legal advice even when there is only a faint chance that the law may be an issue or problem for you.

A lawyer can give you a legal opinion about your options in a particular situation, negotiate with other people on your behalf, and advise you about your legal rights and responsibilities.

■ Examples where a lawyer can help

A lawyer is a valuable resource who can help you in many ways, such as when you:

- Start, expand or close down a business
- Prepare a will
- Need tax planning advice
- Enter into a special relationship, such as a marriage or business
- Buy or sell a house

You should definitely contact a lawyer if you are experiencing a tragedy in your life, such as:

- Marriage breakdown
- Someone's mistake causes an accident
- You are being investigated or charged with a crime
- You lose your job unfairly
- A member of your family dies
- You are involved in a lawsuit
- You do not feel comfortable with paperwork someone wants you to sign

■ Legal situations you can likely handle yourself

Not all legal situations require the assistance of a lawyer. For example, you can probably go to traffic court, small claims court, or negotiate an apartment lease on your own.

There are legal self-help books and "kits" on the market that purport to eliminate the need for a lawyer. Be careful, however, because some of these products may not cover your specific fact-situation or may be based on the law in a different legal jurisdiction, such as another province or even the United States. Many self-help books on the law (like this one) can make you a better consumer of legal services — not a legal expert.

If your situation or problem is in any way complicated, confusing, or involves high stakes, consider contacting a lawyer for assistance or advice.

2. How do I find a good lawyer?

As with many things in life, it pays to shop around. Whether you are looking for the "best of the best" or the cheapest deal in town, do some research and don't necessarily sign up with the first lawyer you meet.

A lawyer's reputation is his or her greatest asset, so find out as much as you can about a lawyer's background. You also need to find someone who is compatible with your personality. If you are the type of person who just wants to settle things and get on with life, you won't want a lawyer who tells you he will fight your case all the way to the Supreme Court of Canada!

It is also important to know that many lawyers today specialize in one or more fields, such as business, real estate, wills, or criminal law. Always be careful to find and choose a lawyer who has direct experience with your problem or opportunity. Not all lawyers handle every conceivable legal issue. For example, most real estate lawyers would not handle divorces. Before you look for a lawyer, determine what type of legal issue you have so you know what type of lawyer you will need.

There are at least three common ways to find qualified lawyers:

■ Word of mouth

Ask your industry colleagues, co-workers, friends, and family if they know any lawyers who have experience with your legal issue. Question them closely, since most people tend to think that any lawyer can deal with any legal problem. Find out as much as you can from acquaintances about their perception of the lawyer's skill, personality, experience, and cost value.

Another source for "word of mouth" referrals is the news media. Newspapers, magazines, and even the Internet may quote "experts" or high-profile lawyers talking about issues similar to your own. Lawyers themselves and other professionals, such as accountants, can also be excellent sources of information.

■ Local law society referral service

In some provinces, the local governing body for lawyers (usually known as the "law society") has a service that recommends local lawyers who practise the type of law you need. There may be a small fee for the referral, but any lawyer you contact through the service will likely provide a 30-minute consultation, free of charge. Ask about a fee, however, before setting up a meeting.

Be aware that law society lawyer referral services will not purport to recommend the "best" lawyers in your community, but only those who have identified your type of legal issue as a preferred area of their practice. As well, be aware these referral services typically give out names on a random basis and that these names are not picked on the favourable opinions of past clients, number of successful cases, or reputation.

■ Telephone book & business directories

Many people find a lawyer with expertise in their problem by looking under "lawyers" in the local business pages of the telephone book. For-profit organizations may also offer a "referral service" through Internet-based or printed business directories that feature paid advertising from lawyers or law firms with experience in specific areas of the law. Many of these lawyers also offer a free, 30-minute consultation. Be certain to ask about the cost of an introductory meeting before you go.

3. What is unique about the lawyer-client relationship?

Unlike most business relationships, lawyers operate under a special "fiduciary duty" in their dealings with clients. This means they owe a duty of good faith to their clients and must act scrupulously. Lawyers are governed by their province's law society and its rules of professional conduct, which impose specific ethical standards and duties. In addition, they are under a duty to meet a certain standard of care or competence in handling your legal matter. If not, they must refer you to a lawyer who has the experience to handle the matter.

■ Your lawyer's duties to you

Lawyers have a duty to provide objective advice about a problem and to defend your interests as you wish. Lawyers must maintain confidentiality in their communications with clients, and must be candid and honest. Lawyers cannot put themselves in a conflict of interest. This means they cannot represent two opposing interests at the same time. For example, a lawyer cannot represent both husband and wife when preparing a separation agreement. Lawyers also cannot persuade clients to enter into investments or business schemes where the lawyer has invested his or her own money, unless the client is referred to another lawyer for independent legal advice.

■ Lawyers are regulated & scrutinized

Because lawyers have significant professional responsibilities and fiduciary duties, they are subject to more scrutiny than most other businesspeople. If lawyers violate their professional responsibilities, they will be disciplined by their law society. In serious cases, a lawyer's right to practise may be suspended or withdrawn altogether ("disbarred"). For lesser violations of a client's trust or rules of conduct, the law society may give the lawyer permission to resign or the lawyer may be reprimanded — a fact that the law society will publish to all other lawyers and the public.

4. What is the difference between a barrister and a solicitor?

Simply put, a barrister is proficient in litigation and can represent your interests in courts, administrative hearings, arbitrations, mediations, and dispute settlement negotiations. The solicitor is skilled in all non-litigation aspects of legal practice, ranging from advising on the best legal structure for your business, to drafting contracts, to creating a personal estate plan.

In Canada, all practising lawyers are both barristers and solicitors. They are qualified to operate in either capacity. That said, most lawyers tend to focus their practice on one or the other.

5. What do I need to know about working with a lawyer?

If you understand the role of your lawyer and do your best to help your lawyer where possible, you can speed up the legal process and, possibly, reduce legal fees. Here are some tips:

■ Preparing for the first meeting with your lawyer

Write down a brief description of the facts and events as best you can. Keep your emotions aside. This will help you put the events into the proper sequence and will help you make sure you do not forget any important details. Gather up and take along all documents and other items related to your situation, such as agreements, letters, transcripts, contracts, and photographs.

Know what you want and think carefully about what you are going to say. Prepare to explain your situation clearly and simply, starting from the beginning. You may want to write down any questions on paper. This can help your lawyer understand your situation and what needs to be done, which in turn will save the lawyer's time (and your money) and make it easier to begin working on your case.

■ What to do at your first meeting

The first time you meet with your lawyer, you will need to explain what has happened or what it is that you want to do. Ask questions, such as how the law applies to your situation and what options you have. You may want to ask about the lawyer's expertise and experience in handling your type of situation or problem.

Be prepared to talk about legal fees at the first meeting. Your lawyer will need some money to begin working for you right away. This is called a "retainer" and is used to cover the lawyer's initial fees and expenses. You may also be asked to sign a document, also called a retainer or, sometimes, an "engagement letter." This is basically a contract that authorizes the lawyer to initiate or defend legal proceedings on your behalf, and outlines the lawyer's scope of authority and what work will be done. It also explains the lawyer's policies regarding payment of fees and expenses.

At the first meeting, you can also ask how long it will take to solve the problem or achieve the desired result, and what you should do next. After the lawyer has had a chance to look at your situation, ask about potential difficulties and what can be done to speed up the process or reduce the legal costs.

If you have a legal aid certificate issued by your provincial government, bring it with you to your first meeting. You should also make sure that your lawyer will accept legal aid.

■ Ongoing lawyer-client relations

Lawyers and clients each have ongoing rights and responsibilities. Lawyers have a duty to keep all client communications confidential and to give an honest and candid legal opinion. Clients have an obligation to be honest and to provide all relevant information. Your lawyer needs to know everything to protect your interests and give you the best possible advice.

After you have chosen a lawyer you should expect to be kept informed of how the case is progressing, and to receive a copy of relevant documents and correspondence. Be sure you read and understand any documents your lawyer sends you. If you do not understand something, ask your lawyer to explain it. Be aware that some types of legal matters, such as lawsuits, often involve lengthy gaps in time during which the lawyer has no information or updates for the client.

As your matter proceeds, many clients make the mistake of paying more for the lawyer's time than they should because they call the lawyer too often or engage in unnecessary chatting. Before you phone your lawyer, ask yourself whether it would be better to write a letter or e-mail. You will still pay for the lawyer's time whatever method of communication you choose, but written communication is often read and handled more quickly than a rambling phone call. If you must call and your question is a minor one, see if you can discuss it with the lawyer's assistant or law clerk. Often assistants know about your case and can help.

6. Does my lawyer have to do what I say?

Yes and no. Problems between lawyers and clients can arise when there is a clash between the lawyer's duty to the client and the lawyer's duty as an officer of the court.

In its simplest form, the lawyer-client relationship is similar to other business dealings. Your instructions to your lawyer are to be followed closely, even if the lawyer disagrees with your decision. It's your money and you are the boss.

Your lawyer is under a duty to consult with you and seek your approval for key steps. For example, your lawyer needs your expressed approval to agree to an out-of-court settlement in a lawsuit or to sign-off on a transaction. In many cases, lawyers will want your approval in writing.

Not all your instructions, though, must be followed. For example, a dishonest client may instruct his or her lawyer to lie, hide, or bend the truth in discussions with opposing parties. Lawyers, however, know they are required by their own rules of professional conduct to disclose any criminal or fraudulent act by a client.

This doesn't mean lawyers can't posture during negotiations ("That's our last offer!"). It also doesn't mean a lawyer is always obliged to reveal facts or correct misunderstandings that may weaken the client's position. Most lawyers, however, will caution clients that it is best to reveal all relevant facts.

7. How do lawyers calculate fees?

Lawyers typically calculate fees in one of three ways — a set hourly rate for the time they spend working on your matter, a flat fee for a specific service, or, in many provinces, a contingency fee based on the outcome of your case.

As mentioned above, most lawyers will ask for some money in advance, a down payment of sorts known as a "retainer." As events unfold, the lawyer may also ask you to pay the cost of court fees, document filing fees, and other out-of-pocket expenses known as "disbursements." Many lawyers will also send out monthly or quarterly bills, which pay for work done to date and help you avoid having to make one large payment at the end. In some cases, such as personal injury lawsuits, a lawyer may agree to do the work without billing the client until the case is over.

Note that many lawyers are open to the idea of negotiating a reasonable payment plan, billing frequency, and even changes to their hourly rates. At the beginning of any case or matter, ask questions about your lawyer's approach to fees, estimated total costs, and what disbursements you might expect. For example, some lawyers levy a small charge for individual photocopies or each page of a fax sent or received on your behalf, while others do not. To later avoid that "nickeled and dimed" feeling, be clear about both the lawyer's fee for services and the disbursements.

■ Hourly Rate

Most lawyers calculate their fees using an hourly rate. This is common when a lawyer cannot say with certainty how much time your legal work will involve. A lawsuit, for example, is particularly unpredictable since opposing parties or even the courts can slow or lengthen the process.

Hourly rates differ greatly from one lawyer to the next, and region to region. There is no official "hourly rate" that all lawyers must charge. Hourly rates are usually set by the lawyer, or the law firm's management, after considering the individual's years of experience, reputation, "going rate" in the marketplace, and office overhead. A lawyer in a large city, for example, will have different costs to cover than a sole practitioner operating out of his or her home in a small town.

Your lawyer will keep track of the time spent working on your file — often right down to the minute. Be aware that different lawyers can take different lengths of time to do what appears to be the same task. Time spent can differ according to lawyer experience and the complexity of your case.

Many people, even sophisticated purchasers of legal services, are uncomfortable with an hourly rate approach. They fear that the "sky is the limit" and their legal costs will run up unreasonably. For this reason, it is very important for you to discuss fees at the beginning of the matter and stay on top of your costs throughout. Your lawyer should be able to give you a reasonable estimate of what it will cost. You can then protect yourself further by asking your lawyer to contact you if something happens to change that estimate.

■ Flat rate

In recent years, more lawyers have been willing to quote a fixed fee for a specific task, such as preparing a will or completing a real estate transaction. Generally, this method is used when a lawyer has a good idea of how long it will take to finish the task.

In some areas of law, such as sophisticated business financings or even property transactions in some western provinces, lawyers may also set fixed fees according to the overall value of the transaction. For example, a lawyer may charge a percentage of the value of the house you buy or sell.

It is often left to you to ask the lawyer if a fixed fee might be negotiated for a specific matter. Even in complicated cases, such as lawsuits, lawyers may be willing to negotiate what is often called a "blended" fee — a mix of hourly rates for unpredictable aspects of the case and a fixed fee for simpler tasks, such as preparing a statement of claim.

■ Contingency fees

A contingency fee is tied to the success or failure of your lawsuit or other transaction. If your lawyer is successful in winning your claim or negotiating a business deal, he or she receives a fee calculated as a percentage of what you are awarded in a court ruling, or the value of what you gain in a deal. If the lawsuit or transaction fails, your lawyer may receive an agreed-upon flat fee, or disbursements only, or perhaps nothing at all.

Sounds like a good deal for the client, right? It can be, but this type of fee arrangement should be considered carefully. While contingency fees are quite common in the United States, they are a recent arrival in Canada. For many years, lawmakers in some provinces have been reluctant to allow contingency fees. Some fear that contingency fees will encourage frivolous lawsuits since clients pay nothing at the start. Others believe that some lawyers may only take on cases that they are reasonably certain will win anyway.

For these reasons and others, contingency fees are set out in advance in a written agreement between the lawyer and client — with court approval required in some cases, such as large class action lawsuits. In fact, a written agreement is required in every province except Québec.

There may also be special requirements in certain provinces. New Brunswick requires that a special form created by the government be used; and British Columbia puts a ceiling on contingency fees. Also, contingency fees are usually not allowed in criminal or family law matters.

If you or your lawyer proposes a contingency fee arrangement, investigate whether it truly is the best deal. The typical contingency fee may be anywhere from 10 to 30 percent of what you may be awarded. Is that a fair amount? If your chances of winning are good, will the lawyer be overly compensated? Ask your lawyer and at least one other lawyer what the estimated costs would be based solely on an hourly rate or fixed fee. Also, find out who pays for any up-front expenses and what you may or may not pay if the case fails.

8. How can I resolve a problem with my lawyer?

There are three common problems between lawyers and clients:

- Communication
- Fees
- Breaches of fiduciary duties or negligence

For each of these problems there is a different approach. Keep in mind that you always have the option of firing your lawyer and getting another one, although this can be expensive and time consuming. The best approach is to talk to your lawyer as soon as possible to see if you can resolve differences. Your lawyer is working for you and should answer any questions you have.

■ Communication

If your lawyer does not return your phone calls or reply to letters or faxes, you have a communications problem. This is the most common complaint clients have against lawyers. Quite often, lawyers cannot update clients because there is nothing new to report. Nevertheless, lawyers should explain this by returning telephone calls, faxes, letters, or e-mails.

Express your concern to your lawyer and ask for an update. In most cases your problem will be resolved at this point. If you cannot obtain a response from your lawyer or if you tried talking to the lawyer and it was not helpful, you can contact the complaints or discipline department of your province's law society. Someone from the law society will call the lawyer and attempt to resolve your problem. If the problem persists, you can file a formal complaint with the law society.

■ Fee problem

If you have a problem with the fees you are charged, first ask your lawyer for an explanation of the account. There may be a good reason the bill is not what you expected. For example, the case might have become more complicated than anyone originally thought. Or, the bill might include disbursements, such as photocopying, courier charges, postage, or court fees that the lawyer has paid on your behalf.

If you are unable to settle your fee dispute, you can have your bill reviewed by an impartial representative of the courts. This is sometimes referred to as "taxing" the bill. If you plan to pursue this route, it is often best not to pay your lawyer's bill until you have had the assessment hearing because some court cases have ruled that payment of the bill signifies implied acceptance of its reasonableness. That said, the courts have allowed assessments of bills that have already been paid, particularly in special circumstances such as fraud that is discovered later.

Be aware that you have to lodge your complaint about the bill quickly. In Ontario, for example, the Assessment Office of the Superior Court of Justice requires that you apply for a review within one month from the day the bill was sent to you. A small fee may be charged for this service.

Your lawyer will receive notice of the review (sometimes known as an *Appointment for Assessment*) either by registered mail or by personal service. In some cases, it may be your responsibility to send it to your lawyer.

When the bill is assessed, an independent court officer will look at it to decide if it is reasonable or excessive. The lawyer has the burden of proving the reasonableness of the bill and will be asked to provide records justifying the time billed or documents proving you were aware of the costs.

Assessors take many things into account, such as the time spent on the matter, its complexity, the skill required, the results achieved, the client's ability to pay, and the expectations of the client.

The assessment officer has the right to reduce the lawyer's bill. Or, the court officer might decide that the lawyer's bill is correct. In that case, you will be responsible for the full amount of the account plus interest and, possibly, the costs of the review.

■ Breach of fiduciary duty or negligence

If you believe your lawyer has breached a fiduciary duty or neglected responsibilities, you have the right to complain to the provincial law society governing lawyers. You even have the right to sue the lawyer in court.

Note that there is a difference between professional misconduct and professional negligence. Professional misconduct occurs when the lawyer does something that contravenes the law society's rules of conduct, such as engaging in a conflict of interest that harm's your best interests, or stealing a client's money.

In contrast, professional negligence occurs when the lawyer makes a mistake, such as failing to start legal proceedings within the required time, or incorrectly certifying that you have good title to your house. The law society will look into cases of misconduct, but you may have to retain another lawyer to recover losses arising from negligence.

If you make a complaint to the law society, you will probably be asked to put the complaint in writing. Your letter will then be sent to your lawyer who will be asked to respond to what you have said. If a further investigation is required, special law society investigators will look into it. If there is convincing evidence of wrongdoing by your lawyer, disciplinary proceedings will be initiated. Note, however, that the vast majority of complaint letters do not lead to the formal discipline of lawyers.

If you believe a lawyer has been negligent and your rights have been prejudiced, it will be necessary to consult a new lawyer. If this lawyer tells you that the first lawyer has been negligent, you may be able to recover your losses from the liability insurance policy (known as "errors and omissions" insurance) that all practising lawyers are required to carry.

If you lost money because of professional misconduct, the provincial law society is also likely to have a special fund available to compensate you, at least partially. In Ontario, for example, clients must apply to the fund and may receive discretionary grants up to $100,000. This fund is separate from the professional liability insurance carried by lawyers. In British Columbia, however, the province's "trust protection coverage" will theoretically cover any amount of shortfall that cannot be recovered from the lawyer, his or her law firm, or insurance coverage. In Nova Scotia, the total of all claims against a lawyer is capped at $300,000 per year.

9. What is the difference between a lawyer and a paralegal?

In some circumstances, provincial laws allow people who are not lawyers to act on your behalf in a legal matter. These people are usually called paralegals or agents. They are often unregulated and uninsured for professional negligence or misconduct.

Unlike lawyers, who have years of legal training and must follow their law society's rules of professional conduct, paralegals and agents are not as highly-trained. If they make a mistake, there is very little you can do other than sue them or their company.

Still, there are circumstances where unsupervised paralegals can be helpful. These can include minor motor vehicle offences where there is no risk of imprisonment or seizure of an automobile, and representation before minor administrative tribunals, such as landlord-tenant matters.

As with choosing a lawyer, consumers should be careful and investigate before they hire an unsupervised paralegal or agent to represent them.

10.   How can I become a lawyer?

The roughly two dozen law schools across Canada accept a limited number of new students each year. Demand for legal education is high. In recent years, there have been three to four applicants for every position in first-year classes. Law school tuition fees have also risen dramatically. With limited space and resources, admission committees often must deny admission to many well-qualified applicants.

■ Law School admission requirements

In most cases, law schools require students to have completed most or all of a full-time university degree. Generally, there are no preferred undergraduate degrees. Law students therefore come from science, business, fine arts, or other backgrounds. In most law schools, a very few spots are held open for so-called "mature" students who may not have a recent university degree but do have significant life or work experience.

Law schools consider many factors when admitting students and no single qualification will guarantee acceptance or rejection. To be fair, schools rely heavily on common selection criteria, such as the Law School Admission Test (commonly referred to as the LSAT). Schools also rely on academic scores or grades from undergraduate programs as a guide to future performance. Other factors, such as letters of recommendation, work experience, and interviews may also affect admission.

■ Law School Admission Test (LSAT)

The LSAT is a half-day-long standardized test required for admission to all Law School Admission Council (LSAC) member law schools in Canada and the U.S. The LSAT provides a standard benchmark that measures the reading and verbal reasoning skills of applicants. The test involves five, 35-minute sections of multiple-choice questions, including reading comprehension, analytical reasoning, and logical reasoning sections. A 30-minute writing sample is administered at the end of the test. The writing sample is not scored, but a copy is sent to any law school that you apply to. The score scale for the LSAT is 120 to 180.

Many resources are available to help students prepare for the LSAT. These include Prep Tests and LSAT courses, which sometimes are held over one or two weekends.

■ Academic record

Along with the LSAT score, an applicant's academic record plays a large part in determining acceptance to law school. Generally, undergraduate performance is an important indicator of how someone is likely to perform in law school. Many law schools look closely at university grades when considering individual applications. Course selection can also make a difference in admission evaluations. Applicants who have taken difficult or advanced courses in their undergraduate study often are evaluated more favourably than students who have concentrated on easier or less advanced subjects.

■ Admission status

Once an application and its supporting documents have been received, many law schools will make a preliminary judgement about what the applicant's admission status will be. At this preliminary stage, many schools use an admission index to evaluate candidates. The index ordinarily is a combination of an applicant's academic record and LSAT score. These index formulas are unique to each school and are followed more rigidly at some schools than at others.

Many law schools do not wait to accept or reject applicants on a specified date. Instead, the schools operate what is known as a "rolling admission process." This means that the school evaluates applications and informs candidates of the school's admission decision on a continuous basis over several months, usually beginning in winter and extending to midsummer for waiting-list admissions. Successful candidates are notified in order of preference.

■ The Bar Admission course

Graduating from law school isn't enough to qualify someone as a practising lawyer. Admission to the practice of law requires successful completion of the provincial Bar admission course, which teaches and tests law school graduates on local laws and the rules of the province's justice system.

The Bar admission program runs throughout the year in most provinces and can involve up to two years of instruction and on-the-job work experience before a lawyer is admitted or "called" to the province's Bar.

Even lawyers who are qualified to practise in one province or country will likely be required to pass the Bar admission course to practise law in a different province.

■ Articling

For an individual to be admitted to the practice of law in Canada, all provincial law societies require a law degree from a recognized law school, successful completion of the Bar admission course, and a period of "articling."

Articling is an apprenticeship under the supervision of a qualified member of the law society. It usually involves working on a full-time basis in a law firm, a court, or the legal department of the government or a corporation. The student is under the supervision of lawyers and learns practical aspects of the occupation. The length of the articling clerkship varies by province.

Articled Students-at-Law, as they are known, may appear on your behalf in certain preliminary civil court proceedings and minor criminal court proceedings.

To Whom Is The Duty Owed?

In a real estate transaction, a lawyer acted for both the purchaser of the property and the bank lending money for the mortgage. The purchaser gave the lawyer documents suggesting that there was a potential problem with the title or ownership of the property. The lawyer immediately notified his banking client about the problem.

There was a delay in closing the deal and the borrower ended up paying a higher rate of interest. He sued the lawyer, claiming the document should not have been revealed to the bank. The lawyer, however, said the borrower knew he represented the bank and that he had a duty to both clients.

Was the lawyer correct?

No, said a court in the case of *Taylor v. Blacklow*, pointing out the dangers when lawyers act for both sides. The lawyer did not have the borrower's permission to reveal the documents to anyone else, including the bank. The judge said the lawyer's duty with regard to the documents was to the borrower only and the lawyer should have returned the documents without comment.

No Money, No Law?

An entrepreneur hires a lawyer to incorporate a new company before a certain date so he can take advantage of an income tax break. He gives the lawyer three post-dated cheques as payment. Unfortunately, the second cheque bounces before the new company can be registered — one day before the client's deadline. The lawyer tells the client he will stop working on the file until it is paid up-to-date. The deadline passes and the client loses the tax break.

Was the lawyer right to stop working until paid?

No. The professional conduct rules of the Canadian Bar Association state that a lawyer owes a duty to a client to not withdraw services without just cause and only upon reasonable notice. While the rules do recognize the failure to pay a lawyer's bill as just cause, they also say withdrawal is not proper where a client's interest may be seriously prejudiced.

MIXING BUSINESS WITH PLEASURE?

While acting for a client in a wrongful dismissal lawsuit, a lawyer learns that her client and the client's husband, Adam, are having marital difficulties and have separated. The lawyer always fancied Adam and, coincidentally, sees him soon after at a cocktail party. One thing leads to another and soon they are having an intimate love affair. When the lawyer's client finds out about it, she sues.

Is there any basis for the client's lawsuit?

Yes. In *Szarfer v. Chodos*, a lawyer in similar circumstances was found liable for breach of his fiduciary duty. The lawyer had to pay medical expenses resulting from the former client's distress over the affair and general damages of over $30,000.

THE LIMITS OF SOLICITOR-CLIENT PRIVILEGE

The wife of an aging client comes to his lawyer for help. Her husband has been declared insane by doctors and there is no hope for recovery. His health has deteriorated and he's expected to die within a year. His wife, hoping to do some planning, wants to know the details of her husband's will.

Can the lawyer reveal the contents of the will?

No. The long-standing tradition of solicitor-client confidentiality forbids revealing details of the lawyer's work for the client. This includes revealing the contents of the will to a close family member, even when the testator or author of the will is insane. Even after the husband dies and before the probate process, a lawyer can only reveal the will's contents to the executor.

Three Tips For Successful Lawyer-Client Relationships

1.   **A good lawyer will try to keep you out of court.** Be wary of lawyers who insist the only way to resolve your problems is to fight it "all the way." The costs of going to court can be four to five times what may be spent negotiating a reasonable out-of-court settlement or using alternative dispute resolution techniques, such as mediation and arbitration.

2.   **Insist on regular updates.** Keep your emotions in check and avoid becoming fanatical about your case. Let your lawyer do his or her job, but always be aware of the next steps, your options, and key deadlines.

3.   **Keep records.** Everything you do and talk about with your lawyer should be written down for your own records. Keep copies of all correspondence and documents in one file. Keep a notepad near your telephone to record key discussion points in case of misunderstandings later. If you give an oral instruction to your lawyer, do like lawyers do and write yourself a dated memo that outlines what you said.

WWW Resources

Provincial & Territorial Law Societies

Law Society of British Columbia	www.lawsociety.bc.ca
Law Society of Alberta	www.lawsocietyalberta.com
Law Society of Saskatchewan	www.lawsociety.sk.ca
Law Society of Manitoba	www.lawsociety.mb.ca
Law Society of Upper Canada (Ontario)	www.lsuc.on.ca
Barreau du Québec	www.barreau.qc.ca
Chambre des notaires du Québec	www.cdnq.org
Nova Scotia Barristers' Society	www.nsbs.ns.ca
Law Society of New Brunswick	www.lawsociety-barreau.nb.ca
Law Society of Prince Edward Island	www.lspei.pe.ca
Law Society of Newfoundland	www.lawsociety.nf.ca
Law Society of Yukon	www.lawsocietyyukon.com
Law Society of the Northwest Territories	www.lawsociety.nt.ca
Law Society of Nunavut	lawsociety.nu.ca

Other Lawyer Associations & Bodies

The Federation of Law Societies	www.flsc.ca
Canadian Bar Association	www.cba.org

Provincial Chapters

Alberta	www.cba.org/Alberta
British Columbia	www.bccba.org
Manitoba	www.cba.org/Manitoba
New Brunswick	www.cba.org/NB

Newfoundland	www.cba.org/nf
Northwest Territories	www.cba.org/nwt
Nova Scotia	www.cba.org/ns
Ontario	www.oba.org
Prince Edward Island	www.cba.org/pei
Québec	www.abcqc.qc.ca
Saskatchewan	www.cba.org/sk
Yukon	www.cba.org/yt

Canadian Law Schools & Universities Offering Non-Practising Law Programs

Akitsiraq Law School	www.law.uvic.ca/akitsiraq/program.html
University of Alberta Faculty of Law	www.law.ualberta.ca
University of British Columbia Faculty of Law	www.law.ubc.ca
University of Calgary Faculty of Law	www.law.ucalgary.ca
Carleton University Department of Law	www.carleton.ca/law/index.html
Dalhousie Law School	as01.ucis.dal.ca/law/index.cfm
Université Laval Faculté de droit	www.ulaval.ca/fd
Laurentian University Department of Law and Justice	laurentian.ca/justice/ENGLISH/INDEX.HTML
Université Laurentienne, Département de Droit et Justice	laurentian.ca/justice/FRANCAIS/INDEX.htm
University of Manitoba Faculty of Law	www.umanitoba.ca/faculties/law
McGill University Faculty of Law	www.law.mcgill.ca
Université de Moncton École de droit	www.umoncton.ca/droit
Université de Montréal Faculté de droit	www.droit.umontreal.ca
University of New Brunswick Faculty of Law	www.droit.umontreal.ca
Osgoode Hall Law School, York University	www.osgoode.yorku.ca
Université d'Ottawa, Faculté de droit – Section de droit civil	www.droitcivil.uottawa.ca
University of Ottawa, Faculty of Law – Common Law Section	www.commonlaw.uottawa.ca/maine.htm
Université du Québec à Montréal Départment des sciences juridiques	www.juris.uqam.ca
Queen's University Faculty of Law	qsilver.queensu.ca/law
University of Saskatchewan College of Law	www.usask.ca/law
Université de Sherbrooke Faculté de droit	www1.usherb.ca/droit
University of Toronto Faculty of Law	www.law.utoronto.ca
University of Victoria Faculty of Law	www.law.uvic.ca
University of Western Ontario Faculty of Law	www.law.uwo.ca/
University of Windsor Faculty of Law	cronus.uwindsor.ca/law

FINANCING LEGAL ACTIONS

Did you know that Canadians who cannot afford a lawyer can sometimes turn to a provincial legal aid system for help? However, the ability to access legal aid differs depending on the province you live in.

In the past few years, budget constraints and high demand for financial assistance have caused some provinces to scale back legal aid programs or look for alternative means to deliver legal aid solutions other than through lawyers in private practice. Often, that means an increasing use of "duty counsel," a government-paid lawyer based in the courts, as well as growth in the number of legal aid clinics. Moreover, the type of cases that are covered can vary widely depending on where you live.

According to Statistics Canada, more than $593 million is spent on legal aid annually. That works out to about $19 for every Canadian. Legal aid plans receive over 800,000 applications for funding, of which about 500,000 are approved. When it comes to spending, civil cases use 55 percent of the legal aid budget, while criminal law cases use the remaining 45 percent.

1. What is legal aid?

Legal aid is a program that helps low-income Canadians receive legal representation and advice. If you qualify or meet your province's financial eligibility requirements, legal aid will pay for a lawyer to represent you or assign one to you from a legal aid clinic or legal aid plan. Legal aid is only available to people with certain types of legal problems. Depending on your situation, legal aid may cover all or some of your legal costs.

2.   Who is eligible?

Each province provides some form of legal aid program delivered through lawyers in private practice, staff lawyers, or a blend of both. Saskatchewan, Newfoundland and Labrador, Prince Edward Island, the Yukon, and Nova Scotia provide legal aid primarily through staffed legal aid clinics. Alberta, New Brunswick, Manitoba, Northwest Territories, and British Columbia mostly provide legal aid certificates that members of the public can use to hire lawyers to defend them. Québec and Ontario rely on a blend of staffed legal aid clinics and certificates to deliver legal aid services.

Eligibility qualifications and services differ across the country. Most plans provide better coverage for criminal law issues than they do for civil law, and financial eligibility is a key criterion for determining who gets funded. Some provinces also require the person applying to contribute to their legal fees or pay the plan back over time.

In Ontario, for example, you must have little or no money left after paying for basic necessities, such as food and housing. Your legal problem must also be serious. People on social assistance almost always qualify for legal aid.

That said, you might be eligible for legal aid even if you have some money in the bank or own a home. The legal aid office will look at your family responsibilities and expenses to determine whether you are eligible for assistance. Depending on your financial situation, Legal Aid Ontario may cover all of your legal costs or may require you to pay for a portion. If legal aid requires you to pay a portion of the legal costs, you may have to make monthly payments or pay a lump sum right away. You will also have to sign a payment agreement that requires you to agree to pay a portion of your legal costs. If you own a home or other property, you may still be eligible for legal aid, but you will probably have to put a lien on your home. This means you will have to repay legal aid before you sell or refinance your property.

In Alberta, legal aid isn't necessarily free. Recipients could be required to repay the plan, provided it doesn't cause undue hardship. Alberta determines financial eligibility by examining income and assets. Needs are determined according to gross family income and size of your family.

The plan will look at your spouse's income and expenses in determining if you qualify. Alberta also considers factors such as assets and liabilities, complexity of the case, nature of the service applied for, and whether the case has merit. If your income is over the allowable limits, you may still be eligible provided you contribute to the costs.

These situations contrast to Québec. Like most provinces, not all legal services are covered, but legal aid is granted for instances set out in provincial legislation covering the topic. That includes family cases, young offenders, prosecutions for indictable offences, and applications involving income security, automobile insurance, employment insurance, or workers' compensation benefits. To be eligible, consumers must establish the existence of a right or need to receive legal aid and lawyers must assess whether the case has a chance of succeeding.

3. What kinds of cases are covered?

If a person qualifies financially, the typical types of cases that may be covered by a legal aid plan include: certain criminal charges, issues regarding family law matters, immigration and refugee matters, some civil cases, and final appeals.

■ Criminal charges

The Canadian Centre for Justice Statistics conducts an annual study of legal aid in Canada. It notes that a series of cost-sharing agreements be-tween the federal and provincial governments determines the extent to which criminal infractions are covered. Most jurisdictions provide coverage for indictable offences, which are more serious than summary offences. Generally, summary offences are only eligible for legal aid coverage if there is likelihood of imprisonment or if the punishment would result in job loss (such as a loss of a driver's licence for someone who makes his or her living by driving). Alberta considers special circumstances, such as language issues or mental health.

Most legal aid programs cover the defence of criminal charges that would likely result in jail time, such as assault, impaired driving causing bodily harm, robbery, welfare fraud, and break and enter.

■ Family matters

The type of coverage available for civil legal aid varies widely across the country. According to the Centre's report, New Brunswick, Saskatchewan, and Yukon Territory limit civil cases to family matters, while family cases constitute most of the cases in Prince Edward Island and Nova Scotia.

Other jurisdictions extend civil legal aid coverage to a broader range of cases. Family matters that may qualify for legal aid include:

- Getting or changing custody of children
- Setting up, increasing, or decreasing child or spousal support payments
- Help if a partner denies access to children
- Getting access to see children or to make a major change to access arrangements that have already been made
- Stopping a partner from selling or destroying the other partner's property
- Negotiating ownership of things like RRSPs or pensions that could provide income

■ Immigration and refugee matters

Immigration and refugee matters that qualify for legal aid include: refugee hearings before the Immigration and Refugee Board, sponsorship and deportation appeals, and detention reviews. However, the coverage for immigration matters varies widely depending on where you live.

■ Civil cases and final appeals

Certain civil cases and final appeals that may qualify for legal aid include: Workers' compensation appeal tribunal cases, Social Benefits Tribunal matters, Employment Insurance appeals, and mental health hearings and appeals.

4. How do I apply for legal aid?

To apply for legal aid you will need to contact the local office where you live. It is a good idea to call the office first to find out when is the best time to visit. A list of legal aid organizations appears at the end of this chapter.

■ What you should bring

When you go to the legal aid office, bring as much information with you as possible. This includes:

- Some form of identification, such as a social insurance card, driver's licence, health card, or immigration document
- Any documents relating to your case, such as court orders, separation agreements, or a copy of any police summons, indictments, charge or any documents related to your case

- Proof of your current income if you have any, such as recent pay stubs, welfare cheque stubs, Employment Insurance statements, or T-4 slips
- An up-to-date bank book or bank statements
- Proof of monthly expenses and bills, including rent receipts or mortgage payments, hydro and gas bills, car payment receipts, credit card statements, and car insurance bills
- The deed to your home (if you own your home)
- Proof of any unusual expenses such as medical costs

When you are at the legal aid office, you will likely be required to fill out an application. The staff at the office will help you with this and may be able to tell you right away whether you are eligible for legal aid. It is important that you inform the staff if your situation is an emergency so that you will be given help immediately.

If your application is accepted, you will eventually be assigned to a lawyer or receive a legal aid certificate. You can take the certificate to any lawyer who accepts legal aid and who agrees to represent you.

5. What lawyer can I use? How does it work?

If you qualify for legal aid, you will be allowed to use the services of a lawyer of your choice. You must make sure that the lawyer you choose accepts legal aid cases. You might want to speak with more than one lawyer to find someone whom you feel comfortable with. Once you have chosen a lawyer it is unlikely that you will be allowed to change lawyers.

The legal aid office in your area can likely direct you to lawyers who can work on your case. Note that not all lawyers accept legal aid work, so if you have a legal aid certificate you need to find a lawyer who takes legal aid cases. There are many considerations when choosing a lawyer. Try to find a lawyer who has experience with your kind of legal problem. If English is not your first language, choose a lawyer who is fluent in your language and who can help you understand your choices.

6. How do I find a lawyer who accepts legal aid cases?

There are a number of ways to find a lawyer who accepts legal aid cases:

- There may be a legal aid office in your city. Legal aid lawyers may be able to take your case and represent you in court.
- You can ask the legal aid office to provide you with a list of lawyers who take legal aid cases.

• You can contact the law society in your province. Officials there might be able to direct you to a lawyer referral service.

• Speak to family or friends. Maybe they can recommend a lawyer.

• If you have been abused, a shelter may be able to refer you to a lawyer. Call or visit your local women's shelter to ask for a list of lawyers who work on family cases like yours.

Once you have the names of a few lawyers you may want to work with, call and ask if they will take your case. Spend a few minutes talking to the lawyer or someone in the lawyer's office. Make a list of all the questions you want to ask to help you decide if this lawyer might be right for you. If you are not comfortable, try another lawyer until you find one that does understand you. After a lawyer has agreed to take your case, in most situations the lawyer-client experience should be essentially the same in a legal aid environment as without legal aid. That said, once you have chosen a lawyer within the legal aid system, it is unlikely that you will be allowed to change lawyers (without some proof the lawyer has engaged in some form of professional misconduct), as the switch would become costly to the justice system.

7.   What can I do if I am rejected for legal aid or do not qualify?

If your application for legal aid is refused, most plans have some form of appeal that allows you to challenge the decision. You will have to find out why you were refused and provide proof or a convincing argument showing that the earlier refusal was unfair or incorrect.

If you do not qualify for legal aid, a Community Legal Clinic may still be able to help you. Community legal clinics are run by lawyers and non-lawyer workers who can help you with various legal issues. Clinics deal with housing, social assistance, pensions, workers' compensation, employment insurance, employment rights, and landlord and tenant issues. You will have to complete a financial test to make sure you qualify for this service. Check the Yellow Pages of your telephone book for community legal clinics.

You will have to demonstrate some financial need to be eligible for legal assistance from a community legal clinic. When you go to a clinic, bring your financial information and the documents that relate to your circumstances. The clinic will assess your financial situation to determine your eligibility.

■ Duty counsel for criminal courts

If you are going to a criminal court and do not have a lawyer, some provinces provide, at the courthouse lawyers called Duty Counsel who may be able to help. In some cases, you may have to qualify financially before getting assistance. Duty Counsel provides information and advice. If you are interested in getting help from Duty Counsel, check with the courthouse first to see if a Duty Counsel is available.

■ Special help for charities and non-profit organizations

The Volunteer Lawyers Service was created to promote free legal services in Ontario to help charitable and not-for-profit community-based organizations. Since 1994, approximately 400 participating volunteer lawyers have helped over 150 organizations through the Volunteer Lawyers Service.

The services provided cover a variety of legal issues. Some of the most common are: assistance with incorporating and preparing by-laws, employment and labour matters, tenant and landlord issues, and help with obtaining charitable status.

Organizations may take an application to their local United Way or Volunteer Centre, or they can contact the Volunteer Lawyers Service directly. Once an organization has received approval for these services, they will be matched with a lawyer who can assist with their request. The organization only has to pay for the out-of-pocket costs, such as government filing fees, photocopying, and so on.

Charities and non-profit organizations are eligible to receive free legal advice and services, provided they meet the following four criteria. The organization:

- Must not have more than 12 full-time employees
- Cannot have gross assets exceeding $2 million
- Must not have annual gross revenues plus operating reserves in excess of $1.2 million (except amounts for designated projects)
- Must be a non-profit or charitable community-based organization serving the public interest

If your organization would like to submit an application or would like more information, you can contact the Volunteer Lawyers Service by mail at: Volunteer Lawyers Service, c/o Law Society of Upper Canada, 130 Queen St. West, Toronto, Ontario M5H 2N6. Call (416) 947-3931 or toll-free 1-800-668-7380, or log on to their Web site at www. volunteer lawyers.org. At this time, the service is only available to non-profit and charitable groups in Ontario.

■ Pre-paid legal insurance plans

Another alternative to legal aid, particularly for the middle-class consumer, is joining a pre-paid legal insurance plan. Like a healthcare plan, these insurance policies provide you with basic legal assistance and advice.

Pre-paid legal membership can be in the range of $25 per month. Some companies even offer it to employees as a benefit. Through a "provider law firm" that deals with plan members, you can access fast answers to most legal problems.

There are different plans available depending on the needs of the individual or business. Some basic services include unlimited telephone calls, opinion letters, review of simple leases, calls by a lawyer on your behalf, and will preparation.

8.   How can I get more information about legal aid in my area?

For more information about legal aid, contact the nearest legal aid office or community legal clinic. Here are some possible contacts:

British Columbia Legal Services Society

Vancouver Regional Centre
Suite 200 (Intake), Suite 1500 (administration)
1140 West Pender Street
Vancouver, BC V6E 4G1
Tel: 604-601-6206 (intake)
604-408-2172 (Lower Mainland)
1-866-577-2525 (toll-free, outside the Lower Mainland)
http://www.lss.bc.ca

Legal Aid Alberta

Edmonton Office
300 Revillon Bldg.
10320-102 Avenue
Edmonton, AB T5J 4A1
Tel: 780-427-7575

Calgary Office

#1100, 665 8th Street SW
Calgary, AB T2P 3K7
Tel: 403-297-2260
http://www.legalaid.ab.ca

Saskatchewan Legal Aid Commission

502, 201-21st St. E.,
Saskatoon SK S7K 2H6
Tel: 306-933-5300
Fax: 306-933-6764
Toll-Free: 800-667-3764
www.saskjustice.gov.sk.ca/legal_aid

Manitoba Legal Aid

Administrative & Winnipeg Area Office
402-294 Portage Avenue
Winnipeg, MB R3C 0B9
Tel: 204-985-8500
Toll-Free: 800-261-2960
http://www.legalaid.mb.ca

Legal Aid Ontario

375 University Avenue Suite 404
Toronto, ON M5G 2G1
Tel: 416-979-1446
Toll-Free: 800-668-8258
www.legalaid.on.ca

The Commission des services juridiques (Québec)

2, Complexe Desjardins, East Tower, #1404
Montréal, PQ H5B 1B3
Tel: 514-873-3562
http://www.csj.qc.ca

Legal Aid New Brunswick

Administrative Head Office &
Fredericton Area Office
356 Queen Street
Fredericton, NB E3B 1B2
Tel: 506-451-1424

Newfoundland & Labrador legal aid Commission

P.O. Box 399 Station C
St. John's, NF A1C 5J9
Tel: 709-753-7860

Nova Scotia Legal Aid Commission

5475 Spring Garden Road Suite 401
Halifax, NS B3J 3T2
Tel: 902-420-6573
Fax: 902-420-3471
www.gov.ns.ca/just/legad.htm

P.E.I. Legal Aid
40 Great George Street
P.O. Box 2000
Charlottetown, PE C1A 7N8
Tel: 902-368-6043
Fax: 902-368-6122

How To Sue Someone

When a person, business, organization, or even the government does something (or fails to do something) that injures you or causes financial loss, you may need to consider launching a lawsuit in one of Canada's civil courts.

A "civil lawsuit" or "action" is a legal proceeding that deals with private or civil rights and obligations. It is different from a criminal action, which involves rights and obligations that affect not only individuals but society as a whole. While there might be criminal aspects to someone's harmful action or inaction, the legal system also recognizes there is often a need to right wrongs that arise in our private dealings with others.

Civil lawsuits must be "filed" or brought to civil courts. The complexity of the procedures that need to be followed to start a lawsuit, and the place where your case will be heard, will depend largely on the amount of your claim. For example, a small claims court action goes to a civil court that deals with problems below a certain dollar value according to province. Capable of handling claims up to $5,000, $10,000, or even $25,000 (depending on your province), a small claims court action offers low-cost filing and document services. Your small claims action can also be heard without the use of a lawyer. That said, you may want to consult a lawyer to ensure you proceed in a timely fashion, your documents are completed properly, and you have covered all your legal points. (In the next chapter, we'll give you some advice on whether a small claims action is right for your situation, or whether you may need to take it to a higher level.)

Canada's civil court system deals with all types of disagreements and areas of "private law," ranging from auto accidents to contract disputes. In many cases, the courts apply the principles of "tort" law, which provide a remedy for anyone who has been harmed intentionally or unintentionally through the fault of another, such as personal injury or acts of negligence.

Tort law recognizes we all may have a duty toward others at times, whether it is imposed by legislation or through centuries of common law. As you will learn, a successful lawsuit requires proof that another individual, business, or government owed you a duty, that duty was violated, and that the individual, business, or government was directly or indirectly at fault for your loss. The civil courts and tort law cases also deal with interesting issues, such as whether the damage to you was foreseeable and whether the other party met a standard of care expected of a "reasonable person" in the circumstances.

Another area of private law that civil courts deal with is contract disputes. In these cases, the courts look closely to see if there truly was an agreement promising to do or not do something. Contract law can be complex, and various factors can destroy or "breach" a contract, including misrepresentation, mistakes, and duress or undue influence.

Unlike the criminal court system, the objective in civil courts is not usually to punish someone. Instead, the aim is to compensate those who have suffered a loss or injury and return them, if possible, to the position they were in before the harm was caused. Civil courts also use different words and phrases than criminal courts. In civil lawsuits, the one starting the action is known as the "plaintiff," the "defendant" on the other hand, is the one accused of the wrongdoing.

It is important to remember in a civil case that, even though illegal acts may be alleged by one side or the other, no one is charged with anything or subject to criminal penalty. No one is found "guilty" in civil courts. You simply win or lose.

1. What is a civil lawsuit?

A civil lawsuit is often started when a dispute arises over the private rights or obligations of two or more people or "parties," and one or all sides refuse to settle the disagreement. A civil lawsuit can be brought against a person, business, organization, or even a government that has caused you injury or financial loss. Your right to sue is not affected by whether the injury or loss was intentional or unintentional. You may, however, receive more compensation from the courts or in an out-of-court settlement if the damage was caused intentionally.

Starting a lawsuit is a very serious endeavour with real consequences for all sides. You are accusing the person you are suing of either failing to take the care or precautions that should have been taken, or doing something that should not have been done. While it is possible to bring a lawsuit without legal representation, in most cases it is advisable to seek the assistance of a lawyer.

You should also be aware that if a court views your lawsuit as frivolous, an abuse of the legal system, or knowingly initiated without merit, you could be held financially responsible not only for the court's expenses, but also for the legal costs incurred by the other parties.

■ Three common categories of civil lawsuits

The most common lawsuits fall into three broad categories:

1. Financial loss from a broken contract: This happens when you have an oral or written agreement with someone who fails to perform certain tasks or obligations. You may also sue for financial loss caused by a defective product arising from implied promises of its quality or performance.

2. Personal injury: You may have been injured in an automobile accident, slipping and falling in a store or on a sidewalk, ill-treated by a doctor or other healthcare professional, or by a defective product or person that hurt you either intentionally or accidentally.

3. Defamation (libel or slander): If your reputation or that of your business was damaged arising from a false statement someone made about you to others, you may sue for damages. Libel is defamation by way of the printed word or some other permanent form, while slander is spoken.

■ What are the legal requirements for a successful civil lawsuit?

Under the law, you or your lawyer must satisfy four requirements to bring a successful civil lawsuit.

1. You must prove that the person you are suing owed you a "duty of care." This means the person you are suing had some obligation to actively avoid or prevent your injuries or financial loss.

2. You must prove that person knowingly or recklessly violated a standard of care that would be recognized by the "reasonable person."

3. You must prove his or her failure to take proper care actually caused your injury or loss.

4. You must prove that you actually suffered an injury.

For most types of civil lawsuits, regardless of how negligent someone was, you will not recover any money through the courts if you did not suffer an injury or loss as a result of his or her actions or inaction.

If your lawsuit is successful, the court may order the person you are suing to pay you money as compensation for your loss or injury. Or, a court may order that specific actions be taken, such as fulfilling a contractual obligation. What or how much you are awarded will depend on a number of factors, including the severity of your injury or loss and the impact the injury has had on your life.

■ Why is a civil lawsuit different in Québec?

A civil lawsuit in Québec is subject to a substantially different system of law than that in the rest of Canada. Québec relies on its Civil Code, which can trace its origins back to the time of Napoleon in France.

The Civil Code is comprised of "Articles" or rules that help judges and citizens interpret the law. Many of the legal principles in Québec's Civil Code are quite similar to those found in the common law system, but there can be significant differences that will require the help of a practising Québec lawyer to understand.

For example, when dealing with situations involving personal injury or negligence, Article 1457 of the Civil Code states: "Every person has a duty to abide by the rules of conduct which lie upon him, according to the circumstances, usage or law, so as not to cause injury to another. Where he is endowed with reason and fails in this duty, he is responsible for any injury he causes to another person and is liable to reparation for the injury, whether it be bodily, moral or material in nature. He is also liable in certain cases, to reparation for injury caused to another by the act or fault of another person or by the act of things in his custody."

Québec law requires that a plaintiff prove three elements and each element must be proven on the balance of probabilities:

- The plaintiff must first prove there is "fault" on the part of the defendant. The courts presume fault once the plaintiff proves the circumstances existed for it. It is unnecessary to prove the defendant intended his act or omission. Fault is defined as a mode of behaviour of a person, who is capable of realizing the nature and consequences of an act or omission, and does something contrary to law or fails to meet a standard of care set out by the courts. It can be proven with evidence of malice, imprudence, neglect, or want of skill.
- The plaintiff must also prove that he or she has suffered damage.
- Even if fault is proven, a plaintiff will not succeed unless he or she can prove the causal link between the fault and damage.

In Québec, the standard of care expected of someone is similar to the "reasonable person" benchmark used in common law provinces. The Civil Code standard, however, is sometimes referred to as "bon père de famille" or the good father of the family.

■ Time limits or special notice requirements

In many circumstances, you must give notice to a potential defendant soon after you have suffered an injury or even suspect you have been hurt. This gives the opposite party an opportunity to investigate your claims. So-called "notice periods" are usually very short, particularly if you are blaming the government for your loss.

In most provinces, notice periods are set out in various pieces of legislation, so you will need to contact a lawyer as soon as possible to ensure you have the legal right to sue. For example, when suing a municipality in Ontario for injury caused when slipping on a sidewalk, you must give written notice within seven days of your injury. In the case of a claim against the provincial Crown, the notice period can range from 10 days after the injury to at least 60 days before the commencement of your action.

▪ Limitation periods

In addition to notice periods, there may also be limitations on how long you can wait before starting a lawsuit. You may be prevented from suing if you begin your lawsuit after the limitation period has expired. You therefore will not be compensated for your injury or loss. Limitation periods can be quite different among the provinces and territories; they also tend to vary depending on the specific kind of injury or loss suffered.

Limitation periods can also differ depending on who caused the injury. For example, if you are suing a physician, surgeon, architect, engineer, dentist, or other regulated professional, the limitation period in some provinces may be just one year from the date you knew or ought to have known about the injury.

Ontario recently changed its mixed bag of limitation periods. The *Limitations Act, 2002* now creates just one basic limitation period of two years from the date a claim is "discovered." The two-year limitation period is applicable to almost all claims, except any specifically excluded by the legislation. To avoid situations where an injury or omission might be "discovered" 30, 50, or 100 years later, the statute also has an ultimate limitation period of 15 years from the date the act or omission occurred.

In Alberta, recent changes to legislation also state no claim arising from negligence can be brought after the expiration of either two years from the date the plaintiff knew or ought to have known there was a claim, or 10 years from the date the action or omission arose — which-ever is shorter.

In Québec, the Civil Code has "prescriptions" setting out limitation periods. A lawsuit to remedy an injury or enforce a personal right must be brought within three years and in cases where there is no prescribed limit, the limitation period is 10 years.

The law governing notice and limitation periods is complex and varies by jurisdiction. Again, if you suffered an injury or loss and are considering bringing a lawsuit, consult a lawyer as soon as possible to ensure you do not miss important deadlines.

2. Who can sue?

Anyone can start a lawsuit, provided that person is of sound mind and at least 18 years old. You are considered a minor if you are under the age of 18. If you are a minor and a plaintiff or defendant in a lawsuit, you will likely require someone to represent you. This person is called a "litigation guardian." Litigation guardians are also required for people who are mentally incompetent. A litigation guardian can be anyone who is capable of suing on his or her own and who is not involved with people on the other side of the case. Usually, a litigation guardian is a relative or parent of the minor or incompetent person. The litigation guardian is there to make decisions about the lawsuit and can be responsible for litigation costs. Note that some provinces allow minors who are plaintiffs to represent themselves in a small claims court where the amount requested is small, less than $500, for instance.

3. Who can be sued?

Anyone can be sued, including a minor. It is unlikely, though, that a minor will have the necessary funds to compensate for the damages he or she caused. You might think you can sue the parents instead, but in most cases parents will not be held responsible for the actions of their children unless it can be shown that the parents were negligent in the child's care. The younger the child, however, the more likely that some responsibility will be attached to parents since they are presumed to have control of younger children.

4. How do I start a civil lawsuit?

As noted earlier, small claims courts may be the right forum for your dispute if the amount of money claimed or in dispute is below the maximum limit set in your province. Otherwise, you must hire a lawyer to take your case to a higher level of civil courts.

In most provinces, there is a "simplified procedure" available to handle claims that are just above the small claims limit, but still require the expertise of higher level judges. In Ontario, for example, the simplified procedure is available in the Superior Court of Justice for claims between $10,000 and $25,000. This procedure removes some time-consuming and expensive steps, such as pre-trial discoveries or fact-gathering sessions. Although the process is simplified, it is still too complicated for most people; you will likely therefore need the assistance of a lawyer.

For injury or loss involving even larger claims, your lawsuit must be filed and launched in your province's civil courts. You will, in all likelihood, need a lawyer.

■ General steps involved in all civil lawsuits

All civil lawsuits involve similar steps, including:

- Contacting a lawyer for legal advice or assistance
- Writing and filing a Statement of Claim

- Waiting for the other party to write and file a Statement of Defence
- Possibly participating in mandatory mediation
- Attending examinations for discovery, where both sides get to probe and question the strength of the opposing side's case
- Issuing pre-trial motions to determine what evidence may be allowed and what issues can be brought up in court
- Participating in a trial and, possibly, appeals to higher courts

In most cases, lawsuits are settled before the trial begins. In deciding whether to sue someone, be aware the person you are suing can make a counterclaim, asserting that you, in fact, caused your own or other's harm or loss. If the counterclaim is successful, you could end up not only losing your own claim, but also paying the defendant's claim and court costs.

It is important to determine whether your claim is valid before you start a lawsuit. Otherwise, you could end up on the costly end of the judgment. A civil lawsuit involves many complicated steps and procedures. Although in some cases it may be possible to proceed without a lawyer, it is a good idea to seek legal advice before getting started.

5.   How long will it take to get to trial?

While the vast majority of civil lawsuits never get to trial because they are settled out of court or abandoned, the typical case often goes to trial within two to five years. It takes this long because the justice system requires that all sides have adequate time to prepare a case; receive sufficient notice of each upcoming stage in the legal action; and be able to explore all opportunities to mediate or settle the dispute before engaging a judge in a courtroom.

Note that small claims actions are often handled more quickly since they involve less preparation and fewer steps (no examinations for discovery, for instance). A typical small claims action will likely be heard by the court within six to nine months.

6.   What is a class action "proceeding" or lawsuit?

Class actions are lawsuits that involve a group of people who have all suffered a similar type of injury from the same cause. Rather than each individual beginning his or her own lawsuit, they join to sue a person, business, or public body for compensation. For example, a group of people may all suffer injuries caused by a defective product or have financial losses resulting from one major accident. Usually, a person or a small group of people begins the lawsuit, with others joining as time goes by. The injured may be formally notified of the lawsuit by mail, or they may simply find out about it in the newspaper.

Legal representation is always required when bringing a class action, and the court must approve or "certify" the class of plaintiffs before it can proceed. The first or main person starting the lawsuit is called the "representative plaintiff." The representative plaintiff could personally be responsible for paying the defendant's costs if he or she loses the lawsuit and does not get financial support from the other plaintiffs.

If you are not the first or main plaintiff, but are notified that you are part of a class proceeding, you have the choice of either remaining in the class or opting out. By opting out, you will not be involved in the proceeding and you will not be entitled to share in any money awarded to other members of the class.

Starting or joining a class action can result in a large settlement for — and even against — you. Also, a class action is usually emotionally difficult. Before bringing or joining a class action, consult a lawyer for advice and detailed information about the process.

7.   What are the costs in a civil lawsuit?

According to recent surveys of Canadian lawyers, it can cost anywhere from $10,000 to $25,000 to take a lawsuit through the traditional litigation process and a trial. (Small claims actions cost considerably less and often involve little more than the nominal filing fee and another fee to serve documents on the opposing side.)

A typical civil lawsuit costs $1,500 to $5,000 to initiate an action and have a lawyer deliver a *Statement of Claim*. Responding to the opposing side's documents and conducting examinations for discovery will likely involve another $3,500 to $5,000. The preparation and presentation of your case at a trial is likely to add another $5,000 to $15,000 to your legal costs. None of this includes any court judgments that may go against you. It is therefore easy to understand why so many lawsuits settle out of court.

That said, in addition to whatever damages or remedies a court awards, a successful party is usually entitled to recover so-called "costs" and some of the "disbursements" incurred in starting or defending a lawsuit. The actual amounts awarded are determined by the trial judge or an administrative officer after the trial has ended. In most cases, however, the costs and disbursements awarded are well below your actual legal bill. Also, the costs that may be awarded can be affected if either party delivered a written Offer to Settle before trial.

Since the costs recovered by a successful party are often less than the amount that is owed to his or her own lawyer, a plaintiff who wins a small judgment may turn out to be a financial loser after paying his or her own expenses.

8.   Are there any alternatives to suing?

There are two common alternatives to starting a lawsuit when people want to resolve a disagreement — mediation and arbitration. Both are covered in detail in the chapter on *Resolving Disputes Without Going To Court*. Here, however, is a brief summary.

■ Mediation

Mediation is a procedure where the goal of the parties in a lawsuit is to reach an out-of-court agreement. Mediation allows an outside mediator to facilitate the discussions, but the parties make any final agreements themselves. Mediation is a practical solution where the parties are in the best position of solving the problem themselves, and where they are willing to work together. Mediation works well when everyone wants a common outcome, such as completion of a contract where there are only a few discrepancies or disagreements. Mediation is less expensive than both arbitration and the more lengthy traditional litigation process. It is also faster than going to court. With mediation, the parties have an opportunity to solve their own problems, which means they are both more likely to be happy with the outcome.

■ Arbitration

Unlike mediation where the parties reach an agreement, arbitration involves an arbitrator who makes a final decision in the same manner as a judge in a traditional court case. Arbitration requires that the parties involved in the dispute all agree to accept the decision of the arbitrator before starting the process. Because arbitration is less expensive and faster than going to court, many contractual agreements include clauses providing that the parties must submit their problems to arbitration and the arbitrator's decision shall be final.

9. What is mandatory mediation?

Many provinces have introduced mandatory mediation programs before a trial is held to provide those involved in a lawsuit an alternative to the traditional court process. With mandatory mediation, it is hoped that individuals and businesses in lawsuits will save time and money. Mandatory mediation may be required in all cases except small claims and family law matters.

In a mandatory mediation session, the parties will have to select a mediator from a list of qualified private sector mediators. The parties will be required to attend and pay for at least one session. In most provinces, the mediator's fees will be set or capped and costs will be divided equally among parties. Those who cannot afford the mediation fees may be able to obtain a legal aid certificate or apply for financial aid from the government.

If the parties have not resolved their problem at the end of the mediation, but feel they would like to continue, they may make arrangements for further sessions directly with the mediator. Even if the case does not settle at the mandatory mediation session, the parties may at any time voluntarily pursue a subsequent mediation session anytime before trial. Cases that do not settle during mediation will continue in the traditional litigation process.

10. What should I know about lawsuits involving automobile accidents?

Your legal options and even your ability to launch a lawsuit when you have been involved in an automobile accident will depend very much on the law in the province where the accident happened.

For example, in Ontario there is a "no-fault" insurance system in which compensation for an automobile accident that does not result in serious injury or death is handled entirely through the individual's insurance company and cannot involve a lawsuit. That said, in a few limited circumstances, it may be possible to get additional compensation by suing the driver responsible for the accident. (See the next question for more information on no-fault insurance regimes.)

If you have been in an automobile accident, you should begin by telephoning the police while you are still at the scene. Depending on the severity of the accident and where it took place, the police will either come to the scene or will tell you to drive to the nearest collision reporting centre or police station to report the accident and file the necessary paperwork for an insurance claim.

If the other driver was at fault, there are generally four circumstances in which you may be able to sue for compensation in addition to your basic insurance coverage.

1. Pain and suffering for permanent and serious injuries: Depending on the province, if your injuries are permanent and serious, you may be able to sue the other driver for your pain and suffering. Injuries can be either physical or psychological. Whether your injuries are permanent and serious is decided by a judge based on medical evidence.

2. Loss of income and earning ability: You may be able to sue the other driver for compensation for both present and future loss of income and earning ability if you can prove his or her negligence led to your loss. There is no requirement here that your injuries are serious or permanent.

3. Health costs, if injuries are catastrophic: You may be able to sue for recovery of healthcare expenses if you suffer a "catastrophic" injury as a result of the accident. For example, if an accident renders you a paraplegic or you suffer a complete loss of vision, you will probably be able to recover your healthcare expenses.

4. Claims of family members: Your family members may be able to sue for loss of your guidance, care, and companionship if the accident caused permanent and serious injury, whether physical or psychological, or resulted in your death.

If you plan to sue after an automobile accident, you are usually required by law to meet certain requirements for notice. For example, in Ontario, you must notify the person being sued within 120 days of the accident. You must also normally begin the lawsuit within two years of the accident.

"No-fault" automobile insurance

In an effort to reduce insurance costs, unclog the courts, and hasten compensation for injuries, several provinces (and insurance companies) have promoted "no-fault" insurance regimes.

Under a no-fault insurance system, accident victims, regardless of fault, are entitled to specific benefits from their own insurance companies. No-fault coverage pays for some or all of the insured person's loss, but also restricts or denies the rights of innocent victims to seek justice through the courts. Also, the no-fault insurance system only applies to compensation for bodily injury and not pain or suffering, or property damage.

Ontario, Québec, and Manitoba have no-fault systems. In Saskatchewan, drivers can give up the right to sue and pay a lower insurance premium if they choose a no-fault insurer. A similar "right to choose" system, offering lower rates to those who give up their right to sue, has been proposed in other provinces such as Newfoundland and Labrador. (Interestingly, there is confusion in legal circles over what to do in "right to choose" jurisdictions when an accident involves two vehicles, one of which is no-fault.)

Benefits of "no-fault" insurance

Under a "no-fault" system, you will receive compensation for your injury much more quickly than under the more traditional fault system where you would have to wait for a decision about who is to blame. In fact, your insurance company is often required by law to pay you weekly benefits shortly after your claim is filed. After paying, however, your insurance company will still determine who was at fault to decide whether or how much to increase your insurance premiums. If you were at fault, your insurance premiums may increase. If you were not at fault, your premiums may not be affected. In either case, you will still receive compensation for your injuries.

No claims for property damage

Unlike claims for bodily injury, insurance claims involving property damage are still based on fault. If you are at fault for an automobile accident involving property damage, you will only be covered if you have purchased additional insurance coverage, such as "all perils" or "collision." These types of coverage are usually not mandatory. If you have purchased this extra coverage, your claim will be paid, regardless of fault, but your insurance premiums may increase.

If the other driver is at fault in an accident resulting in property damage, you will usually be covered under either direct compensation for property damage coverage or your uninsured automobile coverage. Both types of insurance are mandatory for drivers and your insurance company will pay your claim. Depending on your particular insurance policy, you may also have to pay a deductible. However, because the other driver was at fault, your insurance premiums will not increase as a result of making the claim.

If the other driver cannot be identified, you will only be covered if you have purchased optional "collision" or "all perils" coverage.

11. I was injured by a defective product. What should I know about product liability lawsuits?

If you suffer an injury or your property is damaged by a product you purchased, you can seek compensation from both the store that sold you the product and the company that manufactured it. Depending on your injury, you may be compensated for your medical costs, financial losses, and for pain and suffering.

If product has a warranty: You should check if the product came with an express warranty or guarantee either from the store or the manufacturer. If it did, you may be entitled to a refund or some other form of compensation by contacting the store or the manufacturer and explaining your problem.

If product does not have a warranty: If you discover that the product did not come with an express warranty, or if you are told by the seller or the manufacturer that the defect you have experienced is not covered by the warranty, you may still be entitled to compensation. Begin by contacting the store where you purchased the item. Under the *Sale of Goods Act* in all provinces, stores have legal obligations to their customers, regardless of whether the product came with a specific warranty or guarantee. Québec's Civil Code imposes similar responsibilities.

First, stores are legally required to sell products that are suitably fit for their purpose. This means the product you purchased must function in the way that was advertised. Second, if you bought the product based on a description, such as found in a catalogue, or if you bought the product based on a sample, such as a piece of carpet, the goods you receive must closely match that description or sample. Third, if the goods are bought by description, such as by catalogue, they must be fit to be sold.

If a seller violates any of these obligations, you are entitled to cancel the contract and receive a refund. If the store is unwilling to refund your money or otherwise compensate you, or if the people there insist you contact the manufacturer, tell them that under the *Sale of Goods Act*, they are required to handle your complaint.

Contact the manufacturer

Although the store where the product was purchased should be your main focus, there are times when you will want to directly contact the manufacturer. First, you may want to contact the manufacturer simply to warn that the product is defective. Second, if a store is unwilling to handle your complaint, you may have to call the manufacturer to explain your problem to the customer service department. Third, if you did not personally purchase the product (for example, you bought it second-hand), a manufacturer may provide your only avenue for compensation. If this is the case, the store where the product was purchased does not have any obligations to you under the *Sale of Goods Act*.

Obligations of consumers to use products properly

Although you may have been injured or your property may have been damaged as a result of a defective product, you may not be able to get compensation if you contributed to the injury or loss. For example, you cannot seek compensation if you failed to follow the safety instructions or directions for use, or if you used the product in a way that it was not intended to be used.

If you have been injured by a product or if your property has been damaged, you should begin by writing a letter to the store explaining the problem and asking for specific compensation. If the store refuses to compensate you, and you cannot get satisfaction from the manufacturer, your only recourse may be to start a lawsuit. For legal advice or assistance, contact a lawyer.

12. What should I know about professional malpractice lawsuits?

Professional malpractice refers to the negligence or misdeeds of professionals in their work. Included in this category are doctors, dentists, chiropractors, optometrists, nurses, lawyers, architects, accountants, engineers, and so forth. In most cases, lawsuits against professionals for malpractice are difficult to prove and can be expensive.

The standard of care professionals must meet

The law does not require professionals to be perfect. If they made a mistake that could have been made by a reasonable practitioner in similar circumstances, then they will not be liable for the injury or loss. To be successful in a lawsuit against a professional, you must prove that he or she failed to provide the standard of service or care that other reasonable practitioners would provide in similar circumstances. For example, if you were not informed by your doctor of all risks associated with a procedure, or if your accountant did not follow accepted practises, you may have grounds for a malpractice lawsuit. The standard of care that must be met will vary with the type of care or service required and the type of professional providing it.

Obligations of professionals

All professionals have obligations to their patients or clients. For example, before administering any kind of medical treatment, medical practitioners have an obligation to advise the patient fully of associated risks, to discuss other options, and to fully explain the treatment. Lawyers have an obligation to act in the best interests of their clients. The obligations that each profession has are based on the law and written guidelines of its governing body.

As a patient or client, you are also required to fulfill certain obligations under the law, such as providing a full medical history to your doctor or telling the truth about the case to your lawyer. If your failure to fulfill your obligations contributed to your injury or loss, the court may not hold the professional responsible and will not compensate you. If you are successful in suing a professional, the court may award you compensation for out-of-pocket expenses, lost income, legal fees, and for pain and suffering, if any.

Filing a complaint

Regardless of whether you decide to pursue a lawsuit against a professional, you also have the option of filing a formal complaint with the organization that governs that profession. If you wish to find out more about the professional standard for a specific profession, contact the organization that governs it. Be aware, however, that a finding of malpractice or negligence by a governing body may not result in a monetary award. Instead, the governing body, in most cases, will be more concerned with the discipline of the professional. If you have suffered an injury or loss and you need legal advice or assistance, contact a lawyer as soon as possible because strict limitation periods may apply.

13. I had a slip or fall and was injured. Who can I sue?

Generally, you can sue the owner of the property where you fell, such as a retail store, school, hospital, city or municipality, or neighbour. Common examples of "slip and fall" incidents include falling on walkways that have not been cleared of snow or ice or that have not been repaired, falling on dirty or slippery floors, tripping on objects left on the floor, or falling as a result of poor lighting.

Limitation periods

In most circumstances, the law requires that you start your lawsuit for a slip and fall injury within a specific period after the date of the accident. The limitation period varies in each provincial or territorial jurisdiction, but it is generally two years. However, if you are injured on a sidewalk or other area owned or operated by a municipality (such as a bus or skating rink), you may have to notify the municipality of your intention to sue within as little as 3 to 10 days of the accident (depending on your province), and you may have to begin your lawsuit within as little as three months of the accident. Other limitations may apply if the property belongs to the federal or provincial government. If you miss these deadlines, you may not be able to recover any compensation for your injury or loss. Check with a lawyer.

Compensation for slip and fall lawsuits

If your lawsuit is successful, you may be able to recover money to compensate for your general pain and suffering, loss of income, expenses such as prescriptions and travel to and from your doctor, and future loss of income.

The amount of compensation you receive will depend on how serious your injury is and how it affects your life. The court will often take into account your age, whether you have any pre-existing injuries or conditions, and whether you contributed to your own injury. If you have sustained injuries, contact a lawyer immediately for legal advice and to avoid missing important notice or limitation periods.

14. What should I know about a lawsuit involving breach of contract?

Under the law, a violation of a contract is called a "breach." It means that one of the parties did something they should not have done or failed to do something they were required to do under the terms of the agreement. A breach of contract or agreement can be grounds for a civil lawsuit, regardless of whether the contract was oral or written.

There are three important considerations you should think about before starting a lawsuit for breach of contract:

1. You must be certain a contract was in fact made. Contracts can be made in any number of situations, ranging from a simple oral agreement with your plumber to a complex business transaction. Of course, the existence of a written contract is easier to prove than an oral contract.

2. You must be able to prove the other party breached an important term of the contract. For example, a simple breach of an agreement occurs when a business hired to pave your driveway fails to do the work or does not complete it satisfactorily.

3. You must be able to show that you suffered a loss because of the breach, a loss such as the cost of completing the original job or repairing the faulty workmanship.

In many cases, you may be able to use the small claims court process, depending on the amount claimed and the small claims limit in your province. See the chapter on *Small Claims Court* for more information.

15. What should I know about lawsuits involving construction claims?

It is not uncommon for disputes to arise in the construction and home renovation business over the quality of workmanship or completion of a project. Those hiring individuals in construction always have the ability to sue, but unlike other businesses, the construction trades have unique remedies available.

For example, in all provinces, trades people involved in the construction business who perform services or supply materials to a project (even a home renovation), are protected by legislation allowing them to place a "lien" against property for unpaid work or materials. This lien prevents the sale of the property until the lien is settled and removed.

Liens

A lien arises when the work is completed at the job site. Subcontractors are protected, even though they may not be one of the parties in a contract with the property owner. In other words, a subcontractor can still have a lien against a property even after the owner has paid the general contractor.

Contractor's trust obligations

A contractor is obligated to pay subcontractors first from any money received from the owner. Legislation, however, also requires the contractor to retain a 10% "holdback." Only after the subcontractors are paid can the contractor use any remaining money, except for the holdback. If the contractor does not pay the subcontractors, they have a legal right to sue the contractor for breach of trust and lien the property.

What if the general contractor goes out of business?

Even if the general contractor goes out of business or becomes insolvent, there may still be an opportunity for subcontractors to collect money owing. Subcontractors may be able to sue the property owner or a third party, such as a bank that distributed funds it ought to have known were trust funds. There may also be an opportunity for the subcontractors to sue the directors and senior officers of the general contractor if they knew or ought to have known their behaviour was a breach of the company's trust obligations.

16. What should I know about defamation (libel and slander) lawsuits?

Defamation (known as libel or slander) involves untrue statements made by someone that are harmful to another individual's reputation. Libel refers to statements that are written or in some permanent form, while slander refers to oral statements. Under the law, both are grounds for a civil lawsuit.

There are four circumstances where a harmful statement does not amount to libel or slander. A defamation lawsuit will not succeed if the statement:

1. Was only made to the person mentioned in the statement and not to anyone else.

2. Was actually true and can be proven so.

3. Was protected by a special type of privilege under the law. For example, a harmful statement given as evidence in a trial is not actionable (protected by "absolute privilege") nor are subsequent news reports of that statement (protected by an absolute or "qualified privilege," depending on the province).

4. Was made by someone who had a moral or legal duty to make it, or who was offering an honestly held personal opinion based on known and provable facts. For example, a former employer called for a reference likely cannot be sued successfully for defamation for expressing a personal opinion about your capabilities.

If you are suing because your reputation was damaged by a defamatory statement, you do not have to prove it actually caused financial loss. In libel cases, once a statement is judged to actually be defamatory, the law immediately presumes your reputation suffered an injury. In part, this is because it is difficult to assess damage to an intangible asset such as a person's reputation.

In slander cases, though, you may have to prove financial loss. There are some limited circumstances however, when you do not have to prove financial loss in slander, such as when the statement damaged your professional or business reputation.

If you are suing a print publication, radio or television station, you or your lawyer must give them notice of your intention to sue usually within six weeks after learning about the defamatory incident. You must then start your lawsuit within three months. If you are suing anyone other than these media outlets, you must normally start your lawsuit within two years.

There are technical requirements associated with proving a defamation case. For more information on pursuing a lawsuit for libel or slander, consult a lawyer as soon as possible to ensure you do not miss any important deadlines.

17. I have been unjustly fired from my job. What should I know about a wrongful dismissal action?

If you have been dismissed from your employment without a good legal reason or have not been given proper notice or sufficient pay in lieu of notice, you may have been wrongfully dismissed. In some provinces, you may be able to sue your employer in small claims court if the amount claimed is within its limits. (See the chapter on small claims court).

Normally, you or your lawyer will try to negotiate with your employer before formally starting a lawsuit or going to a trial. In many cases, employers do not want the expense of going to court and may prefer to settle the matter with an employee.

If you decide to sue your employer, you can ask for three types of compensation:

> **1.** You can claim you were wrongfully dismissed and ask for the amount of money that equals the notice period to which you were entitled.
>
> **2.** If your employer fired you in a way that was cruel or humiliating, and you suffered mental distress as a result, you can ask for special compensation called "special damages."
>
> **3.** If your employer fired you in a malicious way or with the intent of causing you personal embarrassment or harm, you can also ask for money to be awarded to you as a way of punishing the employer for their actions (called "punitive damages").

Claims for mental distress must be documented by medical reports. Nevertheless, successfully punishing an employer with punitive damages happens only in very extreme cases. The chances of winning in court will depend on the details of your situation. Consult a lawyer if you believe you were wrongfully dismissed and you want to know your legal options or start a lawsuit.

18. The person being sued has died. What now?

If you begin a lawsuit against an individual who later dies before the matter comes to trial, you will have to get a court order to allow the matter to proceed. Otherwise, your lawsuit will also die. If you want to assert a claim against an individual who died before you started any court action, you will have to sue the estate itself, or the executor of the deceased.

19. How can I enforce a civil court judgment?

After a trial, the winning party will have to take steps to collect the judgment ordered by the court. This person is called the creditor and the unsuccessful party who must pay the judgment is called the debtor. If you are the creditor, you or your lawyer should communicate with the debtor to make sure the person knows how and where to pay you. If you have trouble receiving payment from the debtor, you may take steps to enforce your judgment.

Enforcing a judgment can take many forms. For example, you can ask for a judgment debtor examination, make an application to garnish the debtor's wages or rents, or make an application to seize and sell the debtor's personal or real property. Enforcing a judgment can be quite complicated, with the creditor or creditor's lawyer handling the process.

■ Structured settlements

A structured settlement is a way of paying or settling a claim for damages in a lawsuit on a periodic basis over a specified period or for life.

As with any legally required or awarded compensation for a wrongful injury or death, the structured settlement payments are free of tax. (If the recipient of the payments uses the money to create a gain, such as interest, investment growth, or capital gain, that portion is taxable.)

Structured settlements are increasingly popular among insurance companies, plaintiffs, and defendants. For the recipient, the structured settlement is a guaranteed flow of tax-free and creditor-proof payments that can last for many years or life. For the insurance company or other individual creating the structured settlement, the cash requirement to buy the annuity may be lower than the damages awarded.

A structured settlement can be very flexible. Payments can be designed to increase at specific points in time, such as when surgery is needed or large medical payments are expected later in life. The payments can be indexed at a fixed interest rate or linked to the Consumer Price Index to offset inflation. They can also include a series of lump sum payments.

About half of all significant cases in Canada are settled with at least part of the settlement paid with a series of tax-free installments over a fixed term or over the lifespan of the claimant.

■ How is a structured settlement created?

The unsuccessful party in a lawsuit (or his or her insurance company) purchases an annuity that exactly fulfills the required payments to the successful party. The annuity is non-commutable, non-assignable, and non-transferable. This means no one (including creditors) can change or stop the annuity under any circumstances.

The annuity payments are generally guaranteed for a specific period by the insurance industry, but the original defendant is ultimately responsible for every payment to the claimant. The "guarantee period" may be for the first few decades on a life annuity or for a fixed term.

In theory, anyone with a life insurance licence can sell a structured settlement annuity. Without specialized experience, though, a structured settlement may be improperly executed, leaving the claimant with significant tax liability. Structured settlement brokers (of which there are about a dozen in Canada) are well known in the legal profession and insurance community. The structured settlement broker will usually prepare all the required documents and help calculate the appropriate structure.

The right to structure a settlement must be negotiated during the settlement process and must be part of the documented settlement agreement. Funds to purchase the annuity must pass from the defendant or his or her agent to the annuity company or its agent. You cannot receive settlement funds first, and then purchase a structured settlement annuity after the fact. The annuity must, in fact, be purchased by the defendant or insurance company. During the weeks leading up to settlement, a claimant should make sure his or her lawyer is preserving the right to structure any part of the settlement.

■ Negative aspects of structured settlements

Structured settlements cannot be changed by anyone after they are signed and the case is closed. You won't be able to take advantage of opportunities for investments or unexpected purchases in the future by "cashing out" all or part of the structure.

While the structured settlement payment schedule can be shown to a lender as "proof of income" when applying for a loan, the actual payments cannot be pledged, assigned, garnished, or otherwise redirected to a lender.

Also, structured settlement interest rates are fixed at the time of purchase. Better rates of return might be available at some time in the future and the claimant will not be able to benefit.

A very important issue is deciding what happens to structured settlement payments when the claimant or recipient dies. Most structured settlement annuities contain some period of guaranteed payments (say, 25 years for a life annuity) and many claimants incorrectly assume the guaranteed payments will automatically go to family or inheritors if they die before the guaranteed period ends.

Often, however, guaranteed payments are set to "revert" to the defendant or insurance company that bought the annuity upon the claimant's death. This can be avoided by negotiating the right to have guaranteed payments continue even after your death (usually, in return for a relatively minor payment).

It is also important that claimants not name their estate as the beneficiary or recipient for guaranteed payments upon their death since the estate itself is subject to attack by creditors and inheritors, as well as probate and lawyer fees. Actual individuals should be named and, in creating the structured settlement, the recipient should retain the right to change the names of recipients for future guaranteed payments.

TOO SCARY FOR WORDS

A newspaper published an article about local homes that were reputedly haunted. With tongue in cheek, the author described the spooky legends surrounding the homes. One house in particular was up for sale and, after the article was published, the owner sued the newspaper claiming the story was defamatory and ruined his chances of selling the property.

Was the homeowner successful in claiming defamation of property?

Yes. In the case of Manitoba Free Press Co. v. Nagy, an article claiming a house was haunted and uninhabitable was accepted by the court as defamation of a property. Like any asset, a home has a reputation and value that needs to be protected. Usually, the courts require a higher degree of proof in cases involving property. The plaintiff must prove that there was malice in making the defamatory statements, that actual damage was suffered, and the statements were untrue.

WAS IT FORESEEABLE?

Sam drives up to a convenience store, leaving the car keys on his seat and the door unlocked. After Sam goes into the store, a teenager jumps in the car and steals it. Later, the police tell Sam his car was involved in an accident with a bus and some of the passengers were injured severely. Sadly, upon hearing of the accident, a relative of one of the bus passengers gets upset and dies of a heart attack.

Does Sam owe a common law duty of care to the bus passenger's relative? And is he responsible for causing the heart attack?

No. The courts are very reluctant to impose a common law duty of care in such distant circumstances unless it was clearly foreseeable that his actions would result in an injury to a third party. Some courts have even taken the position that Sam doesn't owe a duty of care to the injured bus passengers, either.

WHOSE BREACH? WHOSE CONTRACT?

Belinda makes a deal with Alice. If Alice will drive Belinda's son to school and back every day, Belinda will give Alice's mother a valuable vase she always liked. After several months of fulfilling her side of the deal, Alice sees that Belinda does not intend to give her mother the vase and stops the daily drives. Alice's mother wants to teach Belinda a lesson and sues for the vase, claiming a breach of contract.

Will Alice's mother be successful in court?

No. The legal principle of "privity of contract" prevents a third party to an agreement, even its beneficiary, from having a right of action. Alice herself will have to sue.

YOUR OWN DAY IN COURT: SMALL CLAIMS ACTIONS

Don't you wish sometimes there was some simple way to resolve a minor dispute, protect your rights, or get "your day in court" without all the expense and hassle of hiring a lawyer and getting into a long battle?

There is — and it is called small claims court. The small claims court system is available in every jurisdiction of Canada and it is one place where people can resolve their own minor legal problems. Common types of claims include someone breaking a legal agreement, damaging your personal property, owing you money, or causing you to suffer a physical injury.

Small Claims Court Limits

Alberta	$25,000
British Columbia	$10,000
Manitoba	$7,500
New Brunswick	$6,000
Newfoundland	$3,000
Northwest Territories	$5,000
Nova Scotia	$10,000
Nunavut	No small claims court
Ontario	$10,000
Prince Edward Island	$8,000
Québec	$7,000
Saskatchewan	$5,000
Yukon Territory	$5,000

Small claims court is a faster and less expensive way of resolving legal problems than going to the higher courts. You do not need a lawyer or any special training to make or defend a claim. Small claims courts hear cases for small amounts ranging from less than $3,000 in Newfoundland and Labrador to $25,000 in Alberta.

Although you do not need any special legal training to bring a lawsuit or defend a claim in small claims court, you will need to know a bit about the legal system itself. For example, you should know what to call the various people or parties involved in the lawsuit since these terms will be used on court documents and at the trial (the person who starts the lawsuit is called the plaintiff and the defendant is the one being sued).

Don't be put off by the need to do a little homework before going to a small claims court. While the wait to get into court is often long (3-6 months in many provinces), most people are delighted to find that this court is truly a "people's court" that will help all sides reach a fair conclusion.

1.   What is a small claims "action" or lawsuit?

If someone has violated your legal rights and caused you to suffer a loss, you may be able to start a lawsuit against them. One of the first questions to ask yourself, however, is whether you are within the limitation period allowed to launch a claim. The type of claim you have will determine the time period that applies. Time limits for starting a lawsuit are usually calculated from the day that the problem took place, or the day you realized or found out about the problem or loss.

There are four common types of small claims and each has specific time limits for starting a lawsuit.

1. Cases involving a broken agreement or contract normally must be started within six years from the day when the agreement was broken.

2. Cases involving damaged property or a personal injury suffered through somebody else's negligence normally must be started within six years from the day that the damage or injury occurred.

3. Cases involving an assault or threat of violence have a four-year time limit from the day the injury or threat happened.

4. Libel and slander cases, where one person has written or said something harmful about someone else, normally must be started within two years.

■ Shorter Time Limits for Special Claims

Certain types of legal actions have even shorter time limits. For example, if you are bringing a lawsuit against an insurance company for refusing to pay your claim, you must start the legal action within one year of making your claim.

If you want to take legal action against a municipality or a government agency, you may have to give them notice of your claim. For example, if you fell on an icy sidewalk or if you were injured due to a badly maintained road, these time periods can be very short and will affect your right to bring a lawsuit. Check on this aspect of your case as soon as possible (that is, within days or hours, if possible). If you are uncertain about whether you are too late to start a lawsuit, consult a lawyer as soon as possible.

2.   Who can be sued?

It is not uncommon for people in small claims court to sue the wrong individuals. For example, a delivery van driver may have backed over your new fence. But it is likely that the driver's employer is really the one who should be sued. By *correctly* naming the defendants you are suing, it will be easier to win the lawsuit and collect any money the court may order the defendants to pay you. In a lawsuit, a defendant can either be the person or business responsible for your loss.

Before you start a lawsuit you will also need to know the proper legal name of the defendant.

■ Suing individual defendants

If you are going to sue a person, it is necessary to find out his or her legal name. You can't just sue "Bob, my neighbour." A person's legal name might appear on a lease, cheque, or other official document. If a defendant is known by more than one name, you should list all of them. For example, you may refer to someone as "Robert Smith also known as Bob Smith."

■ Suing a business

If you are going to sue a business, the name you use for the defendant will depend on the type of business. There are three types of business entities: corporations, partnerships, and sole proprietorships.

If the defendant is a corporation, you should use its full legal name, which will probably end with the word corporation, incorporated, limited, or an abbreviation of one of these terms. The full business name usually appears on company letterhead, cheques, business cards, or contracts.

If you want to sue a partnership or one of the partners in a partnership, you should list the partnership as the defendant, rather than the name of any individual partner. Even though you are not required to list individual partners as defendants, if you are suing a partnership but want to be able to collect money from one of the partners personally, you may want to name that partner as a defendant in the statement of claim and deliver a copy to that partner as well.

If the business you are suing is not a corporation or a partnership, and it is operated by a single person, it is called a sole proprietorship. For a sole proprietorship, you can check to see whether the business name is registered with the provincial government. If the business name is registered, you can use the name of the business as the defendant in your lawsuit.

If the business name is not registered, you should use the name of the owner of the business as the defendant. You may wish to include both. For example, you may sue "John Smith, carrying on business as John's Cleaning Service."

To obtain more information about the full legal name and address of a business, partnership, sole proprietorship, or corporation, you can do a search through the government ministry that oversees corporations in your province. It usually entails a small fee. This office is listed in the Blue pages of your telephone book.

■ Children or minors

Minors are usually treated differently in court and most often need an adult to represent them as a litigation guardian or personal representative. The rules vary according to province and age, so you must check with the small claims court in your jurisdiction.

A litigation guardian can be anyone who is capable of suing on his or her own and who is not involved with people on the other side of the case. A litigation guardian is usually a relative or parent of the minor.

A litigation guardian carries a very responsible role. He or she is there to make decisions about the lawsuit for the minor. In small claims court, the litigation guardian can represent the minor and can negotiate with the other side on behalf of the minor. The litigation guardian does not, however, have the right to settle the matter without going to court first to have a judge approve the settlement agreement. Note, however, that a litigation guardian may also be personally responsible for any legal costs of the lawsuit.

3. How do I file my Statement of Claim?

To start a lawsuit in small claims court, you must fill out a special form called a "Statement of Claim." The Statement of Claim form is available at the small claims court in your area, and you must fill out all relevant sections.

■ Plaintiff and defendant information

This identifies who is involved in the lawsuit. Be sure to fill in all the information requested on the form, including the proper legal name and address of the defendant. If you are suing more than one defendant, include the name, address, and other required information on the form for each.

■ Amount of claim

Indicate in the pre-printed form how much you are suing for. The most you can sue for is the maximum that the small claims court in your jurisdiction allows. Most provincial forms already state that you will be asking for compensation for costs — that is, the expenses you paid to bring your case to court. Costs include the fee for filing the statement of claim, photocopying charges, and postage. Compensation costs can even include lawyers' fees. The judge may order the defendant to pay you some or all of these costs if you win the case.

■ Type of claim

The form will also ask you to indicate the type of claim. This is where you will need to check the box that best describes your situation, such as contract or damage to property. If the boxes don't fit your situation, check the box marked "other," and write your matter out in the blank space. For example, if you are suing because of an assault, you should check other on the form and write in the word, "assault."

■ Facts of your case

The form will also require you to set out the facts of your case and describe what you are claiming. It is best if you write a separate, short paragraph for each claim. Number your paragraphs and list all the facts in the order that they happened. Do not include arguments or opinions. Always list the date when something happened and the names of the people involved. When referring to yourself, write or make reference to "the plaintiff." Refer to the person you are suing as "the defendant."

Be brief in writing out the facts of your case. Include only what is necessary for the defendant and the judge to know and why you are claiming the amount you have written on the form. If you need more space than is provided, attach extra sheets of paper. Be sure to write clearly and legibly.

If you are relying on a contract, a receipt, or a letter, attach a copy of the document to your claim. If you do not have a copy, indicate the reason you do not have the document. For example, if a store refused to give back your receipt, write that as the reason you do not have the receipt. If you tried to settle the problem before going to court, include a copy of any related letters you wrote.

■ Pre-judgment interest

The claim should also include a request for pre-judgment interest, which is interest on the amount of money or loss you claim in the lawsuit. Pre-judgment interest is calculated from the day the problem occurred until the day that the judge decides the outcome of the case. The judge will decide whether to grant pre-judgment interest, but your claim must request it.

The rate of pre-judgment interest will usually be the rate used by the courts at the time of the lawsuit, unless another rate has already been agreed upon by you and the defendant.

The staff at most small claims court offices can also provide you with information on how to complete the statement of claim.

■ Filing the Statement of Claim

Usually, you must go to the court building in person and pay a required fee. To verify that your claim has been filed and that the lawsuit is underway, the small claims court office will give you a claim number to use whenever you are referring to your case. The office staff will also sign and stamp your statement of claim so you can then deliver it to the defendant.

Where you file a claim is also important because this is the place where the trial will be held. Although there are many small claims courts throughout the country, you are normally required to go to the small claims court in the area where the problem occurred, or to the court nearest to where the defendant lives or carries out business.

If this is not possible or convenient, you may file an Affidavit or statement sworn under oath to be true (in front of a Commissioner of Oaths, usually a lawyer) at the small claims court where you want the trial to be held. This document states the reason why you want to have your action in that place. The staff at the court can give you the Affidavit form and printed instructions on how to complete it.

Next, you need to deliver a copy of your claim to the defendants.

■ Serving a Statement of Claim

In most provinces, the plaintiff is responsible for delivering a copy of the statement of claim to the defendant. This is known as "serving" the defendant. There are two main ways to serve your statement of claim.

The first: deliver it to the person you are serving. This is called personal service. If you personally serve the statement of claim on the defendant, then, depending on the province, the defendant has a specific number of days in which to file his or her *statement of defence* with the court.

The second: mail it to the defendant's last known address. In some provinces, you will require a receipt indicating that the document was received, so it is best to use registered mail.

If the defendant is a business, you can leave the statement of claim with anyone at the defendant's work place who appears to be in control of the office. You may also use registered mail to serve the statement of claim on a business.

■ Getting an Affidavit of Service

Regardless of whether the defendant is a person or business, you must prove that you served the defendant with a statement of claim by filling out and filing a form called an Affidavit of Service. This form is also available from the small claims court.

Fill out the Affidavit of Service, by explaining how you served the defendant. Then sign it and swear that what you say is true in front of a Commissioner of Oaths, such as a lawyer or a notary public. Staff at the small claims court may also be able to commission your affidavit.

If you have tried to serve the defendant but have been unsuccessful, you may ask a judge to let you serve the statement of claim another way. For example, you may want to serve it by posting it on a door or sending it by fax. Ask the small claims court staff in your region for instructions on how to apply to the court to request permission to serve the claim in another way.

4. What happens if I am being sued in small claims court?

If you receive a *Statement of Claim* from small claims court, it means someone is suing you for the reasons stated on the forms. How you respond to these forms will affect whether the person can collect the money that is claimed.

First, do not ignore a statement of claim. If you do not respond to a statement of claim, the plaintiff may win the case automatically when he or she appears before the judge. Second, read all the papers you receive very carefully to find out what the lawsuit is about and how long you have to respond.

If you do not agree with all or part of what is stated in the statement of claim, you can fight the lawsuit. To fight a lawsuit, you must fill out a special form called a *Statement of Defence*. This form is available at the small claims court office. There are time limits for responding to the claim against you.

■ File a Statement of Defence

If you have received a *statement of claim* but do not file a *statement of defence*, the judge may assume you agree with the claims in the statement of claim and may sign a *default judgment*.

A default judgment usually allows the plaintiff to win the lawsuit because you did not fight it. With a default judgment, the plaintiff is allowed to collect money from you right away. If there is a default judgment against you, but you had a good reason for not filing a statement of defence, you may still be able to fight the lawsuit after the fact if you get permission from a judge.

■ I did not file a defence. Can I set aside a default judgment?

If you want to file a statement of defence after a default judgment has been signed, you will require a judge's order setting aside the judgment. You will need to visit the small claims court, fill out the appropriate forms indicating why the judgment should be set aside, and pay a fee.

In most jurisdictions, you must fill out what is often called a *Notice of Motion*, and an *Affidavit in Support of Motion*. You must swear in front of a commissioner of oaths that the information in the Affidavit is true. The staff at the small claims court office will give you a time and date to appear in front of the judge. You must then deliver a copy of the Motion and Affidavit to the plaintiff at least seven days before the date you are scheduled to appear in front of the judge. If you serve the Motion and Affidavit on the plaintiff by mail, you must allow 12 days for the service.

When you appear in front of the judge, you must explain why you were late in filing your statement of defence. For example, if you recently moved, and the statement of claim was forwarded to your new address late, then you should explain this to the judge. Or, if you were out of the country or in hospital and did not know the statement of claim was at your home, this should be explained to the judge.

You must also be prepared to tell the judge what your defence is, so that the judge is satisfied there is a good reason to set aside the plaintiff's default judgment.

The judge will decide if your reasons are good enough. If the judge agrees with you and signs an order allowing you to file a statement of defence, you will have to file it within the time allowed by the judge. After you file a statement of defence you will be notified of a trial date.

■ What should a Statement of Defence say?

To file a defence, use the standard Statement of Defence form available at the small claims court office and fill in the appropriate information. You'll need to indicate how you are responding to the claim.

The form usually includes a space for you to describe your response to the lawsuit. If you do not admit any of the plaintiff's claim, or if you deny that you owe any money to the plaintiff, you should say you dispute the full claim made by the plaintiff.

If you admit that you owe some of the amount claimed, but not all of it, then you should state what part of the plaintiff's claim you agree is owed.

At this point, you may want to explain how you wish to pay the amount you are admitting you owe the plaintiff. You should make sure any payment plan you propose is one you will be able to carry out until the debt is paid off. If the plaintiff accepts your payment plan, he or she will get a judgment from the court for that amount and the plaintiff will be paid according to your plan. If the plaintiff does not accept the payment plan, he or she will still get a judgment for the amount that you have admitted you owe, but the payment terms will still have to be worked out.

If you have admitted you owe part of the amount claimed, the plaintiff may still proceed to trial to prove the entire amount.

■ Reasons for disputing the claim

Your statement of defence should also provide your reasons for disputing any claims. Write a separate, short paragraph on each point you are making. Begin by listing all the facts that you agree with. For example, if the plaintiff's statement of claim says that you entered into an agreement and that is true, then you should say so. After you have agreed with some statements, note which statements you disagree with.

Then, list the facts that you are going to use to prove your side of the case. You do not have to follow the statement of claim in filling out this part of your defence, but can write down your own version of the events. Make sure your statements are clear and readable and are as brief as possible. If you run out of space, attach extra pages to the statement of defence.

If you are relying on documents different from ones that are attached to the statement of claim, attach a copy of the new ones to your statement of defence. These might include contracts, leases, receipts, payment records, cancelled cheques, and similar documents. If you are relying on documents you do not have, explain why.

After you have filled out the statement of defence, you will need to file it at the small claims court office and pay a fee. The court will then notify you of a trial date. The staff at the small claims court office can provide printed information on how to fill out the statement of defence. If you need legal advice and assistance with a statement of defence, consult a lawyer.

After a statement of defence is filed, the court will send it to the other people involved in the lawsuit. The small claims court office may set a date for a trial or a pre-trial conference. A trial date will only be set upon the request of the plaintiff and payment by the plaintiff of any fee to set an action down for trial.

Everyone involved in the lawsuit will receive by mail a notice informing them of the trial date or any pre-trial conferences. You should read the notice carefully. It will tell you the date, time and location of the trial or the pre-trial conference.

5.   Can a defendant also make a Statement of Claim?

Defendants who are sued sometimes have a claim of their own against the plaintiff or against somebody else. If you are sued, you may "counter-claim" and file a claim by filling out a separate form.

Sometimes, two people have a reason to sue each other. If someone is suing you and you have a reason to sue him or her, you can start a separate lawsuit against that person. In most cases, however, both lawsuits can and should be heard at the same time so all the issues can be resolved at once. For both lawsuits to be heard together by the same judge, the defendant of the first lawsuit needs to file a counterclaim.

■ Claiming against someone other than the plaintiff

Sometimes a plaintiff does not sue the right person. If you are being sued and you believe that another person is responsible for all or part of what the plaintiff is claiming, then you may be able to bring that third person into the lawsuit. You may *cross-claim* to bring the third person into the lawsuit by filing the appropriate form and providing details of the claim.

6.   What is involved in a pre-trial conference?

After the Statements of Claim and Defence have been served and filed, the case may go to a judge for review. In most provinces, a judge can order that a pre-trial conference be held before a lawsuit goes to trial.

At a pre-trial conference, the plaintiff and the defendant meet with each other in front of a judge, usually in the judge's office. The purpose of a pre-trial conference is to resolve or simplify the issues in the lawsuit, to speed up the lawsuit, to help reach a settlement instead of going to trial, to prepare each side if there is going to be a trial, and to ensure that everyone in the lawsuit knows all the important facts and evidence.

If you go to a pre-trial conference, be prepared to talk about the lawsuit. Also, bring all the important information and documents available. If you are not prepared when you attend a pre-trial conference or if you do not show up, the judge can order you to pay the other side's expenses for having to come to the pre-trial conference needlessly.

If a person does not show up at the pre-trial conference, the judge can also strike that person's claim or defence and immediately give judgment for the other side. It is very important, therefore, to show up or to notify the other side and the court if an emergency prevents you from attending.

Attending a pre-trial conference will usually make the trial easier. It may even help you settle the lawsuit. In most cases, a lawsuit settles before it goes to trial because settling saves both sides the time and expense of a trial. For more information about pre-trial conferences, contact the small claims court office.

7.   What is a motion?

Sometimes before or during a trial, issues arise that need to be resolved before the trial can continue. To resolve such issues, one of the parties can make a motion, or a request to the court for the judge to make a decision about the issue. For example, during a trial one of the parties involved might discover that somebody else might be responsible for the plaintiff's loss and should be added to the lawsuit. That party would then make a motion to the court and ask the judge to allow them to serve a claim on that person. The judge's decision on a motion may affect how the trial continues, but it may not determine the ultimate outcome of the lawsuit.

To make a motion, you will need to fill out the appropriate forms. In most provinces, you must file what are often called a *Notice of Motion* and an *Affidavit in Support of Motion*. The forms are available at the small claims court office. A Notice of Motion requires you to fill in the names of the parties and select the type of Motion you are bringing. An Affidavit in Support of Motion requires you to explain why you are making the motion and to set out the facts that support your motion.

To fill out the affidavit, you should describe the issue that needs to be resolved, how you think the issue should be resolved, and the facts that you think prove your point. Then, you must swear that the affidavit is true in front of a commissioner of oaths. Lawyers are commissioners of oath. In some cases, staff members at the small claims court can also swear your affidavit.

You must file the Notice of Motion and affidavit at the small claims court office. The staff at the court office will give you a time and date to appear in front of the judge. Before the motion, you must deliver copies of the Notice of Motion and affidavit to the other side under deadlines specified by the court.

A motion may be heard in the judge's office or in the courtroom. Check the lists posted at the courthouse to see where your motion is being heard. At the hearing, both sides will be able to speak to the judge about the motion. If the other side is making the motion and you agree with it, then say so. If you do not agree, you will have to tell the judge what part of the motion you do not agree with and why. The judge will make a decision about the motion. Then the trial can continue.

If you feel that a serious error was made by the judge in granting or denying a motion, it may be possible to have it reviewed. This can be a complicated procedure, however, and you should consult a lawyer about this.

Because small claims court is intended to be fast and straightforward, you should only bring a motion if it will make a difference to the lawsuit. Before you bring a motion, try to resolve the issue with the other side or see if they will consent to the motion without a hearing. The final decision will be up to the judge.

8.   What is an offer to settle?

Most lawsuits are settled before they go to trial. If you are involved in a lawsuit, you may want to settle the matter to save time and money. Sometimes, there are rules and penalties that may apply if the lawsuit has to be decided by a judge.

An *offer to settle* usually includes a statement by the plaintiff or defendant about how he or she is willing to resolve the lawsuit without going to trial. An offer to settle can be made by anyone involved in a lawsuit at any time. An offer to settle can be withdrawn as long as it has not been accepted by the other side.

If you make an offer to settle, and the other side accepts it, then a settlement agreement has been made. If someone makes you a reasonable offer and you do not accept it, you may have to pay extra costs after a trial. The consequences of not settling will depend on who made the offer and whether the amount awarded by the judge is more or less than the offer.

An offer to settle should be made in writing. It should include the date, what you are offering, how long the offer is open, and your signature. Always keep a copy of any offer you make or receive. If you want to accept an offer made by the other party, do so in writing and keep a copy of the signed offer. Any final agreement to settle a lawsuit should be set in writing and signed by everyone involved.

9.   How should I prepare my small claims case?

At the trial you will have an opportunity to explain your side of the issue and respond to the claims of the other side. Before you go to court, you should have a good understanding of both sides of the case so you can speak to the judge clearly and answer any questions that arise.

After you understand your position and the position of the other side, develop a strategy to prove your side of the case. You can develop a strategy by organizing how you will present the facts, evidence, and what the law says about an issue. Such a strategy should not be complicated or fancy because it is the method that will help the judge understand the facts of your case and why you believe your side should win.

In thinking about your strategy, think about the facts from the judge's point of view. The judge needs to know who was involved, what happened, when it happened, who was at fault, and how much money was involved. If you can answer these questions clearly, you are well on your way to having an organized case.

■ Tell Your Story Using Facts, Not Emotion

Use the facts to prove your case. To help you decide what facts to tell the judge, write down only the important ones in the order that they occurred. Remember, you likely know more facts about the situation than the judge will really need to hear. Then, look over these facts and take out anything that will not help the judge understand your position.

You can also use "evidence," such as written documents or testimony from a witness. Examples of written documents that may be important are contracts, letters, invoices, receipts, photographs, or hospital records. An example of helpful witness testimony might include having someone explain the scene of an accident or describe the damage to property. If possible, take photographs of things that cannot be brought to court. The witness can then testify that the photograph correctly represents the real place or thing. Keep in mind that a witness can only give evidence at trial about something he or she actually saw, heard, or did. Only bring a witness who can contribute something important to your side of the case.

Normally, you cannot just bring evidence to the trial on your own. Instead, copies of documents that will be used as evidence should also be given or sent to the other side at least 14 days before the trial. As well, keep copies of the evidence for your own records, and the original documents to show the judge at trial.

You can also help your side of the case by telling the judge how the law has dealt with similar issues in the past. If you have consulted a lawyer or have researched examples of this, mention it at the trial. If you plan to refer to specific cases, provide copies of these examples for the judge and the other side.

Refer to your notes during the trial to assist you. Write out the order in which you want to present your evidence. This way, you will be less likely to forget to say or present something. Practise what you plan to say ahead of time with a friend or by yourself. The more prepared you are, the more effective you will be.

■ Witnesses

There are three important things to do if you want to have someone testify at your trial. First, decide if the witness is necessary to your case. Second, make sure the person will show up. And third, prepare your witness to testify in court.

Well before the date of trial, meet with the witness. Go over what it is he or she will say. Ask the questions that you will need to ask at trial. Think about what kind of impression the person will make: Will the person get nervous and forget things? Does the person stick to the same story? If you think that the person will not make a good impression, do not have that person testify.

Personally arrange for a witness to come to the trial if you think that the person is necessary for your case and will make a good impression. Asking the person to come voluntarily is the easiest way to get a witness to come.

If a witness does not want to testify, or if that person cannot take a day off work, ask the staff at the small claims court for a special form called a Summons to Witness, which is an official request by the court. There is a $10 fee for each Summons to Witness. You will then have to deliver the completed Summons form to the appropriate person.

Anyone who receives a Summons to Witness must attend the trial. That person's employer must also allow the individual to go to court during work hours. You will have to pay a fee for the witness to attend the trial, as well as pay the witness's travel expenses. You may get these expenses back from the other side if you win your case.

■ Preparing a witness

Before the trial date, spend some time preparing the witness. Review the facts that the witness knows and make sure the person can testify to those facts. Try asking the witness questions. Have that person answer as if in front of a judge.

At trial, the other side will be allowed to ask your witness questions. They will try to make the witness look unreliable and bring out facts that hurt your case. Prepare your witness for this so he or she is not surprised at trial. Make sure your witness understands that he or she must always tell the truth in court. It is illegal to tell the witness what to say or to ask the witness to withhold the truth.

As a plaintiff or a defendant, you will be the main witness for your side. This means you will need to go into the witness box, swear to tell the truth, and then, explain your side of the issue. It is important, then, that you practise what you will say to the judge before you testify.

Also, prepare to answer the questions the other side might ask. If you do not understand a question the other side or the judge asks, say so. Remember — you must always tell the truth in court.

■ Organization is key

It will be easier for the judge to understand your side of the case if you are well-organized. Do this by putting your papers in proper, usually chronological, order.

To organize your papers, file them in three sections using a three-ring binder or a divided file folder. In one section put copies of letters you have written or received about the lawsuit. In the second section put the statement of claim, statement of defence, and any counterclaims. The last section should contain all the evidence you plan to use at trial. Evidence is anything you use to prove your side of the case, such as a contract or receipts. If available, always have the original document ready to show the judge.

At trial you may need to refer to something in your file. Organizing your papers ahead of time makes a good impression and avoids wasting the judge's time.

10. What actually happens on the day my case is heard?

Whether you are the plaintiff or the defendant, knowing what happens at court and what to do when you arrive will help ease your nerves and keep you better prepared. This knowledge can also increase your chances of succeeding at trial. One of the best ways to prepare is to arrive at least half an hour early so you can get familiar with the court.

When you first arrive, find the courtroom where your trial will take place. Look at the posted lists outside the door of each courtroom to find your name. If you are not on the list, go to the court staff office and ask a staff member to help you find the right room.

Once the doors of the courtroom open, tell the clerk at the front of the room that you are present and ready for trial. Then, take a seat. When the judge arrives, everyone will be asked to stand. The judge will enter and sit on a raised platform at the front of the courtroom.

If you arrive, and the judge is already in the courtroom, it means that a trial is in process. In this case, enter the courtroom quietly, sit down, and wait until your name is called. If there is a break, you should tell the clerk that you are present.

When your name is called, walk to the front of the courtroom. If you are the plaintiff, stand at the right. If you are the defendant, stand at the left. State your name for the judge, who should always be called "Your Honour."

If the plaintiff or defendant does not show up for trial, the judge will decide whether the case will go ahead without that person, or whether the trial date will be moved ahead.

■ Who speaks first at the trial?

Generally, plaintiffs present their side of the case first. If the plaintiff is testifying for his or her own case, the court clerk will ask the plaintiff to swear to tell the truth. The plaintiff will then begin by explaining his or her position. The plaintiff should then tell the judge all the important facts in the order that they happened, and show the judge any evidence. The defendant will then be allowed to ask the plaintiff questions. If the plaintiff has a witness, the plaintiff will ask the witness questions first, and then the defendant will have a turn to question that witness.

Once a plaintiff has finished making his or her case, it is the defendant's turn to tell the other side of the story, show evidence, and call witnesses just as the plaintiff did. A plaintiff will be able to question the defendant and the defendant's witnesses.

Whether you are speaking to the judge or asking a witness questions, always be courteous. Do not get angry or interrupt even if you feel the other side is not telling the truth.

You may interrupt the other side *only* when making an objection to a question that was asked of a witness. Do not make an objection unless you feel it is necessary. Stand up and tell the judge you object to the question and explain why. For example, if the question has nothing to do with the case, or if the other side is yelling at your witness, you may object. The judge will consider your objection and decide what will be done about it.

Before making a final decision on who wins the case, the judge will usually ask both the plaintiff and the defendant to summarize their positions.

The judge can decide not only whose position is correct, but also if any party will have to pay the other's costs. If asked to summarize your case, do not make a big speech or repeat all the evidence. Just outline for the judge why you feel you have proved your case.

If you lose a lawsuit, you may have the right to appeal. Consult a lawyer if you require legal advice or representation..

■ Interpreters

If your language ability prevents you from understanding the court proceedings, or the judge does not understand you, or if any of your witnesses need an interpreter, arrange to bring one who has the proper skills to translate from your language to English. The interpreter however must not be connected with the lawsuit, and if possible, should not be a member of your immediate family. If you do not know someone who can act as an interpreter, there are services from which you can hire a court-qualified interpreter. However, this can be costly because small claims court does not provide interpreters.

If a trial has started and the judge feels that a party or a witness cannot properly understand due to language difficulties, the judge can order that the party provide an interpreter.

When using an interpreter, you must give all your evidence in your own language. You cannot testify partly in English and partly in your language. Speak slowly so the interpreter can translate for the court.

Consider carefully whether you or your witness need an interpreter. Keep in mind that you want the judge to have the best possible understanding of your case.

■ Judge's role

The judge's role in small claims court is less formal than the role of a judge in the higher courts. In fact, in some jurisdictions, the person hearing the case is actually a lawyer, or even a court clerk, who will review the facts with a judge after the trial.

The judge will usually listen to both the plaintiff and the defendant and, if necessary, the judge will ask questions that will help the plaintiff and defendant focus on the important facts.

The rules in small claims court are more flexible. Since you are not expected to be represented by a lawyer, and the purpose is to resolve issues relatively quickly, the judge can let participants show any evidence that the court thinks is important to the case.

Ask the judge to explain anything that you do not understand. Always be courteous and respectful when addressing the judge. Once both sides have presented their case, the judge will make the final decision.

11. Can I appeal a small claims court decision?

After the trial is over and the judge has decided the case, one party usually feels satisfied and the other disappointed. If you lost your case, this does not mean that the decision was wrong. But if you believe that the judge made a serious mistake, you may consider appealing the judge's decision, provided you do so within the permitted time frame, which is normally 30 days. Ontario, for example, specifically prohibits an appeal if the amount of money at stake is less than $500. Most other provinces will only allow an appeal from small claims divisions if there is a dispute over the interpretation of the law itself.

An appeal from small claims court goes to a higher provincial court. The rules for making appeals and appearing in such a court are complicated. Appeals can also be expensive and time-consuming. Only consider an appeal if you believe that the judge made a serious error in the case, and there is a substantial amount of money or significant legal rights involved.

An example of an error made by a judge might involve a refusal to let you tell your side of the case before making a judgment, or if the judge did not allow a necessary witness to testify. Contact a lawyer to get advice about making an appeal.

■ **What is a court award of "costs"?**

"Costs" are the expenses of bringing a lawsuit to court. Usually, the winning side in a court case has its costs added to the amount of the judgment. This may not cover all expenses, but can include some or all of the following:

- Fees paid to the court to file documents like a Statement of Claim or a Statement of Defence
- Fees paid to the court to file a motion
- Witness attendance fees
- Transportation costs to attend court
- Costs of photocopying papers or having photographs developed
- Postage for serving documents
- Compensation for attending court when the other party didn't show up
- Cost of hiring a necessary interpreter

If the winning party was represented in court by a lawyer or a paralegal agent, that person may be awarded legal costs for the representative's attendance. This usually does not cover the entire legal bill, only the representative's court time. In exceptional circumstances, however, a judge may order that the winning party's entire legal bill be paid by the losing party.

An award of costs by a judge can be affected by whether a settlement offer was made. If the judge feels that the winning party should have accepted the settlement offered by the other side, the judge may decide not to award the winning party its costs. If the judge feels that the losing party should have settled the case, the winning party can be awarded double the amount of its costs. These decisions are made when the judge feels that one of the parties has wasted the court's time and inconvenienced the other side.

Sometimes, after a motion or a pre-trial conference, a judge will order a party to pay certain costs to the other side forthwith. This means that the party that has been ordered to pay costs must pay the amount ordered to the other side right away. If the party does not pay, it may not be allowed to go ahead in the lawsuit and judgment may even be ordered against that party.

If you want to check whether an order of costs has been made against you, contact the staff at the court. Use the case claim number as your reference.

12. How do I enforce a small claims court judgment?

This is one aspect of small claims court that can be very frustrating for the average citizen. Sometimes, a small claims court will award you damages or decide in your favour, but the opposing party will still make it difficult to collect your money or enforce your right. Enforcing a small claims judgment sometimes takes a great deal of patience.

Once each side presents its case at trial, the judge will make a final decision called a judgment. A judgment may be oral or written. At the end of a simple case, the judge will usually give an oral judgment by just telling the parties his or her decision. Sometimes, a judge will want more time to consider the result and the decision will be sent by the court to the parties in writing.

If you win a lawsuit, the judge will normally order the other person to pay you for damages you suffered and for your court costs. The person who loses the lawsuit and is ordered to pay money is called the debtor.

The creditor is the person who won the lawsuit and who must be paid by the debtor. The terms debtor and creditor may be used on official court documents, which are necessary to enforce the judgment if the debtor does not pay.

The judgment can state that the debtor must pay the money owed right away, or it can allow the debtor to pay the money over a period according to a payment schedule. Often, though, the judgment doesn't say anything about when the money must be paid.

If you are a creditor, speak to the debtor to make sure that the person knows how and where to pay you. Sending a letter to the debtor is a good idea. The letter should confirm the amount owing, including all the interest to date, and when you expect to receive payment. If one side is ordered to pay money and fails to do so, the person who is owed will often have to take steps to collect the money by applying to the court to enforce the judgment.

■ Collecting money owed

Even though there is a judgment that says the debtor owes you money, it may be hard to get the debtor to pay. If the debtor does not pay, it is up to you to take steps to collect the money. The staff at the court can provide information and forms to assist you in collecting the money. If you do not want to collect the money on your own, you may hire a private collection company, a lawyer, or a paralegal agent to do it for you. Before you spend time and money trying to collect on a judgment, however, you should determine if the debtor has assets and is likely to pay.

To collect the debt by enforcing the judgment, you will need to know about the debtor's finances, including where the debtor works, where the debtor keeps bank accounts, if the debtor is owed money by tenants, what personal property the debtor owns, and if the debtor owns land.

Generally, there are three ways to enforce a judgment through the court. First, the court can help you with garnishment by collecting money from a person who owes money to the debtor, such as an employer or a tenant. Second, the court can help you have the debtor's personal property sold and collect the money that is received from the sale of the property by seizing and selling it. Third, the court can help you collect your judgment by selling or putting a lien on the debtor's land.

Sometimes, a judgment states that the defendant has to return the plaintiff's personal property. If the defendant does not return the property, the plaintiff can ask the court for permission to take the property back, often referred to as a writ of delivery.

If you are unsure whether it is worth the time and expense of collecting a debt on your own, consult a lawyer or a private collection agency.

If you do not have financial information about the debtor, you can request a special meeting to examine the debtor's financial situation, commonly referred to as a judgment debtor examination, and ask questions about his or her finances. You must request such a hearing through the court.

Since it may take months to arrange such a hearing, you might want to negotiate with the debtor about entering into a settlement agreement. You might possibly settle for less money, but you could get paid right away.

■ Judgment debtor examination

If you want to collect a debt through the court, you will need enough information about the debtor's finances to decide how the debt can be collected and if it is worth paying the costs of collecting. If you do not have sufficient information about the debtor's finances and cannot obtain the necessary information on your own, you can request a judgment debtor examination.

A judgment debtor examination is a meeting involving you, a judge, and the debtor. Both you and the judge will be able to ask the debtor questions about his or her finances. This includes how much money or property the debtor owns, how the debtor earns it, and where it is kept.

To obtain a judgment debtor examination, you must obtain a certificate of judgment, swear an affidavit, and deliver a notice of the examination to the debtor. Expect to pay a fee for the hearing.

To get a certificate of judgment, you will need to fill out a form from the court. Provide all the information requested, including the date of the judgment, the amount of the judgment, the amount of pre-judgment and post-judgment interest, and the amount of costs. There is a fee for obtaining a certificate.

To complete an affidavit, you need to provide information from your statement of claim. At this stage, the plaintiff is now the creditor and the defendant is now the debtor. Include information such as the date of judgment, the court where the judgment was made, and the amount still owing on the judgment. Once you complete the affidavit, you will have to sign it, and swear that it is true in front of a commissioner of oaths. A staff member at the small claims court office might also be able to do this for you.

Then, you must complete a notice of examination form. The small claims court office staff will give you a time and date for the debtor hearing, which can be several months later. The notice tells the debtor to attend court on a given time and date to provide information about his or her finances.

Finally, you will have to deliver the notice to the debtor. Depending on the amount owing, you may want to pay a private collection company to handle the debtor examination for you.

■ Preparing for the debtor hearing

The hearing is a chance for a creditor to find out about the debtor's finances, because once you know how much money the debtor has, or where the debtor works, you can take steps to collect it. Write out your questions in advance so you will not forget to ask anything important.

Generally, you can ask questions about a debtor's financial situation, including:

- Why the debtor has not paid you
- How much the debtor earns
- How much the debtor owes other people
- How much other people owe the debtor
- Who these people are
- Whether the debtor sold any property since the judgment was made

At the end of the examination, the judge will usually order the debtor to pay off the judgment either in one lump sum payment, or in several payments over time.

If the debtor fails to attend the hearing, normally the judge will reschedule the examination for another day. If the debtor misses more than three times, the judge can decide that the debtor is in contempt of court and can issue a warrant for the debtor's arrest.

If a judge orders someone to pay you money, and the debtor refuses to pay, you can usually collect it through the court where the trial occurred. If the debtor does not live or carry on business in the same area where the small claims court is located, you will need to collect the money in the area where the debtor lives. To do so, you will require a document that confirms the judgment and allows you to transfer it from one court to another.

Referred to as a *certificate of judgment,* it is prepared by the creditor and brought or mailed to the court where the judgment was made so the

court seal can be put on it. If you are unsure about how to obtain a certificate of judgment, the staff at the small claims court office can provide
you with the form and printed information on how to complete it.

◼ Garnishment

If you have a judgment that says you are owed money and the debtor
refuses to pay, a common way to collect is by garnishment. Garnishment
orders are issued by the court. They allow the creditor to collect money
directly from someone who owes the debtor money, such as an employer
who owes wages. This person or business is called the garnishee. Depending on where you live you will need to obtain some type of court execution
order to allow you or the sheriff to act on the order.

To apply for garnishment, you will usually need to do four things:

- Obtain a certificate that confirms the judgment
- Fill out a garnishment notice
- Swear an affidavit
- Deliver the garnishment notice to the debtor and the garnishee

To get a certificate of judgment, you will need to fill out a form from
the court. Provide all the information requested, including the date of
judgment, the amount of the judgment, the amount of pre-judgment
and post-judgment interest, and the amount of costs. There is a fee for
obtaining a certificate.

The garnishment affidavit should include information about the
case, including the name and number of the case, the date that the
judgment was made, the court where the judgment was made, how
much you are owed, and whether any of the debt has been paid. You
will also need to state the name and address of the garnishee and
explain why you think the garnishee owes the debtor money. Once you
fill in the affidavit, you will have to swear that it is true in front of a
commissioner of oaths. A lawyer or a staff member at the court office
can normally do this for you.

When you submit your documents, you will be required to pay a
fee and obtain a notice of garnishment, which must be provided to the
debtor and the garnishee. It instructs the garnishee to pay the court
office. Once the court office receives payment, you will have to request
that it pays you.

A notice of garnishment may be good for 12-24 months, depending
on provincial law. If you can not collect all the money within that time,
you will have to request another notice before the first one expires.

Depending on the amount of money owed, you might want to pay a private collection company to handle the garnishment for you.

Generally there are three different things you can garnish:

1. Wages: Garnishing wages generally allows a creditor to collect money from the debtor's employer, who will in turn deduct the amount from the employee's wages. Under the law, if you garnish someone's wages you can only collect a percentage from each paycheque. Normally the employer will give the money to the court office. You will then have to request that the court office release the money to you.

2. Bank Accounts: Garnishing a bank account allows a creditor to collect money from the debtor's bank. The bank will give the full amount or as much as the debtor has in the bank, to the court office. Then you will have to request that the court office release the money to you.

3. Rent: Garnishing rent is only available if the debtor is a landlord. Garnishing rent allows you to collect rent money directly from a tenant who owes rent to the debtor landlord. The tenant will have to pay rent to the court office until the amount of money owed is paid off. You will have to request that the court office release the money to you.

■ Challenging a Garnishment Order

Sometimes there are mistakes or problems with a garnishment situation. For example, the garnishee may not be paying the creditor, the creditor may be garnishing from the wrong person, or the debtor may claim that the creditor has already been paid in full.

If there is a problem with the garnishment, the debtor, the creditor, or the garnishee can each ask the court to schedule a garnishment hearing, which is usually held in front of a judge. The judge will hear each person's story and decide how to solve the problem.

■ Seizure of a debtor's personal property

If there is a court judgment that states you are owed money and the debtor refuses to pay, you may be able to recover the debt by selling the debtor's personal property. Examples of property that can be sold are cars, government bonds, some equipment, furniture, or jewellery. Note that not all property can be sold to collect a debt: clothing, beds, stoves, refrigerators, or other necessities are usually excluded.

To collect a debt by having a debtor's property sold, you will need to obtain an execution order, known as a writ of seizure and sale, which directs a sheriff to seize and sell the personal belongings of a debtor.

■ Obtaining a Writ of Seizure and Sale

You will need to swear an affidavit stating how much money is still owed and then ask the court to issue the order. Such orders last for a specific period. You will need to request that the Writ of Seizure and Sale be renewed before the first writ expires.

You may also be able to recover the debt by selling or putting a lien on the debtor's land. If you have attempted garnishment or seizure and sale of personal property, such as a vehicle, but were unsuccessful and the debtor owns land, it may be possible to have the land sold so the proceeds of the sale go toward the debt to you.

Most amounts awarded in a small claims court judgment are too small to force a debtor to sell land. If you are unable to sell the debtor's land, you will have the option of putting a lien on it. Putting a lien on the debtor's land is often a good way to get the debtor to pay, because your lien may discourage other lenders from extending the debtor credit. You can normally register the judgment with the provincial land registry so when the debtor sells the land, you must be paid from the proceeds.

To get the debtor's land sold or to put a lien on it, you will need to obtain a writ of seizure and sale of land, which is a form stamped and signed by the clerk of the court. You will need to swear an affidavit stating how much money is still owed and ask that the writ be issued to the sheriff. Describe the land and any buildings on the land, giving the exact address. Attach a copy of a land title search, which is a record of who owns the land. To do a land title search, contact your local land registry office. State whether there are any mortgages on the land. If the debtor lives there with a spouse, give the name of the husband or wife.

■ Costs of enforcing a judgment

Enforcing a judgment will cost you money. Regardless of whether you initiate a debtor examination, attempt garnishment, or use the court or sheriff's office to collect the debt, you will be responsible for paying costs and fees associated with these processes. You are entitled to collect all costs of enforcing the judgment from the debtor. If you do not collect any money from the debtor, you will probably not be able to get money back for the costs of trying to collect.

13. I owe money.
How can I change the payment schedule?

If you were sued and lost, you were probably ordered to pay the other person an amount of money. This person is called a creditor and you are called a debtor. If you are currently paying off a debt to a creditor and something happens that prevents you from making your payments, such as illness or unemployment, you may be able to have your payment plan altered.

If you cannot meet your payment schedule, do not just ignore the debt. Explain your situation to the creditor and ask to change the payment plan. If the creditor agrees, put the new plan in writing and make sure both of you sign it. A signed agreement is evidence that the creditor agreed to the changes.

If the creditor will not change the payment plan, you can ask a judge to do it. You will however, need to make a motion at court to have a judge revise your payment plan.

■ Changing a garnishment order

Through garnishment, the creditor is allowed to collect a percentage of your wages until the debt is paid off. The creditor can collect money directly from your employer, who will deduct the amount from your paycheques. Your employer is not allowed to fire or suspend you because of the garnishment.

Depending on how much you earn and how much you owe, it may take a long time for the debt to be paid off by garnishment. The creditor may agree, however, to accept a lower amount in a lump sum in exchange for ending the garnishment. If the creditor does so, ask for the agreement to be put in writing for both of you to sign so you are protected from any false claims. As well, ask the creditor to obtain a court direction that the garnishment be terminated. This should be given to your employer, for without it your employer cannot stop garnishing your wages.

■ Consolidating judgments

If you owe money to more than one creditor, it may be difficult for you to pay off all your debts. To make things easier, you may want to ask a judge to consolidate the judgments. Consolidating judgments means that all debts are added together and treated as one. This will make your finances less confusing because you will only be making one payment.

To consolidate judgments, you will need to make a motion in court. At the motion you will appear in front of a judge where you can explain whom you owe money to, how much you owe, and how you want to pay it off. The creditors will also be asked to explain their positions.

If the judge agrees with you, the judgments will be consolidated. The judge will order you to make payments to the sheriff by a certain date, or give you a payment plan to follow. The sheriff will then divide your payment among the creditors until all your debts are paid. If you are in violation of the consolidation order for a period of at least 21 days, the consolidation order will end.

If you are unsure about how to have your judgments consolidated, the staff at the court office may be able to provide you with more information.

Pop Quiz! Test Your Understanding

1. A plaintiff is the person:
    a) Who rules on a lawsuit
    b) Who defends a lawsuit
    c) Who starts a lawsuit
    d) Who swears in a witness

2. The time limit for launching a lawsuit for a breach of contract is normally:
    a) Two years from the date the agreement was breached
    b) Six months from the date the agreement was breached
    c) Unlimited
    d) Six years from the date the agreement was breached

3. A pre-trial conference takes place:
    a) After a judgment is rendered
    b) Before the trial starts
    c) During the trial
    d) Before you file the lawsuit

4. A garnishment order allows you to:
    a) Sell the debtor's land
    b) Collect a portion of the debtor's wages
    c) Sell the debtor's personal belongings
    d) None of the above

5. A small claims court judge should be called:
    a) Your Honour
    b) Hey, Buddy
    c) Mr. or Mrs. Justice
    d) My learned colleague

True or false

6. Small claims courts in Canada have a cap on the amount of damages you can claim according to each province.

7. A debtor is the person who owes money.

8. The defendant presents his or her case first.

9. I can only name one person in a lawsuit as a defendant.

10. The rules in small claims court are usually as stringent as superior courts.

Answers

1. c
2. d
3. b
4. b
5. a
6. True
7. True
8. False, the plaintiff usually presents first
9. False, you are entitled to sue everybody who is at fault
10. False, rules in small claims court are normally more flexible

Canada's Small Claims Courts

British Columbia

Robson Square Provincial Courts
Suite 100, 800 Hornby Street
Vancouver, BC V6Z 2C5
Tel: 604-660.8989
http://www.ag.gov.bc.ca/courts

Alberta

Provincial Court, Civil Division
Court House Annex
P.O. Box 1830, Station M
603 - 6 Avenue SW
Calgary, AB T2P 0T3
Tel: 403-297-7217
http://www.albertacourts.ab.ca

Saskatchewan

The Provincial Court, Small Claims Division
Provincial Court Building
Fourth Floor, 1815 Smith Street
Regina, SK S4P 3V7
Tel: 306-787-5375

or

The Provincial Court, Small Claims Division
Provincial Court Building
220 - 19 Street East
Saskatoon, SK S7K 2H6
Ph. 306-933-7053
www.plea.org/freepubs/scc/sccpdf.pdf

Manitoba

Provincial Courts, Small Claims
373 Broadway, 2nd Floor
Winnipeg, MB R3C 0T9
Tel: 204-945.3138

Ontario

Court Operations, Small Claims Court
3rd Flr., 47 Sheppard Avenue East
Toronto, ON M2N 5N1
Tel: 416.326.3554
Fax: 416.325.8912

Québec

Court of Québec
1 rue Notre-Dame E., Room 1.04
Montréal, PQ H2Y 1B6
Tel: 514-393-2304
www.justice.gouv.qc.ca/english/publications/
generale/creance-a.htm

New Brunswick

Small Claims Court
15 Market Square
Saint John, NB E2L 1E8
Tel: 506-658-2560

Nova Scotia

Provincial Courts
Provincial Court House
5250 Spring Garden Rd
Halifax, NS B3J 1E7
Tel: 902-424-8718
www.gov.ns.ca/just/regulations/regs/
sccforms.htm

Prince Edward Island

Small Claims
P.O. Box 2000
Charlottetown, PE C1A 7N8
Tel: 902-368-6002
www.gov.pe.ca/courts/supreme/rules/
annotated/a-rule74.pdf

Newfoundland

Provincial Courts, Small Claims
Box 68, Atlantic Place
St. John's, NF A1C 6C9
Tel: 709-729-1368; 709-729-1389
        709-729-1395

Nunavut

Nunavut Court of Justice
P.O. Box 297
Iqaluit, Nunavut, X0A 0H0
Tel: 867-975-6100
Fax: 867-975-6168

Northwest Territories

Northwest Territories Courts
4905 - 49 Street
2nd Floor, Court House
P.O. Box 550
Yellowknife, NWT X1A 2N4
Tel: 867-920-8760

Yukon

Small Claims Court
P.O Box 2703, J-3
Whitehorse, YK Y1A 2C6
Tel: 867-667-5619
Fax: 867.393.6212

GETTING JUSTICE

Resolving Disputes Without Courts: Mediation & Arbitration

I s it possible to resolve a dispute over money, a broken contract, and even matrimonial property rights without the considerable costs, time, and stress of going through a court trial? It most certainly is and that's why everyone involved in a legal disagreement needs to know about and consider using mediation and arbitration.

What may surprise many North Americans accustomed to our litigious ways is that mediation and arbitration are time-honoured methods of resolving disputes elsewhere in the world. In fact, some cultures frown on going to court and actually prefer the speed, low cost, and privacy of these "alternative dispute resolution" options.

Increasingly, mediation and arbitration clauses are inserted by drafters of legal agreements and contracts to avoid the financial pain, delays, and other suffering that often accompany court litigation. In certain types of disputes, such as marriage breakdowns or insurance claims, mediation and arbitration are becoming increasingly common.

As you will see, mediation involves a neutral third party meeting with each of the people involved in the dispute, as a group and individually, to work out the issues and make non-binding recommendations. Arbitration also involves a neutral intermediary, but typically involves binding rulings.

In Canada, federal and provincial lawmakers have enacted laws in recent years to provide a framework for conducting mediations and arbitrations, as well as the authority for the courts to enforce binding decisions. While mediators and arbitrators are unregulated and should be chosen with care, many participants in alternative dispute resolution sessions tend to be satisfied with the process – considering it more favourably than court.

MEDIATION

1.   What is mediation?

Mediation is a structured and facilitated process to help solve disagreements between people, businesses, and even countries without the need of going to court. It is actually a form of negotiation, chaired by a neutral person called a mediator. The mediator has no personal interest in the outcome.

Often, the mediator is a trained professional who has learned to help people who have disagreements listen to one another, to understand the dispute from the other's perspective, and to help them work out solutions tailored to their needs.

Mediation is an alternative to litigation that is actively encouraged by lawyers, social workers, and judges. Mediators generally have backgrounds as lawyers, social workers, or psychologists.

Research has found that, generally, parties who mediate their own agreements have a greater tendency to actually stick to them. Why? One theory is that the parties have actively participated in the process and feel they had control over their own destinies, as opposed to court orders that involve a judge imposing a decision neither party may be happy with.

Mediation can take place with or without lawyers. Whether someone's lawyer attends is a decision that can be made by the parties and their lawyers together. If the disputing sides are able to resolve their disagreement with the help of the mediator, they can later write up the agreement in the form of a contract with their lawyers.

Even if the parties decide to mediate, each should continue to have a lawyer who will provide independent legal advice to ensure each party is aware of his or her rights and responsibilities along the way. As well, all parties must be aware of the consequences of any agreement reached before signing it.

Unlike a lawyer in litigation, the mediator does not represent one side or the other. A mediator's job does not involve giving legal advice. The mediator's role is to try to bring the parties to agreement. By doing so, the mediator faces many challenges including:

- Creating an objective and safe psychological and emotional environment such that each party feels he or she is being heard without prejudice or judgment
- Allowing each party to speak freely and express his or her position with respect to the various issues
- Identifying the contentious issues
- Getting the parties to go below the surface of the contentious issues in an attempt to have them express the underlying reasons for maintaining their positions
- Helping the parties to understand where the other is "coming from" emotionally and psychologically
- Offering various compromise solutions for positions where the parties seem to be at an impasse
- Encouraging the parties to come up with their own solutions

2. When is mediation appropriate?

The three most common reasons why people choose to mediate instead of going to court are:

1. The parties can reach their own agreement

2. Mediation is much less expensive than court

3. Mediation can occur quickly, while a trial could take years

Mediation is not appropriate when one of the parties has reason not to settle for less than what was initially demanded. This may be the case, for example, when the disagreement is a test case involving an issue that no court has ever decided.

Mediation may also not be appropriate where one of the disputing parties has far greater resources. This may result in the weaker side settling for a bad deal or being unfairly persuaded to settle. In family disputes, moreover, mediation is usually not recommended where there is a history of domestic violence. If, however, these people want mediation, attendance with their lawyers is a good idea.

Mediation is most effective when all involved have carefully considered what is likely to happen if they are not able to settle the dispute. Each side in the dispute should have spoken to a lawyer, at least for a consultation, and asked that lawyer to explain what the possible outcomes could be if a court were to make the decision. Everyone should have a reasonable understanding of what the courts might decide and what it will cost to go to trial before mediation starts.

If you feel your situation would be resolved best through mediation, speak with your lawyer about selecting a mediator.

Generally, the parties split the cost of mediation equally. That means both parties are splitting the cost of one professional, which is considerably less expensive than each side paying for its own lawyer. As well, the mediation process is generally outside the realm of the courtroom, which is another cost saver.

3.   How is a qualified mediator selected?

The mediation profession is not regulated in any province. Mediators do not have to take required courses or pass any tests to practise mediation. As a result, you cannot go to any one source to obtain information about their qualifications.

There are many different courses that a mediator may have attended, including courses offered by local universities. Some educational programs offer diplomas or certificates. For example, a person can receive a Master's degree in law specializing in mediation.

When choosing a mediator, the parties should each consult their lawyers and ask them to suggest specific mediators. Organizations such as Family Mediation Canada certify mediators who have completed the requirements established by that organization.

Once you have found a prospective mediator, ask him or her to provide a résumé, as well as the names of lawyers or others who have referred cases to that person. It is a good idea to ask mediators whether they have ever mediated a dispute like yours, what they charge, and how and where they conduct mediations. It is important that all sides have confidence in and feel comfortable with the mediator.

Remember that mediation only works when both parties consent to participating in the process. Although the choice of mediator is important, choosing the mediator should not become part of the dispute. Agreeing on a mediator should be the first step toward reaching a final agreement.

4.   What happens in the mediation?

For mediation to be useful, everyone must come prepared. This requires each side to make sure that any reports, invoices, financial statements, or other documents they feel are helpful in supporting their position are made available in the mediation. These are the same documents that the parties would exchange if the case went to court. The documents should be put together in a logical order and a copy made for everyone who is attending the mediation. Your lawyer will be able to help you or actually prepare the documents on your behalf.

The best preparation for mediation is to understand what it is that you really want to get out of a settlement and to understand what it is that the other side is likely to want. Mediation is also effective when everyone is in agreement that mediation is a useful process and is appropriate in the circumstances. Mediation is pointless if either side is merely going through the motions and intends to fight in court anyway.

Mediation usually takes place at the office of the mediator or at another neutral place provided by the mediator, such as a meeting room in a hotel.

■ Mediator's role

The mediator usually takes time before the first session to meet with the parties individually. The purpose of the initial meeting is to give the mediator the opportunity to hear the positions of each of the parties and to identify the issues that are in dispute.

The mediator will be clear with each one of the parties that he or she is not representing any person or viewpoint, and will not be taking sides. The mediator will also explain how the process works so that everyone has the same understanding of what will happen when all parties are together.

The mediator may also explain that she or he may meet individually with the parties from time to time during the mediation. The mediator will explain that anything participants tell him or her in private will not be shared unless the individual agrees.

The main role of mediators is to ensure they are neutral participants. The mediator is trained to assist the parties to listen to one another and make sure the participants feel they are being heard. The mediator helps the parties exchange opinions without needless conflict and, hopefully, solve one problem at a time. The mediator will, with the agreement of everyone, give suggestions if he or she feels the discussions are stalled.

■ Lawyer's role

The parties may attend mediation with or without their lawyers. If you are in attendance with a lawyer, you are still one of the primary participants in the mediation. The lawyers' role will be to provide guidance on legal aspects of possible settlement options, not to speak for you or argue your case at length.

■ Your role and that of other parties

Your main role, and the role of other parties, is simply to bargain in good faith. Mediation can be successful if the participants have considered what will likely happen if they do not settle their dispute in mediation. For example, if the parties know the alternative to reaching an agreement in mediation is a lengthy trial with the final decision made by a court, both parties may be more likely to compromise and negotiate to reach an agreement.

■ The mediation agreement

Many mediators require that the disputing parties enter into an agreement regarding the mediation process itself. The parties, for example, must decide if the mediation is confidential. If so, it is called a closed mediation. If the discussions will be set out in a report that the mediator provides to all the parties, it is an open mediation.

The "Mediation Agreement" will also specify what fees will be charged for the mediation and who will pay the fees. Policies for cancellation of meetings will also be included. Most agreements require participants to agree that the mediator may meet with them individually and she or he may provide suggestions to the parties if discussions are stalled. The Mediation Agreement is usually signed at the first meeting, when all the parties are together.

■ Rules

The mediator will usually start the mediation by talking about the ground rules. Often, the mediator will set basic rules, such as allowing only one person to speak at a time and not using the mediation for personal attacks. The mediator will also invite the parties to set their own ground rules.

■ Settlement

If the parties are able to settle their differences in mediation, the mediator will record their agreement in a memorandum, which is sent to all parties to review with their lawyers. The memorandum will state that the agreement is not final until each of the participants has had an opportunity to obtain legal advice.

If the lawyers are at the mediation, they may agree to write up the details of the settlement between themselves and have the parties sign the agreement at the next mediation meeting.

5.   Is the mediation agreement final and binding?

The agreements of the parties in mediation are made final only after each side sees his or her lawyer for legal advice. Once that happens, they can agree that either the lawyers or the mediator will draft the contract that the parties sign to end their dispute. It is important that the contract contain a certificate from the lawyer for each side saying that independent legal advice was given. The contract is then binding. If either side makes an agreement that is in the contract and then does not honour the deal, a court can make decisions based on the contract.

The mediator cannot give legal advice to any party.

■ Who Writes the Final Agreement?

The question of who writes the agreement can vary depending on the mediator. Usually, the practice of mediators is to send a letter to the parties and their lawyers which reports on the agreement that was reached. This report, often called a "Memorandum of Understanding," will state that the agreement is final once each side has discussed it with that side's respective lawyers.

Some mediators will actually write the agreement in the form of a contract. The mediator will do this only if that is what the parties want. Sometimes, the parties want the mediator to prepare the contract because it may save some expense. Yet even if the mediator writes the contract, it is still necessary for everyone to take the agreement to a lawyer to get independent legal advice before signing.

■ Can there be a partial agreement?

In the course of the mediation, everyone can agree to write up an agreement on some of the matters that have been settled. This contract can state, for example, that when all is settled the interim agreement will be part of the final agreement. Or it might state that the interim agreement will only be binding until a certain date.

■ What if the mediator's report is never made into a final contract?

If the parties agreed that the mediation is private or "closed", the mediator cannot be asked later to reveal what happened. In other words, if the Memorandum of Understanding never becomes a final contract, all the mediator can say is there was or was not an agreement. So, if the mediation is private and a party changes his or her mind after receiving independent legal advice, the details of the proposed settlement cannot be disclosed by the mediator if the parties later go to court.

If the mediation is "open" (not private), the mediator can write a report that outlines what happened and what each party proposed, accepted, and rejected. The mediator should not give any opinion as to whether either party was "fair" or "reasonable." In an open mediation the parties can use the report of the mediator, if they decide to go to court.

Arbitration

6. What is arbitration?

The definition of arbitration given by the American Arbitration Association is used in most provinces:

> The submission of a dispute to one or more impartial persons for a final and binding decision. Through contractual provisions, the parties may control the range of issues to be resolved, the scope of the relief to be awarded and many of the procedural aspects of the process.

Arbitrations are usually legally binding. That is, the parties or various sides in a dispute agree beforehand, usually by signing an agreement, to have any dispute settled by an impartial third person and to be bound by that decision. In many cases, even a court cannot interfere with the decision.

That third person is often referred to as a third party neutral, arbitrator, or arbitral tribunal. The parties in an arbitration have wide latitude as to how the process will be conducted. If everyone agrees, they have the option of:

- Introducing elements of informality
- Simplifying the procedure so it is far removed from the requirements of the courtroom setting
- Permitting the matter to be presented through written arguments and documents without the attendance of witnesses

• Ensuring the arbitrator's award or decision is final and there is no right to appeal to the courts in any circumstances

Or, the parties may agree that:

• The arbitration procedure will be more stringent than that found in the court system

• A panel of arbitrators and not just a single arbitrator will hear the case and render a decision

• Either party, as of right, may appeal the arbitrator's or panel's award on any issue of fact or law or mixed fact or law

In many provinces, there is legislation governing such arbitrations. In Ontario, for example, the *Arbitrations Act, 1991* governs private "domestic" or commercial arbitrations, and arbitrations conducted in accordance with other statutes. The names may differ slightly in other provinces, such as British Columbia's *Commercial Arbitration Act*.

7. When is arbitration appropriate?

Simply put, arbitration is appropriate in any case where everyone agrees to submit his or her dispute to arbitration. Most likely these parties have decided they cannot resolve the dispute among themselves, that conciliators or mediators will not assist them, and they need an impartial person to impose a decision that will be binding upon them, whether or not they like the decision rendered.

Why choose arbitration over a lawsuit? In a lawsuit, only one disputant, the plaintiff, can insist that the dispute be decided in the court system. If the dispute is to be decided by way of arbitration, then all disputants must agree to this process. One aggrieved party alone cannot insist that a dispute go to arbitration unless it was previously agreed by all involved that disputes be settled by arbitration, or there is some agreement, after the dispute arose, to have it arbitrated.

In a lawsuit, the disputants cannot select the judge. The disputants are bound by the court's rules of procedure. The court will decide the timetable for the various steps and the date of hearing. In a lawsuit, legislation, common law, and the rules of procedure will determine what decisions of the trial judge can be appealed or reviewed.

Arbitration offers much greater flexibility. The disputants will be able to select their arbitrators and set the date when the dispute will be heard. The parties will determine whether the hearing will be held in private or whether it will be recorded or transcribed. They will often even have considerable latitude in determining the procedure and steps that will be taken leading up to the arbitration hearing and during the arbitration.

Disputants opting for arbitration will also have to select the place where the arbitration will be conducted. It must be noted, however, that disputants selecting arbitration must refer to the applicable arbitration legislation in their jurisdiction to determine the extent to which they can structure and draft their own arbitration process.

Finally, once a dispute is resolved, the decisions or awards of arbitrators can be enforced, just like they can in court judgments.

8.   How is an arbitrator selected?

One of the primary considerations in selecting an arbitrator is deciding if you want someone known primarily for his or her understanding of the law, or someone thoroughly familiar with the subject matter surrounding the dispute. Or, do you want someone who is well-versed in both?

Most arbitrations resemble the procedure, form, and format of a courtroom hearing. There may be lawyers with witnesses testifying and cross-examined. During the hearing, one party or the other may make a motion for interim relief or on a procedural matter. If the arbitration takes on this air, then you may want to have an arbitrator who is familiar with legal procedure, legal precedent, and legal reasoning. A person trained in the law, such as a lawyer, would be well-suited for arbitrating in such circumstances.

Other times, disputes are deeply steeped in a particular area of knowledge, such as construction, accounting, medicine, or technology. Here, disputants may feel better with an arbitrator who has great familiarity with the subject matter. With such an arbitrator, basic terms do not have to be explained and the arbitrator may be better able to relate to the experiences presented. In some instances, it may be possible to find an arbitrator who is versed both in the law and has experience in the subject area in which the dispute has occurred.

Under some provincial statutes, if the number of arbitrators is not specified in the arbitration agreement, then there will be a single arbitrator. If the disputants have difficulty agreeing on the one person who will act as the arbitrator, and if the arbitration agreement does not provide a procedure for the appointment of an arbitrator, then one of the disputants can apply to the court to appoint one.

The opportunity to select arbitrators is one of the attractions in this process of settling disputes. In the court system, disputants cannot "forum shop" or look for judges who tend to rule in favour of certain types of disputants or have the best appreciation of the law that will arise. In the public court system, the judge fulfills the task and dispenses justice on the basis that he or she is impartial, unbiased, has no conflict of interest, and is capable of appreciating the facts and applying the law.

In an arbitration, however, the disputants can select whomever they want. While all disputants must agree on the person selected, the issue as to who is best suited for the task will depend on the circumstances, dispute, kind of arbitration, and ultimately, the agreement between disputants.

9. What happens in the arbitration?

Preparing for an arbitration should be done in much the same way as a lawyer would prepare to take a case to court. While the atmosphere, rules, procedures, and evidence may be somewhat more relaxed in an arbitration, it is best to prepare as if you had to meet the stringent requirements imposed in a court of law.

A disputant or party may wish to consult a lawyer for advice on how to prepare. Often, each party in the dispute hires and is represented by a lawyer during the entire arbitration. Representing yourself is generally not a good idea in an arbitration, but if you do, here are five important matters to consider:

1. Determine, specifically, what the question or issue is that is being brought to the arbitrator. You may need to refer to the arbitration agreement and any related agreements for answers.

2. Who will be called as witnesses during the arbitration? Does your arbitration even permit witnesses to be heard under oath or are witnesses required to swear affidavits that set out their story? Help your witnesses prepare by asking them to give you a brief written account of their perspectives. The witnesses should be told that they will be cross-examined by the other party.

3. If you call witnesses, the other side may also call witnesses. Be prepared to cross-examine the witnesses called by the opposing side.

4. What statute law or legal precedent exists that will help make your point and get the result you desire?

5. Assume you will have an opportunity to make an opening statement at the beginning of the arbitration and closing submissions at the end. Prepare a general outline in advance.

■ Duties and powers of an arbitrator

All provincial arbitration legislation has provisions dealing with the duties and powers of the arbitrator. For example, in most provinces, the statute has provisions dealing with, among other things:

- The duty of an arbitrator
- Disclosure requirements of an arbitrator
- Acceptable challenges to an arbitrator
- Termination of an arbitrator's mandate
- Removal of an arbitrator on application to the court
- Scope of the arbitration agreement or jurisdiction of the arbitrator
- Powers of the arbitrator to order the detention, preservation, or inspection of property or documents of the disputants, and to grant certain injunctive and other related forms of relief

In general, an arbitrator or arbitral tribunal must decide a dispute in accordance with the law, including the law of equity (that is, fairness), and can order specific performance ("do what you promised to do"), injunctions, and other equitable remedies. Legislation may allow this to be varied so the tribunal can have no "limits."

In some jurisdictions, for example, the parties could decide to empower the arbitrator to make a decision on any basis whatsoever or to decide based on facts and evidence learned by the arbitrator.

For instance, Alberta's *Arbitration Act* states that the arbitral tribunal "may, if the parties consent, use mediation, conciliation, or similar techniques" and can resume their roles as arbitrators without disqualification. There is no statutory prohibition, however, against the parties agreeing, for example, to conduct a so-called Mediation-Arbitration. In contrast, arbitrators in Ontario cannot conduct any part of the arbitration as a mediation or conciliation process so as to ensure impartiality.

The American Arbitration Association defines a Mediation-Arbitration as:

> A process that employs a neutral, selected to serve as both mediator and arbitrator in a dispute. Mediation/Arbitration combines the voluntary techniques of persuasion and discussion, as in mediation, with an arbitrator's authority to issue a final and binding decision.

In most cases, the arbitrator conducting an arbitration:

- Determines the time, date and place of arbitration
- Determines the meeting place for hearing witnesses, experts, or parties, or inspecting documents or property

- May require that the parties submit their statements within a specified period, or may permit the parties to submit their statements orally
- May conduct the arbitration on the basis of documents
- May appoint an expert to report on specific issues
- May issue a notice requiring a person to attend and give evidence at the arbitration
- May, in deciding the dispute, take into account any applicable usages of trade
- May award costs of an arbitration, which include the parties' legal expenses and arbitration expenses
- May award prejudgment and post judgment interest.

An arbitrator or arbitral tribunal is also usually empowered to award costs of the arbitration. Subject to legislation and any arbitration agreement between the parties, the decision of an arbitrator may be appealed to a court of law. In some cases, the parties may opt out of all of the appeal provisions set out in the applicable statute.

10. Is the arbitrator's decision final and binding?

Unlike a mediator, the arbitrator makes a decision as to who is right or wrong and what relief will be awarded to the aggrieved party. Although a decision or the award of an arbitrator is usually binding and enforceable, just as a court order, it is important to consult the appropriate legislation. Three sources of legislation that may apply are:

1. Provincial domestic arbitration legislation
2. Provincial international commercial arbitration legislation
3. Federal commercial arbitration legislation

Sometimes, however, the parties may wish to go through a process similar to an arbitration but not want the decision of the arbitrator to be final and binding. In such cases, the goal is to have the neutral third party make a non-binding assessment of each party's respective rights and an evaluation of the compensation.

It is probably best to refer to such cases as an "evaluation" rather than an arbitration, and to refer to the individual making the evaluation as a neutral third party rather than an arbitrator. Avoiding the words "arbitration" and "arbitrator" will help you avoid misunderstanding or being drawn inadvertently into some legislative arbitration framework.

In the case of an evaluation, the parties usually present written material and documents to the neutral "evaluator" for his or her review. The evaluation is non-binding and is usually used to assist parties in reaching a settlement.

Web Resources	
ADR Atlantic Institute	www.adratlantic.ca
ADR Institute of Canada, Inc.	www.adrcanada.ca
ADR Institute of Ontario, Inc.	www.adrontario.ca
ADR Institute of Saskatchewan Inc.	www.adrsaskatchewan.ca
Alberta Arbitration & Mediation Society	www.aams.ab.ca
American Arbitration Association	www.adr.org
Arbitration & Mediation Institute of Manitoba Inc.	www.amim.mb.ca
British Columbia Arbitration & Mediation Institute	www.amibc.org
British Columbia International Commercial Arbitration Centre (BCICAC)	www.bcicac.com
Family Mediation Canada	www.fmc.ca
ICC International Chamber of Commerce, International Court of Arbitration	www.iccwbo.org
Institut de médiation et d'arbitrage du Québec	www.imaq.org
JAMS/Endispute	www.jams-endispute.com
The Network Interaction for Conflict Resolution	www.nicr.ca

Section Two
RELATIONSHIPS

RELATIONSHIPS

COUPLES

Most of the time, even when marriage and parenthood are less than blissful, families manage to keep their personal problems out of the hands of lawyers and judges. When things do go wrong, however, a wide variety of laws and legal authorities can become involved. During these times of great stress and heartache, it is critical to be aware of your rights and responsibilities.

In Canada, the federal and provincial governments split jurisdiction in many areas of family law. The federal government, for example, has the constitutional authority to govern the general laws of divorce in Canada and works with provincial governments on child and spousal support, and custody issues. The provinces, however, have exclusive jurisdiction over division of marital property, adoption, and child welfare.

Whether the topic is child support or same-sex marriages, family law "rules" in each province and territory are constantly changing. This is one area of law where advice from a lawyer experienced in family law is essential.

Getting Married

1. What happens when an engagement is broken?

Nothing, in most provinces. If someone has breached his or her promise to marry, only Alberta still specifically allows a lawsuit to be launched. B.C., Manitoba, and Ontario specifically prohibit these types of court actions.

A common legal question is what happens to the engagement ring? The general rule is that whoever ended the engagement forfeits the ring. If the ring's giver breaks it off, the receiver gets to keep the ring. If the recipient, however, breaks the deal, the ring has to be returned.

2. What is required by law to get married?

To be legally married, you and your future spouse must follow the rules and procedures established by the provincial government where you plan to marry.

You must have reached the age of majority in that province, or have the written consent of a parent, guardian, or the court to marry if younger (see the table below). Exceptions are often made for girls who are pregnant or are already mothers. Generally, marriages of those below the age of 16 are voidable — that is, valid until someone challenges them in court and points out the flaw.

Blood tests and medical exams are not required in Canada. Most provinces do not require that you meet any residency requirements, but some may require that you wait anywhere from 24 hours to 15 days between getting a marriage licence and actually getting married.

Both people must be mentally competent. Those under the influence of liquor or drugs will not be granted a licence to marry or have their marriage solemnized.

Neither person can be already married. If you are divorced or widowed, you must provide proof in the form of a divorce or death certificate.

You and the person you are marrying cannot be closely related.

In every province except Québec, you must obtain a marriage licence first. This can be done by visiting your local city hall, civic centre or, sometimes, a church official. You and the person you are marrying will have to show your passports, birth certificates, or citizenship cards, then fill out an application form and pay a small fee. If you or your future spouse have been previously divorced, you must each provide proof of divorce, usually in the form of a *Certificate of Divorce* obtainable from the court where the proceedings took place.

A marriage licence will usually be prepared and given to you while you wait. In some provinces, the marriage licence will be sent to the official conducting the ceremony.

Before conducting a marriage ceremony in Québec, an "officiant," such as a minister or civil official, must "publish the bans" — that is, post a notice for 20 days before the date fixed for the marriage at the place where the marriage is to be held. In theory, any interested party can oppose the marriage for good reasons.

Then, *after* the wedding ceremony, you file a "Declaration of Marriage" and apply for a Marriage Certificate. The Declaration establishes the legality of the marriage and enables the spouses to obtain a Certificate of Marriage. You and your witnesses sign the Declaration at the end of the wedding ceremony and send it to the Registrar of Civil Status for inscription in the register of civil status of Québec. The Marriage Certificate sets out the surnames and given names of the spouses, the date and place of the marriage, the registration number, and the date of issuance. The Marriage Certificate proves that the marriage is legal and ensures the civil rights of spouses, children, and heirs.

Publication of "banns" or "bans" is also a permitted substitute for a marriage licence in Manitoba and Ontario.

Important Ages

Province	Age of Majority & Marriage Without Without Consent	Minimum Age for Marriage with Parental Consent	Age Where Consent of Child Required For Adoption
Alberta	18	16	12
British Columbia	19	16	12
Manitoba	18	16	12
New Brunswick	19	12 for girls; 14 for boys	12
Newfoundland & Labrador	19	16	12
Nova Scotia	19	16	12
Ontario	18	16	7
Prince Edward Island	18	16	12
Québec	18	16	10
Saskatchewan	18	16	12
Northwest Territories	19	15	12
Nunavut	19	15	12
Yukon	19	15	12

3. Who can perform a legal marriage ceremony?

Marriage licences in most provinces expire after three months, so the ceremony must be held within this time. In Newfoundland & Labrador, though, the licence is valid for only 30-60 days, depending on what you request.

To be legally valid, someone who is registered to perform marriages must conduct the marriage ceremonies. This includes most ministers, priests, and rabbis, as well as judges and justices of the peace. Marriage ceremonies presided over by judges and justices of the peace are usually conducted in judicial chambers. There must also be two people over the age of majority to witness the ceremony.

4. What is the legal significance of marriage?

Before entering into marriage, you should be aware of the many rights and obligations arising from marriage that will affect you, your spouse, and your children in the event of a marriage breakdown.

On separation, your property rights and the distribution of your joint assets will be governed by your province's "Family Law" or "Marital Property" Acts. In all provinces, these laws attempt to equalize the net family property of the spouses. In other words, the assets acquired since your marriage will be divided evenly after settling the marital debts, or they will be subject to other arrangements made before or after the marriage as set forth in a so-called "domestic" or "marriage" contract between the parties.

There may also be rights and obligations for financial support for the spouses and their children after a marriage break-up. If you want to change any of the provisions or rights established by the laws of your province, you should consider entering into a marriage contract. If you need additional information about the legal consequences of entering into a marriage, consult a lawyer.

5.   What are domestic or marriage contracts?

If spouses separate and divorce without a marriage contract, their property will normally be allocated according to the laws of their province of residence. The laws are complex but, in general, they require an equalization of the net family property. This equalization is ordinarily calculated at the date of separation.

To do this, the spouses calculate the increase in their net worth since marriage and then equalize the difference. There is an exemption for the "value" of property calculated at the date of marriage in respect to most property. Essentially, the property owned by each spouse at the date of marriage is given a dollar value (based on its worth at the date of marriage). The dollar value at the date of marriage is then subtracted from the value of each spouse's total property at the date of separation.

Before marriage or separation, however, couples can enter into a marriage contract to decide for themselves how property will be affected. A marriage contract can also deal with other matters such as spousal support.

A marriage contract sets out what will happen financially if a couple separates. It allows couples to set their own terms, and prevents them from being bound by the terms of the province's marital property laws. There are some restrictions on the right to contract in family matters, however. For the most part, these restrictions arise in respect of children of the marriage and possession of the matrimonial residence.

■ Why enter into a marriage contract?

There are three reasons why a couple may decide to have a marriage contract. First, a spouse who is substantially wealthy or has an asset base that is increasing in value may wish to avoid having to account for any increase in wealth on marriage breakdown. When a person has a great deal of money, or expects to receive a lot of money in the future, he or she may want to make sure that any increase in net worth will not be equalized. Specific assets can also be protected, such as pensions or real estate. Such assets can also be kept intact if the marriage fails.

Second, a marriage contract can be used to establish arrangements — in advance — for financial support if the relationship ends. For example, one spouse may want to make sure that the other spouse will provide adequate spousal support or child support if the relationship ends. Alternatively, the other spouse may wish to limit the amount and duration of any support paid. Income tax obligations may be a concern that can be addressed in respect of spousal support. Either way, spouses can come to an agreement about support while they are still on friendly terms.

Third, a marriage contract can be used to make arrangements for dividing property and money earned during the marriage, or to make special arrangements about particular matters such as partnerships or corporations in which one or both may have an interest. Again, this allows couples to decide on a division of property different from that provided by the law, and to reach an agreement while they are on good terms.

■ Limits of marriage contracts

Although spouses can make any kind of financial arrangements in a marriage contract, a marriage contract cannot make any rules about who will get custody of children or which spouse will have access to children. Also, a marriage contract cannot put any limits on the rights of a spouse to live in the matrimonial home.

■ Requirements for legally binding marriage contracts

To create a legally binding marriage contract, both spouses must be completely open and honest about their financial situation. This requires a detailed disclosure of significant assets and liabilities. The contract must be in writing and signed by each party in the presence of a witness. The contract must be entered into voluntarily and not under any duress. Each party must also understand the contract.

It is in the interest of both parties that each receives independent legal advice. Some aspects of the contract may eventually be subjected to judicial review and, in certain areas, particularly where the rights of children are involved, the terms of the contract can be overridden.

While it is the policy of the courts to uphold marriage contracts, practically speaking, attempts to create one-sided contracts should be avoided. Unfair contracts may tend to create resentments that can contribute to marriage breakdown. Unfair contracts also encourage litigation on marriage breakdown, which is the very thing they are supposed to deter. Although a marriage contract becomes legally binding once signed, the parties can change the terms by further agreement at any time.

A marriage contract is an important legal document so you must get independent legal advice before you enter into one. A lawyer can tell you what rights you normally have under the law and what rights you may be giving up by signing a marriage contract.

Note that your contract will be stronger if you and your spouse each consult a different lawyer before signing it. This will prevent spouses from later saying they did not understand what they were agreeing to in the contract.

A lawyer can also ensure that the contract is clear and complete. While the failure of a marriage is rarely a pleasant experience, a clear and fair marriage contract may make the separation much easier. Since most consequences of a marriage contract will only come into play if there is marriage breakdown, once you and your future spouse have signed a marriage contract, put it away and get on with your marriage.

6. What is involved in getting a marriage annulled?

An annulment is a declaration by the court that two spouses were never legally married. It allows some spouses to end a marriage without divorce.

Although many people would prefer annulment to divorce, the grounds for annulment are very specific. In fact, very few marriages are ever annulled by the courts. Even if you do seek and obtain an annulment, you should be aware that there might still be obligations for support and division of property under your provincial family laws.

■ Grounds for annulment

A marriage under the federal *Divorce Act* can be annulled for a number of reasons, which usually relate to a legal defect in the marriage ceremony or a disability of one of the spouses. For example, spouses can seek an annulment if one spouse:

- Was already married to someone else at the time of the marriage ceremony
- Was under the age of 18 or 19 at the time of the marriage ceremony and married without parental permission
- Lacked the mental capacity to understand the basic meaning of marriage

A marriage can also be annulled if one spouse was unable, or refused to consummate the marriage; if the marriage was entered into under duress, fear, or fraud; or if the spouses were too closely related to each other by blood or marriage.

Although there is no time limitation on when spouses can obtain an annulment in most provinces, annulments are most often used to end new marriages. In Québec, for instance, you cannot annul a marriage three years after the fact.

Note that religious annulments are not recognized by civic or judicial authorities. If you want to find out whether a marriage can be annulled, or if you need advice about a particular situation, a lawyer will be able to provide additional information and specific legal advice.

7. Do I have to change my name after marriage?

Upon marriage, both spouses may continue to use their own surnames — the law does not automatically give both spouses a single last name. In every province, either person in a marriage must apply for a change of surname, usually upon proof of one year's residence there.

Many people do change their names when they get married, or change the last names of their children when entering another marriage. Some people also change their names for personal or professional reasons. The steps required to change your name are different in each province and depend on the reason, whether the change is due to a shift in marital status or something else altogether.

In most cases, you make the change by submitting a form to your provincial government. The consent of children over 12 will likely be needed. There may also be special rules for women who assume a married name. A fee may also be involved.

■ How to change your name upon marriage or divorce

Upon marriage or divorce, both men and women have the right to change their last names. When you get married, you can change your name to your spouse's or to a combination or hyphenation of both. In some provinces, however, there may be a limit on the number of hyphenated surnames (for instance, Smith-Lee-Jones may not be allowed). Also, you can change your name back to its original when you get divorced.

Both men and women can apply to have their last names legally changed by changing the names on their birth certificates and having the government issue a change of name certificate. To do this, you need to complete a change of name application form, available by calling your province. There is usually a fee to change your name after a divorce.

Women in most provinces have the option of assuming their spouses' name without changing their birth certificates. To do this, you can automatically assume your married name and use your marriage certificate as proof of marriage, and change of name, when applying to update your business and government records. Your birth certificate will not change, which means that after a divorce, you may use it as proof if you re-assume your original name. Some places may also require proof of divorce to change their records.

SEPARATION & DIVORCE

8. What is "separation"?

A separation is recognized in law as soon as two spouses are living separately and apart under circumstances where there is no reasonable prospect that they will reconcile. This usually means one spouse has moved out of the family home.

Even if the spouses are still in the same residence, in some circumstances they could be legally separated if they are considered to be living "separate and apart" and have ceased to engage in any conjugal relationship. If possible, seek legal advice before separating. The things you do at the time of separation can have a significant impact on who gets custody of the children, possession of the family home, and division of property.

■ What happens when you separate?

Once spouses begin to live separately, important legal rights and obligations arise that affect finances, property, and children. Separation is the first step in what can be a complex and sometimes costly sequence of events.

Once a couple separates, five basic rights arise:

1. You can apply to equalize net family property or, on an interim basis, apply to obtain possession of property or to preserve property

2. You can apply for financial support for yourself and your children

3. You can apply for custody of the children

4. You can apply for visitation rights

5. You can apply to live in the family home without your spouse even if you are not the one who owns it. Obtaining an order that would require your spouse to live somewhere else is called "an order for exclusive possession" and is mainly used for spouses who are experiencing abusive situations

■ What property can you take upon separation?

When a married couple separates, the spouses will need to know what they are each entitled to. Ordinarily, separating couples will agree on the personal property to which each is entitled. In the absence of agreement, each spouse is entitled to take anything that he or she owned before marriage.

It is important to remember that, ordinarily, your provincial family legislation does not change rights of ownership in respect of either personal property or any other asset. For example, bank accounts owned by each spouse will remain his or her separate property. Ordinarily, the proceeds of a joint bank account will be divided.

Usually when spouses separate they will sell or otherwise dispose of their matrimonial home. Generally speaking, the equity in the home at the time of separation is treated as belonging to both spouses regardless of whose name is on the title. For example, if the house is registered in the name of the husband alone, the equity in the home will still belong to both spouses.

The status of the matrimonial home differs according to province. For example, Ontario's family law legislation gives spouses an equal right to possession of the couple's matrimonial home, even though it may be owned by only one of them. The spouse of the owner of the matrimonial home must be a party to any transaction involving the home (such as a sale or mortgage) and must execute both the agreement and the transfer or mortgage, in question.

Family law legislation in British Columbia also provides certain protections to a spouse who may have an unregistered interest in land. Western provinces have "homestead" laws that prohibit the sale of the family home without the consent of the wife. In Alberta and Manitoba, the law prohibits either husband or wife from disposing of a homestead without consent of the non-titled spouse. A disposition includes, among others, a transfer, a mortgage and a lease over three years.

All this does not require the owning spouse to sell the home and, indeed, any post-separation increase belongs to the owning spouse who also assumes the risk of any decline in value.

There are occasions when one spouse may leave the matrimonial home while the other remains. Under certain circumstances the court can order that the contents of the home remain in the home until the matrimonial affairs have been settled. In the absence of a court order, it is not unusual for a parent departing with a child to take the possessions necessary to look after the child. If you are about to separate or have recently separated, a lawyer can help you understand your legal rights and ensure your interests are protected.

■ What is a separation agreement?

A separation agreement is a written agreement between two spouses who have separated or are about to separate. The agreement generally establishes the rights for each spouse, including who lives in the family home, how property will be divided, who will pay the family debts, who makes child and spousal support payments, who has custody of children, and what kinds of visiting rights the other parent will have.

Writing a separation agreement is completely voluntary and is not required under the law to establish a legal separation. With or without an agreement, a separation is legal as soon as two spouses are living separately and at least one spouse does not intend to move back in together.

Still, a separation agreement resolves most of the issues of separating and makes the separation easier. When possible, spouses who separate should try to reach an agreement and formalize it in a separation agreement as soon as possible. Although reaching an agreement shortly after separation helps spouses get on with their lives, separation agreements can be made before or after a formal divorce.

Unlike restrictions on marriage contracts, parties to a separation agreement can agree on possession of the matrimonial home and on custody of children and rights of access.

■ Requirements for a legally binding separation agreement

To create a legally binding separation agreement both spouses must be completely open and honest about their financial situations. This requires a detailed disclosure of their significant assets and liabilities. The agreement must be in writing and signed by each party in the presence of a witness. The agreement must be entered into voluntarily and not under any duress. Each party must understand the agreement.

It is in the interest of both parties that each receives independent legal advice. Some aspects of the agreement may eventually be open to review by a judge and in certain areas, particularly where the rights of children are involved, the terms of the agreement can be overridden.

While it is the policy of the courts to uphold separation agreements, practically speaking, one-sided agreements should be avoided. Unfair agreements may create resentments that lead to court proceedings. Unfair agreements also encourage litigation on marriage breakdown, which is the very thing they are supposed to deter. Although a separation agreement becomes legally binding once it is signed, the parties can vary the terms by further agreement at any time.

■ Enforcing a separation agreement

By entering into a separation agreement, each spouse will have the same rights and obligations as if a court ordered the terms of the separation agreement. If you are concerned your spouse is not going to fulfill some of the obligations in the agreement, file it with your provincial government. This will help enforce any schedule of payments under it. Responsibility for enforcing registered agreements in most provinces comes under the justice or attorney general's ministry or department. All these jurisdictions have a so-called Maintenance Enforcement Program.

In Ontario, the Family Responsibility Office can help enforce your agreement without cost to you under the *Family Responsibility and Support Arrears Enforcement Act*. This office is funded by the government and has significant powers to enforce support payments. You can also file an agreement with the family law court in your province. Most other provinces have similar agencies. For example, in British Columbia, it is called the Family Maintenance Enforcement Program. In New Brunswick, it is the Family Support Orders Service. In Nova Scotia it is the Director of Maintenance Enforcement.

■ Preparing a separation agreement

Although it is possible for spouses to prepare their own separation agreement, most are prepared and negotiated by lawyers. The rights and obligations in separation agreements are very important so each spouse should be certain of his or her legal rights before signing. If you are not each represented by a different lawyer when an agreement is prepared, you should at least consult with your own lawyer before signing.

9.   My lawyer recommends mediation. What is it?

As discussed in Section 1, mediation is an alternative to litigation that involves the intervention of a third party professional who acts as a facilitator to help parties reach their own agreement.

Mediation can be particularly useful in separations and divorces because mediators work to reduce the litigiousness of disagreements. As a neutral third party, the mediator's role is to try to bring both parties to an agreement.

Mediation can also be financially advantageous. Generally, the parties split the cost of mediation 50-50, meaning both spouses are splitting the cost of one professional. This is considerably less expensive than each party having to pay for his or her own lawyer.

For more information on mediation, please see the discussion in Section 1.

■ Do I still need a lawyer if I mediate?

Even if you and your spouse decide to mediate, you should each continue to have your own lawyer. The lawyers will provide ongoing independent legal advice to ensure that both of you are aware of your respective rights and responsibilities along the way. As well, you must be aware of the legal consequences of any agreement you come to, and each lawyer must review the agreement and discuss it with the relevant party before signing. It is not the mediator's role to give legal advice, so each party must have his or her own lawyer for that purpose.

Mediation is a viable, affordable, effective, and often preferable alternative to litigation. Consider mediation if you think you and your spouse are capable of reaching an agreement with the help of a third party professional. Settling your differences through mediation can help you save time and money.

10. How can I get a divorce?

To get a divorce under Canadian law you no longer have to prove that one spouse did something wrong. Most divorces are granted on the basis of "marriage breakdown."

This is proven simply by showing that you and your spouse have lived "separate and apart" for one year. You do not, however, have to wait one year after separation before seeking a divorce. You can start proceedings immediately. The only limitation is that the court cannot grant a divorce judgment until spouses have been separated for a year.

Where divorce is sought on the grounds of physical or mental cruelty that makes the continuation of marriage intolerable, or upon the grounds of adultery, the divorce judgment can be granted within the year of breakup. It is usually easier, less expensive, and less painful, though, to wait a year and then divorce on the grounds of "marriage breakdown."

Before commencing a divorce petition, the court requires that one of the parties has to have been resident in the province for at least one year.

Also, it is not necessary for both spouses to apply for a divorce: a divorce can be granted when just one spouse seeks it.

■ What if we are not apart for a full year?

The law allows a trial reconciliation period during the one-year separation. If you and your spouse decide to give your marriage another try at any point during the one-year separation period, you can move back in, and not affect your application for divorce, if you live together for one period not exceeding 90 days. If the attempted reconciliation does not work out, you will still be eligible for a divorce one year after your original separation date.

Although the court will generally grant you and your spouse a divorce if you show that your marriage has broken down, the judge will also want to make sure you have made suitable arrangements for your children. Consult with a lawyer if you and your spouse are considering a divorce.

■ The divorce process

Once you have decided to get a divorce, you must follow a number of procedures for the courts to actually grant it, including filling out forms, filing documents with the court, and possibly going before a judge to resolve contested issues between you and your spouse. In most cases, these procedures will be handled by your lawyer and explained to you in more detail. The following information should give you a general overview of the procedure.

■ The divorce petition

A divorce generally begins with a petition. The petition is a document that contains information about you and your spouse, including the grounds for divorce and whether you and your spouse actually have a marriage contract. It may also include claims under provincial family legislation relating to questions of property, including equalization of net family property, custody of children, and who will live in the family home. It may also include claims for spousal and child support.

Your divorce petition is the document that the judge eventually hears and considers before making a formal order giving you and your spouse a divorce. A divorce petition can be filled out and filed by one or both spouses. Spouses will normally only file together if they agree on how to split family property, who gets custody of the children, and how much child and spousal support will be paid.

■ Responding to a divorce petition

If your spouse files for divorce, you will be served with a divorce petition. In most cases you will only be allowed 20 days to file a response with the court. Most people consult a lawyer for advice and assistance so they can respond appropriately. If you do not respond within the 20-day period there can be serious consequences. The court may proceed with the divorce without you and give your spouse everything he or she asked for in the petition.

■ Uncontested divorces

If you and your spouse both want a divorce, and you agree on things such as how property will be divided, who will have custody of children, and any support payments, the divorce procedure is relatively simple. In most cases you will not have to go to court to get the divorce.

After filing all your documents with the court you are simply required to wait until a judge has signed your divorce papers and returned them to you in the mail. Under the federal *Divorce Act,* special provisions have been made for the support of children. Subject to certain complexities, the Federal Child Support Guidelines set out tables showing the amount of support that must be paid for each child depending on who has custody and the income of the non-custodial parent. Before granting a divorce, the judge must first be satisfied there has been compliance with the Guidelines.

■ Contested divorces

If there are things you and your spouse cannot agree on, you may eventually have to go to court to resolve these issues and to get a divorce. In some cases there can be many court hearings, called "motions," to resolve temporary issues about custody of children, child support, and spousal support. There may also be a trial to make a final decision on any issues that have not been agreed on.

■ When is a divorce final?

Once a judge has signed your divorce papers, there is a one-month waiting period before your divorce becomes final. This waiting period gives you and your spouse a chance to cancel the divorce if you decide to get back together.

Getting a divorce can be a confusing and complicated process. Even if you and your spouse both want a divorce, and you agree on property, child custody, and support, you should consult a lawyer to make sure you both know your legal rights. If you and your spouse do not agree on how to divide property, how much support needs to be paid, or who will have custody of your children, a lawyer will be able to provide you with specific legal advice and help you take the proper steps to protect your rights.

■ Foreign divorces

A foreign divorce will be recognized in Canada if you file an application or petition with a Canadian court to have the foreign divorce judgment declared "executory" or enforceable in this country. Nevertheless, you will likely need a lawyer's help.

If the judgment was properly obtained in accordance with the laws of the foreign jurisdiction and your ex-spouse was aware of the process, the petition will likely be granted.

■ Do I need a lawyer to get a divorce?

Couples who are both seeking a divorce and completely agree on everything, including how to divide family property, who will have custody of the children, and how much child and spousal support will be paid, might be able to complete a divorce without a lawyer.

In most provinces, there are agents or non-lawyer paralegals that can help complete the documents, if necessary. Standard forms and samples can also be obtained at some bookstores.

Although it may be possible to complete your divorce without a lawyer, both spouses should make sure they fully understand their rights and obligations before agreeing to the terms of a divorce. At a minimum, each spouse should get independent advice from a lawyer before finalizing an agreement or signing any documents.

11. In a divorce, how are assets, property, and debt divided?

Contrary to what many people might think, the court does not just divide property in half when married spouses divorce. If you and your spouse do not have a marriage contract and cannot agree on how property will be divided, your property will be handled according to the detailed rules and calculations under your provincial family or marital property legislation.

■ By agreement between spouses

The easiest way to settle property issues is by reaching an agreement. If you and your spouse can reach an agreement on how to divide property to your mutual satisfaction, you do not need to follow the rules set out in your provincial family or marital property legislation. Most couples who are separating, however, use the legislation as a guideline. An agreement on how to allocate property can be reached directly between the spouses who are separating, through their lawyers, or through the assistance of a mediator who stands between the parties and helps them reach a deal. Spouses negotiating their own allocation of property should each get their own legal advice to make sure they know what they are entitled to under the laws of their province, and to make sure the agreement will be legally binding.

Even if a mediator is used, the parties should each have independent legal advice to make sure they are comfortable with the deal reached through mediation. By reaching an agreement first, you can avoid the financial and emotional costs of a trial or other court hearings.

■ Division under family or marital property laws

If you and your spouse do not reach your own agreement, your property rights will be determined according to the rules set out in your provincial family or marital property legislation. Although there are specific pieces of property that may belong to each spouse, it is actually the value of all the property you and your spouse own, minus the value of all property owned by each on the date of marriage, that is "divided."

The courts will not normally decide who gets each specific item. This is usually decided by original ownership. Generally speaking, the value of all property is equalized between the spouses by a cash payment. This can include the transfer of land, cars and personal possessions, money in the bank, business interests, investments, and pensions.

In general, the adjustment of property claims under your provincial family or marital property legislation is intended to let each spouse keep the value of what he or she brought into the marriage, plus half the value of property acquired, or that increased in value, during the marriage. Still, there are special rules about some types of property, especially the "matrimonial home" or principal residence, as you will see below.

■ Calculating the value of family property and equalization payments

These six steps will give you a basic understanding of how assets are dealt with under your provincial family or marital property legislation. The process is fairly complicated and requires legal advice.

1. List your property and its value as of the separation date

The first step in determining property rights under your provincial family or marital property legislation is for each spouse to make a list of his or her assets. This may include personal property, real estate, bank accounts, shares in corporations, and pensions including Registered Retirement Savings Plans (RRSPs). Property belonging to a spouse must also be valued as of the *date of separation*, which ordinarily is the date that the spouses ceased living together.

The value of most assets can be easily determined by reference to current fair market value. There are some assets, however, where the determination of value can be quite complex, such as pensions or shares in companies that are not traded publicly. You may very well require the assistance of an accountant as well as a lawyer. If you and your spouse own property together, you count half of the value of the property as your own.

Not all property is taken into consideration. For example, money or assets received after marriage as an inheritance or a gift from a person other than your spouse is exempt under most circumstances. Money received under life insurance policies or as compensation for personal injuries is also exempt. Consult a lawyer for details in any particular case, as there are limitations on exemptions. For example, money from these sources may lose exemption if it has been used to purchase a matrimonial home or to pay down a mortgage on a matrimonial home.

2. Subtract your total debt as of the separation date

The next step is to add up all your debts on the date of separation. If you and your spouse have debts together, count half the debts as yours. Then subtract your total debt from the total value of things you owned on the date of separation. This will give you a total value of your property as of the day you and your spouse separated.

3. Calculate the value of your property less debts as of the date married

Next, make a list of everything you owned and all your debts on the day you and your spouse married. Add up the value of everything you owned at the date of marriage. Remember that "value" means value as of the date of marriage — and not current value. Subtract the value of all your debts on the day you were married. This will give you a total marriage date value of your property.

4. Subtract the value of pre-marital assets

You are now in a position to determine your "net family property." In summary, you total the value of your property at the date of separation. Then calculate the value of your property less debts existing at the date you married. Then deduct any debts on the day you and your spouse separated. The result is your net family property. It cannot be less than zero. In other words, it cannot be a negative number.

5. Subtract any compensation for personal injury, inheritances, and proceeds of life insurance

In determining your net family property you are entitled to deduct the value of any inheritances or gifts from people other than your spouse that you personally received while you and your spouse were married, any money you may have received from court as compensation for personal injury; and any proceeds from a life insurance policy. There are a few other things you may be able to subtract from your total, but there are exceptions, so you should consult a lawyer for more information.

6. Deduct the lower "net family property" from the higher, and divide by two

You and your spouse will each have your own total net family property. The court will compare these two totals and require the spouse who has the higher total to pay the spouse with the lower total half the difference.

For example, if a wife has a net family property of $20,000 and the husband has a net family property of $30,000, the difference is $10,000. Half of $10,000 is $5,000, so the husband would have to pay the wife $5,000.

■ Equalization payments

The money that the spouse with the higher total has to pay the spouse with the lower total is called an "equalization payment." The purpose of an equalization payment is to put both spouses in an equal position. The result is that both spouses end up owning the same total value of property.

There can be many issues about the value and ownership of a spouse's assets. There may even be issues about the equalization payment. In some circumstances, such as a marriage of less than five years duration, the court can order a lesser payment to prevent an unconscionable result. To protect your rights, spouses who are separating should each consult a lawyer for specific advice.

■ The "matrimonial home"

The "matrimonial home" is the legal term used to describe the family home in which you and your spouse were living at the time of separation. Unless spouses have a marriage contract setting out what happens to the matrimonial home, the special rules set out in your provincial family or marital property legislation will apply. These special rules are especially important if one spouse owned the home before the marriage and it continues to be a matrimonial home at the time of separation.

For example, in Newfoundland and Labrador, and New Brunswick, a matrimonial home is owned by both spouses equally, no matter whose name is on the title. In other provinces, if the title to the home is in only one name, the legislation helps decide who owns the house or how its value will be split.

If you and your spouse own more than one home, each home may be considered a "matrimonial home." A second home can include a cottage or chalet or simply another home in another place. If you and your spouse regularly use more than one home together, then each can be considered a matrimonial home.

■ Special rules for the matrimonial home

Regardless of actual ownership, each spouse is generally regarded as having an equal interest in the matrimonial home.

For example, Ontario's family law legislation gives spouses an equal right to possession of the couple's matrimonial home, even though it may be owned by only one of them. The spouse of the owner must be party to any transaction involving the home (such as a sale or mortgage) and must execute both the agreement and the transfer or mortgage in question.

Family law legislation in British Columbia also provides certain protections to a spouse who may have an unregistered interest in land. In Alberta, the *Dower Act* prohibits a married person from disposing of a homestead without consent of the non-title spouse. A disposition includes a transfer, a mortgage, and a lease over three years.

Even if one spouse owned the matrimonial home before marriage, any increased value of the home still has to be divided with the other spouse upon separation, if that home was occupied, as a matrimonial residence, as of the time of separation. If the spouses owned more than one matrimonial home, the value of each must be allocated equally as of the time of separation if these properties were ordinarily occupied as matrimonial residences.

■ Gifts and inheritances

Provincial family or marital property legislation typically excludes certain gifts and inheritances received from third parties in calculating the spouse's net family property.

Gifts and inheritances will be excluded from a spouse's net family property if they were received from a third person after the date of marriage. However, gifts received from the spouse are part of net family property. Gifts and inheritances received before the date of marriage may be subject to deduction but will not be simply excluded from the calculation. Therefore any growth in their value will be subject to sharing.

This is contrasted with gifts from third parties where any increase in the gift's value is not shared. In addition, the donor must have expressly intended to give the gift or inheritance to the spouse alone, rather than to the entire family.

Gifts and inheritances are not excluded from net family property if they have become intermingled with other family assets, such as the matrimonial home or family money. For example, if a spouse purchased property with gift money, that spouse would have to show that the property was bought exclusively with gift money. This could be particularly difficult if the money was withdrawn from the family's joint account. If the spouse cannot prove that the property was bought exclusively with gift money, the new property will not be excluded from the spouse's net family property. The onus to prove the gift is upon the person making the claim of having received the gift.

Furthermore, gifts and inheritances cannot be excluded from the spouse's net family property if the other spouse can prove the couple had a common intention to share the gift or inheritance, such as purchasing and sharing real estate with inheritance money. Finally, interest or other income arising from a gift or inheritance during the time of the marriage will only be excluded from the net family property if the gift's donor expressly stated in a document that it was to be excluded. Such a document could be a will or a simple written statement.

If a court finds that a gift or inheritance does not belong exclusively to one spouse then that gift or inheritance or a part of its value will be included in the spouse's net family property. If the gift or inheritance is not shareable, then if it is sold or transferred into another asset, then that asset belongs to the one spouse alone. Also, any proceeds of sale of such excluded property or traced property should also qualify as excluded property. Speak with a lawyer for legal advice on your specific situation.

■ Is marital property treated differently in Québec?

Yes, Québec divides property based on three types of "matrimonial regimes":

- Partnership of Acquests
- Separation as to Property
- Community of Property

As in other provinces, Québec residents can change the way the law is applied to them through a marriage contract entered into before or during marriage. If there is no contract, the law decides the regime based on the year of marriage. Couples married before July 1, 1970, must follow the regime of community of property. Those married after July 1, 1970, are under the regime of partnership of acquests.

■ Partnership of Acquests

The partnership of acquests works as follows:

- Any assets acquired before marriage or received during marriage by inheritance remain the private property of each person
- Any other assets are considered "acquests" and will be divided
- At the time of divorce, any assets on hand are also considered "acquests" and each spouse is entitled to one-half the value while conserving his or her own private property

■ Separation as to Property

As to property, couples with marriage contracts usually adopt the regime of separation. In this case, there are no acquests or common property unless they are bought jointly in both names. Each person is the sole and exclusive owner of assets registered in his or her name.

■ Community of Property

With this regime, assets the spouses owned before marriage and acquired during marriage are both considered joint or common property at divorce. This regime is not often used since it followed the outdated notion that the husband manages most of the assets during the marriage. In a division after divorce, each party keeps his or her private property and has a right to one-half of the common community property.

■ Family Patrimony

In all cases in Québec, "family patrimony" laws apply to assets such as the family home. Even if there is a marriage contract treating all property as separate, the net value of any assets included in family patrimony rules will be divided unless the spouses legally opted out of the application of these provisions by 1990. These rules not only apply to the family residence, but also to the net value of secondary residences, family furniture, vehicles, and pension plans.

CUSTODY OF CHILDREN

12. Who gets custody of the children?

If you are separating and have children, custody and visitation rights will probably be among the most important concerns. "Custody" means having legal care and control of children.

Usually, the children live all the time, or most of the time, with the parent who has custody. Sometimes one parent will have custody and sometimes parents will have what is called joint or shared custody. Parents with joint custody share in the important decisions about how the children are raised and may take turns having the children live with them. In recent years, concepts have developed such as "split custody," where one or more child of the marriage remains with each parent. A parent who does not have custody will usually have rights to visit with the children at set times, and rights to ask about the children. This is sometimes called "access."

In most circumstances, the courts will not interfere with an agreement made by parents about custody and access. Whenever possible, parents should try to reach an agreement they can both accept. Asking the courts to resolve custody disputes is usually expensive, unpredictable, and emotionally draining.

If parents are unable to reach an agreement, a court can decide for them. The judge will decide who will get custody and visitation rights based on what the court thinks is in the best interests of the children. The court will consider the love, affection, and emotional ties between the children and each parent, how well each parent can give guidance, education, and the necessaries of life, and how long the child has lived in a stable home.

In most cases, the parent who has custody of the children during the separation is more likely to get permanent custody of the children after divorce. The court rarely disrupts the children's home environment if they have settled into a steady and stable routine with one parent.

As part of the process of deciding what is in a child's best interests, a court often orders an assessment by a professional such as a psychologist. The psychologist will usually meet with the children and parents several times to conduct tests and make observations. The psychologist will then make a recommendation to the judge as to which parent should get custody. The court usually takes these recommendations seriously, so it is very important to participate actively in the assessment if one is ordered.

13. How does joint custody or "shared parenting" work?

For some couples, the best possible option is joint custody. This can mean that the children live part of the time with each parent or that the children live with just one parent. When there is joint custody, both parents legally have care and control of the children.

Because joint custody requires a lot of co-operation, there may be hesitancy on the part of the court in making an order if there is significant friction between parents. Split custody is a variant of joint custody, which usually requires the consent of both parents. Courts do not ordinarily order split custody without agreement as it is in the best interests of children to remain together.

Making decisions about custody of children can be very difficult. However, these decisions are extremely important. If you want to have custody of your children or access rights, consult with a lawyer.

Since 1998, lawmakers have been discussing changes to the *Divorce Act* that would do away with the concept of "custody" and provide for a "shared parenting plan." This would require the sharing of child raising responsibility and would put an end to disruptive custody disputes.

14. What are my visitation and access rights as a parent?

A parent who is not given custody of a child can still have rights to visit the child and take part in the child's life. These are called "access rights" and allow you to visit with your children and know about their health, education, and general welfare. You and your spouse can either agree on visitation yourselves, or you can ask the court to give you an access order. Access orders can be open or they can be specifically structured depending on the circumstances.

In some cases a parent who does not have custody will only have occasional access rights while, in other cases, a parent who does not have custody may have the children every weekend. A typical access order provides that the parent who is given access will be with the child on alternate weekends and perhaps one evening in between. Long weekends will be divided equally, as will Christmas vacations and March breaks. An access parent will usually have the child for two or three weeks in the summer to coincide with his or her own vacations. Where appropriate, however, the non-custodial parent may be denied access. A lawyer can help you understand your rights and establish the best possible arrangement for you and your children.

15. What rights do grandparents have to visit or take custody of children?

Across Canada, there are no clearly defined rights for grandparents when it comes to visitation rights or custody. Only in Newfoundland and Labrador does the law provide grandparents with a right of custody or access to children. Some others, including New Brunswick, Nova Scotia, Ontario, Prince Edward Island, Saskatchewan, and the Yukon, allow people other than parents to apply for custody and access.

From the courts' standpoint, the only important issue involves the best interests of the child, and it often doesn't matter what the grandparents want.

16. Can custodial parents take their children anywhere?

When one parent has custody of the children and the other parent has visitation rights, problems sometimes arise when the parent with custody wants to travel abroad or even move. The parent that only has visitation rights usually will not want the parent who has custody to move to a distant place, which makes regular visitation difficult or impossible.

The law generally allows parents who have custody to move with the children as long as the move is reasonable in the circumstances, and in the best interests of the children. If the parent who does not have custody asks the court to stop the other parent from moving, the parent who has custody will usually have to prove that the benefits of moving are greater than the loss of the children's ability to visit with the other parent.

17. What can be done when a parent takes or abducts his or her children without permission?

Abduction occurs when a parent takes a child out of the possession and against the will of the child's other parent. Both family law and criminal law can deal with the act of abducting one's own children. The courts consider this a serious matter, especially if the parent who has rightful custody of the child has a court order or a signed agreement.

■ Family law remedies

Family law can help prevent the abduction of children by their parents. Courts may restrict the issuing of passports, for example, or set restrictions on access to the children. If a parent fears that a child may be abducted by the child's other parent, he or she should certainly consult a lawyer immediately.

If one parent has taken a child against the will of the other, then a pre-existing custody order is not necessarily required to initiate proceedings. However, courts usually deal with parents who abduct their own children after an interim custody order has been granted to the child's other parent. Generally, a custody order should be sought in the province in which the child is ordinarily resident before the abduction. A court in the child's usual province of residence has the power to grant custody even if the child has been taken out of that province.

Courts have the power to order the police to enforce a custody provision that has been contravened by a child's parent. All provinces are bound by a custody order that has been made under Canada's *Divorce Act*. If a custody order has been made under provincial law, then the other provinces are not necessarily bound by that order. Nevertheless, provinces generally co-operate to enforce provincial custody orders that are deemed to be in the best interests of the child.

Locating and seeking the return of a child who has been abducted from Canada to another country can be particularly difficult because it requires co-operation with the other country's government. For participating countries, the Hague Convention *On the Civil Aspects of International Child Abduction* enforces custody orders for children under the age of 16 who have been taken from their habitual country. A custodial parent should be well advised to protect their custodial rights if the non-custodial parent wishes to take the child on a holiday to a country where the non-custodial parent was born, and if that country has not become a party to the Hague Convention.

Courts will consider factors such as the child's habitual place of residence and how long the child has been in the new place of residence. If a court finds that a child has been wrongfully removed under the habitual country's laws, and that it would not be contrary to the child's best interests, then the child will be returned.

The provincial office for the Attorney General or Minister of Justice should usually be contacted to initiate a proceeding under the Hague Convention. Another agency that deals with the abduction of children by parents is the Federal Orders and Agreements Enforcement Unit, under the Federal Department of Justice. In addition, provincial police forces work with the Missing Children Registry of the RCMP.

■ Criminal law remedies

Parents or guardians may also be charged under the Criminal Code for abducting their own children who are under the age of 14. The criminal offence of abduction occurs when a parent takes the child out of the possession of and against the will of the child's other parent, or otherwise contravenes a custody provision made by any Canadian court.

The essential element of the criminal charge of abduction is the intent to deprive the other parent of possession of the child. An abduction has occurred when an offender could foresee that his or her act would certainly deprive the other parent of possession of or the ability to exercise control over the child.

The child's consent or lack of consent is not relevant to the criminal charge of abduction. An abduction occurs when a child is taken against the will of the child's parent or guardian, even if the child takes an active or leading role.

A valid defence to the criminal charge of abduction can be based on the accused's honest but mistaken belief regarding the legal effect of a custody order. It is extremely difficult to prove that an honest mistake was made, however. Offenders may also plead that they were protecting either the children or themselves from immediate harm, usually from the other parent. This matter becomes very complicated when both parents have joint custody and the child spends equal time with each parent.

If no custody order has been made then the consent of the Attorney General is necessary before the criminal charge of abduction can be laid against a child's parent or guardian. The abduction must be reported to the police and a missing person report filed. A Canada-wide arrest warrant will then be issued for the offending parent or guardian. This process may be faster than proceedings under family law. The *Criminal Code* does not provide for the return of a child to his or her parent or guardian, however.

Abduction is a very serious offence under the *Criminal Code*. The term of imprisonment for abduction of a child under 14 is up to 10 years.

The criminal offence of abduction does not automatically terminate an offender's existing right to custody of his or her child under the *Children's Law Reform Act*. Nevertheless, because custody rights are granted in accordance with the child's best interests, the criminal conduct will be relevant to the court in considering an offender's custody rights.

When an abduction occurs it is important that the custodial parent take immediate steps to get sound legal advice. For legal assistance in the case of a child's abduction, contact the police and consult a lawyer immediately.

CHILD & SPOUSAL SUPPORT

18. How do I get child or spousal support?

Courts in each province have the power to make orders for child and spousal support. They may award both periodic and lump sum support payments, but the courts treat child and spousal support as separate issues. In some provinces, there may be no right to spousal support for unmarried couples.

To seek an order for child or spousal support at a court, you must file an application with the courts. A lawyer can help you do this. Family law courts in each province can also provide you with information about other methods of addressing your dispute, such as mediation. Except for emergency situations, you or your lawyer should bring an application for child or spousal support to the family law court in the municipality in which you live. In some cases, the courts may be able to issue an "interim support order" while you are awaiting your application hearing.

19. Up to what age must children be supported?

Child support is generally available for any child under the age of 18 or 19, depending on your province's age of majority. In some cases, child support does not have to be paid for children who are 16, 17, or 18 if they have chosen to move out of the family home and no longer live by their parent's rules. Child support can also be required for children over the age of 18 or 19 if they are unable to withdraw from parental support, such as children who are still in full-time attendance at school or unable to support themselves because of disability.

Generally speaking, child support obligations relate to birth parents. It is important to remember, however, that anyone who treats the child of another as his or her own may also assume a legal obligation of child support. A typical illustration would be where a man marries a woman who has two young children from a previous marriage. In the course of marriage the man may form a close bond with those children and come to be regarded as a "father" for the purposes of paying child support.

20. For taxation purposes, how are child support payments treated now?

At one time, the person who paid child support could subtract it from his or her taxable income. The person who received the child support had to add it to his or her taxable income.

The *Income Tax Act* has been changed and child support that is paid according to a written agreement or a court order made on or after May 1, 1997, is neither deducted from the payer's income nor added to the recipient's income.

For people with agreements before May 1, 1997, these tax rules do not apply and are not retroactive. That said, the parents can agree to have the tax rules apply to their existing order if they don't want to change the amount but simply want the new tax treatment. Also, if they get a new order or agreement changing the amount of child support, then the newer tax rules will apply.

21. How is the child support payment calculated?

Child support can be agreed to between the parents or set by the courts. Until recently, the amount of child support was determined on a case-by-case basis. Now, the initial amount to be paid is based on federal and provincial government guidelines.

These guidelines are based on a set calculation that determines the amount of support. The calculation is based on the actual income of the parent who does not have custody and the number of children being supported. The rules determining "income" can be complex but are usually calculated on a spouse's total annual income.

There are also issues involving "add-ons" such as daycare and undue hardship that may have to be resolved. For example, a parent who does

Monthly Support

Income	1 Child	2 Children	3 Children	4 Children
$10,000	79	119	132	146
20,000	163	285	390	476
30,000	266	446	568	672
40,000	345	570	748	894
50,000	429	700	917	1,094
60,000	507	823	1,076	1,283
70,000	572	927	1,212	1,444
80,000	639	1,031	1,346	1,603
90,000	706	1,136	1,480	1,761
100,000	773	1,240	1,613	1,919
125,000	940	1,500	1,948	2,315
150,000	1,108	1,761	2,283	2,711

not have custody and who earns $25,000 per year would have to pay $222 per month for one child or $360 per month for two children. If a parent who does not have custody earns $80,000 per year, he or she would have to pay $639 per month for one child or $1,031 per month for two children.

22. Can I change the amount of child support I am receiving or paying?

If parents have separated or divorced and their children live all or most of the time with one of the parents, the other parent is usually responsible to pay child support to help provide for the children. The amount of child support will generally depend on how many children are being supported and the amount of money being earned by the parent paying the child support. Payments, from the parent who does not have custody to the parent who does, are usually made through a government office and sometimes directly from one parent to the other.

In situations of joint or shared parenting or split custody, the responsibility for child support may be reduced depending on the extent of parenting assumed by each parent and by their respective incomes.

At any time, either parent can apply to the court to have the amount of support changed if there has been a significant change in circumstances. For example, you may want to reduce the amount of child support you are paying if your income suddenly declines.

Although the new guidelines are usually closely followed, many factors affect how much child support should be paid. A lawyer can help with your particular situation. There are special rules that may change the guideline amount where the payor spouse is earning over $150,000 annually, or where there are "special or extraordinary expenses."

The rules also change where the "child is over the age of majority." There are special rules to adjust payments in the case of shared custody or split custody. There is also relief available for cases where the payor spouse is experiencing "undue hardship" based on a relative standard of living test. If you require legal assistance with regard to a child support order, consult a lawyer.

23. What is "spousal support" and who gets it?

Spousal support is money paid by one spouse to the other following a separation or divorce. Its general purpose is to compensate one spouse for any financial losses suffered as a result of the marriage and to assist that spouse until he or she becomes financially independent. It is not intended to punish or blame one spouse for the breakdown of the relationship. Spousal support can either be based on an agreement made between the spouses or it can be set by the courts.

Spousal support is not available for everyone and will depend on several different factors. In Québec, for example, there is no right to spousal support for unmarried couples.

The court will generally look at the length of time the spouses were married and the roles that each played during the marriage. If a spouse is unable to support herself or himself, and can show that he or she is in this position because of the marriage, that person will usually be entitled to spousal support provided the other spouse has income. Spousal support is often awarded where there is a significant difference in the incomes of spouses.

■ Calculating spousal support

The amount of spousal support generally depends on the need of the spouse seeking support, the ability of the other spouse to pay, and what kind of lifestyle and standard of living the spouses enjoyed during marriage. Though spousal support can be a lump sum payment, most of the time it is an ongoing weekly or monthly payment.

The extent of the obligation to pay spousal support will depend on many different factors. Where the marriage had been of short duration it is more likely that any support ordered will be paid over a short period. Where both spouses worked throughout the marriage any support ordered may be for a limited term. On the other hand, where the marriage was a "traditional marriage" in the sense that the wife remained in the home, raising the children without significant employment outside the home, the support obligation may be without time limitation.

24. Can I change the amount of spousal support I am receiving or paying?

After a court makes a spousal support order, either spouse can apply to have it increased or decreased if there has been a material change in circumstances. For example, you may be able to reduce your payments if you recently lost your job, if your spouse recently remarried, or if your spouse was able to get a job. Much will depend on the circumstances of each case and whether the "material change" was foreseeable. This is an area where legal advice should be sought before making any application.

Since spousal support is assessed on a case-by-case basis, it is important to know your rights. A lawyer can help you determine whether spousal support should be paid and in what amount.

25. How are support orders enforced?

The enforcement of court-ordered support payments is generally a provincial or territorial matter and methods vary in each jurisdiction. To ensure that payments are made, child support and spousal support orders issued by the courts are usually sent to so-called maintenance enforcement agencies.

In Ontario, the Family Responsibility Office co-ordinates and monitors all support payments by either arranging for the paying spouse to send payments to the office on a regular basis, or in some cases, by automatically deducting the payments from the supporting spouse's pay. In both situations, the office forwards the payments to the receiving spouse. Although the money is supposed to be forwarded right away, there are sometimes administrative delays. All other jurisdictions have similar programs under names such as the Family Maintenance Enforcement Program, Family Support Orders Service, and Director of Maintenance Enforcement.

If you have reached an agreement for child support or spousal support without a court order, you can file your agreement with these provincial enforcement agencies and ask them to enforce it. They will do so as long as the agreement is capable of being filed with the court. This means the agreement may be enforced, where it is filed, as if it were an order of the court.

Once support has been ordered by the court, or you have filed your support agreement with the proper provincial authorities, you will receive a package of forms to fill out and return. These forms ask for information about you and your spouse including where your spouse works. If the supporting spouse does not send cheques to the government as required, the enforcement office can take a number of steps to get the support money.

If the supporting spouse is employed, the enforcement authorities will deal directly with his or her employer to have the money taken directly from the supporting spouse's paycheque. This is called garnishment. In some jurisdictions, the amount garnished may not exceed a set amount of the supporting spouse's net income.

If the spouse does not have a regular employer, the government can sometimes take money from the spouse's other sources of income, such as a bank account, income tax refund, pension, or even a disability payment. In some circumstances, it can also take steps to sell property owned by the spouse and put that money toward support payments. The government can also suspend the driver's licence of a defaulting payor spouse.

If your ex-spouse owns a business, it may become responsible for the payment. Provinces such as B.C., Manitoba, and Ontario allow the assets of the corporation to be seized. In Ontario, a court can even force someone who is financially connected to the ex-spouse, such as a current spouse, to file financial information and documentation to help find hidden assets.

If you need to enforce an order or agreement for child support or spousal support, obtain assistance from a lawyer or the provincial enforcement authorities listed in your telephone book.

Common Law Relationships

26. What is a "common law" relationship?

When two people live together and are not married, they may be considered to be living in a "common law" relationship — usually after a period of three years. If you are living in a common law relationship, you will have a number of rights and obligations arising under family law, tax law, welfare and family benefits, and employee benefit plans. Different rules apply for each of these areas of law. Also, depending on the province where you live, the rules of a common law relationship may be applied even to same-sex relationships.

■ Family law issues

If you are considered to be living in a common law relationship under family law, you may have an obligation to financially support your spouse if you separate. There are two ways for a common law relationship to arise under family law.

First, a common law relationship can legally arise when two people have been living together in a conjugal relationship for three continuous years in Saskatchewan, Ontario, New Brunswick, and Prince Edward Island. In Nova Scotia, common law relationships arise after one year (or when you have a child).

Second, a common law relationship can also legally arise when two people have been living together in an ongoing relationship for any period and they have a child together.

Sometimes it may not be clear if two people have been living common-law. The law tries to decide whether two people have been living together by looking at whether they cohabit. Incidents of cohabitation will include whether one person was financially supporting the other, whether they have had a sexual relationship, and whether they shared household expenses and child raising duties.

■ Tax law issues

Under tax law, a common law relationship legally arises when two opposite sex spouses have been living together for 12 months, or when two people have a child together. If you are considered to be a common law spouse under tax law, you will have certain rights and obligations when filling out your yearly income tax return. For example, you may be able to claim a dependent spouse credit if you are financially supporting your common law spouse.

■ Welfare and family benefits issues

If you are considered a common law spouse for the purpose of welfare and family benefits, you must include your common law spouse's income on your application for benefits. Under welfare and family benefits rules, a common law relationship legally arises when two people live together as a couple for any period, however short, and share financial responsibilities. Someone could become your common law spouse on the day they move in with you under these rules.

■ Employee benefit plan issues

If you are considered a common law spouse under your spouse's employee benefit plan, you may be entitled to benefits such as prescription medication, life insurance, and dental coverage. Employers can make their own rules about when a common law relationship arises. Some employment benefit plans let common law spouses share in the benefit plan if they have been living together for just six months. Others may require 1-, 3- or 5-year cohabitation periods. Check with your personnel department.

A lawyer can give you advice if you need additional information about how living with someone can affect your legal rights. .

27. What is a "cohabitation agreement"?

A cohabitation agreement is a written contract that can be made between common law spouses. Its purpose is to establish the property rights of each spouse if they separate. Without a cohabitation agreement, the only right that a common law spouse may have on separation is the right to make a claim for financial support. Unlike married spouses, common law spouses do not have any automatic rights to share property when they separate.

The law does not require common law couples to sign cohabitation agreements, but it is often a good idea for two reasons. First, it gives you and your spouse the opportunity to discuss what you each expect if the relationship ends. Second, it lets you create rights that the law does not otherwise provide for. For example, you might both agree to split property equally if you separate. Or you might agree that neither of you has the obligation to support the other financially. The only terms you cannot put in a cohabitation agreement are child custody and access arrangements.

To create a legally binding cohabitation agreement, you and your spouse must be completely open and honest about your financial situations and you must both sign the agreement in front of a witness. There cannot have been any pressure or threats involved in signing the agreement.

Although it is possible to write your own cohabitation agreement, it is best to contact a lawyer to make sure your agreement properly protects your interests and is legally binding. The agreement will also be stronger if you and your spouse each talk to different lawyers before signing the agreement. This will prevent one spouse from later saying that he or she did not understand what was agreed to in the cohabitation agreement.

If you and your common law spouse decide to get married, a cohabitation agreement is not cancelled. After you are married, your cohabitation agreement automatically becomes a legal marriage contract.

28. What are my rights upon break-up of a common law relationship?

Unless you have signed a cohabitation agreement, common law spouses generally have fewer legal rights than married spouses upon break-up of a relationship. Under your provincial family or marital property legislation, a couple is considered to be living in a common law relationship if they have been living together intimately for at least three years or if they have been living together for less time and have had a child together.

■ Rights common law spouses do not have

There are two important rights that common law spouses do not have if they separate. First, common law spouses do not each have an equal right to live in the family home. Second, common law spouses do not have an automatic right to equalize their net family property acquired during their relationship. In most cases, both the home and other property go to the person who is the owner on title. Each person usually keeps everything he or she personally owns and nothing more.

B.C., Saskatchewan, Ontario, New Brunswick, Nova Scotia, Newfoundland and Labrador, the Northwest Territories, and the Yukon all make special provisions for some kind of sharing of the matrimonial home between married people, but not for common-law partners. Common law partners also have no control over the owner's decisions regarding the home, while a married person needs the other's signed consent.

Only in Manitoba does a common law partner have a right to live in the home and then only if the couple has cohabited for one year or more and has a child from the relationship.

Where one, or both, of the common law spouses has made a significant contribution to the property of the other, there may be a right in respect of property based on principles of trust or unjust enrichment. Generally speaking, the longer the relationship between unmarried cohabitees or common law partners, the more likely there is a remedy. In some circumstances, it may be possible to be given the right to live in the family home or the right to divide property. This involves going to court and convincing a judge that you made a significant contribution to the home or to the property. It is best to consult a lawyer, as this is a complex area of law.

■ Rights common law spouses do have

There are other rights that common law spouses share with married spouses, including child support, spousal support, and rights to CPP pension credits.

■ Custody of children and child support

Common law spouses have the same rights and obligations as married spouses to care for children. This includes rights to custody of children and obligations to financially support children. If the parents cannot decide who will have custody of the children, the courts will decide based on what is in the children's best interest. If the parents cannot agree on child support, a court can order support payments based on the federal and provincial guidelines.

■ Spousal support

Common law spouses may also have rights to financial support as long as a claim is made within two years of separation. The court will look at whether one spouse needs to be financially supported and whether the other spouse has the ability to pay. If both spouses are employed and earning a similar amount of money, the court will generally not order one spouse to support the other.

■ Right to spouse's CPP credits

Common law spouses also have a right to each other's Canada Pension Plan credits if they have lived together for one year. Most people earn these credits while they are working. When you and your spouse separate, the credits earned by both of you while you were together are divided evenly. For more information, call the Human Resources and Social Development office in your area.

■ Separation Agreements

When common law spouses separate, they can deal with all the issues of their separation by entering into a formal separation agreement. This agreement can set out how property will be divided, who the children will live with, and how much child support and spousal support will be paid. Although it is possible to write your own separation agreement, consult a lawyer to make sure that both you and your common law spouse understand your legal rights. A lawyer can also make sure your separation agreement is clear, complete, and legally binding.

29. Are same-sex relationships treated differently?

Until recently, same-sex couples across Canada could not legally marry and were not treated the same as unmarried opposite-sex couples. Courts in provinces such as B.C. and Ontario now support the position that human rights legislation should provide for the prevention of discrimination based on sexual orientation. Based on an even earlier Supreme Court of Canada decision, the law in all provinces must also recognize same-sex couples for the purpose of spousal support. As with opposite-sex couples in common law relationships, the rights of same-sex couples in many provinces now hinge on whether they marry.

■ Custody and Adoption

Another area where same-sex couples have similar rights or obligations relates to children. While the biological parent will often be given custody, the other person may be required to pay child support, may be entitled to visiting rights, and may apply for custody or adoption of the children. Whether a custody or adoption application is successful will depend on what the court decides is in the "best interests" of the children.

■ Protect yourself

Because of limited legal protection for people in unmarried same-sex relationships, same-sex couples may choose to take steps to protect themselves from the consequences of a break-up. For example, they can put property in both of their names jointly, instead of in just one person's name. If their relationship ends at some point in the future, the property may then be divided equally between them.

Also, same-sex couples can write a kind of cohabitation agreement that sets out each person's right to property.

Same-sex rights are presently in a state of flux. If you want to prepare a cohabitation agreement or you have separated from a partner, consult a lawyer for advice and assistance.

ADOPTION

30. What is involved in adopting a child?

Provincial governments have many rules and guidelines for the adoption of children. These procedures must be followed to legally adopt a child.

Any child under the age of majority (18 or 19) can be adopted by married or unmarried adults, step-parents, or any other person (including a single individual) a court believes will honour the best interests of the child. Many provinces allow same-sex adoptions. In some provinces, the adopted individual must be younger than the adopting individual. If an adult (someone who has attained the age of majority) is to be adopted, there may be restrictions on who can adopt (usually, only the person or couple who tended to the individual when he or she was a minor).

In most jurisdictions, consent for the adoption will be required from a child over the age of 12 and also any living parent or guardian of the child. In some circumstances, written permission may also be required from someone else who is providing financial support to the child or who has custody of or access to the child. That said, the court may dispense with the need for consent.

To adopt a child, you usually must live in the same province as the child and you must usually be at least 18 or 19 years old, depending on your province's age of majority. As mentioned above, you do not have to be married but, if you are, your spouse must also agree in writing that he or she wants to adopt a child. Two people can only adopt a child together if they are married or living in a common law relationship.

Depending on the province, the child must be at least three or seven days old before written permission for adoption can be given and, again depending on the province, the natural parents then have 21 or 30 days to change their minds and cancel the permission. If permission is cancelled within the prescribed period, the child must be returned to the natural parents. If the period has gone by and the child has been placed with an adoptive family, the natural parents cannot normally change their minds about the adoption.

In some situations, the court can decide that written consent of the natural parents is not needed. If a child has been neglected or abused, the court can allow the child to be adopted without the parents' consent.

31. Who can help me adopt a child?

There are generally two ways to adopt a child, depending on the prov-ince. The first is through a local Children's Aid Society, provincial Child Welfare office, or similar public agency. To adopt a child through a public agency, you must first apply and go through a standard screening process. If your application is approved, the agency will try to match you with a suitable child. A social worker will visit with you and the child and help you apply to the court to make the adoption final. Usually the child has to have been in your care for six months before the court gives the adoption order.

The second way to adopt a child is through a private agency licensed by a provincial government. The process is very similar to going through the public agency. In most cases, a social worker will conduct a home study to make sure the adoption is suitable for the parents and the child. Note that there are no provincial caps on adoption fees, which can range from $6,000 to $20,000.

If you want to adopt a member of your own family, such as a grand-child or step-child, you do not need to go through a public or private adoption agency, but you still need to go to court to get a formal adop-tion order. A lawyer may be able to help you deal with all of the require-ments if you would like to adopt a child.

32. How do I adopt a child from abroad?

Since it can be very difficult and time consuming to adopt a child in Canada, many people choose for personal or humanitarian reasons to adopt a child from abroad. This is a complicated process which will require you to consult an immigration lawyer.

Children adopted from abroad immigrate to Canada in the "family class" category. The adoptive parents sponsor the child to come to Canada after the child has been adopted according to the laws of the child's home country. An adoption that is legally completed in a foreign country is given automatic legal recognition in most jurisdictions in Canada.

To sponsor the immigration of an adopted child, you must be a Canadian citizen or permanent resident 19 years of age or older. You must promise to provide support for the child for 10 years, and you must demonstrate that you are able to provide financial support. Remember: children eligible to be sponsored must be adopted outside Canada according to the laws of their home country. Adoption laws vary from country to country and you should consult an immigration lawyer to help you through the process.

The following is a brief summary of the typical procedure that would be followed to adopt a child from another country:

- First, contact the adoption authorities of the province where the child will live to determine the provincial adoption requirements. In some provinces, the government may want to conduct a "homestudy" of the adoptive parents. This will depend on the adoption laws of the country where the child lives. The provincial adoption authorities will usually need to issue a letter of approval.
- Second, begin the immigration process by submitting a sponsorship application for a "family class" immigrant. This application to the federal government should include an Undertaking form, a Financial Evaluation form, and the processing fee per child.
- Third, the adoptive parents complete an application for Permanent Residence on behalf of the child. This application should be submitted to the visa office in the child's home country.

When the sponsorship application is approved, a visa officer will decide whether the child can be admitted into Canada as an immigrant.

Three conditions must be satisfied before the immigrant visa is issued. First, the child must meet all the basic immigration requirements, including a medical check. Second, the provincial child welfare authority must approve the adoption. Third, the foreign authority must allow the transfer of the child to the adoptive parents. The child can travel to Canada once an immigrant visa is issued. Sponsors should not attempt to go abroad intending to return to Canada with the child until the immigration process is complete.

The adoptive parents can apply for Canadian citizenship for the child after he or she arrives in Canada and is granted permanent residence. You can obtain more information about international adoption from an immigration lawyer, the provincial social services ministry, or a Canada Immigration Centre.

33. How can I search adoption records or find a birth parent?

Adoption records are normally kept confidential until the adopted person is 18 or 19 years old, depending on the jurisdiction. If an adopted person of this age wants to find his or her natural parents, he or she can usually declare this desire with a provincial adoption disclosure registry.

These agencies are in all provinces and territories. If the natural birth parents also register, the Adoption Office will arrange a meeting. If the natural parents do not register, the child can ask the Adoption Office to do a search for any surviving natural relatives. There is usually a long waiting list for this search.

In some provinces, such as B.C. and Saskatchewan, identifying information about birth and adoptive parents or children may be automatically disclosed unless one of the parties involved specifically refuses. In Nova Scotia, so-called reunions are assisted by the government unless they pose a risk to the health, safety, or well-being of a person involved. In the Northwest Territories, children adopted after 1998 will be able to access a wealth of information not just about birth parents, but also other relocated children and the parents and grandparents of the adopting parent and natural parent.

In late 2005, the Ontario government was planning amendments to its adoption information disclosure law that would allow adoptees over the age of 18 to obtain copies of their original birth records that would provide them with their original birth name(s) and might also identify birth parents. It would also provide birth parents with access to information from their child's birth records and adoption orders once the adoptee has reached 19, allowing them to know their child's given name(s) after adoption. All parties would have the right to put a "no contact" notice on their file.

Although adopted children may not be able to find out who their natural parents are until they are 18 or 19 years old, they can still find out some information. If the child gets permission from adoptive parents, they can ask the Adoption Office to give them the social and medical histories of their birth parents. The actual names of the birth parents are not part of this information.

Child and Spousal Abuse

34. What can I do to stop child or spousal abuse?

There are several things you can do if your spouse is abusing you or your children. These include seeking shelter, having criminal charges laid, getting a peace bond, getting a family law restraining order, or getting an order for exclusive possession of the family home. No one should have to remain in a dangerous or abusive situation. The law and community support agencies make it possible to quickly improve your situation.

■ Seeking shelter

If you or your children are being abused, the first priority should be for your immediate safety and the safety of your children. There are many shelters that can provide a safe and supportive environment while you decide how to deal with the situation. The shelters are listed in your telephone book.

■ Having criminal charges laid

Whether you have left for a shelter or remain in your house, you can call the police. Many police forces have a policy whereby they must lay charges for domestic assault situations. Other police forces will not automatically lay charges, but want to see some evidence of physical abuse before they do.

If the police are not willing to lay a criminal charge against your spouse you can take steps to have a criminal charge laid yourself. To do this, you have to meet with a justice of the peace and lay what is called an "information." The information is a document that sets out what happened. If the justice of the peace thinks there is good reason to believe you were assaulted, your spouse will have to face criminal charges. You can arrange to meet with a justice of the peace at most court offices.

■ Peace bonds

If you do not want to lay a criminal charge against your spouse, you may want to get a peace bond instead. This is a court order that requires your spouse to be on good behaviour and keep the peace. To get a peace bond you will have to meet with a justice of the peace and explain what happened. The bond will usually last for one year. If the rules of the peace bond are broken, your spouse may be sent to jail.

■ Restraining orders

Another option is to get a family law restraining order. This has generally the same effect as a peace bond. The advantage of a restraining order is you can get one quickly from your local family court without your spouse knowing. Once the court has granted you a restraining order, you should give a copy to your local police department.

■ Exclusive possession of the family home

If you or your children are being abused and you want to get your spouse out of the family home, you can go to court and ask the judge for what is called "exclusive possession of the matrimonial home," together with the contents of the home. This is a court order that requires your spouse to live somewhere else. It gives you the right to live in the family home without your spouse — even if your spouse is the legal owner of the home. The court can also order your spouse to pay you money for the upkeep of the house.

■ Getting help

Domestic assault is a serious crime. Every person is entitled to be safe in his or her own home. By using some of the options discussed in this section you can significantly improve your situation. Consult a lawyer for legal advice.

35. What happens when the justice system intervenes in cases of child abuse?

Social workers with your province's children's aid or child welfare offices are authorized by law to conduct investigations and prepare custody and access reports. These reports are an investigation on all matters concerning custody of or access to the child and the child's support and education.

A custody/access report focuses on the interests of the children based on their needs and wishes, and the family's ability to meet those needs. It provides a picture of the family history, current situation, and parenting plans for the future. It can also provide recommendations to help the family make decisions about ongoing parenting plans.

If a decision is made to provide services, social workers collect and evaluate information from family members and others who have been involved with the family to help understand what parenting arrangement would be best for the children. They assist families to look at various options that will meet the needs of the children and the family. They may prepare reports for the court with recommendations that consider the interests and wishes of the children.

The social worker will arrange to meet the family. Some interviews may be at the social worker's office and some may be at the family's home. The children will be observed with family members and may be interviewed privately, if appropriate. The number and location of interviews will be determined by the social worker.

The social worker will ask the family to sign release forms that will be sent to "collateral sources." These may include the children's school, daycare provider, doctor, community agencies, police, and counsellors. The forms will allow such sources to share information with the social worker that will assist with the evaluation.

Social workers who prepare social work reports regularly interview and observe children. It is best if this is done in a comfortable and familiar environment. The social worker understands that the children may be experiencing many different feelings about the separation and family situation. Depending on their ages, the social worker may have the children participate in structured play, draw pictures, or tell stories to express their feelings.

Parents often want to know, "Will the social worker ask my children where they want to live?" Children's thoughts, feelings and experiences are important and will be discussed, but the social worker will not ask the children to choose between parents.

■ Helpful Hints

There are some things parents can do that may help make the custody/access report process less stressful for both themselves and the children. These include:

- Asking the social worker questions about the process, and writing the questions down
- Preparing school, health, and other information that might be helpful, such as names and telephone numbers
- Asking for information about reading material, separation and divorce workshops, counselling, and other resources and
- Telling the children about the process. Social workers can suggest approaches for different age levels

During the process, the parties involved in the custody/access case may decide to come to an arrangement concerning the children. The social worker may help arrange a settlement or disclosure meeting that may include the parties involved and their lawyers.

Once a report is completed, it is filed with the court and copies are sent to the lawyers. The report becomes part of the court record. Each party usually has the right to send a formal dispute of the report.

We'll Get Married If...

After moving to Calgary together, William tells Annie he will marry her after he finds a "good job." Over the next few years, William has a string of jobs he says are "not good enough yet." Annie's patience runs out and she decides to sue for breach of promise to marry. William, however, says he hasn't breached his promise and just hasn't found the right employment.

Will Annie succeed?

No. In the few jurisdictions like Alberta where a breach of promise to marry is allowed, a marriage proposal is a valid and binding contract that will be upheld by a court. The courts may also recognize that a contract can be conditional. In this case, William needs to find "a good job." Over the years, courts have upheld conditions such as finishing one's education, obtaining parental consent, the death of a parent or other relative, settling a relative's estate, converting to another religion, reaching retirement, and acquiring a home.

Courts, however, will not support a contract that is contrary to public policy, such as promises to marry conditional on the death of another spouse, grant of a divorce, or in exchange for sexual intercourse.

If Annie had been successful, a court would likely have awarded her damages for the breach of contract, but still would not have required William to marry her.

Is a Platonic Relationship a Marriage?

Alicia and Sam were in their retirement years when they decided to get married. Both agreed the marriage was based solely on their need for companionship and neither wanted sex. In fact, Sam was physically unable to have sex. Soon after marrying, they had a big fight and decided to ask for an annulment of the marriage on the basis that it had not been consummated.

Will they succeed?

No. In the 1979 Ontario case of Norman v. Norman, the court said an annulment is not the right remedy. The husband's inability to consummate the marriage was not the reason for its failure. After agreeing to enter into a platonic marriage, neither spouse could complain about the lack of sexual intercourse.

Parental Pressures?

The mother and step-father of a young woman told her they had found the perfect husband. After they met, the woman said she didn't like him, but her parents continued to pressure her. In the end, she agreed to the marriage. Soon after the ceremony, however, she changed her mind and asked for an annulment claiming she did not give her consent to the marriage.

Will the young woman succeed?

Yes. In a similar Ontario case in 1988, *S.(A.) v. S.(A.)*, the court found the young woman was under duress. In other words, she believed she had no free choice in the matter. Even though a "reasonable person" might not agree, all that matters is the woman's honest belief that she could not resist. Duress is a subjective test.

Marriage of Inconvenience?

Raj told his friend, Helena, he would soon be forced to leave Canada because his immigration visa was expiring. Helena, a Canadian citizen, suggested they get married so Raj could stay.

Is the marriage valid?

No. Most provinces forbid "marriages of convenience." Typically, these marriages are considered void — as if they had never happened — because there is no intent to marry in good faith.

Are a Homemaker's Contributions Important?

While living together in a 12-year common law relationship, Alice took care of their children and domestic chores, such as painting the fence and shovelling snow, without compensation. Dan owned the home, eventually paid off the mortgage and bought a houseboat and van with money he earned. Alice and Dan then separated.

Is Alice entitled to compensation for her contributions to the common law relationship?

Yes, said the Supreme Court of Canada in the 1993 case of *Peter v. Beblow*. Generally, noted the court, a common law spouse owes no duty to perform work or services for the other party to the relationship. So, homemaking and childcare services in a common law relationship may give rise to claims against the other spouse. In this case, the court ruled that Alice's contributions helped Dan pay off his mortgage and freed cash for other purchases, such as his boat and van.

WHEN DOES SUPPORT END?

Sven and Gilda were married in Europe in the 1950s and moved to Canada in 1960. They separated in 1973 and divorced in 1980. Gilda had a Grade 7 education and no special skills or training. During their marriage, she cared for the house and three children. She also worked six hours a day cleaning offices.

After their separation, Gilda was awarded custody of the children and received a small amount of money each month for spousal and child support. She continued to clean offices. Sven later remarried in 1984, but continued to pay support to his ex-wife.

Gilda was laid off from work in 1987 and, from that time on, was only able to get part-time cleaning work. In 1989, Sven asked the court for an order terminating the spousal support, saying his ex-spouse had more than enough time to become financially independent.

Will Sven be allowed to end the spousal support payments?

No. In the Supreme Court of Canada case of *Moge v. Moge*, the court said a wife in a similar situation was entitled to ongoing support for an indefinite period. While the court said it would not generally interfere with agreements between couples that ended spousal support after a stated period, the judges believed a door must be left open for spouses who sacrifice future employment prospects for their family or further their partners' careers.

In this case, the woman's work within the home had "undeniable value" and her ability to become self-sufficient had been compromised by her marriage. The court said people still have an obligation after a marriage breakdown to contribute to their own support, but that the courts will also take into account the advantages conferred on the other spouse during the marriage.

Young & Old

C hildren and seniors can be among the most vulnerable members of our society. The law recognizes this and may set out different rules and protections for the young and old.

In the eyes of the law, you are a child (referred to as an "infant" in some legal circles or a minor) until you reach the "age of majority." After that point, you are largely responsible for your own decisions and can do what you wish, within the bounds of the law.

Each province establishes its own age of majority at either 18 or 19 years old. This is an important age to reach since it opens up a world of new rights and obligations. For example, depending on your province's age of majority, you can marry at 18 or 19 without parental or court consent. Below that age, you need written permission from a parent or a judge to get married.

Not all the rights of an adult may be available to you upon reaching the age of majority. For example, in some provinces the age for purchasing, obtaining, and consuming liquor is 19.

This doesn't mean to say you have no rights of your own as a child. Children are protected in many ways by federal and provincial laws. For example, children over 12 and not mentally incompetent cannot be adopted in most provinces without their written consent. As well, federal criminal laws are applied differently to children, depending on their age.

As for seniors, as they say, you are as young as you feel. In many cases, there is no "official" age at which you become a senior, though most people consider 60 to 65 to be a critical threshold. As you will see, seniors, too, have special rights and protections.

CHILDREN

1.   How long is a parent responsible for caring for a child?

Both parents are legally responsible for financially supporting children to the best of their ability and according to need until the child reaches the age of majority. That responsibility continues past the age of majority if the child is enrolled, for example, in a full-time education program at university or college.

Parents are not financially responsible for a child who reaches the age of 16 and withdraws from parental control (moves to his or her own apartment, for instance).

This doesn't mean to say parents must give children everything they ask for — only what they need and what the parent can reasonably afford.

2.   Are a child's rights different if born out of wedlock?

Courts no longer make any distinction between children born in a marriage and those born out of wedlock.

3. Is a parent responsible for a child's actions that cause damage?

When property has been damaged or a person injured owing to the actions of a child, the common law position of the civil courts is that a parent is not responsible for the actions of a child when committed without the parent's knowledge, participation, or sanction.

If a parent was negligent and failed to exercise reasonable supervision and control over the child, the courts will likely hold parents responsible for any damages caused. In most cases, it will be up to the parent to prove that there was no negligence.

In criminal law, the child alone will be held responsible to the extent allowed under the *Youth Criminal Justice Act*. This law, which deals with the criminal actions of youths, applies only to children 12 to 17 years of age. Below this age, no criminal action will follow. After age 18, the individual is considered an adult in the eyes of criminal courts.

4. Can a child sue or be sued in civil court?

A child can sue or be sued by anyone in a civil lawsuit, but he or she will have to be represented in court by a "litigation guardian." Each province sets out its own rules for litigation guardians.

Children and parents can also sue each other, and children can even sue in some provinces for pre-natal injuries suffered, such as during a mother's substance abuse during pregnancy.

5. How old does a child have to be to get a job?

Depending on the province, child labour provisions generally do not allow children under the ages of 14, 15, 16, or 17 to be employed. In some provinces, written government or parental permission can allow exceptions.

In some jurisdictions, children under the age of 16 are prohibited from working anywhere that can be dangerous to their health or well-being, such as a construction site. Children may also be prohibited from working during normal school hours and may be limited in the total number of hours they can work each day.

6. Can a child be a party to a legally enforceable contract?

In the past, the common law held that minors, infants, and children could not be a party to a legally enforceable contract. In many provinces, however, there is recognition in legislation that children do form contracts that must be enforced for their benefit or that of others when renting an apartment, buying insurance, or ordering goods.

Children will likely be held responsible for any liabilities arising from contracts for necessities, such as food, shelter, or simple debts. Newfoundland and Labrador, for example, allows a child who entered into a simple contract before the age of 16 to be held responsible after he or she passes the age of 16.

Some provinces, such as B.C., allow children (or an adult acting on their behalf) to ask a court to give them contractual capacity to enter into a contract that would usually be considered unenforceable. In Manitoba, a child over the age of 16 with no parent or guardian can enter into a contract to perform work or a service. In Alberta, Newfoundland and Labrador, and New Brunswick, a child is able after the age of 16 to sign an enforceable life insurance contract.

Some provinces prohibit lawsuits against children after they pass the age of majority based on contractual obligations entered into while they were still minors. That said, some provinces also allow an adult who has entered into a contract with a minor to request a written reaffirmation or repudiation of the contract after the child reaches the age of majority. In some jurisdictions, that must happen within one year for the contract to be enforceable.

CHILD SAFETY & ABUSE

7. What is child abuse?

Child abuse happens when any person, even a parent, guardian, or caregiver mistreats or neglects a child resulting in injury, significant emotional or psychological harm, or serious risk of harm to the child.

Abuse can be physical, sexual, emotional, psychological, or even financial. A child may experience more than one type of abuse. The abuser may also be a sibling, relative or stranger. If anyone is abusing children, there are several things that can be done by police or child protection authorities, and they must be done quickly.

Physical abuse includes hitting, pinching, slapping, pushing, punching, kicking, burning, shooting, stabbing, or cutting someone. For children, sexual abuse is sexual touching or sexual activity. Emotional or psychological abuse can include threats to harm you or someone you know, breaking your belongings, or stalking. All are crimes in Canada.

Another serious form of abuse is neglect. This occurs when a child's parents or other caregivers are not providing the basic necessities needed for emotional, psychological, and physical development. Examples of basic necessities include food, clothing, shelter, cleanliness, medical care, and protection from harm. Emotional neglect is another category of abuse and it happens when a child's need to feel loved, wanted, and safe is not met.

Other forms of abuse that are not usually considered crimes, but can be acted upon, include humiliation, vicious insults, screaming, and name calling.

8. What is the difference between disciplining a child and abuse?

There is no concrete answer to this question since it depends on the degree of force and the circumstances involved. The Criminal Code permits the "corporal" punishment of children by teachers, parents, and guardians when needed to correct children's behaviour. For example, spanking is a common form of punishment.

The Criminal Code does not grant anyone a right to use force nor does it provide a licence to hit children. The law says individuals acting as parents are "justified in using force by way of correction toward a pupil or child, as the case may be, who is under his care, if the force does not exceed what is reasonable under the circumstances." The key issue at all times will be what was reasonable force.

9. Who has a legal obligation to report child abuse?

Anyone who has a reason to believe that a child has been or is likely to be abused or neglected has a legal duty under each province's child protection laws to report the matter to the police, child welfare authorities, or both.

Professionals who work with children, such as doctors, nurses, lawyers, teachers, police, and social workers, have a specific obligation under the law to report promptly any suspicion that a child is or may be in need of protection. A professional who fails to report may be liable for a fine in many provinces.

Most of the reporting "hotlines" are listed in your telephone book in the government pages. You will not have to give any details or proof of an actual offence before calling, but you will be asked for as much information as you can provide. If a civil action is brought against any person who made a report, that person will be protected unless he or she acted maliciously or without reasonable grounds for his or her suspicion.

Usually, you will be asked to provide several things:

- Your name and phone number (you may call anonymously)
- How you know the child and your relationship to the child
- Your immediate concerns about the child's safety
- Location of the child
- Child's age
- Examples of what you've seen that have raised your concern
- Information on the family, parents or alleged offender

After you give your report, a child protection officer or social worker will review your comments to determine if the child needs protection. The police may also be notified, if necessary. In fact, if you believe a child is in immediate danger, call the police yourself as soon as possible.

SENIORS

10. At what age is someone considered a senior citizen?

There is no generally accepted age that determines when one becomes a senior citizen. It is an important question, though, since seniors may be entitled to a variety of benefits ranging from shopping discounts to government benefits.

Basically, a private organization, such as a social club or retail outlet, can make its own rules for determining "seniors" status. Federal and provincial governments may also make their own rules. For example, some government services for senior citizens are available as soon as an individual attains 55 years of age. Government financial benefits, however, often don't come into play until a person is at least 60, 62, or 65, depending on the type of benefit.

11. Can I be forced to retire? Are mandatory retirement ages legal?

Canada's federal and provincial human rights codes protect Canadians from age discrimination. In some jurisdictions, however, these laws specifically exempt those who are 65 years of age or over. As a result, a person could be forced to stop working for a company or government agency. That said, this doesn't mean you are prohibited from working for an employer who doesn't care about your age or working in a self-employed situation.

Lately, some provinces have been reviewing the concept of mandatory retirement. Mandatory retirement has been specifically prohibited in New Brunswick since 1973, Manitoba since 1974, and Québec since 1982.

Jurisdiction	Retirement Rule
Federal	The Canadian Human Rights Act allows mandatory retirement after age 65 for federally regulated industries, but it is not the policy in the federal civil service itself
Alberta	No mandatory retirement
British Columbia	Mandatory retirement at age 65, if required by employer
Manitoba	No mandatory retirement
New Brunswick	Prohibited unless specifically outlined under terms of employment for a retirement or pension plan
Newfoundland and Labrador	Retirement age must be specifically outlined under terms of employment for a retirement or pension plan. Otherwise, mandatory retirement not enforceable until age 65.
Northwest Territories	No mandatory retirement
Nova Scotia	Mandatory retirement at age 65, if required by employer
Nunavut	No mandatory retirement
Ontario	Mandatory retirement at age 65, if required by employer
Prince Edward Island	No mandatory retirement
Québec	No mandatory retirement
Saskatchewan	Mandatory retirement at age 65, if required by employer
Yukon	No mandatory retirement

12. Can family members or others take away a senior's authority to make financial, health, or other decisions?

When situations causing serious illness or diminished mental abilities arise for any individual (whether a senior or not), that person's capacity to make decisions may be reduced. The law recognizes that a substitute decision-maker may be needed.

This substitute can be a family member or anyone chosen by a court, a government agency or, increasingly these days, anyone chosen by the affected individual in advance. Just as you can assign your decision-making authority to a lawyer or someone else through a "power of attorney," you can also assign general or specific financial and health decisions to a substitute decision-maker in the event of your mental or physical incapacity.

Granting of this decision-making authority is not to be taken lightly. The decision-maker must be trusted to make decisions in your best interests. In some cases, it may be best to assign joint authority to both a family member and a lawyer or other professional.

A lawyer can help you draft clear directives for a substitute decision-maker. In some provinces, you may be required to draft different documents for different purposes. For example, Ontario requires three different types of power of attorney for health care and two powers of attorney for property.

13. How can seniors get assistance in finding shelter, food, and other basics?

Each province has some type of initiative to encourage affordable housing for seniors. The type of housing available will depend on the area where you live. Eligibility for assisted housing is often tied to financial need and the rents are either capped or tied to income. To access subsidized seniors' housing, you will need to complete an application and may be put on a waiting list.

For seniors who require care services, such as meals and light nursing, there are rental units called "Care Homes" in which you can rent an apartment or room, or share a room with someone else, as well as receive care services. These housing units are more commonly called "retirement homes" or "supportive living apartments."

Retirement homes are rental housing, although you may also purchase nursing services and other help from the landlord. Most retirement homes are run by private individuals or businesses under a provincial licence. Your rights as a tenant in such establishments are usually governed by the landlord-tenant or retirement home legislation in the province in which you live.

Essentially, you have the same rights as tenants in other rental housing. One difference in most jurisdictions is that landlords in retirement homes must give you a tenancy agreement before you rent the apartment or room. The tenancy agreement must tell you what you are required to pay as rent. It must also include which care services will be provided to you and how much you must pay for each of these services.

The landlord must also give you an *information package* that tells you what other services are available in that retirement home and how much each service costs. The landlord of a retirement home cannot usually evict you or tell you to move, unless he or she follows the rules in your jurisdiction's *Tenant Protection Act.*

14. How can a senior get benefits from the Canada Pension Plan (CPP)?

The Canada Pension Plan is administered by the federal government and provides a benefit plan for all retired workers. Workers pay a portion of their wages into the Canada Pension Plan fund until they retire.

Canada Pension Plan benefits are normally paid to workers when they retire at age 65. If a worker retires between the ages of 60 and 65, he or she may still be eligible for benefits, although the amount may be reduced. If a worker dies before anything is paid out, the benefits may also be paid to a worker's spouse. If the worker becomes disabled and can no longer work, the Canada Pension Plan may also begin paying benefits before the worker turns 65.

The amount of benefits that someone is eligible for depends on how long the person or the person's spouse worked and paid into the plan.

To start receiving benefits when you retire, you will need to fill out an application form available from the Human Resources and Social Development centre in your area and provide a proof of age document, such as a birth certificate.

15. What is Old Age Security (OAS)?

Old Age Security is a benefit paid to most senior citizens. The OAS Program is administered by the federal government through Human Resources and Social Development. Eligibility for OAS benefits depends on your age, how long you have lived in Canada, and your marital status.

You are normally eligible to receive OAS benefits one month after your 65th birthday. Because payments are not automatically sent to you, you will need to apply for the benefit by filling out an application form available from a Human Resources and Social Development centre. Spouses and widowed spouses may also be eligible for a benefit from the age of 60 if their income is below a certain level.

Eligibility for OAS benefits will also depend on the total number of years that you have lived in Canada and whether you currently live in Canada. If you presently live in Canada, you are eligible for benefits provided you lived here for at least 10 years since you turned 18 years old. If you reside outside Canada, you must have lived here at some point for at least 20 years since your 18th birthday to be eligible for benefits. If you do not qualify in either of these categories, you may still be eligible for benefits depending on agreements that may exist between Canada and the countries where you lived.

Your eligibility for OAS benefits also depends on your marital status and the income of your spouse. This includes whether you are married, separated, widowed, or have been living common-law for at least one year.

In addition to regular OAS benefits, a Guaranteed Income Supplement benefit is paid to seniors whose income or combined income with their spouse is very low. To receive the guaranteed income supplement benefit, you will be required to re-apply each year.

Most provinces and territories also offer income supplements, housing allowances, and health benefits to low-income seniors.

16. What is a "reverse mortgage" and what should seniors know about it?

A reverse mortgage is a somewhat controversial financial tool that allows homeowners to access the money or equity they have invested in their homes. It allows homeowners who have little or no income to continue living in their home while they use their property as a source of income. A reverse mortgage can only be obtained by a homeowner who is at least 62 years old and, generally, whose home is entirely paid for.

A reverse mortgage may be a good option for homeowners who need cash to pay for living expenses, but do not have liquid assets. With a reverse mortgage, a percentage of the value of the home is converted to cash and is used to purchase an annuity, which provides the homeowner with a guaranteed income. The cash advance is registered against the title of the home as a mortgage, but no mortgage payments need to be made. The money from the reverse mortgage can be paid in a lump sum or in regular monthly instalments.

With a reverse mortgage, the lender pays the homeowner in cash. Only after the homeowners' death will the home be sold and the bank collects the mortgage amount owing plus interest. Any money that is left over after the home is sold and the bank is paid will be available to beneficiaries or dependants of the homeowner.

While many seniors have benefited from reverse mortgages, others believe it can impoverish an individual's estate. Advice from an independent financial advisor is a good idea before agreeing to a reverse mortgage.

17. What is "elder abuse"?

It is estimated that 4 percent of Canada's elderly suffer physical and mental abuse at the hands of others. Elder abuse occurs when a person in a position of trust or authority harms a senior. This person may be a family member, neighbour, nurse, landlord, or caregiver.

Abusive situations include:

- Someone who is hostile or threatening to a senior
- Someone who makes the senior fearful or ashamed
- Physical violence
- Neglect of the senior's needs
- Someone who coerces seniors to give money or takes advantage of them

If a senior is being abused, that senior or anyone else can call the police. Some police forces have officers who deal specifically with elder abuse.

If anyone believes that a senior or any other adult is not mentally capable and is personally at risk of serious harm, or that the senior's money or property is at serious risk, that individual may report this to the provincial Public Guardian office. This is the government agency responsible for assisting adults who need support in financial and personal decision-making.

A Public Guardian or Public Trustee can investigate allegations of abuse of vulnerable adults in the community and, in serious cases, will become the senior's or the adult's guardian to help or protect that person. The Public Guardian and Trustee may also get help from the police or other social services.

Senior Web sources: Elder Abuse

http://fp.kwic.com/~jpreston/projects.htm
• A listing of Ontario elder abuse community task forces.

http://www.bccrns.ca
• Site of British Columbia's Community Response Network to
support and assist abused adults.

http://www.advocacycentreelderly.org
• A legal clinic for low-income senior citizens.

http://www.attorneygeneral.jus.gov.on.ca/english/family/pgt
• Office of Ontario's Public Guardian and Trustee.

http://www.cacc-acssc.com
• Canadian Association for Community Care, a non-profit organization comprising
home care and support home agencies, long-term care facilities, meals programs,
and community groups.

http://www4.gov.ab.ca/just/trustee/other.cfm#ORG021
• Listing of Canada's Public Guardians.

http://www.elderabusecenter.org
• American organization combating elder abuse.

Senior Web Resources: Financial Information

http://www.hrdc-drhc.gc.ca/isp/common/cpptoc_e.shtml
• Federal government Web site for information about Canada Pension Plan.

http://www.hrdc-drhc.gc.ca/isp/common/oastoc_e.shtml
• Federal government Web site for information about Old Age Security.

http://www.hrdc-drhc.gc.ca/isp/oas/ispb184.shtml#g
• Federal government Web site for information about the Guaranteed
Income Supplement.

http://www.hrdc-drhc.gc.ca/menu/seniors.shtml
• A special Web page for seniors set up by Human Resources and Social
Development Canada that addresses a range of senior issues, from pensions
to care giving.

Pension facts and figures

• The maximum monthly benefit for CPP and QPP in 2005
was $828.75.

• The maximum monthly benefit for Old Age Security in
2005 was $473.65.

• The maximum monthly benefit for a single person seeking
the guaranteed income supplement in 2005 was $562.93.

When Can You Take Your Pension?

Blanche has worked in Canada for 30 years. She turns 60 this year and is considering early retirement.

What are her options when it comes to the Canada Pension Plan (CPP)?

At 60, Blanche could begin receiving a reduced CPP early, wait until she's 65 and receive the full amount, or wait until she's 70 and receive more each month than she would at 65. The amount of her pension will depend on her earnings over the course of her employment.

What Help Is Out There?

Bob lived and worked in Canada for most of his life. He turned 65 and began collecting his Canada Pension Plan. He is finding it hard to meet his bills, however. He has no RRSPs (Registered Retirement Savings Plans) or private pension plan, and is running out of savings.

Is Bob eligible for other assistance?

Bob could apply for Old Age Security (OAS). He must be over 65, and be a Canadian citizen or a resident at the time of his application and have lived in Canada for at least 10 years since turning 18. Bob may also be eligible for the Guaranteed Income Supplement (GIS), which he must apply for and renew each year. To qualify for GIS you must be entitled to OAS. The amount you receive will depend on your income and that of your spouse.

ANIMALS

Do animals have rights? For many years, Canadian lawmakers viewed animals only as property and offered little in the way of legal protection against abuse or mistreatment. Recently, however, there has been a shift toward a more caring and protective approach — one that recognizes we have relationships with our animals.

At all levels of government, from municipal by-laws to provincial hunting laws to the federal *Criminal Code*, there is a recognition that animals may indeed have some rights or, at the very least, that society has fundamental obligations in the handling and care of animals.

In the criminal law, particularly, there is an acknowledgement that the penalties for abuse or mistreatment must be serious enough to deter offenders. Many argue that morally reprehensible behaviour threatens not only animals, but also the moral and physical welfare of society. Studies of criminal behaviour have concluded that acts of intentional cruelty can lead to increasing incidents of violence. Research even shows that many serial killers and mass murderers have a history of animal abuse.

Recently, the federal government debated amendments to the Criminal Code that could strengthen our anti-cruelty laws and recognize the seriousness of animal abuse by:

- Consolidating laws related to cruelty to animals and no longer treating offences as property crimes
- Making it illegal to brutally or viciously kill animals
- Raising the penalty for intentional cruelty to a maximum of five years' imprisonment with no set limit for fines

- Providing that anyone convicted of animal cruelty may be prohibited from owning an animal for any period a judge considers appropriate
- Giving judges the authority to order anyone found guilty of animal cruelty to pay restitution to the animal welfare organization that cared for the animal.

With the laws affecting animals largely unchanged since 1892, these amendments were much anticipated by animal lovers but have failed to make it into law to date. That said, most of us would admit that all animals are not treated equally. Some such as are our pets are beloved friends, while others are used for food, clothing, entertainment, and scientific experiments. For the time being, it will likely be a difficult challenge for the law to find a middle ground in the treatment of animals that will satisfy everyone.

1. How can I help a neglected pet or stop cruelty to animals?

If you discover that an animal is being neglected or treated cruelly, there are at least three ways you can help.

■ Report it to municipal or regional authorities

Local by-laws may provide minimal requirements for the care of so-called "companion animals" or pets. The types of animals covered will be listed in the by-laws and this may vary, depending on where you live. Some typical by-law requirements include the:

- Need to provide proper care and attention to the animal's needs
- Need to ensure that fresh water is available at all times
- Minimum or maximum length of a leash for an animal
- Requirement for some form of shelter from the weather

To find out what by-laws are in place in your community, contact your municipal or regional animal control office or a non-profit humane society. If you believe that local by-laws have been violated, report it to the local animal control office as soon as possible. These public officers have powers under the by-law, such as the authority to warn the offender to stop the cruel behaviour, or to charge that person with violating the by-law.

If an individual is charged, the case will be heard by a Justice of the Peace. If an individual is found guilty, the Justice of the Peace can order the person to pay a fine or to be imprisoned.

It is useful, though not necessary, to have a detailed written or visual record, such as photographs of anything you see, and also a record of when it happened. When you make a complaint, you may be asked to give a verbal or written account of what you witnessed or believe is happening.

▪ Report it to an animal protection organization

Organizations such as the Society for the Prevention of Cruelty to Animals (SPCA) or a Humane Society are often authorized under the law to take action to protect animals in "distress." Animals in distress include those:

- Needing proper care, water, food, or shelter
- Injured, sick, in pain, suffering, or being abused
- Suffering undue or unnecessary hardship or neglect

These organizations can usually issue orders under the law requiring that the animal's owner take necessary action to remedy the problem. In some cases, they can immediately remove the animal from the situation and provide the care that is needed.

▪ Report it to the police

You may be able to have an individual or company criminally prosecuted under the *Criminal Code* for cruelty to animals. The *Criminal Code* gives the police and humane organizations the authority to investigate complaints of animal cruelty and to lay charges where appropriate. Be aware that the police are not always familiar with this part of the *Code*, but you are entitled to make a complaint and have them investigate it.

The *Criminal Code* sets out eight different offences for cruelty to animals. The most common are:

1. Willfully causing or permitting unnecessary pain, suffering or injury to an animal or bird.

2. Owning or having custody or control of an animal, and abandoning the animal in distress or willfully neglecting or failing to provide suitable and adequate food, water, shelter, and care.

3. Participating in the "fighting" or "baiting" of animals.

Depending on how serious the charge is, the owner may have to pay a fine, go to jail, or can be prohibited from owning any animals for a period of up to two years.

2.   What if the police or local humane society will not help a neglected or abused animal?

If the police or local humane society is not helpful in prosecuting a cruelty charge, any member of the public can go before a Justice of the Peace and initiate the laying of a charge. To do this, you must go to your local office for the Justice of the Peace (look in your phone book) and outline or swear what is called an "information." An information is a simple legal document containing details of the alleged offence.

When you meet with the Justice of the Peace, you will have to explain what happened and swear an oath that you have good reason to believe a criminal offence has been committed. If the Justice of the Peace is satisfied that an offence was committed, he or she will issue a "summons" to the alleged offender. The summons is a legal document that orders the person or company you accused to come to court on a specific day to offer a defence to your accusation.

3.   Can I prevent animal abuse in circuses or public shows?

In most provinces, local municipalities pass by-laws on the prohibition, regulation, and licensing of exhibitions, menageries, circus riding, and other similar kinds of shows.

In an increasing number of municipal jurisdictions, from British Columbia to Newfoundland, there are by-laws prohibiting the keeping of particular species of animals or "exotic" pets within the jurisdiction. There are several reasons why these by-laws are enacted:

- Concerns about the cruel ways that performing animals are often trained
- Stressful and impoverished conditions in which the animals live
- Concerns about the well-being of the general public, whose safety may be threatened when exposed to wild, dangerous, and sometimes sick animals

If you are concerned about circuses or other shows abusing animals in your community, contact a municipal councillor. Your municipal councillor may be able to help you contact the municipal clerk or a committee responsible for by-laws. Animal protection groups can also help you collect necessary information.

If your local by-laws do provide for the protection of animals and you feel that a circus or show is in violation of the laws, notify the local animal control office as soon as possible to investigate your complaint.

If your local by-laws do not prohibit the maintaining of certain species of animals or do not provide for minimum standards for the treatment of animals, you could try to bring about a change in your local by-laws. Again, your municipal councillor will be able to guide you on how to begin the process.

In some cases, the poor treatment of circus and other animals may actually constitute a criminal offence. If the situation is bad enough, call an animal protection organization, such as the Humane Society, or the police to have the responsible individuals charged criminally. The *Criminal Code* has several sections dealing with cruelty to animals.

The *Code* gives the police and local Humane Society the authority to investigate complaints of cruelty to animals and lay charges when appropriate. For example, it is a criminal offence for the owner or a person with custody or control of an animal to fail to provide it with suitable and adequate food, water, shelter, and care. Depending on the seriousness of the charge, the offender may have to pay a fine or go to jail. If you decide to contact the police or the Humane Society, do it quickly since a circus or travelling show is usually in town for only a short time.

4.   Can a student be forced to participate in the dissection or vivisection of animals in schools?

If a student is being forced to perform dissections or vivisections, the student may have the right to refuse to participate. First, the student should speak with the teacher responsible for the assignment and ask for an alternative project. If the teacher is unwilling to provide one, the student should contact the head of the school department or the principal. Many schools do provide alternative experiments.

If exploitation of the animals is a violation of the student's sincerely held beliefs and no alternative experiment is provided, the student may be able to rely on the fundamental protections in our Constitution or in human rights laws.

■ Constitutional or *Charter* Rights

The *Canadian Charter of Rights and Freedoms* protects people from government actions that offend their constitutional rights, such as the right to freedom of conscience and religion, as well as the right to freedom of opinion, belief, and expression.

If the school is considered to be an agent of the government and it will not provide an alternative experiment, offended students might be able to rely on *Charter* rights. They may be able to claim the school has an obligation to provide an alternative experiment or procedure that does not violate their conscience and beliefs.

Not all schools, however, may be seen as an agent of the government in the eyes of the law. To decide whether a school is sufficiently connected with the government such that it falls under the *Charter*'s rules, a student will likely have to consult a lawyer. If it is sufficiently connected with the government to make a *Charter* claim possible, then the student and a lawyer will have to decide whether a formal challenge is truly worthwhile.

■ Human rights legislation

If a school is not sufficiently connected with the government to be considered its agent under the *Charter*, a student may still be able to rely on the *Canadian Human Rights Act* if a federally regulated institution is involved, or the provincial *Human Rights Code* for provincially regulated schools. Both of these laws provide, among other things, that everyone has the right to not be discriminated against or harassed based on religion or creed. Complaints of this kind are generally made through a human rights commission or tribunal, not the courts.

For more information about pursuing a human rights claim, refer to the chapter on Human Rights actions.

5. What can I do about hunters trespassing on my property?

■ Put up "No Hunting" signs

All property owners have the right to keep hunters off their property using trespass laws. One way to do this is by putting signs around the edge of your property indicating clearly that hunting is not permitted. The signs may have to be posted in a particular way, as set out in your province's trespass legislation (some jurisdictions don't have a trespass law and rely on the common law or historical precedent). For example, under trespass laws in most jurisdictions, signs posted on your property must be clearly visible in daylight under normal conditions from the approach to each ordinary point of access to the premises. You could use large signs, for example, that have the word "hunting" written on them or a picture of someone hunting and then a slanted red line through the word or the picture to indicate no hunting is allowed.

■ Erect marking systems

Instead of signs, you could also use a special marking system to tell people that hunting on your property is prohibited. Ontario, for example, has a system of red or yellow markings. These markings must be posted and large enough that a circle 10 centimetres in diameter can fit wholly inside the marking. Like any trespass sign, the markings must be clearly visible in daylight under normal conditions from the approach to each ordinary point of access to your property.

Under the Ontario marking system, red markings mean that entry of any kind on the premises is prohibited. Yellow markings mean that entry on the premises is prohibited, except for certain activities. To ensure the markings you use are correct, obtain legal advice or contact your provincial government department or ministry responsible for natural resources, which usually oversees hunting. You can also contact the provincial Justice Department or Attorney General, which may administer trespass laws.

■ Hunting dogs

Often, hunters use their dogs to go on ahead of them and flush the hunted animals out. Even when it is not hunters themselves, but their dogs that enter your property, this may also be considered trespassing.

■ Taking action against a trespasser

Where either a hunter or a hunter's dog is on your property, you should call the police or the local natural resources office. If you have posted proper signs or markings on your property, you, a person authorized by you or a police officer can arrest the trespasser without a warrant. Be careful, however, since anyone making an arrest who is not a police officer must promptly call for the assistance of a police officer.

If a person has trespassed and has since left the premises, only a police officer can go after that person and make the arrest. Under the law, the trespasser may be ordered to pay a fine or even go to jail.

Your provincial government, such as a Ministry of Natural Resources, might also be of assistance. These Ministries regulate hunting, trapping, and other uses of wild animals. Their authority is often set out in legislation, such as a *Fish and Wildlife Conservation Act*. These laws require hunters to respect property rights, and violators may be ordered to pay a fine or go to prison.

A Pet's "Best Interests" or An Owner's Rights?

A breeder of Miniature Dachshunds sells a puppy to an individual for $650. The breeder cautions the new owner to take good care of the dog or she will take it back.

Five years later, the breeder is contacted and asked to take care of the dog for a few weeks while the owner is away. The breeder is shocked to see the dog is three times its proper weight and suffering from physical neglect. She decides to refuse return of the dog to the owner, claiming he breached the condition of sale. The owner sues, noting he has not been convicted of neglect by the authorities and claiming the dog is his property to do with as he wishes.

Does the dog owner have an absolute right of possession?

No, said a British Columbia provincial court judge in Watson v. Hayward (2002 BCPC 0259). While a domestic animal is personal property, ruled the judge, provincial laws protecting animals from cruelty can override those rights, even when an individual has not been convicted of neglect or another offence. The judge noted other court cases that have found certain pet adoption agreements do create a limited property interest in an animal if certain conditions of care are not met. In this case, though, the court ruled the overriding interest was the "best interests" of the dog and the breeder was awarded custody.

A "Defective" Pet?

After a dog was treated for canine hip dysplasia, the owner of the Golden Labrador Retriever sued the seller to recover veterinary expenses. The owner argued he had purchased a "defective dog."

Who is responsible for the bills… the owner or the seller?

The owner. In the case of Gandy v. Robinson, [1990] N.B.J. No. 565, the trial judge acknowledged that while there is a contract of purchase and sale for the dog between the people involved, there is also a contractual relationship of sorts between the dog and its owner.

There was no evidence to suggest the seller had knowingly sold a defective animal and no guarantees of future fitness were offered at the time of sale. The court went on, however, to note that another contract was "drawn up between man and dog over 10,000 years ago." If a dog is a loving companion, provides protection, and does what dogs are supposed to do, owners in return will provide it with food, water, shelter, companionship, and care. In this case, the court said the dog's health care costs were covered under the "contract" between owner and dog, in return for the pet's performance of its tasks.

Proposed Criminal Code Amendments, 2003 and 2005

Cruelty to animals

182.1

In this Part, "animal" means a vertebrate, other than a human being, and any other animal that has the capacity to feel pain.

Killing or harming animals

182.2

(1) Every one commits an offence who, willfully or recklessly,

- (a) causes or, being the owner, permits to be caused unnecessary pain, suffering or injury to an animal;
- (b) kills an animal or, being the owner, permits an animal to be killed, brutally or viciously, regardless of whether the animal dies immediately;
- (c) kills an animal without lawful excuse;
- (d) without lawful excuse, poisons an animal, places poison in such a position that it may easily be consumed by an animal, administers an injurious drug or substance to an animal or, being the owner, permits anyone to do any of those things;
- (e) in any manner encourages, promotes, arranges, assists at or receives money for the fighting or baiting of animals, including training an animal to fight another animal;
- (f) builds, makes, maintains, keeps or allows to be built, made, maintained or kept a cockpit or any other arena for the fighting of animals on premises that he or she owns or occupies;
- (g) promotes, arranges, conducts, assists in, receives money for or takes part in any meeting, competition, exhibition, pastime, practice, display or event at or in the course of which captive animals are liberated by hand, trap, contrivance or any other means for the purpose of being shot at the moment they are liberated; or

(h) being the owner, occupier or person in charge of any premises, permits the premises or any part of the premises to be used in the course of an activity referred to in paragraph (e) or (g).

Punishment

(2) Every one who commits an offence under subsection (1) is guilty of

(a) an indictable offence and liable to imprisonment for a term of not more than five years; or

(b) an offence punishable on summary conviction and liable to a fine not exceeding ten thousand dollars or imprisonment for a term of not more than eighteen months or to both.

Failing to provide adequate care

182.3

(1) Every one commits an offence who

(a) negligently causes unnecessary pain, suffering or injury to an animal;

(b) being the owner, or the person having the custody or control of an animal, willfully or recklessly abandons it or negligently fails to provide suitable and adequate food, water, air, shelter and care for it; or

(c) negligently injures an animal while it is being conveyed.

Definition of "negligently"

(2) For the purposes of subsection (1), "negligently" means departing markedly from the standard of care that a reasonable person would use.

Punishment

(3) Every one who commits an offence under subsection (1) is guilty of

(a) an indictable offence and liable to imprisonment for a term of not more than two years; or

(b) an offence punishable on summary conviction and liable to a fine not exceeding five thousand dollars or imprisonment for a term of not more than six months or to both.

Note: As of the time of publication, the proposed amendments in Bill C-15B were not yet passed into law.

Web Resources

Canadian Federation of Humane Societies	www.cfhs.ca
Yukon SPCA	users.yknet.yk.ca/adoptapet
British Columbia SPCA	www.spca.bc.ca
Alberta SPCA	www.albertaspca.org
Canadian SPCA	www.spca.com
Ontario Society for the Prevention of Cruelty to Animals	www.ospca.on.ca

Section Three

MONEY MATTERS

Spending Money

We are consumers nearly every day of our lives. We get our car repaired at the corner gas station, we buy an article of clothing, or hire someone to fix our roof. What if those goods or services we buy are not what we expected?

Consumer law is all about ensuring that you get fair treatment in the purchase and sale of goods and services. Canada has some of the best consumer protection laws in the world. In fact, all provinces and the federal government have laws that deal with the sale of commercial goods and almost all these governments have laws specifically to protect consumers. The courts also have become much more protective of the average consumer in their rulings.

In the bad old days when only the common law applied, the rule was always "buyer beware." Today, legislation clearly spells out the ground rules for selling and buying goods. Provincial laws determine exactly when and how the title to goods is transferred from the seller to the buyer and what remedies are available when disputes arise. These laws can also help protect the seller, too.

1.   What are the general principles of consumer protection laws?

Consumer laws are really just another form of contract law. Generally, the rights of individual consumers hinge on the "conditions" (essential terms) and "warranties" (promises) of a contract of sale. Some provincial laws refer to "express warranties" (conditions) and "implied warranties" (warranties).

The "contract" can be in writing or oral. For significant purchases, of course, it's always best to do business in writing since it's easier to prove what was promised. In fact, Alberta, Newfoundland and Labrador, Nova Scotia, P.E.I., Saskatchewan, and the Territories all have laws requiring contracts, over a certain value to be in writing and signed by a purchaser to be enforceable. The value ranges from $1,000 in the Yukon to just $30 in P.E.I.

The conditions of a contract are quite different from the warranties. A breach of a condition, such as changing the contracted price or selling goods without proper ownership rights, is a serious infringement of a sales contract that makes it "void" in the eyes of the law. The consumer can refuse to go through with the deal, ask for a refund, or demand a replacement product, since the contract is not enforceable.

By contrast, a warranty is a representation or promise by the seller which you relied on, such as a promise that a product is this year's model and not last year's. A breach of a warranty must only be remedied or fixed by the seller (usually at no cost to the consumer), but does not necessarily destroy the contract and your obligation to accept and pay for the goods once repaired.

The *Sale of Goods* laws in all provinces provide basic conditions and warranties that apply automatically in every commercial or consumer transaction. For example, there is an implied condition that the seller has a right to sell the goods and there is an implied warranty that the goods will be free from claims by a third party unknown to the buyer at or before the contract was made. Québec doesn't have a *Sale of Goods Act*, but its Civil Code provides for similar conditions and warranties. While buyers and sellers are free to strike any deal they want, *Sale of Goods* laws often forbid any attempts to "contract out" some fundamental consumer rights.

Sale of Goods laws normally apply only to purchases of goods and not services. Most provinces, however, have other laws that may apply to goods and services. These may include a *Consumer Protection Act, Direct Sellers Act, Fair Trading Practices Act,* or *Unfair Business Practices Act.* Some of these laws may also require that consumer contracts be written in "plain English" or "plain language" that is understandable to the average citizen.

Consumer protection legislation in Manitoba, Saskatchewan, Nova Scotia, New Brunswick, and the Territories do apply to services. Alberta's *Fair Trading Practices Act* applies to all consumer transactions, including both supply of goods and services. In Newfoundland and Labrador, P.E.I., and B.C., the consumer protection laws focus more on direct sales contracts, executory contracts, and credit contracts.

Consumer protection laws in Manitoba, Nova Scotia, New Brunswick, Saskatchewan, Ontario, and the Territories are even more far-reaching than the *Sale of Goods Acts.* They set out specific conditions and warranties that must be implied in every consumer sale and the implied warranties cannot be waived by the buyer or seller.

Manitoba, Nova Scotia, New Brunswick, and Saskatchewan and the Territories include additional warranties that goods must be new unless otherwise stated by the seller, that goods are of merchantable quality, and that goods match the description under which they are sold. Again, these warranties cannot be waived in the contract.

2. Does a business have to accept the return of a product I am unsatisfied with? Can I get my money back?

The answer to these questions depends on what is wrong with the product. If the goods you purchased do not work as advertised, are defective in a way that you did not know about at the time of purchase, or what you ordered was different from what was delivered, you likely have a right to a refund or, at least, a replacement.

If the defect is a breach of a "condition" or fundamental term of the sale, you can choose to treat it as an event that voids or nullifies the contract. You can return or refuse the defective product and the seller should return your money. If the defect is a breach of a warranty or a misrepresentation of what was promised, the seller is only obligated to either repair or replace the product.

Problems in returning products can arise if the seller advertises something "as is," sells on the basis of "no returns/final sale" or points out defects before you purchase. In that case, you are usually obliged to inspect the goods before purchase and decide for yourself if it's what you want.

If, however, you simply don't want the product anymore, don't like the colour, or you saw it for a better price elsewhere, you will have to rely on the business's refund and return policy.

Sellers are free to set the conditions of sale so long as they make their policy clear at the cash register or through signage in the store. One store can require returns within 10 days, another can allow 30 days, and yet another can charge you a "restocking" fee for returns of otherwise good merchandise.

Some retailers follow the dubious practice of stating their return policy on the back of the sales slip (which does you no good after you've bought), so it's always wise to ask about returns and refunds before you buy.

3.   The salesperson made promises I relied on that are not in writing or in a contract. Is the business still responsible?

Oral promises, they say, are not worth the paper they're written on. In most cases, statements or representations by salespeople should always be in writing to help you later prove what was promised.

That said, many jurisdictions have consumer protection legislation that says oral statements of a salesperson that are relied upon by the consumer can be considered enforceable "warranties" in a sales contract. In other words, a business will have to honour those promises or provide some form of remedy.

Also, the law is clear that businesses are also responsible for any statement a salesperson makes while acting within the scope of his or her actual, usual, or apparent authority. In court, the onus will be on the supplier to prove that the salesperson was acting outside the scope of his or her authority.

Finally, it is worth noting that a seller is also responsible for statements or promises that a manufacturer or distributor makes on packaging, signs, or documents accompanying the product.

4. A business sent me unsolicited goods in the mail and then an invoice. Do I have to pay?

No. Most jurisdictions have legislation that specifically prohibits attempts to charge you for unsolicited goods, such as books or credit cards. You are not obligated to pay any invoice and you are not responsible for sending the goods back.

Some book-of-the-month clubs used to cause problems for consumers by sending unsolicited goods and then charging for the books if you didn't send them back within a set period. These days, most reputable book or record clubs merely send you a catalogue each month and ask you to pick a minimum number of products per year. Others, though, may entice you to join their club with special prices and then lock you into a contract that involves them sending "special" products regularly. Read the agreement closely before you sign.

It is also worth noting that criminals may try to send you or your business fraudulent invoices for directories, Web site listings, office supplies, or other products you have not ordered or received. You are under no obligation to pay the invoice, no matter how "official" it seems to be.

5. Can a business be held criminally liable for its practices?

The federal *Competition Act* provides several criminal penalties for certain types of business practices. For example, it is against this law for businesses to conspire or plot to prevent, limit, or lessen competition in the trade of goods or services. This might happen if two or more businesses in town decided to charge everyone the same price for a good or service and drive any competition out.

The penalty for a conspiracy conviction can be imprisonment for a term of up to five years and a fine not exceeding $10 million per offence. Other criminal offences include:

- Price discrimination (giving discounts or rebates to one purchaser which are not given to others buying goods of like quality and quantity)
- Predatory pricing (selling products for unreasonably low prices)
- Reckless or knowingly misleading representations in advertising or contracts

Prosecution of these offences is not common, though the competition authorities do tend to pursue large businesses, such as department stores or national chain stores.

Note that the federal competition law also allows any person who has suffered a loss from these criminal activities to sue in civil court to recover the loss plus legal costs. This is a relatively new right for consumers. An interesting aspect of this law is that evidence from any criminal proceeding (such as a voluntary plea of guilt or no contest) can be used in the private lawsuit — making a consumer's case very easy to win when a criminal prosecution by the federal government has been successful.

Competition authorities can also investigate and stop business practices that are not illegal or criminal, but contrary to consumers' interest. These include unreasonable refusals to deal with specific consumers and any abuse of dominant market position.

6.   What is misleading advertising?

As we all know, some advertisers can be a bit too enthusiastic about their products and "over-sell" the benefits. "The best you can buy…" "The leading widget in the world…" "The only tool you will ever need…"

As reasonable consumers, many of us know these claims are not all true and cannot all be believed. In law, these claims are often called "puffery." And few businesses are ever charged with misleading advertising for their exuberance.

Some businesses, however, do make claims that are knowingly false in an attempt to make us buy their products or try to fool us into believing a product or service does what it cannot actually do. Some businesses try to get us into their stores with very low prices available in low (or no) quantities and then push a more expensive product on us (a ploy called a "bait-and-switch"). Others may claim "fire sale" or reduced sale prices that are really their everyday, ordinary prices. When serious enough, these misleading advertisements and pricing claims can be prosecuted in criminal court and the businesses sued in civil courts.

The federal *Competition Act* can apply to advertising cases in both civil and criminal courts. It is against the law to make any false or misleading representation to the public for the purpose of promoting a business interest, particularly if it is done deliberately or recklessly. If it's not deliberate or reckless, the federal government may simply tell the business to "cease and desist," pay a fine, and publish information notices to the public telling of its errors.

7. What must be disclosed in a promotional contest or draw?

The federal *Competition Act* has specific requirements for disclosure in any promotional contests. The rules of the contest must be easily available to the consumer and disclose the number and value of prizes. The rules must tell you the chances of winning. Also, since gambling via lotteries is only allowed by governments, contests will usually offer a "no purchase required" method of entry and require that potential winners answer a skill-testing question.

A new provision in the competition law forbids businesses from sending so-called "deceptive prize notifications." In these schemes, a consumer receives a notice that suggests he or she has already won a prize. The "sting" in this scam comes when the "winner" must pay money or incur a cost to collect the prize. A business can avoid prosecution under this provision by consulting a lawyer and making specific written disclosures to consumers.

8. What can I do about defective goods I bought?

If you purchase a defective product, you are often entitled to compensation from either the store that sold you the product or from the manufacturer that designed and made the product.

Generally, a consumer who purchases goods or services is entitled to sue for damages for breach of the contract if the quality, fitness, or performance of the product does not match the express or implied terms of sale. Sometimes, the implied terms can be what are reasonable or normally expected in trade practice or common use.

■ Compensation under a warranty

First, you should check if the product came with a warranty or guarantee either from the store or the manufacturer. If it did, you may be entitled to a refund or some other form of compensation by contacting the store or the manufacturer and explaining your problem.

■ Compensation under the *Sale of Goods Act*

If you discover, however, that the product did not come with a warranty or if the seller or the manufacturer tells you that the defect you have experienced is not covered by the warranty, you may still be entitled to compensation. Under the *Sale of Goods Act*, businesses have three legal obligations to their customers, regardless of whether the product came with a specific warranty or guarantee.

First, they are legally required to sell products that are suitably fit for their purpose. Essentially, the product you purchased must function in the way that it is supposed to function.

Second, if you bought the product based on a description, as found in a catalogue for instance, or if you bought the product based on a sample, such as a carpet swatch, the goods you receive must correspond to that description or sample.

Third, if the goods are bought by description (a catalogue description for example) they must be fit to be sold. The *Sale of Goods Act* applies to every consumer sale of goods, even if a seller told you before you purchased the item that the *Sale of Goods Act* would not apply, or if you signed a contract that said that the Act did not apply. Legislation prohibits exclusion of these statutory warranties and conditions from contracts for the sale of products to consumers.

If a seller violates any of these obligations, you are entitled to cancel the contract and receive a refund. If the store is unwilling to refund your money or otherwise compensate you, or if they insist that you contact the manufacturer, tell them that under the *Sale of Goods Act* they are required to handle your complaint.

■ When to contact the manufacturer

Although the store where the product was purchased should be your main focus, there are a few instances where you may want to contact the manufacturer. First, you may want to contact the manufacturer simply to warn it about the defective product. Second, if a store is completely unwilling to handle your complaint, you may have to call the manufacturer and explain your problem to its Customer Service department. Third, a manufacturer will be your only avenue for compensation if you did not personally purchase the product. If this is the case, the store where the product was purchased does not have any obligations to you under the *Sale of Goods Act.*

■ Compensation in a negligence claim

If you get no satisfaction by this stage, your only option may be a civil lawsuit claiming negligence in the manufacture of the good. If the damages are small enough, you may be able to pursue this in small claims court without a lawyer.

You will have to prove there was a failure to exercise reasonable care in the design or manufacture of or instructions for the product that resulted in injury to a foreseeable user (you) or your property. If there was an unintended defect in the way the product was made, a court will still likely hold the manufacturer responsible since its processes or employees should have caught the error.

You may also be able to sue when a retailer, distributor, or manufacturer recklessly or carelessly makes false statements about the safety or use of the product. This is called a negligent misrepresentation. The court will look closely to see if you relied on that statement and that it caused you damage.

If you have experienced a loss or injury, contact a legal clinic or consult a lawyer for more information on beginning a lawsuit for compensation.

9. What can I do about unsatisfactory services I bought?

If you purchase a service that is carried out in an unsatisfactory way, you may be entitled to compensation from the person or company that provided the service.

Common services include house painting, vehicle and appliance repair. Although you may not have signed a written contract, you still have certain rights and protection under the law. Purchasing a service always forms a contract, whether formally written or not. It is best to always put the contract in writing to avoid uncertainty and confusion about what you are agreeing to.

■ Compensation under a warranty

First, check if the service came with a warranty or guarantee from the seller of the service. If it did, you may be entitled to a refund or some other form of compensation by contacting the person or company who performed the service and explaining your problem.

■ Compensation under the law

If you discover that the product did not come with a warranty or if the seller tells you that your problem is not covered by the warranty, you might still be entitled to compensation. Under the law, service providers are required to meet three specific standards:

- They must perform the service with a reasonable amount of care.
- They are required to perform the service within proper industry standards.
- They are required to use materials of reasonably good quality.

■ Compensation in a breach of contract or negligence claim

If you get no satisfaction by this stage, your only option may be a civil lawsuit claiming a breach of contract or negligence in performance of the service. If the damages are small enough, you may be able to purse this in small claims court without a lawyer.

For a breach of contract claim, you will have to prove that what was promised in writing or orally was not performed or delivered. Typically, a court will award you damages or financial compensation for the breach. In rare cases, the court may award "specific performance" and require the contract be fulfilled.

In a negligence claim, you will have to prove there was a failure to exercise reasonable care in the delivery of the service that resulted in injury to a foreseeable user (you) or your property. If there was an unintended defect in the way the service was rendered, a court will still likely hold the service provider responsible.

You may also be able to sue when a service provider recklessly or carelessly makes false statements about the service. This is called a negligent misrepresentation. The court will look closely to see if you relied on that statement and that it caused you damage.

■ Steps to take to protect yourself

To protect yourself against unsatisfactory services, it is important to put your agreement in a written contract. Write out the services you are paying for, how the services are to be performed, and for what price. You should also specify exactly when the repair will be completed.

10. What can I do about dishonest businesses and practices?

Although most sellers and retailers make honest claims about the products and services they are selling, sometimes a dishonest seller may overly exaggerate. To protect consumers from such misleading sales claims and unfair business practices, governments have *Business Practices Acts*, which identify what unfair business practices are and the rights for consumers who have been victimized.

■ Business Practices Act

Eight provinces have legislation to control unfair business practices. Most *Business Practices Acts* list these examples of false, misleading, or deceptive consumer representations, including:

• A seller stating that a product or service has sponsorship or approval that it really does not have

• A seller stating that a product or service has a particular standard, quality, or style that it really does not have

• A seller indicating that a product is new when it is not, or

• A seller or repairperson stating that a particular repair or replacement is needed when it is not

The law also takes into account whether the consumer was subject to undue pressure to purchase the product or service, whether the price was excessively high, and whether the consumer was unable to protect his or her interests because of a disability or illiteracy.

■ Signing a contract

Be careful when signing any contract to ensure that the written document contains the promises or guarantees that the seller told you about. If the seller won't write these "extras" in, then they are not really available. Never sign a contract you don't fully understand.

■ Cancelling a contract

If you have been convinced to buy a product or service based on a false, misleading, or deceptive sales pitch or advertisement, the *Business Practices Act* gives you the right to cancel the contract. Under the law, cancelling a contract is called "rescission."

To rescind a contract, write a letter to the sales person or company within six months of entering into the agreement. In your letter, describe your problem and indicate that you wish to rescind the agreement because of an unfair practice under the *Business Practices Act*.

If the company or sales person refuses to handle your complaint, your next step is to bring a civil lawsuit. You can also contact the provincial Ministry of Consumer and Commercial Relations for assistance and more information on your rights.

11. What should I know about co-signing or guaranteeing a loan?

Banks and other financial lenders will often require someone other than the borrower to co-sign or guarantee the loan. Although many people are familiar with these practices, consumers are often unaware of the legal consequences.

■ **Co-signing for a loan**

If you co-sign a loan for someone, such as your child or your spouse, you are equally responsible for the repayment of the loan. This means the lender can demand payment from you before, instead of, or after approaching the borrower.

■ **Guaranteeing a loan**

On the other hand, if you guarantee a loan for someone else, the bank or other lender must first demand payment from the borrower before asking the guarantor. Despite this difference, both co-signers and guarantors are equally responsible for the full amount of the loan if the original borrower does not repay the loan. If you have signed a continuing guarantee, you may even be legally responsible for all future loans taken out by the borrower.

Co-signing or guaranteeing a loan can have major financial consequences. It can cost you money and affect your own credit rating. To better protect yourself, have a lawyer review the agreement before you sign it. You might also want to ask the lender to keep you informed of all activity on the loan account.

12. What should I know about buying or leasing a new vehicle?

There are both advantages and disadvantages to buying and leasing a new vehicle. Depending on your preferences and particular financial situation, one option may be more or less suitable for you. Although leasing usually has the short-term benefit of lower monthly payments, buying has the long-term benefit of full vehicle ownership.

■ **What is leasing?**

Leasing a vehicle can be compared to a long-term vehicle rental. By signing a lease contract, you are agreeing to pay an amount each month for the use of the vehicle over a specified number of years. The number of years you agree to is called the "term" of the lease. During the lease, you do not own the vehicle. At the end of the term, you may have the option to simply stop making payments and return the vehicle to the leasing company, or you may be able to fully purchase the vehicle for a specified price.

■ **How are the monthly payments calculated?**

Your monthly lease payments will generally be equivalent to the vehicle's depreciation, which means the decline in the value of the vehicle over time. So, for example, if the depreciation on a $30,000 vehicle over a three-year lease term is $10,000, it means that three years later, the vehicle will only be worth $20,000. Your lease arrangement would finance that $10,000 depreciation by spreading out the $10,000, plus the interest, over the three-year term in the form of your monthly payments.

■ Advantages of leasing

Leasing is a better option than buying in three specific circumstances. First, leasing is beneficial for people who want to change their vehicle for a new vehicle every two years or so. Generally, leasing will be extremely expensive over the long run for someone who intends to keep the same vehicle for more than two years. Second, leasing may be a better choice if you are using the vehicle for business. By leasing, you can deduct the lease payments as an expense rather than deducting the depreciation, which tends to be less.

Third, leasing is a more affordable short-term choice in many cases. Although leasing can become more expensive in the long run, your down payment will be less and your monthly lease payments will generally be lower than monthly loan payments on the purchase of a vehicle.

■ Disadvantages of leasing

Although leasing has its advantages, there are a number of drawbacks:

1. You do not own the vehicle, and you may never own the vehicle unless you pay a large sum at the end of your lease, usually called a "buy back." You are basically paying rent on the vehicle for a certain period.

2. There may be certain restrictions on the use of the vehicle, and you may not be able to use it in another province or country.

3. You may have to pay penalties at the end of your lease if you exceed the mileage limitations, and you will have to pay penalties if you want to end the lease early.

4. You are obligated to maintain the vehicle in accordance with the maintenance schedule set out in the lease contract.

5. If you decide that you do not want to continue leasing the vehicle, you are obligated to pay for the full term of the lease. If you try to break the contract, the leasing company will normally sue you.

6. There are often "hidden" or "forgotten" costs at the end of the lease, such as administrative and "wear and tear" costs that could result in a lease costing more than you first thought.

Before signing a lease agreement, make sure you fully understand your obligations. Ask about a number of details, such as your responsibility on the residual value, gap insurance, residual value insurance to protect you if your vehicle depreciates faster than projected, and whether the lease is open or closed. For more information on leasing a vehicle, you can call the Automobile Protection Association.

■ Advantages of buying

Although buying a vehicle may require a larger down payment and possibly higher monthly payments, your money will be going toward a vehicle that you will eventually own. Buying a vehicle has a number of other advantages, including no restrictions on how and where you can use the vehicle. If you are using the vehicle for business, you can deduct the depreciation of the vehicle and the interest on any money you borrowed to finance it.

13. Is a used vehicle an option?

For many prospective vehicle buyers, a used vehicle is a much more affordable alternative to a brand new one. However, before making a purchase, carefully consider both the benefits and disadvantages of buying a used vehicle.

■ Two main benefits

First, and most obvious, the purchase price of used vehicles is less than that of new vehicles. Also, unlike new vehicles, you do not have to pay federal GST on used vehicles bought privately.

Second, used vehicles retain more of their value over the years. Not only are new vehicles significantly more expensive, but they also depreciate at a faster rate than older vehicles. This means they lose more value in their early years. For example, a used vehicle purchased for $10,000 may be worth $6,000 three years later. A new vehicle, however, purchased for $30,000, may only be worth $20,000 three years later. Buying a used vehicle means you will lose less of your money to depreciation.

■ Disadvantages

Despite the up-front financial savings, a used vehicle may require more repairs. And, unlike new vehicles, most used vehicles will not include a manufacturer's warranty for repair and service. In fact, often drivers decide to sell their vehicle specifically because maintenance is required, or because the warranty has expired.

■ Used Vehicle Information Packages

In Ontario, the provincial government has a service called the Used Vehicle Information Package. This package contains a variety of information, including a complete history of the vehicle and whether there are any liens registered against it.

If you are buying a used vehicle privately, and not through a car dealership, the seller is required by law to provide you with a copy of the Used Vehicle Information Package for the vehicle you are buying. If you are buying a used vehicle from a car dealership, contact the Ontario Ministry of Consumer and Commercial Relations or a Driver and Vehicle Licence Issuing Office to obtain a copy of the Package before buying the vehicle.

Make sure that the name of the person selling the vehicle is the name registered in the Package and that there are no outstanding liens on the vehicle. If you buy a vehicle that has a lien registered against it, you may be held responsible for the outstanding debt. It is not necessary to conduct a search for liens under the *Personal Property Security Act* if you have a copy of a recent Used Vehicle Information Package.

Once you buy a used vehicle, you are required by law to take the Package to a Driver and Vehicle Licence Issuing Office to register as the new owner and pay retail sales tax within six days of the sale. If you purchased the used vehicle from a car dealer, you will be required to pay both Provincial Sales Tax and the GST. However, if your vehicle was purchased privately, you are only responsible for paying Provincial Sales Tax. The tax will be based on either the purchase price of the vehicle, or the average wholesale value of the vehicle listed in the Used Vehicle Information Package, whichever is greater.

You will be required to bring a number of documents with you when you go to register as the new owner, including the entire Used Vehicle Information Package, the vehicle portion of the Application to Transfer, which should be given to you by the seller, a Safety Standards Certificate, valid vehicle insurance information, and driver's licence or other identification. If you are transferring your licence plates from your old vehicle to your new one, you will have to bring the plate portion of the registration permit. If you are buying new plates, you will have to bring at least $90 to purchase a plate and a validation sticker for one year.

It is not advisable to purchase a vehicle that does not have a Used Vehicle Information Package available. This may mean that the vehicle has come from another country or province, and often such vehicles have suffered considerable damage in an earlier automobile collision. If a Package exists, but the seller did not give it to you, you may be required to buy the Package before you can register the vehicle.

For now, this information service is only available in Ontario, though some private businesses do advertise services purporting to track a used vehicle's history.

■ Tips when shopping for a used vehicle

• Inspect the vehicle during the daytime

• Take the vehicle for a test drive. If the steering is pulling in one direction, the vehicle may require an alignment. If the brakes squeal, the vehicle may require new brake pads. If blue smoke is coming from the exhaust, the vehicle may need expensive engine repairs. If you notice a general lack of control or excessive bounce when driving, the vehicle may require steering repairs or new shocks.

• Check the odometer for kilometres travelled over the life of the vehicle. You can also check the Used Vehicle Information Package for a record of the kilometres each time the vehicle was sold. It is illegal to tamper with a vehicle's odometer.

• Check with the mechanic who prepared the Safety Standards Certificate. Although the vehicle is road-worthy, it may need extensive repairs.

14. How do I sell a used vehicle?

To sell a used vehicle, you must comply with any rules established by your provincial government.

For example, if you are selling a used vehicle privately in Ontario, you are required by law to purchase a Used Vehicle Information Package and make it available to prospective purchasers. This package contains information about the history of the vehicle and whether anyone has a claim to the vehicle. You can obtain the Package for a cost of $20 from any Driver and Vehicle Licence Issuing Office or from the Ministry of Consumer and Commercial Relations.

In Ontario, you must give the Package to the buyer when the vehicle is eventually sold. Once you find a buyer, record your name and signature as well as the sale price and date on the bill of sale portion of the Package. The buyer must then take the Package to a Driver and Vehicle Licence Issuing Office to be registered as the new owner and pay the retail sales tax.

In all jurisdictions, as a seller, you must also complete and sign a section on the back of your car registration documentation, sometimes referred to as the *Application to Transfer*. You will give the vehicle portion to the buyer, and keep the plate portion of the registration permit for yourself. You will use this plate portion if you decide to put your licence plates on a new vehicle.

As a seller, you must remove your licence plates from the vehicle you are selling. You can keep them and use them on your next vehicle. Even if the buyer asks you to, it is best not to leave your licence plates on the vehicle you are selling. If you give your plates to the buyer and the buyer does not have his or her own vehicle insurance, your insurance will have to pay for the damage if the buyer is in a car accident.

You should be careful not to misrepresent the condition or previous use of the car. It is all right to give a positive description of what you are selling, but any important stated fact that the buyer later discovers is not true may entitle the buyer to return the vehicle.

The safest method to accept payment for your used vehicle is in the form of cash, certified cheque, or money order. A regular cheque may bounce, leaving you without your vehicle and without payment.

15. What should I know about motor vehicle repairs?

Many provinces have *Motor Vehicle Repair Acts* to protect consumers when they take their vehicle to a dealership, used car lot, neighbourhood garage, muffler shop, auto body shop, or gas station. The laws generally say you must be given a clear estimate for work and repairs, and a minimum warranty for all parts and labour. Anyone who works on or repairs the vehicle for a fee must obey this law.

■ The right to a written estimate

If you ask for a written estimate you cannot be charged for any work or repairs unless you accept this estimate and authorize the job. Estimates must include:

- Your name and address, and the name and address of the garage or shop
- A complete identification of your vehicle
- A description of the work or repairs to be done
- A list of the parts to be installed
- Information about whether these parts will be new, used or reconditioned

- The price of these parts
- The number of hours that will be billed
- The hourly rate
- The total labour costs
- The total amount that will be billed
- The date the estimate is given
- The date after which the estimate is no longer good

The garage cannot charge you for providing an estimate unless you are told in advance that there is a cost and what the cost will be. By law, the fee for providing an estimate includes the cost of diagnostic time plus the cost of reassembling your vehicle. It also includes the parts a garage or shop might damage and have to replace while providing an estimate.

If you authorize someone to work on your vehicle and the work is completed, you cannot be charged for the estimate, even if you were told about the costs of providing an estimate from the start. The only exception is when the garage or shop has to wait a long time for your authorization. If this happens and your vehicle has to be reassembled and moved to free up repair space, you can be charged for both the estimate as well as the repairs.

■ How much can you be charged?

There is a limit to how much you can be charged for work or repairs on your vehicle. First, you cannot legally be charged for work or repairs unless you authorized the job. Second, if you received a written estimate, you cannot be charged more that 10 percent above that estimate. If you authorize a job by telephone, the garage or shop must record your authorization in writing.

■ You can get parts returned to you

When you authorize a garage or shop to work on your vehicle, you should say whether you want your old parts returned to you. Unless you say you do not, the garage or shop must offer to return old parts, and the garage must give the old parts to you in a clean container if you do want them.

■ Posted signs required

In most jurisdictions, every garage or shop must post signs stating the following five things:

- Whether they charge for estimates
- That written estimates are available upon request

• That old parts can be returned to you after the work or repairs are done

• How labour costs will be calculated, including the hourly rate and any pre-set or minimum time charged for labour, and

• The telephone of the Ministry of Consumer and Commercial Relations, unless this telephone number is printed on the invoice or repair order

The signs should be posted in a conspicuous place where the customers can see them.

■ Warranty on all work or repairs

The law says that your garage or shop must give warranties on all new or reconditioned parts and the labour needed to install them. This warranty must be for a minimum of 90 days or 5,000 kilometres, whichever comes first.

During the warranty period, if your vehicle breaks down or becomes unsafe because of the work done by the garage, take it back to the garage or shop that did the job. If this is not practical, you can have your vehicle repaired somewhere else. By law, the original place must reimburse you for the cost of the work or repairs it charged you. In practice, however, it is not always easy to get your money back.

■ What if the garage or shop disobeys the law?

If the garage or shop does not obey the law, you may have to take the garage or shop to Small Claims Court and prove that your vehicle broke down because of the work the garage did or failed to do. If found liable, the garage or shop will also owe you towing costs if your vehicle had to be towed.

You may also have the option of contacting the provincial consumer ministry and making a complaint. These Ministries have the power to investigate the situation. A person or company that violates the law may be convicted and fined. This might not help you in recovering any money that the garage may owe you, however.

16. What should I know about door-to-door or "direct" sales?

Under the consumer protection or fair trading laws in all provinces, sales of products or services made door-to-door (usually defined as "away from the seller's principal business location") give rise to special consumer rights and what are known as "cooling-off" periods.

Many provinces now provide cooling-off periods for certain types of transactions, particularly those that are considered high-pressure sales. For example, condominium purchases, fitness club memberships, and pre-paid funeral services. Cooling-off periods may range from two days to as much as 30 days, depending on the province and type of sale.

■ Right to cancel contract

Generally, you can cancel a "direct sales" contract in writing within 10 days of signing and receiving a copy of the contract. Remember, a direct sales contract is one made away from the seller's place of business. In some provinces, the sale must involve face-to-face contact, so telephone sales or Web sales may not count (check with your provincial consumer and business affairs ministry or local Better Business Bureau). Notice of cancellation can usually be given in person, by registered mail, courier, or even fax.

Note that in Manitoba the cancellation period is seven days.

■ Extended Right to cancel contract

In some jurisdictions you may be able to cancel a contract in writing at anytime if an "unfair practice" led you to purchase the product or services. This includes if you were misled, cheated, or taken advantage of by a salesperson. Under the law in many provinces, an unfair practice can involve a number of behaviours including a seller making false or misleading statements, such as saying something you own requires servicing or replacing when it does not, or stating that the product or service is better than it really is.

Unfair practices can also include situations where a seller takes advantage of a buyer's reading problems, language difficulties, or mental or physical disabilities. This also includes excessive pressure and charging an excessively high price.

Before signing a contract, make sure you take your time and read it completely from beginning to end, including any sections on the back of the contract. If the seller doesn't want to let you take the contract to review before signing, this may be an indication that the contract isn't what the seller is telling you it is. Don't ever be pressured into signing a contract you don't fully understand. If it is an important contract, or one that involves a large sum of money, consider having a lawyer review it before you sign.

17. What should I know about home repair contractors?

Because home repairs can be expensive, it is important to inform yourself fully of the risks and protect yourself from disreputable practices. To begin, you should contact at least three contractors for cost of repair estimates. You can also contact the Better Business Bureau, your local Chamber of Commerce, or your local municipal building inspectors for information on the reliability of various home repair contractors. For each contractor, ask about the types of warranties and guaranties on offer.

If you hire someone to perform any home repairs, ensure that your agreement is in writing and is clear to both you and the contractor. Make sure your written agreement includes a total cost for the repairs, the start date, and the date on which the repairs will be completed. Your contract should also list the specific details about the kinds of repairs you are paying for, and whether the price includes any extra costs for related services, such as electricians and plumbers.

Once a cost is established, try to negotiate a down payment of no more than 10 percent of the total cost. Monitor the progress of the repairs as time goes by. This will allow you to correct any problems as they arise. Following the completion of the work, you are entitled under the *Construction Lien Act* to hold back 10 percent of the total cost for 45 days from the date of completion. This 10 percent can be used to pay any unpaid sub-contractors or material suppliers if they did not receive their share from the contractor.

If a contractor breaks either an oral or a written contract to perform home repairs, you may be able to sue for compensation. If the cost of the repairs is under the small claims limit, you can begin your lawsuit in Small Claims Court. If the work was done in accordance with the terms of your contract, however, the contractor can sue you for the money owed or register a lien against your property. A lien on your property can affect your ability to sell it.

18. What should I know about model and talent agencies?

There are many modelling and talent agencies and most are legitimate businesses, working hard to represent their clients. There are, however, a growing number of unscrupulous agencies that take money for services not delivered, make promises of work that never appears, and overcharge for photo portfolios and for computer and television listings that are not needed. Some people have lost hundreds or even thousands of dollars without ever getting work as models or actors.

Be very careful about signing contracts or giving money to agencies that approach you. It is very rare for legitimate modelling and talent agents to approach people on the street or to call them on the phone. If you have been approached with promises of work, or a screen test, make sure all such promises are put in writing. Don't sign a contract or give the agency any money or your credit card number before you have checked out the contract and the agency itself.

If you have been the victim of misrepresentation or unfair consumer practices, you may be able to cancel the contract and get your money back by filing a complaint under your jurisdiction's unfair business practices law.

19. When should I make a formal consumer complaint to the government?

If you have been the victim of a consumer scam or bad business practice, you have rights and remedies under the law. You should therefore let both the seller and government authorities know about it. Two business practice categories should always prompt complaints:

■ Unfair Practices

"Unfair practices" are misrepresentations made to a consumer by a business to get the consumer to buy a product or service. Unfair practices include businesses:

- Stating that used goods are new or unused
- Stating that goods or services are sponsored or approved when they are not
- Stating there is a price advantage when there is not
- Stating that a service or repair is needed that isn't
- Failing to state important facts about the goods or services
- Promising that an item can be returned or a refund obtained when it can't

■ Unconscionable Consumer Representations

An "unconscionable consumer representation" happens when a business takes advantage of a consumer because of the consumer's weaker position. For example, if a seller knows that a buyer cannot read English and has that person sign an English language contract that spells out something different from what was promised, this would be an unconscionable consumer representation. Other examples include:

- If the seller knows that the goods or services will not be of any use to the consumer

• The seller knows that the consumer will not be able to pay

• The seller uses undue pressure to get the consumer to sign an agreement or to purchase goods

• The seller takes advantage of a consumer's disability, illiteracy or ignorance in order to make the sale

■ Rights and Remedies

If you have been the victim of either an unfair practice or an unconscionable consumer representation, the *Business Practices Act* in some provinces ensures you have the right to cancel your contract within six months of signing it and to receive back any money you paid. You can make a complaint about your contract to your provincial consumer ministry if you have cancelled the contract within six months and not received your money back. You are also entitled to go to court to claim the money.

Even if more than six months has passed, you may be entitled to go to court and sue the business for your money on the basis that it took money from you under an invalid or improper contract.

All in the Family?

John was the primary cardholder for a credit card and authorized the issuance of a subsidiary card for his son, Dan. Unfortunately, Dan decided to engage in a fraudulent scheme and deposited a $20,000 cheque into the credit card that later bounced. Before the cheques could be returned for non-sufficient funds, Dan made over $15,000 in purchases and cash withdrawals — well beyond the $2,200 credit limit. John says he was a victim of fraud, too, and should not be liable for Dan's activities.

Is John correct?

In a 1996 case, an Ontario court said John was responsible for the debt. According to the credit card agreement, cardholders are jointly and severally liable for all indebtedness, even when expenditures happen through fraudulent activities of only one of the cardholders.

IS A PROMISE A PROMISE?

A husband and wife were enticed by advertisements to attend a seminar about a "Home Buying Club." The club's owner told them he provided a catalogue and warehouse where members could select and order home furnishings at low manufacturer's prices. During the presentation, he guaranteed that items shown would be available if ordered.

The couple was impressed, bought a membership in the club, and signed a contract. When they tried to order a TV, they were told it was discontinued by the manufacturer. They were then invited to buy another, more expensive model.

The couple decided to ask for the membership fee back, citing the promise that there were no discontinued items. The club's owner refused, pointing to the contract, which said there was no guarantee items would be available.

Should the couple get their money back?

Yes, said a B.C. court in the 2002 case of *Roa* v. *Bonanza Ventures Ltd. (c.o.b. UCC TotalHome)*. The judge believed the couple's testimony that the club owner promised no items were discontinued and that they relied upon that statement. More important, the court ruled the contract itself violated the province's consumer protection laws on several fronts, such as restricting the rights of purchasers to deal with manufacturers in case of a warranty claim. As for the contract clause stating that "orders are contingent on the manufacturers' ability to complete such order," the judge concluded members could end up paying for services they never receive since the only service the club offered was buying items from a manufacturer. The couple was entitled to a refund.

IS A DEAL ALWAYS A DEAL?

A man paid $225 for membership in a fitness club and signed a contract to pay monthly dues of $8, plus GST. The contract expressly stated that dues may increase "to reflect a higher cost of living."

A few years later, the club tried to increase the monthly fee to $18. The customer refused, citing the low annual increases in cost of living published by Statistics Canada. The club agreed to increase his dues to $10.

About six months later, the club announced an increase to $21. The man again refused, citing a nominal 0.8 percent increase in the cost of living as an example. He offered $10.10, but was refused and told his membership was terminated with 30 days notice.

Did the fitness club have a right to cancel the contract?

No, according to the 2002 B.C. case of Phillips v. Ron E. Zalko Projects Ltd. While there was no definition of "higher cost of living" in the contract, and everyone recognized the club must operate at a profit, the court ruled the business had to stick to the deal it made and the government's cost of living numbers were a reasonable guideline.

WWW Resources

Canadian Legislation	legis.ca
Consumer Connection	strategis.ic.gc.ca

INVESTING MONEY

T he Toronto Stock Exchange estimates that more than 50 percent of Canadians are invested in the stock market through individual equities or mutual funds. Canadians earned more than $32 billion in investment income according to the last census. As well, more than half of us invest in RRSPs (Registered Retirement Savings Plans), socking away an individual median average of $2,600 a year in 2003. Creating wealth, however, is no easy task and consumers must be diligent in their investing pursuits.

There is a broad range of investing options, from stocks and bonds to mutual and segregated funds. As well, investors must decide whether they hold their investments inside registered accounts that generate favourable tax treatment, or outside registered accounts that also have tax consequences. That's why it's important that consumers investigate their options thoroughly and understand how an investment works before they put their hard-earned dollars at risk.

INVESTOR PROTECTION

1. Why is the Canadian Deposit Insurance Corporation important to my financial health?

The Canadian Deposit Insurance Corporation (CDIC) is a federal Crown corporation, created in 1967, to protect the money you deposit in member financial institutions in the event they fail. You do not apply for deposit insurance; eligible deposits held with CDIC member institutions are automatically protected.

CDIC member institutions include banks, trust companies, and loan companies. Although insurance companies, credit unions, or investment dealers are not eligible for CDIC membership, they can provide other forms of protection for your money (see below). All CDIC members display the CDIC sign in their branches.

2. What does CDIC insure?

CDIC insures eligible deposits you make with its members. These deposits include:

- Savings and chequing accounts
- Term deposits, such as guaranteed investment certificates (GICs) and debentures issued by loan companies

- Money orders and drafts
- Certified drafts and cheques
- Traveller's cheques issued by members

To be eligible for deposit insurance protection, your deposit must be payable in Canada, in Canadian currency. Term deposits must be repayable no later than five years after the date of deposit.

3.   What doesn't CDIC insure?

Not all deposits and investments offered by CDIC member banks, trust companies, and loan companies are insurable. For example, CDIC does not insure:

- Foreign currency deposits, such as accounts in U.S. dollars
- Term deposits with a maturity date of more than five years from the date of deposit
- Debentures issued by chartered banks
- Bonds and debentures issued by governments and corporations
- Treasury bills
- Investments in mortgages, stocks, and mutual funds

■ Basic deposit insurance protection

By law, the maximum basic protection for eligible deposits is $60,000 per person, including principal and interest, at each member institution.

Separate protection

In addition to basic coverage, CDIC insures certain classifications of deposits separately. These are:

- Coverage for joint deposits
- Coverage for deposits in trust
- Protection of deposits held in RRSPs
- Protection of deposits held in RRIFs
- Payment of insured deposits if a CDIC member fails

4.   What happens if a member institution fails?

If a CDIC member institution fails, CDIC automatically makes payment of insured deposits based on the records of the member institution. You do not need to file a claim for your CDIC payment. CDIC writes to the insured depositors advising them of how and when they will receive payment.

CDIC may choose to pay all insured depositors by transferring insured funds to another CDIC member, or by mailing each depositor a cheque for the insured amount. The decision of which form of payment will be used depends on the circumstances of the individual case.

The terms of deposits at the failed CDIC member, such as the maturity date of term deposits and the interest rate, are void once the failure occurs. If CDIC makes payment by transferring insured funds to another institution, your payment will be placed in a savings account until you decide about reinvesting it and provide instructions to the new member institution.

CDIC makes payment of insured deposits as soon as possible, normally within two months. The payment includes principal and earned interest on eligible deposits, to a maximum of $60,000 per depositor. No interest will be paid from the date the Court officially closes the failed member institution, except in extraordinary circumstances, where, for instance, CDIC takes more than six months to repay insured depositors.

For more information contact a CDIC member institution directly, or contact the Canadian Deposit Insurance Corporation at 1-800-461-CDIC (1-800-461-2342) or info@cdic.ca.

5. Are other types of financial investments or holdings protected by law?

■ Investment Dealers

In Canada, all investment and securities dealers, as well as independent brokerages, are governed by a self-regulatory organization known as the Investment Dealers Association (IDA). The IDA's role is to investigate breaches of its own by-laws, regulations, or policies. The IDA will take disciplinary action against member firms or registered employees, using fines, suspensions, or expulsions from the association.

The IDA itself, however, does not compensate investors for losses and, if your investment firm refuses to return your money, the only recourse may be to sue in civil court. All IDA members do belong to the Canadian Investor Protection Fund, which provides up to $1 million coverage against losses by each individual client arising from an investment dealer's insolvency.

The Fund makes some distinctions in its coverage. For example, the limit for the total of losses in each client's general accounts (that is, cash, margin, short sale, options, futures, and foreign currency accounts) is

$500,000. Separate coverage is provided for certain types of accounts to another maximum of $500,000. Separate accounts include

RRSPs, LIRAs, RRIFs, LIFs, RESPs, joint accounts, and genuine trust accounts.

The Fund does not cover customers' losses resulting from changing market values of securities, regardless of the causes of such losses. It should be noted the IDA does provide an inexpensive arbitration process for settling disputes between member firms and clients.

■ Mutual Funds

The Mutual Fund Dealers Association (MFDA) is a self-governing organization for the mutual funds industry in Canada. Securities commissions in each province regulate the funds or fund manufacturers themselves, but the MFDA has been set up to create an investor protection fund (in effect, as of July 2005). Again, any investments in mutual funds will not be protected by the MFDA from normal market losses.

INSURANCE INVESTMENT PRODUCTS

6. What are segregated funds?

While sometimes considered similar to mutual funds, segregated funds, or guaranteed investment funds as they are sometimes called, are actually a form of life insurance. When an investor purchases segregated funds, he or she is entering into a contract called an "Individual Variable Annuity Contract." The contract is designed to provide the contract holder with an opportunity to set aside money by making premium payments in the form of deposits. These deposits will be allocated to one or more funds selected by the contract holder with the assistance of a life insurance licensed representative. The contract will be based on the life of a person, called an annuitant, who is named by the investor in the application.

The most important feature of segregated funds contracts is they allow contract holders to participate in the potential growth of financial markets while at the same time, the contract guarantees certain payments to contract holders, or their beneficiaries, as a buffer against downside risks experienced in these markets from time to time.

7. What are the key features of segregated funds?

Segregated funds have a number of important features that vary from contract to contract. Careful regard should be given to the terms set out in the information folder for the segregated funds. The information folder must be supplied to any prospective purchaser of segregated funds.

The segregated funds contract may be registered as a Registered Retirement Savings Plan or a Registered Income Fund under the *Income Tax Act*, in which case the contract holder must also be the annuitant. In addition, the contract may be designated as a locked-in RRSP or locked-in retirement account, or a life income fund under certain pension legislation.

Before investing in segregated funds, whether for registered retirement savings plans or otherwise, one should review the sales and management fees along with all other terms contained in the information folder. A life insurance licensed advisor should be able to satisfactorily answer questions before you sign the application.

■ Deposit maturity guarantee

The deposit-maturity guarantee is applicable on the deposit maturity date, which is generally on the 10th anniversary of the investor's deposit. The issuer of the contract guarantees that the value of the investor's units will be no less than the guaranteed minimum amount, which, depending on the terms of the specific segregated funds contract, will be between 75 percent and 100 percent of the original amount deposited.

The deposit-maturity guarantee will be subject to reduction if the contract holder has made cash withdrawals during the 10-year contract. Naturally, investors are hopeful that market conditions over a 10-year period will have trended upward. If the segregated funds chosen by the investor have indeed fared well, the contract will mature at an amount higher than the original amount deposited and a new guaranteed minimum amount will be established for the next 10-year period.

One of the features of a segregated funds contract is a "reset feature." With certain exceptions for individuals who are beyond the eligible age stated in their contract (usually, an age ranging from 65 to 85), a contract holder can reset the clock and lock-in gains in favourable markets. In this way, a higher guaranteed minimum amount is established for the investor, but then a further 10-year period is commenced in respect of the deposit maturity guarantee.

■ Death-benefit guarantee

The other guarantee available in a segregated funds contract is a death-benefit guarantee. This guarantee provides that, upon written notification of the death of the annuitant, the beneficiary is entitled to receive the greater of the market value of the policy, or 100 percent of the net deposits, less proportionate market value reductions for withdrawals and fees. Accordingly, if market conditions at the time of death of the contract holder are less favourable than at the time of the deposit, the contract issuer will top up the value of the contract to the deposit value, less applicable service charges.

■ Protection from creditors

Creditor protection may be possible because provincial insurance laws provide that life insurance contracts, including annuity contracts such as segregated funds, may be exempt from seizure by creditors if the owner has designated certain related persons as the beneficiary of the contract. The beneficiary can be a spouse, child, parent, or grandchild of the annuitant. Because creditor protection can be lost under certain circumstances, it is advisable to discuss your individual situation with a lawyer.

■ Avoidance of estate taxes and fees

The second feature that attracts many investors to segregated funds is the opportunity to avoid estate administration taxes, also known as probate fees. If the death benefit is paid directly to a beneficiary, it is not included as part of the estate of the contract holder and accordingly, provincial estate administration taxes on this amount may be avoided. Once again, this may depend on whether the contract is held in the name of the individual or as part of a trust in a registered plan. Legal advice should be sought to determine if estate administration taxes could be avoided.

8. What is a Universal Life Policy?

Universal Life is a type of insurance policy that covers both the insurance and investment needs of individuals. It involves a term insurance policy attached to a tax sheltered investment account. Under a provision of the *Income Tax Act*, the investment account that goes with the insurance is tax sheltered so that beneficiaries do not have to pay taxes on the growth of funds inside the account. Accordingly, this kind of policy can be an excellent estate planning tool that may provide a large lump sum to help beneficiaries settle up the capital gains taxes resulting from the death of a taxpayer.

Universal Life policyholders pay an annual amount, only part of which is for the annual insurance premium. The balance, the amount of which is determined by the policyholder's cash flow, is the investment portion. Expenses and administration fees are deducted from the investment portion. The maximum amount policyholders can add to the plan is defined by tax legislation, and depends on an actuarial calculation related to the amount of insurance coverage and the policyholder's age.

The type of investor for whom a Universal Life Policy is most suitable is the one who has contributed the maximum to his or her RRSP, and who has investments outside the retirement account. Income on investments outside an RRSP is generally subject to tax, but can become tax sheltered inside a Universal Life policy.

Another feature of a Universal Life Policy is its flexibility in terms of deposits and withdrawals. A Universal Life Policy allows the policyholder's annual deposit to be the minimum amount required to keep the insurance in force, the actuarial maximum, or any amount in between. Also, the policyholder can withdraw funds at any time, although taxes are payable when funds are withdrawn.

For example, business owners may put surplus cash in the plan when the business is thriving. In years when the cash flow is down or equipment must be purchased or facilities renovated, they can withdraw the necessary funds leaving only enough in the plan to pay the insurance premiums. Once again, Universal Life Policies are generally considered most suitable for those who have maximized RRSP and pension contributions and eliminated or largely reduced non-deductible interest debt.

RRSPs & RESPs

9. What are RRSPs?

The federal government has established special tax rules for retirement investments. These rules were created to encourage people to save for their retirement. Investments made under these special rules are called Registered Retirement Savings Plans, or RRSPs for short.

RRSPs are tax deferral plans that allow you to put a percentage of your income into an investment account. RRSPs are registered with Canada Revenue Agency. You will not have to pay tax on the income you contribute to your RRSP until you withdraw the money. The *Income Tax Act* describes eligible investments for an RRSP. The money that you put into an RRSP can be invested in mutual funds, GICs, term deposits, stocks, bonds, or mortgages. The RRSP planholder is responsible for ensuring that the investments held in the RRSP are eligible investments.

10. What are the benefits of RRSPs?

There are many benefits to investing in an RRSP.

First, your RRSP contribution for a particular year is included on your income tax return as a deduction. This reduces the amount of tax you have to pay in the year that you make the contribution, because it reduces your annual taxable income for that year.

The second advantage of RRSPs is that they defer some income taxes. You will not have to pay tax on the money you invest until you withdraw it. If you withdraw the money during your retirement or at a time when you have very little income, you will be in a lower tax bracket and you will pay less income tax than if you had paid tax on the money when you earned it.

The third advantage is that RRSP investments are tax sheltered. This means that any increase in the value of your investment will not be taxed while the money is in the RRSP. Because your RRSP is tax sheltered, it grows faster than it would if you had to pay tax on the earnings every year. Any gain in your investment will be added to the principal amount you contributed. The entire investment is tax sheltered and you will not have to pay tax on it until you start making withdrawals.

Fourth, RRSPs are a good way to save for your retirement or for some other time when you need to supplement your income. For example, if you decide to take time off to raise your children or if you quit your job to start your own business, you can use your RRSP as a source of income. You should understand the terms and conditions of your RRSP and any restrictions that may apply, such as the ability to withdraw money immediately. Some RRSP plans, such as GIC investments, lock in your investment for a certain period.

Canada Revenue Agency also allows you to contribute to an RRSP on behalf of your spouse. The contributing spouse may deduct the contribution amount from his or her taxable income. A withdrawal from the plan is taxed in the hands of the planholder. Note that if a withdrawal is made from a spousal plan within three years of a contribution being made, the amount withdrawn may be taxed in the hands of the contributing spouse.

The advantage of contributing to a spousal plan is the ability to split income at retirement to minimize the tax liability when money is withdrawn from each spouse's plan. This results in two smaller incomes that will be taxed at a lower rate than the rate that would be applied to a single larger income. The overall result is that you will pay less tax.

▪ Locked-in RRSP

A locked-in RRSP holds funds transferred directly from a pension plan. If you change jobs, the pension plan that your former employer offered may allow the value of your pension benefit to be transferred directly to a locked-in RRSP. The funds held in the locked-in RRSP are administered under the same federal or provincial pension legislation as the pension plan. You may not withdraw from or contribute to a locked-in RRSP.

11. How much can I contribute to an RRSP?

The federal government sets a limit on the amount of money you can contribute to your RRSP each year, which is determined by your earned income. Canada Revenue Agency shows you how much contribution room you have available on the Notice of Assessment it sends you after you file your previous year's tax return.

You can contribute 18 percent of your earned income from the previous year, up to a maximum set dollar limit. The government has recently approved increases in the RRSP limit. For 2006, the maximum is $18,000. That will increase to $19,000 in 2007, $20,000 in 2008, $21,000 in 2009, and $22,000 in 2010, after which it will be indexed.

For example, if your "earned income" in 2005 is $45,000, you can contribute a maximum of $8,100 to your RRSP, which is 18 percent. If your earned income was $200,000 in 2005, however, you can only contribute a maximum of $18,000 to your RRSP, which is less than 18 percent, but at the maximum level.

12. What happens if I don't make the full contribution?

You can add your unused RRSP contribution amount to your current contribution limit. For example, if you could have deposited $10,000 last year, but you only contributed $9,000, then you can carry forward $1,000 to your contribution limit for this year. The contribution limit that is shown on your Notice of Assessment includes the amount of your unused contribution. You can also find out what your RRSP contribution limit is by contacting Canada Revenue Agency TIPS hotline. If you belong to a company pension plan or deferred profit sharing plan, your RRSP contribution limit will be lower than these general limits. If you contribute more than the amount allowed, you may have to pay a penalty.

Check the details of the RRSP investment you decide to buy to determine whether your investment suits your needs. If you are unsure how to calculate your contribution limit, or if you do not know what type of investment is best for you, contact an investment advisor or an accountant for advice.

13. Can I borrow money to make an RRSP contribution?

You can usually borrow money from a bank or a lending institution to contribute to your RRSP. If you do not have enough money available to make an RRSP contribution, it is probably worthwhile to borrow the money. If you use your tax refund to pay off some of the loan, you can reduce the amount of interest you will have to pay. The money you will save in income tax and the return on your RRSP investment will probably be more than the amount of interest you will have to pay in the loan. Although it will cost money to take out a loan, over the long term you will earn income and build up retirement savings and this will outweigh the immediate expense of the loan.

■ Factors to consider

The decision about whether to borrow should be based on a calculation of several factors related to your particular situation. These factors include:

- How much income you earn each year
- The amount of tax you pay each year
- The amount of interest you will have to pay on the loan

14. What happens to my Registered Pension Plan when I leave my job?

When individuals leave their employment, they may be entitled to receive a portion of the assets in the company's pension plan. They must then determine what do to with these funds.

The first step is to gather necessary information from the company's personnel department. There will be certain options regarding the type of plan into which the funds may be transferred. Under pension legislation, you may be prevented from immediately withdrawing pension benefits from your employer's plan on your departure from the company. This legislation is commonly referred to as "locking-in" legislation.

■ Purchase of Locked-in RRSP

If your pension benefits are locked-in, then you have the option of transferring the pension funds into a locked-in RRSP. Locked-in RRSPs are subject to the same restrictions on withdrawal of funds as the original pension plan. For example, you cannot usually access the locked-in plan funds until you are within 10 years of the retirement date set out in the plan documents.

With a locked-in RRSP, you cannot make additional contributions, but you can decide how your retirement savings are invested. This makes a locked-in RRSP a popular choice with people who are leaving an employer's registered pension plan. If you were to have any additional RRSP room available, you would be advised to open another RRSP account, and in fact many people have both a regular RRSP and a locked-in RRSP.

If you have locked-in RRSP funds, they must be transferred to a Life Income Fund, or an annuity when you reach 69 years of age.

■ Purchase of LIFs or LIRFs

In the case where the employee is within 10 years of the retirement date set out in the pension plan document, he or she can use the plan funds to purchase a special retirement account that will provide a lifetime income or an annuity.

Two types of special retirement accounts are Life Income Funds (LIF) and Locked-In Retirement Funds (LIRF). A Life Income Fund and a Locked-In Retirement Fund are types of Registered Retirement Income Funds, but with additional restrictions.

Like any other Registered Retirement Income Fund, a minimum amount must be withdrawn each year. As well, under an LIF or an LIRF, there is a maximum amount that can be withdrawn until age 80. Thus, the funds remain "locked-in" just like a pension or locked-in RRSP. Also, with a LIF the investor is required to purchase an annuity upon reaching 80 years of age.

■ Purchase of Life Annuity

If the employee is within 10 years of the retirement date set out in the pension plan document, and he or she does not want to purchase a special retirement account, that person can purchase an annuity. An annuity provides a fixed sum of money regularly over a specified period.

A Life Annuity can be purchased from an insurance company and individuals can defer receiving payments until the age when they want to begin withdrawing funds. This would be the earliest date permitted by law, but no later than age 69.

The amount of income you receive annually will be determined when you purchase the annuity contract. With this option, you have no control over your funds. You cannot allow for changes in the rate of inflation or take action to affect the return on your invested funds. You surrender control of the funds to the issuer of the annuity in exchange for steady future payments.

Before deciding on a payment option, it is advisable to discuss the various choices with a financial advisor who will consider all of your financial circumstances.

15. Can I borrow money from an RRSP to buy a home?

The RRSP Home Buyers' Plan (HBP) allows you to borrow money from your RRSP to buy or build a home. There are five main rules that apply to the plan.

■ Maximum withdrawal of $20,000

First, you can withdraw a maximum of $20,000 from your RRSP. If you have money in more than one RRSP, you can withdraw money from all of them, up to the limit of $20,000 in total. If you have a spouse who is also eligible for the HBP, you can each withdraw $20,000 from your RRSP, for a total of $40,000. The money you withdraw must have been in your RRSP for at least 90 days.

■ Must be a first-time homebuyer

The HBP is only available to first-time homebuyers. You are only eligible if:

- Neither you nor your spouse currently own a home
- Neither you nor your spouse has owned a home in the past five years. In most cases, a homebuyer can only use the plan once in a lifetime.
- You will live in the home as your principal residence

■ Must enter into an agreement to buy or build a home

You must also enter into an agreement to buy or build a home before you can sign up for the HBP. Both new and existing homes that are located in Canada are eligible for the plan. You must intend to live in the home within one year of buying it. The home can be detached or semi-detached, a townhouse, a condominium, a mobile home, shares in a co-operative housing corporation, or an apartment in a duplex, triplex, four-plex, or apartment building.

■ Specify that the withdrawal is to buy a home

When you withdraw the money from your RRSP you must specify that you are making the withdrawal to buy a home. You must fill out a

Canada Revenue Agency form called Form T1036. This form is available from a Canada Revenue Agency office.

■ Repay the money to your RRSP over 15 years

You must repay the money you withdraw from your RRSP over a period of not more than 15 years. You will not have to pay income tax on the money you withdraw as long as you replace it within 15 years. Because you already received the tax benefit for the money you withdraw, your replacement payments must be made with your after-tax income. The repayment period begins two years after the year in which the withdrawal is made. If you do not make a payment or allocate part of your tax refund to your homebuyers' plan, the government will add that year's amount you owed to your income.

16. How are funds withdrawn from RRSPs taxed?

Depending on the type of RRSP investment you purchase, you may be able to withdraw money at any time. When you withdraw money from your RRSP, it will be taxed as income. You must include the amount you withdraw on your tax return as part of your total income for the year. This will probably increase the amount of income tax you must pay.

Many people wait until they retire to withdraw money from their RRSP. This is because when you retire, your income usually decreases, so that when you add your income for the year to the amount that you withdraw from your RRSP, your total income is still low enough to keep you in a lower tax bracket.

Even if you are not retired, but your income is very low, you may want to withdraw money from your RRSP as a supplement. Depending on the income you earn and the amount of money you want to withdraw, this may affect the tax bracket you are in. If you are unsure about how to calculate your own tax rates, contact an accountant, a tax lawyer, or a financial advisor.

17. How long can I contribute to an RRSP?

When you reach the age of 69, you are no longer allowed to contribute to your RRSP. According to the rules of Canada Revenue Agency, you must start to take minimum annual withdrawals from the total amount you saved. These withdrawals will be taxed as income. You must decide what type of withdrawal you would like to make by December 31st of the year you turn 69. You have three options:

■ Cash withdrawal

First, you can withdraw the entire amount from your RRSP in cash. This withdrawal will be treated as income, and you will be taxed accordingly. If you do not make a decision about what you would like to do with your RRSP funds by December 31st of the year you turn 69, your RRSP will be de-registered and the entire amount less withholding tax will be paid to you. This amount will be considered taxable income for the year following the December 31 deadline, and you will be taxed accordingly.

■ RRIFs

If you have saved a large amount of money in your RRSP, it may be better to choose an option that allows you to make smaller periodic withdrawals. Doing so keeps you from having to pay a single large lump-sum tax payment. Instead, this spreads the tax payments over a longer period.

One way to withdraw money slowly is to transfer your money into a Registered Retirement Income Fund (RRIF). You have the option of leaving your money in the same investment it was in when you had the RRSP. You can still earn the same rate of interest on your investment, and the money you make on your investment is still tax sheltered as long as it is in your RRIF.

The main difference between a RRIF and an RRSP is that with an RRIF you cannot contribute to the investment and you must withdraw a minimum amount every year. The income you receive from your RRIF is included on your personal income tax form, and is taxed at your personal rate. The minimum annual withdrawal for people under the age of 71 is determined by a calculation that uses the age of the RRIF owner and the amount of money in the RRIF at the beginning of the year. After age 71, the minimum withdrawal amount is determined by a standard payment schedule, which is available from your investment advisor. There are no limits on the maximum withdrawal you can take from your RRIF.

■ Annuity

An annuity is a fixed annual allowance provided by an investment. An annuity can provide a guaranteed regular income for the rest of your life or for a specified number of years. The amount of income provided through an annuity is generally determined at the time of purchase and depends on a number of factors, including the following five:

• the amount of money deposited
• the current interest rate

- your age
- your sex, and
- the number of years for which the company promises
to make payments

You decide how often you want to receive payments, monthly or annually for example, and whether you want your payments to be indexed to help offset inflation. Although none of the RRSP proceeds will be taxed at maturity, when you set up the annuity the annuity payments themselves will be taxed as you receive them. Note that currently up to $1,000 per year of the annuity income may be exempted through the pension income tax credit.

There are three general kinds of annuities:

1. "Term certain" or "fixed term" annuities, payable to you or your estate for a fixed number of years.

2. "Single life" annuities, payable to you as long as you live.

3. "Joint and survivor" annuities, payable as long as you or your spouse is alive.

If funded with RRSP money, legislation requires a "term certain" annuity to expire by the time you or your spouse turn 90. On the other hand, a "joint and survivor" annuity guarantees an income for the lifetimes of the annuitant and his or her spouse. This could be well beyond age 90 in the case of one or even both spouses. This type of annuity can also have a minimum guaranteed payment period to provide a death benefit if both annuitants die prematurely. A "single life" annuity with no minimum number of payments offers the highest amount of income but no death benefit.

The available options, and their effect on the monthly annuity payment you will receive, should be discussed with your life insurance licensed financial consultant. A decision about which annuity to pick hinges on factors like your cash-flow requirements, your estate plan and related factors. As well, because an annuity also locks in your investment, and if interest rates are low, you cannot move your money to a more lucrative investment. Therefore, you should consider the prevailing interest rates to determine whether annuities alone, or a combination of annuities and Registered Retirement Income Funds, might provide greater flexibility and returns.

You can obtain more information about what you must do with your RRSP when you reach the age of 69 from the Canada Revenue Agency or a professional, such as an accountant, a financial advisor or a tax lawyer.

18. How can I use RESPs to save for my child's education?

Registered Education Savings Plans, often called RESPs, are designed to help people save for post-secondary education costs. All RESPs are registered with the Government of Canada because they provide the contributor with tax benefits. In most cases, it is parents who invest in RESPs for the education of their children. When evaluating the various options available for education savings, one should consider issues of flexibility, control, and taxation. Two alternatives for education savings are the Registered Education Savings Plan (RESP) and the informal "in trust for" account.

■ Registered Education Savings Plan (RESP)

The RESP offers investors the option of investing in two different plans, individual or family.

An individual plan is ideal for an investor who intends to set up a plan for one beneficiary who may or may not be related to the investor. The family plan is well suited to those who are saving for multiple beneficiaries or who are concerned that the earnings in the plan may be forfeited if a beneficiary does not attend a post-secondary institution. This choice gives them the flexibility of transferring the entire earnings in the plan to one or more beneficiaries who are related to the contributor by blood or adoption.

Whether an investor chooses an individual or family plan, contributions for RESPs are as follows: the annual contribution limit is $4,000 per beneficiary with a lifetime contribution limit of $42,000.

To assist families, and as an incentive to save for post-secondary education, the federal government created the Canada Education Savings Grant (CESG). Beneficiaries of an RESP may qualify to receive up to $400 free per year to a lifetime maximum of $7,200 through this program. In addition to age restrictions, the beneficiary must also have a Social Insurance Number and live in Canada to qualify for this government grant.

As the money is intended for post-secondary education expenses, the contributor will have to repay the grant portion if the beneficiary does not attend a post-secondary institution and another qualified beneficiary is not appointed.

If the beneficiary does not pursue a post-secondary education, the contributor may withdraw the RESP earnings in cash. Doing this, however, would be disadvantageous because the contributor will be charged an additional 20 percent penalty tax in addition to his or her income tax rate. The better choice is to transfer the earnings in the RESP to an individual or spousal RRSP. The rules permit up to $50,000 in RESP earnings to be transferred to RRSPs provided there is contribution room.

The RESP contributor is free to select both domestic and international investments with no foreign content restrictions. Although the contributions to RESPs are not tax deductible, payment of tax is deferred while the earnings in the plan are allowed to compound tax-free. It is the beneficiary who pays tax on the earnings on both the contributions and the grant payments, but not until the money is withdrawn from the plan to pay for college or university. This is advantageous because in most cases, the student's tax rate will be lower than the tax rates of the contributors and the amount invested will grow at a much faster rate.

■ Informal "in trust for" account

An alternative to the Registered Education Savings Plan is the informal "in trust for" account. The "in trust for" account can be a flexible savings vehicle because the funds can be used for any purpose that benefits the beneficiary. It is referred to as informal because no formal trust document is signed, but a beneficiary is designated. Accordingly, all savings and earnings must be used for the benefit of the beneficiary.

An informal "in trust for" account may be used by itself or in combination with an RESP. The RESP can be used to shelter earnings and qualify for the federal government grant, while an informal trust account can be used to make contributions beyond RESP limits. As is the case with RESPs, informal trust accounts allow for complete flexibility in selecting securities for the plan, without any restrictions on foreign content.

Unlike RESPs, where tax payments are deferred while earnings in the plan compound tax-free, informal trust accounts do not give earnings tax shelter. Instead, they allow a contributor to divide some of the taxable income in the plan with the beneficiary. Interest and dividends are taxed in the contributor's hands, while capital gains are taxed in the hands of the beneficiary.

The subject of education funding and the most advantageous route to take, given your unique set of circumstances, should be discussed with a financial planning consultant.

Investing In Capital Markets

19. How are public companies governed?

Unlike the United States, Canada does not have a national securities regulator to oversee capital markets and publicly traded companies. Rather, we have 13 different securities regulators that set rules governing public companies. The Canadian Securities Administrators is an umbrella organization for these regulators and is working on harmonizing Canada's securities laws.

Most public companies are considered "reporting issuers," a term used by securities regulators. These companies must make continuous and timely disclosure to their shareholders, the securities regulators, and to the investing public. An important principle of securities regulation is that all material information about a reporting issuer is available, so that investors can make informed investment decisions.

Continuous disclosure obligations of a public company include annual and quarterly financial reporting as well as providing information in connection with meetings of shareholders. Reporting issuers must also immediately issue press releases when there is a material change in their affairs. The public record of a reporting issuer, containing all electronic filings made with securities regulators in Canada, is available to the public free of charge on the SEDAR website at www.sedar.com. If you want to find out more about a public company, the SEDAR Web site provides access to documents such as annual reports, financial statements, information circulars, and press releases.

When a company issues new securities to the public it must provide a prospectus, which is a document containing detailed information about the company and the securities for sale. Generally, companies cannot sell their securities in a province until a prospectus has been accepted for filing by the local securities commission. By accepting the prospectus, the securities commission is not endorsing or recommending the security as a good investment. Accepting the prospectus means only that the prospectus meets the securities law standards for disclosure of information.

A securities commission can take enforcement action against public companies when they do not comply with their obligations under securities legislation.

A securities commission may issue a "cease trading order," which prevents trading of a company's shares. This means that the company cannot sell its shares and also, investors cannot buy or sell the shares while the cease trading order is in effect. A cease trading order may be issued for a number of reasons, most often when a company fails to file financial statements or other disclosure documents as required by law.

Enforcement actions are taken by regulators for activities of a company or individual that does not comply with the law. These actions may result in various sanctions imposed on companies or individuals. Nonetheless, they generally do not involve obtaining money compensation for individual shareholders or investors.

Shareholders or investors who want to claim damages or compensation for any wrongful activity of a public company must bring their own civil proceedings.

Shareholders of all companies, whether public or private, have rights that arise from corporate law, which is the law under which the company is created. Companies can be created either under the federal *Canada Business Corporations Act* or through similar legislation at the provincial level.

The basic responsibility for management of a company's affairs, sometimes called "corporate governance" issues, rests with the board of directors. The board of directors is accountable to the shareholders of the company that elect them. The right to vote at meetings is one of the basic rights of shareholders owning voting shares.

20. What is the role of a securities commission?

Canada has a number of provincial securities commissions, such as the Ontario Securities Commission and the Québec Securities Commission. Commissions are mandated to protect investors from unfair, improper, or fraudulent practices and to foster fair and efficient capital markets. They do this by:

1. Registering and supervising those in the business of advising on or trading in securities.

2. Supporting self-regulation of the securities markets and overseeing the self-regulatory organizations.

3. Ensuring that investors have access to the information they need to make informed investment decisions.

4. Conducting investigations and bringing enforcement actions for serious infractions of securities law.

In Ontario, for example, anyone who sells securities or gives advice about securities must be registered with the Ontario Securities Commission. Different types of registration can be held by an investment representative or the sponsoring firm. Individuals or firms that are registered are called "registrants." The type of registration determines what kinds of products investment representatives are licensed to sell or the types of services they can provide.

The OSC sets competence standards for registrants and makes and enforces rules for operation of the securities markets. The securities commission oversees self-regulatory organizations, called SROs, which have responsibility for direct regulation of registrants or other market participants in specific areas of market activity. These SROs have their own rules and by-laws that members must follow. The Toronto Stock Exchange and the Investment Dealers Association of Canada (IDA) are self-regulatory organizations.

If you would like to find out whether a person or firm that you are, or will be, dealing with is registered, contact the Ontario Securities Commission. Staff can tell you if a person is registered and in which category.

They can also tell you which regulatory organization has responsibility (the IDA or the OSC) and where to send a complaint. The OSC does not give an opinion on whether a registered company or individual broker is reputable. You can, however, find out whether there are any current or past *formal* proceedings against an individual or company. Information is not given out about complaints in progress.

21. Who regulates financial institutions?

Banks and insurance companies can also be public companies whose shares are listed on a stock exchange and subject to securities laws. The regulation of financial institutions is split between the federal government and the provinces. Banks and banking products are regulated by the Office of the Superintendent of Financial Institutions, a federal organization. Federally incorporated insurance companies are also regulated by OSFI. The provinces have a say in the regulation of various parts of the financial services industry, including certain insurance companies, pension plans, loan and trust companies, credit unions, mortgage brokers, and co-operatives.

22. What is an investment advisor?

Investment advisors, also referred to as salespersons, brokers, or dealers, are people who are trained to provide investment advice and buy and sell securities. To be registered as an investment advisor, the individual must be at least 18 years old, and must have successfully completed the Canadian Securities Course and the Conduct and Practices Handbook Course offered by the Canadian Securities Institute. The individual must then complete a 90-day in-house training program.

After those three elements are completed, the individual must become registered as an investment advisor with the Investment Dealers Association of Canada or the relevant stock exchange. Following registration, the investment advisor must operate under supervision for six months and complete an additional course within 30 months of registration.

23. What can an investment advisor do?

An investment advisor can help you manage your investment portfolio. Investment advisors provide investment advice and guidance to clients by recommending a mix of investment options, including bonds, mutual funds, and stocks that are appropriate for the clients' needs. This level of appropriateness is known in the securities industry as "suitability" or the "know-your-client rule." It is important to discuss your investment objectives with your advisor so he or she can invest your money in ways that make you comfortable.

You can set limits on the level of risk you are willing to accept and on the types of investments you are prepared to make. All investments come with some risk, but your investment advisor can structure your portfolio so it matches your comfort level and investment objectives.

Investment advisors are usually paid by taking a commission when they buy or sell securities on your behalf. An investment advisor cannot buy or sell a security in your account without consulting you, unless you grant the advisor permission in writing. Also, you must receive a confirmation of all trades made in your account as well as regular account statements.

24. What is insider trading?

The policy behind monitoring insider trading is to ensure that investors compete on a level playing field. Therefore, trading and informing others based on knowledge of important information about a public company, called material information, is only prohibited where that information has not been generally disclosed to the public.

Insider trading occurs in two circumstances. First, it is considered insider trading when a person buys or sells the securities of a public company while knowing undisclosed material information about that company. Second, it is considered insider trading when someone who knows undisclosed material information about a public company informs other people about such information.

An insider of a public company includes:

• Every director or senior officer of a public company

• Any person who beneficially owns, directly or indirectly, more than 10 percent of the voting rights of the public company, or exercises control or direction over more than 10 percent of the voting rights of the public company, or a combination of both

• A subsidiary of the public company is considered an insider of the public company

• If a company is considered an insider of the public company, the directors and senior officers of the insider company are also considered insiders of the public company

When someone becomes an insider of a public company he or she is required to file an initial insider trading report with the System for Electronic Disclosure by Insiders. Insiders must file insider-trading reports within 10 days of a trade.

People in a special relationship with a public company are prohibited from purchasing or selling the securities of the company if they have knowledge of specific confidential information, which, if disclosed, would likely materially affect the value of that company's securities significantly.

The classes of people who are considered to be in a "special relationship" with a public company include:

• Anyone who is a director, officer, or employee of the public company and/or its affiliates

• Anyone who is engaged in or proposing to engage in any business or professional activity with the public company

• Anyone who obtained inside information while belonging to one of the classes of such persons

• Anyone who obtained material information from a person whom the recipient knew or ought reasonably to have known was in a special relationship with the company

• Any person in a "special relationship" with a public company who tips inside information to a third party may be liable to the person who sold or bought the securities from that third party

There are substantial statutory penalties for persons and companies where there has been a breach of the law, including situations where required documents or notices contain misrepresentations about an insider's trading activities. These penalties include fines up to $1,000,000 or triple the amount of any profit made by such contravention. Penalties can also include prison terms of up to two years.

Where a public company is found to be in breach of the law, the directors and officers who authorized, permitted, or agreed to the events are also held to be guilty and can be liable to the same penalties as the public company.

Insiders and their affiliates and associates are also held accountable to the public company for any direct benefits or advantages received or receivable as a result of making use of inside information. Advantages include any gains from the purchase or sale of securities of the public company on the basis of such information or communication of such inside information.

A company is considered an affiliate of another if one is a subsidiary of the other or if both are subsidiaries of the same company.

A person or company is an associate of a public company in any of the following six circumstances:

- The person or company beneficially owns more than 10 percent of the voting rights attached to all voting securities of the public company
- Any partner of such person or company
- Any trust or estate in which such a person or company has a substantial ownership or other beneficial interest, or serves as a trustee or in a similar capacity
- Any relative of such person
- Any person of the opposite sex married to such person or has the same home, or is living with this person in a conjugal relationship outside marriage
- Any relative of a person mentioned above who has the same home as that person

Insider trading is a very complicated area of law. If you require legal advice, consult an investments and securities law lawyer.

25. What is a prospectus?

A prospectus is a document that provides relevant information about a company. It allows investors to evaluate company securities before making a purchase.

A prospectus must be given to anyone to whom securities are "distributed" (given, sold, etc.) so he or she can assess the merits and risks of the investment.

A prospectus is required when securities are to be "distributed" to the public. A distribution occurs in any of the following four situations:

- When there is an initial issuance of securities from a company's treasury
- When there is a resale of securities returned to the company
- When there is a sale by a person holding 10 percent or more of a company's shares
- In certain circumstances, when there is a resale of securities issued under special exemptions (for example, a sale to a company founder or close relatives)

26. What is in a prospectus?

A prospectus must contain full, true, and plain disclosure of all material facts relating to the securities of the company. A material fact is a fact that significantly affects or would reasonably be expected to have a significant effect on the market price or value of the securities.

A prospectus includes recent financial statements of the company and generally contains verifiable facts. The inclusion of a forecast is possible and is guided by additional policies. Any future-oriented financial information included in a prospectus must be prepared in accordance with the Canadian Institute for Chartered Accountants Handbook, and projections can only be included in certain circumstances.

27. How does the prospectus process work?

The prospectus process involves the filing of a preliminary prospectus with the appropriate provincial securities regulatory authorities where the purchasers live. The preliminary prospectus can be used by the company and its securities dealer, called an underwriter, to market the securities.

The securities regulatory authorities will review the preliminary prospectus and provide comments to the issuer. After receiving the comments, the issuer will make any amendments necessary and then file a final prospectus. The time period during which the securities regulatory authorities review the preliminary prospectus is called the waiting period.

The issuer must make amendments to the preliminary prospectus if any adverse change in the affairs of the issuer occurs during the waiting period. Also, during the waiting period, the selling activities of the issuer and its dealer are limited to distributing the prospectus and using very limited advertising regarding the extent of the offering.

A dealer, upon receiving an order or subscription for a security offered in a distribution, must send the purchaser a copy of the final prospectus before or within two business days of entering into a written confirmation of the sale of a security. The purchaser is then entitled to a "cooling-off" period. The purchaser has two business days from receiving the final prospectus to withdraw from the obligation to buy the securities. This provides the purchaser with an opportunity to review the final version of the prospectus. To withdraw from the obligation to buy, the purchaser must give notice not to be bound to the dealer who sold the securities.

28. What happens if the prospectus has a misrepresentation?

If the prospectus contains a misrepresentation, anyone who purchased its securities is deemed to have relied upon the misrepresentation in deciding to make the investment.

The purchaser has a legal right to sue for damages against any of the following:

- The company or any selling shareholder on whose behalf the distribution was made
- Every person who was a director of the company at the time the prospectus was filed
- Each underwriter of the offered securities
- Every person or company whose consent was required to file the prospectus, such as lawyers and accountants, but only with respect to reports, opinions, or statements made by them
- Every other person who signed the prospectus, such as promoters

Instead of suing, a purchaser who relied on misrepresentations contained in the prospectus may elect to exercise his or her right of rescission against the company or any selling security holder or underwriter. The right of rescission means that the purchaser can return the securities and get back the money paid.

29. What constitutes a misrepresentation?

A misrepresentation can include any of the following:

- An untrue statement of a material fact

- An omission of a material fact that should be stated
- An omission of a material fact that is necessary because the omission makes another statement misleading

If a prospectus contains a misrepresentation, the company or those selling the securities have no defence unless the purchaser bought the securities with knowledge of the misrepresentation.

A director or officer who signed the prospectus and who believed that the prospectus did not contain any misrepresentations does have certain defences. Such a director or officer may withdraw his or her consent to the filing of the prospectus before the purchase of securities and may rely on a due diligence defence.

To succeed in proving due diligence, the defendant must prove three things:

- That he or she actually believed that there were no misrepresentations in the prospectus
- That there were reasonable grounds to believe that there were no misrepresentations
- That he or she had conducted reasonable investigations to support such a belief

The company's lawyers and the underwriters co-ordinate and assist in the due diligence process, which is largely completed before the filing of the preliminary prospectus.

For legal assistance with the issuance or examination of a prospectus, consult an investments and securities law lawyer.

Stocks, Bonds & Mutual Funds

30. What are equity investments?

Stocks, shares, and equities are all words used to describe investments that represent an ownership interest in a company. One share usually represents a very small percentage ownership in a company. Companies typically sell shares to raise money. If you invest in shares, your investment is tied to the fortunes of the company. If the company prospers, the company's share price may increase. If the company is unsuccessful, the company's share price may decrease.

There are several types of shares that a company can issue, and each type has different benefits and risks. The two main types of shares are common shares and preferred shares.

31. How do preferred shares work?

Preferred shareholders are paid dividends, or payments made by a company from its profit, in priority to common shareholders. Therefore, the dividend is typically fixed so shareholders know what they will receive.

In the case of liquidation, preferred shareholders have a claim on the assets of the company in priority to the common shareholders. For example, if the business fails and the assets of the business are sold, then the proceeds are distributed to creditors and preferred shareholders before common shareholders. In short, preferred shares provide greater security of a return than common shares.

The disadvantage of preferred shares is that even if the company experiences tremendous growth and the company's share price increases, preferred shareholders do not share in the additional growth because their dividends are fixed. Preferred shareholders typically only have the right to a return of capital invested. Also, there is no guarantee that dividends will be paid in any particular year. The decision as to whether to pay dividends rests with the directors of the company.

There are many types of preferred shares, some of which provide voting rights in certain cases.

32. How do common shares work?

The other main type of share is a common share. The advantage of common shares is that if the company does very well, then the shareholder could earn a larger return on the investment in the form of higher dividends and an increase in the price of the shares. The disadvantage of common shares is the risk of not receiving any dividends if there is not enough profit.

Also, investors who own common shares are subordinate in priority to investors who own preferred shares or debt (bonds, etc.) with respect to claims on the assets and dividends of the company. Common shareholders are entitled to a residual interest in the company's assets after the holders of debt and preferred shares are paid.

Common shares usually grant the owner voting rights at the annual shareholders' meeting.

In general, common shares offer the potential for larger returns than preferred shares, but they also come with more risk than preferred shares.

33. What is a "Blue Chip" stock?

Stocks in large, stable corporations are known as Blue Chip stocks, a reference to shares with a record of continuous dividend payments. They are typically very solid investments in secure, highly rated companies. As with other companies, even Blue Chip companies from time to time decide not to pay dividends for any particular year. Instead, the company may decide to reinvest its profit back into the company. If this happens, investors will not receive any dividend payments.

34. What is the Dividend Tax Credit?

Investments that pay dividends are given preferential tax treatment. If you invest in the common or preferred shares of a Canadian corporation, the dividend income you receive will be eligible for the Dividend Tax Credit. Dividends from Canadian corporations are subject to less tax than both interest income and capital gains. This means that investing in dividend-paying Canadian stocks may reduce taxes and improve the after-tax yield of your investment.

An accountant, a tax lawyer, or an investment advisor can help you calculate the tax advantage of owning shares in Canadian corporations and can advise you on which investments are eligible for the dividend tax credit.

35. What are the risks of buying stocks?

Whenever you buy shares, it is important to remember that there is no reward without some risk. There is no guarantee that you will make money with stocks and there is always a possibility that you could lose money. In fact, if the business fails, investors could lose their entire investment, which is the price paid for the shares and any gain in the shares' value over time.

You should evaluate how much risk you are willing to accept, and determine whether your investment matches the level of risk you are comfortable with.

36. What are bonds?

A bond is a loan. When you buy a bond, you are loaning your money to the company or government that issued the bond. The company or government promises to pay you a specific amount of interest for a specific period, and it also promises to repay the loan.

Investing in bonds, especially those issued by the Canadian government, provincial government, or the U.S. government, is usually a fairly safe way to invest. Bonds also offer some certainty about the amount of return on your investment.

There are many different types of bonds, and each offers different benefits and risks.

■ Canada Savings Bond

A common type of bond is a Canada Savings Bond. These bonds are issued by the Government of Canada and they are typically sold each fall. Canada Savings Bonds are sold in a variety of denominations. There are two kinds of Canada Savings Bond. One pays interest each year. The other reinvests the interest you receive or compounds the interest. When the bond matures, or when you redeem it, you receive the face value of the bond, plus any interest that is owed to you. Canada Savings Bonds can be cashed at any time by the owner at any bank in Canada. Canada Savings Bonds are considered very safe investments.

■ Treasury Bill

Another common type of bond is a Treasury Bill. Treasury Bills are commonly known as T-bills. T-bills are sold at a discount, which means you pay less than the face value of the T-bill when you buy it. Your return on the investment is the difference between the price you pay for the T-Bill and the face value of the T-Bill, which you receive when the T-bill matures.

■ Corporate Bonds

Companies can also issue bonds. Like government bonds, corporate bonds constitute a loan that you make to a company. The company promises to pay you interest for the loan and to repay the amount of principal you invested. There are many kinds of corporate bonds and each offers different features and advantages. If you want to buy or sell corporate bonds you will have to do so through an investment advisor or discount broker.

You can obtain more information about the variety of bonds that are available for sale from your investment advisor or from a bank.

37. What are mutual funds?

A mutual fund raises money by selling shares or units to individual investors. The fund uses this pool of money to purchase a variety of investments. The mutual fund makes money by trading a variety of securities. As an investment, mutual funds offer three main advantages:

■ Professional Management

Mutual funds provide an affordable way for individual investors to benefit from professional investment management.

■ An easy way to diversify investment

They are an easy and low-cost way for individual investors to diversify their investment portfolios. All investments come with some risk, but by purchasing several investments and diversifying your investment portfolio, you can lower your overall investment risk. It can be expensive for investors to try to diversify their individual portfolios on their own. But because mutual funds represent ownership in a wide variety of investments, buying shares in a mutual fund will help an investor diversify his or her investment portfolio and minimize the overall investment risk at a relatively low cost.

■ Liquidity

Most mutual funds are very liquid investments. It is fairly easy for investors to buy or sell mutual fund units. There are a wide variety of mutual funds available. You can contact an investment advisor for more information about what mutual funds are available and which are suitable for your investment objectives.

38. How do I decide which mutual fund to invest in?

There are many types of mutual funds available and the fund you select should reflect your personal investment objectives.

When determining which fund is best for you, there are four main things to consider: the history of the fund, the current management of the fund, the philosophy of the fund, and the fees and risks associated with the fund.

■ History of the company or fund

Mutual funds are sold by many investment companies, banks, and other lending institutions. You may want to consider whether the company or fund has an established history of making good investments and achieving a satisfactory level of returns.

■ Fund managers

The management team of any fund has a direct impact on the success of the fund because its decisions determine what securities are bought and sold.

■ Focus or management style

You may want to invest in companies that focus or specialize in a particular industry or sector of the economy or region, such as high tech companies or Far East funds. You may also wish to invest in funds with a particular philosophy. For instance, if you feel strongly about protecting the environment or preventing cruelty to animals, you might invest in ethical or green funds.

■ Fees and risk

Investors should consider what fees the company charges for managing money and what commissions or fees are charged by the investment advisor that sells the funds. Funds are usually sold on a load or a no-load, no-commission basis. A fund with a front load means you are charged when you buy the mutual fund. A fund with a back-end load means you are charged when you redeem your units. Most funds also charge monthly management fees. You should also decide what level of risk you want to take with your investment. Risk levels should be discussed with your investment advisor.

39. How do I complain about an investment advisor?

If you have a concern about the way your account has been handled, you may first try to discuss the problem with the company the investment advisor works for. Raise your concern with the investment advisor, the advisor's branch manager, or the company's compliance officer. If you are not satisfied, you can make a complaint to the Investment Dealers Association, your provincial securities commission, or the relevant stock exchange.

As well as filing a complaint with a regulatory body, you may also be able to arbitrate your dispute with your investment advisor. An arbitrator listens to both sides of the dispute and provides a decision that is binding on both parties. Arbitration is a time- and cost-effective alternative to court proceedings. More information on the arbitration option is available from the Investment Dealers Association.

Alternatively, after you file a complaint with the Investment Dealers Association, the securities commission, or the relevant stock exchange, you may also be able to start legal action against the investment advisor and the firm that person works for. You will have to show that your case involves more than a decline in an investment's value.

Investment Quiz

1. You earned $100,000 in 2005. The maximum RRSP contribution you can make for 2006 is:

a) $9,000

b) $18,000

c) $50,000

d) Depends on how much contribution room you have available.

The correct answer is d. You can contribute up to 18 percent of your earned income to a maximum of $18,000 for 2006. However, if you have unused contribution room from prior years, that carries forward into the future and means you could possibly contribute more than the $18,000 in this case.

2. How much does the Home Buyer's Plan allow each individual to borrow from his or her RRSP?

a) $10,000

b) $15,000

c) $20,000

d) $25,000

The correct answer is c. The plan allows each spouse to borrow up to $20,000 to buy his or her first home.

3. If you borrow money from your RRSP to buy a house, how long do you have to repay it before paying tax on the money?

a) 5 years

b) 7 years

c) 10 years

d) 15 years

The answer is d, 15 years.

4. At what age do you have to stop contributing to your own RRSP.

a) 62

b) 65

c) 69

d) 71

The correct answer is c.

5. Investment income earned in an RRSP is taxed at your personal rate.
True or False.

The answer is false. The RRSP is a tax-sheltered vehicle. The money is not taxed until removed from the RRSP.

6. Which three characteristics do RESPs have?

a) An annual contribution limit of $4,000, a lifetime limit of $42,000, a maximum $400 a year grant from the federal government.

b) An annual contribution limit of $7,200, a lifetime limit of $50,000, a maximum $200 a year grant from the federal government.

c) Unlimited annual contributions, a lifetime limit of $100,000, no federal grants unless you earn under $30,000.

The correct answer is a.

6. A segregated fund:

a) Avoids estate taxes

b) Provides creditor protection

c) Includes a death benefit

d) All of the above

The correct answer is d.

7. A mutual fund is best described as:

a) A risk-free investment

b) A basket of stocks or bonds managed by a portfolio manager

c) An annuity

d) A share in a single company

The correct answer is b.

8. Canadian banks are primarily regulated by:

a) The Toronto Stock Exchange

b) The Ontario Securities Commission

c) The Office of the Superintendent of Financial Institutions

d) The Mutual Fund Dealers Association of Canada

The correct answer is c.

Investor Web Resources

The Canadian Securities Administrators	www.csa-acvm.ca
The Investment Dealers Association	www.ida.ca
The Investment Funds Institute of Canada	www.ific.ca
The Toronto Stock Exchange	www.tse.com
The Montréal Stock Exchange	www.m-x.ca
The Winnipeg Commodity Exchange	www.wce.ca
The System for Electronic Disclosure by Insiders	www.sedi.ca
Investor Education Fund	www.investored.ca
The Ontario Securities Commission	www.osc.gov.on.ca
The Alberta Securities Commission	www.albertasecurities.com
The British Columbia Securities Commission	www.bcsc.bc.ca
Commission des valeurs mobilières du Québec	www.cvmq.com

PROTECTING MONEY

At first, insurance might seem to be a form of legalized gambling. You and the insurance company make bets on whether a catastrophic or damaging event will occur, and then you wait and see who wins. Insurance contracts, however, are a complex area of law that deserve close scrutiny and consideration by those buying insurance. In some cases, such as tax planning, insurance can be a valuable tool for dealing with at least two certainties in life — death and taxes.

When it comes to auto insurance in Canada, some provinces such as Alberta, Ontario, Québec, Nova Scotia, New Brunswick, Prince Edward Island, and Newfoundland have private insurance schemes serviced by private companies or insurers. Other provinces have a public system run by a government insurer, including British Columbia, Saskatchewan, and Manitoba. In those provinces, the government insurer provides the minimum policy and drivers can buy additional insurance from either the government or private insurers. Each province sets minimum standards for coverage that drivers must purchase, and benefits in the event of an accident.

Home insurance is generally designed to protect you from losses resulting from damage caused by events that are difficult to predict or prevent. Unlike standard automobile insurance policies, there is no standard home insurance policy. Policies can vary widely depending on the insurance company and type of coverage.

Life insurance allows you to provide your dependants and loved ones with financial protection and support after your death or severe injury. It can also help to cover the costs of funeral expenses, capital gains taxes, loan repayments, or other obligations arising at death.

Auto Insurance

1. What are the basic requirements for auto insurance coverage?

Automobile owners are required by law to carry a minimum level of automobile insurance. Most provinces require drivers to purchase four types of insurance coverage, and all are included in most standard insurance policies. These are:

■ Third party liability of $200,000

Third party liability coverage insures you if the driver of your vehicle injures someone or damages someone else's property. Although the minimum is $200,000 in every province but Québec (where the minimum is $50,000), most owners purchase liability insurance of between $500,000 and $1 million dollars or more.

■ Uninsured motorist

Uninsured automobile coverage insures you if you are injured or your vehicle is damaged by drivers who do not have their own insurance.

■ Accident benefits

Compulsory in all jurisdictions except Newfoundland, statutory accident benefits provide coverage for a number of benefits if you are injured or killed in an automobile accident. This coverage applies regardless of who was at fault for the accident. Accident benefits are various and include income replacement, long-term disability, medical and rehabilitation expenses, attendant care, death, and funeral benefits.

■ Direct compensation for property damage

Direct compensation for property damage insures you against damage to your vehicle caused by another vehicle. This insurance may have no deductible, which is the amount of money you must pay toward the total cost of the damage or loss. A claim for this compensation does not affect your premiums.

2. Are there other kinds of auto insurance coverage available?

In addition to mandatory coverage, in many provinces you can purchase a number of extra types of insurance coverage, such as increased accident benefits, collision, specified perils, comprehensive, or all perils insurance.

Here are other types of optional coverage:

- "Collision insurance" covers property damage to your own vehicle in the event it is in a collision with another vehicle or object. Collision coverage is generally claimed where you are at fault or the damage is the fault of an unknown individual.
- "Specified perils insurance" covers damage to your vehicle caused by certain specified perils such as fire, theft, explosion, earthquake, lightning, and so forth.
- "Comprehensive insurance" covers damage to your vehicle as a result of things other than a collision, such as fire, lightning, theft, or vandalism, and includes the perils covered by specified perils insurance.
- "All perils" insurance offers a combination of collision and comprehensive coverage.

As well, different provinces have specific types of coverage that one can add to the basic coverage. For example, in Ontario, you can buy coverage that will index your income replacement benefits to the cost of living. You can also purchase coverage that will increase the maximum of your income replacement benefit from $400 to $600, $800, or $1,000 per week. You can also purchase increased coverage for medical, rehabilitation, death benefits, and benefits for caregivers.

3. What do I do if I have an accident?

If you are in an automobile accident, try to call the police from the scene. By law, in most provinces, you are required to report to your insurance company any accident that involves any personal injury or major property damage (usually over $1,000) within seven days of the accident, unless you are injured and unable to report. In some major cities, drivers can drive or be towed to a designated collision reporting centre to file a report.

Often, it's better to be safe than sorry so call the police right away to ask for advice on whether you can leave the scene.

4. What is no-fault automobile insurance?

"No-fault" insurance means your own insurance company will always pay your benefits under your policy regardless of whether you or another driver was responsible for the accident. That said, if you caused the damage, your insurance company will still consider you "at fault" and your insurance premiums will likely increase.

Many provinces have "no-fault" insurance schemes allowing accident victims to claim compensation regardless of who caused the damage. These schemes range from Québec's and Manitoba's "pure no-fault" system to the "threshold no-fault" system in Ontario. Other provinces may also use very basic "no fault principles" in determining eligibility for benefits.

Ontario's system, for example, only requires "no fault" payments of accident benefits as compensation for bodily injury and not for property damage. To recover for property damage, an individual has to claim damages from the individual at fault (or his or her insurer) or sue in court.

Ontario's system does allow accident victims to sue for additional compensation for personal injuries through the courts when certain "thresholds" are passed. The thresholds can be financial (specified level of medical expenses) or descriptive (involving severe injuries, loss or impairment of bodily functions). For example, seriously injured claimants (or personal representatives if the person is killed or incapacitated) may sue for pain and suffering, but not for lost income and other economic losses.

The benefit of a no-fault system for bodily injury is that you will receive compensation for an injury more quickly than under a fault system, where you would have to wait for a decision about who was at fault. In fact, in Ontario, an insurance company is required by law to pay weekly benefits within 14 days of a claim being filed.

After paying, your insurance company will still determine who was at fault to decide whether to increase future insurance premiums. If you were not at fault, your premiums will not be affected. In either case, you will still receive compensation for your injuries.

5. Does no-fault insurance apply to claims for property damage?

No. Unlike compensation for bodily injury claims, insurance claims involving property damage are still based on fault. If you are at fault for an automobile accident involving property damage, you will only be covered if you have purchased additional coverage such as "all perils" or "collision." These types of coverage are not mandatory in any province. If you have purchased this extra coverage, your claim will be paid, regardless of fault, but your insurance premiums might increase.

If the other driver is at fault for the accident, and that person caused property damage, you will usually be covered under either your direct compensation for property damage coverage or your uninsured automobile coverage. Both types of insurance are mandatory. Your claim will be paid by your insurance company. Depending on your particular insurance policy, you may or may not have to pay a deductible. But because the other driver was at fault, your insurance premiums will not increase as a result of making the claim. If the other driver cannot be identified, you will only be covered if you have purchased optional collision or all perils coverage.

Auto Accident Benefits & Options Canadian Provinces & Territories

Insurance coverage for accident benefits is compulsory in all provinces and territories except Newfoundland and Labrador. The following chart offers a cross-country perspective on the benefits and litigation options available.

Alberta

Insurance System: Private insurers

Right to sue for pain and suffering? Yes

Right to sue for economic loss in excess of no-fault benefits? Yes

Compulsory minimum 3rd-party liability: $200,000 in benefits is available per accident. If a claim involving both bodily injury and property damage reaches this figure, the payment for property damage will be capped at $10,000.

Medical payments: $10,000/person, rehabilitation included, amounts from medical and hospital plans excluded; chiropractors $500/person per occurrence; time limit 2 years.

Funeral expense benefits: $2,000

Disability income benefits: 80% gross wages; maximum $300/week; 104 weeks temporary or total disability; 7-day wait; unpaid housekeeper $100/week, maximum 26 weeks.

Death benefits: Death anytime; head of household

$10,000 plus $2,000 each dependant after first and 1% of total principal sum for 104 weeks, no limit; spouse $10,000; dependent child according to age maximum $3,000.

Note: *In Alberta, "insureds" involved in accidents in Québec can receive from their own insurer the equivalent to the benefits available to Québec residents from the Societe de l'assurance automobile du Québec. Similar arrangements were implemented June 1, 1998 for accidents involving Alberta "insureds" in Saskatchewan and Manitoba.*

British Columbia

Insurance System: Government administered (government and private insurers compete for optional and excess coverage).

Right to sue for pain and suffering? Yes

Right to sue for economic loss in excess of no-fault benefits? Yes

Compulsory minimum 3rd-party liability: $200,000 in benefits available per accident. If a claim involving both bodily injury and property damage reaches this figure, the payment for property damage will be capped at $20,000.

Medical payments: $150,000/person, rehabilitation included, excludes amounts payable under surgical, dental, hospital plan or other insurer.

Funeral expense benefits: $2,500

Disability income benefits: 75% gross wages; maximum $300/week; 104 weeks temporary disability, lifetime total and permanent; 7-day wait; homemaker up to $145/week, maximum 104 weeks.

Death benefits: Death anytime; head of household $5,000 and $145/week for 104 weeks to first survivor plus $1,000 and $35/week for 104 weeks for each survivor after first, no limit; spouse $2,500; dependent child according to age; maximum $1,500.

Manitoba

Insurance System: No fault, government administered (government and private insurers compete for optional and excess coverage).

Right to sue for pain and suffering? No

Right to sue for economic loss in excess of no-fault benefits? No

Compulsory minimum 3rd-party liability: $200,000 in benefits is available per accident. If a claim involving both bodily injury and property damage reaches this figure, the payment for property damage will be capped at $20,000.

Medical payments: No time or amount limit; includes rehabilitation

Funeral expense benefits: $3,803

Disability income benefits: 90% of net wages; maximum income gross $58,500/year; 7-day wait; indexed.

Death benefits: Death anytime; depends on wage and age; minimum $43,466; maximum $292,500 plus $20,646 to $38,032 to dependants according to age.

Impairment benefits: Up to $108,664

Note: *Lawsuits are not allowed for injuries sustained in automobile accidents in Manitoba. Victims and dependants resident in Manitoba are compensated by their government insurer for injuries whether or not the accident occurs in Manitoba. Residents of Manitoba involved in accidents in Québec can receive from their own insurer the equivalent to the benefits available to Québec residents from the Societe de l'assurance automobile du Québec. Collision insurance is compulsory in Manitoba (deductibles for all-perils claims vary according to type of vehicle). Policyholders may purchase coverage for economic loss greater than maximum accident benefits.*

New Brunswick

Insurance System: Private insurers

Right to sue for pain and suffering? Yes

Right to sue for economic loss in excess of no-fault benefits? Yes

Compulsory minimum 3rd-party liability: $200,000 in benefits is available per accident. If a claim involving both bodily injury and property damage reaches this figure, the payment for property damage will be capped at $20,000.

Medical payments: $50,000/person, including rehabilitation, excluding health insurance plans; time limit 4 years.

Funeral expense benefits: $2,500

Disability income benefits: 104 weeks partial disability; lifetime if totally disabled; maximum $250/week; 7-day wait; unpaid housekeeper $100/week, maximum 52 weeks.

Death benefits: Death within 2 years; head of household $50,000 plus $1,000 each for all dependants beyond first; spouse $25,000; dependent child $5,000.

Newfoundland

Insurance System: Private insurers

Right to sue for pain and suffering? Yes

Right to sue for economic loss in excess of no-fault benefits? Yes

Compulsory minimum 3rd-party liability: $200,000 in benefits is available per accident. If a claim involving both bodily injury and property damage reaches this figure, the payment for property damage will be capped at $20,000.

Medical payments: $25,000/person, including rehabilitation, excluding health insurance plans; time limit 4 years.

Funeral expense benefits: $1,000

Disability income benefits: 104 weeks partial disability; lifetime if totally disabled; maximum $140/week; 7-day wait; unpaid housekeeper $70/week, maximum 12 weeks.

Death benefits: Death within 2 years; head of household $10,000 plus $1,000 each for all dependants beyond first; spouse $10,000; dependent child $2,000.

Northwest Territories/ Nunavut

Insurance System: Private insurers

Right to sue for pain and suffering? Yes

Right to sue for economic loss in excess of no-fault benefits? Yes

Compulsory minimum 3rd-party liability: $200,000 in benefits is available per accident. If a claim involving both bodily injury and property damage reaches this figure, the payment for property damage will be capped at $10,000.

Medical payments: $25,000/person, excluding medical and hospital plans; time limit 4 years.

Funeral expense benefits: $1,000

Disability income benefits: 80% gross wages; maximum $140/week; 104 weeks temporary disability; lifetime if totally disabled; 7-day wait; unpaid housekeeper $100/week, maximum 12 weeks.

Death benefits: Death within 2 years; head of household $10,000; spouse $10,000; each survivor after first $2,500; one survivor; spouse or dependant; principal sum increased by $1,500.

Nova Scotia

Insurance System: Private insurers

Right to sue for pain and suffering? Yes

Right to sue for economic loss in excess of no-fault benefits? Yes

Compulsory minimum 3rd-party liability: $200,000 in benefits is available per accident. If a claim involving both bodily injury and property damage reaches this figure, the payment for property damage will be capped at $10,000.

Medical payments: $25,000/person, including rehabilitation, excluding health insurance plans; time limit 4 years.

Funeral expense benefits: $1,000

Disability income benefits: 104 weeks partial disability; lifetime if totally disabled; maximum $140/week; 7-day wait; unpaid housekeeper $70/week, maximum 12 weeks.

Death benefits: Death within 2 years; head of household $10,000 plus $1,000 each for all dependants beyond first; spouse $10,000; dependent child $2,000.

Ontario

Insurance System: No fault system with private insurers offering coverage.

Right to sue for pain and suffering? Yes, if injury meets a specific threshold (special deductible also applies). A lawsuit is allowed only if the injured person dies or sustains "permanent serious" disfigurement or impairment of important physical, mental or psychological functions. The court is directed to assess damages, then deduct $15,000 ($7,500, if a Family Law Act claim).

Right to sue for economic loss in excess of no-fault benefits? Yes. Injured person may sue for 80% of net income loss before trial and 100% of gross after trial. Also can sue for medical, rehabilitation and related costs when the injury is catastrophic.

Compulsory minimum 3rd-party liability: $200,000 in benefits is available per accident. If a claim involving both bodily injury and property damage reaches this figure, the payment for property damage will be capped at $10,000.

Medical payments: $100,000/person ($1-million if injury "catastrophic"), including rehabilitation, excluding health insurance plans; attendant care $72,000 ($1 million if injury "catastrophic").

Funeral expense benefits: $6,000

Disability income benefits: 80% of net wages up to $400/week, $185/week for those not employed (104 weeks maximum; longer if victim is unable to pursue any suitable occupation); 7-day wait for employed people, otherwise 26 weeks.

Death benefits: Death within 3 years; $25,000 for spouse, $10,000 for surviving dependant or for loss of dependant.

Note: *Ontario "insureds" involved in accidents in Québec can receive from their own insurer the equivalent to the benefits available to Québec residents from the Societe de l'assurance automobile du Québec. Policyholders may purchase coverage for economic loss greater than maximum accident benefits.*

P.E.I.

Insurance System: Private insurers

Right to sue for pain and suffering? Yes

Right to sue for economic loss in excess of no-fault benefits? Yes

Compulsory minimum 3rd-party liability: $200,000 in benefits is available per accident. If a claim involving both bodily injury and property damage reaches this figure, the payment for property damage will be capped at $10,000.

Medical payments: $25,000/person, including rehabilitation, excluding health insurance plans; time limit 4 years.

Funeral expense benefits: $1,000

Disability income benefits: 104 weeks partial disability; to age 65 if totally disabled; maximum $140/week; 7-day wait; unpaid housekeeper $70/week, maximum 12 weeks.

Death benefits: Death within 2 years; head of household $10,000 plus $1,000 each for all dependants beyond first; spouse $10,000; dependent child $2,000.

Québec

Insurance System: No fault government administration for accidents involving bodily injury. Private insurers offer coverage for property damage.

Right to sue for pain and suffering? No

Right to sue for economic loss in excess of no-fault benefits? No

Compulsory minimum 3rd-party liability: $50,000 in benefits. Liability limits relate to property damage claims within Québec and to personal injury and property damage claims outside Québec.

Medical payments: No time or amount limit; includes rehabilitation.

Funeral expense benefits: $3,582

Disability income benefits: 90% on net wages; maximum income gross $49,000/year; temporary 3 years; permanent life-time; 7-day wait, indexed.

Death benefits: Death anytime; depends on wage and age; minimum $47,775; maximum $245,500 plus $22,692 to $41,804 to dependants according to age; if no dependants — $17,916 to parents

Impairment benefits: Scheduled up to $134,652

Note: *Lawsuits are not allowed for injuries sustained in automobile accidents in Québec. Victims and dependants resident in Québec are compensated by the government insurer for injuries whether or not the accident occurs in Québec. In Québec, accident victims who are not residents are entitled to compensation only to the extent that they are not responsible for the accident (unless otherwise agreed*

between the Societe de l'assurance automobile du Québec and authorities of the victims' place of residence) and additional compensation may be available from their own insurers.

Saskatchewan

Insurance System: Right to choose no-fault coverage (government and private insurers compete for optional and excess coverage).

Right to sue for pain and suffering? No

Right to sue for economic loss in excess of no-fault benefits? Yes; injured people may sue for economic losses that exceed no-fault benefits. However, regarding loss of income, they may recover only with respect to gross income losses that exceed $52,058/year; award is net of income taxes.

Compulsory minimum 3rd-party liability: $200,000 is available for any one accident; however, if a claim involving both bodily injury and property damage reaches this figure, payment for property damage would be capped at $10,000.

Medical payments: $526,970/person; includes rehabilitation.

Funeral expense benefits: $5,270

Disability income benefits: 90% of net wages; maximum income gross $54,893/year; 7-day wait; indexed.

Death benefits: $47,427 minimum with spouse or dependants; $10,539 if no spouse or dependants; death educational benefit $31,618

Impairment benefits: Scheduled up to $131,743

Note: *Collision insurance is compulsory in Saskatchewan (deductibles for all-perils claims vary according to type of vehicle).*

Yukon

Insurance System: Private insurers

Right to sue for pain and suffering? Yes

Right to sue for economic loss in excess of no-fault benefits? Yes

Compulsory minimum 3rd-party liability: $200,000 in benefits is available per accident. If a claim involving both bodily injury and property damage reaches this figure, the payment for property damage will be capped at $10,000.

Medical payments: $10,000/person, rehabilitation

included, amounts from medical and hospital plans excluded; time limit 2 years.

Funeral expense benefits: $2,000

Disability income benefits: 80% gross wages; maximum $300/week; 104 weeks temporary or total disability; 7-day wait; unpaid housekeeper $100/week, maximum 26 weeks.

Death benefits: Death anytime; head of household $10,000 plus $2,000 each dependant after first and 1% of total principal sum for 104 weeks, no limit; spouse $10,000; dependent child according to age; maximum $3,000.

Source: Insurance Bureau of Canada

HOME INSURANCE

6. What are the different types of home insurance?

There are three main types of home insurance:

- "Basic named perils" insurance covers your home and its contents for only the specific risks that are listed in the policy and is generally cheaper than comprehensive coverage
- "Broad" insurance generally provides more coverage than the "basic named perils" policy, but less than the "comprehensive" policy. With "broad" coverage, you obtain comprehensive coverage for your house and basic named perils coverage on its contents.
- "Comprehensive" insurance covers your home and its contents for all risks, except for any that are specifically excluded in the policy

Most policies of home insurance, as well as tenant and condominium insurance, also provide coverage for your legal liability to others because of bodily injury and property damage unintentionally caused by you and other members of your household.

Although home insurance generally covers the contents of your home, you may require extra coverage or your coverage may be limited if you own special or expensive property such as jewellery, antiques, or art work. Talk to your insurance company or broker for information on whether your expensive or special items are covered in your policy. Without the proper coverage, you may not be compensated in the event of a loss.

7. What is tenant insurance?

If you rent an apartment, you can buy tenant insurance to protect the contents of your apartment, such as furniture, clothing, and electronic equipment. Your tenant insurance will also protect you if you accidentally damage the apartment unit itself. For example, if you or your property is the cause of a fire that results in extensive damage to the building, you may be required to pay for the cost of repairs, which should be covered under your policy.

8.   Can I insure a condominium?

If you own a condominium unit, you can purchase condominium insurance to protect against loss or damage to your unit and its contents, as well as injury to your guests or workers hurt in your unit. You are also protected if you are responsible for damage to common areas of the building (lobby, swimming pool, or parking garage) or other units (water leaking from a shower to a suite below). Many policies also protect you from special assessments made against all owners arising from a claim made against the building.

By law, condominium corporations are required to insure the building as a whole and common elements against damage or loss, but are not required to provide coverage for the property, upgrades, or belongings within your unit.

9.   How can I save on home insurance?

You may be able to reduce the money you are paying for home insurance. First, many insurance companies offer discounts for people who install smoke alarms, sprinkler systems, or home security systems. A discount may also be offered for long-time customers who have been loyal to a particular insurance company or for customers who have both their vehicle insurance and their home insurance with the same insurance company.

Second, you can lower your premium by raising the amount of your deductible. Third, you should regularly calculate the value of the items you are insuring to avoid paying for more insurance than you actually need. In many cases, however, people are under-insured because they do not properly re-calculate the replacement costs of insured items.

Life Insurance

10. Do I need life insurance and if so, how much?

How much life insurance you require, or if you require any at all, depends on your personal situation., Consider several things when evaluating whether to buy life insurance.

■ Dependants

Do you have dependants and wish them to be financially secure if you were to die? As a general rule, you may want to leave your dependants enough money to cover specific expenses and maintain their current lifestyle. Your dependants should be left with enough money to pay off your debts and funeral expenses and to pay for food, shelter, clothing, and education costs, at least during the transition period.

■ Support obligations

If you are a single parent, making or receiving support payments, how will these payments be kept up in the event of death?

■ Outstanding mortgage

If you have a mortgage on your home, do you want it paid off in the event of your death?

■ Legacy

Would you like to leave money to certain charities?

■ Tax obligations

What capital gains taxes or other financial obligations would arise at death?

11. What are the main sources of life insurance?

If you decide you need life insurance, you need to know what the four main sources of life insurance are, and what types of life insurance you can choose from. You may find you already have some group life insurance sponsored by your employer, union, or association, or you have monthly survivor benefits or the lump-sum death benefit paid under the Canada Pension Plan. You may also have creditor insurance, which was purchased when you applied for a mortgage or loan.

In addition to these three sources of life insurance, you can purchase an individual policy directly from an agent or insurance company. Once you know what your source of insurance is, you will need to decide what type of policy is best for you.

12. What types of life insurance are there?

While there are many variations, there are two main types of life insurance: term insurance and permanent insurance.

In both cases, you are usually required to make monthly payments called premiums. Premiums are paid throughout a person's lifetime or for a specified period, depending on the type of insurance policy.

■ Term insurance

This is the simplest and least expensive kind of life insurance characterized by fixed premiums for a defined period or term. The amount of the policy is paid out to the beneficiary if you die during that period. If you survive the term, the policy expires. Term insurance is often sold in 1-, 5-, 10-, or 20-year terms and is often available in renewable and convertible forms. A renewable term insurance policy allows you to renew the insurance policy at the end of the term, at an increased cost, but without having to take a medical and prove your insurability. A convertible term insurance policy allows you to convert your policy into a cash-value type of policy without having to prove insurability. It is best to buy term insurance that is both renewable and convertible, unless you are sure your needs for insurance are temporary.

■ Permanent insurance

The second type of life insurance is called permanent, whole life, or cash-value insurance. Permanent insurance provides protection as long as you live, provided you continue to pay the premiums. The premiums are usually a set amount so permanent insurance is more expensive than term insurance in the early years but less expensive in later years. The cash value that usually develops from the higher early premiums is given to you if you terminate the policy or you can borrow it to meet your other financial needs. Universal life is a popular type of permanent insurance that typically provides you with some flexibility with the level of premium payments and some options for the investment of the cash value.

As a general rule, permanent needs such as funeral expenses, capital gains taxes, and long-term needs of a disabled dependant should be covered with permanent insurance, while temporary needs such as mortgage payments and education costs for dependants should be covered with term insurance.

For more information on the type and amount of life insurance you may require, consult with a tax lawyer or an insurance agent.

13. How are life insurance benefits paid?

Insurance proceeds are paid, usually in a lump sum, to the person or group of people you have chosen to receive the benefits; these people are called beneficiaries. The amount paid is almost always tax-free and is not subject to probate fees if paid to a beneficiary. If you have not chosen a beneficiary, the proceeds of the insurance policy will go to your estate. Once the proceeds of life insurance are included in the estate, they will be subject to taxation. Therefore, it is advisable to always name a beneficiary in your life insurance policy.

Insurance Facts and Stats

• Fraudulent claims represent approximately 10 to 15 percent of claims, costing $1.3 billion per year in Canada

• More than one quarter of all personal injury claims contain elements of fraud, which costs the industry $500 million annually

• 92 percent of Canadians do not approve of submitting false or exaggerated insurance claims

• Nearly one in four Canadians knows someone who has committed personal injury insurance fraud

• Since 1991, bodily injury claims have more than doubled from 75 per thousand collisions to 163 in 1998

• 1.4 percent of all deaths in Canada are attributed to vehicle collisions

• More than one-third of accidental deaths are caused by such collisions

• More than 70 percent of accidental deaths of young people aged 15 to 24 are due to automobile collisions

• The odds of a death by collision are 30 times higher for these young people than for the rest of the population

• There are more than 220,000 injuries and over 28,000 acute care hospital injury admissions every year due to automobile collisions

Sources: Canadian Coalition Against Fraud (1997) and The Fraser Institute (1998).

Taxes

D eath and taxes. The two certainties in life and it's no different for Canadians. Both federal and provincial governments, as well as some municipalities, collect taxes as a source of revenue to pay for social and economic programs. The federal and provincial governments each can create certain types of tax laws, though the federal government through Canada Revenue Agency, generally controls the tax collection process (except in Québec, where the provincial government has its own income tax collection process).

The main law for taxing income is the *Income Tax Act*, which sets out rules for both individuals and businesses. The *Income Tax Act* usually undergoes important changes every year when the federal government sets its annual budget. These changes will affect how much tax you pay from year-to-year.

In addition to the *Income Tax Act*, other laws cover the taxation of importing, exporting, the sale of goods and services, and property. As well, Canada is a signatory to many international treaties with other countries that govern the taxation of individuals and businesses doing business or earning income internationally.

The Canadian tax system relies on self-assessment by taxpayers. This doesn't, however, mean our tax system is voluntary. All taxpayers are responsible for reporting their total income and determining their total tax owing.

Canada Revenue Agency enforces the tax law by performing a small number of audits on individuals and businesses each year. If Canada Revenue Agency finds that someone made errors in calculating or reporting the amount of tax owed, that person is "reassessed" and, if the error was deliberate, a penalty is levied. If someone is found to be intentionally evading the law, he or she may be prosecuted by the Department of Justice for tax evasion or for a criminal offence.

As with any complex area of law or regulation, it is also wise to consult a knowledgeable tax lawyer or tax accountant.

1.   What types of income are taxable?

Individuals and corporations are taxed on their total income after subtracting allowable deductions. There are four general types of income that are taxed:

- Employment earnings, which usually only apply to individuals
- Profit made from a business activity
- Investment income from property or investments
- Capital gains on the sale of capital property

Different rules apply to each type of income, which affect the amount of tax you have to pay. To file a tax return and claim deductions, you need to know what type of income you earned.

■ Employment income

Employment income is usually a person's wages or salary paid by an employer. It can also include any vacations, gifts, or added perks you receive from your employer as part of your employment. Generally, there are few expenses that can be deducted from employment income, although there are exceptions for people in sales.

■ Business income

The law makes a distinction between employment income and business income. Business income can be earned by an individual, a partnership, or a corporation, and includes any money you earn from a profession, trade, or any other business where you expect to make a profit. Some types of rental income may also be considered business income. For example, if a landlord offers uncommon services such as laundry or housecleaning, or if a landlord runs an office with employees who manage the rental properties: this type of income can generally include business expense deductions.

■ Income from property

The law also requires a taxpayer to pay tax on income from property, which includes interest from investments and loans, and can include rent from investment properties. Generally, expenses cannot be deducted from this type of income unless they are directly related to earning the income. A common deduction from property income is interest on a loan that was taken to purchase the property. There are also rules specific to property income that prevent you from transferring property income to a spouse or child for the sole purpose of reducing the amount of tax you have to pay.

■ Capital gains and losses

The law applies different tax rules to capital gains and losses. Generally, if you sell capital property, such as stocks on the stock market, for more than you paid, the amount of the difference is considered a capital gain. If you sell something for less than you paid, the amount of the loss is considered a capital loss. If you have a capital gain, only 50 percent of it will be taxed. If you have a capital loss, 50 percent of it can be subtracted from any capital gain you made that year and your net capital gain is reduced. The capital loss can be carried back or carried forward.

Some types of property are exempt from being taxed for capital gains. The most common capital gain exemption is the sale of your principal residence. A principal residence is the home where you ordinarily live or where your spouse, former spouse, or child ordinarily lives.

Other examples of income generally not considered a capital gain include proceeds from the sale of business inventory, land bought with the intention of making profit on its resale, and profit made on the sale of personal property that costs less than $1,000. If you sell personal property for more than $1,000, you will only have to claim a capital gain on the amount you received above the $1,000 original cost.

You will need to determine your total capital gains and losses before filing your tax return. When you sell stocks or other investments through a broker, you will usually receive a receipt for tax return purposes that lists your capital gain or loss. For more information about capital gains and losses, consult a tax lawyer, accountant, or a tax filing service.

2.   Are there different tax rules for residents and non-residents of Canada?

The *Income Tax Act* sets out different taxation rules for residents and non-residents. The *Act* also has guidelines that determine whether individuals and corporations are residents of Canada for income tax purposes. It is important to know whether you are a resident or non-resident for Canadian tax purposes because it will affect how much tax you have to pay.

Individuals and corporations that are considered residents must pay tax on their income from all sources, no matter where it was earned. Non-residents usually only pay tax on income earned in Canada and are levied a 25 percent withholding tax on income they make from interest or dividends in Canada. Also, non-residents may not be entitled to capital gain exemptions on the sale of their homes.

■ Defining "resident" for tax purposes

There are also different resident tax rules for individuals and corporations. An individual is considered a resident based on many factors, including:

- How much time the person spent in Canada during the year
- Reasons why the person was in Canada
- Where the person's regular home is located
- If the person owns property in Canada
- If the person is a member of a club in Canada
- If the person has a family in Canada

Generally, if an individual visits Canada for at least 183 days in a calendar year, for tax purposes that person is deemed to be a Canadian resident for the year.

Different rules apply to corporations. A corporation is considered a resident in the place where its central mind and management or head office is located. Companies that incorporated in Canada after April 26, 1965 are automatically considered to be resident in Canada, and will have to prove otherwise.

Consult a tax lawyer or an accountant if you are unsure whether you are considered a resident for income tax purposes.

Tax Rules for Individuals

3. Do I have to file a tax return?

You must file a tax return if any of the following applies:

- You have to pay tax on income earned during the previous calendar year
- The tax authorities requested you file a return
- You sold or otherwise disposed of property, such as real estate or shares
- You have a taxable capital gain or are reporting a capital gains reserve you claimed on your previous year's return
- You have to pay back a portion of your Old Age Security or Employment Insurance benefits
- You have not repaid money you withdrew from your RRSP under the Home Buyers' Plan or Lifelong Learning Plan
- You are contributing to Canada Pension Plan (CPP). For instance, your net self-employment income and pensionable employment income, was more than $3,500

You also need to file a return to be eligible for a tax refund, Goods & Services or Harmonized Sales Tax credit, Child Tax Benefit payments, tuition or education payments, RRSP contributions, or if you have incurred a non-capital loss that you want to be able to apply in other years.

4. How do I file a tax return?

Filing a tax return involves submitting forms to the Canada Revenue Agency which report your income for the year, any deductions and credits you are claiming, and the calculation of the tax you owe for the year.

If you are going to prepare your own tax return, you can obtain a tax return kit from Canada Revenue Agency or from the nearest post office. Since there are usually changes to the tax laws each year, it is important to use a current year's form. You can also purchase a computer program that will ask you to input information and will then calculate your taxes. These programs usually are set up in a simple question and answer format, and are programmed to check for any deductions or credits you may be entitled to.

Regardless of who prepares your return, you will need copies of all the tax receipts from your income sources, including any T4 forms for employment income, T5 forms for interest earnings, and T3 forms for trust income or mutual fund income. Generally, your employer and investment company will send these to you. It is also a good idea to compile any receipts for credits or deductions you will be claiming, such as RRSP contributions, medical expenses, donations, tuition, or rent.

■ Making changes to your tax information

To make a change to any tax return that you have already filed, you can complete a special form called a T1 Adjustment Request, which is available from Canada Revenue Agency. You can also write a letter to Canada Revenue Agency with the details of the changes you want to make, as well as your Social Insurance Number, name, address, and daytime telephone number. Attach any supporting documents or receipts.

For additional information on how to file a tax return, call Canada Revenue Agency. This number is listed in the Blue pages of your telephone book. For assistance in filing a tax return, consult an accountant or a tax filing service.

5. Why do others pay a different tax rate than me?

The federal and provincial governments each levy and collect income tax. The taxes are combined so that the taxpayer only files one tax return, and pays the combined tax total, which the governments then divide. The amount of tax you are required to pay depends on the amount of income you earned during the year and the deductions and credits you claimed. In most cases, you are also required to pay tax on investment income earned in the year, even if it is not received until the next calendar year.

■ Tax brackets

Depending on the amount of income you earn, you will fall within one of three tax brackets. Each bracket is taxed at a different rate. The system is based on what is called graduated tax rates. This means that if your income increases so that you enter a new tax bracket, only the amount of your income that falls in the higher tax bracket gets taxed at the higher rate.

■ Rates of tax

There is a federal and a provincial tax rate that together are called the combined tax rate. In addition to the combined rate there may be surtaxes that primarily apply to incomes in the highest tax bracket.

■ Deductions and credits

There are two main ways to reduce the amount of tax you pay: first, by claiming deductions and second, by claiming credits.

Deductions are amounts you can subtract directly from your income before calculating tax. There are fewer deductions for employed individuals than individuals who carry on a business. Some common deductions for individuals include support payments made to an ex-spouse, contribution amounts to a Registered Retirement Savings Plan (RRSP) up to your annual maximum, and moving expenses if you had to move more than 40 kilometres because of work.

The second way to reduce the amount of tax you pay is through tax credits. Tax credits are subtracted from the amount of tax you owe. The most common credit that everyone can claim is a basic personal tax credit, which allows you to subtract an amount set by the federal government. There are also credits for medical expenses, which equal over 3 percent of your net income or $1,813 for 2005 (whichever is smaller), and credits for college or university tuition.

6. When does my tax have to be paid?

If you earn income from employment, your employer is obligated to deduct tax installments from every paycheque and remit them to Canada Revenue Agency. If your employer has not deducted enough during the year, you will have to pay more tax when you file your tax return. If your employer deducted too much because you have deductions or credits to claim, you will usually get money back after you file your return for the year.

If you earn income from a source other than an employer, you will usually pay the tax you owe when you file your tax return or when you are asked to make quarterly installment payments.

You are required to pay tax on certain types of investment income you earn during the year regardless of when you actually receive it.

Under the law, you are required to file your tax return and pay any taxes owing by April 30th of the following year. If you, your spouse, or a common-law partner is self-employed and carried on a business in the year of the return, the forms may be filed on or before June 15th. If you have a balance owing, however, you still have to pay it on or before April 30th.

7.   How do I get a tax refund?

Generally, you are entitled to receive a tax refund if you have paid more tax during the year than required. Taxes that are withheld by an employer are typically based on your estimated income for the entire year. The employer usually calculates the taxes you will owe based on tax tables provided by Canada Revenue Agency. In most cases, employers do not consider whether you have deductions or tax credits to claim or if there are circumstances that cause you to have taxable income less than the estimated amount.

Even if you are entitled to a refund, you will not receive it unless you file a tax return. When you file your tax return, you or your accountant will calculate the correct amount of taxes you owed and will determine whether you should receive a refund. Once you file your tax return, Canada Revenue Agency will review and process it. It usually takes four to six weeks before you receive your refund. The earlier you file a return, the quicker you'll get the refund.

If you think you are owed a refund for any year from 1985 onward, you may still be entitled to the refund. You can file a tax return or adjustment for the relevant year with all receipts for deductions and credits attached. If you are unsure whether you are entitled to a refund or if you need assistance, consult an accountant or a tax filing service.

8.   What happens if I do not file a return or I pay late?

Normally, if you do not file a tax return and are required to, make false statements in completing your tax return, or leave out important information so you underreport your income, the *Income Tax Act* imposes penalties. In circumstances of willful fraud or tax evasion, you can be criminally prosecuted.

■ Penalties for filing taxes late or paying too little

Under the law, you are required to file your tax return and pay all taxes owing by April 30th of the following year. If you do not file a return and are required to pay taxes, you will be assessed a penalty of 5 percent of the amount owing plus 1 percent for each month it is past due, up to 12 months. You will also be charged compound daily interest on any outstanding tax. If you cannot afford to pay the entire amount you owe at once, you may be able to arrange a payment plan with Canada Revenue Agency.

▪ Penalties for fraud and evasion

If you are suspected of fraud or tax evasion, you may be prosecuted for a criminal offence. If you are found guilty, the penalties can include a fine of between 100 to 200 percent of the amount of tax evaded, or up to 5 years in prison.

If you are found to owe more than you calculated, you can usually appeal this decision. If you are charged with a criminal offence under tax law, consult a lawyer immediately.

9.   How does a RRSP help me shelter income?

The Canadian government has established special tax rules for investments that encourage people to save for their retirement. Investments made under these special rules are referred to as a Registered Retirement Savings Plan or RRSP.

RRSPs are tax deferral plans registered with Canada Revenue Agency that allow you to put a percentage of your earned income into an investment account. You will not have to pay tax on the income you contribute to your RRSP until you withdraw the money. The money that you put into an RRSP can be invested in mutual funds, term deposits, stocks, bonds, or mortgages. You should make sure that the investment you would like to buy is RRSP eligible.

There are many benefits to investing in an RRSP. First, RRSPs usually reduce the amount of income tax you have to pay. Your RRSP contribution for a particular year is included on your income tax return as a deduction. This reduces the amount of tax you have to pay in the year you make the contribution, because it reduces your annual taxable income for that year. Essentially, you do not pay tax on the money you invested until you withdraw it. If you withdraw the money during your retirement or at a time when you have very little income, you will be in a lower tax bracket and will pay less income tax than if you had paid tax on the money when you earned it.

The second advantage is that RRSP investments are tax-sheltered. This means that any increase in the value of your investment will not be taxed while the money is in the RRSP. Because your RRSP is tax-sheltered, it grows faster than it would if you had to pay tax on it. Any gain in your investment will be added to the principal amount you contributed. The entire investment is tax sheltered, and you will not have to pay tax on it until you start withdrawing money.

Third, RRSPs are a good way to save for your retirement or for some other time when you need to supplement your income. For example, if you decide to take time off to raise your children or if you quit your job to start your own business, you can use your RRSP as a source of income. You should make sure your RRSP allows you to withdraw money when you want. Some RRSP plans lock in your investment for a certain period.

Finally, RRSPs allow you to split your retirement income with your spouse by allowing the person with the larger income to make contributions to the spouse's RRSP. The result is that each spouse's RRSP will be about the same amount, which means that both spouses can withdraw money. The couple will therefore be taxed on two smaller incomes rather than one single larger income. The overall result is that the couple will pay less tax.

10. What is the child tax benefit?

The Child Tax Benefit is a tax credit for families raising children under 18 years of age. It is a tax-free monthly payment to the parent who is primarily responsible for caring for the children. If you are married, however, both spouses must file a tax return each year to keep receiving the benefit.

The amount you are entitled to receive generally depends on the number of children you have, the age of your children, your family income, and whether you are married. The amount you are eligible for decreases as your family income rises above $35,000.

To begin receiving the Child Tax Benefit, you must fill out forms available from Canada Revenue Agency. For additional information about the Child Tax Benefit, contact Canada Revenue Agency.

11. How are child and spousal support payments affected by tax law?

Generally, child support payments are not deductible by the person paying or taxable in the hands of the person receiving the money. In Canada, though, there are two sets of rules for periodic payments required under child support orders or written agreements — one set for agreements made before May 1, 1997 and another for those after April 30, 1997.

Support payments must be required by court order or written agreement. The requirement can include payments for a spouse or common-law partner, or support for a child. Lump sum or one-time payments are not considered support payments because they are not periodic. In all cases, the payor and recipient must live apart.

The support agreement or court order must be registered with tax authorities through a completed Form T1158, *Registration of Family Support Payments.* A copy of the order or agreement must also be included.

■ Two sets of rules

If the child support order or agreement was made before May 1, 1997, then the parent who pays child support can deduct the payment amounts from his or her income before taxes are applied. The parent who receives the payments must also include the child support payments as income for tax purposes.

If the child support order or agreement was made after April 30, 1997, then the parent who pays the child support cannot deduct the support payments for tax purposes. The parent who receives child support payments also does not include it as part of his or her total income and therefore does not have to pay any tax.

Obviously, there are tax disadvantages for one parent or the other, depending on when the agreement arose.

■ Changing support agreements made before May 1, 1997

If you have a child support order or agreement that was made before May 1, 1997, you may be able to change the order or agreement so that the new tax rules apply. If you elect to make changes, usually it will cause the parent paying support to pay more tax for the year and the parent receiving the support to pay less tax. If you want to change an order or agreement and the other parent does not agree, you will usually have to go to court. Consult a lawyer if this is the case.

■ Spousal support

Generally, periodic spousal support payments continue to be taxable in the hands of the recipient and deductible for the payor when there is a written agreement or court order. Any voluntary payments outside those required by the order or agreement may not be deductible. Consult a tax lawyer or accountant for specific advice.

12. What are the tax rules for gifts and inheritances?

There are tax rules for giving gifts while you are still alive and for leaving someone an inheritance. The law applies different rules to cash and most personal property than to property that can have a capital gain or loss, such as stocks or land.

These rules may affect how you arrange your finances and property to minimize the amount of tax you pay. If you receive a gift or an inheritance, you will not usually be taxed. Although there are no direct taxes on received gifts and inheritances, there are usually tax consequences for the person who gives a gift or leaves an inheritance.

■ Gifts

Generally, you cannot avoid paying tax by giving someone a gift. For example, if you give a gift of cash to someone close to you (such as your spouse or your child who is under the age of 18), any income generated from the gift will still be considered part of your income for tax purposes.

If you give someone other than a spouse a gift of property, such as land, it will be considered for tax purposes to have been sold at fair market value. Fair market value is the estimated value that something would sell for in the market at a given time. If the fair market value of an item exceeds the amount you initially paid for it, then you have a capital gain that you have to pay tax on.

■ Gifts of property to a spouse

If you give a gift of property, such as jewellery or land to your spouse, you may be able to defer paying tax. If your spouse sells the property, tax will be paid by the transferring spouse on any capital gain made. The capital gain will be calculated by using your purchase price and the selling price used by your spouse. If you give a gift of farm property to a child, you may be exempt from paying tax and should consult a tax lawyer for additional information.

■ Tax on property owned at time of death

There are also rules for the property that you own at the time of your death. If you own property or investments, under the law you will be considered to have sold them at fair market value just before you died. Since a tax return must be filed for the year in which you die, if the value of the property or investments has increased since you acquired them, your estate will be considered to have received a capital gain. Your estate's personal representative (also known as "executor" or "executrix") will be responsible for paying tax on the capital gain with money from your estate. There are tax rules that defer the capital gain on death if your will gifts property to a surviving spouse.

■ Tax implications if you receive a gift

If you receive a gift or inheritance from someone other than a spouse, you will usually be considered to have acquired it at fair market value.

In the future when you sell it, your capital gain or loss will be based on the value of the item when you acquired it. It is very important to consider the tax consequences of gifts and inheritances before you give away your belongings. Consult a lawyer or estate planner to minimize the amount of tax you or your family will have to pay.

13. What income taxes apply after someone dies?

Although there is no "death tax" in Canada, there are two main types of income tax that are collected after someone dies. First, there are taxes on income or capital gains earned during the last year of life. Second, there is interest or capital gains made on money in the estate. You can minimize the amount of taxes payable by arranging your finances and property with the help of an estate lawyer.

■ Who is responsible for paying a deceased person's taxes?

After a person dies, someone has to be responsible for paying the deceased's taxes. Most people write a will and appoint a personal representative—the "executor" or "executrix"—to act upon their death. This person carries out the instructions in a will and is responsible for administering the estate. One of the responsibilities of a personal representative is to file the deceased's last tax return and pay any taxes owing, using money from the deceased's estate.

■ Duties of a personal representative

When someone dies, a personal representative is normally required to file a tax return for the deceased by April 30th of the following year. If the person died after October, the tax return may be filed within six month's of the person's death. The tax return will include all income and capital gains made from January 1st of that year until the day of the person's death. Generally, any income or capital gains that are made after the person's death will usually be considered income of the person's estate. The personal representative will be responsible for paying taxes on such income with money from the estate.

■ Taxes on property owed at time of death

Even if a deceased person did not sell any property or receive any capital gains during the last year, he or she will usually have to pay tax on property owned at the time of death unless it is being inherited by a spouse. This normally applies to property such as land or investments and not to personal use property.

Generally, property not being inherited by a spouse will be considered, for tax purposes, to have been sold immediately before the deceased's death. The sale will be considered to have been made at fair market value. See the above section on Gifts for an explanation of "fair market value."

■ Tax implications for inheritances of property

If an individual inherits property from a deceased spouse and that surviving spouse sells it or later dies, taxes must be paid on the full capital gain from the time the deceased spouse first acquired the property.

There are many tax rules that apply when someone has died. For more information, consult a tax lawyer or an estate lawyer.

TAX AUDITS & INVESTIGATIONS

14. What triggers a Canada Revenue Agency audit or investigation?

Canada Revenue Agency may choose to audit an individual or business even if there is no apparent reason to do so. Generally, Canada Revenue Agency can only audit someone up to three years after a tax return has been filed, unless there is misrepresentation or fraud involved.

■ Reasons for investigating a taxpayer

There are four main reasons that Canada Revenue Agency chooses to investigate or audit someone:

• If there is an inconsistency in the reporting, such as not including income that an employer has reported, Canada Revenue Agency will investigate the situation and may reassess the tax return
• Canada Revenue Agency may target a group of businesses or individuals to audit as part of an initiative to raise levels of compliance within the group
• Canada Revenue Agency may be informed of non-compliance by an outside source or from another government investigation, and may choose to audit based on this lead
• Canada Revenue Agency may also audit someone who is financially linked to someone who is already being audited, such as a business partner

15. What is involved in a tax audit?

If you are audited, your tax return will be reviewed and your records will be examined. Canada Revenue Agency might determine that you owe more or less tax for that year. Most audits are not criminal investigations, but are done to determine whether the taxpayer paid enough tax. In extreme cases, an audit will be done to investigate whether a taxpayer has been intentionally evading taxes, which may result in prosecution similar to a criminal prosecution.

■ Canada Revenue Agency audits

If Canada Revenue Agency is going to audit you or your business, you will usually receive a written notice. Then an auditor may contact you to set a date to start the audit. If you are being audited, you may want to consult a lawyer or an accountant about your rights and the process before you meet with the auditor.

The auditor will review your income tax return, and will usually want to see bank account statements, original receipts, your books or records, and financial statements from your business. The auditor has the legal authority to inspect any documents that relate to the tax return under review. The auditor also has the authority to enter a business premises without a warrant and require the owner or manager to provide reasonable assistance. An auditor does not, however, have the authority to enter your home unless you agree to it or the auditor gets a warrant from a judge.

An audit normally takes up to two weeks to complete, although a simple audit of an individual will take substantially less time. If the auditor finds errors in your return, the auditor will usually first give you a chance to provide further information that might explain the situation before finalizing the audit.

If the auditor finds that your tax return was incorrect, you will usually receive a Notice of Assessment or Reassessment, which corrects the tax return and shows if you owe any tax money. In rare cases it is possible for the Assessment or Reassessment to find that Canada Revenue Agency owes the taxpayer money. If you are found to owe more tax than you thought or if you are charged a penalty, you have the right to appeal.

16. Can I appeal a reassessment or tax decision?

If you disagree with an assessment or reassessment of your tax return by Canada Revenue Agency, and you want to appeal, consult a tax lawyer or tax accountant. In simple cases, you may be able to make an appeal on your own, although you may still want to consult a professional for advice.

■ First step to appealing

If you disagree with an assessment or reassessment, first contact the General Inquiries telephone line of Canada Revenue Agency to discuss the matter with a representative. If the matter is not resolved at that stage, you can object to the assessment or reassessment by writing to the Assistant Director of Appeals at your local Canada Revenue Agency office or tax centre. The letter should outline all the reasons why you object to Canada Revenue Agency's assessment.

■ Formally objecting to a decision

Objections must be received within 90 days from the date the Notice of Assessment or Reassessment was written. Individual taxpayers may be able to file an objection within one year of filing a return even if the 90-day period has passed. Call Canada Revenue Agency to determine your deadline for appeal. Once your objection has been received, an independent review will take place and you will usually be able to present information about your objection to an appeals officer who will make a decision.

■ Appealing to the Tax Court of Canada

If you do not agree with the appeals officer's decision, you have the right to appeal to the Tax Court of Canada within 90 days. There are two ways to make an appeal to the Tax Court: an informal procedure and a general procedure. The type of procedure you use will depend on the amount of money in dispute. If you choose the informal procedure, you do not require a lawyer, although some people are represented by other professionals, such as accountants. Generally, decisions made through the informal procedure are final and you have no right to an appeal.

The general procedure is a formal trial before a judge. A lawyer represents most people who go through the general procedure. Decisions made in a general procedure may be appealed to the Federal Court of Appeal and to the Supreme Court of Canada.

There are formal documents that must be filled out in order to make an appeal through either the informal or general procedure. For information on how to make an appeal, contact Canada Revenue Agency or consult a lawyer.

17. How long should I keep my tax records?

Generally, it is recommended that you keep records for at least seven years. The tax authorities can review and reassess your income tax returns for the previous three years and, in some cases, even farther back.

Canada Revenue Agency can also arbitrarily assess or guess your income if you have not kept all your returns and supporting documentation. Common records to keep include:

- All T-slips
- RRSP contribution slips
- Medical receipts
- Charitable donation receipts
- Self-employed and business revenue and expense records

Are Legal Fees Deductible?

Anne and her child were in desperate financial circumstances. Her ex-husband had not been paying child support, so she went to court to get a support order and won. When completing her tax return, she attempted to deduct her legal costs. The tax authorities denied the deduction, taking the position the legal costs were like any other personal or living expenses one is required to pay. Anne appealed to a higher authority.

Should Anne be allowed to deduct legal expenses?

Yes. After many years of denying the deduction of legal fees when establishing the right to support, Canada Revenue Agency is now required to allow individuals to deduct expenses incurred to establish the right to spousal support and obtain an increase in spousal or child support amounts. You can also deduct legal fees incurred for enforcing pre-existing rights to either interim or permanent support amounts under a pre-existing written agreement or court order. The costs of defending against the reduction of support payments are also deductible.

The issue of whether legal fees can be deducted is very complex and differs greatly for individuals and businesses. For example, an individual defending a personal injury lawsuit is not allowed to deduct legal fees. An employee who earns commission income and is defending a lawsuit arising from normal business risks, however, may be able to deduct legal expenses. As always, consult with a tax professional.

WWW Resources

Canada Customs & Revenue Agency	www.ccra-adrc.gc.ca
Canadian Taxpayers Federation	www.taxpayer.com
Tax Court of Canada	www.tcc-cci.gc.ca

Buying & Selling A Home

I t is the dream of almost everyone to one day own a home. As financial institutions like to remind us, it is one of the biggest purchases most of us will ever make. Whether we are buying or selling a property, there is no denying it is an emotion-packed life event and the legal aspects of what we are doing are often not given full consideration until it is too late.

For example, how do you know the seller has a legal right to sell the property? What conditions should you put in every offer and agreement to purchase? What can you do to protect yourself from a buyer or seller who backs out of the deal? Whose name should be on your title of ownership?

The stakes are often high in real estate and the courts are reluctant to rescue someone who makes a bad deal, such as buying at too high a price or getting a furnace that dies one month after the purchase.

For many people, the purchase or sale of a home is their first significant encounter with lawyers, legal jargon, and major contractual obligations and responsibilities. From the moment you see your dream house (or dream purchaser) everything seems to be on the fast track with lawyers, real estate agents and lenders looking for information, money, and your signature. Sometimes, it seems beyond your control.

Of course, it's not beyond your control. It is in fact to your advantage to be as familiar as possible with the process of buying and selling a home. Fortunately, with many thousands of properties changing hands each year, there are also lots of experienced lawyers and real estate professionals available to offer advice and assistance.

1.   Do I need a real estate agent to buy or sell a property?

Real estate agents or realtors are individuals licensed in their province to negotiate the purchase or sale of property. Agents must undergo training before acquiring a licence and abide by a strict code of professional standards.

That said, there is no legal requirement for property buyers or sellers to hire real estate agents. Most people, however, prefer the services and assistance of a professional. Sellers, particularly, can find it difficult to attract a constant flow of potential buyers since they may not have access to the local real estate association's multiple listing service, where agents post information about available properties. Also, real estate agents representing buyers may ignore or show less interest in properties sold by non-agents since the amount of their sales commission can be uncertain.

Note that selling your home without the assistance of a real estate agent could save you a substantial amount of money. You will have to cover your own advertising costs, but they may amount to much less than the commission payable to a real estate agent. Commissions can vary from about 3 to 8 percent of the selling price.

If you decide to contact a real estate agent, look for someone with a good reputation who is familiar with your neighbourhood and type of home. As in any business relationship, question potential agents on their marketing methods, commission structure, and how long your agreement with them will last. All aspects of your relationship with the agent can be negotiated, including the commission.

If you decide not to use a real estate agent, be certain to have a lawyer review any "offers to purchase" you receive or plan to make. Although most real estate agents can explain the basics of your obligations in an Agreement of Purchase and Sale, have a real estate lawyer review the agreement before you sign it. For example, both a lawyer and a real estate agent will likely insist you make an agreement to purchase conditional on a satisfactory home inspection or approval of financing.

2.   What does a real estate agent do for a seller?

When you are selling your home, a real estate agent can help you determine its fair market value, advertise your home to potential buyers, arrange for interested buyers to view your home, and guide you through the process of negotiating an agreement.

Most sellers sign a listing agreement with the real estate agent. This is a written contract between the seller and the agent that sets out most of the duties and obligations of the relationship. It includes how the real estate agents will market the property and how much they will be paid for their services.

Most real estate agents are paid a commission or percentage of the selling price. Commissions can vary from 3 to 8 percent — a fee that is sometimes split equally with an agent acting on behalf of the buyer. If your property does not sell, you do not have to pay anything.

■ Multiple listing agreement & exclusive listing agreement

Selling your home with a real estate agent will generally involve signing a listing agreement. There are two main types of agreements — Multiple

Listing Agreements and Exclusive Listing Agreements. Most people choose multiple listings, since all member agents of the local real estate board receive information about the listing, and are entitled to share the commission if they bring a purchaser to buy the property. This is often the most effective way to sell a home, although the commission for a multiple listing will usually be higher than the commission for an exclusive listing since two agents are sharing the fee.

An exclusive listing agreement means your home will only be offered to prospective purchasers through the company with which you list. Other agents are not automatically entitled to a commission if they bring a buyer, unless your agent agrees to co-operate with them. Although it may take longer to find an interested purchaser, the commission payable to your real estate agent will usually be lower than for a multiple listing.

3.   What does a real estate agent do for a buyer?

If you are buying a home, a real estate agent can help you find the right type of home at the right price, help prepare your offer to purchase, and present it to the owners. In most cases, there is no direct cost to a purchaser for the agent's services. The agent you work with will normally be paid part of the commission paid to the listing agent by the seller. What many people may not realize is that both the listing agent, and the purchaser's real estate agent, are supposed to be working for the seller. In other words, under the law even the agent for the buyer has a responsibility to assist the seller get a fair deal.

Unlike a seller, a buyer sometimes does not sign a written agreement with a real estate agent before house hunting begins. That said, there is a growing trend in many provinces for real estate agents to ask buyers to sign what is called a "purchaser agency agreement." These agreements generally commit the purchasers to using only one agent for their search. Although agents with this type of agreement may provide better service to the purchasers, it is not usually necessary to sign a purchaser agency agreement.

4.   What are the legal obligations of real estate agents?

Real estate agents are held to certain standards and ethics under provincial laws. Overall, agents are required to use reasonable care when carrying out their duties. For example, they must perform the obligations in their agreement (for example, advertising the property on the market or multiple listing service) and they must present all offers from potential buyers to the seller. Real estate agents are also under an obligation to be completely honest at all times and to always follow your instructions or seek your approval. If you have a complaint about a real estate agent, contact the real estate board in your area for more information.

5. What is the role of a lawyer in a real estate transaction?

The general role of real estate lawyers is to protect your legal rights throughout the process of selling or buying a home. Most important, your lawyer will review your Agreement of Purchase and Sale to ensure it meets your needs, and you fully understand the legal rights and obligations you have agreed to.

■ Lawyer's role before your offer has been accepted

Before making an offer on a home, you may find it useful to have your offer reviewed by a lawyer. The lawyer can explain the legal concerns that generally arise from the purchase and sale of a home (such as unseen defects or financing issues) and advise you on your rights and obligations. If necessary, the lawyer can make changes to the offer to reflect your needs.

■ Lawyer's role once your offer has been accepted

Once an offer has been accepted, the lawyer for the purchaser will be responsible for a number of land title searches and administrative tasks. Most important, the lawyer will make sure that the person selling the property is the registered owner. For example, in some provinces, matrimonial property laws prevent the sale of a family home without consent from both spouses even though only one may be shown as the legal owner. The lawyer will also perform other administrative tasks, such as:

- Transferring billing information with the utility companies
- Finding out if there are any other mortgages, liens, or easements registered against the land
- Checking with the municipality to make sure there are no unpaid taxes
- Ensuring the property complies with the zoning requirements
- Checking a survey of the property to make sure the home is accurately described in the Agreement of Purchase and Sale

Increasingly, lawyers are offering clients a way to avoid the time and expense of searching property records with what's known as "title insurance." This one-time, low-cost coverage is most often used for properties that lawyers believe have a "clean" chain of title transfers over the years or present little risk of being challenged. Like any insurance policy, title insurance protects owners from undetectable problems such as forgery, fraud, or missing heirs claiming rights of ownership.

If you are buying a home with another person such as your spouse, your lawyer will also explain the different legal options for registering the legal title. For example, you may want to register the home under one spouse's name only. Or, you may want to register the home together as joint tenants or tenants in common. How you register can affect how the property is dealt with over time.

Joint tenants share undivided ownership in a property (usually for life) and each individual's interest in the property automatically transfers to the surviving joint tenant upon death. Tenants in common, however, have their interests transferred to their estate or heirs. In some provinces, such as British Columbia and Ontario, a purchase of land by two or more people is presumed to be a purchase by tenants in common unless otherwise stated in writing.

6.   What is a lawyer's fee in a real estate transaction?

Unlike most transactions with lawyers that involve an hourly fee, real estate lawyers generally charge a set or flat fee for their work, plus the actual expenses they incur on your behalf, such as title search fees and registrations (known as disbursements).

Different lawyers will charge different fees for handling real estate transactions. Your lawyer's fee will depend on the level of service provided, complexity of your transaction, and the region or province in which you live. Before hiring a lawyer, ask how much the legal fees will likely be, along with an estimate of disbursements.

7.   What is an Agreement of Purchase and Sale?

As it suggests, an Agreement of Purchase and Sale is a written, enforceable contract between a seller and a buyer for the purchase and sale of a particular property. The buyer agrees to purchase the property for a certain price, provided that a number of terms and conditions are satisfied.

The Agreement begins as an offer by the purchaser and becomes a legally binding agreement only if the seller accepts the offer and signs it. At this point, the Agreement cannot be cancelled without agreement from both the buyer and the seller.

Because all agreements for the purchase and sale of land must be in writing to be legally enforceable, the Agreement of Purchase and Sale provides a general layout for addressing problems that may arise, such as the forfeit of a deposit if the buyer backs out.

Most local real estate boards and the licensing body for realtors have established standard Agreements of Purchase and Sale forms. Although these forms contain standard terms and conditions, the agreement can be changed if both the buyer and the seller agree and write their initials alongside any additions or deletions.

8. What are common terms in the Agreement of Purchase and Sale?

Most standard Agreements of Purchase and Sale begin with some basic information about the buyer, seller, and property. In the Agreement, the seller is referred to as the "vendor." There will also be an area to record the deposit paid by the buyer to the seller's real estate agent, who will hold it "in trust" until the terms of the agreement are met.

The next section in the form is usually a blank area for purchasers to identify in writing any special arrangements. For example, the buyer may agree to assume the seller's existing mortgage rather than getting separate financing through a bank. A clause can also be included here making the agreement conditional on the sale of the purchaser's current house or on the purchaser arranging financing.

■ Fixtures & chattels

The next section typically deals with "fixtures" and "chattels." Fixtures are improvements made to a property that are attached or cannot be removed easily without causing damage to the property. Hot water heaters, built-in cabinets, and lights are examples of fixtures. Fixtures are assumed to be included in the sale of the home, unless they are specifically excluded in the agreement.

Chattels are moveable items of personal property contained on the property and must specifically be listed in the agreement if they are to be part of the sale of the home. For example, if the seller agrees to include a refrigerator, stove, or gardening equipment in the sale, these items must be specifically identified in the Agreement. If there is any doubt whether an item is included or excluded, it should be clearly specified in the agreement.

▪ Dates, searches & requisition date

Next, are a series of clauses dealing with relevant dates. The first of these is usually a clause establishing that the buyer's offer will be void unless the seller accepts it before a certain date. It is not unusual for sellers to have only a few hours to consider the offer.

A deadline is also set in the Agreement for all searches to be done on the property. This is commonly referred to as the "requisition date," and is generally at least one month before the "closing date" of the transaction. Before this date, it is the buyer's responsibility to do a number of searches to ensure there are no problems with the property. These include searching the registered ownership of the property through the land registry office, checking that the property complies with zoning regulations, and searching for outstanding municipal work orders or builders' liens.

The buyer and the seller also must identify a date for the closing of the transaction. This is the very important date when the sale is finalized and the buyer takes physical possession of the property.

▪ Conditions

The Agreement will also establish so-called "conditions" that must be met before the sale can be completed.

First, the buyer's entire offer to purchase the home is usually conditional on the seller being the legal and registered owner of the property.

Second, if the buyer's lawyer discovers any problems while doing the various document searches, the buyer (or the lawyer) must send a letter explaining the problem to the seller's lawyer before the requisition deadline. If the seller is unable to fix the problem, then the entire Agreement may come to an end unless the buyer specifically chooses to take the property with the particular defect.

Finally, the Agreement will state that, unless the buyer makes an objection in writing before the requisition date, the buyer cannot complain later about any defects in the seller's ownership of the property. For this reason, it is very important for the buyer's lawyer to perform all the necessary searches to ensure there are no hidden problems that may arise at a later date.

Other clauses in the Agreement may deal with technical issues relating to future use of the property, production of documents, insurance, tax arrangements, adjustments, and spousal consent. Your lawyer or real estate agent can provide a more detailed explanation of these terms.

Completing an Agreement of Purchase and Sale can be complicated and technical. Before the Agreement is final, it may change several times as the buyer and the seller negotiate its terms, and counteroffers are presented. To be certain you understand all the terms, it is best to have your agreement reviewed by a lawyer before your purchase or sale of land is finalized.

9. What is the difference between an offer and a counteroffer?

It is quite common for a homebuyer to make a conditional offer to a seller for the purchase of a home. This means the buyer offers to purchase the home, but only if certain conditions are first satisfied. Buyers will often offer to purchase provided they are able to sell their current home or arrange suitable mortgage financing. A buyer may also include a condition to buy the home subject to a satisfactory home inspection, or subject to a zoning change or other municipal approval. To be legally binding, the condition must be specifically written into the offer to purchase.

Conditional offers can very effectively reduce risks for the purchaser. They are less attractive to sellers, however, and may not be accepted. For example, in "hot" real estate markets, sellers may not accept conditional offers because they don't want to wait in uncertainty.

In reply to a conditional offer, the seller might make a counteroffer instead of simply refusing the conditional offer. A counteroffer will agree with some of the conditions wanted by the prospective buyer, but exclude the rest. Seek the assistance of your real estate agent and your lawyer in preparing either a conditional offer or a counteroffer.

10. What is an appropriate deposit?

When an offer to purchase is made, the purchaser usually gives the seller a deposit toward the purchase price. The deposit assures the seller that you are serious about the purchase and intend to complete the deal if the offer is accepted.

■ Deposits for re-sale properties

Deposits for re-sale properties can be any amount, although 2 to 5 percent of the purchase price is typical. An offer with a high deposit may be viewed as more attractive than one with a small deposit. Although the deposit will be credited to the purchase price and deducted from the amount due on closing, it is not normally paid directly to the seller. In most cases, deposits are made payable to the listing agent "in trust." The listing agent will place the money in a secure trust account until the closing date. Once the deposit has been credited to the purchase price on closing, the seller will usually authorize the agent to deduct commission from the deposit.

■ Deposits for new homes

For new homes, the deposit is usually payable directly to the builder and not held in trust. Builders may require higher deposits than normally paid for re-sale properties. This allows the builder to use the money toward ongoing construction costs. Because there is a risk that the buyer may lose the deposit, non-government agencies across Canada such as the Ontario New Home Warranty Program, will insure deposits (ranging from $10,000 to $60,000, depending on the province).

If the builder fails to complete construction of your home and files for bankruptcy, you can make a claim against the Warranty Program to recover your deposit. Since deposit coverage is limited, purchasers should be cautious about giving larger deposits. Or they might make such deposits over the coverage limit payable to the vendor's lawyer in trust.

11. What happens if I change my mind after signing an offer or purchase agreement?

Any offer or counteroffer can be withdrawn before the other party formally accepts it (that is, with his or her properly witnessed signature). It can also be withdrawn if there is a time limit on the offer or counteroffer and it passes without being accepted.

An agreement for sale may also be terminated if it becomes impossible to perform through no fault of either party (lawyers say such a contract is "frustrated"). An example is property destroyed in a flood or a fire before the buyer has taken possession. Purchasers of new condominiums in some provinces have a cooling-off period to back out of purchase agreements (10 days in many jurisdictions, for example).

Once the offer or counteroffer has been formally accepted, however, the buyer and seller are bound legally by its terms. If you walk away from a deal you will not only lose your deposit, but may also be liable for any damages suffered by the other party, such as the lost opportunity to sell to someone else, expenses arising from a delayed move, or the seller's loss of deposit on another home intended for purchase. The legal remedy, called "specific performance" (making you complete the purchase), is an unlikely event, but a court could still hold you responsible for the entire purchase price, plus expenses and court costs.

12. Why is a professional home inspection important?

In recent years, many purchasers have decided to make their offers conditional on a satisfactory home inspection by a professional home inspector. This can be especially important if you are buying an older home.

Professional home inspectors will thoroughly check for defects and assess what repairs may be needed in upcoming years. This will include assessing the state of the roof, plumbing, insulation and electrical, and heating and cooling systems. If you purchase a property conditional on receiving a satisfactory home inspection and the inspection reveals problems, you have a legal right to terminate the contract. Some purchasers who find problems will try to negotiate a reduction in the purchase price to cover the cost of repairs instead of cancelling the agreement, although the seller has no obligation to accept this.

To obtain the right to conduct a home inspection, you must include a specific written provision in the offer to purchase. In most regions, there are commercial inspection services and homeowners associations who will perform an inspection for you. Fees range from about $200 to $400, depending on your area and type of home. Home inspectors are often listed in the business pages of the telephone book. Since these services are not closely regulated, you should seek recommendations from your lawyer, real estate agent, or friends to ensure you hire a reputable person or company.

13. What is a property or land survey?

A survey is a detailed drawing of a property, including the exact dimensions of the land and location of buildings, fences, driveways and adjacent roads. It will also show easements (a legally enforceable right-of-way) that utility companies, neighbours, or others may have over the property.

A survey is very important to a purchaser because it shows whether the size of the property stated on the listing and in the purchase agreement is accurate. It will also show whether the property's buildings encroach onto adjoining properties, whether the neighbour's buildings come onto your property, and whether the property conforms to municipal requirements, such as the minimum distances of buildings from the property line or street.

A recent survey is often required by your financial institution or mortgage lender. In many cases, a survey that is 15 or 20 years old will be sufficient, as long as there have been no significant changes to the property.

If you are buying a home, ask whether the sellers already have a survey. If they do, you can include a clause in your offer that the seller must provide you or your lawyer with the survey shortly after the agreement is accepted. If the seller does not have a survey, you may want to include a clause that the seller provide you with an up-to-date survey at the seller's cost.

If you are purchasing a new home, the builder will usually provide you with a copy of the survey. Make sure, however, that this is written into the agreement.

If there is no recent survey for the property you are purchasing, you might need to have one done by an appropriate professional. A survey can cost from a few hundred dollars to several thousand dollars, depending on the size and shape of the property and the number of buildings or other improvements on it. If you do not know a professional land surveyor, your lawyer or real estate agent can usually refer you to one.

14. What are easements and restrictive covenants?

Even though you are the legal owner of a property, other people may have legal rights to access it or there may be certain restrictions on what you can do with your property.

Rights and privileges over your property that are given to others are called "easements" or rights-of-way. Restrictions on your land are called "restrictive covenants." Because these rights and restrictions are legally attached to the land and not the owner of it, they continue to exist over the property even with new ownership.

Easements may arise from a written agreement or can arise informally by permitted use. For example, if children have been allowed to cut across your property to get to school for a number of years, you might not have the right to build a fence and keep them out. Common easements include the rights given to utilities for maintenance of water, sanitary, and storm sewer lines, or rights given to telephone companies for line maintenance. Formal easements over your property are normally registered on title at the local land registry office.

A restrictive covenant is a written contract that places limitations on what can be done on your property. For example, a subdivision may have a restrictive covenant preventing the storage of boats or trucks in the driveways, or prohibiting satellite dishes or clotheslines. As your lawyer may tell you, some restrictive covenants are not legally binding, particularly if they are considered arbitrary or contrary to public interest.

15. How do zoning and municipal by-laws affect the purchase or sale of property?

Although you may own a particular piece of property, you may not be free to use and develop it as you wish. For example, your neighbour in a residential subdivision probably cannot sell the property for heavy industrial use. Through zoning by-laws the government regulates the development and use of land, and the general layout of all townships and municipalities. Zoning governs where buildings can be constructed, where residential subdivisions can be developed, and where schools, parks and factories can be built.

Zoning by-laws also govern the use of each individual plot of land. As a result, you may be required to seek municipal approval before making certain changes to your property. For example, to build a deck, construct an addition, or move your driveway, you will likely have to obtain a permit from your local municipal authority. You will also be limited to certain uses of the property. You may not, for instance, be allowed to open a retail business from a residential home.

The law also regulates the subdivision of land. This means you cannot sell part of your property without obtaining a municipal approval. To subdivide your property, you would need to make an "application for severance" to your local municipal authority. A lawyer can provide you with additional information about zoning and other by-laws and help you get severances or change the permitted uses.

16. What additional costs should homebuyers be aware of?

In addition to the purchase price, legal fees, and disbursements, you will normally incur a number of additional expenses, including land transfer tax, GST, and adjustments.

■ Land Transfer Tax

One of the largest additional expenses when purchasing a property is the provincial land transfer tax. The amount the purchaser pays is set by each province, usually calculated according to a schedule geared to your purchase price. There is no tax payable by the seller. A first-time homebuyer may qualify for a rebate of the tax from the provincial government. Your lawyer or real estate agent can provide more information about land transfer taxes and the first-time buyers' rebate.

■ GST on the purchase price

The Goods and Services Tax (GST) does not apply to the purchase of used homes. If you buy a new home, however, GST will be payable. Currently, the GST is 7 percent of the purchase price, but most purchasers who buy a property for their own personal use (rather than as an investment property) are entitled to a GST rebate of up to 2.5 percent, depending on the price and area. Many builders include the GST in the purchase price, while others charge the GST on top of the purchase price. If you are buying a new home, make sure you know the total purchase price, including the GST.

■ GST on transaction costs

Even if GST is not payable on the purchase price of your home, GST is payable on other transaction costs, such as legal fees and disbursements, real estate commissions, appraisals, home inspections, and survey fees. GST is not payable on Land Transfer Tax or mortgage insurance fees.

■ Provincial Sales Tax

If your purchase includes appliances, furniture, or other items that are left in the home, you may also have to pay the retail sales tax on the value of these items in provinces with sales taxes.

■ Adjustments

On the closing date of your purchase or sale, the money due on that day will be "adjusted" to reflect the ongoing expenses of the property that have already been paid by the seller for any subsequent period that you own the property. For example, the purchaser will usually reimburse the seller for prepaid property taxes for the remainder of the year. Sometimes, if an oil furnace heats a home, the seller will fill the tank before closing and the purchaser will pay the seller the cost of the full tank.

■ Determine your total expenses

In addition to taxes and adjustments, purchasers are also responsible for a number of general administrative costs including legal fees, document searches, and registration costs. Purchasers may also need to pay for mortgage insurance if they have less than a 25 percent down payment or for a survey of the property if the seller is not able to provide one.

It is very important to know in advance how much money you will actually receive from the sale of a property and how much you will need for your purchase. Your lawyer will be able to calculate most of these costs for you and provide an estimate of the total.

17. What is title insurance?

When you buy a home, you are essentially buying the legal ownership or "title" of a property. Title insurance is an option for homebuyers who want additional protection when purchasing. Buyers pay a one-time insurance premium that will compensate them if there is a problem with the title, including zoning problems or ownership issues. When purchasing title insurance, buyers will usually receive reduced legal and document searching costs.

Though title insurance provides protection for homebuyers, there are two reasons why a lawyer is still required. First, title insurance policies can only be obtained through a lawyer and not by buyers directly. Second, title insurance policies provide varying amounts of protection and coverage and never cover all possible risks associated with buying a home. Generally, they provide buyers only with protection against risks such as zoning problems, outstanding work orders against the property, and problems that a land survey would reveal. Some policies also protect against lawyer error. The cost of title insurance may vary, but generally it's about $250. Your lawyer can provide you with more information about this option.

18. What is unique about new home purchases?

There are several differences between buying a new home and buying a resale home. First, the offer to purchase a new home is considerably longer and more complicated than a resale Agreement of Purchase and Sale. Second, the text is often written in very small print and there is not much space to make changes.

For this reason, it is important to take the offer to a lawyer before signing it. Your lawyer will explain the agreement to ensure it is acceptable. With your lawyer's advice and assistance, you might also be able to delete or change terms that are heavily weighted in favour of the builder.

If you are unable to consult a lawyer before signing the offer, you can choose to insert a written clause into the contract stating that your acceptance is conditional on your lawyer reviewing the agreement and finding it satisfactory. Some builders will not accept agreements with substantial changes to standard clauses. In these circumstances, it is important to assess the reputation of the builder and how the builder has dealt with past purchasers.

▪ Delays and extensions to the closing date

When buying a new home, be prepared for possible delays and complications. Although many new homes are complete and ready to move into by the scheduled closing date, it is not unusual for the closing date to be delayed or extended. This can happen because of strikes, shortages of labour or materials, or the builder's inability to meet the original delivery date.

New homebuyers generally have less certainty about closing dates and moving dates. Usually, a delay does not automatically void or cancel an agreement between a buyer and a builder. Almost all builder contracts include a clause that allows the automatic extension of a closing date for up to 120 days. After 120 days, buyers then have a 10-day window to cancel the entire contract. If the buyer chooses not to cancel the contract, the closing date can be extended again for another 120 days. Once this second 120 days has elapsed, the contract is automatically cancelled unless both the buyer and the builder agree to further extend the closing date.

■ Deposit protection and warranties

In all provinces and regions (except the Northwest Territories), all newly constructed homes and condominiums must be enrolled in a New Home Warranty Program. In addition to setting specific guidelines for how builders must deal with purchasers, the most important part of the program is the insurance plan. This protects purchasers from having to live in an unfinished or structurally defective home if the builder is unable or unwilling to complete the work that needs to be done. It also protects purchasers from unauthorized substitutions of materials, and from losing their deposits up to a specific amount (ranging from $10,000 to $60,000, depending on the province) if the builder goes bankrupt.

Purchasers usually have to pay an enrollment fee, ranging from $500 to $1,000, depending on the purchase price of the property. If a builder fails to honour its warranty for service and repair, the cost or repairs may be covered by the Warranty Program. For certain problems, the buyer may be able to make a claim for compensation against the Program rather than having to sue the builder.

Depending on your region's or province's Warranty Program, you can receive coverage for anywhere from 5 to 10 years. During the first year, the builder is generally responsible for repairing defects in material or quality of work. During the remaining years, the builder is typically responsible for repairing any major structural defects in construction that significantly affect the use of the home.

If for any reason the builder is unable or unwilling to return to make the necessary repairs, the Warranty Program will pay for someone else to handle the repairs. Buyers of new homes should be aware, though, that the Warranty Program does not cover every kind of defect in a new home, such as normal wear and tear or defects in cabinetry or appliances installed by the homeowner. These programs also do not typically cover cottages, homes built on existing footings or foundations, converted buildings, homes lived in or rented by the builder before they are sold, or homes built by their owners.

■ Additional costs

Buyers should also be advised of a number of additional costs involved in new home purchases. Apart from the Warranty Program enrollment fee, GST is payable on new homes. In many cases, this is already included in the purchase price. Since this is a very significant expense, the Agreement of Purchase and Sale should clearly state if the GST is included and how rebates are to be handled.

Other extra charges in new homes can include lot levies, sewer impost charges, hydro meter installation, curb charges, gas hook-up charges, water hook-up charges, tree charges, and "super mailbox" charges. If you are buying a new house, be sure you know what is included and the additional costs you will be responsible for on closing.

19. Do first-time homebuyers enjoy any special benefits?

Both federal and provincial governments have programs to assist first-time homebuyers.

■ First Home Loan Insurance Program

Since 1992, new homebuyers who meet certain financial conditions can purchase a new home with a down payment of only 5 percent. The remaining 95 percent of their mortgage is insured by Canada Mortgage & Housing Corporation or other lenders. The maximum amount that can be borrowed varies across the country, from $125,000 to $300,000.

■ RRSP Homebuyer's Plan

The RRSP Homebuyer's Plan was introduced by the federal government and allows first-time homebuyers to withdraw up to $20,000 tax-free from each of their RRSPs to use toward the purchase of a home. To qualify as a first-time homebuyer, purchasers must not have lived in a home owned by themselves or a spouse in the previous five years. If you and your spouse qualify under the plan, you can each withdraw up to $20,000 from your RRSPs for a total of $40,000.

Before you are entitled to withdraw the money from your RRSP, you must have entered into a written agreement to purchase or build a home you intend to occupy as your principal residence. The purchase of a cottage, for example, would not qualify for this program because it is not a principal residence.

Money can be withdrawn from your RRSP provided it has been in your RRSP for at least 90 days. So, if you have signed an Agreement of Purchase and Sale and have at least 90 days until your closing date, you can open an RRSP and make a contribution, receive the tax deferred benefit and then withdraw the same money and put it toward the purchase of your home.

Money withdrawn under this federal program must be paid back to your RRSP within 15 years. Most people deposit 1/15th of the amount withdrawn back to the RRSP over each subsequent year. If you do not pay the full amount back to your RRSP within 15 years, the amount outstanding will be subject to tax when you file your income tax return the following year.

■ Provincial Home Ownership Savings Plan

Nova Scotia offers first-time homebuyers a Home Ownership Savings Plan. This program provides a tax credit for contributions up to specified amounts each year. The savings you accumulate can then be used toward the purchase of a home. To qualify, you must earn less than $40,000, or if you have a spouse, your combined income must be less than $80,000. You can obtain additional information about this program from your lawyer, your bank, and the provincial government.

■ Land Transfer Tax rebates

Depending on your province's tax laws, first-time homebuyers may also be eligible for a land transfer tax rebate on purchases of newly built homes.

20. In whose name should the title of ownership be held?

When your lawyer is preparing to transfer the title to your property, you will likely be asked who will actually own it. You may choose to list one name alone, fellow investors (a parent, for example) or, particularly in a marriage, both spouses. The issue of whose name is on the title is frequently important when one individual is putting up most or all of the money for the purchase.

Lawyers have several options in setting out title. For example, one person may have a 75 percent interest and another may have the remaining 25 percent. Most lawyers will recommend that married or common law couples own their home equally as joint tenants. This will make them each full owners; and the survivor will become the sole owner if the other dies first. This arrangement prevents the property being tied up in probate proceedings and may result in significant tax savings. (Be aware, however, that there are still administrative and legal costs associated with transferring title to a surviving joint tenant.)

It is also important to know that matrimonial property laws in some provinces can override your decisions on who holds title. For example, in Newfoundland and New Brunswick, a matrimonial home is owned by both spouses equally regardless of the name on the title. In other provinces, the matrimonial home is a special asset and its value will be split by the spouses even though only one name is on the title.

Adding a child or other third party (such as a relative or business) as joint tenant can be risky. The danger here is that your property could become enmeshed in that person's own financial or marital woes. That said, a lawyer may be able to help structure an agreement to avoid such difficulties.

For business or tax planning reasons, you may want your property owned by one spouse alone. Your lawyer should also discuss the estate planning consequences with you. When property titles are held in joint tenancy, it can make drafting your will more complex. For example, if you want to pass your property on to a child or someone else, the wills of both joint tenants must address this wish.

If your property is already in one individual's name and you are considering transferring it to a joint tenancy, seek the advice of your lawyer. The provincial government may levy a fee based on the value of the property. GST may also be owed if the added name on the title is not a spouse.

21. When can I move into my new home?

Under normal circumstances, purchasers can move into newly purchased homes on the closing day of the transaction. The closing date will be agreed to by both the buyer and the seller and will be set out in the Agreement of Purchase and Sale. On the closing day, the purchaser will pay the remaining balance of the purchase price in exchange for the deed to the property and, usually, the keys to the home.

The actual closing of the transaction will normally take place at the local land registry office to allow the buyer's lawyer an opportunity to conduct one final search on title to ensure that nothing new has been filed against the property. The buyer and seller will each need to meet with their respective lawyers before the closing date to complete the necessary paperwork.

On the closing date, the lawyers will not be able to formally transfer the ownership until the purchaser's lawyer receives the funds to pay the balance of the purchase price. Sometimes funds will be available for the lawyer to pick up from a mortgage company or a bank early in the morning, but it is often mid-afternoon or later when the funds are received and the transaction can be completed.

Sellers often move their belongings out on the actual closing date and may not be done until late in the day. The bottom line is that purchasers should not expect to move into the new home early in the morning. In most circumstances, your lawyer will be able to let you know in advance when your purchase or sale is likely to be completed.

For purchasers of newly built homes, delays and extensions often arise for a number of reasons. In these circumstances, the builder will usually have a right set out in the sale agreement to periodically extend the closing date.

22. What are condominiums? How are they different from houses?

The word "condominium" refers to a specific kind of legal ownership and includes any type of construction, though typically apartment-style buildings, townhouses, and lofts. Each owner of a condominium unit owns legal title to his or her own unit. All the owners together own a number of facilities in the building called "common elements." Common elements can include gardens, parking areas, party rooms, pools, elevators, and recreational facilities.

In most condominium corporations, each owner is responsible for the maintenance and repair of his or her own unit. The corporation itself is responsible for the maintenance and repair of the common elements and the overall building structure.

Condominiums and condominium corporations are created legally when two documents are registered — the description and declaration. The description includes building plans and a property survey. The declaration is the equivalent of a constitution or charter for the condominium corporation, and may include restrictions that apply to condominium residents. For example, the declaration may include a prohibition against keeping pets.

In addition to these two documents, condominiums also have by-laws and rules dealing with matters such as duties and powers of the condominium Board of Directors, and the rights and obligations of any residents (such as tenants) and owners of the condominium.

Each condominium development becomes a condominium corporation once the declaration and description are registered. All condominium owners are owners in the corporation and given rights to vote on certain matters. The directors of the corporation, who are elected by the owners, handle the day-to-day running of the condominium or delegate it to a management company.

To pay for the general maintenance and upkeep of the common element facilities, condominium owners pay monthly common expenses (also known as "maintenance fees"). Each resident's common expenses will usually depend on the size of the unit and facilities offered. Condominiums with swimming pools and entertainment centres, for example, will generally have higher monthly common expenses than buildings with no facilities. Monthly fees can be significant, so it is important to keep this in mind before purchasing a condominium unit.

Buyers of condominiums should take extra care to investigate the financial situation of the condominium corporation before finalizing a purchase agreement. You or your lawyer should examine the documents that condominium corporations make available to prospective purchasers (known variously as the Status Certificate, Estoppel Certificate, or Disclosure Statement in some provinces), and review the financial statements and current budget.

Pay particular attention to the amount of money held in the reserve fund. Ensure there are sufficient funds to cover ongoing maintenance and repair of the condominium's major capital items, such as expected roof or parking garage repairs. A condominium purchaser's Agreement of Purchase and Sale must be conditional on the purchaser receiving this package, having a set number of days to review it, and being satisfied with its contents.

23. What's different about buying a new condominium?

Buying a newly built condominium unit can involve complicated issues. Often a buyer of a new unit may have to deal with an interim closing date, a final closing date, and occupancy fees. These arise because the new condominium project cannot be legally registered until the building is fully constructed. The builder also cannot give full legal ownership and title to the new buyers until registration. While buyers can move into units without full legal title, they cannot own their units or obtain a mortgage loan until after registration.

Your province's *Condominium Act* has rules about purchasing and moving into a condominium before it is registered. On the interim closing date, buyers are permitted to move into completed units even though the condominium is not yet registered and the buyers do not yet have legal ownership. Instead of paying the balance of the purchase price, purchasers pay an occupancy fee, which is similar to rent, until the final closing date for legal ownership. This fee covers expenses such as taxes, maintenance, and interest on the unpaid balance due on closing.

When the condominium is registered, the purchaser can obtain mortgage funds. The builder will also give the buyer full title or legal ownership of the unit. After this final closing date, purchasers will not need to pay any occupancy fee, but will pay their mortgage, realty taxes, and common expenses instead.

Because the purchase of a new condominium can be complicated, condominium legislation usually provides buyers of new condominiums with a 10-day "grace period" from when the agreement is first accepted. During this period buyers can cancel the deal. This is intended to allow purchasers time to review the condominium documents and seek legal advice. This 10-day period does not apply to resale condominiums. If you are purchasing a condominium, your lawyer can help you better understand all the documents and obligations that apply to the condominium corporation and your unit.

24. What are co-operatives and co-ownerships?

Co-operatives and co-ownerships are two forms of housing that are different from condominiums. Although co-operatives and co-ownerships involve buildings with several units, their legal structure or organization is different from condominiums.

■ Co-operatives

In a co-operative, a corporation owns the land and building, including all units. Each purchaser in a co-operative buys shares in the corporation as opposed to buying a specific unit. Purchasers in a co-operative do not own their units but are given the right to occupy them by the corporation. So, the legal interest of the co-operative dweller is that of a shareholder of the corporation that owns the property. For this reason, the co-operative dweller is often referred to as a tenant-shareholder. The legal interest of the tenant-shareholder is different from that of the condominium owner, who has a so-called "fee simple" or fully entitled landowner interest in a particular condominium unit. As well, the provincial condominium legislation does not apply to co-operatives. The rights, duties and liabilities of a tenant-shareholder in a co-operative are governed by the following documents:

1. Incorporating documents of the corporation

2. By-laws of the corporation

3. Where applicable, a shareholders' agreement among the tenant-shareholders

■ Mortgages and taxes in co-operatives

Since the units are not owned by the individual tenant-shareholders, mortgage financing is initially secured for the building as a whole. It is often referred to as a "blanket mortgage" and the corporation is usually the mortgagor.

Each tenant-shareholder contributes toward the blanket mortgage. If one tenant-shareholder is in default, the others must increase their payments to meet the deficiency or else risk a foreclosure or power of sale proceedings against the whole building. After a co-operative has been in existence for some time, there is often no financing at all remaining on the building.

There is one tax bill, which applies to the entire property, and all tenant-shareholders are also jointly liable under the tax bill. The amount that each tenant-shareholder has to pay for mortgage and tax is based on the number of shares each one purchases. The number of shares purchased is usually determined by the size of the unit and when the shares were purchased.

■ Selling shares of a co-operative

An individual who wants to sell his or her shares in a co-operative follows a different process than does a condominium owner selling his or her unit. Whereas a condominium unit owner is generally free to sell the unit to a prospective purchaser without consulting fellow unit owners or the condominium corporation, the new purchaser in a co-operative must be approved by the corporations' Board of Directors before acquiring shares.

Unlike the sale of units in condominium corporations, the marketing of an interest in a co-operative to the public requires compliance with the province's securities laws because it is a sale of shares rather than a sale of real property. That said, although no interest in real property is being transferred when an interest in a co-operative is sold, land transfer tax is payable on the sale price of the shares.

▪ Co-ownerships

An alternative to co-operatives and condominiums is co-ownerships. This method of selling interests in property is less common today. In a co-ownership situation, each person who wants to live in a building buys an ownership interest in the real property, becoming an "owner in common" with every other purchaser. Instead of owning a specific unit, the purchaser has the right to lease a particular unit for 21 years less a day with the understanding that a new lease would be granted by the other co-owners at the end of that time.

In the co-ownership system, buyers are legally bound by the terms in their contract rather than by any legislative provisions. Like the co-operative, co-ownership involves only one mortgage and one tax bill for the entire property, with each person responsible for his or her proportionate share of the costs.

▪ Financing of co-operative and co-ownership interests

With co-operatives and co-ownerships, it can be difficult to arrange individual financing to assist a purchaser in the acquisition of an interest. It is not uncommon for the vendor (that is, the current shareholder) to finance the purchase by way of a vendor take-back mortgage.

25. What do I need to know about financing my purchase?

Most people need to take out a loan to finance the purchase of a home. Although the loan itself is often referred to as a mortgage, the "mortgage" is actually what the bank takes as legal security for giving the loan. By placing a mortgage on your home, the bank has legal rights to your home and can sell it if you are unable to repay the mortgage loan.

Financial institutions and lenders offer different mortgages with a variety of different features and legal obligations.

Open mortgage   An open mortgage gives you the flexibility to make extra payments on your loan beyond your regular payments. You can also pay it off completely at any time without penalty. Open mortgages usually have slightly higher interest rates and a shorter term.

Closed mortgage   Closed mortgages have a lower interest rate, a longer term, and reduced flexibility. In closed mortgages, you can only make regular payments and cannot pay off your mortgage at any time without penalty. If you are expecting a promotion to a higher paying job in the near future or if you think interest rates are going down, you may prefer the flexibility and shorter term of an open mortgage.

Fixed and variable interest rate   A mortgage can also have a fixed or variable interest rate. A fixed interest rate means you lock in at a certain rate for a set term. A variable interest rate means your interest fluctuates with changing market conditions. The benefit of a fixed interest rate is the security and certainty of a set interest rate. The drawback of a fixed interest rate is that it is usually higher than the variable interest rate. If you think interest rates are on the rise or if you dislike risk, you may prefer a fixed rate of interest. If you think interest rates will go down and you do not mind risk, a variable interest rate may be better for you.

Short- or long-term   A mortgage can be for a short or a long term. A term is the length of time that your agreement with the lender exists. Terms usually range anywhere from six months to 5 or 10 years. During this time, you agree to pay a certain interest rate on a certain schedule. When rates are low, short-term mortgages usually have lower interest rates than long-term mortgages. When interest rates are high, short-term mortgages usually have higher interest rates than long-term mortgages. If you think interest rates are going to drop, you may want to opt for a short-term. If you think interest rates are going to rise, you may want to lock in a long-term.

Amortization period   The term of a mortgage (six months or five years) is different from the amortization period of a mortgage. The amortization period is the total length of time you will be making payments on your mortgage before it is completely paid off. The tradi-- tional amortization period in Canada is 25 years. The length of your amortization period affects the amount of your monthly payments and the total amount of interest you will have paid on your mortgage loan once it is completely paid off. Shorter amortization periods result in higher monthly payments, but greater total savings because you pay less interest. Longer amortization periods result in lower monthly payments, but more is spent on interest. The term and amortization period

are usually not the same. At the end of the term, if the amortization period is longer than the mortgage term, you will still owe
money to the lender and will either have to repay it entirely or
arrange new financing.

■ How much should you borrow?

When buying a home, an accepted guideline is that the purchaser spend
no more than 25 percent of the household's gross monthly income on
principal, interest, and taxes. Most lenders, though, use their own formula
to calculate the amount they think you can reasonably handle, taking into
account existing debts and various other expenses in owning a home. Your
real estate agent or local bank branch can help you determine what mortgage loan you can qualify for based on current interest rates.

■ Buying a home with less than 25 percent down

In the past, lenders would only give loans for up to 75 percent of the
value of the home with the remaining 25 percent down payment from
you. With mortgage insurance, however, first-time homebuyers can
obtain a loan for up to 95 percent of the value of the home with as little
as 5 percent down (for homes ranging from $125,000 to $300,000,
depending on where you live). A first-time homebuyer is someone who
has not owned a home in the last five years.

If you have had a mortgage loan previously, you can still get a mortgage loan for up to 90 percent of the value of the home. Mortgage insurance gives lenders greater protection from the risk of homebuyers who
become unable to repay their mortgage loan. If you are considering purchasing a home with less than a 25 percent down payment, your lender
will require you to arrange the necessary mortgage insurance. Common
mortgage insurers include Canada Mortgage and Housing Corporation
and GE Capital Mortgage Insurance.

Mortgage insurers usually require the home be used for full-time,
personal occupancy and that mortgage and tax payments do not exceed
30 percent of your gross monthly income. You will also be subject to a
credit check and will have to provide proof of income. You will also need
to obtain an appraisal of your home's value, usually prepared by your
financial institution.

The actual premiums for mortgage insurance vary. The general range
is from 0.5 to 3.5 percent of the value of your loan. This premium can
be added to your mortgage loan and paid off as a regular part of your
mortgage payments. If you have the money, though, you can pay the

premium in a lump sum to avoid interest costs. In provinces with sales tax, there is also usually tax on these premiums that must be paid at the time the insurance is purchased.

■ Reducing mortgage interest

Many financial institutions do innovative things to satisfy customers. For example, you can usually negotiate a weekly or bi-weekly payment schedule of payments, as well as the right to make additional lump sum payments in addition to regular payments. Many consumers are often so glad to be approved for the mortgage that they forget to negotiate the best deal before signing. A lawyer or even the lender can offer suggestions for reducing your cost of borrowing.

■ Renewing a Mortgage

Renewing a mortgage loan can be done with your existing lender or elsewhere if you prefer the services and interest rate of another lender. The interest rate is the main issue when you renew your mortgage loan so you may want to consider your options with other lenders to find the best arrangement. Although your existing lender may charge you a fee to switch your mortgage to another lender, you may be able to negotiate with your new lender for the fee to be covered. In any event, make sure you begin switching your mortgage loan at least 60 days before the expiry of your term to give yourself enough time to make the necessary arrangements.

26. What if I can no longer afford to pay my mortgage?

For one reason or another, many people experience financial difficulties. During this time, they may be unable to make mortgage payments. The most important advice is to consult your bank or other financial institution and explain your situation clearly. Often, the bank will come to some sort of arrangement to accommodate your needs. For example, the bank may agree to temporarily reduce regular payments.

If you stop paying your mortgage payments and do not make other arrangements with the lender, it will likely begin legal action to take possession of your home. Whatever your problems, it is always a good idea to advise your bank and request a temporary solution until you become more financially stable.

If your home is not worth more than your mortgage loan and you cannot make your payments, you may want to consider walking away from the home under a "quit claim deed." If your mortgage lender agrees, you may be able to transfer title of the house to the lender in return for a complete release of all your obligations. The lender then becomes the full owner of the property.

If you cannot reach an agreement with your bank, the lender may begin action to take your property. Before this happens, though, contact a lawyer to review all your options.

27. What does it mean to "default" on my mortgage?

A mortgage default means you violated one or more terms of your mortgage agreement, which is a contract that lists all the terms and obligations. The most obvious default is failure to make a required regular payment, but other things can be classified as defaults, including:

- Failing to have adequate insurance on your property
- Failing to pay property taxes
- Putting another mortgage on the property
- Failing to keep the premises in a reasonable state of repair
- Selling the property without the bank's consent

Because the home is the bank's security for the mortgage loan, it has an interest in maintaining the home's value. The above actions can jeopardize the value of the property.

Lenders have a number of options once a mortgage has gone into default. The lender may first send you reminder letters or call. It will usually send you a demand letter, which demands payment of the outstanding balance. If you fail to pay, the bank can eventually take possession of the property and sell it under the terms of the mortgage agreement or by foreclosure. Any costs incurred by the lender when selling your home is added to the amount you already owe.

If you cannot make the mortgage payments, but your home is worth more than the outstanding balance of the mortgage loan, you may want to sell the property yourself. This way, you will be able to pay off the financial institution and still keep the equity, which is the difference between the loan and the amount you received when it sold.

If you cannot make your mortgage payments and cannot reach some agreement with your financial institution, seek advice from a lawyer. Your lawyer may be able to delay or prevent you from losing your home. As always, if you are experiencing financial difficulties, it is a good idea to contact the lender before allowing a default to occur.

28. Can the government take or expropriate your land?

Under rare circumstances, the government may be able to buy the property from you for a fair market price, but without your consent. This is called expropriation and it involves taking private property for public use. Common examples of expropriations occur when a municipality widens a road or a school makes an addition to its facilities. Under these circumstances, the municipality or school will serve a notice of application to the registered owners of the property. The property owners can then request a hearing to determine whether the expropriation is fair and reasonable. Eventually, the relevant provincial ministry either approves or rejects a proposed expropriation.

In addition to fair compensation for the price of the expropriated property, landowners may also have a right to compensation for losses including a loss of tenants, business losses, mortgage prepayment losses, and other specific losses. A lawyer versed in municipal law or your local municipal office can provide you with additional information about expropriations.

AIR RIGHTS OR NO RIGHTS?

A company erected several high transmission towers on the edge of its property. Next door was a flying school. The aviators went to court claiming their neighbour was obstructing the airspace. The towers interfered with landings and take-offs.

Should the towers be allowed to stay?

Yes, said the court in *Atlantic Aviation* v. *Nova Scotia Light & Power*. A landowner, ruled the judge, has a right to "erect structures on his land in the exercise of his use and enjoyment of his land, even if the obstructions interfered with the free passage of aircraft taking off and landing on an adjoining airfield." Even though planes were in danger, it was a lawful, reasonable, and necessary use of the airspace.

AIR RIGHTS REVISITED

A property owner was out walking on his grounds when he suddenly noticed a small airplane circling overhead at about 1,000 feet. Irritated, the landowner yelled at the pilot to go away, but the plane continued to fly overhead for long after. Later, the landowner discovered the pilot had been taking photographs of his property and was offering them for sale. The landowner sued for trespass.

Did the landowner have the right to prevent the plane from flying over his land?

No, said an English court in *Bernstein of Leigh* v. *Skyview & General*. In a decision still followed by Canadian courts, the judge said a landowner only has rights to airspace in so far as is practical and necessary to protect buildings or use land. The courts will not allow a property owner to claim rights all the way to the heavens.

AN EASY EASEMENT?

For many years, trucks servicing a rural business drove along a private dirt road owned by a neighbouring landowner. Occasionally, the landowner objected, but the road was used off and on for over 20 years. The business decided to apply to the court for a legal declaration that it had a right of easement to use the road.

Was a right of easement created after 20 years?

No, the court ruled in Temma Realty v. Ress Enterprises Ltd. because there was no "continuous, uninterrupted, open, peaceful use, and enjoyment of the way with the knowledge of and without objection from the owner." Most serious was the fact in this that the landowner had blocked the road for 16 months before the legal action began. The court said it could not allow "neighbourly accommodation" to become a legal right against the true owner.

Must You Tell The Bare Truth?

An agreement was signed to purchase a beautiful lake front property in British Columbia and the happy purchasers excitedly put down a $100,000 deposit. Shortly after the deal was signed and before closing day, the purchasers learned from a neighbour that a property next door was used in summer as a rowdy nude beach. Quickly, they stopped payment on the down payment and refused to close. In court, they argued the vendor had an obligation to reveal information about the nude beach since it was a "latent defect" that could affect the value of the property.

Was the vendor obligated to reveal this information?

No, said a B.C. appeal court in the case of *Summach* v. *Allen*. "The presence of nude bodies next door or parading in front of one's house may or may not be a defect," said one appeal court judge. "This requires a subjective test. To allow defects to be determined by individual preferences would open the floodgates of litigation by remorseful purchasers and create an impossible standard of disclosure for vendors."

There are two types of property defects — patent and latent. Patent defects are obvious flaws you should detect when inspecting a property with ordinary care, such as a damaged roof. Sellers do not have to alert buyers to patent defects.

While the law on latent defects is more complex, vendors do have a duty to disclose latent defects that render a property dangerous. Any defects which vendors know (or ought to know) would render the premises unfit for habitation must also be disclosed. That said, sellers have no legal obligation to volunteer information about latent defects that only affect the value of a property.

WWW Resources

Alberta New Home Warranty Program	www.anhwp.com
Alberta Real Estate Association	www.abrea.ab.ca
Appraisal Institute of Canada	www.aicanada.org/welcome.htm
Association des courtiers et agents immobiliers du Québec	www.acaiq.com
Atlantic New Home Warranty Program	www.ahwp.org

WWW Resources

British Columbia Homeowner Protection Office	www.hpo.bc.ca
British Columbia Real Estate Association	www.bcrea.bc.ca
Canada Mortgage & Housing Corporation	http://www.cmhc-schl.gc.ca
Canadian Condominium Institute	www.cci.ca
Canadian Real Estate Association	crea.ca
Garantie des maisons neuves de l'APCHQ (GMN)	www.apchq.com/1Grandpublic/Garantie
Manitoba Real Estate Association	www.realestatemanitoba.com
National Warranty	www.nationalhomewarranty.com
New Home Warranty Program of Manitoba	www.mbnhwp.com
New Home Warranty Program of Saskatchewan	www.nhwp.org
Nova Scotia Association of Realtors	www.nsar.ns.ca
Ontario New Home Warranty Program	newhome.on.ca
Ontario Real Estate Association	www.orea.com
Real Estate Council of Ontario	www.reco.on.ca
Saskatchewan Real Estate Association	www.saskatchewanrealestate.com
Yukon Real Estate Association	www.yrea.yk.ca

Quick Glossary

Amortization Period: The period over which you pay back your mortgage loan.

Conventional Mortgage: A mortgage loan up to 75 percent of your property's appraised value or purchase price.

High-Ratio Mortgage: A mortgage loan for over 75 percent of the home's appraised value, which must be insured.

Mortgagee: The lender of mortgage money.

Mortgagor: The borrower.

Principal: The amount of money borrowed and still owing on a loan.

Second Mortgage: A mortgage loan secured by all or part of any equity remaining after a first mortgage. In a foreclosure situation, the first mortgage has priority over any funds recovered.

Title: The legal ownership in a property.

Vendor Take-Back Mortgage: The seller provides some or all of the financing.

MONEY MATTERS
Renting A Home

Each province has its own set of rules and regulations that govern the relationship between residential landlords and tenants, usually called the *Residential Tenancies Act* or *Tenant Protection Act*. The associated laws set out the obligations of each party to the rental or lease agreement.

Disputes between landlords and residential tenants are normally dealt with through a provincial agency set up to deal with landlord-tenant matters. The laws vary widely, but generally cover tenancy agreements, rent amounts and increases, security deposits, and tenancy termination.

The definition of what is covered as a residential premise differs according to province and many of the acts exclude certain types of premises, such as hotels, seasonal homes, co-ops, university residences, and hospitals. It is therefore important that you check the law of your province. Commercial tenancies, on the other hand, are governed largely by the same laws used for any business agreement.

1. How can a landlord evaluate potential tenants?

Most landlords require tenants to provide information about their finances, employment, and credit history to determine if the tenant is able to pay rent on an ongoing basis. A landlord may also require tenants to give references or even have someone else co-sign the lease as a security measure.

2. Is it illegal for a landlord to discriminate?

Although landlords can usually assess potential tenants on their ability to pay rent, it is illegal for a landlord to discriminate against tenants on personal characteristics, such as those set in provincial human rights laws. For example, it can be illegal to discriminate against tenants based on marital status, race, religion, sex, sexual orientation, or language. Other factors could also come into play, such as pregnancy and whether prospective tenants have children.

If a landlord refuses to rent for any of these reasons, people should contact their provincial human rights commission to determine their rights.

3. Do leases need to be written and signed?

Except in British Columbia, a written lease is not required by law. It is good practice, however, to have a written lease that sets out key terms of the tenancy arrangement, and many landlords will require new tenants to sign a lease to ensure they will be responsible for certain obligations. If there is a written lease, many provinces require that a copy be provided to the tenant within 21 days of the start of the tenancy relationship.

Many landlords use a standard lease that requires the tenant to live in the rental unit for at least one year, to pay a set amount of rent on time each month, and follow other rules about how the tenant may use the premises. Whether a lease gives the landlord or tenant rights or obligations depends on the terms of the lease and what the law allows.

■ Terms of a lease are not necessarily valid

Residential landlords and tenants have rights and obligations set out by both provincial law and previous court cases. Although terms of a lease may attempt to limit a tenant's rights, they may not necessarily be enforceable by law. For example, even if a lease states a landlord can evict a tenant without a reason by giving the tenant a reasonable notice period, the tenant may still have the right to stay to the end of the lease period. For legal advice on the validity of a lease, you should consult a lawyer or contact a legal clinic in your area.

■ Lease advantage for tenants: provides certainty

The primary advantage of a written lease is that it provides tenants with certainty as to their accommodations in terms of length of rental and price. Nonetheless, tenants are at risk of being evicted if the landlord or the landlord's family wants to move in; if the landlord sells the premises; or plans major repairs or renovations that require a building permit and vacant possession. These are referred to as "no fault" reasons since the eviction is not based on the behaviour or conduct of a tenant. Depending on your province's laws, landlords may be permitted to break a lease provided they give some type of adequate notice. Manitoba requires 90 days notice from a landlord, while Ontario requires only 60 days notice.

■ Lease disadvantage for tenants: inflexibility to move

If a tenant wants the flexibility of moving without having to give much notice, a written lease will usually be a disadvantage since the tenant may be legally responsible for paying the entire amount of the lease if he or she is leaving before it expires. Although landlords are required to make all efforts to find a replacement tenant for the premises, if unsuccessful, the landlord may be able to sue the outgoing tenant who broke the lease. In most provinces, if an annual or fixed-term lease expires and you continue to stay in the rental unit, it automatically turns into a month-to-month lease.

4. What are the rights of a tenant living with children?

Tenants with children cannot be discriminated against as long as there is no illegal overcrowding. Tenants have a responsibility, however, to ensure that their children do not unreasonably disturb other tenants by making excessive noise or committing illegal acts.

5. Do tenants have rights if they only rent a room?

It depends on the province. In many provinces, rooming houses, board-ing houses, and rooms in landlords' houses have special exemptions from landlord-tenant legislation. For example, in Ontario, tenants who rent a single or shared room have the same rights as most other residential ten-ants. If they share a kitchen or a bathroom with the owner or the owner's immediate family members, special rules apply.

6. Does a tenant have the right to keep pets?

Generally, tenants have the right to keep pets as long as they do not seriously disturb other tenants or cause damage to the premises. Still, a landlord can refuse to rent to someone who has a pet.

7. When can the landlord enter a premise?

Under the law, a tenant has the right to privacy and the right to quiet enjoyment of the premises. In some provinces landlords can enter a premise without notice in an emergency, although most provinces require that the landlord provide 24-hour notice before entry.

8. What happens if a landlord enters illegally?

If a landlord or his or her employee is illegally entering the tenant's unit, the tenant may first attempt to resolve the problem with the landlord in person or in writing. If the landlord or the employee is not entering to do valid work, or if tenants fear for their safety, they can call the police for protection. If the problem continues, a tenant can also complain to the provincial organization that oversees tenancy issues.

9. Who can change the locks?

Most provinces have a blanket prohibition on parties changing the locks, unless there is consent from both parties and the landlord provides the tenant with a new key. In British Columbia, however, tenants can change locks if they prove that the landlord is illegally entering the premises.

A tenant who wants the locks changed because of safety and security concerns should write a letter to the landlord stating all their concerns. A practical solution may be to get permission to change the locks or to install an additional lock and provide the landlord with a key.

10. What are the rights and obligations for repairs?

■ Duties of landlords and tenants

Generally, landlords are responsible for maintaining their rental premises in a good state of repair. This includes complying with all health, safety, and maintenance standards set by the local municipality. Tenants are responsible for keeping their unit clean and for repairing any damage they or their guests cause to the unit or the premises.

■ A landlord's duty to maintain the premises in good repair

A landlord's obligation to maintain the premises is ongoing, and does not just arise when the tenant complains or when the disrepair becomes severe. Although a tenant has the obligation to keep the premises clean, it is the responsibility of the landlord to repair damage due to reasonable wear and tear over time. This includes: fixing broken appliances, leaking faucets, peeling paint, and clogged pipes, and ensuring a proper supply of water and other utilities included in the tenancy agreement. A landlord is also responsible for preventing and ridding pests and insects from the tenant's unit and the entire premises.

■ A tenant's legal options if a landlord is not maintaining the premises

If a landlord is not maintaining the premises properly, a tenant has four legal options:

- Tenants can write a letter to the landlord detailing all repairs that are needed, keeping a copy of the letter for their records
- If the landlord refuses to address the problems, the tenant can contact the local municipality responsible for building standards. Since problems of disrepair, safety, and infestation are usually violations of a by-law, if a tenant calls the municipality, an inspector will normally make an appointment to inspect the premises. If the inspector finds that a by-law has been violated, that person will usually write a report ordering that the repairs be completed by a given deadline
- If the landlord does not comply with the order, that person can be fined or charged with an offence, and the tenant can use the report as evidence in a legal action against the landlord
- Even if the landlord repairs the problem, a tenant can still request an abatement of rent. An abatement of rent is a reduction in rent for the months that the premises were in disrepair. Applying for an

abatement of rent will likely involve a hearing in front of some type of tribunal, board, or arbitrator who will review the evidence of disrepair, hear arguments from both sides, and determine if the tenant should receive a deduction in rent.

11. Can a tenant move out when there is a lease?

A tenant who breaks a lease can be held responsible for paying the rent up to the end of the lease. Tenants sometimes have the option, however, to sublet or assign their unit and avoid having to pay the landlord for the remaining months of the lease.

■ Subletting rules

Tenants who only want to move out temporarily can arrange to sublet their unit. Subletting is when a tenant rents out his or her unit to another person for a period that is less than the length of the lease. The original tenant is responsible for collecting the rent from the subletter and ensuring it is paid to the landlord. If a tenant rents on a month-to-month basis, he or she can only sublet the unit for less than one month and not any longer, or the tenant and the sub-tenant may lose their rights to the unit.

Generally, if tenants want to sublet their unit, they require the landlord's approval. In some cases the ability to sublet depends on the length of the lease. The landlord must have a good reason for refusing a sub-tenant. Depending on the province, the landlord must respond to the sublet request within 7 to 14 days, depending on the province. A failure to respond has different ramifications in different provinces. In Alberta, the landlord is deemed to have consented if there is no response, while in Ontario if the landlord rejects a sublet, the tenant can apply to the Ontario Rental Housing Tribunal to determine if the sublease should be allowed. In some provinces a landlord can charge extra rent.

■ Assigning a lease: transferring it to someone new

If tenants want to move out before the lease expires and do not want to return, they can assign their lease to another person, who will then become the tenant. Assigning a lease transfers all the tenant's rights and obligations to another person. The new tenant, called the assignee, will be required to pay the same rent that the original tenant was paying, and the terms of the original lease will apply.

12. Can a landlord raise rents?

The ability of a landlord to raise rents depends on whether the province or territory has rent controls in place. The landlord must also provide notice of rental increases to the tenant. As well, landlords must often wait a minimum period between rental increases.

Province	Rent control system?	Notice time requirement before a rent increase
British Columbia	• Rent review system	• Weekly renters: 12 weeks • Monthly renters: 3 months • All other tenancies: 180 days
Alberta	• No	• Weekly renters: 12 weeks • Monthly renters: 3 months • All other tenancies: 180 days
Saskatchewan	• No	• Weekly renters: 3 weeks • Monthly renters: 3 months
Manitoba	• Government sets annual guidelines • Rents can only be raised once every 12 months	• All tenancies: 3 months
Ontario	• Government sets rent guidelines each year • Landlords can apply to a tribunal for increases above the guidelines Landlords can raise rents only after 12 months since a tenant moved in or since the last increase	• All tenancies: 90 days notice in writing
Québec	• No ceilings on rent increases • Landlords are restricted in raising rents during a lease that is less than 12 months	• If the lease is for less than 12 months or the duration is undetermined, the notice of change of conditions must be given at least 1 month and not more than 2 months before the end of the term. For leases of 12 months or more, the notice must be given at least 3 months and not more than 6 months before the end of the lease. For the lease of a room, the notice must be given at least 10 days and not more than 20 days before the end of the lease.

New Brunswick	• No	• Monthly renters: 2 months
		• Yearly renters: 3-12 months
Nova Scotia	• No	• All tenancies: 4 months
	• Rents can only be raised once every 12 months	
Newfoundland	• No	• All tenancies: 3 months
Prince Edward Island	• Government sets rent increase annually	• All tenancies: 3 months
	• Rents can only be raised once per year	
Yukon	• No	• Not allowed in first year of a tenancy agreement
		• All tenancies: 3 months
Northwest Territories	• No	• No more than one increase every 12 months
		• All tenancies: 3 months
Nunavut	• No	• No more than one increase every 12 months
		• All tenancies: 3 months

13. Can a landlord require a security deposit?

Except in Québec, landlords are permitted to request that tenants provide a security deposit ranging from half a month's rent to a full month's rent. Generally, landlords are not allowed to charge tenants additional fees or charges above rent. For example, a landlord cannot charge a key deposit. Landlords who collect security deposits must pay interest on the money, usually at a rate declared by the province.

14. What are tenants' rights and responsibilities when moving out?

A tenant's right to move out will depend on whether there is a lease and whether the tenant gave the landlord proper notice. The tenant will also be responsible for leaving the unit in a satisfactory condition, or the landlord may take legal action against the tenant.

■ Tenants' notice to move out

Tenants who want to move out are normally required to give notice to the landlord in writing. The length of notice required depends on how often the tenant is required to pay rent. Generally, a tenant is required to provide a landlord with notice when he or she plans to move. It can range between one and three months depending on the length of the lease and the province.

15. What is a tenants' association?

Many rental buildings have tenant associations which work to improve the premises or solve problems that are common to many tenants. Tenants have the right to organize and join a tenants' association without being harassed or interfered with by the landlord.

16. What are a roommate's rights and obligations?

While the law sets out the rights and obligations that both landlords and tenants have, it usually says little about rights and obligations that roommates have toward each other.

If you and another person wish to rent an apartment as roommates, you should ensure that both of you sign the lease with the landlord. Understand, however, that if your roommate does not pay his or her share of the rent, you may have to pay it. Also, if your roommate leaves without giving notice, you may be responsible for the whole lease.

If your roommate leaves the apartment, you may be able to find someone else to replace that person. The landlord must approve this person as a tenant for him or her to be added to the lease.

Because the law is not clear about the legal obligations of roommates, be very careful about entering into such an arrangement with anyone.

17. When can a landlord evict a tenant?

Contrary to what many people believe, tenants can be evicted at any time of year, even if they have children, as long as the landlord has a valid legal reason for the eviction, such as a breach of the lease, major repairs requiring a vacant premises or demolition of the property. Nonetheless, tenants who pay their rent on time and live up to their other obligations have an ongoing right to live in the rented premises without interference by the landlord. Special rules often apply to tenants living in subsidized housing, who have fewer rights than most other tenants.

If a landlord tries to evict a tenant and the tenant disputes the eviction, the landlord will have to prove (often, in front of a government rental housing tribunal) there is a valid legal reason for the eviction. Common reasons for evicting a tenant include: non-payment of rent, continually paying rent late, significantly disturbing others in the building, damaging the property, committing an illegal act on the property, and overcrowding. Tenants are normally responsible for any children or guests in the home, and may be evicted for their actions as well.

Landlords must go through a series of legal steps and make certain official notices to the tenant before eviction can happen. The landlord will usually have to apply to the provincial agency that oversees disputes between landlords and tenants for an eviction order, and the tenant must be given notice of the landlord's eviction application and information on how to challenge or appeal it. Even if tenants are ordered to vacate the premises, only a sheriff can force them to leave. If a landlord locks tenants out of their homes without the sheriff present, the tenants can contact the police for help to re-enter the unit.

18. How do you evict a tenant?

A landlord must take a number of steps to evict a tenant. First, the landlord is required to give the tenant a notice form that lets the tenant know the reason for eviction and when the landlord can start legal action. The type of notice form and the number of days that a landlord must wait before taking formal action depend on the reason for eviction. It also varies across the provinces from 48 hours in Alberta in the case of a tenant causing significant damage or engaging in a physical assault, to one month in other provinces. Notice forms and instruction kits are usually available at your local landlord-tenant agency.

Once a landlord has given the tenant a notice form and the required notice period has passed, the landlord can apply to the provincial landlord-tenant agency for a hearing before some type of tribunal or arbitrator. The landlord must fill out a form and file it at the agency and there could be a fee involved. The staff at the agency will set a date for the hearing.

The tenant must then be notified of the hearing and will have a chance to present his or her version of the dispute, often within a certain period.

In some provinces, a mediator may contact both the landlord and the tenant to help them resolve the issues. If the matter is not resolved through mediation, it will normally go to a hearing.

If the eviction is allowed, the person assigned to oversee the dispute will sign an Order that the landlord is required to give to the sheriff's office, which the sheriff then uses to evict the tenant. A landlord cannot evict a tenant or change the locks without the sheriff present.

19. What can a tenant do to defend against an eviction?

If a tenant receives an eviction notice, he or she must act quickly to avoid being evicted. In some provinces, action by the tenant must be taken within just five days.

Tenants must respond by filing a dispute form with the provincial landlord-tenancy agency as quickly as possible. A dispute form advises the agency that the tenant contests the landlord's reasons for eviction. The eviction notice given to a tenant usually states the required response time.

If the tenant does not dispute the eviction, the government agency or tribunal will likely approve the eviction order. Sometimes, however, tenants do not find out they are being evicted until they receive a notice from the sheriff or a copy of an eviction order. If this happens and the tenants did not have a fair chance to dispute the eviction, they may be able to stop the eviction and have a new hearing scheduled or appeal the decision.

20. What happens if a tenant did not dispute on time?

If the tenant does not respond in time, the agency overseeing the dispute may make a decision without holding a hearing and may order the eviction. The tenant could also be ordered pay any arrears of rent owing plus the landlord's legal costs.

21. Can a tenant get an eviction order set aside?

If there is a good reason to stop the sheriff from going through with the eviction, a tenant has to apply for the eviction order to be set aside within 5-10 days from the date it was signed, depending on the law in many provinces. If the 5-10 days have passed since the eviction order was signed, tenants can still apply for it to be set aside but the eviction may still occur, making it very difficult for tenants to get back into their home. Your provincial or territorial rental authority can provide you with instructions on appealing an order. Also, eviction orders often come with some instructions for appeals.

Depending on the complexity of the issues involved, a tenant may want to contact a legal clinic for advice and in some cases representation at the hearing.

22. What happens to a tenant's property after eviction?

Only a sheriff can evict tenants from their homes — and only after the landlord has obtained an eviction order. If a sheriff evicts a tenant, the tenant will normally be required to leave immediately without being given an opportunity to take personal property. In some jurisdictions, tenants only have 48 hours to return to the unit and remove all their belongings, unless the landlord allows more time. If the landlord will not give the tenant more time to retrieve his or her things, and the tenant does not remove the property within the 48-hour period, the landlord has the right to dispose of it. This means that the landlord has the legal right to sell or throw away the tenant's property. If a tenant has been evicted and needs more than 48 hours to move belongings, a local legal clinic may be able to assist the tenant in negotiating with the landlord. Legal clinics are listed in the Blue pages of the telephone book.

If the sheriff comes to evict you, it is a good idea to take important documents such as identification, passports or immigration papers, and any necessary medications, prescriptions, and eyeglasses. If you have nowhere to go, take a change of clothes for yourself and any others living with you, and contact a local emergency shelter.

23. How can a landlord collect arrears of rent?

Under the law, a tenant who does not pay rent is considered to be in arrears. If the landlord wants to evict the tenant and collect the outstanding rent, the landlord has to apply to the provincial landlord tenancy agency for an order terminating the tenancy and requiring the tenant to pay the money owing. Sometimes, landlords can avoid the time and expense of legal action by having the tenant sign a written agreement stating that the tenant will pay the arrears according to a set payment schedule. Still, if the tenant defaults on any of the payments, the landlord will usually have to apply to the agency to evict the tenant and then take steps to collect the arrears from the tenant after that person has moved out.

If you are a tenant who is asked to sign an agreement to pay arrears of rent, make sure the terms of the agreement are reasonable for your situation. This way you will not default on the agreement and give the landlord the right to evict you.

A landlord who obtains an order from the agency stating the amount of arrears that the tenant owes can generally enforce it through the sheriff's office. The landlord will also be entitled to garnish the tenant's wages or seize and sell the tenant's property to pay off the debt.

WWW Resources

Canadian Mortgage Housing Corporation: its site includes excellent provincial fact sheets for renters and landlords, which can be accessed on the buy or rent a home button on the upper left side of the page. http://www.cmhc-schl.gc.ca

Landlord Tenant Legislation

B.C. Residential Tenancy Act	http://www.qp.gov.bc.ca
Alberta Residential Tenancies Act and Regulations	http://www3.gov.ab.ca acts_regs.cfm#Residential_Tenancies Saskatchewan Residential
Tenancies Act	http://www.qp.gov.sk.ca
Manitoba Residential Tenancies Act	http://web2.gov.mb.ca
Ontario Tenant Protection Act, 1997	http://www.e-laws.gov.on.ca
Québec	http://www.rdl.gouv.qc.ca
New Brunswick Residential Tenancies Act	http://www.gnb.ca
Nova Scotia Residential Tenancies Act	http://www.gov.ns.ca
Prince Edward Island Rental of Residential Property Act	http://www.gov.pe.ca
Newfoundland and Labrador Residential Tenancies Act	http://www.gov.nf.ca
Northwest Territories Residential Tenancies Act	http://www.iijcan.org

Provincial Organizations

British Columbia Residential Tenancy Head Office	http://www.rto.gov.bc.ca
Alberta Government Services	http://www3.gov.ab.ca
Saskatchewan Office of the Rentalsman	http://www.saskjustice.gov.sk.ca
Manitoba Residential Tenancies Branch	http://www.gov.mb.ca
Ontario Rental Housing Tribunal	http://www.orht.gov.on.ca
Québec Régie du logement	http://www.rdl.gouv.qc.ca
New Brunswick Office of the Rentalsman	http://www.gnb.ca
Nova Scotia Residential Tenancies Office	http://www.gov.ns.ca
Price Edward Island Office of the Director of Residential Rental Property	http://www.irac.pe.ca
Newfoundland and Labrador Residential Tenancies Division	http://www.gov.nf.ca
Northwest Territories Rental Office	http://www.justice.gov.nt.ca

Landlord and Tenant Guides and FAQs

British Columbia	http://www.pssg.gov.bc.ca
Alberta	http://www3.gov.ab.ca
Saskatchewan	http://www.saskjustice.gov.sk.ca
Manitoba	http://www.gov.mb.ca
Ontario	http://www.orht.gov.on.ca
Québec	http://www.rdl.gouv.qc.ca
New Brunswick	http://www.legal-info-legale.nb.ca
Nova Scotia	http://www.gov.ns.ca
Prince Edward Island	http://www.irac.pe.ca

LOSING MONEY

"How can I put a stop to all these bills and calls from collection agencies? Maybe I should just declare bankruptcy!" For many Canadians, the pressures and crises of life can make us feel that we have few options when dealing with unruly debt. In many cases, however, there are options. But you may not like the tough decisions that will have to be made.

Whether it's student loans, credit card debts, or mounting business losses, Canada's bankruptcy and insolvency laws may be able to help you stop those collection calls and start your financial life with a relatively clean slate. You will discover, however, that declaring bankruptcy is an extreme option that should only be used as a last resort.

Financial advisors like to tell us over and over that recognizing the warning signs of financial difficulty — especially at an early stage — and then doing something about it, are important steps toward preventing unmanageable debt and, worse, personal or business bankruptcy.

Everyone should look at how he or she uses credit cards. Warning signs include only making the minimum monthly payments, sometimes missing payments, using your credit cards for necessity rather than for convenience, and borrowing from one credit card to make a payment on another.

Everyone should also watch how he or she manages money generally. You may be heading for financial difficulty if you are spending more than you are earning each month, can't keep track of what money you are spending, don't know what money you owe or when your bills are due. If you are well past this stage, then read on ...

1. What is personal bankruptcy?

Filing for personal bankruptcy is a legal process that allows individuals facing overwhelming financial difficulties to clear their debts and make a fresh start.

Bankruptcy is not intended for people who intentionally or recklessly set out to defeat or duck their creditors. Rather, it is intended for those who unexpectedly become unable to repay their debts. They might have genuinely made some poor spending or borrowing choices, have suddenly lost their jobs, or encountered health or marital problems.

To be eligible to file for bankruptcy, you must owe at least $1,000 and you must not be able to pay your debts as they become due. You must also be unable to pay off your debts even if most of your assets were to be sold. In law, this means that you are technically "insolvent."

■ Advantages and disadvantages of bankruptcy

The benefits of declaring bankruptcy are that you are no longer responsible for your current debts, you will not receive any harassing phone calls from your creditors, and you can make a clean financial start.

The main disadvantage of bankruptcy is that your bankruptcy stays on your credit record for seven years. It also means that your creditors will not be able to collect the money that you owe them. As a result, you will have difficulty getting a credit card or a loan after you have filed for bankruptcy.

It will take a while before people trust you enough to lend you money again. This may not be a bad thing. If bankruptcy is due to bad budgeting or poor credit choices, this will force you to learn to live within your budget.

2. How do I file for personal bankruptcy?

To file for personal bankruptcy, you must generally follow a six-step legal process. The length of time from the day you file for bankruptcy to the day your debts are cleared is about nine months.

■ Find a trustee in bankruptcy

The first step is to find a licensed trustee in bankruptcy. You can contact trustees through the Yellow Pages of your telephone book or get a referral from an accountant. A trustee is generally an accountant who is licensed by the government to handle bankruptcies. The trustee will oversee the sale of most of your assets and the distribution of proceeds to your creditors. The trustee also deals with all phone calls and inquiries from your creditors.

■ Meet with the trustee

The second step is to call the trustee and arrange a meeting. To prepare for your meeting, gather together as much of your financial information as possible, such as your most recent credit card statements and loan documents.

At your first meeting, the trustee will explain the bankruptcy procedure, consider your financial position, and advise you whether bankruptcy is the best option. You may also discuss the trustee's fee for handling your bankruptcy. The fee ranges from $1,000 - $1,500.

The person filing for bankruptcy must pay this fee. If you do not have enough money to cover the fee up front, your trustee can make other arrangements with you. The trustee may be able to collect the fee from your tax refund, or may accept monthly payments. If your income after expenses exceeds certain levels, you will be required to pay a portion of the excess to the trustee while you are in bankruptcy.

■ Filing paperwork

If you decide to pursue bankruptcy, the trustee will complete the necessary paperwork to officially file for bankruptcy. Your trustee will also notify your creditors and the phone calls to you will stop. Once the documents are complete, your trustee will file them with the federal government's Office of the Official Receiver.

After your documents have been filed, you are considered to be an "undischarged bankrupt" and are officially "in bankruptcy." All creditors' legal claims against you will stop, and your trustee will handle all calls and questions.

■ Attend a creditors' meeting

The fourth step may be for you to attend a meeting with your creditors approximately three weeks after filing for bankruptcy. This meeting will only be scheduled if more than 25 percent of your creditors request it. At this meeting, your creditors are informed of your financial situation.

If this is the first time you have declared bankruptcy and your creditors are large companies such as credit card companies, or large department stores, they will probably not require a meeting.

■ Financial counselling seminars with the trustee

The fifth step is for you to attend two mandatory financial counselling sessions with your trustee. Your first counselling session will generally take place within three weeks of filing for bankruptcy.

You and your trustee or an associate will go over possible reasons for your financial difficulties, your financial management skills, and how you plan to budget in the future. Your second counselling session will generally take place about four months after you filed. During this session, you and the trustee will again discuss financial planning strategies and effective budgeting.

■ Final discharge

The sixth and final step in a personal bankruptcy procedure is your "final discharge." Being discharged from bankruptcy means you are out of bankruptcy and your debts are officially cleared. If it is your first time filing for bankruptcy, you will normally receive an automatic discharge approximately nine months after you initially filed.

If it is not your first time filing for bankruptcy or if one of your creditors objects, it can be more difficult to have your debts discharged. Your trustee will make a discharge application to the court, and you may have to attend a hearing in court where a judge will hear your case. If you recklessly accumulated debts, or broke some of the rules (such as not attending financial counselling sessions), the judge can refuse to give you a discharge, or can order that as a condition of discharge you make monthly payments for some period.

Being discharged from bankruptcy generally marks the end of your bankruptcy procedure. Still, your bankruptcy stays on your credit record for seven years from the date of discharge. This will affect your ability to get loans and other kinds of credit in the future.

3. Will I lose everything if I file for bankruptcy?

Filing for personal bankruptcy results in a number of significant consequences:

- You may have to give up some of your personal belongings
- You will have to fulfill a number of obligations to your trustee in bankruptcy

• You will remain responsible for certain debts that are not cleared by bankruptcy

• Your credit rating will state that you filed for bankruptcy (for seven years)

Although some of your personal assets and belongings may be sold by your trustee to partially satisfy your debts, usually personal items and household goods are not affected.

You are allowed to keep any necessary and ordinary clothes up to a value of $1,000; household furniture, utensils, equipment, and food up to a value of $2,000; and any items you need for employment including tools, equipment, books, and a car, up to a value of $2,000.

Also, you can keep things owned entirely by your spouse. If you and your spouse own things jointly, you may have to sell the portion that you own. It is a good idea to discuss these issues with your trustee before you file for bankruptcy.

■ Duties under the *Bankruptcy and Insolvency Act*

The second important consequence of bankruptcy is you will have to fulfill certain duties set out in the *Bankruptcy and Insolvency Act*. To begin, when you meet with a trustee in bankruptcy, you must provide a complete list of all your assets and debts.

You must also give the trustee all your credit cards, and advise the trustee of property that you have sold or given away in the last five years and whether you have paid relatives or non-arms length persons within the last year. If you have done any non-arm's length transferring of assets or payments, it may be a good idea to see a bankruptcy lawyer before going to see a trustee.

Once you have filed for bankruptcy, you also have an obligation to keep the trustee informed of any changes in your financial or personal situation, whether you become employed or change your address, for instance. You must attend a meeting with your creditors if one is required, and assist the trustee in handling your estate. You may also have to pay a portion of your regular income to the trustee in order to pay your creditors. These obligations end once you are discharged, which happens about nine months after filing.

4.   Will bankruptcy remove all debts?

Declaring bankruptcy will eliminate most, but not all of your debts. The following five debts are not cleared by bankruptcy:

• Secured debts are not significantly affected by bankruptcy. A secured debt is one where the creditor secured one or more of your assets as collateral as a requirement of the loan made to you. For example, you may promise to give a creditor, such as a bank, your car or your home if you do not repay a loan. A secured creditor can seize these assets, but once they are sold, any outstanding balance will be discharged.

• Child and spousal support payments are not eliminated by bankruptcy.

• Court fines and penalties are not cleared by bankruptcy.

• Any debts you incurred by fraud or by causing bodily harm to another are not cleared by bankruptcy.

• Student loans are not cleared by bankruptcy unless you graduated from school at least 10 years before the date you filed for bankruptcy.

5.   What will happen to my credit rating?

Another consequence of bankruptcy is its effect on your credit rating. Your credit rating is a record of your credit history maintained by credit bureaus such as Equifax and TransUnion Canada.

These credit bureaus track how you handle credit generally and whether you make regular payments on time. Based on this ongoing information, you are given a credit rating. Your credit rating tells banks and other lenders how good you are at handling credit, and is usually checked by lenders before they decide whether to give you a credit card or a loan.

Bankruptcy gives you the lowest possible credit rating and the fact that you went bankrupt remains on your credit record for seven years after you are discharged from bankruptcy. As a result, lenders may be reluctant to give you loans or credit cards for quite some time.

Once you have been discharged from bankruptcy, make sure you send a copy of your discharge order to the credit bureaus so your credit record can be updated. As time goes by, you can gradually work toward rebuilding a good credit rating. It may be difficult to get credit for a while, and it will generally depend on whether you have a steady income and how well you are able to convince lenders that you have become more financially responsible.

6.   Can I transfer ownership of assets, such as my house or car, to my spouse or a friend before I declare bankruptcy?

Any attempts to transfer property or other assets, flee Canada, or otherwise hide assets to avoid creditors are considered "acts of bankruptcy."

Your creditors may be able to have all your assets seized and sold, as well as have any fraudulent transfers undone.

Generally, creditors and courts will look suspiciously upon any transfers of assets that happen within six months of their attempts to recover your debt or declaration of bankruptcy. That said, a court may still look beyond that six-month timeframe if a case is made by your creditors that you knew bankruptcy was likely.

7. Are there alternatives to bankruptcy?

If you have a steady income and you discover that your credit rating is satisfactory, you might be in a financial position that is manageable. Rather than filing for bankruptcy, you might be able to manage your debts, perhaps by consolidating them into one loan and making monthly payments on time. Here are four alternatives that usually have less serious consequences than bankruptcy.

■ Loan consolidation with a bank

You may be able to combine all your debts into one consolidated loan with either your bank or another financial institution. A consolidation loan is always a good idea because your interest rate will be lower than the interest rate on your credit cards, and you will only have to make one payment on your loan each month instead of many different payments for each of your credit cards.

■ Informal arrangement with creditors

You could try to make an informal arrangement with your creditors to pay a lesser amount or make your payments over a longer period. Often this is done with the help of credit counselling agencies. You may want to discover how your credit rating will be affected before agreeing to such arrangements. Sometimes creditors agree to reduce your debt or extend the repayment term, but will still report you to the credit bureau.

■ Consumer proposal

Another option is a "consumer proposal" under the *Bankruptcy and Insolvency Act*. This is a legal process that allows you to make an offer to your creditors to change your payment schedule, or compromise your debts. For example, you may offer to pay less each month over a longer period. Or, you may offer to pay only a percentage of what you really owe. Your proposal must offer creditors at least what they would get if you filed for bankruptcy, and your plan must not extend beyond a five-year period. If your creditors accept such a proposal, you will be able to manage your financial situation without filing for bankruptcy.

■ Credit counselling

A fourth option is credit counselling. There are a number of credit counselling services across Canada that can help you consolidate your loans. Before enrolling with a credit counselling service, make sure you ask about its services and fees. Often credit counselling services are useful in helping you decide whether bankruptcy is the right option.

There are many options to consider when you are experiencing financial difficulty. Consult with a trustee in bankruptcy, a lawyer, or an accountant for more information.

8.   How do I make a consumer proposal?

To make a consumer proposal, you must find and meet with a licensed bankruptcy trustee. This person will help you prepare your proposal and will present it to your creditors. You are also required by law to have two financial counselling sessions with the trustee to discuss financial management and budgeting. You will have to pay a fee of $50 to the government for this service, as well as a fee to the trustees for their services. The amount of the trustee's fee will depend on the complexity of your proposal.

Once you have filed your proposal, any legal action against you by your creditors is stopped. If your creditors accept your proposal, you make monthly payments to the trustee rather than making payments to each creditor yourself. If your proposal is not accepted, you are not automatically forced into bankruptcy and your creditors can begin or continue legal action against you. The failure to attempt a proposal instead of choosing bankruptcy can be held against you when you apply for discharge from bankruptcy.

9.   What are the legal limits on collection agencies?

Collection agencies are either hired by creditors to collect debts on their behalf or these agencies purchase debts at a discount and keep the entire amount if they are able to collect it.

If a collection agency phones you, this probably means you have more severe financial difficulties than you think. You should consider credit counselling or at least work out your budget and consider what realistic payments you can make. You can try to negotiate a payment schedule or payment of a reduced lump sum amount. The collection agency should stop calling if you are able to reach an agreement.

Although collection agencies can be very persistent, the law places limits on their behaviour. In fact, collection agencies cannot:

- Add any extra fees or amounts to the money you owe
- Harass, intimidate or threaten you in any way, whether by mail, over the phone, or in person
- Call you on Sundays or between 9 p.m. and 7 a.m. on any day
- Tell you false or misleading information. For example, they cannot send you false notices or agreements, or tell you they have started a court action when they have not.

If you need help dealing with a collection agency or if you think the collection agency is breaking the law, you can make a complaint to the provincial government department or agency that licenses collection business. You may also be entitled to bring an action against them in Small Claims Court. Contact a lawyer for more information.

10. Can I get any help with a student loan repayment?

A student must begin to repay a student loan six months following graduation, or after completion or termination of full-time enrollment as a post-secondary student.

During these six months, the student must visit the bank that issued the loan. The bank will determine the outstanding amount and interest rate for the student loans, and establish a repayment schedule that can last for up to nine and a half years. Note that interest on the loan accrues during the six months following graduation even if payment is not due.

The federal and most provincial governments offer interest relief programs for borrowers who can demonstrate financial need — including those with low incomes following graduation, single parents with young children, or victims of severe medical conditions or trauma. Eligibility is based on gross family income and financial assets and the monthly student loan payments. Interest relief is usually available for an initial period of 30 months throughout the life of repayment and an additional 24 months within the first five years of repayment for those who qualify.

Most interest relief programs only temporarily cover the interest of a student loan and borrowers are expected to continue to eventually make payments toward the loan principal. The bank that issued the loan and the school's financial aid office will have information on interest relief programs.

Some provinces will also consider forgiving or reducing part of the loan if you have an acceptable record of attempting to make payments.

Typically, if a borrower fails to make any payments for 90 days after the repayment schedule begins, then the loan may be deemed inactive by the bank that issued it. The bank may then seek payment of the loan from the government. A student loan is considered to be in default when the government has paid the bank's claim for an inactive loan.

If a borrower becomes in default for a student loan there are significant penalties that will affect his or her ability to borrow money in the future. The government ministry may turn over responsibility for recovery of a defaulted loan to private collection agencies.

Furthermore, the ministry will report the default to a credit bureau and place the person's name on a "Restricted List" until the default is cleared. People on the list are not eligible for future financial assistance from the government.

Finally, the provincial and federal governments can withhold a defaulted borrower's income tax refund and apply the proceeds toward a student loan debt. A school's financial aid office will have information on the process for addressing and clearing default of a loan.

■ Bankruptcy and student loans

Courts generally look harshly toward a debt incurred by a government student loan. The principle behind this consideration is that the failure of a borrower to repay a student loan endangers the program for other needy students. Consequently, borrowers should be aware that it is difficult to discharge a student loan by filing for bankruptcy.

Under Canada's *Bankruptcy and Insolvency Act*, the debt incurred by a government student loan will no longer be released by an order of discharge if such an order occurs either before or within 10 years after the date upon which the bankrupt borrower ceased to be a full-time or part-time student.

Only after this period may a court, upon application, release the student loan debt. For such an application to be successful, the bankrupt borrower must demonstrate that he or she:

- Acted in good faith with respect to the student loan debt
- Has and will continue to experience financial difficulties to an extent that he or she will be unable to pay liabilities under the student loan

11. How can I repair my credit?

Equifax and TransUnion Canada, the two major credit reporting services in Canada, collect credit and debt information from banks, lenders, credit card companies, leasing firms, courts, and others. Credit bureaus do not report on your annual personal income, family income or how much you have in the bank — only your debt, available credit, and the public record (bankruptcies, court judgments, etc.).

Your credit history is kept on file for six years from the date of last activity. Records of credit inquiries by lenders and others needing credit approval is kept on file for three years.

This credit information is only as good as what is supplied to these private agencies. In other words, it is often up to you to correct an error or misstatement in your record. For example, someone else's debt may be recorded as yours because of a filing error or a case of mistaken identity. Some businesses advertise "credit repair" services and say they can fix bad credit reports for a fee. In most cases, you can do it yourself at little cost.

The first step to repairing your credit is to see what your personal report says. Both credit bureaus in Canada will give you access to your credit report via mail or even the Internet. Next, identify any errors you see in your report and tell the credit agency why it is incorrect. In most cases, you can fill out a form provided by the bureau.

Usually within 30 days the credit bureau will send you a written response outlining what action it has taken to remove the errors or confirm that the information it has is correct. In some cases, you may have to go back to the source of the information, such as a bank or credit card company, to have the error corrected.

Paying off any outstanding loans or unpaid debts will improve your credit score. Another step you can take to "repair" your credit rating is to reduce the number of credit cards you have. High interest credit accounts offered by department stores, hardware stores, and gas companies are often viewed as undesirable by major lenders, such as banks. And, your credit rating will improve if you pay your bills promptly and always meet payment due dates.

If you are rejected for credit by a business or lender, find out why. It may have nothing to do with an error in your credit report. Rather, the creditor may simply have higher requirements for income or credit scores.

WWW Resources

Office of the Superintendent of Bankruptcy Canada	www.osb-bsf.ic.gc.ca
Canada Student Loans Program	www.hrdc-drhc.gc.ca/student_loans
Equifax	www.equifax.ca
TransUnion Canada	www.tuc.ca

Taking Care of Business

Many of us spend a great deal of our life either as an employee or an employer. Yet, a good many employees and employers have only a basic understanding (or basic misunderstanding) of their rights and obligations in the workplace.

Employees have a variety of common law and legislative rights and responsibilities in the workplace. So, too, do employers. Before delving any deeper into this area of law, however, it is important to confirm that you are indeed dealing with an employment relationship and not, say, an independent contractor relationship.

What used to be called the "master-servant" relationship usually arises from either an oral or written agreement ("You're hired. See you on Monday!"). From this basic contractual beginning, the employee agrees to work on a full time or part time basis for an employer for either a set or indeterminate period. In return, the employer agrees to pay a specific salary or hourly wage. Unionized workers are part of a "collective agreement" which also establishes an employer-employee relationship.

The distinguishing factor in these relationships is that the employer has the right to decide where, when, and how the employee's work will be done. An independent contractor or self-employed individual, however, is in a "business relationship." This relationship can also be based on an oral or written agreement to perform specific work in return for payment. One main difference between employees and independent contractors is that the self-employed contractor or "freelancer" has the freedom to decide where, when, and how that work will be done. In fact, the independent contractor does not even have to do all the work and may subcontract it out (subject to an agreement, in some cases). In most cases, the independent contractor works for a variety of clients or businesses at one time.

The law applying to employees is substantially different from that used for business relationships with independent contractors or those who are self-employed.

From a basic legal standpoint, the employee's responsibilities include:

- Showing up on time for work
- Putting in the required hours
- Behaving honestly
- Following the employer's instructions

- Keeping trade secrets
- Doing the job to the best of one's ability

More complicated, however, are the employers' responsibilities. Much of this section, therefore, focuses on the varying rights and responsibilities in the employer-employee relationship.

1. What laws govern the employment relationship?

The rights and responsibilities of workers and their employers have developed mostly over the past century or so — first, through the common law created by judges' interpretations and, more recently, in provincial and federal legislation.

In the early days of employment law, the employer's basic responsibilities included simply paying the agreed-upon wage and providing a reasonably safe workplace, while the employee was expected to show up at work on time and perform the required labour.

We all know, however, that today's workplace is more complicated than that. In fact, in the absence of a written employment contract or legislation, both employees and employers often find there are grey areas that erupt into disputes later. Employees, for example, often wonder whether they can take on a part-time job. (Moonlighting is generally permitted by common law unless there is an employment contract saying otherwise. So long as it does not interfere with an employee's work or involve a competitor, an employer would have a difficult time establishing this was a breach of the employment relationship.)

Once individuals are in a formal "employment relationship," they are protected by a variety of federal and provincial laws. Each province, for example, legislates basic working conditions, such as minimum wages, hours of work, rest periods, eating periods, overtime pay, paid public holidays, vacation with pay, pregnancy or parental leave, and termination or severance notice and pay. Many of these are minimums, it should be noted, and an employee may be entitled to additional protection.

Other laws affecting the workplace govern health and safety, human rights, retirement, benefits, workers' compensation, and unemployment insurance, to name a few. With variations in the law across Canada, as always, specific employment situations should be referred to a lawyer.

2. How do I know if I am an "employee"?

Minimum employment standards only apply to people who are considered employees. It does not protect workers who are independent contractors or freelancers. You are generally considered to be an employee if you have a supervisor who can tell you what to do and how it should be done, and if you work only for that employer and are not genuinely in business for yourself.

To find out whether you are an employee or an independent contractor, carefully consider the following factors:

	Employee	Independent Contractor
Location of work	Usually at the employer's place of business	Usually works from own office
Pay frequency	Regularly	Usually paid for finishing a job and must provide an invoice
Work schedule	Regular hours and days	Decide own work schedule based on contract load
Number of employers	One employer	May work with multiple companies at one time and may have multiple clients or customers
Duration of employment	Ongoing position or a set period	Usually hired to finish a certain project
Equipment	Uses tools or equipment provided by employer	Brings own tools or equipment
Replacement work	Usually cannot hire someone to do his or her job, for example, if that person has to be away	Can usually either hire their own employees or can arrange for a sub-contractor to do the job
Tax status	Income tax deducted from wages and submitted by employer to Canada Revenue Agency	Responsible for calculating and submitting own income tax

3. What are the minimum employment standards?

■ A minimum wage

Employment standards legislation sets out the minimum wage that applies in your province. A minimum wage is the lowest amount that an employer can legally pay an employee per hour. As of 2005, it ranged from a low of $6.25 an hour in Newfoundland and Labrador to a high of $8.50 in Nunavut. In most provinces it generally ranges from $6.50

to $8.00. The amount can also depend on the type of job, if gratuities are involved, and worker experience. For example, firms that employ persons who serve alcohol can pay a lower minimum wage, while homeworkers must be paid an amount higher than minimum wage.

■ Hours of work

Employment standards legislation sets the maximum number of hours that most employees are allowed to work and establishes the amount employees must be paid for working overtime, which is regular wage plus one half of that amount, often called time-and-a-half. Most provinces use an eight-hour day and a 40-hour week as the standard before overtime pay must kick in. But there are some exceptions. In Ontario, for example, overtime kicks in at 44 hours and the maximum workweek is 48 hours.

When it comes to length of workweeks and overtime, many provinces have different rules for some occupations, so check with your local employment standards office.

■ Public holidays

Most employees are entitled to paid time off for public holidays. Each province determines what days constitute a public holiday. Generally, they include New Year's Day, Good Friday, Victoria Day, Canada Day, Labour Day, Thanksgiving Day, Christmas Day, and Boxing Day. Some provinces include Remembrance Day or have created additional days, like Family Day in Alberta and National Holiday in Québec.

Some provinces, such as Saskatchewan, Manitoba, and New Brunswick, exclude Boxing Day as a public holiday. Generally if a major paid holiday, such as Christmas or Victoria Day falls on a weekend, then employees get another day off, usually the following Monday or a day off at some other time.

If an employee is asked to work on a public holiday, normally the employer must pay at least time-and-one-half or more and could be required to give that worker another day off.

■ Vacations and vacation pay

Generally, most employees who have worked at the same place for at least one year have the right to take at least two weeks of paid vacation every year. If an employee does not take a vacation, the employer is legally obligated to pay the employee vacation pay, which is a percentage of an employee's gross salary for the year. Generally, it is between 3 or 4 percent of the employee's annual salary and can rise up to 6 percent for long-time employees.

If you do not receive vacation pay you believe is owed you, talk to your employer. If your employer refuses to give you vacation pay, contact the employment standards office in your area.

■ Maternity and parental leave

Most women employees are entitled to a period of maternity leave, usually about 17 weeks. As well, new parents, whether by birth or adoption, are normally entitled to anywhere from 35 to 52 week parental leave, depending on the province. Both the mother and father can take parental leave.

■ Other types of leave

A number of provinces have started allowing additional types of leave that grant employee's additional days off. For example, many provinces now provide bereavement leave to deal with the death of a close family member, while some allow emergency or family responsibility leave to deal with illness involving a family member, but the length of time and rules around such leave vary.

4.   Can employers pay women differently than men?

A number of provinces have added equal pay provisions in their labour legislation that prevent employers from paying men different wages than women for the same job, with the exception of seniority systems.

As well, more provinces are adopting pay equity legislation. Under pay equity legislation, if there is a group of primarily female workers, the value of their jobs can be compared to groups in the company of primarily male workers based on the tasks and skills they both perform.

5.   What can I do if I am not paid?

It is against the law for an employer not to pay employees for their work. Employers are required to pay employees regularly, according to their usual practice or according to any agreement they have with the employees. If you have completed work and have not been paid or only paid in part, first request payment from your employer in writing. If your employer refuses to pay you, contact your employment standards office for help.

Your employment standards office can help you collect unpaid wages. There is no fee for this service. Employment standard officers can investigate the situation and order your employer to pay the money owed. You can also sue your employer for the wages owed.

6.   What happens to employees if a business is sold?

If a business is sold to a new owner, there are rules that the new owner must follow regarding existing employees. Generally, an employee should not lose any rights or money because the business was sold.

■ Employee rights under a new owner

If the employee keeps his or her job, the employee is usually entitled to maintain his or her seniority with respect to all the benefits and rights that were enjoyed before the business was sold.

■ Employee rights if fired or constructively dismissed by the new owner

If an employee is fired or constructively dismissed, the new employer will be responsible for giving the employee a reasonable notice period, or pay, instead of notice. Under the law, a "constructive dismissal" happens when the employer does not officially fire the employee but instead imposes a fundamental change in the employee's working conditions or benefits. For example, the new employer may significantly reduce pay or benefits, or demote an employee.

Often, the new employer is also responsible for giving employees severance pay. If you work for a business that is sold and lose your job without proper notice or pay in lieu of notice, or lose significant rights or benefits in your job, this may be considered wrongful or constructive dismissal. You may be able to sue both the former and new employer. For more information or advice, consult a lawyer.

7.   Are all employees covered by employment standards laws?

Even if you are considered an employee, you may not be covered by your provincial employment standards legislation. For example, if you work for the federal government, an airline, or a bank, you are usually considered an employee under federal authority and governed by the Canada Labour Code, which is not provincial legislation. The Canada Labour Code has different, but similar types of provisions.

As well, depending on the province in which you live, certain categories of jobs may also not be covered by employment standards for minimum wage, hours of work, overtime, vacations, and statutory holidays. These categories include agricultural workers, professionals and students training to be professionals, such as doctors, engineers and teachers, as well as outside sales people who earn commissions from sales made outside their employer's place of business.

8. How are employees treated in businesses operating under federal authority?

If federal law regulates your employer, you are considered an employee under federal authority and are covered by a different set of rules than most other employees in Canada. Employees under federal authority include employees of the federal government, banks, airlines, railways, telecommunications, Aboriginal bands, interprovincial transportation, post office, and radio and television stations. The Canada Labour Code sets out the main rules that apply to your employment, including hours of work, vacation entitlement, paid holiday, maternity and parental leave, and minimum wage.

■ Hours of work

Generally, an employee under federal authority is not supposed to work more than 8 hours a day and 40 hours a week. There are certain exemptions allowing up to 48 hours per week and situations where an employer can apply for a permit to have a longer work week. If the employee works more than 40 hours a week, the employer generally must pay time-and-a-half for every hour over 40 hours worked.

■ Vacations

An employee under federal authority has the right to take two weeks vacation after the first year of working or to get an amount equal to 4 percent of the yearly salary as vacation pay if the employee does not take a vacation. After the employee has worked for six consecutive years, the employee has the right to three weeks vacation or 6 percent vacation pay.

■ Paid public holidays

Employees under federal authority are entitled to nine paid public holidays. They are: New Year's Day, Good Friday, Victoria Day, Canada Day, Labour Day, Thanksgiving Day, Remembrance Day, Christmas Day, and Boxing Day. If employees have to work on a public holiday, they are entitled to two-and-a-half times their regular wage for the day.

■ Maternity and parental leave

Employees under federal authority can take maternity and parental leave after six months of employment. A natural mother has the right to 17 weeks of maternity leave. Natural or adoptive parents have the right to 37 weeks of parental leave.

■ Minimum wage

All employees under federal authority must be paid at least the hourly minimum set by the province in which they work, unless they are being trained or they are in a licensed apprentice program. If you are unsure about your rights as an employee under federal authority, contact the Federal Labour Standards office listed in your telephone book.

9.   Must employers provide pay statements?

Under law, employers must give employees pay statements showing regular wages and vacation pay. Pay statements should be given to an employee every time the person is paid and should include:

- The employee's wage rate
- The amount of time worked
- The total amount earned
- Any deductions from the employee's gross amount
- The net amount paid to the employee

For vacation pay, the statement should also show how the vacation pay was calculated. If you have questions about pay statements, contact the employment standards office listed in your telephone book or consult with an accountant.

10. What deductions from pay must an employer make?

An employer must make certain regular deductions from an employee's pay. The deductions that are required by law are income tax for most employees, employment insurance premiums, and Canada Pension Plan contributions. If an employer plans to deduct an amount not required by law, the employee must authorize the deduction in writing ahead of time.

If an employer must pay severance pay to an employee, pursuant to a judgment or a settlement for wrongful dismissal, then only income tax and, in some cases, employment insurance, can be deducted.

For additional information about deductions, contact the Canada Revenue Agency. For assistance in making deductions or submitting remittances, contact an accountant.

Unions

11. What is a union?

A union is an organization of employees. The history of unions dates back to trade associations of the late 1800s.

The structure of trade unions and of their relationship to employers differs significantly from one country to the next. In Canada the structure of trade unions is very similar in all provinces and in the federal jurisdiction. There are small variations in the law from province to province while the laws governing union management relationships are usually set out in labour relations legislation.

Labour laws usually define what constitutes a trade union. For example, the Ontario Labour Relations Act defines a trade union as "an organization formed for purposes that include the regulation of relations between employees and employers."

Labour laws usually grant trade unions the right to engage in collective bargaining and enter into collective agreements. Most trade unions active in Canada are large national organizations representing thousands of employees. Small, local, independent organizations can be trade unions, however, if they follow the requirements of the local legislation and rulings by the provincial labour boards.

12. What do unions do?

Unions have two main functions. They:

- Represent particular groups of employees in establishing their conditions of employment, as set out in a collective agreement
- Ensure that employers comply with the agreement

The group of employees represented in industry is usually on a plant-by-plant basis, in construction on a trade basis, and in retail on a store or group of stores basis. Special unions tend to represent large groups of employees in the governmental sector, in teaching, fire fighting, and the police.

▪ Starting a union

Unions arise when a number of employees concerned about work conditions either approach an existing union or form their own, by establishing by-laws, electing officers, and signing up members. The group then seeks union certification through the provincial labour board. For example, in a company that has both plant workers and office workers, the concerned employees may include a few plant workers seeking to represent all the other plant workers. In this example, the entire group of plant workers is called the "bargaining unit" and the few plant workers who seek to represent them will likely be part of the union organizing committee.

The concerned employees who formed a union must then do certain things to convince the local labour board to certify the union's right to represent the bargaining unit. First, they must show that a certain percentage of employees in the bargaining unit support the union. The percentage of support required varies from 25 percent in Saskatchewan to 45 percent in British Columbia. Check with your local labour relations board to determine what percentage of support you need to move forward.

To show support, the union will collect membership cards or applications for membership signed by individual employees who are part of the bargaining unit. Once it obtains the necessary percentage of the bargaining unit's support, the union will submit its application for certification to the local labour board.

After an application has been submitted, labour boards will usually order that a certification vote be held at the workplace within a specified time.

During days leading up to the vote, labour boards often contact the employer and the union to determine which employees are part of the bargaining unit and therefore entitled to vote.

Many labour boards have extensive rules as to which groups may form their own bargaining unit. In the industrial sector in Ontario, for example, plant employees and office employees are usually separate, as are full-time and part-time employees and security guards. Each of these separate groups would be part of separate bargaining units although, except for security guards, they could all be part of the same union. Rules about groups and bargaining units are both complex and evolving. For more information regarding these rules, contact your labour board directly.

Once it has been decided which employees form the bargaining unit, a voters' list is created. Sometimes disputes arise between employers and the union as to which employees form part of the bargaining unit. Sometimes employers want supervisors excluded from the bargaining units or want as small a bargaining unit as possible. The union, on the other hand, might want to include all employees and get the biggest possible bargaining unit.

The vote is usually conducted by secret ballot and is normally overseen by a labour board officer. Most provinces require more than 50 percent of the employees to vote in favour of union representation before a union can be certified. The union is the bargaining unit's representative.

■ Choosing the union leadership

The union leadership at the workplace is usually elected by the employees in that bargaining unit. Depending on the union and the size of the employee group, a union committee may be elected and a number of union stewards chosen. Stewards are the employees' day-to-day representatives. They are regular employees, but most collective agreements give them special rights to carry out the task of representing employee concerns. More senior union officials in district, provincial, and national offices will be full-time paid union personnel. There will probably be a mix of elected officials and appointed professional staff.

■ Terminating a union's representation rights

The provincial labour board is also involved in situations where union representation rights are terminated. Employees may apply to their local labour board for a vote to terminate a union's right to represent them. Usually such applications may be made only during very specific time periods, such as during the last two months before a collective agreement is to expire or where no collective agreement has existed for a year.

If employees wish to apply to terminate the union's right to represent them, they must submit a formal application to the labour board. The application must be supported by a minimum number of the bargaining unit members, which varies according to province.

Most labour board legislation specifically requires that employers have no involvement in an employee application for decertification. To obtain forms for applying for decertification or for more information about the creation of union representation rights, contact your local labour relations board.

13. What is a collective agreement?

Collective agreements are deals negotiated by unions and employers. Collective agreements provide certain terms and conditions of employment for a group of employees called the bargaining unit, who are represented by a trade union. The collective agreement establishes the rights of employees and the union at the workplace.

Any term or condition of employment can be the topic for negotiations and be dealt with in the collective agreement. For very large bargaining units, the collective agreement may be hundreds of pages long. In a typical manufacturing plant or retail store, collective agreements are more usually about 30 pages long. Collective agreements often deal with the following:

- Wage rates
- Health benefits
- Layoff rules
- The right to challenge employer disciplinary actions
- Vacation entitlement
- Holidays
- Bereavement leave
- Jury duty leave
- Promotion selection rules
- Occupational safety provisions

The collective agreement will also require that union dues be deducted from all the employees, by the employer, and sent to the union.

■ Negotiating a collective agreement

Within a short time after the union receives certification by a labour board, the union will begin the collective bargaining or negotiating process with the employer. The purpose of the negotiations is to reach a consensus on a collective agreement.

In negotiations the employees will be represented by an elected committee and a professional trade union staff member who is employed for this purpose.

Once a tentative agreement is reached between the employer and union representatives, union members usually have an opportunity to vote on it. Normally if 50 percent of the union members who actually vote accept the agreement, it then becomes legally binding. If the union members do not accept the agreement, the employer and the union representatives may continue negotiating. Alternatively, the union may call for a strike vote. Most strike votes require 50 percent support from those voting. Very rarely, where a union can neither obtain a ratification or authorization to strike, it will abandon its right to represent the employees.

Typically, the entire process takes as long as six months for the first collective agreement to be negotiated. Renewal agreements take a few months to negotiate as well, but while these are negotiated the old agreement remains in force.

Collective agreements are most often for a two-year period. As the expiry of the period of agreement nears, the union and the employer will begin negotiations for a renewal.

If the employer and the union cannot agree to a first or renewal agreement, then the union can recommend that employees engage in a strike to put pressure on the employer. There are complex rules that govern both the approval process and legal timing of a strike. Employers can also lock out employees to put pressure on the union, but lockouts are in fact rare. While a collective agreement is in force, it can be changed only by voluntary, mutual agreement, which normally requires labour board approval.

14. What are an employee's rights under a collective agreement?

Collective agreements deal with many employee rights. Six examples of common rights found in most collective agreements include:

- Seniority
- Seniority layoff
- Just cause discipline
- Vacations
- Holidays
- Grievance and arbitration procedures

■ Seniority

Many rights in a collective agreement are based upon an employee's seniority.

Seniority is approximately the same as an employee's length of service. Note that certain periods may not count toward an employee's seniority even though they are part of the length of service. For example, if an employee is promoted to a management position and later returns to the bargaining unit, some or all the period in management may not count toward the employee's seniority even though it is part of the employee's length of service.

Length of service is also used in situations where the employee is pursuing his or her personal rights, such as in calculating how much vacation an employee is entitled to.

Often, the length of service for the purpose of determining seniority does not begin until an employee completes a probationary or trial period of employment.

■ Seniority layoff

Seniority is often used as a consideration in situations where there is a competition between two or more employees, or there is a choice to be made between employees. Such situations include times when someone is to be laid off or transferred. Common in collective agreements is a rule that if a layoff is required, employees will be selected in reverse order of seniority. Employees most recently hired will therefore be the ones most likely laid off. It is a "last in, first out" rule.

The layoff rule will usually be modified, however, to allow the employer to retain the services of employees who are especially needed because of their skills and abilities. For example, if the company only had one electrician, he or she would probably not be laid off because of this general rule.

The seniority rule can be applied either on a bargaining unit basis, or on a department or classification basis.

Where there is a surplus of employees in a particular department or job such that some people must be laid off, unionized employees may have seniority-based rights allowing them to claim someone else's job even though the other employee works in a different department. This process of displacing a junior employee is called "bumping." The extent of bumping rights should be clearly dealt with in the collective agreement, although in fact many collective agreements are unclear about the exact procedure.

■ "Just cause" discipline

The third right commonly found in collective agreements is the requirement that discharge or discipline of employees must be for just cause. This rule probably will not apply until the employee finishes a probationary period of employment.

The single most common dispute between unions and employers is what constitutes just cause for discipline. Many thousands of arbitration cases have been held to resolve such disputes.

The collective agreement may have specific rules in which case such provisions answer the question. For example, many agreements say that an employee absent without leave for more than three days is considered to have terminated his or her employment.

In most situations, a particular disciplinary decision is only determined through the experience of a seasoned advisor.

■ Vacation

A fourth right commonly found in collective agreements will usually ensure that employees are progressively entitled to more vacation with each year of service. Thus, an additional week of entitlement might be added after, say, five years of service and another week after 14 years.

The amount of vacation pay an employee receives is often a slightly separate issue from the amount of time off he or she is entitled to.

Vacation pay is usually a percentage of the previous year's earning. Most commonly, an employee will receive 2 percent of the previous year's earnings as vacation pay multiplied by each week of vacation the employee is entitled to.

Collective agreements vary widely as to whether an employee must take vacation, when it must be taken, and how it is scheduled. At a minimum, most agreements require that an employee actually take at least two weeks vacation each year.

■ Holidays

A fifth right included in most collective agreements typically provides for 9 to 13 holiday days per year. Usually, employees must qualify for the holidays, following such rules as having to work the scheduled workday before and after a holiday.

■ Grievance and arbitration procedures

The sixth right that is included in almost all collective agreements is a grievance and arbitration procedure. There are many variations.

The purpose of the procedure is to resolve collective agreement disputes between employees and the union on the one side and the employer on the other.

15. How does the grievance and arbitration process work?

Every collective agreement usually contains some kind of grievance and arbitration procedure.

Essentially, arbitration is only pursued if the dispute is not resolved during the grievance process.

Grievance procedures usually have two or three steps or stages involving progressively higher levels of management and union representation. Also, the grievance and arbitration clause sets time limits for each stage.

■ Types of disputes covered

The most common dispute is whether a discipline or discharge was proper. Examples of other disputes that can be resolved using the grievance and arbitration procedure include a claim by an employee that the wage rate set out in the agreement has not been paid, that an overtime assignment was wrongly made, or that a safety shoe allowance has not been paid.

Employees are usually required to first discuss most complaints with their supervisor. If the supervisor cannot resolve the problem, then the dispute will proceed to higher levels of the grievance process as necessary.

■ Steps from grievance to arbitration

The right to go to higher levels in the grievance procedure and ultimately to arbitration almost always sits with the trade union, not the employee. The union may therefore decide for many reasons not to pursue the employee's complaint.

In situations that impact many employees, unions usually have the right to submit a group complaint, often called a policy grievance. In a policy grievance, no particular employee involved in filing the grievance is named.

If the matter is not resolved at some level of the grievance process, the union may take the matter to arbitration. Arbitration is a type of informal court. The arbitrator is the judge, but unlike the courts, this judge is paid by both the union and the employer in equal amounts, regardless of who wins the case. The arbitrator can be selected by agreement or, if either the union or employer asks, by the provincial ministry of labour.

In earlier generations, it was common to find three-person arbitration boards consisting of a neutral arbitrator, an arbitrator appointed by the union, and an arbitrator appointed by the employer. Not surprisingly, most decisions were two-to-one. Today a single arbitrator is more commonly used.

At an arbitration hearing, both sides present their case. Facts must either be agreed to, or proved by witnesses and other evidence such as documents. Following the hearing, which can take many days if the situation is complex, the arbitrator will usually take some time to consider the problem and then issue a written decision. The arbitrator's decision is legally binding and final.

Termination of Employment

16. Can an employer end an employee's job at any time?

Contrary to what many employees think, an employer can end a non-union employee's job at any time and for any reason. Nonetheless, the employer is required by law to give the employee a minimum amount of notice or pay instead of notice, unless the employee was fired for willful misconduct or neglect of duty.

There are three basic ways to be dismissed:

- You can be fired
- You can be laid off for long enough that your employment is considered terminated

• You can be put in a position where you are made to accept a lesser position or made to quit

■ Getting fired

Many employees who lose their jobs are fired. Generally, it is proper practice for an employer to give an employee a termination letter stating that his or her job has ended and when that person's last day of work is.

■ Getting laid off

Some employees who work for companies that do not always have enough work, or whose plant shuts down from time to time, get laid off. Employees are usually informed of a lay off with a written notice. In many cases people who have been laid off have not lost their jobs permanently and will usually have the right to return to their jobs if the company gets new work or re-opens the plant.

If you have been laid off in Ontario for more than 13 weeks, your employment will be considered terminated and you will have the same rights as if fired. If you are laid off, but you continue to receive fringe benefits from your employer, you will not be considered terminated until 35 weeks after you were first laid off. Speak with a lawyer if you have been laid off to determine if the lay off was really a constructive dismissal.

■ Constructive dismissal

Sometimes employees are not fired directly, but can lose certain rights or even be made to quit their jobs. This is called *constructive dismissal.* Under the law, those who have experienced constructive dismissal are considered to have all the same rights as those who are fired. Situations of constructive dismissal include:

• If the employer decides to substantially change an employee's job description without the employee's consent
• If an employer reduces an employee's pay
• If an employee is made to quit because of harassment or intimidation

For additional information about termination, contact the employment standards office listed in your telephone book or speak with a lawyer.

17. What are my rights if I am fired?

Under employment standards law most workers have the right to receive a minimum amount of notice or pay instead of notice, unless the employee was fired because of willful misconduct or neglect of duty.

As well, the employee must have worked for the company for a minimum period, ranging from 30 days in Newfoundland and Labrador and Manitoba, to 6 months in New Brunswick and P.E.I. (Other provinces require three months.) In some circumstances, employees may also have the right to receive minimum severance pay depending on the size of the company, and the province in which they live.

Companies regulated by federal law, such as banks, airlines, or transportation companies, have different minimum termination and severance pay rules. As well, if you belong to a union, or you have a written employment contract, the rules are different again. To find out about your rights, ask your union representative or read a copy of your employment contract. Contact a lawyer if you have legal questions or need advice.

18. What is the proper notice period or pay in lieu of notice?

Most employees have the right to be given notice about their dismissal if they are fired without a good legal reason. This means being told you will be let go in a stated number of weeks and that you can still work during this period. If your employer wants you to leave right away, you have the right to be paid in place of the notice.

■ Notice requirements set by legislation

Provincial legislation sets out notice periods, which are based on years of service. They differ according to province and range from no notice required for recent employees to eight weeks or more for long-time employees.

■ Notice requirements set by the courts

Although each province's employment standards legislation sets out minimum notice requirements, court cases have established that almost all employees are actually entitled to longer notice periods. To determine if an employee is entitled to longer notice time, the courts will consider many factors, including:

• If there was an employment contract that gave the employee more rights
• The importance and value of the job
• The number of years the employee worked with the company
• The employee's age and the likelihood of the employee finding similar work in the future

Claims for wrongful dismissal can involve substantial amounts of money. If you think you are entitled to additional pay because you were not given enough notice, consult a lawyer.

■ Mass terminations

Some provinces like Québec, Saskatchewan, Nova Scotia, and Ontario have created provisions creating payouts and special notice requirements for group layoffs involving a large number of people. In these instances, a minimum notice period is set based on the number of firings and can range up to 16 weeks (Ontario).

■ Severance

Among the provinces, only Ontario has a severance clause, stipulating that if you lose your job through no fault of your own and have worked for at least five years for a company whose annual payroll is at least $2.5 million, you usually have the right to severance pay. Generally, severance pay is equal to one week's pay for every year you worked, to a maximum of 26 weeks. Federally, the *Canada Labour Code* also provides for severance pay for employees with 12 months service or more.

If you are entitled to severance pay, your employer is usually required to pay you the entire amount within two weeks after your job ends. Your employer is also required to pay all wages and vacation pay owed to you within seven days of termination.

19. What is proper notice for federal employees?

If you work for a company that is regulated by federal law, such as an airline, bank, or transportation company, you are not covered by the same laws as most other employees. Instead, you are generally covered by the *Canada Labour Code*. The *Code* sets out three main rights for most employees who lose their job without a good legal reason. First, they have the right to be given notice. Second, they have the right to severance pay. Third, they have the right to be paid money owing in a timely manner.

■ Notice requirements under the *Canada Labour Code*

If you have worked for at least three months, you are usually entitled to receive two weeks' notice if the employer fires you without a good legal reason. A good legal reason normally means willful misconduct or neglect of duty. If your employer wants you to leave right away, however, you have the right to receive two weeks pay instead of notice.

■ Severance pay eligibility

To be eligible for severance pay generally depends on how long you have been employed and if you were fired without a good legal reason. If you have worked between one and three years, you have the right to receive five days of wages as severance pay, unless the dismissal is for just cause. If you have worked for more than three years, you have the right to receive two days of pay for every year you worked, unless the dismissal is for just cause.

■ Employer required to pay within 30 days of termination

Other than notice or severance pay, if your employer owes you regular wages, vacation pay, or overtime when your job ends, you have the right to receive full payment of all money owed to you within 30 days of termination.

For additional information about your rights on termination under the *Canada Labour Code*, contact the Federal Labour Standards office listed in your telephone book.

Contact a lawyer if you require legal advice or assistance.

20. What is wrongful dismissal?

It is important to determine if you were wrongfully dismissed because you might be entitled to money from your employer. If you were fired, you may be entitled to notice or pay instead of notice and, in limited situations, possibly severance pay. Under the law, if your employer refuses to pay you what you are entitled to, then you have been wrongfully dismissed. If your employer gave you proper notice or paid you all the money you were entitled to, it is not considered wrongful dismissal even if there was no cause for firing you. If the employer had a good legal reason or cause for firing you, then you are not entitled to notice or pay instead of notice, and you are not considered wrongfully dismissed.

21. What is "just cause" for firing an employee?

An employee can be fired without proper notice if there was "just cause." Cause for firing an employee may include:

- An illegal act at the workplace, such as stealing or damaging property or violent behaviour
- Misrepresentation of important qualifications, such as saying you have a degree that you have not earned

• Insubordination, such as refusing to do work assigned to you
• Sexually harassing other employees
• Constantly being late for work
• Fraud

22. What is not "just cause" for firing an employee?

Sometimes an employee does something wrong — but this wrong does not constitute a good legal reason to be fired without notice or pay. Reasons for firing an employee that are not cause under the law include:

• If an employee does something minor and corrects the mistake
• If an employee's work is not up to standard and the employer does nothing to address the problem
• If your employer does not like you
• If your employer discriminates against you because of your sex, race, religion, disability, age, or sexual orientation, unless permitted by law

Claims for wrongful dismissal can involve substantial amounts of money. If you think you were wrongfully dismissed, consult a lawyer.

23. What are my options if wrongfully dismissed?

If you have been dismissed from your employment without a good legal reason and have not been given proper notice, or pay instead of notice, you have been wrongfully dismissed and have rights under the law. You also have the right to sue your employer. In many cases, employers do not want the expense of going to court and prefer to pay the employee to settle the matter. Few cases actually get to trial, and those that do often settle during litigation. Normally, you or your lawyer will want to try negotiating with your employer before starting a lawsuit or before the lawsuit goes to court.

■ Suing for wrongful dismissal

If you decide to sue your employer, you can ask for three types of compensation:

• You can claim you were wrongfully dismissed and ask for the amount of money that equals the notice period you were entitled to.
• You can ask for special compensation if your employer fired you in a way that was cruel or humiliating, and because of this you suffered mental distress.

- You can ask for money to be awarded to you as a way of punishment if your employer fired you in a malicious way or with the intent of causing you personal embarrassment or harm.

Usually, claims for mental distress and employer punishment are only allowed in very extreme cases. The chances of you winning in court will depend on the details of your situation. If you think you were wrongfully dismissed and you want to know your legal options or start a lawsuit, consult a lawyer.

Employment Insurance

24. What is Employment Insurance (E.I.)?

Employment insurance is a program run by the government of Canada to reduce the financial hardship that many experience when they lose their jobs or are unable to work. Most employees pay employment insurance premiums as a deduction from their pay.

You are usually entitled to receive benefits in three general circumstances:

- If you lose your job through no fault of your own, you can collect general benefits
- If you need time off during pregnancy or to care for a child, you can collect maternity or parental benefits
- If you cannot work because of sickness, you can collect sickness benefits

There are many rules established to determine if a person is entitled to collect benefits. Contact the nearest Human Resources and Social Development office for assistance. Office locations are listed in the telephone book.

25. Who is eligible for general benefits?

If you are an employee who pays employment insurance premiums and you lose your job through no fault of your own, you may be entitled to receive general employment benefits. Eligibility is based on the reason your job ended and how long you had been working there.

Generally, you will be eligible for employment insurance benefits unless you quit without a valid reason or were fired for doing something wrong. There are several valid reasons to quit a job and still be entitled to employment insurance benefits, including when:

- You face sexual harassment or other types of harassment
- You need to move with a spouse or dependent child to another part of the country
- You experience discrimination
- The working conditions are dangerous to your health or safety
- You have to care for a family member and cannot be employed at the same time
- You get hired for another job which then falls through
- Your wages or salary are reduced suddenly
- You have to work excessive overtime or your employer refuses to pay you for overtime work
- You have a difficult relationship with your supervisor, but are not the main cause of the problem

On the other hand, there are several reasons for being fired that could make you ineligible for employment insurance, including when:

- You did not follow your supervisor's instructions
- You stole something
- You were persistently late for work after being warned
- You got into a physical fight with someone during work

If you are unsure about the reason you were fired, check your record of employment, which is a form that your employer must give you when your job ends. This record must include the reason you were fired.

To qualify for employment insurance benefits you must have worked for a certain period before you lost your job. The qualifying time is based on the region in which you live and its unemployment rate. The amount of qualifying time is calculated in hours, but generally, you need to have worked between 10 and 20 regular workweeks within the last 52 weeks.

There are also special rules for people who are in the workforce for the first time or who were out of the workforce for some time before their last job. If you are in this situation, you will generally have to work more hours than most other workers before qualifying for benefits.

To find out how many hours you need to work to qualify for general benefits, contact the local Human Resources and Social Development centre listed in the telephone book.

26. How do you apply for benefits?

Most employees whose employment ends or who need time off to care for a new child or an illness are entitled to at least one type of employment insurance benefit. There are four different types:

- General benefits
- Maternity benefits
- Parental benefits
- Sickness benefits

To apply for any type of employment insurance benefit, you will need to fill out a form from the Human Resources and Social Development centre in your area. To maximize the amount of benefits you receive, submit your application to the local centre as soon as you leave your job. For maternity, sickness, or parental benefits, the nearest office will mail you a copy of the application form if you call. You can then have someone else submit it for you if necessary. If your application is accepted, you will have to wait about four weeks from the time you applied before you will receive the first payment.

To fill out the application form, you need your Social Insurance Number and your record of employment. A record of employment is a form that your employer is required to give you when you leave your job, stating how long you worked and how much you were paid. If you have questions about your application, contact the employment insurance officer who is assigned to your file or the Human Resources and Social Development Canada centre where you applied. The nearest centre is listed in the Blue pages of your telephone book.

27. How much money will you receive?

If you qualify for employment insurance benefits, then, in most circumstances, you will receive 55 percent of your salary to a maximum of $413 per week.

Your benefits can be reduced in a number of situations. First, if you have collected a certain amount of employment insurance benefits in the past, you may only be entitled to as much as 50 percent of your salary to a maximum of $413 per week.

Your benefits could also be reduced if you have other income while collecting benefits. You are allowed to earn up to 25 percent of your weekly benefits or $50 per week, whichever is more, without reducing the amount of your benefits. Beyond that amount, your benefits will usually be reduced one dollar for every dollar you earn. Other forms of income that might cause your benefits to be reduced include money from a wrongful dismissal lawsuit, money made from your own business, retirement income from a government or employment pension, and termination pay. Even if you receive these payments after you have finished collecting benefits, you may be required to pay back all or part of the benefits you collected. (Note that income from private RRSPs and disability pensions will not reduce your benefits.)

Your benefits may be increased if you are part of a low-income family and have dependent children under the age of 18.

Finally, if you worked on and off over the past 26 weeks, you may still be entitled to receive employment insurance benefits, but the amount will be based on a special calculation.

28. How long will general benefits last?

If you are receiving general employment insurance benefits, they will last between 14 and 45 weeks depending on where you live, how long you worked before you lost your job, and whether you stop collecting benefits for a period. Typically, a person who worked for a long time and lives in an area with high unemployment will receive more than someone who has worked a shorter time and lives in an area with lower unemployment.

There are circumstances where your benefits can be put on hold for a short time. This might happen if you get some temporary work or enroll in a course. In both of these circumstances, your benefits will be suspended. For example, if you are entitled to 20 weeks of benefits, and you take a temporary job after collecting only 8 weeks, you still have 12 weeks of benefits that you are eligible to collect. After the job is over, if you do not have any work and need to start collecting benefits again, you will usually be able to receive the 12 remaining weeks. Still, you must use up the remaining benefits within one year from the day you originally applied for benefits or you will not be able to collect all of what you are eligible for.

29. What must I do to continue receiving benefits?

Employment Insurance benefits are paid to people who are looking for work and who are not earning income. You are not entitled to receive benefits without meeting these two requirements. To make sure you meet these requirements, you must follow Human Resources and Social Development reporting system.

The reporting system requires you to fill out a card, called a claimant report, and file it with the Human Resources and Social Development office that is handling your claim.

You will be required to explain how you have been looking for work, which includes reading the paper, making calls, and applying for jobs that are suited to you. You are also required to report any other income or employment you get while receiving benefits, which can reduce the amount of benefits you are entitled to. You should also be aware that if you leave the country your benefits may be suspended for as long as you are out of Canada.

You can file a claimant report in person, by mail, or by a telephone with touch-tone service. You should receive claimant report cards in the mail before you receive your first employment insurance payment.

If touch-tone filing is available in your area, you will get information about it in the mail a couple of weeks after you apply for benefits. If you choose to use touch-tone filing, you will only be able to receive your cheques by direct deposit. If you arrange for direct deposit, your benefits will be put straight into your bank account.

If you make a false statement at any time while applying for benefits or reporting your situation, there can be penalties that include losing your benefits, having to pay back money you collected, and even being prosecuted for a criminal offence. If you forget to report something or make a mistake in reporting, tell your employment insurance officer immediately. As long as you come forward on your own and they have not started to investigate you, the officer can decide not to penalize or prosecute you.

30. How do maternity and parental benefits work?

Generally, an employee who is pregnant, just gave birth, or adopted a child is entitled to a leave of absence. In some cases, employees have the right to get their jobs back when the leave is over, but employers are not required to pay employees during their time off.

There are two types of leave available to employees that employment insurance will provide benefits for: maternity leave for pregnant women and parental leave for both mothers and fathers. The amount of time you are covered and can be away from work depends on the province in which you live.

■ Maternity leave

Most women employees are entitled to a period of pregnancy leave, usually about 17 weeks. When leave actually begins varies by province, from a high of 17 weeks before the baby is due to a low of 11 weeks. Mothers may also be eligible for parental leave after birth.

To obtain maternity leave you must have worked for the employer for a required period (ranging from 13 weeks in Ontario to a year in Alberta and Nova Scotia). You must also give the employer notice before the leave starts and usually provide a medical certificate indicating the baby's due date.

▪ Parental leave

If you are a new parent, whether by birth or adoption, you are normally entitled to anywhere from 35 to 52 week parental leave, depending on the province. Both the mother and father can take parental leave.

Parental leave normally begins from the day the pregnancy leave ends or the day the child is born or from the day the adopted child is brought home. Since a natural mother also qualifies for pregnancy leave, she can often combine pregnancy leave with parental leave. There is a two-week waiting period, however, before benefits are payable. This means that the total number of weeks where payments will be made is 50.

▪ Job protection: Federal workers

Employees returning from maternity or parental leave do not necessarily have to be re-instated in their last jobs. However, pregnant women working for federally regulated employers may take the entire 50 weeks and must be re-instated, while fathers and adoptive parents have job protection for 35 weeks.

▪ Job Protection: Provincial workers

Job protection rules for employees returning from maternity or parental leave are different in each province. Generally, the employee must be reinstated to his or her job or a comparable position at the same level of pay and often the same level of seniority. Employees are also normally entitled to participate in the benefit plan during their absence and their pensions should not be affected provided they continue to make necessary contributions.

▪ The amount of weekly benefits

The amount of weekly benefits you are entitled to is 55 percent of your insurable weekly earnings to an annual maximum salary of $39,000. This gives a weekly benefit maximum of $413.

31. What are sickness benefits?

Most employees are eligible for employment insurance if they are sick or injured. There are rules to determine who qualifies for sickness benefits, how much you are entitled to, how long you can collect the benefits, and how to apply.

Generally, to qualify for sickness benefits you must be unable to work because of sickness or injury, and you must have worked for at least 20 weeks during the last 52. If you become sick or injured and are already receiving another kind of employment insurance benefit, you may also be eligible for sickness benefits. However, you will generally not be eligible for sickness benefits if you are receiving workers' compensation.

In most cases, you are entitled to 55 percent of your salary to a maximum of $413 per week. Usually, you can receive up to 15 weeks of sickness benefits. If you return to work and then have to leave again due to the same sickness or injury, your benefits may be reinstated. Note that your benefits will have to be used up within one year from the day you originally applied for benefits or you must re-apply.

Before you apply, you will need a medical certificate signed by a doctor to submit with your application. The medical certificate should explain your condition, why you cannot work, and how long you will be off work.

Application forms for sickness benefits are available at a Human Resources and Social Development centre. If you are too sick to go in person, you can have the office send you an application and then have someone else submit it for you. You should apply for sickness benefits as soon as you stop working. If you wait to apply, you may not get as much money as you would if you applied right away. If you were too sick to apply, note this on the application and you might be able to collect the full amount.

Contact the Human Resources and Social Development centre in your area if you have questions about sickness benefits or if you want to apply. The number and address is listed in the Blue pages of your telephone book.

32. What if I have been refused benefits?

If you have been refused employment insurance benefits, you have the right to appeal the decision. Before appealing, find out the reasons behind the decision and see if there is any wrong or missing information in your application. Speak with your employment insurance officer and give that person any new information that may affect the decision.

If your officer still refuses to approve your application, you have 30 days from receipt of the original decision to submit an appeal. To appeal, write a letter to the Human Resources Centre that notified you of the decision. In the letter, clearly state why you are appealing.

The Board of Referees is a three-person panel that holds an informal hearing that you attend. At the hearing, you will have a chance to explain your side and someone from the employment insurance office will be given an opportunity to explain the original decision. After hearing all the information, the Board of Referees will make a decision. If they disagree with you, you may have the right to appeal the decision to an "umpire," who is usually a judge. Because this type of appeal is more complicated, you should consult a lawyer. If you are unsure how to appeal a decision, call the Human Resources and Social Development centre listed in the telephone book.

Privacy In The Workplace

33. Are cameras allowed in the workplace?

The use of surveillance cameras in the workplace in Canada is steadily increasing. Often, surveillance cameras are installed to deter employee theft, vandalism, assault and sexual harassment. Hidden cameras are also used to secretly record suspected criminal or improper activity. Video surveillance is common in retail stores, financial institutions, manufacturing plants, casinos, and wherever cash or inventory is found. More disturbing to some, however, is that employers are now using hidden and even openly disclosed surveillance cameras to routinely record job activities. Does the employer have that right? Generally speaking, Canadian courts have not looked favourably on employers who install surveillance cameras to spy on employees without good reason.

■ Surveillance in the non-unionized workplace

In the non-unionized workplace, employees enjoy a general right to privacy unless they give it up in their employment contract or otherwise waive the right expressly. That said, in civil court, employers have used surveillance tapes in wrongful dismissal cases to prove they had "just cause" to dismiss an employee, when a worker pushed or threatened a manager for instance.

Surveillance may infringe upon an employee's right to privacy if cameras are installed only to monitor the general conduct, behaviour, or efficiency of a specific employee or group of employees. If, however, the camera is installed as an investigative aid for a specific time to monitor an area for suspected criminal activity, the surveillance is likely justified.

The key question is often whether there is a reasonable expectation of privacy. An employee who works in plain view of the public does not have a reasonable expectation. Similarly, employees and the general public who use the front lobbies of businesses, customer service areas, waiting rooms, or parcel pick-up areas would have little expectation of privacy. In washrooms, change areas, and locker rooms, however, it is reasonable for anyone (employee or customer) to expect privacy. Simply put, an employer would likely not be allowed to target particular workers without cause, but may be able to target general areas in the non-unionized workplace with surveillance.

In criminal matters, Canada's *Charter of Rights and Freedoms* has been used to protect workers' privacy in non-unionized settings. A worker "caught on tape" committing a crime could argue at a criminal trial that he had a reasonable expectation of privacy in his circumstances (for example, in a workplace washroom) and that his right to privacy had been infringed so as to "bring the administration of justice into disrepute." The worker could then ask the judge to exclude from evidence the videotape that showed him, for example, committing theft or vandalizing his employer's property. If the court held that the worker's privacy rights had been infringed and then excluded the videotape, the accused might be acquitted.

■ Surveillance in the Unionized Workplace

Unionized employees should look to their collective agreement to see if it prohibits management's use of video surveillance to observe workers. In a unionized workplace, video surveillance has been used successfully to monitor employees' performance and investigate workers suspected of criminal activity. When unions grieve on behalf of workers disciplined by the employer, management will often tender videotapes as evidence. The tapes are used to prove discipline was justified because the employee broke a workplace rule or regulation, engaged in behaviour that violated the collective agreement, or committed a criminal act.

In a union dispute, a labour arbitrator, not the courts, will lay down the rules governing the use of surveillance. Labour arbitrators usually consider the following questions when deciding whether they should take a look at management's surveillance videotape of a unionized worker:

- Was it reasonable, in all the circumstances, for management to request video surveillance of the worker?
- Was the surveillance conducted in a reasonable manner?
- Were other alternatives open to management to obtain the evidence it sought?

If the first two questions are answered "yes" but the third is answered "no," then the surveillance videotape will probably be viewed.

34. Does an employer have to give notice, such as using signs, that there is video surveillance?

Employers who want video surveillance in a general area should post notices and signs in conspicuous places that are easily readable, even from a distance. Wherever they are placed, the signs and notices should clearly convey the message that the area is being monitored. The purpose of the signage is to remove any reasonable expectation of privacy. Signs and notices should be written in both of Canada's official languages, English and French. Multilingual signs should be used in retail stores, banks, or businesses in areas where other languages are spoken. For greater impact, the signs and notices can even be hung beneath a camera attached to a video monitor displaying a live action picture.

35. Is audio surveillance allowed in the workplace?

Many surveillance cameras are capable of recording not only pictures, but also sound. Recording private communications without the consent of those speaking or without legal authority (such as a warrant issued to police by a judge) is a criminal offence. A key aspect of this area of law is the expectation of privacy of those involved in the conversation. If there is a reasonable expectation of privacy, then permission or legal authority must be sought to record or listen in on conversations using electronic devices.

Generally in Canada, surveillance cameras can only be used to record video, not audio communications. Even in public places, there is likely a reasonable expectation in some circumstances (such as a quiet discussion between two people) that a conversation is private.

36. Can an employer conduct a body search of an employee suspected of theft? Can a locker or car be searched?

The Canadian *Charter of Rights and Freedoms* protects everyone from unreasonable or unauthorized search and seizure by government authorities, such as police. In the workplace, however, the *Charter* does not often apply to the private employer-employee relationship.

That said, the Canada Labour Code, Canadian Human Rights Code, provincial human rights codes, and collective agreements between labour and management can each affect the issue of whether employee searches are reasonable or whether evidence they uncover can be used against the employee.

Generally, employers have no greater right than other citizens to search someone's personal belongings or body without justification or permission. An attempt to search someone's body without a reasonable excuse could be considered an assault under the law. A search of a worker's car or gym bag without permission could be considered trespass. An employee, however, cannot prevent a search of any property that belongs to the employer, such as a work desk, computer, or locker.

While an employer usually cannot search a person's body, it may be quite reasonable for a manager who suspects theft, substance abuse, or some other misdeed on the job to ask the employee for his or her co-operation in emptying pockets, purses, or knapsacks. The employee does not have to comply, but the employer would be free to draw conclusions based on the refusal.

Even with permission, a search of an employee's clothed body should always be done by someone of the same sex to avoid later allegations of improper touching. Also, any search of a person or property by an employer should be done with one or more witnesses on hand.

Where criminal behaviour is suspected, an employer would be wise to contact the police and delay any searches until the proper authorities are on site.

Sexual Harassment

37. What is sexual harassment?

Sexual harassment generally refers to unwanted sexual comments or actions. If it takes place at work or outside work by your co-workers or your employer, your provincial human rights code and the Canadian *Human Rights Act* make this conduct illegal. Some types of behaviour could also be offences under the *Criminal Code*.

There are at least five types of behaviour that are considered sexual harassment if they are unwelcome. Sexual harassment can take the form of spoken words, gestures, showing offensive or obscene pictures, physical contact, or intimidation. The following are examples of each.

■ Spoken words or sounds

Spoken words or sounds that are offensive may be considered sexual harassment if they occur on an ongoing basis. For example, it may be sexual harassment if someone is:

- Always talking about sex
- Telling jokes about sex or about gender roles

- Making whistling or kissing sounds
- Making sexual comments that are embarrassing
- Using vulgar language
- Making sexist remarks or insults
- Questioning someone about his or her sex life
- Making sexual threats or put downs

■ Gestures

Obscene or threatening gestures can sometimes be considered sexual harassment. These may be obvious or subtle and may be made by someone's eyes, face, hands, or other parts of the body. Even an idea or thought that is made known to others by a gesture can be sexual harassment. This could happen when someone gives you looks with a sexually suggestive meaning, holds or eats food in an obscene or embarrassing way, is always flirting with you when it is unwanted, or sends you offensive or suggestive notes.

■ Obscene pictures

Showing obscene pictures or making someone look at something offensive is also a form of sexual harassment. If someone posts sexually explicit photographs or symbols, displays pornography, exposes parts of his or her body, or shows another person obscene cartoons or drawings, it may be sexual harassment.

■ Physical Contact

Unwanted physical contact or threats of physical contact can be considered sexual harassment. There does not always have to be direct contact. It could just be that someone stands too close to you on an ongoing basis and makes you feel invaded or uncomfortable, or that someone corners you. It may be sexual harassment if someone brushes up against you, pinches you, or touches you in an inappropriate way. If someone tries to force you into sexual touching or touches you without your consent, it may also be considered sexual assault under the *Criminal Code*.

■ Intimidation

Sexual harassment can also take the form of intimidation. Examples of intimidation include:

- Repeated requests for a date
- Offering or asking for sexual favours
- An employer making an employee wear revealing or suggestive clothing

Sexual harassment can take many forms, but will usually make the employee being harassed feel very uncomfortable in the workplace.

38. Are you being sexually harassed?

Not all sexual comments or actions in the workplace are sexual harassment. Sometimes it is difficult to decide what is and what is not sexual harassment. People who work together often date each other without it considered sexual harassment. The following information will help you determine if your situation is actually sexual harassment under the law.

There are five things to consider when deciding if the situation is sexual harassment:

- Is the behaviour sexual?
- Is it unwelcome?
- Is it ongoing?
- Is it forced?
- Is it being used to punish or reward someone?

■ Sexual behaviour

The first thing to consider is whether the behaviour is sexual. The comments or actions must involve something about sex. It does not have to be obvious, however, and often it is very subtle. For example, someone may never talk about sex, but the way they talk about other things may be sexually suggestive.

■ Unwelcome behaviour

The second thing to consider is whether the behaviour is unwelcome and unsolicited. Unwelcome means that the person being harassed has let the harasser know that the behaviour is unwanted or it should have been obvious to the harasser that the conduct was unwanted. This does not necessarily mean the person being harassed has to directly say anything about the behaviour. The person being harassed could just walk away when a comment is made or tear up a written note. A response such as this is enough to show the harasser that the behaviour is unwelcome.

Unsolicited means that the person being harassed did not willingly participate in the behaviour or encourage it. For example, if two people are telling sexual jokes and making sexual innuendoes, one of them cannot later claim that it was sexual harassment, because they both willingly participated in the behaviour.

■ Ongoing behaviour

The third thing to consider is whether the behaviour has been ongoing. Usually a one-time comment or action will not be considered sexual harassment unless it is very serious. For example, if someone tells an offensive joke once, it is not sexual harassment under the law. Yet, if someone continues to tell offensive jokes after being told to stop, it is more likely to be considered sexual harassment.

■ Forced participation

The fourth thing to consider is whether someone was forced to participate in sexual behaviour. This could be where an employer forces an employee to have sex to get a promotion or to avoid being fired. In this type of case, the employee may participate in the behaviour but can claim sexual harassment because he or she did not willingly participate.

■ Rewards and punishment

The fifth thing to consider is whether there is a reward or punishment based on the employee's reaction to sexual advances. Rewards usually involve raises or promotions, while punishments usually involve demotions, decreases in pay, or employees forced to do different kinds of work that they do not like. If an employer repeatedly asks an employee out on a date and the employee refuses and is then fired, this is clearly sexual harassment. It may also be sexual harassment if the employee goes on the date to keep from getting fired.

If you are unsure whether your situation is sexual harassment, a lawyer can help you to decide and help you deal with the situation. Additional information may also be obtained from your local Human Rights Commission.

39. What can I do if I am sexually harassed?

You have several options if you are being sexually harassed. The option you choose will depend on your particular situation and the place you work. In all cases, harassers can be held responsible for their actions. In most cases, the employer is also responsible for dealing with the problem in a fast and proper way. The main options for people being sexually harassed include talking to the harasser, complaining to the employer, complaining to the Human Rights Commission, suing the harasser or employer, or having criminal charges laid. If you are unable to resolve the situation quickly and in an informal way, discuss your options with a lawyer.

■ Talk to the harasser

The first option is to talk to the harasser. Depending on the situation, you may feel comfortable enough to tell the harasser that you do not like what is going on. Sometimes if you let the person know in private that you would rather not hear his or her jokes or comments, that person will stop. It is usually best to first try to solve problems informally if possible.

■ Talk to a manager or supervisor

If you have tried talking to the harasser, or feel that the problem is too serious, then you may want to talk to a manager, supervisor, or human resources about the problem. It is usually best to put your complaint in writing and keep notes of any related meetings you have. If your company has a complaints system for sexual harassment, follow the proper procedures.

   If you make a complaint to your employer, the employer will usually tell the harasser about the complaint and give that person a chance to explain the situation. If the employer believes that there was sexual harassment, the employer can do several things. Usually, the employer will tell the harasser to apologize and stop the harassment. In addition, the harasser may be given a warning that is put on file. That person may also be suspended with or without pay, or may be fired if the harassment is very serious.

■ Complain to a Human Rights Commission

If your complaint has not been dealt with properly by your employer, or the problem is very serious, you may be able to make a complaint to your provincial Human Rights Commission. Commissions investigate complaints. If there is sexual harassment they can award compensation and order employers to rectify the situation.

   To make a complaint to a Human Rights Commission, you should call the Commission and speak to an investigator. The Commission will send you forms to fill out with the details of your situation. If the investigator thinks your case is strong, it will be sent to a hearing. Many cases do not make it to a hearing because there is not enough evidence to prove them, or the complaint forms did not include all the proper information. On the other hand, a case might also get resolved before a hearing. But if your case does go to a hearing (which works a lot like a trial), commission representatives will hear each side's story, listen to any witnesses, and make a decision.

   In some provinces you might be entitled to have your case sent to mediation, which is faster than the normal complaint process. Mediation is a meeting between the person making the complaint and the person being accused of harassment and, in some cases, the employer. At the meeting, there is a person called a mediator who helps the two sides find a solution to the problem.

■ Sue the harasser and/or the employer

The fourth option if you are being sexually harassed is to sue the harasser or the employer. If you suffer a financial or emotional loss because of the sexual harassment, you may be able to sue the harasser and you may also be able to sue the employer. Employers are responsible for ending the sexual harassment promptly and effectively once they are aware of it or when they should have been aware of it. If the employer fails to do this, you may be able to recover some or all of your loss from the employer. Employees who were fired or forced to quit as a result of the sexual harassment use this option most often. You may be precluded from suing only the harasser for the sexual harassment, unless you can argue it was a constructive dismissal, assault, or some other civil wrong. The legal issue surrounding sexual harassment lawsuits is very complicated. You should therefore consult a lawyer for assistance.

■ Bring criminal charges

The fifth option applies only to certain types of sexual harassment. If you are forced into any sexual act against your will or you are touched in a sexual way without your consent, the harasser may be guilty of sexual assault. You can contact the police and report the situation. If appropriate, the police can then lay criminal charges.

■ Deciding what to do

Before deciding on an option, write down a list of what happened, when it happened, and who was involved. This way, you will have a clear idea of what you are claiming and it will make it easier for someone hearing your complaint to understand your situation. If your situation is not quickly and completely resolved through an informal process, seek the advice of a lawyer.

40. What must employers do in sex harassment cases?

Even though harassers are responsible for their actions, the employer is also responsible in most cases for dealing with the situation in a prompt and proper way. The employer is responsible if the employer knew or should have known about the sexual harassment. If the employer fails to deal with the situation properly, the employee who was being harassed may be able to sue the employer.

In some situations, an employer can even be held responsible for dealing with sexual harassment by someone who is not an employee or if an employee sexually harasses someone outside the workplace. For example, if someone comes to fix the photocopier and sexually harasses an employee or if an employee is travelling to a work-related conference and sexually harasses someone at the conference — the employer may be responsible for dealing with such situations.

Even though an employer may have a policy against sexual harassment and may have steps in place for making complaints, the employer may still be responsible if sexual harassment happens. Employers are responsible for making sure that the policy or complaints procedure will actually help someone who has been harassed.

An employer who becomes aware of sexual harassment should immediately investigate the situation in a confidential and discrete way. The employer must take reasonable actions to resolve the problem, but must also deal fairly with the harasser. Someone who is being accused of sexual harassment should always have a chance to explain his or her side of the story before the employer takes action against that person. An employer should also tell the person making the complaint that the alleged harasser will be told about the complaint.

41. Can an employer prevent sexual harassment?

All employers have a legal responsibility to try to prevent sexual harassment at work. How an employer can do this will depend on the size of the company and the people who work there. A few small steps can often go a long way toward preventing sexual harassment.

It is usually a good idea for an employer to write a sexual harassment policy and create a complaints procedure. Even small companies can benefit from having a system in place to deal with sexual harassment. Managers and employees should know that sexual harassment is unacceptable and will be taken seriously when their company has a sexual harassment policy and complaints procedure.

Sexual harassment policies usually include a purpose statement, a definition of sexual harassment, statements indicating who the policy applies to, what the penalties are for breaking it, and how complaints should be made and dealt with. To be useful, the policy should be clearly posted in the workplace.

Sexual harassment policies can help prevent sexual harassment and may even protect an employer from being found responsible for any harassment incidents if the employer can prove it acted diligently to prevent problems.

A good way to make the policy work is to ensure that managers and supervisors understand it and are going to enforce it. At large companies, the employer may want to hold a special meeting to go over the policy. For smaller companies, an employer may want to discuss the policy at a regular meeting with managers or supervisors. It is also important that managers and supervisors talk to the staff about the policy.

Letting employees know that sexual harassment is unacceptable is a big part of preventing it. If you need specific information about employers' responsibilities or about writing a sexual harassment policy, consult a lawyer.

Test your knowledge

1. Parental leave covers:
    a. Pregnancy
    b. The time after a child is born
    c. Time away to grieve the death of a parent

2. If you are wrongfully terminated you are:
    a. Out of luck
    b. Entitled to notice
    c. Allowed to sue your employer
    d. A and b
    e. B and c

3. A public holiday is:
    a. A day when everyone gets together
    b. The third Friday of every month
    c. A day set out in legislation that employees are entitled to take off
    d. A day set out in legislation that all employees must work

4. A collective agreement is:
    a. The document an employer gives you when you're terminated
    b. An agreement negotiated between management and the union
    c. The document that governs the establishment of a union
    d. The legislation under which unions apply for certification

5. You must wait how many weeks before you can collect employment insurance:
    a. Four
    b. Two
    c. Six
    d. None
    Answers: 1. b; 2. e; 3. c; 4. b; 5. b

Provincial employment standards sources

Canada	labour.hrdc-drhc.gc.ca
British Columbia	www.bcest.bc.ca
Alberta	www.gov.ab.ca
Saskatchewan	www.labour.gov.sk.ca
Manitoba	www.gov.mb.ca
Ontario	www.gov.on.ca
Québec	www.cnt.gouv.qc.ca
New Brunswick	www.gnb.ca
Nova Scotia	www.gov.ns.ca
Prince Edward Island	www.gov.pe.ca
Newfoundland and Labrador	www.gov.nf.ca/labour/Labour/
Yukon	www.yuwin.ca

Employment information

Workrights.ca: www.workrights.ca
A Web site created by the Canadian Labour Congress that includes a range of information on employment standards and work issues.

Human Resources and Social Development:
http://www.hrdc-drhc.gc.ca
Includes a wealth of information about employment insurance and how the system works.

Provincial labour boards

Canada	www.cirb-ccri.gc.ca
British Columbia	www.lrb.bc.ca
Alberta	www.gov.ab.ca
Saskatchewan	www.sasklabourrelationsboard.com
Manitoba	www.gov.mb.ca
Ontario	www.gov.on.ca
Québec	www.crt.gouv.qc.ca
New Brunswick	www.gnb.ca
Nova Scotia	www.gov.ns.ca
Newfoundland and Labrador	www.gov.nf.ca
Prince Edward Island	www.gov.pe.ca
Yukon	www.gov.yk.ca
Northwest Territories	www.justice.gov.nt.ca
Nunavut	www.gov.nu.ca

STARTING, MANAGING & GROWING A BUSINESS

To start and manage your own business is a life's dream for many people who have an entrepreneurial itch. Even those who need the security of full-time employment may be interested in the tax advantages and extra earning potential of a part-time or home-based business.

In Canada, it is quite easy to get the most basic form of business — a sole proprietorship — up and running. In fact, roughly two million Canadians claim self-employed status and many thousands more have small businesses on the side or go on to launch private and public corporations. That said, even the basic form of business requires some planning, good record keeping, and an awareness of potential liabilities.

It is important to know that owning and running a business today can be a complex, stressful, and challenging task. Recent surveys of Canadian owners of small and mid-sized businesses reveal they must cope daily with worries about keeping customers happy, staffing issues, taxes, government red tape, and finding capital to grow.

The good news, according to these surveys, is that most business owners would not have it any other way and many recommend others pursue their dreams of owning a business.

Understanding how businesses operate is also valuable information for consumers and investors. For example, you may want to sue a corporation and its management for some foul deed, but your lawyer is telling you the executives themselves likely won't pay a cent. Do you know why their liability is limited? Or, your spouse, cousin, or a friend may ask you to invest in a new business as a shareholder or even as a director of a corporation. Are you aware there may be significant legal and financial risks?

Businesses today have a powerful influence on our economy, government policies and even our daily lives. Knowing how the law views businesses can make you a wiser consumer, investor, and entrepreneur.

1. What are the different forms or structures available for businesses in Canada?

If you have decided to start a business or already have one, it is important to decide what legal form of business will work best for you. There are three main forms to choose from — sole proprietorships, partnerships, and corporations.

If you are going to start a business alone, you can choose between a sole proprietorship and a corporation. If you are going to start a business with at least one other person, you can choose between a partnership and a corporation.

There are important legal differences between the three forms. For example, both sole proprietors and partners of a partnership are not considered legally separate from the business. The owners are personally responsible for every aspect of the business and any profit or loss must be included on the personal income tax return of each owner.

In comparison, a corporation is considered legally separate from its owners. In fact, the law considers a corporation to be a legal entity, much like a person. The owners of a corporation do not usually have personal liability for the debts of the business or for any lawsuits that arise and the corporation is taxed separately from its owners. (That said, tax authorities and creditors may not let owners hide behind a "corporate veil.")

There are many factors to consider when choosing the legal form that is best for your business. As your business grows, the advantages of the corporate business form may outweigh the disadvantages. A lawyer can help you determine which form of business is best for your situation.

Sole Proprietorships

2. What are the advantages & disadvantages of sole proprietorships?

A sole proprietorship is a business owned by one person. It is the simplest type of business to start.

There are several important features of a sole proprietorship.

- The business and the owner are considered to be one entity under the law

- The sole proprietor personally owns all the assets of the business
- The sole proprietor is not considered an employee of the business.
- Because of this, the sole proprietor is not eligible for employment insurance if the business fails.
- The sole proprietor is not paid a salary, but can take any amount of money from the business through personal drawings

As you might imagine, owning a sole proprietorship has several advantages and disadvantages.

■ Advantages

One of the advantages of being a sole proprietor is you can be your own boss. You make business decisions without having to ask anyone else for approval. You also get to keep the profits from the business and have the freedom to end your business when you want. Although you need to keep separate accounting records for the business, you only need to file one personal income tax return.

■ Disadvantages

The owner of a sole proprietorship is personally responsible for all aspects of the business. If the business is sued, so is the owner. If the business owes money, the owner is personally responsible for the debt. If the owner cannot pay the debts of the business, he or she may have to claim personal bankruptcy. Sole proprietorships are usually best for businesses that do not have significant exposure to liability or lawsuits. The only way to transfer ownership of a sole proprietorship is to sell the entire business to someone else. Otherwise, the life of the business ends if the sole proprietor closes the business or dies.

3. Do I have to register a sole proprietorship?

The business name of a sole proprietorship must be registered unless it is the proper name of the sole proprietor. For example, if you call your business by your own name, John Smith, you do not need to register the business name. However, if you decide to call the business John's Ice Cream, then you must register the business name.

In some provinces, such as Ontario, you must register the name of your sole proprietorship within 60 days of creating your business or be fined up to $2,000. There are two other reasons why you should register. First, you will need to show your copy of the business name registration when you set up a bank account for your business. Second, since the law requires that you register your business name (unless you are using your own name), it helps to ensure a particular name is not used by another business. The goodwill or familiarity that goes with a particular business name is very important and valuable. If you do use the name of another business, you can be sued in civil court to change it and pay compensation to the other business.

The registration fee for a sole proprietorship is not expensive, often between $50 and $100, depending on the province. The registration form is often quite simple and you will likely be able to complete it on your own. Some provinces even allow registration online. If you need advice about your business name or choosing a sole proprietorship as your form of business, contact a lawyer.

4. How do I choose a business name for a sole proprietorship?

There are several guidelines to follow when you choose a name for a sole proprietorship. The name should be distinctive and describe your business. The name must not be misleading and cannot include obscene words. The words "corporation," "incorporated" or "limited" cannot be used since these words are reserved for corporations only.

You must be careful not to copy or come too close to copying another business name. If your business name is too similar to a name that is already used by another, you can be sued and will have to change your name. To make sure your business name is not already being used, conduct a name search.

▪ Conducting a name search

There are four types of name searches. You can do two of these searches for yourself or you can pay a search company to do it. The first search is to look in your telephone book, trade directories, and even on the Internet for similar names. Second, you can usually conduct a free search yourself at provincial or federal government offices where businesses are registered. These records, however, are not always up-to-date.

A third type of search may be conducted through your provincial government's own name search service. If available in your province, you fill out a form and formally request a search of government databases for a small fee. A fourth type of search is the NUANS search. NUANS stands for New Upgraded Automated Name Search. A NUANS search is the most thorough type of search. There is a nominal fee involved. The NUANS search will reveal all registered business and corporation names and trademarks that are similar to the business name you propose to use. This search is necessary if you want to conduct business outside your own province. Lawyers or name search companies listed in your telephone book can perform a NUANS search.

5. How do I register and protect my business name?

After you ensure that the name you want is not used, you can register your sole proprietorship with the provincial government. There are several steps in registering your business name and keeping the registration valid.

To register the business name of a sole proprietorship, obtain an application form that asks basic information about your business, such as its name and address, and the name of the owner. After completing this form, submit it together with a small application fee. If there is a problem with your application, the government will contact you. If you register in person, the registration can be completed the same day.

When a business name is registered, it is added to the public record of businesses. A business name registration is only valid for five years in most provinces. If you plan to use the name for longer than five years then you must renew your registration before it expires. The government will not notify you when your business name expires. It is your responsibility to record the date for renewal.

Also, if a change is made to your business, such as a new owner takes over or the address of the business changes, you must file a new registration within 15 days of the change. There is no fee for filing these changes.

Cancel your business name if you want to stop doing business under your registered name or want to stop doing business altogether. This is done by filing another form with the government. There is no fee for filing a cancellation.

Partnerships

6. What are the advantages & disadvantages of partnerships?

A partnership is an unincorporated business carried on by two or more people who intend to share the profits. Partnerships have several important features:

- A partnership can be created by an express agreement or can be created when people are simply acting in a way that seems like a partnership

• Partners can be held responsible for the actions and business debts of the other partners

• Partners personally own all the assets of the business

• Partners are not considered employees of the business. Because of this, partners are not eligible for employment insurance if the business fails.

• Partners are not paid a salary, but can take money from the business through personal drawings

There are two main types of partnerships:

1. General partnerships, where all partners share the profits and losses of the business.

2. Limited partnerships, where the limited partners are not involved in the daily operations and are only responsible for losses up to the amount they contributed to the business.

It is important to put a partnership agreement in writing because it will outline issues including how the profits or losses will be divided and will describe any limits to the legal responsibility of the partners. Being a partner in a partnership has several advantages and disadvantages, including important tax implications.

■ Advantages

There are three main advantages to forming a partnership.

1. A partnership allows two or more people to work together, and bring different skills and resources to the business.

2. A partnership is fairly easy to establish. The actual registration of a partnership is not expensive or complicated. As noted above, it is a good idea to decide how the partnership will be run — then put it into a partnership agreement.

3. If the partnership suffers a loss but the partners have other employment income, the loss can be used to reduce each individual's taxable income and lower the tax owed by each partner.

■ Disadvantages

There are five main disadvantages to forming a partnership.

1. Because the partnership is not considered to be separate from its owners, the partners are personally responsible for liabilities of the partnership. If the business fails, the partners will be personally responsible to pay all the debts and obligations of the partnership.

2. Because each partner is an agent for the business and for the other partners, each is personally responsible for the actions of the other partners. If one of the partners makes a bad business decision or acts negligently resulting in the partnership owing a debt, all partners are personally responsible to pay it back.

3. Because a partnership is based on the individual partners and is not a separate legal entity, then if one of the partners dies, the partnership ends. This means the remaining partners have to re-establish the partnership.

4. Because a partnership is not a separate legal entity, it is difficult to buy or sell a partnership interest. Buying or selling a partnership interest involves rewriting the partnership agreement and determining exactly how the partnership will change.

5. Although the resolution of disagreements among partners is generally covered under a written partnership agreement or case law, the settling of disputes is usually very difficult. There is no legislation that sets out rules for settling partnership disputes. If disagreements are not resolved by the partners themselves, they will usually have to turn to outside help, which can be time-consuming and costly.

7.   How do we choose a partnership name?

There are several guidelines to follow when choosing a name for your partnership. The name should be distinctive and describe your business in some way. The name must not be misleading to the public and cannot include obscene words. The words "corporation," "incorporated" or "limited" cannot be used because these words are reserved for corporations only.

You must be careful not to copy or come too close to copying another business name. If your name is too similar to one that is already being used by another business, you may be sued and have to change it. To make sure your business name is not already being used, you should conduct a name search.

For information on how to conduct a name search, see the previous section on sole proprietorships.

Although by law most partnerships must be registered, there are at least three other important reasons for registering a partnership name. First, by registering a name you are giving notice that the name is being used. This will help prevent others from using your business name. Second, by searching and registering a business name you can ensure you are not using someone else's business name. This is important because if you do use someone's business name you could be forced to stop or even be sued. Third, by registering a business name you are helping establish the goodwill or familiarity that goes with a particular business name. This is important in securing new business and can increase the value of your business if you decide to sell it. For assistance in determining the form of business you should have, or for help with your partnership legal issues, consult a lawyer.

8. How do we register a partnership name?

The law requires that the business name of a partnership be registered unless it is the name of one of the partners. If you do not register the name of your partnership in Ontario within 60 days of creating your business, you may be fined up to $2,000.

To register the business name of a partnership, obtain an application form from your provincial government that asks basic information about your business, such as the name of your business, its address, and the names of the partners. Submit the completed form and a small application fee. If you submit the form in person, the registration can be completed the same day. If you submit the application by mail it will take about a month to be registered. If there is a problem with your application, the government will contact you.

A registered business name is added to the public record of businesses and is valid in most provinces for five years. If you plan to use the name for longer than five years then you must renew your registration before it expires. The government will not notify you when your business name expires and it is your responsibility to record the date for renewal.

Also, if a change is made to your business, a new partner is added or the address of the business changes, for instance, you must file a new registration within 15 days of the change. There is no fee for filing these changes.

Cancel your business name if you want to stop doing business under your registered name or you want to stop doing business altogether. This is done by filing another form with the government. There is no fee for filing a cancellation.

9. Why is a partnership agreement important?

If you decide to form a partnership, you should put a partnership agreement in place. A partnership can exist without a formal, written agreement but you may run into problems in the future.

A partnership agreement establishes rules about how the business is going to be run. It usually includes who the partners are, what bank the business will use, how the profits or losses of the business are to be divided among partners, what the capital contribution of each partner will be, the role and responsibilities of each partner, and how the partnership can be dissolved. Establishing these details at the beginning of a business relationship can help avoid disagreements later.

Many of these details can be decided between the partners before they approach a lawyer to finalize the agreement. Nonetheless, creating a partnership agreement is a detailed legal process. You should have a lawyer help you create the agreement, or at least have a lawyer review the agreement before you sign it.

10. How do we know if our business is a partnership?

Sometimes, two or more individuals may engage in a business activity yet there will be uncertainty as to whether they are actually in partnership. This can become an important issue if the activity creates unpaid debt or results in a claim of liability. If there is a partnership, all participants will be responsible equally. If not, then only one participant may be on the hook.

In law, the question of whether a partnership exists must be determined by the real intentions of all the parties and their conduct. In determining their "real relationship," a court will look at the substance rather than the form of their relationship. The court will consider everything that is available, such as formal contracts, documents, advertisements, correspondence, and evidence of witnesses. The factors that must be present to find that a partnership exists are:

- The formal registration of a partnership
- Contribution by the parties of money, property, knowledge, skills, or other assets used in the business
- Joint property interest in the property of the business
- Mutual right of control or management of the enterprise
- Expectation of profit
- Right of each party to participate in the profits

■ A "view to profit"

Provincial legislation may also state that a partnership exists if the parties carry on a business in common with a view to profit. Therefore, even if the parties intend to form a partnership and address themselves as partners or use the word "partnership," a partnership will not exist unless they intend to share profits. If profit is to be generated, but is not to be common to the partnership but individual to the participants, then the necessary common profit element will not be found to exist. For example, two individuals may join forces to market their services, but not share equally in profits generated by each person. This approach would likely not be seen as indicative of a partnership.

■ Formal registration

If there is no other evidence, the formal registration of a partnership will likely be sufficient to determine that a partnership has been created. It is important to understand that it is not necessary to formally register a partnership to create it nor is registration absolute proof that a partnership exists.

■ Contribution of each party

Another factor that the court considers is contribution. Some form of contribution by each of the parties and an indication of interdependence are normally enough to allow the court to decide that a partnership has been created.

CORPORATIONS

11. What are the advantages & disadvantages of incorporating a business?

The main feature that makes corporations different from sole proprietorships and partnerships is that corporations are legal entities separate from their owners. The corporation is responsible for its own debts, assets, and lawsuits. The legal responsibility of the shareholders, directors, officers, and employees of the corporation is limited, which means, with few exceptions, these people cannot be held personally responsible for the debts and obligations of the corporation. This is why "Limited," "Incorporated," "Corporation," or one of their abbreviations must be included in the full legal name of the corporation. These words give notice to the public that the business is a corporation and its owners, directors, officers, and employees have limited liability.

Corporations are also owned by shareholders. As the name suggests, they own a percentage of the entire corporation through their shares. Shares of corporations can generally be bought and sold fairly easily, unless restrictions have been placed on the transfer of shares.

■ Advantages

First, there is the advantage of limited personal liability for the people who own and run the corporation. This means the shareholders cannot be held responsible for the debts and obligations of the corporation unless they provided a personal guarantee.

Second, a corporation has an unlimited life. Because the corporation is a separate legal entity, it will continue to exist even if the shareholders die or leave the business, or if the ownership of the business changes.

Third, the corporate form of business makes it easier for a business to grow and expand. Through the issuance of shares, corporations may be able to access money they need for expansion. This makes the corporate form of business more suitable for large business ventures than sole proprietorships or partnerships.

Fourth, there may be tax advantages to running your business as a corporation. Examples of corporate tax advantages are tax deferral strategies and income splitting. Corporate taxation is a complicated matter and it is important that you talk to an accountant or a tax lawyer to determine which advantages apply to your situation and how best to structure your business. Finally, a corporation may appear more stable and sophisticated to the public. This may help you acquire new business.

■ Disadvantages

First, you have to file two tax returns – one for the business and one for your personal income. Unlike sole proprietorships and partnerships, any losses from the corporation cannot be deducted from the personal income of the owner. Second, the registration and set-up fees for a corporation are higher than the set-up fees for a sole proprietorship or a partnership. Incorporating a business is also a more complicated process than starting a sole proprietorship or partnership. You should contact a lawyer to help you incorporate your business. Third, the government requires corporations to maintain proper corporate records, or what is called a minute book. A minute book contains the corporate by-laws and minutes from annual meetings. To determine whether you should incorporate your business, consult a lawyer who can help you evaluate your specific situation.

12. How do I choose a name for the corporation?

All corporations must have and use a corporate name. The corporate name may either be the corporate number which is issued by the government upon incorporation, or a distinctive corporate name which has been properly searched and appears on the "Articles of Incorporation." In addition to having a corporate name, it is possible for corporations to register and use other business names.

The name of a corporation is strictly regulated in all Canadian jurisdictions to avoid names that are too general or misleading. Also, the Québec Charter of the French Language requires that a corporation carrying on business in Québec use a French version of its name.

■ Using a corporate number as name

In some cases, companies do not want to use a descriptive name for the business and simply choose to use the corporation number followed by the words Incorporated, Corporation, Limited, or one of their abbreviations (for example, 123456 Alberta, Ltd.).

■ Using a descriptive corporate name

If the company does want to use a descriptive corporate name, then the proposed name must be searched. A formal NUANS (New Upgraded Automated Name Search) search must be conducted and submitted to the government. A NUANS report will show all businesses and trademarks that have similar names to the one you propose to use.

While you will need the formal search, it is a good idea to first conduct searches using the telephone book, Internet, and trade directories. If you do not find a name too similar to the one that you propose to use, then you can go forward with a NUANS search. The NUANS search is usually conducted by a private search company and involves a small fee. You must be careful not to copy or come too close to copying another registered business name. If your corporate name is too similar to a name that is already being used, you may have to change your business name — and you may be sued.

■ Business names for corporations

A corporation may also want to use an abbreviated version of its legal corporate name, or a totally different name for advertising or marketing purposes. For example, a shorter name on a storefront sign can attract more public attention. To legally use a different name from the corporate name, it must be properly registered to the corporation. It is important to understand that a registered business name does not replace the legal corporate name, but is used in addition to the legal corporate name.

Although corporate names do not expire, business names are only valid for five years. If you plan to use a business name for longer than five years then you must renew the registration before it expires. The

Ministry will not notify you of the expiration date. It is your responsibility to renew your business name.

■ Names must be registered

Corporations are legally obligated to register all names they use. If a corporation does not register one of the names being used and a legal problem arises, the limited liability of the corporation may not be valid under the unregistered business name. This means the owners and the employees of the corporation may be held personally responsible for corporate liabilities.

Incorporating a company and selecting corporate and business names for a corporation are complex legal issues. Consult a lawyer for more information and assistance.

13. What is involved in incorporating a business?

The legal form of business you choose has an important effect on the entire nature and structure of your business. A lawyer can help you decide if you should incorporate and which corporate structure is best for you. Before you register your corporation, you must choose a corporate name, draft your Articles of Incorporation, and submit a processing fee.

■ Articles of Incorporation

The Articles of Incorporation must be drafted. This is a document that sets out important information about the structure of your corporation, such as the minimum and maximum number of directors your corporation is allowed to have, the different classes of shares, and the names of the incorporating directors. Two original sets of the Articles of Incorporation are to be submitted to the relevant federal or provincial government agency, along with any incorporation fee.

In British Columbia and Nova Scotia, two separate documents must be registered. First, there is the "Memorandum," which sets out the company's name, its authorized capital, and any restrictions on its business and powers. Second is the "Articles," which govern the conduct of the company's internal affairs. In other jurisdictions, the information in the Articles is dealt with in by-laws passed by the directors and shareholders following incorporation.

14. Should the business be incorporated federally or provincially?

If your business will be located or operate regularly in more than one province or in foreign countries, it may be best to incorporate under federal law. This allows you to carry on business in any province without being licensed, although a simple registration may still be required in some provinces.

If you plan to operate mostly within one province, a provincial incorporation will likely suit you. If you do business in another province, however, you may have to register there and may be required to obtain an extra-provincial licence.

You will likely need a lawyer to register in a province outside of where you live. Some jurisdictions have residency requirements. Most Canadian laws require that a majority of the directors of a corporation be Canadian residents. The federal law has been amended recently to reduce the Canadian residency requirement for corporations in most industry sectors to 25 percent, except where there are fewer than 4 directors, in which case at least one must be a resident Canadian.

In Alberta, at least half the directors must be Canadian residents. In British Columbia, a majority of the directors must be Canadian residents and at least one director must also be resident in that province. In Ontario, a majority of the directors must be resident Canadians, but if the corporation has only one director, that person must be a Canadian resident. If there are two directors, one must be Canadian. Québec, New Brunswick, Nova Scotia, and the Yukon impose no residency requirements for directors.

Foreign investors can deal with the residence requirement for directors by finding Canadians to represent them on the board of a subsidiary. Some jurisdictions (federal, Ontario, and Alberta) allow a "unanimous shareholders agreement" which gives the powers of the directors to manage the business in whole or in part to shareholders.

Also, some U.S. investors can easily incorporate in Nova Scotia where a unique "unlimited liability company" form of business exists that offers certain U.S. tax advantages and different residency requirements. A lawyer can explain whether this form of business is right for you.

15. Can I incorporate a business myself?

The incorporation of a business in Canada can be done very quickly and a routine incorporation can easily be completed within a week by anyone familiar with the various forms required by either federal or provincial governments.

Most people feel more comfortable hiring an experienced lawyer or even a paralegal (non-lawyer) to do the paperwork, but it is not a requirement. With a careful review of the government forms to be filed, reliable name search results and a clear understanding of the best structure for your business, it is possible to do it yourself.

If you have never done it before, however, it may be more prudent to hire an experienced person. These days, lawyers can be found in the business pages of the telephone book who charge a flat fee of $500 to $1,000, plus the filing fees. Some online services claim a fee as low as $99.

The cost of establishing a Canadian corporation is relatively modest (under $400, and cheaper if done online). Also, some law firms have so-called "shelf" corporations that are already incorporated and can be activated immediately, if required.

16. What are corporate shares?

The owners of a corporation are called shareholders. Every corporation must decide what type of shares it will have, and what the rights and restrictions of the different shares will be. Different rights can be given to different types or classes of shares. For example, people who hold one type of share may be allowed to vote while people holding another type may not. If different people have the same type of shares, their rights must be the same. This means that if you plan to have only one type of share, then all shareholders must have the same rights.

■ Share specifications in Articles of Incorporation

The different classes of shares and the rights attached to each must be specified in the Articles of Incorporation. You must also specify any restrictions you want on the shares of the corporation, even if you only want to have one class of shares. For example, you might want to restrict who is allowed to own shares. Additionally, private corporations are restricted in the number of shareholders permitted and are not allowed to offer their shares to the public. The legal issues involved in structuring a corporation's shares are complex. Consult a lawyer for more information and assistance before you incorporate your business.

17. What is the difference between common and preferred or special shares?

If you hold common shares, you are a part-owner in the corporation. Common shareholders, however, risk losing all or part of their investment if the company fails. The business's creditors and preferred shareholders come ahead of common shareholders in claiming assets of the company, if the company fails.

In both private and publicly traded companies, there may also be different classes of common shares, where some carry voting rights but pay no dividends and others offer no voting rights but pay dividends.

In most corporations, preferred shareholders receive a higher dividend than common shareholders. As a result, preferred shares are often valued higher than common shares. Most preferred shares do not carry voting privileges.

18. Can I transfer shares in a private corporation to someone else?

Private corporations (which differ from those that sell their shares on public stock markets) have 50 shareholders or less with shares that are not offered to the public. Most small corporations and family-run corporations are privately held corporations.

One of the benefits of the corporate form of business is that the ownership of the corporation can be transferred easily by the purchase and sale of shares. If shareholders of a privately held corporation do not want to own a part of the corporation any longer, their shares can be sold to someone else including another corporation or a partnership. If a shareholder wants to split income with family members for tax purposes, he or she will be able to do so by transferring shares. If you are an owner of a privately held corporation and want to sell or transfer your ownership, do note the following several steps:

■ **Restrictions on the transfer of shares**

Before you transfer or sell shares, make sure you follow any rules that are set out in the Articles of Incorporation and in the corporate by-laws. There may be restrictions on who can buy or sell shares or on how many shares can be transferred. For a privately owned corporation, the Articles of Incorporation usually require that the other shareholders agree to the transfer of shares. It is also common that the shareholders of the corporation will have to pass a resolution that approves the transfer of shares. You should review the Articles of Incorporation of your corporation or contact a lawyer to help you determine what restrictions apply to your situation.

■ **Price of the shares**

Before selling or buying shares, the price will have to be determined. Unlike the shares of a public corporation where the price is determined in the stock market and listed in the newspaper, the price of shares for a privately held corporation is determined by the shareholders. There is no single formula for determining the price of shares. If you have a shareholders agreement, the formula to be used for your corporation may be found there. If no formula or price has been put in place, consult a lawyer, business valuator, or accountant for help.

■ Effect of transferring shares

Transferring shares does not change or nullify the legal structure of the corporation. In many privately held corporations, however, the owners of the corporation also take an active role in running the day-to-day affairs of the business. If a shareholder leaves the business, then there may be some significant changes in the way the business is run. Also, there may be tax implications when transferring shares. Before you buy or sell shares of a privately held corporation, consult a lawyer.

19. What is the difference between a shareholder, director, and officer?

Corporations are managed and directed by officers and directors, and owned by shareholders. Each group has a different role and responsibility in the corporation.

■ Shareholders

Shareholders are the owners of the corporation. Holders of shares that carry voting rights exercise control through votes – often annually in large companies, but more often in small businesses. They elect the directors who guide and control the overall business operations. Shareholders are also asked to vote on important issues, such as the sale or dissolution of the business. They generally do not participate in the day-to-day operations of the business unless they are also directors or officers. Shareholders also influence control of the corporation through the purchase and sale of corporate shares, giving them greater or lesser voting rights.

■ Directors

Directors are elected by the shareholders to guide the business operations of the corporation. Directors select the officers who manage the daily business activities. Directors approve budgets and important contracts. They also decide when to issue shares and when to declare a dividend.

■ Officers

Officers are the day-to-day managers of the corporation. Officers include the president and vice-president of the corporation. The duties of the various officers are established by the directors and by the by-laws of the corporation.

The maximum and minimum number of directors is stated in the Articles of Incorporation. Each privately held corporation must have at least one shareholder and at least one director. Typically, corporations have one or more officers who are approved by the directors. In a small corporation, it is possible for one person to hold all these positions and to perform all the duties. Often, however, when a corporation begins to grow, more people will be needed to manage and direct it.

20. Why is a shareholder agreement important?

A shareholder agreement exists between shareholders of a corporation and details the rights and obligations of each shareholder. It is often used in corporations where there are not very many shareholders. Shareholder agreements cover topics such as how shareholders can transfer shares, how disputes between shareholders will be resolved, and how shareholders may vote in annual or special meetings.

Every shareholder agreement should be tailored to the specific requirements of the corporation. The guidelines in shareholder agreements should be simple and easy to follow. Contact a lawyer to help you structure your shareholder agreement.

21. Do directors and shareholders face any personal liability in a corporation?

One of the main benefits of the corporate form of business is that shareholders, directors, and officers of a corporation are not usually held personally responsible for the debts and obligations of the corporation. Nonetheless, if a shareholder or director has personally guaranteed a loan or debt, he or she will be held personally responsible for it.

Directors of a corporation can be held personally responsible in other situations as well. For example, if the corporation has not paid its corporate income tax or the GST and PST on sales, directors may and probably will be held personally responsible. Often, directors buy Directors & Officers (D&O) liability insurance to protect themselves in case this type of situation arises. In comparison, shareholders are not responsible for these debts unless they have personally signed a guarantee.

Be careful if you have been asked to be a director for a corporation or if you are not involved in the day-to-day business of the corporation in which you are already a director. It is important to be aware of all your legal responsibilities as a director so seek the advice of a lawyer.

22. What is legally required to maintain a corporation?

After your business has been incorporated and you receive your certified Articles of Incorporation, the corporation must follow several legal requirements:

■ Minute book

First, prepare a minute book, which is a chronicle of resolutions and a resource of important corporate documents. Examples of documents that must be kept in the minute book are the Articles of Incorporation, the rules and by-laws of the corporation, registers of the directors, shareholders, number of shares issued, and the minutes of director and shareholder meetings.

■ Share certificates

Share certificates may also be kept in the minute book. Share certificates are the actual pieces of paper that show who owns shares in the corporation.

■ Shareholders and directors register

Create a shareholders' and a directors' register. A shareholders' register is a list that records each class of shares issued, who holds the shares and how many shares each person owns. A directors' register is a list that records the name and address of each director, the date each director was elected, and, if applicable, the date on which his or her term as director ended.

■ Seal

You may want to buy a seal with the name of your corporation imprinted on it. A seal is stamped on documents and may be required for some business and banking procedures.

Incorporating a business and formulating the proper corporate records are complex and detailed legal matters. Consult a lawyer for assistance.

23. What government regulations affect businesses?

Corporations, partnerships, and sole proprietorships must comply with various federal, provincial, and even municipal government regulations and laws concerning business licences, tax collection, employee records, and details of business transactions. There are also administrative requirements such as keeping business records and more formal requirements for corporations, such as keeping minute books and holding annual meetings.

■ Business licence

Whether you conduct business from a commercial office or from your home, you might be required to obtain a business licence. Business licences are issued by your municipal licensing board and are usually inexpensive. Specialty licences or provincial or federal licences can also be required. For example, if you sell liquor, you will need a provincial liquor licence. If you own a restaurant, you will need a licence to sell food. A lawyer can help you determine what type of licence, if any, you will need for your business.

■ Taxes

Most businesses will need to register to collect the Provincial Sales Tax (PST) for those provinces that have a sales tax and the federal Goods and Services Tax (GST). You can register for a PST number with your provincial government taxation branch. You can register for a GST number (known as a Business Number) through Canada Revenue Agency. Businesses with total sales of less than $30,000 in a moving 12-month period are not required to register for or collect the GST, but also cannot deduct any GST they have paid, or apply for GST refunds.

■ Business accounting records

All businesses are required to maintain proper records of business transactions including sales records, bank statements, expenses, and cancelled cheques. An accountant or a bookkeeper can help.

■ Employees

A corporation with employees is required to deduct employment insurance premiums, Canada Pension Plan contributions, and income tax from employee salaries. These deductions, along with your employer's contribution to employment insurance and the Canada Pension Plan, must be submitted to Canada Revenue Agency by the 15th day of every month. Canada Revenue Agency sets the deduction amounts. If your business has employees, you may also need to register with a provincial occupational health and safety agency.

You may also need to register with the provincial workplace safety or worker compensation board. These provincial agencies provide funds for people who are injured at work. Contact your provincial worker compensation or workplace safety and insurance board for a free information kit.

In addition to these general regulations, there are many specific government regulations that may apply to your corporation depending on the type of business you conduct. If you are uncertain which regulations apply to you, contact a lawyer for advice.

Commercial Tenancies

24. What law applies to commercial landlords and tenants?

Unlike residential tenancies, the law governing commercial leases generally treats landlords and tenants as equals, without giving tenants any additional protective rights. Although commercial landlords and tenants are free to enter into any type of agreement, they normally follow a standard commercial lease format.

A landlord or tenant who breaches the lease can be sued. Another remedy for a landlord when a tenant breaches a lease is for the landlord to have the tenant's personal property confiscated and sold. The sale proceeds are then applied against the outstanding amounts owed to the landlord under the lease.

The costs associated with a lease are often a significant part of a business's operating budget. Also, the location of a business can be vital to its success. Before commercial landlords and tenants sign a lease, they usually consult their lawyers.

25. How do landlords seek increases in commercial rents?

Normally, a landlord and tenant negotiate the amount of rent and any rent increases and include those details in the lease. If a landlord wants to raise the rent more than the lease allows, the landlord will have to wait until the lease expires. To protect a tenant from a steep rent increase or eviction, many leases give the tenant the right to renew the lease for a pre-set amount of rent. For advice about commercial rent increases, consult a lawyer.

26. Can a commercial landlord evict tenants?

Most commercial leases state the reasons why and how a landlord can evict a commercial tenant. Normally, there are two main reasons why a landlord is entitled to evict a tenant: for non-payment of rent and for failure to perform a material or key requirement of the lease.

▪ Eviction for non-payment of rent

If a tenant fails to pay rent, the landlord is entitled to re-enter the premises, which usually includes changing the locks and preventing the tenant from using the premises any longer. Unless the lease requires the landlord to give the tenant notice, the landlord may be able to terminate the lease immediately and evict the tenant if the tenant does not pay the rent on time.

■ Eviction for failure to perform other obligations

A commercial lease may also contain other obligations that the tenant is responsible for. If the tenant does not perform such obligations, the landlord may be able to terminate the tenancy and take over the premises but must do so in compliance with any legislation that a province has governing commercial landlords, such as the *Commercial Tenancy Act* in British Columbia and the *Commercial Tenancies Act* in Ontario.

It is not always clear whether the lease has been breached. In some cases the landlord may apply to a court to have a judge decide if the tenant has breached the lease, and if so, to have the lease terminated. If a landlord applies to court, the tenant will be given the opportunity to appear at trial to argue his or her side.

A landlord who wants to evict a commercial tenant or take the tenant to court should first consult a lawyer.

27. What can a landlord do if the tenant is in arrears?

Paying rent on time is usually the main obligation of a commercial tenant. Most commercial leases state what a landlord can do if a tenant does not meet this obligation. Normally, a landlord has three possible options:

• To terminate the lease and sue for arrears and future loss
• To sue the tenant for arrears and maintain the tenancy agreement
• To seize the tenant's goods and furniture and sell them to pay off the arrears

■ Landlord's right to terminate the lease

First, it is common in commercial leases that the failure to pay rent entitles a landlord to re-enter the premises, which usually means that the landlord can change the locks and prevent the tenant from using the premises again. Unless the lease requires the landlord to give the tenant notice, the landlord may be able to terminate the lease and evict the tenant as soon as the tenant does not pay the rent on time, even if it only happens once. Or, the landlord may choose to apply to court to have the tenancy terminated and the tenant will have an opportunity to explain why the rent was not paid. If the tenant has temporary financial difficulties and otherwise acted in good faith, a judge may not terminate the tenancy.

◼ Suing a tenant for arrears of rent

Second, a landlord also has the option of suing the tenant for the arrears of rent. Even though a landlord can usually terminate the tenancy immediately, the landlord and tenant may disagree about how much rent is owed. If the landlord does not apply to terminate the lease or does not terminate it by taking over the premises and changing the locks, then the lease continues even though the tenant is being sued for arrears. If the judge finds that the tenant is in arrears, the tenant will be ordered to pay the landlord.

◼ Distress: a landlord's right to sell the tenant's property

Third, if a landlord wants to collect arrears of rent but does not want to terminate the tenancy by taking over the premises and changing the locks, or does not want to sue the tenant, the landlord usually has the right to seize the tenant's goods and furniture and sell them to recover the arrears. Under the law, this is called distress. If the entire amount from the sale of goods and furniture is not recovered, the landlord may be able to sue the tenant for the remaining amount owing. The landlord no longer has the right to terminate the tenancy once the arrears are recovered.

Before taking steps to evict a tenant or collect arrears, a landlord should consult a lawyer.

28. What constitutes a breaching of a lease?

Under the law, a lease may be considered breached if a landlord or tenant fails to live up to one or more of the lease obligations.

A tenant is commonly considered to have breached the lease if he or she moved out before the lease expired. Generally, if a commercial tenant wants to vacate the premises earlier than the lease allows, the tenant will have to get written agreement from the landlord or the tenant may be responsible to pay rent for the entire duration of the lease. Under the law, a landlord is required to seek a new tenant, but if the landlord cannot find one, or loses any money because the old tenant breached the lease, the landlord may be able to sue the tenant. If a tenant wants to vacate the premises early, a lawyer should be consulted about the possible consequences and options.

Many commercial leases do not require the landlord to do anything other than allow the tenant to use the premises. Still, if the landlord does not meet certain obligations that are in the lease, such as providing utilities or maintenance services he or she may have violated the lease. Even if a landlord violates the lease terms in some way or interferes with the tenant's business operations, the tenant normally does not have the right to stop paying rent. Instead, the tenant may apply to court to have a judge order the landlord to fulfill the obligations or sue for damages suffered.

A landlord or tenant who wants to break a lease or start legal action should first consult a lawyer.

29. What are the tenant's rights and responsibilities when moving out?

Unless the lease states otherwise, a tenant is generally required to leave the rented premises in the same condition as it was found, minus reasonable wear-and-tear. If the tenant installs fixtures or furnishings that need to be removed at the end of the tenancy, the tenant is normally responsible for ensuring any damage due to installation or removal is repaired. If a tenant renovates a unit according to a requirement in the lease or with permission of the landlord, the tenant will usually be able to leave the premises in the renovated condition, as long as there is no unreasonable damage to the property. Fixtures installed by the tenant do become the property of the landlord.

If the tenant damages the property or leaves the premises in a way that causes the landlord a financial loss, or does not comply with the terms of the lease, the landlord may be able to sue the tenant. Tenants who are unsure of their obligations when moving out should consult a lawyer.

Tax Rules for Businesses

As noted elsewhere in this guide, the Canadian tax system relies on self-assessment by taxpayers, including businesses. All taxpayers are responsible for reporting their total income and determining their total tax owing.

Canada Revenue Agency enforces the tax law by performing a small number of audits on individuals and businesses each year. If Canada Revenue Agency finds that someone made an error in calculating or reporting the tax he or she owed, that person is "reassessed." If the error was deliberate, a penalty is levied. If someone is found to be intentionally evading the law, that person may be prosecuted by the Department of Justice for tax evasion or a criminal offence.

As with any complex area of law or regulation, it is also wise to consult a knowledgeable tax lawyer or tax accountant.

30. Is a sole proprietorship different from other businesses for tax purposes?

A sole proprietorship is an unincorporated business that is owned by one person. Sole proprietorships are treated differently from other types of businesses for tax purposes. Income in the hands of a sole proprietor is treated the same as personal income and is included on the sole proprietor's personal income tax return.

Note that a sole proprietor is required to keep separate personal records and business records. If you are a sole proprietor, you are required to pay personal income tax on net business income earned during the calendar year, even if you do not receive some of the revenue until the next calendar year.

▪ Fiscal period

You may be eligible to apply to use a different fiscal period other than a calendar year for calculating and paying taxes, but you will not usually be able to defer taxes this way.

▪ GST and PST

As a sole proprietor you may also be required to collect and remit Goods and Services Tax (GST) and Provincial Sales Tax (PST).

31. Is a partnership different from other businesses for tax purposes?

When two or more individuals join to do business for profit but do not incorporate, they have formed a partnership. Partnerships are treated differently from other types of businesses for tax purposes.

Usually the business profits of a partnership are divided between the partners. The partnership itself does not pay taxes and there is no separate tax return for the partnership. Instead, any net partnership income in the hands of a partner is treated the same as personal income and is included in the partner's personal income tax return. Each partner pays income tax for the calendar year in which the partnership earned it, even if the partner does not receive payment until the next calendar year.

▪ Fiscal period

As a partner, you may be able to apply to use a different fiscal period other than a calendar year for calculating and paying taxes, but you will not usually be able to defer taxes this way.

■ GST and PST

A partnership may also be required to collect and remit Goods and Services Tax (GST) and Provincial Sales Tax (PST).

32. How is a corporation taxed?

The tax rules for a corporation and its owners are different from other types of businesses. Under the law, a corporation is considered a separate legal entity and is required to pay taxes on net income. A corporation's income is the profit that remains after deducting business expenses and before paying out dividends to its shareholders.

■ Tax filing requirements

As a separate legal entity, a corporation is required to file a separate tax return within six months of the end of its fiscal period, even if no taxes are owed. Corporations in many provinces are required to file two tax returns — one for the federal government and one for the provincial government. Generally, a corporation is also required to report and remit taxes in monthly installments, by the end of each month.

■ Tax implications of receiving profit or drawing a salary

If you want to draw money from your corporation, there are different tax consequences depending on how you are paid. Generally, there are two ways to get paid by a corporation. You can usually draw a salary as an employee of the corporation, or, if you are a shareholder, you can receive dividends. Since each has different tax consequences, an accountant or tax lawyer can advise you on which is better in your situation.

■ Reduced tax rate for small businesses

If you draw a salary, the amount of your salary is considered an expense of the corporation. This means that the corporation can deduct the amount of your salary from its income before taxes are applied. If you draw a salary, you may also be able to reduce the amount of tax you pay personally by making RRSP deductions and deducting the contributions from income.

■ Paying out dividends

If you own shares in a private corporation, the other way to draw money is to receive dividends. The overall tax implications of paying dividends instead of a salary will depend on the applicable corporate tax rate and your available tax credits and deductions.

One of the differences between salaries and dividends for business tax purposes is that a corporation can deduct salaries as an expense before taxes but must pay dividends from after tax income. If you receive dividends, you will not be able to use the RRSP deduction to reduce your taxable income. Still, because of the dividend tax credit you personally pay less tax on dividend income than if you were paid a salary.

33. Do I have to register my business with Canada Revenue Agency?

Most businesses are required to collect and remit federal taxes and will need to register with Canada Revenue Agency to do so. It assigns each business one "Business Number" to simplify correspondence.

To apply for a Business Number, complete a form available from Canada Revenue Agency. Once you are assigned a Business Number, you can use it as a reference number for collecting and remitting GST, import or export taxes, payroll deductions, and corporate income tax.

Generally, a business is only required to register for GST if it sells taxable goods or services, and if its total revenue from all sources is more than $30,000 annually. If your business is not registered and your revenues total more than $30,000 in any four consecutive quarters, you will usually be required to register for GST within one month.

Some types of businesses do not have to register, regardless of their annual revenue. These include most health related services, daycare services, financial services, tuition for educational programs, and services provided by charities that have annual revenues less than $175,000.

If you do not register, you will still have to pay GST on your business expenses, and you will not be able to recover the GST you pay to your suppliers or contractors.

Finally, businesses pay other taxes and premiums that are administered by other government offices that do not use the Business Number assigned by Canada Revenue Agency. These taxes and premiums include provincial sales tax, workplace safety and insurance, and employer health taxes. For more information on these taxes, contact your provincial government.

34. What are allowable business expenses for deductions?

Sole proprietors, partners, and corporations can usually reduce the amount of tax they pay by deducting allowable business expenses from their income before applying taxes. Allowable expenses only include business expenses that were incurred for the sole purpose of earning business income — and not your own personal or living expenses.

■ Types of deductible business expenses

Some of the main types of business expenses that can be deducted from business income include:

- Accounting and legal fees
- Expenses for advertising
- Fees and licences necessary for business
- Employee salaries
- Interest and bank charges
- Up to 50 percent of meals and entertainment that you pay for the purpose of earning business income
- Rent, if you run a business out of your home you can usually deduct the business-related portion of rent, mortgage payments, insurance, electricity, and cleaning supplies
- Office supplies
- Business telephone expenses
- Business travel expenses

■ When can expenses be claimed?

Business expenses can only be claimed in the year they are incurred and only during the period that the business existed. If Canada Revenue Agency audits you or your business, you will usually have to provide dated receipts or purchase agreements for every expense you deducted from your income. Deducting business expenses can substantially reduce the amount of tax that you or your business pays.

35. What are an employer's responsibilities for taxes?

An employer normally has four main tax obligations:

1. To collect and remit deductions from employees' paycheques.
2. To make contributions in addition to employee deductions.
3. To report employee earnings.
4. To pay tax on the income you earn.

■ Employee taxes to be deducted from payroll

Employers are required to deduct income tax, Canada Pension Plan contributions, and Employment Insurance premiums from an employee's paycheque. Employers are also required to contribute an amount in addition to the employee's contribution to Canada Pension Plan and Employment Insurance. For Canada Pension Plan contributions, the employer matches the amount deducted from the employee's paycheque. For Employment Insurance, the employer contributes slightly more than the employee.

■ Employee deductions and employer contributions

The amount of employee deductions and employer contributions depends on the employee's income. To find out how much you have to deduct or contribute, call Canada Revenue Agency to get a copy of the Payroll Deduction Tables. Canada Revenue Agency will also provide you with various forms that you and the employee will need to fill out before the employee is paid for the first time.

An employer is required to fill out special forms when reporting employee earnings. To report salaries, wages, and taxable benefits, an employer is required to fill out a T4 form and give the employee their copy by the end of February of the following year. To obtain these forms and for more information call Canada Revenue Agency.

Employers may also be responsible for paying employer health tax (only in Ontario) and workplace safety and insurance premiums, which are calculated as a percentage of the business's total payroll expense and are administered by provincial government offices. If you are starting a new business or hiring new employees for the first time, contact an accountant to determine if you have to register with the Workplace Safety & Insurance Board and to find out how much tax you have to pay.

■ Deadlines for remitting employee income tax deductions

There are deadlines for remitting income tax deducted from employee paycheques. Generally, the deadline is the 15th day of the following month or penalties may apply. If the 15th day falls on a Saturday, Sunday, or holiday, payment is due by the next business day after the 15th. Some small business employers may be allowed to remit deductions on a quarterly basis. Canada Revenue Agency will automatically notify you if you qualify for this program.

36. What should I know about collecting and remitting Goods & Services Tax (GST)?

Collecting and remitting GST may allow a business to reduce the amount of GST it pays on business expenses. Only businesses which register with Canada Revenue Agency can collect the GST from customers and recover the amount of GST they paid on business expenses. There are two main ways of calculating how much GST to remit — the General Method and the Quick Method.

■ General Method

The general method requires you to keep track of the GST collected from each business transaction. Then, you add up the GST you paid on allowable business expenses (called your input tax credits) and subtract that amount from the total GST you collected from customers. The difference is remitted to Canada Revenue Agency.

Allowable business expenses which are eligible for input tax credits include merchandise, advertising services, office furniture, equipment, rent, and office supplies. If your business collects less GST than it pays, you can apply to Canada Revenue Agency for a GST rebate.

■ The Quick Method

Most small businesses with annual sales of $200,000 or less can also calculate how much GST they owe by the Quick Method. Although the Quick Method may not necessarily save you money, it may simplify your accounting procedures.

The Quick Method does not require you to track GST collected on each sale or service performed and you do not have to claim input tax credits. Instead, you simply pay either 2.5 percent or 5 percent of your total sales to Canada Revenue Agency. The rate will depend on your annual sales, the type of business, and where your business is located.

The total amount of your annual revenue will determine when you have to report and remit GST. If your revenues are $500,000 or less, you are only required to report annually. If your revenues are between $500,000 and $6,000,000 you are required to report quarterly. And, if your revenues are more than $6,000,000 you are required to report monthly.

For additional information on how to collect and remit GST, contact an accountant or call Canada Revenue Agency's Business Inquiries Department.

37. What do I need to know about collecting and remitting Provincial Sales Tax (PST)?

Every province except Alberta has a retail sales tax on most goods and services. To collect retail sales tax you are required to obtain a vendor permit from the provincial government and remit tax regularly.

■ Who is exempt from paying PST?

You must have a vendor permit to be exempt from paying retail sales tax on your own business expenses. Generally, businesses that manufacture, sell, or import goods or services are eligible for a vendor permit and should collect and remit retail sales tax. If you sell goods that are not taxable or if you only sell taxable goods occasionally, you will normally not require a vendor permit. Goods and services that are not taxable include the sale of fresh fruit, dry cleaning services, and generally the sale of goods and services by religious, charitable, and non-profit organizations.

■ Different rates of PST

Different rates of retail sales tax are applied to some goods. In Ontario, for example, the PST rate is usually 5 percent on less than one month of accommodation in hotels, camps, or clubs. For admission to amusement places or for alcoholic beverages sold at a licensed establishment in that province, the rate is usually 10 percent. To apply for a vendor permit and for more information on how to collect and remit retail sales tax you can contact the Retail Sales Branch in your area.

Tax Audits & Investigations

38. When does Canada Revenue Agency investigate?

Canada Revenue Agency may choose to audit an individual or business even if there is no apparent reason to do so. Generally, Canada Revenue Agency can only audit someone up to three years after a tax return has been filed, unless there is misrepresentation or fraud involved.

For a detailed discussion on tax audits, see Section III, Tax Audits and Investigations.

Business Bankruptcy

39. What is a business bankruptcy?

A business can choose to become bankrupt when it owes over $1,000 and is insolvent. A business is insolvent when it is unable to make payments on its debts as they become due, or if it would be unable to pay off its debts even if the business assets were sold.

A business can go bankrupt in one of three ways. Most common is a business that voluntarily declares bankruptcy. In other cases, a business will become bankrupt if it makes a proposal to its creditors that is not accepted by them. Finally, and most rare, the creditors of a business can sometimes push the business into bankruptcy by filing a petition with the court.

A business bankruptcy will be handled by a licensed trustee in bankruptcy who will handle the sale of the business's assets and the distribution of proceeds to creditors. Usually, the assistance of a bankruptcy lawyer is required. The situation should also be reviewed with a lawyer before the trustee is engaged.

40. What are the ramifications of a business bankruptcy?

The effect or ramifications of business bankruptcy depends on whether the business is a sole proprietorship, a partnership, or a corporation.

If your business is a sole proprietorship or a partnership, it is important to recognize that the bankruptcy of your business will result in your personal bankruptcy as well. As a result, most of your personal assets, such as your car and home, could be sold to satisfy business debts, and the bankruptcy would appear on your personal credit record.

If your business is a corporation, your business can go bankrupt without involving your personal assets, unless you have personally guaranteed a loan or you are a director and the company has failed to make payments such as GST, Retail Sales Tax, or remit employee source deductions. Before filing for bankruptcy, make sure you fully understand the effect of your business's bankruptcy on your personal situation.

During a business bankruptcy, business owners sometimes have an opportunity to buy back the business equipment and start the business all over again, free of most debts. Nonetheless, a deliberate business failure with a view to buying assets back can be considered fraud that carries criminal consequences.

When a business goes bankrupt, the trustee takes all assets and sells them to pay off as many of the debts owed to the creditors as possible. Often if the business has a secured creditor such as a bank with a *General Security Agreement*, the bank will appoint someone called a Receiver to conduct the sale and the trustee will merely monitor matters for unsecured creditors. This is generally done through some form of public sale process, such as a solicitation of bids, tenders, or auction, although private sales are also common. The public sale of assets can be a very complicated procedure. Consult a lawyer or an accountant for specific legal and financial advice before choosing how to proceed.

41. Are there alternatives to a business bankruptcy?

Bankruptcy is only one of several available options for a business facing financial difficulties. Instead of bankruptcy, you may want to consider making an informal or a formal proposal to your creditors. Or you may wish to sell the business with or without the help of a secured creditor.

■ Proposal to creditors

First, you may want to make a proposal or arrangement with your creditors to pay lower monthly payments over a longer period, or perhaps a reduced amount altogether. This is a good alternative for a business that has a steady income flow and some prospects for the future. If you have only a small number of creditors you may want to make an informal proposal by calling your creditors and explaining your situation. If you have a large number of creditors, you may have to call a trustee in bankruptcy and arrange to make a formal proposal under the *Bankruptcy and Insolvency Act.*

A proposal to creditors is a contract between the business and its creditors. The trustee will help you and the creditors negotiate terms that you both find reasonable. The proposal must be approved by the court, and accepted by two-thirds of your creditors at a meeting of creditors. If your proposal is not accepted, your business will automatically become bankrupt.

■ Receivership and buy back

Instead of making a formal proposal to your creditors, you may decide to allow a secured creditor to place your business into receivership so your secured creditor can sell it. A secured creditor is a person or institute that loaned you money in return for your written promise to give it rights to specific property (called collateral) if you do not repay the loan. If you fail to make payments on your loan, the secured creditor may appoint a receiver to take control of and sell the property you promised it. A secured creditor must give you 10 days notice of its intention to appoint a receiver. If you receive notice that business assets will be sold, contact a lawyer immediately for more information and advice. It may be possible for you to buy back your business assets — but you will have to outbid any competition.

Filing for bankruptcy may or may not be a suitable choice for your business depending on your particular situation. Consult a lawyer, a trustee in bankruptcy, or an accountant for more specific information and advice.

42. What are a creditor's options for recovering debts?

The term "creditor" is used to describe anyone owed money, including banks, credit card companies, and family or friends who loaned you money. Under the law, creditors can enforce a number of legal rights against you if the money you owe them is not paid. Their particular rights depend on whether they are a secured creditor or an unsecured creditor.

■ Rights of secured creditors

A secured creditor loaned you money in exchange for your written promise to give it rights to your property if you do not pay back the loan. The property you have given rights to is called "collateral" or "security." For example, a bank or leasing company may give you a car loan on condition that it can take the car if you are unable to repay the loan. Or, a bank may give you a loan to buy a home when you give it the right to take the home if you default on your mortgage loan payments.

If you stop making payments, the secured creditor must generally give you some period of advance notice before actually taking or selling the collateral. The period will vary depending on the type of collateral. Once secured creditors have taken the property and sold it, they will have the right to sue you if the sale did not generate enough proceeds to repay the debt in full. Conversely, if they receive more than the amount of the debt, they must give you the difference.

■ Rights of unsecured creditors

Unlike secured creditors, unsecured creditors lend you money without taking collateral. As a result, they do not have the automatic right to take specific property if you stop making payments. Instead, they must sue you and obtain a court judgment against you. The judge will give the creditor a judgment against you if the creditor shows that you failed to repay the loan.

Once creditors have a judgment, they can ask the sheriff to take your property, such as a car, and sell it to pay off the debt. They can also ask the sheriff to garnish money from your wages, or from your bank account. This means that money could be deducted from your pay-cheque or withdrawn from your bank account without your permission. Only 20 percent of your net wages after deductions can be garnished, and garnishments for support orders must be paid first.

If a creditor is threatening to sue you, or has a judgment against you, try to talk to the creditor and arrange a payment schedule where you can pay the debt over time. To protect yourself, make sure the payment schedule is in writing and signed by both you and the creditor. If you are unable to pay and unable to reach an agreement with the creditor, consult with a lawyer for more information and advice.

43. I sold goods to a business and now it is bankrupt. Can I get my goods back?

When a business goes bankrupt or a receiver is appointed for it, an unpaid supplier has a right to serve written notice of repossession of the goods within 30 days after the goods are delivered to the purchaser. The actual act of repossession must take place within 10 days after the notice is delivered or the right is lost.

The supplier bears the cost of recovering the goods. The goods must actually be in the possession of the purchaser or receiver, be identifiable as the specific goods sold, be in the same condition as when they were sold (that is, not incorporated into another product or good), and not have been resold to someone else.

If you are able to recover the goods, you cannot also seek payment for the goods. As well, if there was partial payment for the goods, the supplier can only recover the unpaid portion of the supplies.

Common Business Questions

44. Should I extend credit to customers?

Many businesses extend credit to their customers. This means the business provides goods or services to the customer without requiring payment right away. The customer then owes the business a debt.

Before you extend credit to your customers, you can conduct a number of searches to check the credit record of the borrower and verify whether other lenders have existing claims on their assets. The type of credit search you will need depends on the type of business you are in and the amount of credit you want to offer. The eight most common searches include:

- a search under the Personal Property Security Act
- a credit search at a credit bureau
- an execution search
- a search under the Bank Act
- a corporate search
- a bankruptcy search

- a search at the Official Receiver's Office
- a vehicle record and driver record search

■ Personal Property Security Act search

In exchange for extending credit to your customers, you can claim a security or lien on a debtor's specific asset (usually the item you sold the customer). If the customer does not pay the debt, you can take possession of the specified asset, sell it, and take the money you are owed out of the proceeds. Any money received from the sale that is more than the amount owed must be returned to the debtor.

A *Personal Property Security Act* search is conducted to determine if there are any registered liens against the personal property of the individual or the business. This is important because the customer may have already used the property as collateral. To conduct this search, visit your local land Registry Office or the provincial Personal Property Security office. Searches in most provinces are inexpensive.

■ Credit Bureau search

A credit search provides information about the credit history and credit rating of the person or business you are searching. It will also give you some information about outstanding loan or credit card payments, if the borrower makes payments on time and if there are outstanding liens. It will also help you determine the level of risk involved in giving credit to the customer.

To conduct this search, visit a credit bureau, such as Equifax Canada or TransUnion of Canada, Inc. Credit information can only be obtained by businesses that are registered members of the Credit Bureau. Membership fees are inexpensive. It is not possible for individuals to be registered, although individuals can request their own personal credit check.

■ Execution search

An execution search reveals whether there is a legal judgment against the person or business. A judgment is a decision made by a court meaning that the court has ordered that person or business to pay a sum of money. The person who is owed money by your customer may have legal claims to his or her property. Also, if your customer is already facing a judgment, it probably means that that person is a credit risk. To conduct an execution search, visit the local sheriff's office in the area where the person being searched lives, works, or owns property. You will be required to fill out a search form and pay a small fee.

■ **Bank Act search**

A *Bank Act* search will reveal whether a bank has taken security on the same property that your customer is trying to give you as collateral. If the bank does have a claim on the property it means it has loaned your customer money and has the right to take possession of and sell the property if the loan is not paid. This is important for you to know for two reasons. First, it shows that the person or business you are going to lend money to already has a debt with the bank and may not be in a stable financial position. Second, it will show you if the collateral you are supposed to receive is already secured. You will need to provide the bank with the name of the person or business being searched together with a small fee.

■ **Corporate search**

A corporate search reveals information about a corporation, including the registered corporate name, any registered business names, the date of incorporation, whether the corporation is active and the names of the directors and officers. This search can be done through the government ministry responsible for businesses in your province.

■ **Bankruptcy search**

A bankruptcy search tells you whether the person or company being searched has filed for bankruptcy in the last five or six years. This search can be done by phoning the Bankruptcy Office in Hull, Québec. There is a small search fee per name.

■ **Search at the Official Receiver's office**

A search at the Official Receiver's office reveals whether the person or company being searched is or has been bankrupt. It also reveals whether it has filed a proposal under the *Bankruptcy and Insolvency Act.*

■ **Vehicle Record and Driver Record search**

Vehicle Record and Driver Record searches reveal information about vehicles and drivers, such as who owns a vehicle and how many vehicles the person being searched owns. To request these searches, complete specific forms that are available at the provincial transportation ministry.

45. Can the law help me collect on business debts?

Sometimes a business is owed money either by an individual or by another business. The person or business that owes you money is called a debtor and you are called the creditor. If you have trouble getting the money you are owed, there are several steps you should follow.

■ Contact the debtor

First, always telephone or contact the debtor in person. The debtor may only need a friendly reminder of the money owed so you should always try to be on good terms with the people you do business with. If a phone call does not work, you can send the debtor a letter detailing what is owed. The letter serves as a formal notice of the debt and it may be required before you try other means of recovering your money.

■ Other options

If a phone call and a letter do not work, you have several options. You can hire a lawyer to try to collect the money on your behalf or you can take the debtor to small claims court if the amount is within the limits of your province (see the chapter on small claims court). Or, you can call a collection agency to take over recovery of the debt. If the collection agency recovers some or all the debt from the debtor, the agency will take a percentage of the money recovered as its fee. Finally, you can consider writing off the debt. Sometimes the amount of the debt is not worth the time, effort, and expense involved in collecting it.

■ If you have a security interest in the debtor's assets

If you have loaned money and have taken the debtor's assets (such as a car or equipment) as security, you may be able to seize and sell the assets. This means you can take possession of the asset, sell it and take the money you are owed out of the proceeds. Any extra money from the sale of the asset must be returned to the debtor.

Debt collection is an important business matter. You should have a debt collection procedure in place to ensure your business does not experience cash flow problems.

46. What happens if I get a garnishment order for an employee?

As an employer, if you receive a court order to garnish an employee's wages, you are required by law to comply and are not allowed to punish or fire the employee because of the garnishment. If an employee's wages are being garnished it is because he or she owes a debt and you will usually be required to pay a portion of the employee's wages to the court until the debt is paid, at which time you will be notified to stop garnishing the wages. If you receive a garnishment order and are unsure of what to do, contact the number provided on the court documents you received advising you to garnish the wages.

47. What should I know when raising money for a business?

Companies often need money from external sources to operate or expand. There are five main ways to raise money for a business: investing your own money; borrowing from friends and family; borrowing from a bank; issuing and selling more shares; and obtaining government funding.

■ Investing your own money

You can invest your own money in the business. If you do not have the necessary funds, you may be able to raise money yourself by taking out a mortgage on your home, or by getting a personal bank loan.

■ Borrowing from friends and family

You may be able to borrow money from your friends and family. If you borrow money, decide with the people you borrowed from whether they are going to be lenders or shareholders. You will owe a different legal obligation to them depending on whether they are lenders or shareholders. If they are lenders, then the business will probably be responsible for paying them the amount loaned, together with interest. If they are shareholders, then they will be co-owners in the business. As an owner, they will not recover any money unless the business is successful. If the business is successful, they will share in the profits.

■ Borrowing from a bank

You may be able to borrow money from a bank. A bank will probably want to take the business assets as security before it processes a loan. This means that if the business does not pay back the loan, the bank can seize the assets, sell them, and take the money it is owed from the proceeds. Any money left over must be returned to you. The bank will likely also require a personal guarantee from the owners of the business. This means that if the loan is not repaid by the business, the bank will be able to collect the money from the owners and their personal assets.

■ Issue and sell shares

If your business is a corporation, you can issue and sell corporate shares. When you sell shares, however, your percentage ownership in the corporation is reduced. Before issuing and selling shares consult a lawyer to discuss the ramifications and best choices in your particular situation.

■ Government funding

Finally, you may be eligible to receive financing from a government-sponsored program designed to help businesses. Contact the provincial and federal governments to find out if there are any business programs that may be available for you.

48. What is involved in buying or selling an existing business?

When a business is bought or sold, an Agreement of Purchase and Sale should be written and signed. A purchase agreement describes exactly what is being bought and sold and for how much. Several things must be determined when you create a purchase agreement.

First, a value must be put on the business. In most cases, an accountant or business valuator can do this. He or she will consider the business profits over the last few years, business assets, and the goodwill or public familiarity of the business.

If you are buying a corporation, you will need to know whether you are buying the assets or the shares of the corporation. When you buy the assets of the corporation, you are buying individual pieces of the business. You can decide which pieces you want. Buying the assets also allows you to select which liabilities you want to take on. Any liabilities you do not take on, such as an outstanding debt or lawsuit, remain the responsibility of the seller of the assets.

When you buy the shares of the corporation, you are buying the entire corporation as a whole. All the assets are included, as are all the corporation's liabilities.

There are complex tax consequences associated with both the purchase of assets and the purchase of shares. Before selling or purchasing a business, consult with a lawyer for assistance.

49. I'm thinking of buying a franchised business, what should I know?

Franchises are a popular way for people to buy a business.

■ What is a franchise?

A franchise is a contract or agreement where a franchisor gives a franchisee the right to start a business under a business system that already exists. Under the franchise agreement, the franchise business usually uses the name or trademark of an existing company and conducts the same type of business as the existing company. The franchisee has a right to use the name or trademark of the existing company and the franchisor gets to have some control over the franchisee's business. The franchisor also has a continuing right to receive payments from the franchisee.

■ Advantages of owning a franchise

There are at least four advantages to owning a franchise.

1. You are able to operate your own business while still having the security of working with a large company.

2. You do not necessarily have to be an expert at running your own business because you will usually receive support from the franchisor. For example, the franchisor may provide such things as ongoing training and business advice.

3. You enjoy the benefit of using the franchisor's reputation. As a result, there is less business risk for you if the franchise has developed a successful product.

4. It is sometimes easier to borrow money to buy a franchise than to start an independent business.

■ Disadvantages of owning a franchise

There are also several disadvantages to owning a franchise. Depending on the franchisor and the franchise agreement, the franchisor may maintain a substantial amount of control over new franchises. In typical franchise situations, the franchisor will set the opening and closing times of the franchise, determine what is to be sold and how it is to be sold and will put restrictions on the ability of the franchisee to sell his or her franchise. Discuss this before you enter into a franchise agreement.

Another disadvantage of franchises is that franchisees usually have to pay an up-front fee simply to begin using the business name. To continue using the name, the franchisee will usually have to pay a set fee either every month or every year. These fees can be substantial. On the other hand, the franchisee gets to use the franchise name in exchange, and sell the franchise product. People will know your business name and you will not have to spend time developing a marketing plan or customer recognition.

In some provinces, such as Alberta and Ontario, franchise sellers may be required to meet certain disclosure requirements and provide a full package of information on your rights and responsibilities.

There are many complicated legal issues involved in buying and operating franchises. Consult both a lawyer and an accountant when planning to enter into a franchise agreement.

50. How are home businesses affected by the law?

The term "home business" generally refers to a business that is run by someone who is self-employed and who operates the business out of his or her home. Home businesses have become very popular. Technology such as fax machines, e-mail, and the Internet has made it easier for many people to run a business from home. You should consider several legal issues if you want to start a home business. Many of these are general issues that are important for all businesses. For example, all businesses must decide what form of business to use and all businesses must obey employment standards and deduction requirements. Home businesses must pay special attention to zoning restrictions, tax issues, and licensing requirements.

■ Employment standards and deductions

If your home business employs other people you will have to follow general employment standards. For example, you cannot pay your employees less than the legal minimum wage, you cannot fire an employee in a way that violates the laws concerning termination of employment, and you must obey occupational health and safety laws. You will also have to deduct employer deductions such as Canada Pension Plan contributions and employment insurance contributions from the employees' paycheques.

■ Zoning restrictions

Check your municipal zoning by-laws to ensure the activity you propose is allowed in your area. Zoning restrictions are particularly important for home business owners because many activities are not allowed in residential areas.

■ Tax issues

There are several tax issues that home business owners must consider. For example, working at home means you might be able to deduct some of your housing costs from your income, which will affect the amount of personal income tax you have to pay. Doing so, however, means that when you sell your home, part of the value will not be considered your principal residence but your office. This means you may have to pay tax on capital gains allocated to the office portion of your home.

One thing you should do to minimize the negative tax implications of working at home is to get a letter of opinion about the value of your house from a realtor when you start the business. Depending on the type of business you operate, you may also have a legal responsibility to collect various provincial and federal taxes.

■ Licences

Depending on the type of business you operate, you may need a licence for the activity you propose. You can contact your local municipal authorities to determine if your business will be affected by local business regulations, municipal business taxes, or licensing requirements.

■ Public perception of a home business

Another challenge is the general perception of a home business. Sometimes, home businesses are not taken seriously or treated as favourably as other businesses. It can be more difficult for home businesses to secure loans and get sales. However, this perception is changing because the number of home businesses is increasing rapidly.

Starting a home business can be a risky and rewarding venture. Because the legal issues that arise with a home business can be very complicated, you should consult a lawyer for assistance and advice.

51. To import or export goods, what should I know?

If you plan to import or export goods for commercial purposes, you must follow several regulations and procedures:

■ Importing

All businesses that plan to import goods to Canada on a commercial basis must obtain an Importer number or a Canada Revenue Agency (CRA) Business Number.

Importers must know what items they are importing and their country of origin. Importers must provide CRA with an invoice that shows the value of the goods they are importing. CRA will usually classify and value the goods according to an international description and coding system. The government classifies imports to compile trade statistics and to determine whether any conditions apply to the imports, such as prohibitions, quotas, anti-dumping, countervailing duties, NAFTA or other preferential tariff treatments.

If any of these conditions apply to your imports, it can affect the quantity of goods you are allowed to import. You may also be eligible to participate in a variety of CRA programs or services for importing businesses. You can obtain more information about government services and classification systems from CRA.

Depending on the goods you plan to import, you might need an Import Permit. Controlled substances such as textiles, clothing, agricultural products, and footwear require permits. The Export and Import Controls Bureau of the Department of Foreign Affairs and International Trade can help you determine what permits and documents you need.

Importers may choose to hire a customs broker to represent them in their dealings with CRA. Only customs brokers who have been licensed by CRA can account for goods and pay duties and taxes.

■ Exporting

There are a variety of government programs and services that can help you start or expand an export business. These programs and services include training and preparedness programs, trade information, export counselling, trade and statistical information, export financing, regulations information, and info-fax services. You can obtain more information about these services from a Canada Business Service Centre. The telephone number is listed in the Blue pages of your telephone book and can be found on the Web. All Canadian businesses that export on a commercial basis must obtain a Business Number from CRA. You can obtain an application form from CRA.

If you export a commercial shipment that is valued at $2,000 or more to a foreign country other than the United States, you must fill out an Export Declaration. If you ship controlled, regulated, or prohibited goods, you must submit a permit or certificate. You can obtain more information about the goods or countries that require an export permit from the Export Controls Division of the Department of Foreign Affairs and International Trade.

52. What is involved in forming a not-for-profit organization or corporation?

Not-for-profit organizations can be unincorporated associations or incorporated entities. A not-for-profit corporation is similar to a for-profit corporation in the following five ways:

- A corporation has perpetual existence
- It exists separate and apart from its shareholders or members
- It may hold real estate in its own name

• It can sue, be sued and contract in its own name as a separate entity

• In most cases, individual shareholders or members of a corporation are exempt from personal liability for the debts and obligations of the corporation

The three main differences between for-profit and not-for-profit corporations are:

• Not-for-profit corporations are without share capital and have members rather than shareholders

• In a not-for-profit corporation the members are prohibited from receiving any financial gain

• Not-for-profit corporations must be established for purposes other than gain for their members. The stated purposes for establishing the corporation are set out in a Letters Patent and may be referred to as the *"objects"* or goals of the corporation. A not-for-profit corporation can have either charitable objects or non-charitable objects.

■ Structure of not-for-profit corporations

Not-for-profit corporations are incorporated by Letters Patent. The issuance of Letters Patent may be withheld when incorporation is considered not to be in the public interest. As with any other type of corporation, a not-for-profit corporation must have by-laws which provide the framework for democratic decision-making and which set out the rules of how business will be conducted. The by-laws also set out the rights and obligations of the corporation members.

■ Board of directors

A board of a non-profit entity must have a minimum number of directors, usually three. The persons named as the first directors in the letters patent of the corporation remain the directors of the corporation until they are replaced by the same number of people appointed or elected in their place. Members elect the directors of a not-for-profit corporation. In turn, directors must elect a president from among themselves. The directors must also appoint a secretary and may appoint vice-presidents and other officers, all of whom do not need to be directors. The appointment, remuneration, functions, duties, and removal of officers are governed by the corporation's by-laws.

■ Members

In addition to directors and officers, every not-for-profit corporation must have members. Each member who signs the application for incorporation becomes a member as of the date of incorporation. Although there is no limit on the number of members of a not-for-profit corporation, there must not be fewer than three. After incorporation, the directors may admit others to membership.

Membership in a not-for-profit corporation is generally not transferable and therefore ceases to exist upon the death or resignation of a member. There may be more than one class of membership and members may be natural persons, corporations, or unincorporated associations.

A not-for-profit corporation is not allowed to pay dividends to its members and no member can receive any profit or gain from the corporation because it must be carried on without the purpose of gain for its members. Any profits must be used in the promotion of the objects of the corporation as set out in its Letters Patent.

■ Auditor and Records

To legally run a not-for-profit corporation, members must appoint an auditor annually and keep proper accounting records with respect to all financial and other transactions. Other required records include books with minutes of all meetings of members and directors, and registers of the members and directors. These records must be kept at the corporation head office and must be available during normal business hours for inspection by the directors.

53. What is involved in establishing a registered charity?

In Canada, there are four "heads" or categories of charities:

- Relief of poverty
- Advancement of education
- Advancement of religion
- Other purposes beneficial to the community

For an organization to be considered charitable, it must be operated for the benefit of the community or a significantly important class of the community. The basic theory for giving charitable and not-for-profit organizations preferential tax treatment is that they are not meant to make profits, but are established to provide public benefits.

A Canadian charitable organization may be incorporated or unincorporated. There are three types of Canadian charities:

- Charitable organizations
- Public foundations
- Private foundations

Each must meet different requirements. For a not-for-profit organization to obtain charitable status, it must file an application with and receive the approval of Canada Revenue Agency (CRA), Charities Division. If the organization wishes to become incorporated, it must also file an application for incorporation either federally or provincially.

■ Advantages of charitable registration

The advantages of charitable status are tax-based. These include exemption from and reduced liability for certain municipal, provincial, and federal taxes and the ability to issue income tax credit receipts for donations. In addition, an organization with charitable status is often seen by the public in a more positive light.

■ Registration

To apply for registration as a charity under the *Income Tax Act* (Canada), various documents must be filed with CRA. If all documentation and information filed is acceptable to CRA, the organization will receive written notice of its registration as a charity within approximately 8 to 12 months, subject to CRA discretion.

Considering the privileges that charities enjoy in our society, an organization must satisfy a number of conditions before it can be registered. It must also continue to meet various obligations to maintain its charitable status. Charities must file an annual information return with CRA and must disburse their funds for charitable purposes in accordance with a specified quota.

All not-for-profit corporations, whether charitable or non-charitable, must have their financial statements audited. And business must not be carried out with the purpose of providing gain for their members. If you require legal advice or assistance with regard to a not-for-profit or charitable organization, consult a lawyer.

WHAT'S YOUR SHARE OF A SHARE'S VALUE?

A small brokerage firm became very successful over the years by offering "star" employees shares in the business. At one stage, two employees decided it was time to move on and, in accordance with their shareholders agreement, offered the shares for sale to the remaining majority owners.

The majority owners showed the four their financial records and, based on the amount of capital or investment in the business, calculated the total value of their shares at $47,000. What the majority owners did not tell their departing colleagues was that the business was about to be sold and the actual value of their shares would soon be over $2 million.

Did the majority shareholders have a duty to their minority shareholders to reveal this information?

Yes. In a recent Ontario case, the court ruled that all "material information" must be disclosed to minority shareholders who are entitled to receive "fair market value" for their shares. The judge said the Ontario Business Corporations Act protects the "reasonable expectations" of shareholders to be dealt with fairly.

This case underlines the law's requirements that directors treat all their shareholders fairly and that any material information affecting the value of shares be disclosed to them. In other words, if you have key information, you can't sit on it. This requirement not only applies to large, publicly traded companies, but also to private and closely held companies with small numbers of shares.

It is also important to know that all minority shareholders in corporations have powerful remedies available under Canadian law to deal with "oppressive" actions by the majority.

CAN A COMPANY COMMIT MURDER?

A journalist wrote a scathing story about a company's environmental misdeeds and ended it with a dramatic assertion that the business "had committed murder." The corporation issued a statement denying the allegation and promptly sued the reporter for defamation.

If the murder accusation proves groundless, will the corporation win its lawsuit?

In all likelihood, no. Canadian courts have held over the years that a defamation action will fail if a corporation itself is not physically capable of an alleged act. For example, actual corporations cannot commit murder or rape. In one defamation case involving the Church of Scientology of Toronto, the court agreed the church was incapable of performing alleged acts. A reporter claimed that church members were practising medicine without a licence. The court ruled that the allegedly defamatory statements were in reference to church members only, and not the corporate entity itself which could not practise medicine. All said, allegations of illegal or improper actions by the people running a corporation (such as a CEO or owner) can still be the subject of a successful defamation lawsuit.

WWW Resources

Canada Business Service Centres	http://www.cbsc.org
Canada Business Service Centres Business Start-Up Assistant	http://bsa.cbsc.org
Office of the Superintendent of Bankruptcy Canada	osb-bsf.ic.gc.ca
Canada Student Loans Program	www.hrdc-drhc.gc.ca
Equifax	www.equifax.ca
TransUnion Canada	www.tuc.ca

Workers' Compensation

Whether they know it or not, most workers in Canada are protected against injuries or illnesses on-the-job by an insurance plan operated by a provincial workers' compensation board (or similarly named equivalent). These public agencies regularly collect contributions or premiums from employers and pay benefits to any insured workers who lose part or all their salary because of a work-related injury or disease.

Workers' compensation also assists employees in recovering so they can get back to their jobs or find new work. According to the Association of Workers' Compensation Boards, about 80 percent of

Canadian workers are covered by insurance under a provincial board plan. The law surrounding workers' compensation can be complex and confusing. Not only do each province's individual laws and regulations come into play, but there are also extensive policy manuals that can affect how a worker or employer is treated.

1. What is workers' compensation insurance?

Workers' compensation is a no-fault system of insurance. This means that benefits are provided to the injured employee no matter how the workplace injury or disease was caused. If an employee is entitled to benefits, however, it is important to know that the system takes away the employee's right to sue the employer. This trade-off applies in all cases, except situations where an employee may sue someone other than the employer for negligence.

2. Who is eligible for benefits?

To be eligible for benefits, you must be employed by an employer that falls under the province's workers' compensation legislation. Generally, the laws apply to most businesses, which are grouped in industry sectors and named in the legislation. Some occupations, such as those in the construction business, have different rules. Some occupations are exempt. Employers in industries covered by the legislation are required by law to register with their local workers' compensation board. Employers who do not register are subject to penalties. Surviving relatives of a worker who dies in a work-related accident or from a work-related disease are also eligible to collect benefits.

3. Who is not covered?

Each province sets out specific categories of people who are automatically not covered. For example, independent contractors and the self-employed are often excluded, as are officers of a corporation, partners in a business, and farmers.

Some provinces, however, do allow these excluded groups to apply for coverage. As well, different rules may apply to officers of a corporation, a partner in a business or a sole proprietor employed in an industry covered by the law. If you are unsure about whether you are covered or if you are eligible to collect benefits, you can call your local workers' compensation board or speak to a lawyer.

4.   What types of benefits are available?

If you are a worker with a work-related injury or disease that causes you to lose wages, you may qualify for different types of benefits. Each province determines what the insurance plan will cover. Depending on your province, the range of categories may include:

- Loss of wages
- Medical expenses
- Survivor benefits
- Vocational rehabilitation
- Physical rehabilitation
- Disability/extended wage loss benefit

■ Loss of wages

Compensation for loss of wages due to injury or disease becomes payable as soon as your income is affected. These benefits continue until you are capable of earning your normal salary again. The benefits are not 100 percent of your regular pay, but range from between 75 to 90 percent of earnings, depending on where you live.

If you return to work, start to earn income, or if your condition improves, workers' compensation will assess your ability to earn the same income as you did before your injury. Depending on how much your situation has improved, your benefits may be reduced or your benefits may end.

■ Medical expenses

Benefits cover a variety of medical expenses ranging from prescriptions and drugs to medical devices, like crutches or canes to counselling and rehabilitation services. Benefits could also cover dental services and chiropractic services, as well as physical therapy, optometry, and prosthetic aids. Check with your local workers' compensation office to determine your coverage.

■ Survivor benefits

If you die form a workplace injury or disease, your dependants can normally collect compensation benefits for a period.

■ Vocational rehabilitation

In some instances, an injury may be of such magnitude that the worker is unable to return to his or her former occupation. In those instances workers are often provided access to vocational services that will help

retrain them for some other occupation. It can also include career counselling, training in work search skills, and assistance in finding a new job.

■ Disability payment

Workers who lose a limb or body function while working are often entitled to a lump sum payment depending on what part of the body is
damaged.

If you have been permanently injured or impaired you may be entitled to non-economic benefits. These benefits are paid to compensate for
the negative effect the injury or disease has had on your life.

Non-economic benefits are in addition to benefits for loss of earnings.
If you are eligible for non-economic loss benefits, you may receive a
lump sum payment or, depending on the amount of the award, monthly
payments for life. Workers, however, have the right to choose to receive a
lump sum payment if that suits them better. The amount you are entitled to is based on a special calculation that takes into consideration your
age and permanent medical restrictions.

Some provinces also provide a retirement income benefit if you have
been receiving loss of earnings benefits for at least 12 consecutive months.
Basically, this is a savings plan for when you reach 65. Since the small
amount given for loss of earnings may make it difficult to save for retirement, and since your employer only has to continue contributing to
group insurance and pension plans for one year following your accident,
this benefit provides assistance by contributing to your retirement savings.

If you are eligible for retirement income benefits in Ontario, Ontario's
Workplace Safety and Insurance Board will set aside an additional percentage of your loss of earnings benefits every pay period. You also have
the choice of contributing to the retirement savings plan. This money
will be invested until you are 65, at which time it will be paid to you or
your surviving family. You will have the choice of a number of payment
schemes and, in the case of a small pension, the board will pay it in a
lump sum.

5.   How do I apply for benefits?

If an injury or disease results from an accident at work, it is the employee's
responsibility to report it to the employer and seek medical attention.
The employer must notify the workers' compensation board of all accidents that may result in benefit entitlement under the law. An accident
form must be filled out, signed by the employee, and then filed with the
board. In most cases, this effectively begins the claim process. In every case,

however, the employee must sign a claim form or else benefits will not be paid.

Apart from the claim process, employers must take the necessary steps to ensure that the employee receives immediate medical attention. The employer must also pay the employee for the day the accident occurred.

6. What is the limitation period for reporting an injury or disease?

The initial accident reporting form must be filed within a certain time specified in the legislation. It ranges from as quickly as three days in Ontario to up to a year in British Columbia. After completing and submitting the forms, the employer should give the employee a copy. You can also obtain copies from the local workers' compensation office.

7. What is the application process?

Once the initial reporting form is received by the workers' compensation board, the worker will be sent a package of information and forms to be filled out and signed. The forms include an approval for the release of medical information to both the employer and the board. Usually the doctor, nurse, chiropractor, or physiotherapist that is treating the injury or disease will have to fill out a form explaining the worker's functional abilities. This information assists the employee and employer in returning the injured worker to suitable employment, if possible.

The employee is responsible for getting the forms filled out and giving appropriate copies to the employer. It is a good idea for the worker to keep an organized file with copies of all forms, and ask the employer for copies of any forms that the employer submitted.

8. How is a claim decided?

Once the board receives the completed form, it reviews the application in a "claim adjudication process." Depending on whether all the appropriate information has been provided, in some jurisdictions, the claim adjudication process may take up to six weeks from the date of injury or disease before the worker receives the first benefit payment.

Most boards try to start payments within the first two weeks of the accident. If a worker has already returned to work before receiving any benefits, then the payment will normally include the entire amount of benefits that the worker is entitled to based on the time he or she was off work.

9.   How do I appeal a decision?

You can appeal if your claim for benefits is denied or you do not agree with other aspects of the decision. Employers also have the right to appeal. Most appeals are handled by a lawyer or other representative, especially if they involve a hearing. Most provinces provide some type of worker advisory service or legal clinics to assist in appeals.

■ Time Lines

There are many steps to an appeal and they can be complex. As well, there are deadlines to follow. Most provinces require an appeal be launched within 30 days, although some allow for 90 days.

Usually, both the employer and worker will each be notified of the relevant appeal deadlines from the Workplace Safety and Insurance Board when an entitlement decision is made.

■ What to do

There are usually four steps in the appeal process:

- Writing a letter to an adjudicator
- Attending mediation if the adjudicator rejects the letter
- Attending a hearing held by the Workplace Safety and Insurance Board
- Attending a hearing held by the Workplace Safety and Insurance Appeals Tribunal

The first step for you or your representative is to write a letter to the adjudicator that made the decision, stating your name, file number, and why you disagree with the decision. The adjudicator will review the matter and may change the decision if you have provided new information or if a mistake has been made.

If the adjudicator does not change the original decision, you will be sent an objection form to complete and return to the Appeals Branch of the workers' compensation board. Once it receives your objection form, the board will consider if there are issues in your case that can be settled through mediation. Mediation is an informal meeting between an employer and worker with a mediator assigned by the board to help both sides find a solution. Mediation will occur automatically if the issue concerns returning to work.

If mediation is inappropriate or does not work, the board will hold a hearing at the request of either the employee or the employer. A hearing is more formal and is conducted by an appeals resolution officer who will hear all sides of an issue and make a decision. Hearings before the board may be conducted orally or in writing.

■ Tribunal appeals

If the board does not change the original decision, workers and employers normally have a further line of appeal to an appeals tribunal that can rule on decisions made by the workers' compensation board. An appeals tribunal acts like a court. A hearing before an appeals tribunal may be conducted orally or in writing.

10. What are my responsibilities while receiving benefits?

Under the law, if you are receiving workers' compensation benefits, you have obligations to the board and to your employer. You are required to comply with all board requests for re-assessments of your medical condition, which may involve examinations by a doctor, providing information about your state of health, and participating in medical rehabilitation programs to improve your condition.

You are also required to report any changes that could affect your eligibility for benefits, such as if you return to work, get other employment, or your condition improves. If you do not properly report information to the board or you do not follow its requests or instructions, your benefits may be suspended or you may have to return money you collected. Employees must also co-operate with their employer and the board in returning to work as quickly and as safely as possible.

The employer will normally be responsible for maintaining your employment benefits such as health insurance, life insurance, or private pension for as much as one year while you are away and receiving injury benefits. Note that if you normally contribute to employment benefit plans, you must keep making regular contributions while you are off work. Otherwise, your employer may suspend your employment benefits until you return.

11. Can I get my job back?

When you are capable of returning to work, your employer is usually required to give you your pre-injury job back or one that is similar. If you are unable to return to pre-injury employment, but can perform some work, your employer must offer you the first available job that is suited to your skills and physical ability. An employer who violates an employee's return-to-work rights is subject to substantial penalties.

If your employer does not offer you suitable work, the Workplace Safety and Insurance Board may stop your benefits if you do not try to find other employment immediately. Most boards will assist you in finding work by providing you with a skills and abilities assessment and, if necessary, a so-called Labour Market Re-entry program. If you are found to be capable of returning to the same or similar work, but cannot get your job back, the Labour Market Re-entry program will establish a plan to help you find a new job. The plan usually sets a deadline when you will stop receiving benefits and may also require you to attend training courses.

If you have been given a plan to find new work or have been assessed as capable of returning to work and do not agree with the assessment or the plan, you can appeal the decisions.

12. For employers, what are the benefits of paying premiums?

Private sector employers are obligated to pay workers' compensation premiums to insure employees for work-related injuries and disease. Most public sector employers, including the provincial and municipal governments, do not pay premiums but are still required to pay benefits, under the legislation, directly to employees.

The chief benefit of paying premiums is that employers covered by workers' compensation cannot be sued for work-related injury or disease. Another benefit is that a valuable employee can receive proper help for recovery and be brought back to the workplace without added financial burden for the employer.

13. What are the costs to employers?

The costs for most employers are the premiums set each year by the provincial workers' compensation board. Premium payments are usually based on the size of the employer's payroll and the established rate for the industry category in which the employer belongs. Rates for industry categories depend on the nature and risk involved in the work. Generally, the higher the risk of accidents in an industry, the more an employer will pay in premiums.

For private sector employers and some public sector employers, the various provincial boards regularly review the frequency and cost of claims. The claims experience, which is the cost of claims made by an employer, is compared to the premiums that the employer has paid into the accident fund and this, in turn, is compared to the performance of all employers in the same industry. This analysis is typically carried on over a moving three-year period. If the employer's claims experience is good, it may receive a premium rebate. If the claims experience is bad, the employer will likely have to pay a surcharge.

14. Are there employers who do not have to pay premiums?

Each province and territory sets the criteria for employers exempted from premiums or registering with workers' compensation or insurance boards. In most provinces, it does not matter whether employees are full-time. There are also types of businesses that do not have to register. Contact your local workers' compensation board for more details.

15. What is an employer's responsibility to prevent injuries?

All employers have legal obligations to prevent workplace injury and disease. Most employers must register with their workers' compensation board and pay insurance premiums to cover injured employees.

An employer's obligation to prevent injury and disease includes maintaining a healthy and safe work environment, taking steps to train employees about occupational risks, and complying with established safety standards. Employers must take every precaution reasonable in the circumstances for the protection of workers.

An employer also has an obligation to register with its workers' compensation board. In some cases, even if an employer contracts out work, it may be responsible for premiums for contractors, subcontractors and their employees if the contractor or subcontractor defaults in its premium payments. To register as an employer, you can obtain the necessary information from your local workers' compensation board office.

16. What happens if someone is injured?

Under the law, an employer has several responsibilities after a work-related injury or disease occurs. Depending on the province, these may include:

- First aid and transportation to a health care facility, if necessary
- Reporting the accident to the local board
- Continuing regular employee benefits for a period while the worker is absent

• Returning the worker to the same or a similar job when the worker is able to return to pre-injury employment, and to a suitable position if the worker is not able to return to pre-injury employment

• The employer is also required to pay the worker his or her regular daily rate for the day of the accident

17. What do employers need to report?

Employers must report accidents to their board if an employee has to obtain health care for a work-related injury or disease or if an employee has to take time off work and cannot earn regular wages because of the injury or disease. To do so, the employer is required to complete a special form provided by the board and file it within the time specified in provincial law, which can vary.

For example, in Manitoba and Saskatchewan, an employer must report within five business days, while in Ontario it's within three days of learning about the worker's condition. Employers who don't report are subject to fines.

18. Must employers continue to contribute to benefit plans after an employee is injured?

If the worker is away due to a work-related injury or disease, the employer may be required to continue making contributions to regular employment benefit plans, such as health insurance, life insurance, and pensions, but it varies according to province.

In Nova Scotia, for example, there's no duty to pay. In Ontario, an employer must contribute for at least one year. If employees also contribute to any of these benefit plans, they will be required to continue contributing while away from work or the employer will not be obligated to provide the benefit.

19. Must an employer re-employ an injured worker?

Under the law, employers are normally required to reinstate a worker after the person has recovered. There are exceptions, such as for very small businesses. If the worker's job is unavailable, the employer is normally required to provide a job that is comparable in responsibility and pay. If the worker cannot perform the essential duties of the pre-injury job, then the employer may be required to offer the person a position that is suitable to his or her skills and physical ability.

20. When do employers have to return injured workers to their job?

Workers' compensation officials will decide when the worker is ready to return to work. Workers and employers must co-operate in the effort to return the injured worker to work as soon as it is safely possible.

Under most compensation schemes and human rights laws, an employer is required to accommodate the worker by helping that person perform the essential duties of the job. Employees must therefore co-operate in the return-to-work effort.

21. What are the penalties for not returning an injured worker to a job?

Employers who do not comply with the return-to-work obligations of the legislation will be fined by their workers' compensation board. As well, employers have limitations on when they can terminate an employee who has returned from an injury or disease.

True or False?

1. Every employee in the country is covered by workers' compensation.

2. Covered workers can apply for compensation benefits for both a workplace disease and injury.

3. An employer has a legal obligation to re-hire an injured worker.

4. A board decision on benefits is final.

5. An employer subject to workers' compensation must report an accident when an employee is injured.

Answers

1. False. The compensation board determines which industries are covered.

2. True

3. True

4. False. Board decisions can be appealed.

5. True

Workers' Compensation Boards

**Workers' Compensation Board
of British Columbia**
P.O. Box 5350
Vancouver BC V6B 5L5
Tel: 604-273-2266   Fax: 604-276-3151
www.worksafebc.com

Workers' Compensation Board of Alberta
P.O. Box 2415
9912-107 Street
Edmonton AB T5J 2S5
Tel: 780-498-4000   Fax: 780-498-7875
www.wcb.ab.ca

**Workers' Compensation Board
of Saskatchewan**
200, 1881 Scarth Street
Regina SK S4P 4L1
Tel: 306-787-4370   Fax: 306-787-0213
www.wcbsask.com

**Workers' Compensation Board
of Manitoba**
333 Broadway
Winnipeg MB R3C 4W3
Tel: 204-954-4321   Fax: 204-954-4968
www.wcb.mb.ca

**Ontario Workplace Safety
and Insurance Board**
200 Front Street West
Toronto ON M5V 3J1
Tel: 416-344-1000   Fax: 416-344-3999
www.wsib.on.ca

**Commission De La Santé Et De La
Sécurité Du Travail**
1199, rue de Bleury
C.P. 6056, Succursale
Montréal QC H3C 4E1
Tel: 514-906-3780   Fax: 514-906-3781
www.csst.qc.ca

**New Brunswick Workplace Health, Safety
And Compensation Commission**
1 Portland Street
P.O. Box 160
Saint John NB E2L 3X9
Tel: 506-632-2200   Fax: 506-632-4999
www.whscc.nb.ca

**Workers' Compensation Board
Of Nova Scotia**
5668 South Street
P.O. Box 1150
Halifax NS B3J 2Y2
Tel: 902-491-8999   Fax: 902-491-8002
www.wcb.ns.ca

**Workers Compensation Board
Of Prince Edward Island**
14 Weymouth Street
Charlottetown PEI C1A 4Y1
Tel: 902-368-5680   Fax: 902-368-5705
www.wcb.pe.ca

**Newfoundland Workplace Health Safety
And Compensation Commission**
146-148 Forest Road
P.O. Box 9000, Station B
St. John's NF A1A 3B8
Tel: 709-778-1000   Fax: 709-738-1714
www.whscc.nf.ca

**Yukon Workers' Compensation
Health & Safety Board**
401 Strickland Street
Whitehorse YK Y1A 5N8
Tel: 867-667-5645   Fax: 867-393-6279
www.wcb.yk.ca

**Workers' Compensation Board
Of The Northwest Territories And Nunavut**
P.O. Box 8888
Yellowknife NT X1A 2R3
Tel: 867-920-3888   Fax: 867-873-4596
www.wcb.nt.ca

**The Association of Workers
Compensation Boards**
6551 B Mississauga Road
Mississauga, Ontario
L5N 1A6   Canada
Tel: 905-542-3633   Fax: 905-542-0039
www.awcbc.org/

TAKING CARE OF BUSINESS

Intellectual Property: Protecting The Intangible

Intellectual property (IP) is the end product of human creativity and expression. Music, writing, paintings, computer software, inventions, industrial processes, and many other original creative endeavours can be intellectual property.

Among the most common types of protection for IP are patents, trademarks, copyright, and industrial designs. Others areas of IP law cover trade secrets, integrated circuit topography registrations, industrial designs and plant breeders' rights.

As with any private property, IP owners and creators (not always the same) have enforceable legal rights preventing others from using or profiting from their creations without permission and allowing owners to sell, license, or transfer various IP rights.

To fully protect your original invention, product, service, or work, you may need to know about different types of IP rights and protections. For example, a newly invented machine may need a patent to protect its method of operation, an industrial design registration to cover its construction, and a trademark to stop other businesses from using its unique name in the marketplace. While the invention itself does not qualify for copyright, the machine's operating manual probably does. Each of these rights exists for different periods and may need to be registered or granted in different countries.

If the law surrounding intellectual property sounds confusing and complex, that's because it is. In most cases, a lawyer or other registered IP professional will be needed to sort through the various registration procedures, application requirements, and protections available. As always, however, it helps to understand the basics of this evolving area of law.

1. What types of intellectual property protection are available?

• Patents cover new inventions such as processes, machines, manufacturing, composition of matter, or any new and useful improvement of an existing invention

• Trademarks protect words, symbols, or designs (or a combination of these) that distinguish wares or services from others in the marketplace

• Copyrights provide protection for artistic, dramatic, musical, or literary works (including computer programs)

- Industrial designs are the visual features of shape, configuration, pattern, or ornament applied to a manufactured article

A lawyer or other registered intellectual property specialist can provide more information and determine which intellectual property category best meets your needs.

2. Why is intellectual property different from other property rights?

This area of law recognizes that original creators in our society should have special rights. For instance, they should be compensated for use of their intellectual property or the authority to stop others from using or selling their invention or work. Unlike almost any other type of property, intellectual property is:

- Intangible
- Often expensive to develop
- Easily copied or distributed to an infinite number

A shrinking global market and the growing use of technologies, such as the Internet, have increased the danger that intellectual property rights will be violated or abused. With effective protection and enforcement of these rights, however, businesses and creative individuals will have an incentive to pursue new scientific, artistic, and business endeavours.

3. What laws affect intellectual property rights?

In Canada, IP rights are granted under the:

- Copyright Act
- Industrial Design Act
- Integrated Circuit Topography Act
- Patent Act
- Plant Breeders' Rights Act
- Trademarks Act

Enforcement or use of these rights may also arise under other legislation, such as the Competition Act, the common law and Québec's Civil Code, including rights given to trade secrets and unregistered trademarks.

Patents

4. What is a patent?

In Canada, a patent is granted by the government for a limited period of 17 to 20 years for the exclusive use, sale, or manufacture of invented products or processes. To be patentable, an invention must be novel and have utility. A third criterion used recently is that the invention must not be obvious to a person skilled in the field of the invention. It is difficult for many inventions to meet this last criterion.

A patent will not keep your invention secret from the world. In fact, it will do the exact opposite and tell everyone exactly how it works. In Canada, 18 months after you file an application for a patent, the Canadian Intellectual Property Office publishes your application. This gives other people the opportunity to learn from your invention.

It is also important to realize that your patent is only recognized in Canada. Generally speaking, patents are obtained on a country-by-country basis, although there are some mechanisms by which an applicant can apply for patents for more than one country in a single application.

5. What can be patented?

You may be able to patent any invention that is a new and useful art, process machine, manufacture or composition of matter, or an improvement on any of these. Most patents are issued for inventions that are improvements on an already existing and patented invention.

In Canada, you generally cannot patent such things as mere ideas, architectural plans, computer programs or methods of medical treatment. There are, however, other kinds of intellectual property protection that you may be able to use.

6. Why obtain a patent?

There are two main reasons why it is a good idea to obtain a patent for your invention. First, a patent gives you the right to stop others from making, using, or selling your invention. Second, you can use the patent to make a profit by selling it, licensing it, or using it as an asset to negotiate funding.

You do not need a patent to make, use, or sell your invention. Nonetheless, if you are going to make your invention public and want legal protection for your rights as an inventor, you will need a patent. Unlike other areas of intellectual property law such as copyright, you cannot claim the exclusive rights to an invention merely because you invented or created it first. The law will only provide you with protection for an invention you make public through a patent. If you do not have a patent, someone could legally copy your invention and sell it for a profit.

■ "First to file" rule

In Canada, the "first to file" rule applies. This means that the first person to file a patent application for an invention will have priority over any later applications filed for the same invention. In other countries, such as the United States, the "first-to-invent" rule is used. In Canada, therefore, it is advisable to file a patent application as soon as the invention is finished. It is also extremely important that the application is completed correctly. It is a good idea to hire a patent lawyer or a registered patent agent to handle your application. If you do not get a patent for your invention before someone else obtains a patent, he or she may be able to prevent you from using your invention.

■ "No public disclosure" rule

In most countries, you will not be able to obtain a patent if you made your invention public before you filed an application for a patent. This means you must not advertise, display, sell to the public, or publish your invention until you have filed an application for a patent.

While making an invention public before filing an application can be a bar to obtaining patent protection, Canadian law allows a one-year "grace period" during which an invention may be disclosed in public, before filing, without jeopardizing the validity of the eventual patent. Most other countries do not allow such disclosures and foreign patent opportunities may be lost where there has been public disclosure, such as in a trade journal, before filing.

7.   Who are patent agents?

Applying for a patent involves many complicated legal and technical issues. A patent lawyer or a registered patent agent can help draft your patent application so it fully protects your invention. Unless you have experience with the patent process, you should hire a registered patent agent to assist you. Many registered patent agents are also lawyers and can represent you in legal matters associated with your patent.

■ What a patent lawyer or registered patent agent does

Patent lawyers and registered patent agents handle your patent application and act on your behalf in communicating with the Canadian

Intellectual Property Office. A patent agent must pass rigorous exams to be registered with the Canadian Intellectual Property Office. You can obtain a list of registered patent agents from the Canadian Intellectual Property Office in Ottawa. Beware of any unregistered patent agents who are not authorized to handle patent applications and are not subject to discipline from the Canadian Intellectual Property Office. For example, some businesses purport to help inventors take their inventions to market, but these businesses may not be fully qualified.

You should find a patent lawyer or registered patent agent that you feel comfortable with. Be sure to discuss the fee before the lawyer or agent begins work on your application. Fees are not regulated by the Canadian Intellectual Property Office. Once you have appointed a patent agent to handle your application, the Intellectual Property Office will communicate with your agent.

8. What do I need to do to prepare for filing a patent application?

Before you spend time and money filing an application for a patent, you may want to hire a registered patent agent or a patent search firm to conduct a preliminary search to see what other patents already exist. Although no search is exhaustive, a preliminary search will help you decide if your invention is truly new and different enough from what others have patented. If your invention is not new and obvious to others (see question 4 in this section), you will not be able to receive a patent for it and you should not file an application.

■ When a preliminary search is not needed

In most cases, it is best to conduct a preliminary search. There are instances, however, when you may not need a search. For example, if you are concerned someone else will file an application for the same invention before you, then you may decide not to wait to conduct a search. Discuss your situation with a lawyer or a registered patent agent. This person can help you decide whether you should conduct a search and whether other inventions are too similar to yours to warrant a patent application.

9. What is required for a patent application?

Again, if you decide to apply for patent protection, consider contacting a lawyer or a registered patent agent for help because the application process and patent laws are complex and a simple error can be fatal to your application.

Although the Canadian Intellectual Property Office does not provide a standard application form for you to fill out, your patent application must still follow a standard format. You or your agent must complete a petition, pay fees, and submit information that describes your design.

■ The Petition

A petition is a request for a patent. This provides the names and complete addresses of all the inventors involved, a title for the invention, and name of the patent agent who will be acting on your behalf.

■ The Patent Application

You must submit detailed information about your invention. There are three parts to the submission:

1. The abstract
2. The specification
3. Drawings of the invention

The abstract is a short technical description of the invention and describes how it is different from other inventions. Consider it a summary of sorts. The specification must include a clear and complete description of the invention and its usefulness. One very important part of a specification is the "claims." Claims are a definition of the boundaries of patent protection you want. They are like a fence around the patented invention that protects it from trespassers. Everything that is not enclosed by this fence is freely available to be copied, manufactured, or sold by the public.

The difficult part of the application is to write the claims so that the invention is defined broadly enough to provide the maximum protection, while also being specific enough to differentiate your invention from what others have done before you. A claim can only cover what you have invented. A lawyer or a registered patent agent will help write the claims for your application.

The final part of the required information involves drawings of the invention. There are specific requirements that must be followed with respect to the size, quality, and detail of the drawings. The drawings should also clearly show all parts of the invention defined in the claims.

10. What happens in the patent application process?

There are four main steps in the application process, which usually takes two to three years to complete.

■ Filing the application

The first step is to file the application with the Canadian Intellectual Property Office. Applications will be accepted for filing whether or not they are complete. If your application is complete, it will be assigned a number and a filing date and the Canadian Intellectual Property Office will issue a filing certificate. Your lawyer or patent agent will keep a record of the number assigned to your application and refer to it in all correspondence with the Intellectual Property Office. Remember, there are fees for filing the application, plus the cost of your agent's services.

If the application is incomplete but still provides certain basic details, it will still be assigned a number and a filing date. However, the application must be completed later within a specific time or your application will be considered abandoned. You must also pay an additional fee to complete the application.

■ Requesting an examination

The second step is to request an examination, which must be submitted in writing to the Canadian Intellectual Property Office within five years of filing your patent application. An examination fee must also be included.

■ Prosecution of examination

After the request for examination has been made, the patent examiner will review your application. The examination process can take up to two or three years. The examiner will review the claims and ensure your invention is new and non-obvious. The examiner will search for so-called "prior art," which is anything of a tangible nature that can be used to dispute your claim of originality, such as a similar invention already in use.

If the examiner has no objections to your application, you will be granted a patent. There is rarely an application that does not involve objections. If the examiner has objections about some aspect of your application, your patent agent will receive a letter of objection from the Canadian Intellectual Property Office. This is not the end of your application, though. You are given an opportunity to respond to the objection and, if the examiner is satisfied with your response, then the application will be allowed. Your patent agent is experienced in responding to objections. A process of receiving and answering objections may be repeated several times.

If the examiner's objections cannot be satisfied, your application will be rejected. You or your agent can appeal this decision to the Patent Appeal Board.

■ Granting of a patent

If the examiner allows your application and indicates a willingness to grant you a patent, your patent agent will receive a Notice of Allowance by mail. You will be required to pay a final fee. The patent will be granted anywhere from 6 to 16 weeks after the final fee is paid.

11. When can I use the terms "Patented," "Patent Pending," and "Patent Applied For"?

After an invention has been patented, it can be marked as "Patented." You do not have to mark a patented invention in Canada, but it is usually a good idea to do so because it lets people know they cannot legally manufacture, sell, or use the patented invention without your permission.

It is also possible to mark inventions immediately after you have filed a patent application but before the patent is issued. The phrases "Patent Applied For" or "Patent Pending" can be used to let people know a patent application has been filed.

These phrases will only serve as a warning. Until a patent is issued, anyone may lawfully use or duplicate the invention. That said, if someone uses an invention without the inventor's permission with the knowledge that a patent is pending, and the inventor later receives a patent, the inventor may sue that individual for using the invention back to the date the application was published.

12. How long does patent protection last?

If your patent application is accepted and you obtain a patent in Canada, you have the right to exclude others from making, using, or selling your invention for a maximum of 20 years from the day you filed your application in Canada.

To maintain your patent application and patent protection over this period, you must also pay an annual maintenance fee. This fee increases as the 20-year period passes. If you do not pay the fee, your patent or patent application will lapse, which means others will be allowed to use the invention without your permission.

13. Can I profit from a patent or patent application?

Assigning and licensing are two different ways inventors can profit from their patents. The process of assigning or licensing a patent or a patent application is complicated. To make sure your rights are protected, contact a patent lawyer for advice about assigning or licensing your patent or patent application. You should also have your lawyer review the agreement before you sign it.

■ Assignment

An assignment is the sale of the ownership of all or some of a patent. When you assign your invention, you give up your rights as the inventor. A benefit of assigning your patent is that you can make an immediate profit without worrying whether the invention will be a success in the market. You can assign a patent or even a patent application, but it must be made in writing. Any changes in ownership should also be registered with the Canadian Intellectual Property Office. This will protect your legal rights and you will still be able to bring a lawsuit against anyone who uses your potential invention without your permission. There is a small government fee for filing an assignment with the Intellectual Property Office.

■ Licensing

Licensing gives someone other than the inventor permission to make, use, or sell the patented invention. The inventor maintains ownership of the patent. In most cases, the owner of the invention will charge a fee or royalty for granting someone a licence. If you are involved in a licensing arrangement, make sure the agreement is in writing and it includes time limits for the licence and the fees or royalties to be paid. Licences should also be registered with the Intellectual Property Office. Again, there is a small government fee for filing a licence with the Intellectual Property Office.

14. How do I obtain a patent in another country?

A Canadian patent does not protect your rights in foreign markets. If your invention will be marketed elsewhere, you should apply for a patent in the appropriate countries. You can apply for a foreign patent either within Canada through the Canadian Intellectual Property Office by filing an international patent application, or you can apply directly to the patent office of the country concerned.

Patent rules in foreign countries may be different from rules in Canada. For example, in many countries you will not be able to obtain a patent for an invention that has been disclosed to the public before the filing date of your patent application. This means you must not, for example, sell, advertise, display, or publish your invention until you have filed an application for a patent. Because the rules elsewhere are sometimes different and complicated, contact a patent lawyer or a registered patent agent to help you deal with foreign countries.

15. What is patent infringement?

Patent infringement occurs when someone makes, uses, or sells a patented invention without permission of the owner. Generally, the patent infringement must occur in a country where the inventor holds a patent. Also, the Canadian Intellectual Property Office itself will not prevent other people from infringing on your patent. It is up to the owner of a patented invention to ensure that no one else uses it.

Your invention is also protected for a period after the patent application is filed but before the patent is granted. This protection is only available for inventions that are successfully patented. If you receive a patent, you can sue someone for an infringement on your patent that may have occurred anytime after the day your application was published. If you can prove that people infringed your patent, the court can order them to stop using your invention and to pay you compensation.

Contact a lawyer if someone does infringe your patent and you wish to pursue legal action. Whether the court agrees that an infringement has occurred will largely depend on the wording you used to define the invention in your patent application. This is why it is so important to clearly define your invention when you file the application.

Also, it is important to be aware that patents are always open to re-examination or other forms of attack. This means that the person who infringes your patent may well argue that your patent is invalid. Again, contact a lawyer for advice if someone has made, used, or sold your patented invention without your permission.

Trademarks

16. What is a trademark?

A trademark is a word, symbol, or picture, or a combination of these, that is used to distinguish a product or service of one business from the products and services of other businesses. It is important to note that there is a difference between a trademark and a trade name. A trade name is simply the name of a business or organization. It is only possible to register a trade name as a trademark if the name is used to identify a product or service.

17. Who can own a trademark?

Companies, individuals, partnerships, trade unions, or lawful associations may all register and own marks so long as they meet the requirements of the Trademarks Act.

18. What can be trademarked?

There are three types of trademarks.

■ Ordinary Marks

The first is words or symbols that distinguish the products or services of a business or individual. An example of a word trademark is "Pepsi." An example of a design trademark would be McDonald's golden arches.

■ Certification Marks

Certification Marks identify products or services that meet a defined standard. One person or business usually owns this type of trademark, but the trademark is often licensed to other people to use if their product or service meets the defined standard. An example of a certification mark is the "wool mark" owned by The Wool Bureau of Canada and used with permission by other companies to indicate clothing made with pure wool.

■ Distinguishing Guise

A Distinguishing Guise identifies the unique shape of a product or a package. For example, the shape of a particular bottle may be a trademark, such as the traditional Coca-Cola bottle.

19. Why register a trademark?

You are not required to register a trademark with Canada's Intellectual Property Office to have a legal right to use it. Many trademarks are established simply because they are used for a long time. However, if there is a dispute about who owns the trademark, it can be difficult to prove your ownership and protect your rights if your trademark is not registered.

The main advantage of registering your trademark is that you will have the exclusive right to use the trademark throughout Canada. In the absence of a registered trademark, your scope of protection is limited to the geographic region within which you have developed business goodwill or a reputation in connection with your trademark.

■ "First use" rule

In trademark law it is very important that you first use the mark to establish your rights as the owner because the first one to use it is the lawful owner. You can use the mark even before your application for registration has been filed. Even if you have a registered trademark, you could be ordered to stop using it if someone else started using a similar or confusing mark before you started using yours.

20. What trademarks cannot be registered?

There are some trademarks that you cannot register for exclusive use, though you may still be able to use them for your products and services. Be aware of these seven restrictions before you apply to register your trademark.

■ Names and surnames

You cannot register a trademark that is essentially a proper name or surname. There are two exceptions to this rule. First, if you can show your products or services have become known and recognized under that name, you may be granted a trademark. The second exception is if your name has another meaning. For example, the word Black may be your last name, but it is also a colour.

■ Descriptive words

You are not permitted to register a mark that just describes some aspect of your products or services. For example, the words "cold" for ice cream or "juicy" for apples could likely not be registered. These words describe general qualities of ice cream and apples, and it would be unfair to allow only one person to use them. Still, if you can show that the mark has become so well known that people think only of your products or services when they hear or see it, then you might be able to register it.

■ Misleading marks

You will not be able to register a mark that is clearly misleading. For example, you likely could not register the mark "air express" for a courier service that uses ground transportation.

■ Place of origin

You will not be able to register a mark that clearly describes the place where the product or services came from or which clearly misleads the public into thinking that the products or services came from a place they did not. For example, the words "British Columbia Wines" or "Danish furniture" likely could not be registered.

■ Words in other languages

Words in another language that are the names of the products or services cannot be registered. For example, "gelato," an Italian word meaning ice cream, and "cervesa," a Spanish word meaning beer, could not be registered.

■ Words that cause confusion

A mark that is confusing with someone else's trademark will not be registered. The Trademark Examiner will consider whether the two marks in question look or sound alike, suggest similar ideas, are used with similar products or services, how long they have been in use, the extent of use, and whether the associated customers are similar.

■ Prohibited marks

Finally, there are several types of marks that are not allowed. For example, you cannot register official government symbols, the coat of arms of the British Royal family, symbols of provinces, municipalities, and public institutions, profane language, racial slurs, or obscene drawings.

Finally, note that the Intellectual Property Office may require a disclaimer for any part of your trademark that is clearly descriptive in nature or which is a name or surname. This means you will not be able to prevent anyone from using the disclaimed portion of your trademark.

21. What should I do to prepare for a trademark application?

Before you spend time and money filing an application for a trademark, there are two things you may want to do. First, make sure you are either using or will be using the trademark in Canada. Second, conduct a preliminary search to see what other trademarks exist.

The law requires that you use your trademark before it can be registered. This means you must use the name, symbol, or design in association with the products or services offered. The Intellectual Property Office will ask you to provide the date of first use on your trademark application. If you have not started to use your trademark, you should apply for a "proposed use" trademark. This is an important distinction.

Second, a preliminary search will help determine whether your trademark could be confused with someone else's. If your trademark is too similar to another's you can consider modifying it before you apply. A search cannot only help you avoid infringing someone else's trademark, it can also help avoid potential lawsuits against you.

■ How to conduct a search

Conducting a search is a very complicated and technical process. Conducting an accurate and thorough search can be even more difficult. You should consider hiring a trademark agent to do a search for you. A trademark agent has the expertise needed to compare your mark to others and determine whether your mark can be registered.

22. What is required for a trademark application?

It usually takes between one and two years to register a trademark. Applying for a trademark is not only a lengthy process, but is also very complicated. If you decide to apply for a trademark, contact a registered trademark agent for assistance.

■ Determine what form of application to submit

Different applications are required depending on whether your application is for a mark that you now use, one you propose to use, and whether it is a word and other variations.

■ Create and fill out the forms

Creating the proper application is complex because the application must be prepared with your specific mark and use requirements in mind. It is important to make sure your application is correct because changes are often not allowed after you have filed it. You may have to file another application and pay another application fee depending on the required changes.

■ Submit drawings if required

If your trademark is anything other than a word or words in block letters, then you must submit a drawing of the trademark. The drawings must be of a specific quality and size.

23. What happens in the trademark registration process?

There are six main steps in the application process. It will usually take one to two years to register a trademark.

■ Filing the application

Your application must be filed with the Canadian Intellectual Property Office. If your application is incomplete, the Office will notify your trademark agent to ask for missing information. If the application is complete, the Canadian Intellectual Property Office will issue a filing date and an application number. Your trademark agent should keep a record of this number and refer to it in all correspondence with the Intellectual Property Office. If there is no missing information, your trademark agent should receive the filing receipt within two to three weeks.

■ The examination

When the application is complete, an examiner will conduct a search to make sure your proposed trademark will not be confused with anyone else's and that your mark can be registered according to the *Trademarks Act*. Often the examiner will find a problem with an application. If this is the case, the Canadian Intellectual Property Office will contact your trademark agent and he or she will have a chance to respond to the problems.

The examiner may request a disclaimer at this point. A disclaimer is a statement that a certain part of your trademark is not exclusively yours. It is still possible to use the disclaimed part of your mark, but you will have no rights to it. If there is a problem with your trademark application and your response to the problem does not satisfy the examiner, the application will be refused.

Your lawyer can appeal this decision to the Federal Court of Canada. If you fail to respond to the Intellectual Property Office by the required date, it will become abandoned.

■ Advertisement

If the examiner is satisfied with your application, your trademark application will be advertised in the Trademarks Journal. There will be a two-month period during which other people can oppose your application. If someone does oppose your application, your lawyer or trademark agent will be notified by mail.

■ Allowance and final registration

If there is no opposition to the application or the opposition is unsuccessful, your application will be allowed. To register your trademark, you must pay a final registration fee. If your application was based upon proposed use, you must send in a declaration that you are now using your trademark. The Trademark Office will send your lawyer or trademark agent a Registration Certificate, which shows proof that your trademark is registered in Canada.

24. When can I use the official trademark symbols ™ or ®?

The owner of a trademark is not required by law to use the trademark symbol. It is a good idea to use a symbol, however, because it can help prevent people from using your trademark illegally for their own products or services.

There are two different trademark symbols you can use. The most common is ®, which indicates the trademark is registered. This symbol should only be used if the trademark is, in fact, registered. The ™ symbol can also be used. Interestingly, this symbol can be used regardless of whether the mark is officially registered or not. Also, if you want to communicate your trademark in French, you can use the letters "MD" if the mark is registered, or the letters "MC" whether it is registered or not.

25. How long does trademark protection last?

A registered trademark is renewable 15 years from the date of registration. After 15 years, you can renew your trademark registration for another 15 years by paying a small renewal fee. There is no limit to the number of times the trademark may be renewed.

26. Can I profit from a trademark?

Assigning and licensing are two ways to profit from a trademark. To make sure your rights are protected, contact a trademark lawyer to advise you about assigning or licensing your mark. Have your lawyer review any agreement before you sign it.

■ Assignments

An assignment is the sale of your ownership in a trademark. Assignments should be made in writing. You should register any change in the ownership of your trademark with the Intellectual Property Office. There is a small fee for filing an assignment with the Office.

■ Licensing

Licensing gives someone other than the owner a temporary right to use the trademark while the owner maintains ownership. In most cases, the owner of a trademark will charge a fee or royalty for granting someone a licence to use the trademark. If you are involved in a licensing arrangement, you should make sure the agreement is in writing, and includes the time limits of the licence and the fee to be paid.

27. How do I obtain a trademark in another country?

A Canadian trademark registration does not protect your rights in foreign markets.

For protection as the registered owner of the trademark in other countries, you should apply to register in those countries. Because the laws are often different in foreign countries and can be very complicated, contact a registered trademark agent to help you register your trademark in a foreign country.

28. What is trademark infringement?

Trademark infringement is when someone uses a trademark without the permission of the owner. The Canadian Intellectual Property Office itself will not prevent other people from infringing on your trademark. It is up to the owner of the trademark to ensure that no one else uses it. For example, you should watch out for new trademarks, products or services in the marketplace that could be confused with yours.

If someone infringes your trademark, you have the right to take legal action against him or her. If the infringement is proven, the court can order that person to stop using your trademark and to pay you compensation.

COPYRIGHT

29. What is copyright?

Simply put, a copyright is a legal right to make public, produce, or reproduce any original written or artistic work, or a substantial part of it, in any material form. Canada's copyright law makes it illegal to copy certain types of original works without the permission of the copyright owner. To be covered by copyright, the creative works must be original and must not have been copied from something else.

30. What can be copyrighted?

Copyright can be given to various types of dramatic, literary, artistic, and musical works, including:

- Architectural works
- Books, articles and other original writings
- Choreography
- Compilations of works, encyclopedias, and dictionaries
- Computer programs
- Engravings
- Films
- Maps and charts

- Music and lyrics
- Paintings and illustrations
- Photographs
- Plays
- Sculptures
- Sound recordings
- Television and radio programs

Note that mere ideas and information itself cannot be copyrighted. Only the expression of an idea is subject to copyright.

31. Who owns the copyright?

In most cases the person who created the work will own the copyright. If an employee creates the work for an employer, however, the employer is the owner unless it has an agreement that says otherwise. For example, freelance contract workers typically own the copyright in works they produce for someone else, whereas employees do not.

When a copyright owner dies, the copyright is treated like other property and becomes part of the estate to be inherited by the creator's heirs. Heirs also acquire the exclusive rights in the work, which means they can authorize the reproduction, publication, or performance of the work. That said, special ownership rules apply if you assign or license your copyright to someone else.

32. How do I get copyright for my work?

The creator of an original work owns the copyright in Canada from the moment it is created. It is not necessary to register your copyright to have protection in Canada. The work does not even have to be published or seen by the public.

Once the work is put in a fixed form, such as written on paper, recorded on video or created in electronic form, you automatically have copyright protection. If you want to register copyright in your works, you can do so with the Canadian Intellectual Property Office for a small fee. Registering a copyright may help if you take legal action against anyone who infringes your copyright.

33. Is my copyright recognized outside of Canada?

Copyright protection is granted throughout much of the industrialized world as long as the creator was at the time of creation a citizen or resident of one of over one hundred countries that subscribe to international copyright treaties. The treaties cover most countries in the world, but if you are unsure about a particular country, contact the Canadian Intellectual Property Office or a copyright lawyer.

While Canadian copyright owners are given protection under the laws of each particular country, some may specifically require registration for copyright protection. Again, contact a lawyer if you are concerned about international copyright protection.

Interestingly, copyright protection for sound recordings does not fall under the above international conventions. To ensure your sound recording has copyright protection in another country, consult a lawyer.

34. Why should I register a copyright?

Although you are not legally required to register a copyright with the Canadian Intellectual Property Office, there are at least two reasons why it is a good idea to do so.

■ Evidence of ownership

Registering your copyright provides evidence that you are the author or creator of the work. It also provides evidence the work is protected by copyright. This makes it easier to take legal action against someone who infringes your copyright.

■ Facilitates assignments or licences

Registering a copyright will help the author or creator sell or license the copyright. A registered copyright also helps protect the rights of people who purchase the assignment or licence. For example, if you buy a copyright and the transfer of ownership is not registered with the Canadian Intellectual Property Office, you might lose ownership rights if the author sells copyright to more than one person. Having a registered copyright helps ensure the copyright you hold is valid.

35. How do I register a copyright?

You must fill out a standard application form and pay a small application fee. You may also have to submit a copy of your work to the National Library of Canada.

■ Application form

A copyright application kit is available from the Canadian Intellectual Property Office in Ottawa. On the application form you must include the full legal name and complete address of the owner or owners of the copyright. The owner is usually the creator or author of the work, but if you want to register an assignment or licence of a copyright, the owner will be the buyer or licensor.

■ Copyright categories

Next, the application form asks you to choose a copyright category for your work. The instruction sheet provides examples of the available categories. You must also provide a title for your work. On the application form you must indicate whether the work has ever been published. The owner or someone authorized to act for the owner must also sign the form.

■ Library Deposit

The final step in registering a copyright is to determine if you need to send copies of your work to the National Library of Canada. Under the National Library Act, copies of any new "library matter" must be sent to the National Library within one week of publication.

36. What happens in the copyright application process?

You are required to submit your application and registration fee to the Canadian Intellectual Property Office. The Office will review the application to make sure it is completed properly. The Office will inform you if any changes need to be made. Once the application has been accepted, the Canadian Intellectual Property Office will send you a Registration Certificate. The entire process may take four to eight weeks. If the Intellectual Property Office has any questions or concerns about your application it may take longer. You will receive a certificate of registration if your application is accepted.

37. Should I use the copyright symbol © to protect my works?

In Canada, the *Copyright Act* does not require that any symbols be used to indicate that works are subject to copyright. If you do distribute your work to the public or internationally, you should use the copyright symbol to let others know that the work is protected.

The copyright symbol consists of a letter "c" in a circle, followed by the name of the owner of the copyright and the year the work was first published. You can use the copyright symbol even if you have not registered your copyright.

Other countries have different requirements. For countries that require copyright registration, it is wise to use the symbol. The United States, for example, has requirements for registration and marking that Canada does not. Contact a lawyer for more information about the need to register and the use of copyright symbols.

38. Can I profit from a copyright?

Assigning and licensing are two different ways that authors or creators can profit from their copyrights. To make sure your rights are protected, contact a lawyer about assigning or licensing your copyright. As well, have your lawyer review any agreement before you sign it.

■ Assignments

An assignment is the sale of rights of ownership in your copyright. Assignments must be made in writing. You should register any change in the ownership of your copyright with the Intellectual Property Office. This will protect your legal rights. You will also be able to bring a lawsuit against anyone who uses the copyright without your permission. There is a small fee for filing an assignment with the Intellectual Property Office.

■ Licensing

Licensing gives someone other than the owner a temporary right or permission to use the protected work while the owner maintains ownership of the copyright. In most cases, the owner of a copyright will ask for a fee, royalty, or other compensation for granting someone a licence to use the copyright. If you are involved in a licensing arrangement, you should make sure the agreement is in writing and includes the time limits of the licence and amount of fee to be paid. Licences should also be registered with the Canadian Intellectual Property Office. There is a small fee for filing a licence with the Intellectual Property Office.

To register an assignment or a licence, send the original agreement or a certified copy of the agreement with your fee to the Canadian Intellectual Property Office. It will probably take six weeks to register, but the assignment or licence is effective as soon as the agreement is made.

39. How long does copyright last?

In most cases, a copyright lasts for the lifetime of the author plus 50 years after the calendar year in which the author dies. Copyright protection always expires on December 31 of the last year of protection. There are no maintenance fees for copyright and copyright cannot be renewed.

There are, however, exceptions to the general rule, including:

■ Government works

Copyright in a work that is published by a government department lasts for the duration of the calendar year in which it was first published, plus 50 years. There is no term for copyright in legislation or court judgments.

■ Works not published before the author's death

In some cases, creative works are not published before the author's death. Copyright in such works will exist for the duration of the calendar year in which it was first published, performed, or delivered plus 50 years.

■ More than one author

Sometimes works are created by more than one person. In this case, copyright will last for the lives of all creators and will continue for 50 years after the calendar year in which the last author died.

■ Author unknown

If the author of a work is unknown, the copyright could last either for the duration of the calendar year in which the work was first published plus 50 years, or for the duration of the calendar year in which the work was created plus 75 years, whichever is earlier.

■ Sound recordings

For sound recordings such as compact discs, records, and tapes, the copyright lasts for 50 years from the end of the year in which the original recording was made.

Photographs

For photographs, copyright exists during the year that the original negative was made, or, if there is no original negative, during the year the original photograph was made, plus 50 years if the owner is a corporation. Otherwise, the term is for the life of the owner of the negative, plus 50 years.

40. What is copyright infringement?

Copyright infringement occurs when someone copies, performs, or displays a work in public without the permission of the owner. A common example of infringement is plagiarism, which is copying someone else's work and claiming it as your own. The Canadian Intellectual Property

Office itself will not prevent other people from infringing your copyright. It is up to the owner of the copyright to ensure no one copies, publishes, or performs his or her work without permission.

41. Is copying of any kind an infringement? What is "fair dealing"?

The Copyright Act has some exemptions allowing copying without permission. For example, a "fair dealing" defence is available for the use or reproduction of a work for private study, research, criticism, review, or news reporting.

"Fair dealing" is not a licence to freely use all of someone else's work. Reproducing even a small part of an original work could still be an infringement of copyright if it could be considered a "substantial" part of the work.

Other exceptions to copyright infringement exist as well. For example, under certain conditions the performance of a copyrighted work by a church, school, or charitable body is not an infringement. A common myth, however, is that libraries and educational institutions are free to make copies of parts of books or articles for student use.

If someone infringes your copyright, you may want to take legal action. The Copyright Act has a limitation period of three years for commencement of an action alleging infringement. If the infringement is proven, a court can order that person to stop using your copyright and pay you compensation. If the infringement is very serious, criminal charges may be laid according to the *Copyright Act*, which provides for fines of up to $1 million and imprisonment for a maximum of five years. If someone has copied your work without your permission and you need legal advice or assistance, contact a lawyer.

42. What are copyright royalties and tariffs?

Royalties and tariffs are fees that are paid to copyright owners by anyone who first uses copyrighted works. When someone other than the copyright owner publicly uses or sells the work, he or she must pay a royalty to the copyright owner as a commission for the use or first sale. Note, however, that if you hold a private performance of someone else's work, such as playing a song in your home, you will not have to pay a royalty.

Tariffs are standard charges that copyright users must pay to use certain copyrighted works. For example, tariffs are paid by cable companies to rebroadcast television programs. The Copyright Board is a federal tribunal that regulates tariffs.

If you want to use someone else's work but cannot locate the owner of the copyright, you can apply to the Copyright Board for permission to use the work. The Copyright Board may charge you a fee and pay it to the owner when he or she is found.

With so many potential users of copyrighted works, from schools to businesses, it can be difficult for copyright owners to track and collect fees that may be owed. To solve this problem, many creators join a "collective." Collectives grant permission for people to use the works that are owned by their members. They collect royalties for their members. There are many collectives that cover different types of works, from music to writing to plays. You can obtain a list of Canadian collectives from the Canadian Intellectual Property Office.

43. Why are moral rights important in copyright law?

Even though authors or creators may license or sell their copyright, they still have "moral rights." These are rights linked to a creator's reputation. Moral rights ensure no other person can change or distort a work in a way that is harmful to the creator's reputation. These moral rights prevail even over those who have purchased the copyright. For example, moral rights dictate that, where possible, an author's name must be identified when reproducing a work.

Authors and creators cannot transfer or sell their moral rights, except when ownership is passed to an heir after the author dies. Moral rights, however, can be waived. This means that while your moral rights are intact, you can agree in writing not to enforce those rights. If you sell your copyright, you will probably be asked to sign a contract that contains a moral rights waiver clause. This will allow the new copyright owner to deal with and change the work without requiring your consent.

INDUSTRIAL DESIGNS

44. What is an industrial design?

An industrial design relates to the visual appearance of a finished article made by hand, tool or machine. If there are only a few such items produced from the design, these might be considered a work of art and be entitled to copyright protection. Generally, though, if the design is used to produce more than 50 "useful" items, it must be registered as an industrial design to obtain protection from imitation. Examples include:

- Shape of a table
- Ornamentation on the handle of a fork

- Containers
- Furniture
- Home appliances
- Clothing items
- Fashion accessories

If someone designs a piece of equipment that functions better than what is already on the market, the new functionality of the equipment is not subject matter for an industrial design. If, however, the appearance of the equipment casing is unusually different and original, then the design may be appropriate for an industrial design application. For example, items that can be registered as industrial designs include fabric patterns, furniture designs, shapes of bottles, and ornamental aspects of equipment casings.

45. Who is the owner of a design?

The owner is sometimes the person who created the design, but if someone was hired to create a design, the owner is the person who hired the creator. An owner can also be someone who acquires the rights to a design. Any assignments of ownership should be registered.

46. Why register an industrial design?

There are several reasons why you should register an industrial design. First, the law requires, in certain circumstances, that you register an industrial design to protect against unlawful imitation of the design. By registering your design with the Canadian Intellectual Property Office, you can protect the investment you made to create or acquire it.

Second, you can prevent other people from making, using, or selling your design for up to 10 years, if it is registered. If you do not register the design and the article is mass-produced for the public, you will have no legal claim of ownership and anyone can imitate or copy the design.

You must apply to register the design in Canada within 12 months from the day you first "publish" the design to the world. For example, a public sale of a designed article is considered a "publication."

■ Different registration rules if design has not been published

There are different registration procedures for industrial designs that have not been published. If a design has not been published, there is no time limit for registration. If you delay, however, someone who has created the same design may register it and you will lose any rights you might have in the design.

47. When can I use an industrial design symbol?

Once an industrial design has been registered, a special mark can be placed on the article to let other people know the article's design is protected. The symbol for a registered industrial design is a capital "D" inside a circle, which should then be followed by the name of the owner. Although the *Industrial Design Act* does not require that industrial designs be marked, it is a good idea to do it.

Marking may deter other people from infringing or copying your industrial design. Also, if someone does copy your design, a court can order that individual to stop using your design and pay you compensation. If the product is not marked to show that the design is registered, then the court may only order the person to stop using your design while you may not be compensated for all the losses you suffered.

48. What should I do to prepare for an industrial design application?

Before you spend time and money filing an application for an industrial design, you should conduct a preliminary search to check out what other industrial designs exist. Although no search is exhaustive, a preliminary search will help you determine if your design is original. If your design is similar to someone else's registered design, you may need to take steps to avoid infringing that individual's rights. Also, if your design is not original, you will not be able to register it.

■ How to conduct a search

Conducting a search is a very complicated and technical process. The searcher will have to check for all possible versions of your design. You can hire a lawyer who is a patent agent or a search firm to do the search for you.

49. What is included in an industrial design application?

The application for an industrial design must follow a standard format and involves three components, as well as paying application and filing fees.

▪ Filing Certificate

The first form is the Filing Certificate. The Filing Certificate includes a checklist that tells you what other forms and documents are required.

▪ Application for Registration of an Industrial Design

The second required form is the "Application for Registration of an Industrial Design." You must provide the generic or common name of the design, such as fabric, chair, or bottle. This form also requires a written description of the design features that are new and original. Your lawyer or patent agent will write a description that identifies important visual features of the design. The description should outline the design, not the article to which it applies or how the article functions or performs.

The wording for the description is very important because it may influence how much legal protection is given to your design. For example, if the description is worded in very specific terms, the legal protection given may only correspond to those specific criteria outlined. This is why it is so important to hire a lawyer or a patent agent to assist you in preparing your application.

▪ Drawings

The final component required includes drawings or photographs of the design applied to the manufactured article. There are specific requirements with respect to the size, quality and detail of the drawings or photographs you provide. The article should be shown clearly and to scale so that the drawings or photographs can be photocopied. The signature of the applicant should also be placed on the lower right corner of each drawing or photograph. It is important to make sure that all aspects of your application are correct, including the drawings, because it is difficult to make changes after you have filed an application.

50. What happens in the industrial design application process?

There are three main steps in the application process and it will probably take 6 to 12 months to register an industrial design.

▪ Initial processing

When your application is submitted to the Canadian Intellectual Property Office, it will review it to ensure it is complete. A filing certificate and application number will be provided to your lawyer or patent agent when the application is received. Your lawyer or patent agent should keep a record of this number and refer to it in all correspondence with the Intellectual Property Office.

If the application is not complete, the Canadian Intellectual Property Office will tell your lawyer or patent agent what is needed. The Intellectual Property Office will assign a due date for the additional information required.

■ Examination

When the application is complete, it will be examined. The examination process usually takes three to six months. The application will be classified according to the type of article your industrial design is intended for and an examiner will also conduct a "prior art" search to ensure your design is not the same as, or similar to, other registered designs.

If there are problems with your application, your lawyer or patent agent will have an opportunity to respond. If the examiner is satisfied with the response, or if there are no problems with the application, then it will be approved. If the examiner's concerns cannot be satisfied, the application will be rejected. Your lawyer can appeal this decision.

■ Registration

After an application is approved, the design will be officially registered. The Canadian Intellectual Property Office will send your lawyer or patent agent a certificate of registration, which is your proof of ownership. You will then have the exclusive right in Canada to apply that design to an article for the purposes of importation, rent, or sale.

51. How long does an industrial design last?

Ten years is the maximum time an industrial design can be protected. Depending on when your industrial design was originally registered, there are two possible ways to protect your ownership rights up to the 10-year maximum.

■ Registered after January 1994

If your registration for an industrial design was approved after January 1994, the registration will be valid for up to 10 years, subject to payment of maintenance fees. After the first five years, you will be required to pay a small government maintenance fee. If you forget to pay the maintenance fee during the first five years, there is a six-month grace period. If you make a request to maintain an industrial design registration in the six months following the five-year period, the maintenance fee increases by a small amount. Your lawyer or patent agent can help ensure that your registration is maintained.

▪ Registered before January 1, 1994

If you registered an industrial design before January 1, 1994, then the registration period was for five years. You could have renewed the registration for an additional five years by sending a letter of request and a government renewal fee to the Canadian Intellectual Property Office.

However, the 10-year registration period has now expired for registrations prior to 1994. The registration cannot be renewed. The industrial design is no longer protected and other people may legally use the design without your permission.

52. Can I profit from an industrial design?

Assignments and licensing are two ways to profit from a registered design. To make sure that your rights are protected, contact a lawyer to advise you and review any agreement before you sign it.

▪ Assignments

An assignment is the sale of all or some of your ownership rights in an industrial design. Assignments should be made in writing. You should register any change in the ownership of your industrial design with the Canadian Intellectual Property Office. This will assist in protecting your legal rights. There is a small government fee for filing an assignment with the Intellectual Property Office.

▪ Licensing

Licensing gives someone other than the registered owner permission to make, use and sell the design. The registered owner maintains ownership of the design. In most cases, the owner of the design will charge some sort of fee or royalty for granting a licence. If you are involved in a licensing arrangement, you should make sure that the agreement is in writing and it includes, among other things, time limits for the licence and the amount of fees or royalties to be paid. Licences should also be registered with the Canadian Intellectual Property Office. There is a small fee for filing a licence with the Office.

53. How can I register an industrial design in another country?

Registering your design in Canada only provides legal protection for design rights in Canada. In the United States, for example, there is a similar type of protection known as "design patent" protection. To obtain protection in other countries, you must make separate design applications.

54. What is industrial design infringement?

Industrial design infringement occurs when someone applies a registered industrial design, or a design not differing substantially, to an article for the purposes of sale, rental, or exposure for sale without the permission of the owner. The Canadian Intellectual Property Office itself will not prevent others from infringing on the rights of the registered owner. It is up to the owner of a registered design to ensure that no one else is using it.

If someone copies or imitates your registered industrial design, you can bring a legal action against the individual or business. There is a limitation period of three years for bringing an action for design infringement. Delay in taking action against an infringer can also result in prejudice to your case. If the infringement is proven, the court can order the infringer to stop using your design and pay you compensation.

Trade Secrets

55. What is a trade secret?

A trade secret is confidential information that is often technical. Common types of trade secrets are product formulas (the carefully guarded recipe for Coca-Cola or Kentucky Fried Chicken, for instance), secret manufacturing techniques, and customer lists. It is usually information that is used in a business and gives it a competitive advantage.

There is no need to file an application to register your trade secret. In fact, publishing any details of your trade secret can affect your ability to protect it. Although the courts will sometimes step in to prevent employees of a business or others from stealing trade secrets, there is no law that specifically prevents competitors from analyzing your product provided they obtain it legitimately.

It is very important that you not let this information become known to your competitors or to the public. Once the secret is out, the owner has no rights of exclusive ownership. That means anyone can then use your trade secret.

56. How can I protect a trade secret?

As the owner of a trade secret, you must take proper steps to protect it. You can try to keep it secret by limiting physical access to the area of your business where the secret is used and only disclose it to employees who need to know. Employees should be clearly advised that they are obligated to maintain secrecy and this obligation should be written into their employment contracts.

It is often extremely difficult to keep a trade secret from being discovered. Instead, you should consider applying for a patent or other type of intellectual property protection in circumstances where the information cannot be kept secret for long.

IS AN INVENTED LIFE FORM PATENTABLE?

A prestigious U.S. university developed a genetically modified mouse that was ideal for cancer research and testing. Recognizing the commercial potential of its work, the university applied for patents for this new version of a life form in countries around the world, including Canada.

Should this unique, invented life form be granted a patent?

No, said the Supreme Court of Canada in a controversial 5-4 decision in the case of Commissioner of Patents v. President and Fellows of Harvard College. Despite the grant of patents for the "Harvard Mouse" in other countries, Canada's top court ruled that complex, higher forms of life do not qualify as inventions. At the same time, though, the court said any new inventive processes used to develop the mouse could be patented. As well, the court said simpler, lower life forms, such as bacteria, yeast, single cells, and genetically modified plants can also be patented.

GEESE WITH RED RIBBONS

A flock of 60 Canadian geese sculpted by a well-known artist was sold to a major shopping centre in Toronto, where it was hung permanently from the ceiling. During one Christmas season, the mall's management decided to decorate the necks of the geese with red ribbons. The artist objected, saying it was an insult to his work and hurt his reputation

As full owner of this artistic work, did the mall management have the right to decorate the geese?

No, said a judge in the case of Snow v. The Eaton Centre Ltd. Although copyright in the geese had been sold to the mall, artist Michael Snow had not waived his moral rights to protect the work. The court agreed with the artist that the alterations to his work might damage his reputation. While minor changes and modifications to most works protected by copyright will not be serious enough to harm the reputation of a creator, any major unauthorized changes may be an infringement of moral rights (for example, digitally altering a photograph without the photographer's permission).

WHO OWNS A PICTURE?
PHOTOGRAPHER OR SUBJECT?

In 1956, a young journalist interviewed famous Canadian pianist Glenn Gould for a magazine article. The reporter took over 400 photographs and tape-recorded their conversations. Almost 40 years later, the writer published a book that featured over 70 of the photos and excerpts from the conversations. The Gould estate claimed the author did not have permission to use the photos for commercial purposes and sued, alleging copyright infringement.

Did Gould's estate have any right to dictate how the photos can be used?

No, said a court in *Gould Estate* v. *Stoddart Publishing Co.* The appeal court judges said there was no evidence the pianist had placed limits on the use of the photos or recordings and Gould had not commissioned or paid for the photos. The journalist was the creator of the works and sole copyright holder

MONSIEUR, THAT'S NOT FUNNY!

In Québec, a television comedy that was a caricature of suburban life became very popular. So much so that an enterprising filmmaker decided to produce a pornographic movie using characters very similar to those in the television program. When challenged in court, the filmmaker said the characters couldn't be copyrighted and, if they were, his satirical use of them was permitted under the law's "fair dealing" defence, which allows excerpts of copyrighted works in commentaries on matters of public interest.

Was the filmmaker correct?

The court in Productions *Avanti Ciné-Vidéo Inc.* v. *Favreau* said: "Non." The characters were subject to copyright law since the television show creator had used talent, imagination and labour in creating them. Second, the court said this was not a satire since there was no criticism involved. And, since the characters represented a substantial portion of the film and the television show, the court said a fair dealing defence could not be used.

WWW Resources

Canadian Intellectual Property Office U.S. Copyright Office	cipo.gc.ca
U.S. Patent and Trademark Office	www.uspto.gov
Canadian Patent Database	Patents1.ic.gc.ca
Canadian Trademarks Database	Strategis.ic.gc.ca
Intellectual Property Institute of Canada	www.ipic.ca
International Trademark Association	www.inta.org
Software Publishers Association	www.spa.org
World Intellectual Property Organization	www.wipo.int

THE INTERNET & COMPUTERS

The Internet is the proverbial double-edged sword. On the one side, the Internet offers all of us unequalled access to information, entertainment, and anything else you can imagine worldwide. On the other side are many uncharted legal issues where there are few borders, few police, and even fewer rules.

The sheer size of potential Internet audiences, conflicting laws in other jurisdictions and questions about cross-border enforcement are just some of the problems to be tackled in settling electronic-based disputes or alleged infringements of others' rights.

The Internet has spawned situations for which there was little or no law before. Can your personal Web site, for example, use hypertext links to a page in an unrelated site without permission? (Courts are split on the issue.) Is it legal to forward e-mail to others without permission? (Technically, no. The copyright resides with the author.) Is a Web site operator or service responsible for what users say on discussion boards? (Yes, but only if it is a moderated activity, say some courts.)

When the Internet first gained popular use, many people thought no country or court could ever create or enforce rules to govern how it was used. The ability to browse Web sites anywhere or make our thoughts available to anyone gave people the idea that the Internet was all about having freedom – the freedom to use or copy the work of others, to say what we think, to like (or hate) whomever we want.

Today, most of us realize the Internet cannot operate without rules. The rights and intellectual property of others must be protected, reputations can be damaged over the Internet as elsewhere, and society still needs to guard against evils such as child pornography and hate literature. The question most often asked these days is: how do we apply the laws built up over hundreds of years to this new medium?

1. Is there a specific law that governs what you can and cannot do on the Internet?

At this time, most provincial and federal legislators in Canada are reluctant to create any new laws that might suggest the Internet is a different legal environment with different rules. Many of the rules and laws that apply to non-Internet situations apply equally to the Internet.

That said, governments are constantly broadening the scope of various laws, from those governing corporations to the regulation of firearms. The law has come to cover new technological changes, such as electronic meetings, form filing, access to records, and even legal authority for using digital signatures in e-mailed documents. Also, individual laws dealing with privacy rights, the use of personal information, rights of intellectual property owners, broadcasting over the Web, and other areas often include specific laws to govern Internet issues.

Courts and lawmakers are starting to develop a body of case law and legislation addressing online rights and obligations. Not all courts and lawmakers agree. Inconsistencies therefore exist between various jurisdictions, but there are some general rules:

- If you create or exercise physical control over Internet content (such as words, pictures, designs, etc.), you will likely be responsible for damage you cause, as would be the case in any other medium
- If it is within your power to exercise control over content and you learn it is infringing another's rights or a law, you will likely be liable if you do nothing about it
- If you directly or knowingly infringe the rights of another, such as violating someone's copyright (downloading music, plagiarizing writings, etc.), you will be liable for damages caused

• If you unintentionally or indirectly infringe the rights of another after exercising due diligence, you may still be liable but there may be a reduction in damages awarded by a court

• If you use the Internet to commit an act elsewhere that is illegal in Canada, you can still be held responsible here

• If there is not a real and substantial connection between a Canadian defendant and the damages suffered by another in a foreign jurisdiction, courts here are unlikely to enforce a claim or judgment

• Of course there are always grey zones, and individual legal jurisdictions may take different approaches.

2. Is any information private on the Internet?

The popularity of the Internet has raised many questions about the privacy of information that is stored on computers and transmitted across the Internet through e-mail messages, for instance. Recently, the federal government and several provinces have enacted laws to protect against the improper collection, storage, use, and disclosure of personal information by businesses and organizations in both the private and public sectors. For example, a Canadian-based commercial Web site that requests your personal information must disclose how it intends to use it, show you what personal information it holds on you, and allow you to remove it from its databases or restrict its use. Other common issues include:

■ Right to privacy

Generally, information such as medical records or personal financial information is private information that cannot be released without your permission. Private information may also be protected indirectly. For example, it is a criminal offence to break into a computer system, whether to steal or change someone's private information or for other unauthorized purposes. If you think this has happened, call the police or contact a lawyer.

■ Privacy of communications

Generally, you also have a right to have your private communications remain private. In most circumstances, it is an invasion of your privacy for someone to monitor or disclose the contents of your private communications. Different rules may apply for e-mail communications that you send or receive on your employer's computer system. Generally, since employers own the computer equipment you are using, they have the right to store or view information, such as e-mails. Check to see if your employer has a policy that describes what kinds of computer activities are permitted.

Even if your employer does not have a policy about Internet and e-mail use, you should assume that your employer can track all the Web sites you visit and read all the messages you send or receive, even after you have deleted them. If you use the computer system at your workplace to send or receive inappropriate messages, your employer could use this as "just cause" in an effort to fire you.

Computer and e-mail use policy

The best way to avoid problems with Internet and e-mail usage at the workplace is for employers to develop a written policy. The policy should include guidelines on topics such as visiting inappropriate Web sites, spreading computer viruses, confidentiality, personal use of software and hardware, and copyright infringement. Most employers will also want to include an explicit right to monitor the electronic communications of their employees. A lawyer can help a business owner write a fair and effective Internet and e-mail policy.

3. Can a legally binding contract be formed online?

Valid online contracts can be created by having each party to the agreement exchange e-mails or by having one party submit an order form on a Web site. Presenting the terms of the contract to a party and then asking that party to click on the words "I AGREE" or something similar may also create online contracts. This is known as a "Web-wrap" or "click-through" contract.

Most of the time, contracts created online are not physically signed by both parties, but each can still print out a copy of the agreement. That said, some Internet businesses do allow secure and encrypted "digital" signatures to be exchanged between parties.

There are two specific concerns that arise when you enter into an online contract. First, is the contract legally binding? And second, who are you entering into an agreement with?

■ Legally binding online contracts

Even though both parties do not usually sign electronic agreements, they may still be legally binding contracts for most types of transactions. There are, however, special circumstances where an online contract will not be legally binding. For example, if a contract is for the sale of land, a long-term lease, or involves the co-signing of a loan, the contract must be made in writing and must have original signatures.

If you are unsure whether your agreement can be created legally online, contact a lawyer before you make the deal, or else create a traditional, formal contract in writing with original signatures. A lawyer may also be helpful in structuring the online contracting process in a way that will ensure the best chance of creating an enforceable contract.

■ Who are you entering into an agreement with?

When you create an online agreement it is important to know with whom you are contracting and where that person or company is located. Many people and companies online are agents for others. For example, you may think you are making an agreement with someone located in Saskatchewan, when you may in fact be buying something from a business in Singapore. If you are entering into an agreement with someone outside your province, it is important to determine whose laws will apply to the transaction in case of dispute.

In Canada, the question as to where electronic contracts are formed has not been determined. It is a similar situation to contracts formed via fax. The courts in Canada have generally held that fax-based contracts are formed when and where the offeror receives notice of acceptance.

Also, take care in how payments are made or received. For most consumer purchases, a credit card will provide the most protection if the transaction goes sour. In some cases, particularly for large commercial purchases in foreign lands, you may wish to discuss secure payment options with your banker.

4. What should a business know about selling goods or services on the Internet?

One of the fastest growing areas of retail sales and services is electronic commerce or e-commerce. The Internet provides a cost-effective way for companies to sell products through order forms on Web sites or via e-mail. Selling goods and services on the Internet poses some risks for both business owners and customers.

That said, electronic commerce on the Internet can be effective and worthwhile if you take the necessary steps to protect your business and reassure customers that it is safe to do business with you through the Internet.

■ Electronic safeguards in your Web site

The first step to take is to build electronic safeguards in your Web site. For example, your Web site creator can design order forms so the computer will reject fake addresses, incorrect credit card numbers, or other information that does not appear to be correct. This will make it more difficult for people to place fake orders with your business.

■ Credit card security

Many people are concerned about credit card security on the Internet. While it is possible for someone to steal a credit card number sent through the Internet, it is probably no more of a security threat than in a restaurant or gas station. In fact, Internet technologies in recent years have made credit card transactions much more secure.

Many commercial Web sites can scramble Internet transmissions using an encrypted or secure Web page. If encrypted information is "seen" as it is sent from one Web site to another, it will not be understandable by the interceptor. You can usually recognize a secure Web page by the closed-lock icon on the status bar at the bottom of your screen or the Web address starting with "https:" rather than "http:"

Businesses that want to accept credit card payments through their Web sites should address their customers' concerns by clarifying the level of security. They can do this by providing information on their Web sites about what has been done to protect credit card transactions. A Web site developer can help implement encryption on any business's site.

■ Clear contracts

Businesses online should also make the terms of an order or contract very clear. Customers should know what they are buying when they agree to the terms. By being very clear and precise, a business will minimize the number of orders that are returned and will be able to prove it had a valid contract.

■ Know the local law

Business owners who market goods and services on the Internet must also be aware of any laws that affect how they can do business, such as restrictions on misleading advertising or various provincial laws giving consumers the right to return defective or misrepresented goods.

For example, Québec has language laws that can affect electronic contracting and Web sites by requiring French translations if the parties or transactions involved have a Québec connection, which might include an office or employees located in Québec. That said, parties to such a contract may expressly agree to have it written in English only.

■ Export controls

Business owners who export goods, services, or technology must be especially aware of special laws that may control what they can do. Even software programs transmitted electronically may be subject to certain restrictions imposed by export control regulations.

Canadian laws may prohibit the export, without an export permit, of controlled technologies such as products that incorporate encryption, and the export of other items to certain countries listed on Canada's Area Control List, or that are subject to embargo by the United Nations. Before offering products and services over the Internet, businesses should get professional advice from a lawyer.

5. What should everyone know about buying goods or services on the Internet?

Shopping on the Internet is an easy way to buy goods and services. You can usually use your credit card online and have products delivered to your door. The same laws governing all consumer transactions protect consumers who buy goods over the Internet. The most important of these laws is located in each province's *Sale of Goods Act.*

■ Internet shopping and the *Sale of Goods Act*

The *Sale of Goods Act* protects people who buy goods, but not people who buy services. According to the *Sale of Goods Act*, you must be able to use any product you buy for the purpose people ordinarily use it for.

For example, if you buy a vacuum cleaner, it must pick up dirt off your carpet. If it does not do what it is supposed to do, you should contact the vendor and request a refund. You should be aware that in non-consumer transactions, the seller might be able to expressly avoid these types of implied warranties.

You must consider two issues when you buy a product on the Internet. First, Internet purchases of goods are usually based on pictures, and second, purchasers are often not familiar with the businesses they are dealing with.

■ Buying something from a picture

You should always be cautious about buying something from a picture. Computer images can be easily changed or enhanced, and when you get your product, it may not be anything like what you saw on the screen. If the item is not like the picture and you are not satisfied with the product, contact the vendor and request a refund.

■ Know who you are dealing with

You should also be careful about buying something from a business you do not know. If it changes its Internet address or does not have its physical address stated on the Web site, it may be difficult for you to contact the company if there is a problem. If it is an international company and there is no local office, it may be difficult to contact the company or return the product if there is something wrong with it. The best way to avoid these problems is to know the company you are dealing with.

6.   Can a computer be used to commit a crime?

A computer crime is any illegal activity that involves a computer as the object of a crime, as an instrument used to commit a crime, or as a hiding or storage place for evidence related to a crime. For example, a computer crime could involve the theft of a computer, using a computer to illegally access someone else's computer system, or storing documents relating to a crime on a computer.

Computer crimes often involve computer hackers, software piracy, stock manipulation, and business fraud. Hackers are people who use computers to enter someone else's private computer systems. Hackers can change information, steal data, or access confidential information. Hacking into a computer system is like breaking and entering into a private residence. It is a criminal offence to tamper with computerized information and to break into a private computer system.

7.   Is "spam" or unwanted e-mail illegal?

Not yet in Canada. The distribution of unwanted e-mail is not illegal nor is it regulated in Canada. That said, Canada's *Competition Act* provides consumers with protection from the advertising of certain products, such as tobacco, and misleading advertising. Also, the *Criminal Code* has sections on fraud and mischief against data that could, in theory, be used against spammers. New federal and some provincial laws restricting the use of personal information, such as e-mail addresses, may also be used against spammers who abuse information in the course of commercial activity.

8.   How are laws against hate propaganda applied to the Internet?

The Internet makes it easy for someone to distribute hateful messages to the public. Such messages are usually referred to as "hate propaganda."

The *Criminal Code* recognizes three offences – advocating genocide, inciting hatred, and the willful promotion of hatred against an identifiable group. These are criminal offences, whether they are committed using a printed copy of a document or distributed electronically over the Internet.

■ Advocating genocide

Advocating genocide means to promote the destruction or elimination of a race of people. The person who makes the statement advocating genocide will be held responsible for the offence. An Internet service provider who unknowingly allows its facilities to be used to post such statements will probably not be held responsible for the statements, but someone who posts the message on the Internet probably will be held responsible.

■ Inciting hatred

Inciting hatred is committed when someone makes hateful statements in a public place against an identifiable group, statements that are likely to lead to a breach of the peace. This is not as likely to apply to the Internet as the other two areas of hate propaganda cited above and below.

■ Willful promotion of hatred against an identifiable group

The third offence, willful promotion of hatred against an identifiable group, is committed when hateful statements directed at a specific group of people are made other than in private communications. Simply saying "I hate everybody" would not be hate propaganda, but saying "I hate everybody who believes in a 'particular' religion" would be.

Since the second and third offences do not cover private conversations, e-mails sent willingly between two people would likely not be hate propaganda. In contrast, statements made during an interactive chat session could be considered hate propaganda because chat sessions involve a larger number of people and the chat forum can be considered a public place.

In addition to criminal penalties for individual offenders who distribute hateful messages to the public, human rights laws can be used to shut down a Web site and prevent hate propaganda from being distributed to the public. If you see hate propaganda on the Internet, contact the police.

9. How are obscenity and pornography laws applied to the Internet?

In Canada, there is very little regulation or control of what is allowed on the Internet. Although there are many sites that contain nudity and sexually explicit material, most of these are not illegal. That said, Web sites that depict sexual exploitation, violence, or images of children under 18 years old will probably be considered illegal.

Although there are no Canadian obscenity or pornography laws that apply specifically to Internet communication, existing laws governing obscenity would likely apply to acts committed or images shown on the Internet.

In Canada, the production or distribution of obscene materials is prohibited. It is also an offence to knowingly sell or expose to public view, or to possess for such purposes, obscene materials. A related provision in the *Criminal Code* makes it an offence to publish, distribute, or possess child pornography, subject to certain limited exceptions. This means a person who knowingly visits a Web site that contains child pornography and views it on his or her computer monitor may be guilty of a criminal offence because a copy of the images may be left on the computer's hard disk.

10. How are copyright and intellectual property laws applied to the Internet?

Copyright laws make it illegal to copy any form of original work without the permission of the author. The author or creator of a work has certain legal rights. These rights apply even if the work does not contain a statement noting that the work is copyrighted. The general rules of copyright also apply to downloading Internet information and using computer software.

Canadian courts have found that a Web page's look, layout, and appearance are protected by copyright. If you copy Internet information or images without the author's permission, you are probably infringing unlawfully on someone's copyright. You can only legally copy someone else's work if you have the author's permission, or if your actions fall within certain exceptions set out in the *Copyright Act* (for example, copying something for private study or research). As a result of international treaties, Canadian copyright law will also protect most copyrighted material that originates outside Canada.

Also, domain names or Web addresses may be protected under trademark law if they meet the statutory or common law requirements for trademarks. For example, trademark owners may be protected from so-called "cybersquatters" who grab domains using trademarked business or product names.

There should be no doubt that copyright, trademarks, and other aspects of intellectual property law apply to the Internet in the same way as other media. For example, you cannot post the works of others on your Web site without permission (adding a line identifying the source is not good enough to escape prosecution). Similarly, you cannot copy a substantial amount of another's work from the Web and claim it as your own.

It's not unusual for Internet users to assume that any material on Web sites is in the public domain. But this isn't so. A work enters the public domain only when its copyright expires (typically, 50 years after the death of the author in Canada and even longer in other countries).

What about messages posted on a discussion board or news forum? Some would argue a posting carries implicit grants of permission for copying, but others say additional publication (such as in print) requires permission. For example, the U.S. and Canadian *Copyright Acts* specifically protect anonymous and pseudonymous works from unauthorized copying. For now, these are unsettled Internet issues.

11. How are copyright and intellectual property laws applied to computer use?

Copyright law protects many forms of expression, including written works, sound recordings, multimedia works, video clips, and computer programs. Courts recognize that a computer program is a creative "art form" and many computer programs meet the "originality" requirement needed to obtain protection under the *Copyright Act*. The fact that a computer program uses well-known programming techniques or contains unoriginal elements may not prevent its protection under copyright law if the program as a whole is original.

When you buy a computer program, you usually only acquire a licence to use that program. Unless permitted under the licensing agreement, it is illegal to copy the computer program, to load the program onto more than one computer, or to modify the program so that it can be used by more than one person on a network. This is often called piracy. For example, if you are buying a computer program for use by three employees, you often must buy three program licences, depending on what the software's end user licence agreement (EULA) dictates.

Copyright infringement can be a serious criminal offence. Depending on the seriousness of the crime, you could be fined or sent to jail. If you have developed computer software or Internet information you would like to protect, contact a lawyer.

12. How are defamation laws applied to the Internet?

The basic elements of defamation law remain unchanged on the Internet. Individuals or entities are still responsible for defamatory statements they publish, just as they are in print or broadcast media, and the same defences apply. Courts have also demonstrated they are not willing to allow Internet defamers to claim anonymity.

While there have been very few cases of "cyberlibel" in Canada, the courts have shown they are quite willing to hold responsible anyone who uses the Internet to defame others, even if the defamer is outside the country.

The flip side of Canadian courts' willingness to hear cases involving defamation originating outside the country is that the Internet makes it even easier for plaintiffs to go "forum shopping." Differences in the defamation laws and damages awarded in Canada, U.S., U.K., and Europe may give allegedly defamed individuals (particularly high-profile plaintiffs) pause to consider where to sue. Now, with the Internet, these plaintiffs may have an easier time making a case for their right to sue anywhere in the world.

Another concern, heightened by the Internet's broad reach, is the issue of damages. Could a defamatory statement available on the Internet prompt a stratospheric damage award because of the huge, worldwide audience? Canadian courts have shown they are not willing to tie damages to the Internet's potential audience without proper proof.

Is a foreign Web site outside the reach of Canadian law?

After battling with Canadian legal authorities over his racist and hateful Web site, a fanatical individual decides to preach to his followers from a Web server located in a country with no laws against promoting hatred. The government decides to prosecute the individual, who is still a Canadian citizen, for promoting hatred against specific groups. He claims the Web site is not based in Canada and not under its jurisdiction.

Is the fanatic correct?

No. In a similar case involving a well-known individual who denied that the Nazis engaged in genocide during the Second World War, the Federal

Court of Canada ruled an individual can be held responsible in Canada where he or she controls or influences material posted on a foreign Web site. Other jurisdictions also agree. In the U.S., a court ruled its injunction prohibiting publication of copyrighted material was breached when a Web site placed hypertext links pointing to other sites that had posted the same information. The bottom line for anyone in Canada is that you cannot circumvent or breach a Canadian court order by using a foreign jurisdiction via the Internet.

Does Foreign Internet Law Apply In Canada?

A Canadian shareholder posts untrue and damaging comments on an Internet message board about a Canadian company that does business around the world. The company files a defamation lawsuit against the shareholder. However, the file was not made in Canada, but in a U.S. state that deems a non-resident to be doing business in its jurisdiction if it commits a tort or wrong there. The shareholder, who neither lives nor does business in the state, ignores the lawsuit and the company wins its case by default.

Can the Canadian business enforce its foreign court judgment in Canada?

No. In one of the few Internet cases heard by a Canadian appeal court, Braintech, Inc. v. Kostiuk, the foreign court's judgment was overturned because the wrongdoer did not have a "real and substantial connection" to the foreign jurisdiction. In this case, the only connection to the jurisdiction was a "passive posting on an Internet bulletin board." Since there was no proof that anyone there saw the alleged defamatory material, the court said it could not simply presume damages occurred in jurisdictions where the defamatory statements are accessible and likely to have been read.

CRIME AND PUNISHMENT

CRIME AND PUNISHMENT

CRIMINAL JUSTICE

remove your
Criminal Record
for you or someone you care about

ERASE IT AND START CLEAN
IT IS EASIER THAN YOU THINK

If you have ever been charged with a criminal offence, whether you were convicted — or it was thrown out of court — **you have a criminal record**.

If you have ever been finger-printed by the police, call the **Pardons Canada Confidential Support-Line** to find out how to access your record. Removing it is easier than you think.

We remove your criminal record and give you proof in writing that your record is gone.

Many people have made regrettable mistakes. **We promote positive behaviour by giving people hope.** Those who are no longer involved in criminal activity have the opportunity to make a fresh start and immediately change their lives. Removing the stigma and shame associated with a criminal past is a vital part of developing an improved self-image for future success.

REMOVE OBSTACLES
AFFECTING YOUR:

- getting a job
- job promotion
- ability to be bonded
- Canadian citizenship
- adoption / child custody
- peace of mind
- apartment rental
- mortgage approval
- educational opportunities
- volunteer work
- USA employment
- USA travel / entry waiver

Pardons Canada

Toll Free **1 (877)** **929-6011**
Support-line **(416)**

Pre-recorded Information (24 hours/day) .... press 2
- Removing criminal records and eligibility
- USA travel, employment and immigration
- How much it costs and paperwork needed

Walk-in Centre, directions and hours........ press 3

Information by Fax...................... press *

Counsellor Support...................... press 0

information, support & guidance

www.pardons.org

Criminal Records Removed
and
U.S.A. Entry Waivers

3-ways to apply

1 Walk-in Centre

45 St. Clair Ave. West, Suite 901
Monday to Friday
8:30 am - 5:00 pm
No appointment necessary

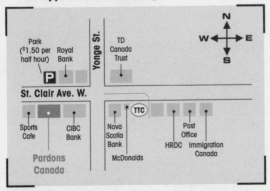

TTC Subway: Yonge Street subway line exit St. Clair station, South side of St. Clair Ave / West of Yonge Street.

2 Mail, Fax or Phone

Pardons Canada
45 St. Clair Ave. W., #901
Toronto, ON M4V 1K9

Fax
(416) 929-3651

Toll Free
1 (877) 929-6011

Telephone
(416) 929-6011

3 The Internet

Email: .... info@pardons.org
Website: .... www.pardons.org

A Resource and Support-line for over 5,400 Organizations

Criminal Records Removed
and
U.S.A. Entry Waivers

3-ways to apply

1 Walk-in Centre

45 St. Clair Ave. West, Suite 901
Monday to Friday
8:30 am - 5:00 pm
No appointment necessary

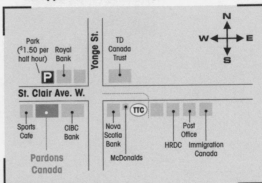

TTC Subway: Yonge Street subway line exit St. Clair station, South side of St. Clair Ave / West of Yonge Street.

2 Mail, Fax or Phone

Pardons Canada
45 St. Clair Ave. W., #901
Toronto, ON M4V 1K9

Fax
(416) 929-3651

Toll Free
1 (877) 929-6011

Telephone
(416) 929-6011

3 The Internet

Email: .... info@pardons.org
Website: .... www.pardons.org

A Resource and Support-line for over 5,400 Organizations

Pardons Canada

45 St. Clair Ave. West, Suite 901, Toronto, ON M4V 1K9

Criminal Records Removed:
- Pardon, Purge, Photograph & Fingerprint Destruction
- USA Entry Waiver, VISA Waiver

www.pardons.org

Tel: (416) 929-6011
Fax: (416) 929-3651
email: info@pardons.org

Criminal Records Removed and U.S.A. Entry Waivers

Those who are no longer involved in criminal activity
have the opportunity to make a positive change in their lives

---

Removing a Criminal Record will enable a person to Pass a Police Clearance for Employment

---

Pardons Canada, a Federal non-profit organization, assists individuals in removing a past criminal offence from public record. As a resource for over 5,400 government and community agencies, we provide free telephone and Internet support, and a walk-in centre.

Many people have made regrettable mistakes. Those who are no longer involved in criminal activity have a real opportunity to make a fresh start and a positive change in their lives. By removing criminal records, we help lift the stigma and shame associated with a criminal past, allowing people to feel that they belong in our society again. People who feel part of a community make better parents, citizens, and neighbours.

Individuals with a criminal record are often at a serious disadvantage when competing for employment, job promotion, volunteer work, getting bonded, apartment rental, child custody, adoption, mortgage approval and educational opportunities. A criminal record also impedes foreign travel, including travel to the U.S.A., and often prevents people from obtaining Landed or Permanent Resident Status and Canadian Citizenship.

Everyday, approximately 250 people in Ontario are charged with a criminal offence and over 5% of all Canadians have a criminal record. **A criminal record is also created when a person has been charged, even if they are not guilty or convicted**. Therefore, a criminal record does exist in cases of acquittals, peace bonds, absolute /conditional discharges, withdrawn, dismissed and diversion charges.

The Canadian Criminal Justice system is extensive. Even people who work in this field are often subject to serious misconceptions about criminal record retention policies, procedures and laws. Pardons Canada is in constant communication with over 1,450 police stations, courts, and probation offices; each with different policies towards record retention and destruction. We are notified daily of policy and regulation changes and remain current with all applicable municipal, provincial, and federal laws.

Pardons Canada offers information, support and guidance. With the applicant's permission, we undertake all necessary steps and procedures for removing a criminal record, including: Pardons, Purges, Photograph & Fingerprint Destruction, and U.S.A. Entry Waivers. We use our computer terminals to easily access and process all the necessary documents and get proof in writing that the criminal record is removed.

Yours sincerely,

Ian D. Levine, National Program Director (ext. 725)

Pardons Canada

Helping You to Help Others — Criminal Records Removed

Recent social and political changes have made criminal record searches common, and in many cases obtaining a criminal record clearance is mandated by law.

Organizations which assist individuals to get their lives 'back on track' can now ensure that the individual's criminal record is removed. Whether you are helping someone find employment, become clean and sober, improve their self-image, or qualify for educational programs, the individual's criminal record will be an obstacle.

Due to the complexity of criminal record retention policies, procedures and laws, even people who work in the 'helping field' are often subject to serious misconceptions. **If a person has ever been charged with a criminal offence, whether they were convicted – or it was thrown out of court – they have a criminal record** and are unable to pass a police clearance. Pardons Canada will help your client remove their criminal record.

- **Receive additional information cards and posters**
- Take part in our 'Community Education Program'
- Call for a **free** one-hour **presentation** at your office (sample documents distributed)

Telephone   **(416) 929-6011 ext. 755**

Telephone Support-line and Resource for over 5,400 Organizations

Canada Employment Centres - HRDC	Correctional Service Canada	Community Legal Clinics
United Way Member Agencies	Adult Learning Schools	'LINK' Community Information
YMCA / YWCA Programs	Metro Community Services	Hospital Programs
Community & Information Centres	Family Assistance Programs	Community Mental Health Services
Elizabeth Fry Society	Immigration / Refugee Centres	Women's Centres
Addiction Treatment Centres	Family Shelters	Gay & Lesbian Groups
University and College Programs	Ethnic & Cultural Centres	Ministry of Public Safety and Security
Board of Education	Support Services for People in Distress	Public Libraries
Ontario Court Programs	Salvation Army	Canadian Human Rights Commission

INTERNATIONAL FINGERPRINTING
www.IFS.ca

United Way
of Greater Toronto

 YMCA

YWCA
of Greater
Toronto

 www.**LEGAL LINE**.ca

Canada

Confidential Telephone, Internet and Walk-in Centre Support

When it comes to criminal law in Canada, the federal government is in charge of creating and legislating most of the crimes and their penalties. When it comes to prosecuting most crimes and administering justice, however, the provinces play a large role. The provinces are also in charge of creating and policing provincial offences, such as workplace health and safety laws and driving offences.

In Canada, if you are charged with a crime it usually means you have been accused of a specific offence under a federal law, usually the *Criminal Code*. The three categories of criminal offences are: summary conviction offences, indictable offences, and hybrid offences. Each category has different penalties and different kinds of trials. Whenever you or someone close to you is dealing with an alleged criminal offence, it is critically important that you speak with an experienced criminal lawyer before making any decisions or engaging the justice process.

Summary conviction offences, such as committing an indecent act, are the least serious type of offences. If you are charged with a summary conviction offence you will not have a preliminary hearing and your trial will be held in the local provincial court, likely before a judge only without a jury.

Indictable offences, such as murder, are the most serious type of offences. The specific indictable offence you have been charged with will determine whether you have the choice of having a preliminary hearing and whether you will have the right to select a trial by a judge and a jury. It also determines which court your trial will be held in. Because of the serious nature of indictable offences, you will require a lawyer to represent you if you are charged with such a crime.

A third kind of offence is called a hybrid offence. For hybrid offences, such as assault, the Crown prosecutor chooses whether the offence will be treated as a less serious summary conviction offence or a more serious indictable offence. The prosecutor's decision will affect where the trial takes place and which penalties apply.

Of course, with so much at stake, you should always consult a lawyer if you have been charged with any criminal offence.

1.   When can the police stop and question me?

The police can stop you under three general circumstances:

- If they suspect you have committed an offence
- If they actually see you committing an offence
- At any time while you are driving to determine whether you have consumed alcohol or drugs, whether you are insured, and whether the car is mechanically fit to be driven

In all cases, once you are stopped by the police, you have the right to know why and the right to speak to a lawyer within a reasonable period.

2.   What should I do if stopped by the police?

Although you have the right under the law to remain silent when questioned by police, it is best to co-operate by at least identifying yourself. In some circumstances, you could be charged with the offence of obstructing the police if you fail to tell them your name. You could also be charged with an offence if you give the police a false name.

If the police continue to ask you questions and they do not allow you to leave, in law it means they are detaining you. When you are detained, you have the right to know why they are detaining or arresting you, and you have the right to talk to a lawyer.

3.   Can the police search me?

The police can generally search you, your clothing and anything you are carrying in five circumstances:

- You agree to let the police search you
- The police have some reason to believe you have committed or you are in the middle of committing an offence involving weapons
- You are in a place where the police are searching for drugs and they believe you have drugs
- You are in a car where there is alcohol
- You are arrested

In all these situations, you have the right to consult a lawyer and you do not have to respond to any police questions, other than providing your name.

If the police find something related to a different offence while they are legally searching you, they can charge you with that offence as well. For example, if the police search you because they believe you have a gun and while searching they find illegal drugs, they can charge you with a drug offence as well.

Although the police cannot conduct random searches, it is best not to become hostile or resist a police search. Resisting a search may result in a charge being laid against you. Instead, contact a lawyer as soon as possible and seek further information and advice.

4. Can the police enter and search your home?

The police can enter and search your home in two general circumstances. First, they can enter and search your home if you give them permission. Second, they can enter and search your home if they have a search or arrest warrant. The police also have the power to enter, but not search, your home in certain emergencies.

▪ Entry with your permission

Permission means that someone who lives in the home allows the police to enter. Generally, only an adult can give permission. If the police ask to enter your home without a warrant, and you do not want them to come in, you should tell them clearly that you do not want them to enter. Otherwise they may think you have agreed to let them in. Note that if you give the police permission to enter and they do not have a search warrant, you can ask them to leave at any time if you change your mind.

▪ Entry with a search warrant

A search warrant gives the police the right to search for and take the things listed in the warrant. The police must have the search warrant with them and you have a right to see it. While searching, the police cannot destroy things unnecessarily. They can also only search in places where the things listed in the search warrant might be found. For example, they can't look inside a drawer if they are looking for a stolen bicycle. Once the police have found the things listed in the search warrant, they must leave your home. They cannot continue to search. Ask for the name and badge number of the officer who appears to be in charge of the search.

▪ Entry with an arrest warrant

An arrest warrant gives the police the right to enter a home to arrest the person whose name is listed on the warrant. An arrest warrant also gives the police a limited power to search a home. If an arrest is made in your home, generally the police can only search the immediate surroundings.

If the police enter your home with a search warrant or an arrest warrant, they can also take other illegal things or evidence of crime that they find during their search. For example, if the police have a search warrant to look for a gun and while they are searching, they find illegal drugs, the drugs can be taken and used as evidence for a drug charge against you.

■ Entry in emergencies

The police also have the power to enter your home in certain kinds of emergencies. There are three general circumstances that are considered emergencies:

- The police can follow someone into your home if that person has just committed an offence or if the police believe that person is about to commit an offence.
- The police can enter if they believe someone in your home is about to harm another person.
- They can enter to give emergency aid to someone inside.

This power to enter your home in an emergency does not give the police the right to search your home. Nonetheless, while they are in your home the police can seize anything illegal or any evidence of a crime they see.

If during a search the police take something from your home, you may be entitled to get it back. Consult a lawyer for further assistance.

Being Charged and Arrested

5. Can anyone lay a criminal charge against someone else?

Although the police will generally lay charges when they believe that an offence has been committed, in some circumstances they may be reluctant to proceed with legal action. If an offence is alleged to have been committed and the police will not lay a charge, any member of the public can take steps to have a charge laid by swearing an information before a Justice of the Peace. An information is simply a legal document that contains the details of the offence and chronicles the progress of the case through Provincial Court.

If, for whatever reason, law enforcement authorities will not lay a charge against someone you believe has committed a crime, you may be able to do it yourself. You will, however, have to convince a Justice of the Peace that the charge is justifiable.

You will have to arrange to meet with a Justice of the Peace in the jurisdiction where you live or the alleged crime occurred. You will have to explain to the Justice of the Peace what happened and swear an oath that you have good reason to believe a criminal offence has been committed.

If the Justice of the Peace is satisfied that an offence was committed, the Justice will issue a "summons," which is a document that orders the person you accused to come to court on a certain day. The Justice may also, in some circumstances, issue a warrant to arrest that person.

At court, the Crown prosecutor will step in and take over prosecution of the person you charged. If you are an essential witness you could receive a subpoena requiring you to attend Court to give evidence on the matter. The subpoena will contain information about the date and relevant courtroom.

6. Under what circumstances can I be charged or arrested?

The police can charge you if they see you committing an offence or if they have a reasonable belief that you have committed an offence. You could also be charged if a member of the public can satisfy a Justice of the Peace that you have committed an offence.

■ Being charged

Although the police will usually both charge and arrest you, for some minor offences you may only be charged, and not arrested. If you are only charged, the police might not take you to the police station. Instead, they will give you a piece of paper that has two dates: one date for fingerprinting and photographs, and the other date tells you when and where to go to court to set a date for trial. If you do not appear for either of these two dates you can be charged with the separate offence of failure to appear.

■ Being arrested

If the police arrest you it usually means the offence is more serious. The police will read you your rights and take you to the police station where you will be fingerprinted and photographed. When you are arrested, the police also have the power to search you.

Even if you are charged with an offence that is not considered serious, the police may still decide to arrest you in addition to charging you. This will happen if you do not identify yourself, if the police believe you might destroy evidence, or if the police believe you might repeat the offence.

In any event, it is best to consult a lawyer as soon as possible if you have been charged with an offence or have been arrested. The police should provide you with a telephone and some privacy when you are speaking with your lawyer.

7. Do the police need a warrant to arrest me?

The police are not required to have a warrant before arresting someone and are given broad power under the law to arrest people without a warrant. In some circumstances, however, an arrest warrant may be issued by a Justice of the Peace to assist the police in carrying out the arrest.

■ Being arrested without a warrant

The police can arrest you without a warrant in five instances:

1. If you have committed a serious offence.

2. If you are in the middle of committing a serious offence.

3. If the police believe you are about to commit a serious offence.

4. If the police believe there is a warrant out for your arrest.

5. Even if the offence is considered relatively minor, the police can still arrest you without a warrant if you refuse to identify yourself, or if the police believe you might repeat the offence or destroy evidence.

8. What are your rights when charged or arrested?

The Canadian *Charter of Rights and Freedoms* establishes a number of rights to protect individuals who are arrested or detained by police. Some of the most important rights are:

• You have the right to remain silent when questioned by the police

• You have the right to be told why you have been arrested or detained

• You have the right to be told you can hire and instruct a lawyer

• You have the right to be told about the availability of duty counsel and legal aid

• You have the right to speak with a lawyer, in private, as soon as possible

It is important to always remember that you have the right to remain silent and the police must inform you of that right upon your arrest.

Regardless of whether you have been arrested or just charged, anything you tell the police can be used as evidence against you. This also applies to any physical tests you are asked to perform or any samples you are asked to voluntarily provide.

Even though you may think that what you are telling the police could not hurt you in court, what you say or write could later become evidence against you. To be safe, consider talking to a lawyer before making any statements to any police officer, or before performing any test or providing any sample.

9. What other constitutional rights do I have?

You also have rights when you have been actually charged with an offence, even if you were not arrested. For example, everyone who is charged with an offence is entitled:

- To have a trial within a reasonable period
- To be presumed innocent unless a prosecutor proves that he or she is guilty
- To be released on bail unless there is a valid reason to be kept in custody
- Not to testify at his or her own trial

If you have been charged or arrested, consult a lawyer to ensure that your legal rights are protected.

10. What happens after I am arrested?

Following an arrest, a person charged with an offence may appear in court a number of times before attending the actual trial. The accused may be required to attend court for a bail hearing, a set date, a preliminary hearing, and pre-trial hearings or motions.

■ Bail hearing

To begin, once you have been arrested and taken to the police station, the police will either hold you in custody or let you leave the police station. Contact a lawyer immediately because it is very important to get legal advice as soon as possible. If the police decide to hold you in custody at the police station, they must bring you to a Justice of the Peace for a bail hearing within 24 hours of arrest, or as soon as possible. At the bail hearing, the Justice of the Peace will decide whether you should be released, or held in custody until trial. You are entitled to have a lawyer represent you at the bail hearing.

If you are released, the Justice of the Peace may impose certain conditions and may require that you have a surety to sign on your behalf. You will also be given a paper that tells you when and where to be in court to set a date for your trial. You are entitled to full disclosure of the Crown's case against you, although you usually have to submit an order form for disclosure. See your Crown office for information.

If you are not released on bail, you will be held in a detention centre until your trial. Note that it is sometimes possible to seek release through a bail review brought in a higher court.

■ Set date for court appearance

If the police allow you to leave, they will give you a paper telling you when and where you have to be in court. In this document you may find conditions attached to your release (for example, not communicating with the alleged victim of the crime). The first court appearance is called your set date because the judge will set a date for your trial. Generally, no date is set for trial until complete disclosure has been received. This may take several weeks and in complicated cases such as a fraud, it may take months. In some cases a pre-trial hearing will be required where the defence and prosecutor along with a judge sort out the legal and factual trial issues. See also question 16 in this section.

■ Preliminary hearing

A preliminary hearing is a court proceeding, but it is different from a trial. In a preliminary hearing, the Crown prosecutor has only to convince the judge that there is enough evidence that a Judge *could* find you guilty. In most cases, a trial will be ordered and scheduled to take place several months later in the province's criminal courts.

Depending on the nature of your case, there may also be pre-trial motions or hearings that take place immediately before your trial. These often deal with a number of technical legal issues, such as the admission of evidence and the protection of your legal rights under the *Charter of Rights*.

The exact procedure from arrest to trial will vary depending on the offence. If you have been charged with an offence, consult a lawyer as soon as possible. See also question 17 in this section.

11. How can I ensure I am released until trial?

If you are arrested and detained at the police station, you have the right to a bail hearing before a judge within 24 hours, or as soon as possible. At your bail hearing, the judge will look at several factors to decide whether you should be released. For example, the judge will consider such things as:

- Whether you are a danger to the public
- How serious the offence is
- Whether you have a criminal record or outstanding charges
- Whether you have ever missed a trial in the past
- If you have a job, a business, or a family in the area

It is always helpful to have a credible friend or family member at a bail hearing to vouch for you if possible.

■ Being held in custody or released on bail

If the judge decides to hold you in custody, you will be held in a local detention centre until your trial. If you are released, you may have to pay money into court as a deposit, a friend or family member may have to agree to supervise you, and there may be certain conditions attached to your release. For example, you may be released on the condition that you do not leave the province. When you are released, you will be given a piece of paper that tells you when and where to be in court to set your date for trial.

■ Appealing your bail hearing

If you are not allowed out on bail, you can ask for a review of the judge's decision. A judge in the province's Superior Court will review your case. If the judge refuses to release you, there is a 30-day wait before you can apply for another review. Bail hearings are very important to anyone who is in custody after being arrested. You should always be represented by a lawyer at a bail hearing.

12. Who can be a surety and what does a surety do?

A surety oversees the accused while he or she is out on bail and is responsible for ensuring that the accused follows the conditions of release, such as adhering to a curfew or an order not to contact a victim. It is the surety's job to make sure the accused shows up in court throughout the trial. The surety must be someone who has regular contact with the accused such as a parent, and can supervise that person. Among the factors the court takes into consideration include the length of time the surety has known the accused and how close the surety lives to the accused. The surety is also required to have enough funds to cover the bail.

Defending a Charge

13. How do I find and pay for a criminal defence lawyer?

Although you are not required to hire a lawyer to defend yourself against a criminal charge, a lawyer will help you to better prepare your defence. Certainly for all serious and technical offences, you will not be able to defend yourself properly without a lawyer. It is best to contact a lawyer as soon as possible after being arrested. If you do not know a criminal lawyer, you can find one at a local legal aid clinic, in the Yellow pages, or possibly through a Lawyer Referral Service sponsored by the local law society.

■ Lawyers' fees

There are a few different ways that lawyers can bill you for their services. They may charge you one flat rate for your case, a fee for each time they appear in court for you, or an hourly rate. The amount they charge you will depend on how experienced they are and on how complicated your case is. If you cannot afford a lawyer, you can apply for legal aid, which will cover the costs of the lawyer's work. Call the legal aid clinic in your area for more information.

14. What is disclosure of evidence?

If you have been charged with an offence, it is important for you to know what evidence the Crown prosecutor has against you so your lawyer can properly prepare your defence. The legal term for your right to know about this evidence is "disclosure." Under the law, the Crown prosecutor must give you a copy of all the relevant evidence against you before the date of your trial. Relevant evidence means anything that you could use to defend yourself. Because the prosecutor often does not provide this information automatically, your lawyer will contact the Crown prosecutor's office before your trial date to formally request disclosure.

Because the obligation to provide disclosure is ongoing, the Crown prosecutor must keep giving you new relevant evidence as it becomes available. Any relevant new information must be disclosed to you as it is received by either the police or the Crown prosecutor. At the same time, you do not normally need to provide the Crown with any information about your defence or your background.

15. What happens during a pleading?

If you have been charged with an offence, you will have to enter your plea in court at the beginning of your trial. To enter a plea means to tell the court whether you are guilty or not guilty of the offence you have been charged with. If you plead not guilty, you are not necessarily denying you committed the offence. Instead, you are requiring the Crown prosecutor to prove in court that you are guilty beyond a reasonable doubt.

If you plead guilty, you are admitting that you committed every offence as described by the Crown prosecutor. Facts in support of the plea will be read into the record, which you will be asked to acknowledge as correct. Because pleading guilty could have very serious consequences, always consult with a lawyer before you enter a guilty plea.

16. What is a "set date"?

If you have been charged with an offence, the police will give you a piece of paper that tells you when and where to be in court to set a date for your trial, or for your preliminary hearing, or "set date."

This preliminary hearing is a court proceeding similar to a trial, where the Crown prosecutor has to convince the judge that there is enough evidence against you to require that you be ordered to stand trial. In most cases, a trial is ordered and scheduled for several months later.

If you plan to hire a lawyer, but have not hired one when you go to your set date, you should tell the judge you are still trying to hire a lawyer. The judge will often give you extra time to find one and order you to return on another day with your lawyer to set a date for trial or for a preliminary hearing.

If you have been charged with a less serious offence, you will generally not be entitled to a preliminary hearing. As a result, you will simply set a date for your trial at your set date. If you have been charged with a serious offence, you will usually have a preliminary hearing first.

17. How do preliminary hearings work?

A preliminary hearing is a court proceeding that takes place before the trial of a serious offence. The purpose of a preliminary hearing is for the judge to decide whether there is enough evidence against the person that a reasonable jury properly directed by the judge could convict. If there is not sufficient evidence, the accused will be discharged. Generally, that is the same as the case being dismissed.

A preliminary hearing is similar to a trial, but usually much shorter. The Crown prosecutor will call witnesses and present evidence against the accused. The defence lawyer will be entitled to cross-examine the Crown prosecutor's witnesses. It is the Crown prosecutor's job to try to show the judge that there is enough evidence to proceed with a trial. Although very few cases are dismissed at this stage, preliminary hearings give the accused the opportunity to see the case against them and may help in the defence plan at trial. They also show the accused the strength of the case against them and may assist in resolving the matter.

If you are charged with an offence where a preliminary hearing is available, you can usually choose not to have the hearing. By doing this, you are accepting that there is enough evidence to go to trial, but you are not admitting guilt. Your lawyer will advise you on whether to have a preliminary hearing. There are some risks involved with taking a preliminary hearing. For example, where the evidence discloses a more serious charge, in some cases you may be ordered to stand trial on that charge as well.

18. Where will a trial be held?

Depending on the offence a person has been charged with, criminal trials in Canada are held in either the lower provincial court or in the higher-level court, known variously as the Queen's Bench, General Division, Superior, or Supreme courts. Generally, the more serious offences are held in the higher-level court before a judge or a judge and a jury, and the less serious offences are held in provincial-level court before a justice only. If your trial is being held in the upper-level court, you will likely have a preliminary hearing before your trial to determine whether there is enough evidence against you to hold a formal trial.

At trial, the Crown prosecutor must prove beyond a reasonable doubt that the person charged with an offence is guilty. If there is any reasonable doubt about whether the person is guilty, the accused must be acquitted.

■ Starting a trial

A trial begins with the charges being read out loud to the court, which in law is called an arraignment. After the charges are read, the person charged will be asked to enter a plea, which means that that person will be asked to declare whether he or she is guilty or not guilty. If you intend to plead guilty, seek legal advice first so you fully understand the possible consequences. It is possible in some circumstances to plead guilty to a lesser or included offence as well.

■ Role of the Crown prosecutor

At trial, the Crown prosecutor and the defence lawyer will each have a chance to present their cases. To prove that you are guilty, the Crown prosecutor must present evidence to the court. This could be physical evidence, such as a gun with your fingerprints on it, or witness testimony, such as a person who testifies that he or she saw you fleeing the scene. The Crown is entitled to rely on both direct and circumstantial evidence. The Crown prosecutor will be the first to present his or her case and call witnesses. When the Crown prosecutor has finished questioning each witness, the defence lawyer can cross-examine him or her. This means that the defence lawyer can ask the witness more questions, usually in an attempt to find flaws with what the witness said. The prosecutor can re-examine the witness in some circumstances to clarify new issues brought up in cross-examination.

■ Dismissing charges

If the Crown prosecutor does not present enough evidence to prove you are guilty, your defence lawyer can ask the judge to dismiss the charges. If the judge dismisses the charges, your lawyer will not need to present evidence in your defence, and you will be free to leave.

■ Role of the defence lawyer

If the Crown prosecutor presents enough evidence to potentially prove you are guilty, your defence lawyer may need to present other evidence to defend the charges against you. In some cases, no evidence will be called by the defence because the Crown's case is so weak. Any witness your lawyer calls can be cross-examined by the Crown prosecutor, which means the prosecutor can ask the witness more questions in an attempt to find flaws with the testimony. You do not have to testify at your trial. If you choose to testify, you should remember that you may also be cross-examined by the prosecutor, who may force you to answer discomforting questions. Your lawyer, however, is there to ensure that the prosecutor does not ask you irrelevant or objectionable questions.

■ Submissions to judge

Once both sides have presented all of their evidence and all the witnesses have testified, each side will be allowed to make submissions to the court. A submission is just a summary of each side's case and may include arguments on the law. The judge, or the judge and jury, will then decide whether the person charged is guilty or not guilty. If you are found guilty, you may be sentenced to a penalty immediately, or at a later date depending on the circumstances of your case. If you are on bail, the bail may be cancelled when you are found guilty, even before you are sentenced.

19. What is the role of witnesses?

The role of witnesses is to tell the court what they know, whether it relates to the person accused, the crime, or the circumstances surrounding the crime. What they tell the court is called their testimony and in law it is considered an important type of evidence.

Usually the Crown prosecutor or the defence lawyer instructs a witness to come to court by issuing a subpoena. A subpoena is a piece of paper that orders a person to come to court on a certain day to speak about certain events relating to the trial.

■ Receiving a subpoena and attending court

If you receive a subpoena to go to court, you must attend. Failing to attend can result in arrest. Once at court, you must testify and respond to questions from both the Crown prosecutor and the defence lawyer. If you refuse to answer questions, the judge may find that you are in contempt of court. This is an offence and means you can be jailed up to 90 days and ordered to pay a fine of up to $100. Although the *Charter of Rights* does offer some protection to witnesses regarding the use of testimony that may incriminate them in another proceeding, there is no Canadian equivalent to the American's Fifth Amendment right to protection from self-incrimination.

■ Testifying in court

Witnesses must take an oath before they testify, which means they must swear to tell the truth. A witness may also choose to affirm or promise instead of taking the oath. Lying under oath is called perjury and is a serious criminal offence under Canada's *Criminal Code*. You could face a maximum penalty of 14 years in prison.

■ What can you testify about?

A witness is questioned first by the lawyer who wanted the witness to come to court and then by opposing counsel. As a witness, you can only testify about things you saw, things you know are true, or in some circumstances, things you heard (like a gunshot). Generally you cannot testify about things someone else told you.

■ Being a witness at your own trial

It is also possible to be your own witness at your own trial and testify before the court. Although you can be your own witness, you cannot be forced to testify at your own trial. In some cases, people who have been charged with an offence choose not testify at their own trial. The reason for choosing not to testify is that both lawyers can question you, which means you are legally required to answer questions from the Crown prosecutor. This can become difficult if the Crown asks you about things that may damage your case. There are other reasons not to testify for which a lawyer can advise you.

20. What are the penalties for criminal offences?

The penalties for criminal offences are set out in the *Criminal Code* and vary depending on each specific offence. For most minor offences (called summary conviction offences) the maximum punishment is a fine of $2,000 and six months in prison. For serious offences (indictable offences), the maximum punishment can range anywhere from two years to life in prison. Some offences under the *Criminal Code* have minimum penalties, meaning the sentencing judge has no discretion to sentence below the set minimum.

■ Factors that affect your penalty

Although the *Criminal Code* establishes a range of penalties, the court will generally also consider your personal circumstances, such as whether this is your first offence and whether you are employed and have a family. See sentencing below for more details. The circumstances in which the offence was committed are also very important. You should have a lawyer assist you at your sentencing hearing.

21. How does sentencing work?

Sentencing is where a judge decides what penalty to give a person who was found guilty at trial. Sentencing can occur immediately following the end of the trial or it can be scheduled for a later date.

■ Sentences and the *Criminal Code*

A judge rarely gives the maximum sentence. Some offences have mandatory minimum sentences, which means you must serve at least a minimum amount of time if you are found guilty.

■ Factors considered in sentencing

Before the judge decides on the penalty, the defence lawyer and Crown prosecutor are given opportunities to tell the judge what they think an appropriate sentence should be.

The judge considers a number of personal factors when deciding a sentence, including:

- Age
- Marital status
- Number and age of children
- Employment status
- The circumstances of the offence
- Past criminal record
- If violence was involved
- Whether the person poses a danger to society
- Whether the crime was planned
- Whether the person co-operated with police

There are many kinds of sentences. A judge may order the guilty person to pay a fine or go to prison. A sentence may include supervision by a probation officer or prohibition from doing or possessing something. For example, a judge usually orders someone convicted of impaired driving to pay a fine and prohibits that person from driving for one year.

22. How do I appeal a conviction?

Appealing a conviction means asking a higher court to review your case and essentially ensure that the court did not make any mistakes in convicting you. Under the law, there is generally no automatic right to appeal your conviction so you must seek permission to appeal from the court. To appeal, you generally have to demonstrate that the judge or jury made a legal error during your trial as opposed to an error of fact. Findings of fact by trial judges and juries generally cannot be appealed. For example, if the judge or the jury came to the conclusion that your story was not believable or you were lying, an appeal court will not dispute that finding.

You can appeal your sentence if the judge made a legal error, or if the sentence was far out of the range of usual sentences for your offence. Appeals from convictions or sentences must be started at least 30 days from when the sentence was imposed. In some cases, you may be able to be released on bail until your appeal is heard.

The rules regarding when someone can and cannot appeal are complex. Consult a lawyer for more information on appealing a conviction.

EARLY RELEASE AND PAROLE

23. What is parole?

Parole, also called conditional release, allows a person convicted of an offence to serve the rest of his or her sentence out of prison. There are three different types of parole:

- **Full parole:** Provides a person with the most freedom. Full parole allows prisoners to leave the prison and return home indefinitely.
- **Day parole:** Allows prisoners to leave prison during daytime hours only. They must return to prison or go to a supervised halfway house each night.
- **Temporary absences:** Unescorted temporary absences allow prisoners a certain number of hours out of prison and without supervision each month. The number of hours they are allowed each month depends on the kind of prison the person is held in. If the person is in a maximum or medium security prison, he or she can have up to 48 hours out each month. If the person is in a minimum-security prison, he or she can have up to 72 unsupervised hours out each month.

■ Conditions attached to parole

Conditions are almost always attached to all types of parole. For example, the person released may have to meet with a parole officer, go to counselling, stay away from drugs and alcohol, or stay away from certain people or places. Failure to respect any conditions will generally result in termination of the parole and a return to prison.

24. Who is eligible for parole?

The point at which a person becomes eligible for parole depends on several factors, including the type of offence that was committed, when the offence was committed, and how long the length of sentence.

In most cases, prisoners are eligible for day parole or unescorted temporary absences after serving one-sixth of their sentences. Prisoners are usually eligible for full parole if they have served one-third of their sentences, or if they have been in prison for seven years. Many prisoners, however, do not get full parole until they have served about two-thirds of their sentence.

Full parole involves a hearing at which the prisoner is present and may be asked questions by the Parole Board. Because parole is a complicated process, consult with a lawyer for more information and assistance.

25. How do I get parole?

Prisoners must apply to the National Parole Board for parole consideration. After applying, prisoners will be interviewed by the parole review board to determine their suitability for release.

■ Factors considered by the Parole Board

The board will consider a number of factors when deciding whether parole should be given. For example, the parole board may look at the person's criminal record, the type of offences committed, and when they were committed. They may also look at how serious the offence was and whether the person feels badly about what they did or understands what they did. The parole board also considers how the person behaved in prison. If a person is not granted parole, he or she may still be eligible to be granted statutory release after serving two-thirds of the sentence. In some cases, the Parole Board can deny a prisoner parole altogether and the full sentence must therefore be served.

COMMON CRIMINAL OFFENCES

26. What is considered theft?

To be found guilty of theft, the Crown prosecutor must prove that you intended to steal the item. For example, if you are charged with shoplifting a book, the Crown prosecutor must prove that you intended to leave the store without paying for the book. If you honestly forgot to pay for the book, or if you honestly forgot you were carrying the book, and the judge believes you, then you cannot be found guilty of the offence.

If someone, such as a store employee, has a good reason to believe that you are stealing, store security can hold you in custody. They cannot hold you for long and they must call the police right away. Although you do not have to answer any questions asked by store security or the police, you should avoid becoming hostile and should identify yourself when asked.

■ Trial procedures and penalties for theft

You can be charged with theft over $5,000 or theft under $5,000, depending on the value of the item taken. Theft under $5,000 is a hybrid offence, which means the Crown prosecutor can choose to treat the offence as a less serious summary conviction offence or a more serious indictable offence. If it is your first offence, the Crown prosecutor will probably choose the less serious summary conviction procedure, which carries a maximum penalty of a $2,000 fine and six months in prison.

Generally, however, the penalty for first time offenders is a small fine and probation or an absolute or conditional discharge. In some areas, the Crown can offer you the alternative of doing community service work and will withdraw the charge if it is very minor. If the Crown prosecutor chooses to treat the offence as a serious indictable offence, your sentence could be much more severe. Theft over $5,000 is a serious indictable offence, and carries a maximum penalty of 10 years in prison.

27. What is an assault?

There are many different kinds of assault under the Canadian *Criminal Code*, including assault with a weapon, assault causing bodily harm, aggravated assault, and several types of sexual assault.

Generally, assault is where one person does something that is forceful or threatens force to another person without that person's consent or permission. There is no requirement for actual physical harm or injury. For example, if you have been seriously threatened with force, or if force has been used against you, the person who committed these acts can still be charged with assault.

■ Sexual assault

Sexual assault means any sexual activity that is done without the consent or permission of one of the people involved. In some cases — where consent is obtained through dishonest means or with an underage victim for example — consent will not matter. Specific sexual assault charges include sexual assault, sexual assault with a weapon, sexual assault causing bodily harm, and aggravated sexual assault.

Both assault and sexual assault apply to violence between spouses and partners. If you believe you have been assaulted, call the police right away.

28. What is possession of a narcotic?

The federal *Controlled Drugs and Substances Act* lists all illegal drugs, including marijuana, heroin, cocaine, amphetamines, and hashish. There has been a movement lately in federal circles to "decriminalize" the possession of small amounts of marijuana that are not intended for sale to others. That said, it is currently illegal to knowingly have any of these drugs in your possession at any time, even if they do not belong to you.

Under the law, the Crown prosecutor must prove certain things before you can be found guilty of possession. First, the Crown prosecutor must prove you had physical custody of the drug, which means that the drug was somewhere on your body or in a place that you control.

For example, your home and your car are places that you control. Second, the Crown prosecutor must prove you knew the substance was an illegal drug.

■ Trial procedures for possession

Possession is a hybrid offence, which means the Crown prosecutor will decide whether to treat your case less seriously, as a summary conviction offence, or more seriously, as an indictable offence. Although the Crown prosecutor's decision will depend on many factors, generally, if it is the first time you have been charged with possession and you only had a small quantity of drugs, your case will be treated as a summary conviction offence.

■ Penalties for possession

The Crown prosecutor's choice between a summary and indictable offence will also affect the penalties that can be imposed if you are found guilty. For the summary conviction procedure, the maximum penalty for drug possession is a fine of $1,000 and six months in prison if it is your first offence. If it is not your first offence, the maximum penalty is a $2,000 fine and one year in prison. However, the penalties usually given by the court for first time offenders possessing "soft drugs," such as marijuana, are fines between $250 and $500 and probation. For more serious drugs, such as cocaine or heroin, the Crown may seek a jail sentence even for first offenders. If the Crown prosecutor proceeds by indictment, the maximum penalty is seven years in prison.

29. What is trafficking?

Trafficking means you were in possession of an illegal drug, and you offered it, sold it, or passed it on to someone else. It is a serious offence under the *Controlled Drugs and Substances Act*, with more severe penalties than possession of a narcotic. Possession for the purpose of trafficking is a separate offence as well.

■ Factors that suggest trafficking

Although it is not always clear whether someone is in possession for the purpose of trafficking, the police often rely on a number of surrounding circumstances to lay a charge. For example, a person might be charged with possession for the purpose of trafficking if he or she has a large quantity of drugs in his or her possession or if that person is caught with several small packages of drugs prepared for individual sale and an accompanying list of names. In the most obvious situation, if a person is caught actually selling drugs or trying to sell drugs, he or she will be charged with trafficking, even if the quantity intended for sale is small. Importing charges will also be laid if a person possessing illegal drugs is caught entering Canada.

■ Penalties for trafficking

The maximum penalty for drug trafficking is life in prison. Most often, the penalty given by the court includes some jail time and probation.

30. Is it legal to carry a weapon, gun, mace, or pepper spray?

Unlike some jurisdictions, such as the United States, Canadian citizens are generally prohibited from carrying mace, handguns, and most other weapons.

■ Prohibited Weapons

The *Criminal Code* definition of prohibited weapons and firearms includes:

- Automatic firearms
- Sawed-off rifles and shotguns
- Silencers
- Large capacity ammunition cartridges
- Knives that open by spring action, gravity or centrifugal force
- Any weapons declared by Order in Council to be a prohibited weapon

Government regulations also list many other devices as "prohibited weapons," including but not limited to:

- Any firearm capable of discharging a dart or other object with an electrical current, commonly known as Taser Public Defenders
- Any firearm designed or of a size to fit in the palm of a hand, commonly known as SSS-1 Stingers
- Any device, liquid, spray, or powder used for the purpose of injuring, immobilizing, or otherwise incapacitating a person such as tear gas or mace
- Any hard non-flexible sticks, clubs, pipes, or rods linked by a length or lengths of rope, cord, wire, or chain, commonly known as Nunchakus

• Any device consisting of a manually triggered telescoping spring-loaded steel whip, commonly known as a Kiyoga Baton or Steel Cobra

By omission, some devices are not considered prohibited weapons, such as batons, truncheons, night-sticks, and billy clubs. Handcuffs and other restraints are also not prohibited or restricted weapons.

The *Criminal Code* contains many offences involving weapons, including those that are not prohibited such as pepper spray. The term "weapon" has been defined to include anything designed, intended, or used to cause death or injury to another person or to threaten or intimidate. For example, the *Code* makes carrying or possessing any weapon, imitation of a weapon, prohibited device, or even its ammunition for a purpose dangerous to the public peace, or for committing an offence, punishable by imprisonment for up to 10 years. Carrying a weapon into a public meeting and carrying a concealed weapon without proper licensing are also offences.

■ Firearms

Firearms, depending on type, fall under the category of restricted or prohibited weapons. As discussed above, if the firearm is prohibited, possession of it is illegal. If the firearm is classified as restricted, the *Code* generally prohibits the possession or transport of it unless the person is licensed to carry the weapon, and then only for certain purposes such as hunting or sharp-shooting. It is even an offence to simply point a firearm, whether loaded or not, at an individual.

31. How can I stop someone from trespassing on my property?

The law of trespass in Canada is formed piecemeal from criminal and tort law, as well as from provincial legislation.

■ Tort Law

Trespass to land is one of the oldest torts known in common law. Historically, it has been held to occur whenever there has been an unauthorized physical intrusion onto the private property of another. The tort has also been recognized when a person remains on an individual's land after permission has been withdrawn. Today, tort writers even argue that the tort of trespass may occur whenever there is an unauthorized "interference" to land, such as causing large amounts of smoke from burning garbage to trail across another's property.

However trespass to land is defined, it is actionable *per se* — that is, without proof of damage. In a typical tort action, any damages awarded will be nominal (that is, small) unless some actual damage is sustained and proven. Not so in trespass. If the incident was for particularly malicious purposes, arrogant, or callous, even punitive damages may apply.

That said, any private person can go onto the property of another during daylight hours if permission to access is implied. For example: where there is a path up to the front door of a residence and there are no signs warning people to stay off the land. This implied permission to enter the property of another can, of course, be revoked instantly by the person in charge of the property. If you are told to leave, you must leave or you could be sued for trespass.

This implied permission does not extend to trespassing at night, which is a criminal offence. Under the *Criminal Code*, anyone who, without lawful excuse, loiters or prowls at night on the property of another person near that person's home is guilty of an offence.

■ Provincial Regulation

Almost every province has trespass legislation. Only Saskatchewan and the territories rely on common law. In some provinces, Privacy Acts, Motor Vehicle Acts, Fish and Wildlife Acts, and even All Terrain Vehicle Acts may give a legal right to an owner to prosecute trespassers.

The purpose of any trespass legislation is to give greater control over entry to or use of an owner's or tenant's premises, to provide penalties and remedies for breaches of the Act, and to facilitate the recreational use of private lands. The legislation, in most cases, does not take away an aggrieved person's right to bring a civil action for trespass, but usually grants the state the authority to seek its own sanctions as a measure to control this sort of behaviour.

While trespassing is typically defined as the unlawful entry onto the private land of another, it also includes performing an unlawful activity on the land of another and refusing to leave when directed.

In some provinces, such as Ontario, there is a reverse onus provision. In this province a person is presumed to be trespassing if he or she is found in a private garden, field, or other land under cultivation, inside lands that are fenced for livestock or cultivation, and on lands where notice has been posted. It is noteworthy that trespass is not presumed in privately owned natural areas if it is not posted as prohibited. This point is in line with the philosophy of encouraging recreational activity on privately held lands.

Offenders may be fined, in some cases up to several thousand dollars. There are a number of defences available to a person charged under provincial trespass legislation. If there is a fair and reasonable supposition that an accused had a right to be on the land, an accused may be acquitted. As noted, there is also an implied permission to approach a door of a building unless there is a notice that warns people to stay away.

■ Criminal Law

The *Criminal Code* makes it an offence to loiter or prowl at night on the property of another person near a dwelling-house situated on that property. "Night" is defined by the *Criminal Code* as between 9:00 p.m. and 6:00 a.m. "Dwelling-house" is defined as a permanent or temporary residence and anything attached to it. The essence of loitering is wandering about apparently without precise destination. It is conduct that essentially has nothing reprehensible about it as long as it does not take place on private property where the loiterer has no business. The substance of prowling is to traverse stealthily — that is, furtively, secretly, and clandestinely — or moving by imperceptible degrees. The Crown need not prove that the accused was looking for an opportunity to carry out an unlawful purpose. Where prowling is made out, the accused is required to prove he or she had a lawful excuse.

32. Can I secretly video or audio tape someone? Is it legal to listen in, tape or "bug" a telephone call?

Generally, it is illegal to secretly record oral communications between two or more people unless you have the consent of at least one of the individuals involved. For pure video recording with no sound, you may have greater freedom to secretly tape people. In British Columbia, Saskatchewan, Manitoba, Newfoundland, and Québec, however, privacy laws may be used to provide a civil remedy for those affected.

■ Criminal Code Offence

There is a general prohibition against interception of private communications of others by use of electronic or other devices. The *Criminal Code* provides that everyone who, by any electro-magnetic, acoustic, mechanical, or other device, willfully intercepts a private communication, may be imprisoned for up to five years. The *Criminal Code* also grants a punitive tort award of up to $5,000 if the aggrieved person has not commenced a separate civil proceeding.

■ The exception: consent

The exception is when there is consent by just one of the parties involved in the communication. The *Code* provides that the offence does not apply to a person who has the consent of the person who originates a private conversation or the person intended to receive it. This consent can be explicit or implied. Implied consent exists if you are actually a party to the conversation. In 1993, Parliament further clarified the meaning of consent by adding a section providing that when a private communication is originated by more than one person or is intended to be received by more than one person, consent to the "interception" can be given by any one of those persons.

■ Police and other agents of the state

For the purposes of recording and intercepting private conversations, police and other agents of the state are governed by the same rules as private citizens. Still, other than in exceptional circumstances, the police must obtain prior authorization from a judge by way of a warrant. The police are also under various disclosure rules specific to covertly obtained audio evidence.

■ Video surveillance

The prohibition against intercepting private communications does not apply to the use of video surveillance equipment where no sound is involved. There is no criminal sanction against photographing or filming people or property open to public view. The *Criminal Code* only applies to the use of video surveillance equipment if it is used to intercept private communications.

■ Cell phones

In 1993, Parliament passed a new criminal law creating an offence for the interception of cellular telephone communications. This section provides that every person who intercepts by any means, maliciously or for gain, a radio-based telephone communication is liable to imprisonment for up to five years if the originator of the communication, or the person intended by the originator to receive it, is in Canada. This reversed a line of cases that held that cellular telephone conversations were not private communications. Note that this section creates an offence only where the interception was made maliciously or for gain.

33. What is stalking? How can I stop someone from following me?

"Stalking" is the term adopted by the public and the media to refer to what the *Criminal Code* classifies as "criminal harassment." It has been the subject of considerable public discussion in recent years and the government has strengthened the law to stop it.

■ The Prohibition

Under the Code, no person shall engage in conduct that causes another person reasonably, in all the circumstances, to fear for his or her safety or the safety of anyone known to that person. This includes:

- Repeatedly following from place to place the other person or anyone known to that person
- Repeatedly communicating with, either directly or indirectly, the other person or anyone known to that person
- Besetting or watching the dwelling-house, or place where the other person, or anyone known to that person, resides, works, carries on business, or happens to be
- Engaging in threatening conduct directed at the other person or any member of that person's family

This section does not apply to someone who is operating with lawful authority or someone who does not know that he or she is harassing another. Although this second defence would appear to be an excuse easily made by a stalker, the *Code* limits the defence by providing that any reckless behaviour is also culpable. The punishment can be imprisonment for up to 10 years. The court will also be particularly severe if there is a previous court order prohibiting contact.

YOUNG OFFENDERS

34. Who is a young offender?

A young offender is someone between the ages of 12 and 17 who commits an offence under federal law, such as the *Criminal Code* or the *Controlled Drugs and Substances Act*. Rather than being treated as an adult, young offenders are handled under a special law called the *Youth Criminal Justice Act*. Although young offenders can still face serious penalties for certain offences, they are not sent to adult prisons and there is generally a greater emphasis on rehabilitation.

35. How is a young offender treated differently?

A young offender is treated differently from an adult in at least three ways:

> • A young offender is given some extra legal rights. In addition to the normal right to consult a lawyer when stopped by police, young offenders also have the right to speak with their parents or guardians, and the right not to be publicly identified.
> • Unlike adults, most young offender's cases are tried in a Youth Court
> • The penalties for young offenders often have more options and more flexibility. For example, police can warn or caution young offenders instead of charging them. The provinces can establish programs that allow Crown attorneys to caution youths instead of prosecuting them. Judges also have a range of sentencing options with custody considered as a last resort. The judge might also order the youth to pay a fine or make restitution to victims.

36. Can a young offender be sentenced as an adult?

Yes. The *Youth Criminal Justice Act* imposes adult sentences upon youths 14 or older for certain indictable offences, such as first or second degree murder and serious violent offences. The provincial attorney general can also bring an application to have an adult sentence imposed.

37. What is an "extrajudicial measure"?

Extrajudicial measures are an alternative to a formal trial for a young offender. Participating in these programs often involves performing community service, enrolling in a training or treatment course, or apologizing to the victim.

Provinces set the criteria for how these measures operate and which offences may be diverted. The type of cases that can be diverted to alternative measures programs usually involve non-violent, minor offences.

In Ontario, for example, first-time offenders charged with offences such as theft under $5,000, possession of stolen goods under $5,000, food and accommodation fraud and fraud under $5,000 are eligible to be diverted to Youth Justice Committees. This contrasts with Saskatchewan, which allows a broader range of charges to be diverted. The type of cases ineligible for diversion in Saskatchewan involve threats, such as incidents involving use of a weapon, violence against others where there is an indictment, and sex assault and abuse cases.

Victims of Crime

38. What can I do if I am assaulted or abused?

If you have been assaulted or abused, you should first escape from the
offender and seek medical attention. You should then call the police and
explain what happened. In most cases the police will arrest the accused
and lay charges. You should also record the names and badge numbers of
the officers who assist you.

To ensure you have an accurate record of the assault, report all your
injuries to both the police and to a doctor in detail, and write down
everything that happened as soon as possible. You may also want to have
photographs taken of your injuries to keep with your written records.
Also try to keep track of all the expenses you incurred as a result of the
assault.

If you are being abused by a spouse or partner, you may want to contact a women's or men's shelter, or call a domestic assault hotline. You will
be able to talk with a counsellor who can advise you of your options and
help you decide what to do. Check your phone book for crisis help lines.

39. What happens once the police arrest an offender?

Upon arrest, the person who assaulted you will be taken to the police
station where formal charges will be laid. Unless the police believe that
the offender is a threat to your safety or may leave the province, the
offender will usually be released to wait for the trial date.

If the police decide to hold the offender in police custody, the offender
will be taken for a bail hearing usually the next day. A bail hearing is a
meeting with a Justice of the Peace who decides whether the offender
should be released. If the Justice decides that the person should be released,
the Justice often attaches conditions. For example, the Justice could order
that the person stay away from you or stay away from certain places. The
Justice might also order the person not to drink alcohol or take drugs. If
the person breaks these rules he or she can be arrested and charged.

If the Justice decides that the offender should be held in custody and
not be released, the offender will generally be held at a local detention
centre until the trial several months later.

40. What happens if the police refuse to lay charges?

The police will always lay charges when they believe a crime has been
committed. If, for some reason, an offence has been committed and the

police will not lay a charge, any member of the public can take steps to have a charge laid by meeting with a Justice of the Peace and swearing what is called *an information*. The information is a piece of paper that contains the details of the offence. When you meet with the Justice of the Peace, you will have to explain the details of the offence and swear an oath that you believe a criminal offence has been committed.

If the Justice is convinced that an offence has been committed, the Justice will issue a summons, which is a piece of paper that orders the person you accused to come to court on a certain day. If the Justice does not believe you or does not believe that an offence has been committed, no legal action will be taken against the offender.

If charges are laid, the Crown prosecutor will step in and take over the prosecution of the person you charged. If you are unsure of how to have charges laid or what options you have, you should consult a lawyer.

41. What if I change my mind about laying charges?

If the police have laid charges against an offender, they cannot be withdrawn unless the police believe they do not have enough evidence to proceed, or a Crown prosecutor determines the charges should not go ahead.

As well, you cannot change your mind about charging an offender and expect to have the charges withdrawn.

That said, if you personally visited with a Justice of the Peace and had charges laid against an offender yourself, you can generally drop the charges at any time before the Crown prosecutor takes over prosecution of the charge.

42. How can I protect myself from spousal assault?

Whether you have involved the police or not, if your spouse or a partner has assaulted you, there are additional ways to use the law to protect yourself. You can try to obtain a peace bond, or a court order preventing a spouse or partner from living in the family home.

■ Obtaining a peace bond

The first way to protect yourself is by obtaining a peace bond. A peace bond is a court order in which your spouse or partner agrees to keep the peace and be on good behaviour for up to 12 months. To obtain a peace bond, you need to go to court and meet with a Justice of the Peace to explain the details of your situation. You must show that you have reasonable grounds to be afraid that your spouse or partner will injure you, your child or your property. The Justice will then decide whether to order your spouse or partner to come to court and sign a peace bond. When issuing a peace bond, the Justice can also attach a number of conditions, such as ordering your spouse or partner to stay away from you.

The only way for a peace bond to help you is if you follow up on it and actually call the police if your spouse or partner breaks any of the conditions. Spouses who refuse to sign a peace bond or violate a condition of the peace bond could be fined or sent to prison. Because a peace bond usually expires after one year, you must reapply if you feel it is still needed.

■ Exclusive possession of family home

Second, you can try to protect yourself by obtaining an order for exclusive possession of the family home. This means you can ask the court to order your spouse to live somewhere else and stay away from the home, even if your spouse is the legal owner of the home.

43. Can victims of crime receive compensation?

There are four ways a victim of crime can be compensated: through insurance; by restitution from the offender; by applying to a provincial victims compensation program; and by suing the person who committed the crime.

■ Insurance

The first way to compensate victims of crime is through insurance. If you are injured, or your car is damaged in an accident, your car insurance company will usually compensate you for damages suffered. You can also seek compensation through your home or property insurer if any personal property is stolen or damaged as a result of a crime.

■ Applying for restitution

The second way to compensate victims of crime is by applying for restitution to the court that found the offender guilty of committing the offence. Restitution means that the offender is required to repay the victim. The court will consider your application when deciding on the offender's sentence. To compensate you, the court can order any stolen property be returned to you or the court can order the person who committed the crime to pay you a sum of money. Still, because the court's main concern during sentencing is not victim compensation, it may be best to try other methods.

■ Victims' compensation schemes across Canada

The third way to compensate victims of crime is through a provincial victim compensation scheme. Awards range between $5,000 and $25,000 and, depending on the plan, can cover claims for everything from medical expenses to lost wages. In most jurisdictions, a special tribunal or government board deals with victims' cases of serious personal injury or death, and can give compensation in several circumstances. These boards can compensate any victim of crime who was physically injured or anyone who was physically injured while trying to prevent a crime. The board can also compensate anyone who was physically injured while lawfully arresting or assisting in the arrest of a person committing a crime. If a victim has died, compensation is still available for the person who financially supported the victim or for the victim's dependants, such as a parent, spouse, or child.

■ Lawsuit

The final way to compensate a victim of crime is to sue the person who committed the crime. A civil lawsuit is held separately from the criminal trial, and can result in an award of damages for injuries suffered. Consult a lawyer for more information if you are considering a civil lawsuit of this nature.

POLICE COMPLAINTS

44. How do I file a complaint against the police?

If you have a complaint against a police officer, there are several things you can do, including starting a civil lawsuit against the officer, laying a criminal charge, or complaining directly to the local police force that is responsible for the officer.

■ Lawsuit

Suing a police officer in a civil lawsuit generally involves preparing for a trial and going to court. If you are able to prove your complaint against the officer, the judge may order the officer to pay damages for the injuries you suffered. In most cases, it will be difficult to prove your complaint and your chances of success will be minimal. In addition, it will be time consuming and very expensive to cover the costs of a formal trial. However, if you decide to pursue this method, make sure you start a civil action against the police officer within six months from when the event happened.

▪ Laying a criminal charge

If you believe a police officer has committed a criminal offence, you can have a criminal charge laid against that officer. To lay a criminal charge, you need to meet with a Justice of the Peace and swear an oath that a crime has been committed and explain the details of the event in question. Depending on the criminal offence in question, you may have a time limit for when charges can be laid.

▪ Filing a complaint with the police

Most provinces have legislation that oversees police and establishes a procedure for making a complaint. You must usually put your complaint in writing to the local chief of police or a public complaints commission that has been established to oversee a force, such as the RCMP or Ontario Provincial Police.

In all jurisdictions, complaints should be made in writing and signed by the complainant. The complaint is then submitted to a special agency overseeing the police (known variously as police services boards, municipal police boards, or police commissions). For your complaint to be investigated you need to: be directly affected by the police actions complained of; submit your complaint within six months of the incident in question; and your complaint must be brought in good faith.

▪ Consequences of filing a complaint

Once a complaint has been submitted to the involved service, the police chief or a designated police commissioner or board will decide whether your complaint will be investigated. This ombudsman of sorts will determine whether your complaint is about the conduct of a police officer or if the complaint is about the policies or services of a police service. The chief or ombudsman will also decide whether you were directly affected by the action complained of, the timeliness of your complaint, and whether your complaint was brought in good faith. If you disagree with any of the decisions you can request the Commission to review them.

▪ Investigation by police service

If an investigation is directed, ordinarily it will be conducted by the public complaint investigators from the involved police service. You may be asked to provide a statement as well as witnesses' names and telephone numbers. The involved officers will also be contacted and will be requested to submit statements and memo book entries. The investigators will obtain all documentary evidence such as radio transmissions, videotapes, and photographs, if there are any. After the public complaint investigation is completed, the investigators will submit a final report to the chief (or other individual) who will then decide, based on the available evidence, whether your complaint is substantiated.

■ Review of decision

If you are not satisfied by a decision arising from your complaint, you can usually ask the commission or board to review the decision, but you often must make that request within a certain time period (typically, 30 days).

■ Discipline of involved officers

If the chief, commissioner, or board finds that the involved officers engaged in misconduct or performed unsatisfactory work, the officers may be disciplined. The nature and degree of discipline will depend on the nature of the complaint and will be decided by the police service.

CRIMINAL RECORDS

45. What is a criminal record?

Not all dealings with the police result in a criminal record. For example, if the police give you a parking ticket, this is an offence under a municipal by-law and is not considered criminal. If you are charged with a provincial driving offence, such as making an improper lane change, this is an offence under provincial traffic legislation and is not criminal.

For a criminal record to exist you must have been a suspect in a criminal investigation and the police must have at least questioned you. In such a case your name and date of birth will be on file with the police. This type of file is called an incident report, and it will be automatically destroyed after a period of about five years, provided that you do not have any more involvement with crime.

If you have ever been fingerprinted in relation to a criminal offence, you have a criminal record, which will appear on police clearance searches. Even if you were not found guilty or if the charges were withdrawn, acquitted, stayed, dismissed, or resulted in a diversion or a peace bond, there is a police record of your arrest, a court record of your trial, and an RCMP record, which includes your photograph and fingerprints.

Once a criminal record exists, it is necessary for you to complete the proper paperwork to have the record destroyed or pardoned.

For more information about removing a criminal record, call the Pardons Canada telephone support line at 416-929-6011 or toll free at 1-877-929-6011 or log onto www.pardonscanada.ca.

46. How do I seal or destroy a criminal record?

Contrary to what most people believe, criminal records are not automatically destroyed or sealed. Instead, you must take active steps to ensure that a criminal record is completely sealed or destroyed. If you were convicted of an offence, you must apply to have your record pardoned, which means it will be sealed and removed from the main repository of RCMP records, and from the police station and courthouse.

■ Pardon for convictions

To be eligible for a pardon, you must wait three or five years after completing the sentence imposed by the court (such as paying fines or completing probation). If the charge was less serious and the court proceeded summarily, then you must wait three years. If the charge was more serious and the court proceeded by indictment, then you must wait five years. Although the waiting period must pass before your pardon can be granted, it is important to start collecting information as soon as possible so you can determine your exact date of eligibility and ensure you have complied with everything that was ordered by the court.

■ Discharges

If you have not been convicted but were found guilty, it means you received either an absolute or conditional discharge. In this case, you will need to have your record purged and destroyed. The waiting period before purging and destroying an absolute discharge is one year, and for a conditional discharge it is three years from the date the court found you guilty.

■ No finding of guilt

If you were fingerprinted, but the charges were withdrawn, stayed, or dismissed, or if you were acquitted outright, you will need to have your photographs and fingerprints destroyed. The waiting period usually ranges from no waiting period to one year from the date of disposition. Whether your file will be destroyed depends on the particular police service and if you have other offences on your record.

   If your criminal record is not destroyed or pardoned, it will be found in almost all police clearance searches. This is because your name, date of birth, and fingerprints are now on file with the local police and the RCMP.

■ Erasing or removing my criminal record

The rules for erasing your criminal record are constantly changing. If you have been accused and charged with a crime and you were fingerprinted, or you attended criminal court, you do have a criminal record.

Even if you were found not guilty, once you have been accused and charged with a criminal offence, a record does exist and you must complete paperwork to have your record destroyed or sealed. It will not go away by itself.

After being charged and fingerprinted, the police and the RCMP will assign a fingerprint number (FPS #) to your name and date of birth before you even go to court.

If you were found not guilty, or you were found guilty but not convicted, you may apply to have all the related police, court, photographs, fingerprints, and RCMP paperwork completely destroyed. Eligibility periods range from no waiting period for withdrawn, dismissed or acquitted to one year for absolute discharges, and three years for conditional discharges. These waiting periods begin as of your final court date.

It is important to start a pardon as soon as possible. As soon as your punishment has been completed, whether it is community hours, a fine, probation or jail, it is in your best interest to start your paperwork as soon as possible.

There are two parts to removing a criminal record. Provincial and federal records must be collected. This information is then used to complete the destruction or pardon application process.

To remove your criminal record, it is necessary to collect your photographs, fingerprints and police, court, and RCMP records. The police, court, RCMP, and National Parole Board all charge fees for their services. It takes between 8–20 months to complete the process.

47. How does a criminal record affect my employment?

Having a criminal record, even in cases where the charges were withdrawn or you were acquitted, can negatively affect your search for employment. A criminal record can also be an obstacle when:

- Seeking a new job or promotion
- Obtaining contracts if you are self-employed
- Getting bonded
- Obtaining a licence

■ Jobs and promotions

Many employers and licensing boards are now conducting mandatory police clearance searches before hiring individuals or allowing applicants into training programs. By signing an application form or an employment agreement, you may be giving permission for a criminal record search to be conducted.

Companies that never before required criminal record searches are now doing so, hindering people who apply for internal promotions. Discovery of a criminal record may not only prevent an employee's opportunity for career advancement within the company, but it may also lead to a person being fired.

In many cases, such as government offices and school boards, financial and insurance institutions, employers conduct police clearance searches on existing employees. Such searches have led to job terminations, even in cases where the employees have been employed for several years.

■ Self-employment

People who are self-employed are not immune to criminal record searches. Many companies that sub-contract work to individuals or to businesses now require criminal record searches on the independent contractor or the owners of the business. This is especially true in situations where the independent contractor will have access to confidential information or will be working with vulnerable people, such as children. Computer programmers, bookkeepers, and nannies are part of just three career fields where criminal record searches are required.

■ Getting bonded

Regarding jobs where bonding is required: it is often too expensive for employers to bond employees who have criminal records. Being bonded means that the employer is paying for insurance against the risk of employees committing crimes such as theft or fraud. If you have a criminal record, the insurance company will charge your employer a premium and your employer may not be able or willing to pay the added cost. As a result, you might not be hired.

■ Obtaining a licence

If you wish to apply for a job or become licensed in a particular industry, it is best to have your criminal record removed before submitting your application.

48. How does a criminal record affect immigration?

A criminal record will negatively affect your ability to immigrate to Canada or remain here. Criminal records will have a different impact depending on whether the individual is a visitor, a refugee, or a permanent resident.

It is illegal to visit Canada if you have a criminal record, unless you have proper immigration status, such as Canadian citizenship or you have acquired special permission from Citizenship and Immigration Canada. If you have a Canadian criminal record, it is best to have it pardoned or destroyed before attempting to enter Canada again. If you have a criminal record from a country other than Canada, you will need to apply for advance permission.

People who were granted permission to enter and be in Canada before they were charged with criminal offences may have their status removed and may be deported from Canada.

Refugees with criminal records can have their status removed and may be deported from Canada. If you have applied to be a permanent resident, your application can be denied. At the very least, the discovery of any kind of criminal record, even where there was no finding of guilt, will result in complications with the immigration application. If your application is part of a family application for permanent residence, the discovery of your record may put every family member's application on hold and may result in the entire family being deported.

If you are a permanent resident, a criminal record can result in your landing status being removed and you being deported. If you have applied for Canadian citizenship, your application can be denied or put on hold. At the very least, discovery of a criminal record will result in complications with your citizenship application. If you wish to apply for permanent resident status or Canadian citizenship, it is best to have your criminal record removed before submitting your application.

49. How can criminal records affect U.S.A. travel and work?

It is illegal to attempt to enter the United States if you have a criminal record, unless you have appropriate immigration status or you have advance permission, called an entry waiver, from the U.S. Immigration Office.

In the past, you may have often passed through U.S. Immigration after answering a few standard questions about your citizenship and the purpose of your visit. It is becoming increasingly common, however, for U.S. Immigration to ask for some identification for the purpose of conducting an RCMP criminal record search. As they are continually enhancing their technology, it now only takes U.S. immigration seconds to conduct a record search. Once you get identified, the immigration officer will download your criminal record into the U.S. Immigration computer system and, as a result, your criminal record will be on file with U.S. Immigration, Department of Homeland Security (DHS). You may also be denied entry to the United States.

After having been denied entry to the U.S., to legally enter at some later date you will require an entry waiver. There are a number of documents that will be required. Also, there are different types of applications depending on what crime you were charged with, and whether you are a Canadian citizen.

Having your criminal record sealed or destroyed in Canada may prevent U.S. Immigration from being able to find the information, unless, of course, you have already been caught at the U.S. border. For more information and assistance in acquiring a U.S. entry waiver, log onto the Department of Homeland Security at www.DHS.gov or to www.pardonscanada.ca.

DO YOU REALLY UNDERSTAND YOUR RIGHTS?

A young offender with subnormal mental capacity was told of his right to legal counsel by police, but said at the time that he simply didn't understand that right. He was later convicted of first-degree murder.

Did the police go far enough in informing him of his rights?

No, according to the Supreme Court of Canada in the case of *R. v. Evans*. The court held that although police read him his rights, he indicated he did not understand his right to legal counsel and that the police offered no additional explanation. A person who does not understand his or her right cannot be expected to assert it. When there is an indication that the accused does not understand his "right to counsel," the police cannot simply rely on reciting that right. They must take steps to facilitate the understanding.

WAS IT A FAIR SEARCH?

An accused arrested for murder indicated he wouldn't provide any bodily samples to the police. He later blew his nose in a tissue that was then thrown in the garbage. The police seized the tissue and had it tested for DNA. The accused was later convicted.

Was that a reasonable search and seizure?

Not while he was in custody, according to the Supreme Court of Canada in *R. v. Stillman*. If the accused was not in custody and discarded the tissue, police can collect and test it because there was no reasonable expectation of privacy in the item. It had been discarded. The situation is different when a person is in custody, especially since the accused's lawyers said their client would not consent to providing samples of his bodily fluids. The seizure was considered unreasonable.

PUBLIC PROPERTY OR NOT?

A small group of citizens, upset over the sale of a controversial book, decide to go down to their local mall and mount a peaceful protest in a public courtyard in front of the book store. After a few minutes, the shopping mall manager arrives and orders the protesters off the property. They refuse, saying they are in a public space along with other shoppers and are voicing their right to freedom of expression.

Can the manager order the citizens to leave the mall?

Yes. In several cases over the years, courts all the way up to the Supreme Court of Canada have upheld the right of those in possession of a property, such as a shopping mall manager, to order anyone off. Even though members of the general public were invited into the mall, that invitation can be withdrawn at any time by a person with the proper authority. The person doesn't even have to own the property, he or she only has to be in possession of it. Therefore, for example, someone leasing a property, a security officer, or even a store employee can order you off.

The same applies to what might be considered truly "public property," such as a government building. Any lawfully authorized person can order a person out of a public building or even off a public street if there's a lawful reason. For example, a peace officer or a public officer can require people to stay out of an area if he or she is administering or enforcing the law.

HEARD IT ON THE GRAPEVINE ... LEGAL OR NOT?

A police officer sitting in a booth at a restaurant overhears two people talking about a crime they committed. After she had heard enough, the officer arrested them and they all ended up in court. The accused argued the officer's evidence was not admissible because their right to privacy was violated and the Criminal Code prohibits unauthorized interceptions of private communications without the permission of the parties.

Are they right? Should the evidence be thrown out?

No. First, the accused were talking about their misdeeds in a place where they had no reasonable expectation of privacy. More important, the Criminal Code law against interception of private communications applies only to the use of mechanical or electronic listening devices, such as a telephone wiretap or a tape recorder secretly left in a room. In the case of R. v. Watson, for example, evidence of a conversation overheard by a police officer by ear was deemed admissible and not an unlawful interception as defined by the Code.

WWW Resources

Canadian Charter of Rights	www.canada.justice.gc.ca/Loireg/charte/const_en.html
Canadian Criminal Code	www.laws.justice.gc.ca/en/C-46
Justice 4 Youth	www.justice4youth.com
Justice for Children and Youth	www.jfcy.org/court
Canadian Resource Centre for Victims of Crime	www.crcvc.ca/
Pardons Canada	www.pardons.org

Victim Compensation

Below is a list of those provinces with agencies that assist victims of crime in recovering compensation.

British Columbia
The Crime Victim Assistance Program
P.O. Box 5350
Station Terminal
Vancouver, BC V6B 1H1
866-660-3888

Alberta
Victims of Crime Financial Benefits Program
10th Floor, J.E. Brownlee Building
10365-97th Street
Edmonton, AB T5J 3W7
780-427-7217

Saskatchewan
Victims Services
6th Floor, 1874 Scarth Street
Regina, SK S4P 3V7
306-787-3500

Manitoba
Compensation for Victims of Crime Program
202-379 Broadway
Winnipeg, MB R3C 0T9
800-262-9344

Ontario
Criminal Injuries Compensation Board
439 University Avenue, 4th Floor
Toronto, ON M5G 1Y8
416-326-2900

Québec
Direction l'indemnisation des victimes d'actes criminels
1199 rue Bleury, 9ième étage
P. O. Box 6056
Succursale Centreville
Montréal, QC H3C 4E1
800-561-IVAC

New Brunswick
Victim Services Program
570 Queen Street
4th Fl., Barker House
Fredericton, NB E3B 6Z6
506-453-2888

Nova Scotia
Criminal Injuries Counseling Program
5151 Terminal Road
P.O. Box 7
Halifax, NS B3J 2L6
902-424-4651

Prince Edward Island
Victim Services
Cambridge Building, 2nd Floor
3 Queen Street
Charlottetown, PE C1A 4A2
902-368-4582

CRIME AND PUNISHMENT
Driving & The Law

Every driver in Canada must have a valid driver's licence to legally operate a motor vehicle on a public road or any other public property. Drivers must carry their licence at all times while driving and must produce it when a police officer asks to see it. Each province manages its own licensing system and the rules for obtaining a licence vary across the country. Many provinces have adopted a graduated licensing system for new drivers that places restrictions on driving conditions.

1.   How do I apply for a driver's licence?

To get a licence, go to the nearest provincial licensing office, which is usually overseen by the government ministry responsible for transportation. Most provinces require that drivers be 16 years of age or over before they can apply for a licence, but there are exceptions. Alberta, for example, allows drivers to obtain a learner's licence at 14, which allows these learners to drive with an adult. In Saskatchewan, you must be 15 years old and enrolled in a driver's education program.

2.   What is graduated licensing?

Many provinces have introduced graduated licensing, a program that eases new drivers into the driving process and requires them to pass various levels and meet conditions before obtaining full driving privileges.

In Ontario, for example, new drivers must successfully pass two levels. First, drivers will need to get a Level One permit, which has conditions or restrictions on where and when new drivers can drive. For a Level One permit, you must take a written knowledge test, an eyesight test at a provincial licensing office and pay a fee for the tests. Level One lasts 8–12 months, depending on whether you have taken an approved drivers' education course.

At the end of Level One, you pay a fee and take a road test. If you pass, you enter Level Two, which has fewer conditions regarding where and when you can drive but still does not give you full driving privileges. Level Two lasts 12 months. At the end you take another road test and, if you pass, you will receive full driving privileges.

3.   What are demerit points?

To keep your licence, you must not abuse your licence privileges. All provincial governments use a demerit or point system to monitor your driving record. If you are convicted of a traffic offence, you will usually receive or lose several points, depending on the province where you are licensed. The number of points varies according to the infraction and is set out in your province's Motor Vehicle Act or its equivalent. Any points that you receive or lose will usually stay on your driving record for up to two years. If you accumulate or lose too many points, your licence will be suspended for a period.

4. How long does my licence last?

To keep your licence valid in most provinces, you have to renew it every five years. Your licence will indicate the expiry date. Governments charge a fee to renew a licence. Elderly people who wish to drive must often meet different requirements to keep a valid driver's licence. Only Ontario requires that when you reach the age of 80 you must take a written test that year and may also be asked to complete a road test. The Ontario licence you receive will be valid for only two years. People with certain medical conditions such as epilepsy, heart conditions, and fainting spells can also have restrictions placed on their driver's licence.

5. Do I need auto insurance?

Please see Section III.

6. What happens if I have an accident?

If you are directly or indirectly involved in an accident that causes property damage, bodily injury, or death, you have certain legal obligations. There are also steps you should take to protect yourself legally if the accident injures someone or causes property damage.

■ Stay at the scene

You must remain at, or immediately return to, the scene of the accident. It is illegal to leave the scene of an accident, whether you were directly or only indirectly involved in the accident.

■ Care for the injured

You must care for the injured person. Call an ambulance if it appears that someone is injured. Do not touch the injured person unless you have medical training or unless the victim's needs are clear. For example, if a car is burning, you can pull the victim from the car. You should also help prevent further accidents by warning approaching traffic about the accident.

■ Call the police

You are legally obligated to call the police when someone is injured or there is significant property damage.

7. What information should I get before reporting the accident?

You should write down everything about the accident, including:

   1. The licence plate of the other car.

2. Its make, model, and year.

3. The other driver's licence number, address, and telephone number.

4. The name of the other driver's insurance company and policy number.

5. The names and phone numbers of witnesses to the accident.

Upon request, you must provide in writing your name, address, phone number, vehicle permit number, and insurance information to all other drivers who were involved in the accident or to police officers or witnesses. Be careful about what you say. Do not admit anything. Do not apologize or make a statement to anyone except a police officer. Do not offer to pay for anything or accept any payments from anyone.

Contact your lawyer or an insurance agent before you accept a payment or sign a release. Keep a record of your medical or mechanical expenses, damaged property, and injuries.

As well, be careful with what you say to representatives of other drivers, including their lawyers or insurance company. Even in minor accidents, it is common practice in the insurance business for a representative of the other driver's insurer to call or contact you shortly after the incident to simply ask how you are feeling. While you may think the insurance company is interested in your well-being, its goal in calling is to determine whether you may have an injury claim. The full symptoms of your injury might not fully surface until well after the accident and any earlier statements — that you "feel fine" or have no injuries — could be used against your claim in future.

Be wary of recommendations about lawyers from tow truck drivers, medical personnel, paralegals, or others who you do not know. In some cases, these people receive commissions or pay-offs for referring accident victims to lawyers or paralegals. Take the time to do your own research and consider the qualifications of several potential legal representatives.

8.   What happens if I fail to remain at the scene of an accident?

It is an offence under both the federal *Criminal Code* and most provincial highway traffic laws to leave the scene of an accident. The offence of failing to remain at the scene of a motor vehicle accident is committed when a driver who is directly or indirectly involved fails to remain at the scene of the accident.

The law requires that you remain at the scene of an accident, or that you immediately return to the scene of the accident. You are legally obligated to give your name, address, telephone number, and insurance information to people who ask for it. The penalties for failing to remain at the scene include a fine of between $200 and $2,000, seven demerit points, up to six months in jail, and a suspended licence for up to two years.

9. Why fight a traffic ticket?

You may want to fight a traffic ticket because the consequences of being convicted can be serious. The penalties for traffic offences can include fines, demerit points, licence suspension, and imprisonment. If you are convicted of a traffic offence, your insurance premiums will also likely increase.

Whether you hire a lawyer or a traffic ticket advocacy service, it may be worthwhile to fight a ticket to simply protect your driving record and avoid or minimize the penalties of a traffic offence. If you fight a traffic ticket, you might be able to reduce the fine, get more time to pay it, have the ticket dismissed, or plead guilty to a less serious offence.

There are several things you should consider when you decide whether to fight a traffic ticket. Think about whether you actually committed the specific offence you are charged with. If you did, was there a good excuse or reason and is that excuse a legal defence? Learn about the offence you were charged with and see what legal defences exist.

10. How do I defend a traffic ticket?

You need to decide whether to represent yourself or hire a lawyer or an agent to represent you. You need to determine what type of traffic ticket you have been issued. You also need to begin preparing your case as soon as possible.

First, decide whether you will hire a lawyer or an agent to represent you. If you could lose your licence, go to jail, or if you are charged with a serious criminal offence, such as impaired driving or failing to remain at the scene of an accident, hire a lawyer to help. A lawyer can also help if you want to plea bargain your charge or if you feel uncomfortable defending yourself. If you want to fight a simple traffic violation, such as speeding, disobeying a stop sign, or parking offences, you can usually represent yourself.

Second, determine exactly what type of traffic ticket you have been issued, whether a provincial offence notice, a provincial offence summons, or a summons. Each type has a different procedure to follow if you wish to fight the ticket.

■ Provincial offence notice

Provincial offence notices are the most common type of traffic ticket. If you have been issued a provincial offence notice, you have three options. First, you can sign the ticket and plead guilty to the charge. Second, you can plead guilty with an explanation. This usually means you will have to go to court and speak with a justice of the peace. The justice of the peace can reduce your fine or give you more time to pay the fine, depending on your explanation. Third, you can dispute the charge by choosing the trial option. If you choose this option you will have to contact the court office and attend court.

If you do not respond to the ticket, it will be reviewed by a justice of the peace, and if the ticket does not contain any fatal flaws, then a conviction will be entered against you. If the ticket contains a fatal flaw, the court can dismiss the ticket. An example of a fatal flaw is if the defendant's name is not on it or there is no offence date or no location or if the officer did not sign the ticket. A minor error such as a misspelled name is not a fatal flaw.

■ Provincial offence summons

A provincial offence summons is usually a pink summons form that is issued for serious offences where there is no set fine. (For example: if you were caught speeding more than 50 km above the speed limit.) You must attend court if you received a provincial offence summons. The maximum penalty for a provincial offence summons can range from $500 to $2,000, depending on where you live.

■ Summons

A summons is usually issued for more serious offences such as failing to remain at the scene of an accident, driving under suspension, or driving with no insurance. The penalties for these offences in Ontario are usually a fine of between $500 and $5,000 or licence suspensions or jail sentences. A summons requires that you attend court on a given date and time. It is an offence to fail to appear in court. If you have received a summons, you have been charged with a serious offence and should therefore contact a lawyer for assistance.

If your ticket is not for a very serious offence and if you decide to fight it on your own, you can prepare your case in several ways. Begin your preparations early, while the details of the incident are still fresh in your mind. Learn more about the charge you face and obtain all the information that the prosecution has against you. This is called disclosure. Decide whether you would like to call witnesses.

Also, decide whether you would like to try plea bargaining with the prosecution. A plea bargain is where you make a deal with the prosecutor that reduces the charge against you. For example, the prosecutor might reduce a charge of careless driving to following too closely, unsafe lane change, or failing to yield. In exchange, you agree to plead guilty to the lesser charge. If you would like to plea bargain, speak with the prosecutor.

11. What defence can I raise when charged with speeding?

The offence of speeding is committed when a driver drives at a speed above the legal limit. It is also an offence to drive so slowly that you block traffic. Speeding tickets are usually the result of a police radar check. It is difficult to fight a speeding ticket if the police have radar evidence against you.

The only possible defence to a speeding ticket is that you were not speeding. This means you must argue that the evidence against you is wrong. You could try arguing that the radar measurement is somehow flawed or mistaken. It is difficult to defend yourself using this argument. Alternatively, you can plea bargain with the prosecutor to reduce the charge against you in exchange for a guilty plea, such as reducing your speeding ticket to a lower speed.

The penalty for a speeding charge is usually a fine, which will be determined based on the speed you were travelling. You may also receive or be given demerit points (the points system differs by province), depending on the speed you were travelling. Your licence could be suspended if you are repeatedly convicted of speeding offences.

12. What defence can I raise when charged with failing to stop at a red light or stop sign?

When a driver goes through a red light or a stop sign without stopping then that person has committed a traffic offence.

The prosecutor must prove that the light was red at the instant you entered the intersection. A car enters an intersection when any part of it crosses over the pedestrian walkway area of the intersection.

If you fight a ticket for failing to stop at a red light or a stop sign, your only defence is that you did stop or that the light was not red when you entered the intersection. If the police officer is unsure what colour the light was when the car entered the intersection, then you can argue that there is reasonable doubt about whether you are guilty. You can also defend yourself by showing that there was some irregularity that caused the sign or the light to be misleading. For example, you might be able to argue that the sign was not visible because of snow or a tree — though this is a difficult defence to make.

13. What defence can I raise when charged with failure to report and remain at the scene?

The offences of failing to report and remain at the site of a motor vehicle accident are committed when a driver who is directly or indirectly involved in an accident fails to report it to the police or fails to remain at or immediately return to the scene of the accident.

The law requires that you report accidents that involve injuries or property damage that exceeds a certain dollar amount, depending on the province. Be careful about estimating the amount of property damage, because people tend to underestimate the extent of damage. You are obligated to report an accident whether you are directly or indirectly involved in it. The penalty for failing to report an accident is usually a fine and demerit points.

One defence to the offence of failing to report an accident is that you did not think the damage was over the reportable amount. There must be no injuries resulting from the accident to use this defence. If the total amount of damage is close to the reportable amount, this argument might be successful.

There are several defences you could use to defend yourself against a charge of failing to remain, but they are difficult to use. If you did not know that the accident occurred — you can use this as a defence. This is especially useful if you were indirectly involved in the accident, although courts are usually skeptical of this defence. If you have been identified as the driver of a vehicle that failed to remain at the scene of the accident, you can argue that it is not certain that you were the driver. It can be difficult to correctly identify the driver of a vehicle that leaves the scene of an accident. You can try using this defence to raise some doubt about whether it was actually you who did not remain at the scene. It is also difficult to use this defence successfully.

Failing to remain at the scene of an accident is a serious criminal offence. Contact a lawyer for assistance if you have been charged with this offence.

14. What defence can I raise when charged with following too closely?

The offence of driving too closely is committed when a driver follows another vehicle at a distance that is not reasonable and prudent. This is a difficult offence for a prosecutor to prove.

The exact definition of a reasonable and prudent distance will depend on the road conditions, and the street or highway you were on. The penalty for following too closely is a fine and demerit points.

As a defence to the charge of following too closely, you could argue that the distance you were following was reasonable. Some people try to argue that their brakes failed. The court is usually very skeptical about this excuse, so unless you have proof it is probably not worthwhile to use this defence.

If you want to fight a ticket for following too closely by arguing you were following at a reasonable distance, prepare your argument well. Know the distance between you and the vehicle you were following, the action you took to avoid the accident, the action taken by the other vehicle that affected your vehicle, and the time span involved.

15. What defence can I raise when charged with driving without insurance?

It is illegal to drive a motor vehicle that is not insured. The law requires that every motor vehicle be insured with at least third-party liability coverage. It is the driver's responsibility to ensure he or she is properly insured. If you are stopped by the police, you must show them your insurance card if they ask for it. If you do not have your insurance card with you, as a courtesy the police will sometimes give you 48 hours to go to the police station and show them your card, but they have no legal obligation to do this.

The penalty for driving with no insurance in Canada ranges from $2,000 to as much as $25,000 in some provinces. Your licence could be suspended for up to one year and your car could be impounded for three to six months.

It is very difficult to defend yourself if you are charged with driving with no insurance. It is no defence that you thought you were insured or that you did not know you had to be insured, although that may help reduce the amount of fine imposed. Also, if you are involved in an accident you may have to personally pay for injuries and damages. If you do not have enough money to pay these costs, you may be forced to sell some of your property. If you do not have any money or any property that you could sell, then the people who were injured in the accident may not be able to get the medical attention they require.

16. When can police stop your vehicle?

The police have the legal right to stop a car at any time for the purpose of checking certain things:

- Whether the driver has consumed alcohol or drugs
- Whether the driver has valid car insurance
- Whether the car is mechanically fit to be driven

The police do not have to suspect that a driver is drunk before they stop a vehicle. In fact, the police have the legal right to conduct random spot checks for impaired drivers and they have the right to pull any car over at a RIDE program check point.

■ Responding to police questions

Once the police have stopped you, they have the right to ask you a number of questions, including whether you have consumed any alcohol or drugs. Although you do not have to answer these questions, it is advisable to co-operate with the police. Refusing to respond may lead the police to suspect you have consumed alcohol and further investigation may result in the police demanding a roadside breath-screening test. If you refuse to provide a roadside breath-screening sample, you can be charged with a serious offence under the Canadian *Criminal Code*.

■ Performing physical tests

The police may also ask you to get out of your car to perform several physical tests, such as walking in a straight line, picking up a coin, and counting backward from 10. Again, although you do not have to perform these tasks, the police may demand a breath sample if you refuse.

17. What are roadside and Breathalyzer tests?

To test a driver's alcohol consumption, the police have the legal right to administer two kinds of breath tests: the roadside breath-screening test and the Breathalyzer test.

The roadside breath-screening test usually takes place at the side of the road after you have been pulled over. This test, which is sometimes called an ALERT test, provides the police with an approximate reading of the amount of alcohol in your body.

The second test is called the Breathalyzer or the intoxicator test. Unlike the roadside breath test, the Breathalyzer is conducted at the police station. The Breathalyzer test is more sophisticated and provides an exact reading of your blood alcohol level.

Refusing to provide a breath sample for either test can result in a serious charge under the Canadian *Criminal Code*. If you have an injury or illness that prevents you from being able to blow enough air into the screening machine, you may have a valid excuse for refusing.

18. Can police order me to take blood and urine tests?

The police will normally demand a breath sample if they believe a driver has consumed alcohol or drugs. In certain situations, however, they have the legal right to request a blood or urine sample under the supervision of a physician.

The police are permitted to request a blood or urine sample if they have a good reason to believe you were driving after having consumed alcohol or drugs and if they have a good reason to believe you will not be able to provide a proper breath sample. For example, if you were in a car accident and were injured or rendered unconscious, you may not be in a condition to give the police an adequate breath sample. A doctor must be satisfied that taking the samples will not endanger your life or safety.

■ Failing a test

If you fail a blood or urine test, you can be charged with other related charges such as impaired driving and driving while exceeding the legal blood alcohol limit. Dangerous driving and criminal negligence may also arise, depending on the facts.

Although you have the right to talk to a lawyer before letting the police take a blood or urine sample, if you refuse to provide a sample, you can be charged with the offence of refusing to provide a sample.

19. What is impaired driving?

Impaired driving means being in control of a vehicle while under the influence of alcohol or drugs. It is commonly referred to as drunk driving. Impaired driving is a serious offence under the Canadian *Criminal Code*.

You do not have to exceed the legal blood alcohol limit to be charged with impaired driving. The only requirement for a charge of impaired driving is that your ability to drive was affected by alcohol or drugs, regardless of how much or how little was actually consumed.

■ How police assess whether you are impaired

The police will make a judgment about your ability to drive safely based on a number of observations, including your appearance, your answers to questions, your physical movement, and whether you or your car smells of alcohol. Under the law, police have the right to stop your car and ask if you have consumed alcohol or drugs before driving. Although you are not required to answer such questions, it is generally best to avoid becoming hostile with police. You are required to provide the police with your driver's licence, car ownership, and insurance papers.

■ Performing physical tests

The police have the right to request that you perform several physical tests, such as walking in a straight line, picking up a coin and following a moving finger with your eyes. You are not required to co-operate with the police, but failing to comply may lead police to suspect you are impaired. They may then demand that you provide a breath sample.

■ When can police request a roadside breath test and a Breathalyzer?

Before asking a driver to perform a roadside breath test, police must generally have a good reason to suspect alcohol has been consumed. Again, for example, this may be based on appearance, movements, or the smell of alcohol. It is important to understand that you do not have the right to consult a lawyer before performing a roadside breath test. You do, however, have a legal right to consult a lawyer before performing a Breathalyzer test at the police station.

■ Penalties

You cannot be charged with an offence for failing a roadside breath test, but you will likely be asked to take the formal Breathalyzer test at a police station. If you fail that test, you can be charged with driving while exceeding the legal blood/alcohol limit.

Other related charges may also arise depending on the facts of your case, such as dangerous driving or criminal negligence in the operation of a vehicle. In some provinces, your driver's licence may be automatically suspended for an extended period (90 days in Ontario, for example).

If you are arrested for impaired driving and you refuse to provide a breath sample or your sample shows your blood alcohol level is over 80 mg, then your driver's licence can be suspended.

If you are found guilty of impaired driving and it is your first conviction of this kind, you will likely be given a fine of $300 to $2,000 and have your licence suspended for 3 to 36 months (usually one year). Jail is also a possibility, with terms ranging up to 6 months for a summary offence and up to five years for an indictable offence. Whether a charge is processed under summary conviction or an indictment is at the discretion of the Crown prosecutor.

For your second offence, you could be jailed for 14 days to 6 months for summary convictions (usually a minimum penalty of 14 days), up to five years for an indictable offence, fined $300 to $2,000 and receive a 6-36 month licence suspension (or up to five years for indictable offences). For a third or subsequent offence, you could be prohibited from driving for 12-36 months, fined from $300 to no limit and jailed for 90 days to 6 months (or up to five years for indictable offences). Add in the offence of driving impaired and causing bodily harm or death and you can lose your licence for up to 10 years, be fined any amount, and go to jail for up to 14 years.

It should be noted that young drivers may face harsher penalties. Ontario has a 0 mg limit for new drivers under its graduated driver licensing system. Prince Edward Island has a 10 mg limit for drivers under 19 years of age. Violations in both provinces are punishable by a 3-month licence suspension.

Manitoba also has a mandatory three-month licence suspension for drivers who fail or refuse a breath test, independent of a *Criminal Code* conviction. The goal of the suspension is to ensure people do not drive during the time between the offence and disposition of the case by the court.

A court may also order you to attend a drug or alcohol rehabilitation program. If you were at fault for an accident and impaired, your automobile insurance policy may not cover damage to your vehicle and you may not be eligible to receive certain other benefits, such as income replacement benefits.

20. What is dangerous driving?

Dangerous driving means driving in a way that endangers other people. It is a serious offence under the Canadian *Criminal Code*.

There do not have to be other people around for a driver to be charged with dangerous driving. The only requirement is that someone drives with reckless disregard for public safety, so that there is a danger to the public who are either present or who might be expected to be present. The police will consider the circumstances, including the nature and condition of the place where the offence took place and the traffic in the area, when they determine whether someone should be charged with dangerous driving.

■ Penalties

If the police lay a charge following an accident, it will likely be for careless driving, dangerous driving, or criminal negligence. Dangerous driving is punishable by a maximum jail term of five years. If you are found guilty of dangerous driving that causes death, the penalty is a maximum jail term of 14 years.

21. What is the difference between careless driving and dangerous driving?

The offence of careless driving is committed when a driver drives without reasonable care or attention to other drivers. If you have been charged with careless driving, you will be convicted if the facts suggest you were driving without proper care and attention. The penalty for careless driving in most jurisdictions is a fine, a possible six-month jail term, up to two years' licence suspension, and usually licence demerit points.

If you are charged with careless driving, the prosecutor will often be willing to plea bargain. A plea bargain is where you make a deal with the prosecutor to reduce the charge against you; in exchange you agree to plead guilty. For example, the prosecutor might reduce a charge of careless driving to following too closely, unsafe lane change, or failing to yield. You should approach the prosecutor to find out whether he or she is willing to plea bargain. Careless driving is an offence under the provincial *Highway Traffic Act* and is not criminal.

Dangerous driving is a criminal offence and is punishable to a maximum of six months or five years in prison, depending on whether the prosecutor proceeds summarily or by indictment. It is committed when a driver drives with reckless disregard for public safety. If you are charged with dangerous driving you should contact a lawyer for assistance.

22. What happens if I drive while my licence is suspended?

It is an offence under both the federal *Criminal Code* and the provincial *Highway Traffic Act* to drive while your driver's licence is suspended.

■ When can your licence be suspended

The Registrar of Motor Vehicles may suspend your licence if you have not paid a fine or if you have accumulated too many demerit points as a result of driving offences. The police may suspend your licence for up to

12 hours if they pull you over and you fail a roadside breath test, and up to 90 days if you fail a Breathalyzer test.

Your licence may also be suspended as a result of a conviction for certain driving offences, such as impaired driving or dangerous driving. In these situations, your driver's licence is automatically suspended for at least one year.

■ Penalties

If you are convicted under your provincial *Highway Traffic Act* for driving while suspended, there are several penalties you may be given. For example, the first time you drive while your licence is suspended the judge can give you a fine of up to $5,000 in some jurisdictions and six months in prison, as well as a longer licence suspension.

If you are convicted a second time or more, the judge can fine you up to $5,000 and can send you to prison for up to six months. The judge must usually give you a minimum fine of $2,000. Also, your licence will be suspended for another six months in addition to the time it is already under suspension. If the suspension arose because you were convicted of a *Criminal Code* offence, the penalties are much more severe: from $5,000 to $25,000 for a first offence, and from $10,000 to $50,000 for a subsequent one.

If you are charged under the *Criminal Code* with driving while disqualified, you could be sent to prison for two years and fined a maximum of $2,000.

If you drive while your licence is suspended and you get into an accident, your insurance will probably not cover the cost of damages, and you can be sued.

Pop Quiz

True or False

1. Driver licence schemes in Canada work on a demerit point system.
2. You have a legal obligation to stay at the scene of an accident.
3. There's no defence for failing to stop at a stop sign.
4. Once the government issues you a driver's licence it's good for your lifetime.
5. You must be 18 before you can get any type of driver's licence.

Answers

1. True
2. True
3. False. You can argue that it was obstructed, but it is a tough argument to make.
4. False. You must renew your licence following a period defined by the province.
5. False. Most provinces allow drivers to get a licence at 16 if not earlier.

Licensing Information

British Columbia	http://www.icbc.com
Alberta	www.gov.ab.ca
Saskatchewan	www.gov.sk.ca
Manitoba	http://www.gov.mb.ca
Ontario	www.mto.gov.on.ca
Québec	www.saaq.gouv.qc.ca
New Brunswick	www.gnb.ca
Nova Scotia	www.gov.ns.ca
Newfoundland and Labrador	www.gov.nf.ca
Prince Edward Island	www.gov.pe.ca
Newfoundland	www.gov.nf.ca
Northwest Territories	www.gov.nt.ca
Yukon	www.gov.yk.ca
Nunavut	www.gov.nu.ca
Young Drivers of Canada	www.yd.com
Canadian Relocation Systems	http://relocatecanada.com

ENVIRONMENTAL CRIMES

C anada's provincial and federal lawmakers protect the environment by prohibiting or controlling a wide variety of potentially polluting activities of businesses, individuals, and others. For example, these laws govern use or disposal of contaminated land, handling of dangerous chemicals or emissions, accidental spills, and those legally responsible for any environmental damage.

Thanks to environmental activists of the past century and greater public awareness of our surroundings, environmental laws these days reach into all aspects of our daily lives. Whether you are considering dumping used engine oil into the sewage system (don't!) or thinking about clearing trees from your land, you may need to consult environmental laws. Penalties for violating environmental laws can include compensation for those who have been injured, fines, and even imprisonment.

Generally, the federal government's authority tends to be specifically defined, while the provincial governments are responsible for a broader range of environmental matters. Federal and provincial environment authorities have sometimes broad powers to investigate environmental offences. These authorities can order companies or individuals to clean up pollution or alternatively, can require them to repay any money spent to clean up or control the environmental damage. Municipalities also play a role in environmental issues through land use planning and by-laws pertaining to noise and nuisances, waste disposal, and sewage.

1.   Who is typically affected by environmental laws?

Everyone in Canada has environmental rights and responsibilities. Some people also have a legal responsibility to know about environmental law because of their activities or business.

For example, people in certain industries have a duty to protect the environment and to follow all environmental laws. These businesses have a direct impact on the environment, through such activities as handling or transporting chemicals or waste, construction, manufacturing, and biotechnology.

People involved in activities such as selling real estate or lending money with land as collateral also need to be aware of environmental issues and laws so they can advise their clients and avoid liability themselves.

In the end, everyone has the right to play an active role in protecting the environment. For example, Ontario's *Environmental Bill of Rights* enables its citizens to provide input into the development of provincial legislation. It also gives citizens the right to request an investigation into an environmental offence, and to sue someone who they believe has broken the law and harmed the environment.

No matter where you live, if you see an individual or a business improperly dumping a harmful substance, you have the right to ask the government (usually the environment department or ministry) to investigate. Depending on the situation, you may also have a right to sue people for the environmental damage they cause.

2.   What do environmental laws do?

In their most basic form, environmental laws make it illegal to release contaminants into the environment. Contaminants can be solids, liquids, gases, noise, vibrations, or radiation that harm the environment or affect peoples' health.

Federal environmental laws establish national standards concerning the regulation of toxic substances and the classification, labelling, transportation and provision of safety information for hazardous or dangerous goods. National standards have been established for specific industries under the *Canadian Environmental Protection Act, 1999* and the *Fisheries Act.* These are the two principal federal statutes that govern polluting activities throughout Canada.

The *Canadian Environmental Protection Act, 1999* has broad powers over areas such as waste disposal or dumping in Canada's territorial seas without a permit. Four air pollution regulations also exist under the Act, which limit the concentration of asbestos emissions, lead emissions, mercury and vinyl chloride.

Another important part of the Act is the regulation and control of "toxic substances." For example, it requires an importer or manufacturer to notify the federal government of the substance before manufacture or importation can take place in Canada. Businesses must also build in a lead time for the introduction of new chemicals or the products of biotechnology into the marketplace.

In most provinces, environmental laws make it necessary to have a licence to dispose of industrial waste or to release substances into the air or water that could harm the environment. Many provincial governments enact laws that follow six basic principles:

1. Preventing pollution is better than fixing pollution.

2. Pollution that has already occurred should not be allowed to spread.

3. Clean-up action should take place as soon as possible.

4. Where pollution does occur, the polluter must pay to clean it up.

5. The original polluter and former property owners can be required to pay for clean-ups, even if they no longer own the polluted land.

6. New owners may have a claim for compensation if they have suffered due to things such as polluted water wells, gasoline emissions in the home, toxic substances buried on the property, and so forth.

3.   What type of pollution is covered by environmental laws?

Most provinces have laws regulating and restricting emissions into the air, water usage and dumping, and waste disposal. There are also industry-specific regulations that establish environmental controls for different substances and activities. In addition to these regulations, a licence or permit is often needed to dispose of waste, use large quantities of water, release any type of water or waste into waterways or release substances into the air. If you fail to obtain a licence or comply with the regulations, you can be prosecuted.

■ Air pollution

Generally, it is illegal to emit contaminants into the air. Contaminants can range from things such as toxic substances to noise and vibrations.

■ Discharging contaminants

If you want to discharge a contaminant into the environment regularly, you will likely need government approval in the form of a permit or certificate. The government will regulate the quality and quantity of discharge to ensure it falls within provincial guidelines and ensure that the overall effect is acceptable for the environment.

■ Releasing water or waste into water

If you plan to release any type of water or waste into a waterway, you will likely need government approval. Most provinces have a number of regulations governing specific industrial wastewater releases.

4. Who is responsible for cleaning up contaminated land?

Environmental laws have rules on who is responsible for the clean-up and who will typically pay for it. The government has broad powers to order a person or company who owns or controls a contaminant to clean up any environmental damage. It can also order the current owner or a previous owner of the property to do the clean-up.

Generally, there are three situations in which contaminated land must be cleaned up:

■ Pollution caused by the current owner of the property

If the current owner of a property causes or permits a spill, a leak or contamination that threatens people or the environment, then the property owner must report it to the ministry and the property owner must pay to clean it up.

■ Pollution caused by some other person or company

If some other person or company, such as the owner of a neighbouring property, owns or controls a contaminant that adversely affects your property, then that polluter is responsible for cleaning up and disposing of the contaminant. If this other person or company does not do the clean-up, then you or the ministry may make arrangements to clean it up. If this happens, then you or the ministry may recover the cost of the clean-up by suing the person or company that owned or controlled the contaminant.

■ Pollution caused by a previous owner of a property

If a previous owner contaminated a property, then either the current property owner or the polluter can be held responsible for the clean-up. If the person who caused the contamination cannot be found or cannot pay for the clean-up, then the current owner will have to pay. The current property owner can then try to recover the cost by suing the original polluter for the cost of the clean-up. Property owners have a legal obligation to inform people who buy their property that it is contaminated. If they do not inform the buyer, they could be sued by the buyer for the cost of the clean-up and any other financial losses.

5. What happens if I buy a property that has environmental problems?

The general rule regarding the purchase of any property is "buyer beware." When you purchase a property, you should investigate what the land was previously used for to determine if it may be polluted or contaminated. In addition to protecting your own health and ability to use the property, you could also be held responsible for any environmental problems that arise in the future.

If you buy a property with some contamination, you may have a choice about when and if to clean it up. But there may be consequences if you wait. For example, the land may become worthless or unsaleable, it may be difficult or impossible to obtain municipal permits, or your neighbours may sue you if the contamination adversely affects them.

When you are considering buying a property, discuss all environmental concerns with your lawyer to ensure you are protected. A lawyer can also help you recover the cost of cleaning up contamination on your property that was caused by someone else.

6. What if my neighbour is causing pollution?

If your neighbour is causing pollution and you are suffering from health problems, or you have suffered property damage or you are subjected to things such as bad smells or loud noises, you have four main courses of action to choose from:

- Speak with and ask your neighbour to discontinue the activities causing the problem. This is not always a possibility, especially if your neighbour is a business.
- Contact your municipality to see if there is a by-law against such activities. If so, the municipality can enforce the by-law, which will

force your neighbour to stop the nuisance. The municipality can even prosecute the neighbour if the nuisance continues

• Lodge a complaint with your ministry or department of the environment. After investigating the situation, the government may issue one of several orders, such as a stop order, or a clean-up order.

• Start a lawsuit. Depending on the situation, it may even be possible to have other neighbours join your lawsuit to help cover legal costs. This is called a "class action" and is permissible when the damages claimed by all the participants are caused by the same thing. In your lawsuit you can ask for compensation or an injunction. Compensation is paid to cover the cost of injuries and expenses that were caused by the actions of the polluter. An injunction is a court order that forces the polluter to stop the activities which cause the problems.

7. How do municipal zoning restrictions help our environment?

Municipal official plans and zoning by-laws restrict the areas where certain activities are allowed to take place. For example, you cannot build an industrial factory in a residential neighbourhood. Any activity on your property must comply with the zoning by-laws of your municipality. In fact, many municipalities are now incorporating clean-up guidelines and contaminated land zoning restrictions into their by-laws. These by-laws will make it illegal to obtain permission to build or change the use of the contaminated land without cleaning it up.

Before you buy land or make plans to build a new building or change an existing building on land you already own, contact your municipal government or an environmental law lawyer.

8. What is an environmental assessment?

An environmental assessment is a formal process in which the federal Canadian Environmental Assessment Agency or the provincial environment ministry evaluates the environmental impact of a proposed development or building. The law ensures that the environmental impact of many large-scale activities is evaluated before the activities are permitted. The environmental assessment process also informs the public about the project and gives interested parties the right to comment before the project is approved.

The Canadian Environmental Assessment Agency deals with projects or properties owned or regulated by the federal government. Most provinces have some type of assessment procedure for activities such as building roads, hydro stations, and landfill sites or major commercial undertakings such as waste-related projects.

9. What powers do environmental officials have?

To ensure that environmental rules and regulations are followed, most provincial governments have the power to send environmental officers to inspect businesses and industry and to investigate potential offences.

■ Inspections

Inspections are conducted to locate and identify pollution, to check water quality, or to make sure businesses and individuals are obeying the terms and conditions of their environmental licences. Essentially, inspections serve to locate problems and have offensive activities discontinued.

■ Investigations

Investigations are different from inspections. Investigations are conducted to locate evidence of an environmental offence. There are two main reasons why environmental officers usually begin an investigation. First, investigations are sometimes started by environment authorities who observe evidence of an offence when responding to a spill or performing a routine inspection of a business or industry. Second, the officer could be responding to a special request.

■ Investigative powers

Environmental officers can enter public property and look around without special permission. Environmental officers do not have to give notice that they will be inspecting a business or industry, especially if it is an emergency situation or if they have legal authority to enter the property. If officers want to enter private property, they must have the permission of the property owner or occupier, or they must have legal authority to enter the premises. For example, an officer may be allowed to enter a property based on an environmental law such as a provincial *Pesticides Act*, which gives officers the authority to inspect certain properties.

In comparison, when officers are investigating an offence, in most cases they are required to have a search warrant. Extensive investigations of offences may last several weeks. In addition, environmental officers who conduct inspections or investigations can take samples of water or waste, and they can take copies of relevant documents. It is an offence to obstruct an environmental officer or to give false information.

10. What happens if there is a spill of a dangerous contaminant?

For most accidental spills, provincial laws require that specific rules and procedures be followed. If you have control of a substance that spills and is likely to harm the environment, you must follow the procedures set out in provincial laws.

Generally, you must report the spill to the appropriate government department, usually the ministry of environment or its equivalent. In Ontario, for example, spills must be reported to an Environment Spills Action Centre that is open 24 hours a day, seven days a week.

Depending on where you live you should also report the spill to your municipality and contact the owner or people in control of the spilled contaminant if they are not already aware of the spill.

There may also be other reporting requirements, depending on the situation and nature of the spill. If you are dealing with a specific toxic substance, check with the government or an environmental law lawyer to find out what regulations apply to your situation.

After a leak or spill, the owner or person in control of the contaminant will usually be required to clean it up. In the event of a major spill, the local environmental ministry or department may choose to handle the clean-up. If necessary, government officials can sometimes enter a contaminated property even without permission of the owner. Afterward, the government will usually try to recover the clean-up costs from the owner or the person in control of the contaminant.

11. How are environmental laws enforced?

Environmental laws are usually enforced in two main ways. First, the environment authorities can issue an order demanding the company or individual to take certain actions. Second, they may choose to charge and prosecute the offender.

Six of the most common types of orders the government may issue are:

• **Stop orders** require an activity to be halted because it is causing or is likely to cause harm to people or the environment. Stop orders are issued to the property owner or to the person responsible for the harmful activity, and they must be obeyed immediately.

Control orders require a person to monitor and control an activity to prevent environmental harm. A control order can also demand that contamination be cleaned up or contained.

• **Preventive orders** demand that a person take precautions to prevent discharges and to clean up or minimize the adverse effects of any discharge that may occur. Preventive orders can be issued even if no contamination has been discharged. Current and former owners and controllers of property or businesses can be subject to preventive orders.

• **Clean-up orders** demand that a person remove contaminants and restore the environment. A clean-up order must be directed to the person who caused or permitted the contamination.

• **Orders to pay costs** demand that a person reimburse the government for the costs of cleaning up the contaminants and restoring the environment. Any person who could have been ordered to prevent contamination or to clean it up can be ordered to pay the government's clean-up costs.

• **Orders regarding waste disposal sites** require owners, operators, and former owners and operators of waste disposal sites, or land where waste was illegally dumped, to clean up the site.

■ Appealing an order

Orders can be appealed, but an order will usually have to be followed while it is being appealed unless the person appealing can show that suspending the order will not damage the environment or health of any person. Orders must be appealed promptly. If a person waits too long to appeal, he or she may lose the right to appeal.

■ Penalties

Depending on the province, penalties for committing an environmental offence can include: paying the cost of the clean-up, fines for the corporation or the individuals involved, jail terms for the individuals involved, revoking licences, and stripping the company of profit it earned as a result of the offence.

12. Who can be held responsible?

For businesses, the directors and senior officers of a corporation have a legal duty to ensure the company's activities comply with the law. The officers and directors can be held personally responsible for environmental offences caused by anyone in the organization, including individual employees, to the point of legal prosecution for environmental damage.

Employees who break environmental laws can also be held legally responsible for their actions. Shareholders who are not officers or employees of the company will not normally be held responsible, unless they have taken an active role in the management of the company.

13. Why is "due diligence" important in environmental law?

In some cases, a corporation or its directors can be held responsible for environmental offences even if they did not intend to commit the offence. This is referred to as "strict liability." Nonetheless, the corporation and its directors may defend themselves by showing they exercised due diligence, meaning that all reasonable care was taken to avoid the harm.

To demonstrate due diligence, a corporation or an individual must show one of two things. Either they must show they did everything within their power to prevent the offence, or they must show that the individual or the directing minds of the company reasonably believed in a mistaken set of facts that, if true, would make them innocent.

The specific requirements of due diligence will depend on several factors, including the potential harm, available alternatives, likelihood of harm, and degree of knowledge or skill that can be expected of the person charged. Overall, the defendant must prove that it was more likely than not that they did everything reasonable to prevent the environmental damage.

To use the due diligence defence, the company or individual must show they established a proper system to prevent environmental harm, and they took reasonable steps to ensure that the prevention system would work effectively. An environmental management system should identify, manage, and control the risk of harm to the environment, and it should document the risks and actions taken.

If you need specific advice about defending an environmental charge, contact a lawyer with environmental law expertise. A lawyer can also advise you about how to ensure that you are complying with the law and how to minimize your exposure to environmental liability before problems arise.

Ontario's Environmental Bill of Rights

The *Environmental Bill of Rights* was passed in Ontario in 1994. It gives every Ontario resident a *formal* right to participate in the environmental decisions of the Ontario government. People now have a formal right to get information on most environmentally significant proposals of any of the Ontario government ministries that are listed under the *Environmental Bill of Rights*. They also have the right to comment on these decisions.

Ontario's *Environmental Bill of Rights* gives Ontario residents the following important rights:

■ Right to Notice of environmentally significant proposals

The formal right to notice of environmentally significant proposals is realized through the Environmental Registry. The Environmental Registry is an Internet Web site where all Ontarians can go to find out about environmentally significant proposals before they are decided. The Registry also provides details on each proposal and how to comment on it within the 30-day comment period.

■ Right to Comment on environmentally significant proposals

Under Ontario's *Environmental Bill of Rights*, people have the right to a minimum standard of 30 days public consultation on most environmentally significant proposals that are put forth by any of the Ontario government ministries covered by the *Environmental Bill of Rights*.

■ Right to Request an Appeal of particular decisions on instruments

Instruments are specific licences to do something environmentally significant usually sought by a private sector company referred to as a proponent. Ontarians now have the entirely new right to appeal decisions made on such instruments.

■ Right to Request a Review of existing government policies

Under the *Environmental Bill of Rights*, any two Ontarians may request a review of existing policies, acts, regulations or instruments if they think the environment is not being protected.

Ontario residents also have the right to suggest new policies to be put in place to protect the environment.

■ Right to Request an Investigation

Under the *Environmental Bill of Rights*, any two Ontarians may request an investigation of contraventions of environmental law. Such a request is best accompanied by as much evidence as possible, including descriptions of the offence, photographs, witness statements, and audio or videotapes.

■ Right to Sue under the Environmental Bill of Rights

Using the *Environmental Bill of Rights*, Ontario residents have the right to sue someone under two circumstances.

■ Right to Protection from employer reprisal

The *Environmental Bill of Rights* protects Ontario residents from retaliation by employers for reporting contraventions of environmental laws or for using any other of their environmental rights. If an employer dismisses, penalizes, or otherwise harasses an employee for these reasons, the employee can seek protection by contacting a lawyer and the Ontario Labour Relations Board. The Labour Relations Board has the authority to order that the employee be compensated or reinstated. For more information on your right to protection from employer reprisal, you can contact the Office of the Environmental Commissioner of Ontario at 416-325-3377 or 800-701-6454.

WWW Resources:
Government Ministries and Agencies

Federal Ministry of the Environment: http://www.ec.gc.ca/
This site includes access to federal environmental laws and regulations and a range of information on environmental initiatives at the federal level.

Canadian Environmental Assessment Agency: www.ceaa-acee.gc.ca
This federal agency manages the environmental assessment process. It assists federal departments and agencies with training and guidance and provides administrative support to independent mediators and panels.

British Columbia Ministry of Water, Land and Air Protection:
www.gov.bc.ca/bvprd/bc/channel.do?action=ministry&channelID=-
95&navId=NAV_ID_province
Information about B.C. environmental issues and links to government information and departments.

Alberta Ministry of the Environment: http://www3.gov.ab.ca/env
Links to Alberta laws statutes involving the environment.

Saskatchewan Environment: www.se.gov.sk.ca/
Government site that features information about environmental issues and services in Saskatchewan.

Manitoba Conservation: www.gov.mb.ca/conservation
Site for environmental information for the province of Manitoba.

Ontario Ministry of the Environment: www.ene.gov.on.ca/
Provides public access to information and laws on the environment for the province of Ontario.

Environment Québec: www.menv.gouv.qc.ca/index-en.htm
Clearing centre for environmental information about the province of Québec.

New Brunswick Department of the Environment and Local Government:
www.gnb.ca/0009/index-e.asp
Site for information about New Brunswick laws and programs pertaining to the environment.

Nova Scotia Environment and Labour: www.gov.ns.ca/enla/
Access to legislation and information about environmental law in Nova Scotia.

Prince Edward Island Department of Environment and Energy:
www.gov.pe.ca/enveng/index.php3
Includes online access to environmental laws statutes and pollution prevention initiatives.

Newfoundland & Labrador Department of Environment: www.gov.nf.ca/env/
Information about Newfoundland & Labrador environmental laws, regulations and the assessment process.

Web Resources
Environmental Organizations

Canadian Environmental Law Association (CELA): http://www.cela.ca
A non-profit, public interest organization that advocates environmental law reforms and provides a free legal advisory clinic for the public.

The Canadian Environmental Network: www.cen-rce.org
This organization provides co-ordination, communication and research services to Canadian environmental groups across the country.

Environmental Defence Canada: www.edcanada.org
A national charity engaged in fighting to protect the environment for future generations.

Canadian Institute for Environmental Law and Policy (CIELAP): www.cielap.org
A national, independent, not-for-profit research and educational organization that examines environmental law and policy issues.

The Environmental Law Centre: www.elc.ab.ca
Based in Edmonton, this non-profit organization provides information about environmental and natural resources law.

Sierra Legal Defense Fund (SLDF): www.sierralegal.org
A not-for-profit environmental advocacy organization.

Section Six
LIFE MATTERS

IMMIGRATION

Although Canada accepts over 200,000 new immigrants each year, all must meet certain entrance requirements. Since the tragedy of 9/11 and the terrorist threat around the world, Canada's immigration policies have toughened significantly. Having an experienced and trusted immigration lawyer has never been more important.

Except in Québec, where the federal government shares jurisdiction with the province, immigration is a federal responsibility governed by the *Immigration and Refugee Protection Act.*

Canada considers immigration applications in four main categories or classes. Under each of these categories, there are different requirements that allow people to stay in Canada. The four categories are:

- Family Class
- Skilled Worker Class
- Business Class
- Refugees

The family class is for immigrants with close relatives already in Canada who have promised to provide financial help or "sponsor" their application. The skilled worker and business classes are sometimes referred to as the independent immigrant category, which includes workers who have occupational skills and experience considered desirable in the Canadian labour market, as well as self-employed people, entrepreneurs, and investors. The refugee class is for immigrants who are unable or afraid to return to their home country.

In most cases, people who want to immigrate to Canada must first apply from another country before they come to Canada. Applications can be submitted by mail or in person to a Canadian embassy, consulate, or commission abroad. You can't just show up at the border and ask to be given citizenship.

That said, applications can be made from within Canada by refugee claimants, live-in caregivers, spouses of Canadian citizens or permanent residents, and other people who have humanitarian or compassionate reasons to be in Canada.

To determine if you meet the entrance requirements and to ensure your application is properly prepared, contact an immigration lawyer and learn what is required to stay in Canada.

1. Can I come to Canada as a visitor?

Canada welcomes most visitors and makes entering the country relatively simple. "Visitors" are those who enter Canada for a temporary purpose and do not intend to remain or become a permanent resident.

Some of the requirements to enter Canada will depend on the citizenship of the visitors. Citizens of the United States, Mexico, most countries in Western Europe and a small list of other countries do not require visas, while visitors from most other countries do require visas.

To visit Canada you must be healthy, obey Canada's laws, have a valid passport, proof of who you are, and a "Temporary Resident Visa," if required. A "Temporary Resident Visa" (which used to be known as a Visitor Visa) is an official document that is placed in your passport. It shows you are allowed to enter Canada as a visitor. A Canadian consulate or embassy can tell you whether you will need a visa to visit Canada. Temporary resident visas must be obtained from outside Canada. Applications can be submitted by mail or in person to a visa office.

You must provide a valid passport or travel document, and two recent passport-sized photos of yourself. You must also provide proof you have enough money to support yourself and your dependants during your stay, and you have enough money to leave Canada. After paying the visa processing fee, you are allowed to enter Canada once using the temporary resident visa.

The date of expiry for visitor status is stamped in your passport or on the document of visitor record. If there is no stamp or documented date of expiry, then your visitor status will expire six months after your date of arrival.

If you want to extend your visitor status, you can apply in writing while the temporary resident visa is still valid. You should allow about one month for the processing of this extension. It is extremely important that you apply well before your visa expires. It is an offence under Canadian law to remain if your visitor status has expired. Applying for an extension only a short time before it expires is very risky.

2. Can foreign students study in Canada?

Students taking a course or program of more than six months must obtain a *Study Permit* before coming to Canada to study. Unless the student is from an exempted country such as the U.S., students may also need a Temporary Resident Visa in addition to the Study Permit.

Students can apply at a Canadian consulate, embassy, or high commission. A Study Permit is valid for the duration of the course of studies. An exemption from applying for the permit is provided for minor children in Canada (such as children of permanent residents) who study at the pre-school, primary, or secondary level, and family or staff members of a diplomatic representative in Canada.

To apply for a Study Permit, you must show a letter of acceptance from the school you plan to attend. You must also prove you can support yourself and that you have enough money to return home. Students may only study at the school they name on the Study Permit. If you want to change academic institutions, you must apply for a transfer.

If you have a valid permit, you can work at a job part-time on the campus at which you are registered as a full-time student. You can also apply to renew your Study Permit from within Canada, if you decide to continue studying in Canada.

If you wish to settle in Canada, meet with an immigration lawyer to discuss whether there are options that might allow you to remain in Canada, or how to make an application to come back to live in Canada. Generally, after pursuing a course of study, such as a Bachelor's degree or a diploma in a certain area, you may be allowed to work in Canada for a period of one year in your area of study.

3.   Can I bring a live-in nanny or caregiver to Canada?

People living in Canada are allowed to bring foreign workers into the country to work as live-in caregivers through a special immigration program. Both the employer and the caregiver must satisfy several requirements to be approved for the Live-in Caregiver Immigration Program.

A live-in caregiver is someone who provides unsupervised care for children, the elderly, or the disabled in a private household.

Employers who would like to hire a caregiver from outside Canada should contact a Canada Immigration Centre. Immigration officers may ask the employer to show they made a reasonable effort to hire a Canadian or a foreign worker who is already in Canada. The employer must have sufficient income to pay a live-in caregiver, and the employer must provide reasonable accommodations for the caregiver in the employer's home.

Employers must find their own caregivers. You can find foreign caregivers through advertisements, personal contacts, or hiring agencies. Once you have found a suitable caregiver, contact an Immigration Centre to have your offer of employment assessed.

When the Immigration office has approved the employer's offer of employment, it will be sent to a visa office in the caregiver's home country, and the visa office will contact the caregiver. The visa office will determine whether the caregiver can participate in the program. To be eligible, caregivers must have completed the equivalent of a Canadian high school education. They must have 6 months of full-time training or have 12 months of paid work experience in a job related to the work they will do as a live-in caregiver. Caregivers must also be able to speak, read, and understand either English or French. If the caregiver is eligible to come to Canada, that person will be issued an *Employment Authorization* document allowing him or her to enter Canada and work as a caregiver.

Caregivers will have to pay for a medical exam, a passport, travel expenses and an application fee. Caregivers can apply at a Canadian consulate, embassy, or high commission outside Canada. Caregivers may also need a Temporary Resident Visa, depending on the country they are coming from.

After the caregiver has worked full-time for two years as a live-in caregiver, he or she is eligible to apply for permanent residence in Canada. Caregivers may include their dependants on their application for permanent residence. The caregiver and all of the caregiver's dependants must pass a security check and a medical exam. You can obtain more information about the Live-in Caregiver Program from a Canada Immigration Centre or from an immigration lawyer.

4. How do I adopt a child from abroad?

Since it can be very difficult and time consuming to adopt a child in Canada, many people choose for personal or humanitarian reasons to adopt a child from abroad. This is a complicated process, and you will need to consult an immigration lawyer.

Children adopted abroad immigrate to Canada in the "family class" category. The adoptive parents sponsor the child to come to Canada after the child has been adopted according to the laws of the child's home country. An adoption that is legally completed in a foreign country is given automatic legal recognition in most of Canada.

To sponsor the immigration of an adopted child, you must be a Canadian citizen or permanent resident aged 18 or older. You must promise to provide support for the child for 10 years, and you must demonstrate that you are able to provide financial support. Children eligible to be sponsored must be adopted outside Canada according to the laws of their home country. Adoption laws vary from country to country and you should consult an immigration lawyer to help you through the process.

The following is a brief summary of the typical procedure that would be followed to adopt a child from another country.

• First, contact the adoption authorities of the province where the child will live to determine the provincial adoption requirements. In some provinces, the government may want to conduct a "home study" of the adoptive parents. This will depend on the adoption laws of the country where the child lives. The provincial adoption authorities will usually need to issue a letter of approval.

• Second, begin the immigration process by submitting a sponsorship application for a "family class" immigrant. This application to the federal government should include an Undertaking form, a Financial Evaluation form and the processing fee per child.

• Third, the adoptive parents complete an application for Permanent Residence on behalf of the child. This application is submitted to the visa office in the child's home country.

When the sponsorship application is approved, a visa officer will decide whether the child can be admitted into Canada as an immigrant.

Three conditions must be satisfied before the immigrant visa is issued:

1. The child must meet all the basic immigration requirements, including a medical check.

2. The provincial child welfare authority must approve the adoption.

3. The foreign authority must allow the transfer of the child to the adoptive parents.

The child can travel to Canada once an immigrant visa is issued. Sponsors should not attempt to go abroad intending to return to Canada with the child until the immigration process is complete.

The adoptive parents can apply for Canadian citizenship for the child after the child arrives in Canada and is granted permanent residence. You can obtain more information about international adoption from an immigration lawyer, the provincial social services ministry, or a Canada Immigration Centre.

5.   What is a "Permanent Resident"?

A permanent resident is a person who has authorization to enter and live in Canada as a resident, but who has not yet been granted Canadian citizenship.

The *Immigration and Refugee Protection Act* establishes residency requirements and obligations with respect to each five-year period after the granting of permanent residency status. A permanent resident complies with the residency provisions if, for at least 730 days in that five-year period, the permanent resident is physically present in Canada or is:

• Outside Canada accompanying a Canadian citizen who is his or her spouse or common law partner or is a child accompanying a parent, or

• Outside Canada employed on a full-time basis by a Canadian business or in the public service of Canada or of a province; or

• Is an accompanying spouse, common law partner, or child of a permanent resident who is outside Canada and is employed on a full-time basis by a Canadian business or in the public service of Canada or of a province.

This residency requirement is substantially different from previous obligations in which retaining residency depended only on satisfactory demonstration of the intent not to abandon Canada as your place of permanent residence.

Once you have been legally admitted to Canada as a permanent resident and have met the residency requirements, you may apply for Canadian citizenship. By that time, you should be able to speak English or French well enough to hold a conversation. Adults over 18 will be given a written exam or an interview by a citizenship judge.

6. What are the travel rights of "permanent residents"?

Permanent residents must carry a "Permanent Resident" (PR) card sometimes referred to as a "Maple Leaf Card," a wallet-sized plastic status card. This card is a proof of status document required by all permanent residents seeking to re-enter Canada on a commercial carrier (for example, an airplane, boat, train or bus). Without a PR card, permanent residents returning to Canada are not permitted to board their carrier. Instead, they must contact the nearest Canadian embassy or consulate to obtain a limited use travel document ($50 each) to re-enter Canada.

The purpose of the card is to increase Canada's border security. It also provides cardholders with convenient proof of their status when re-entering Canada.

7. How do I become a Canadian citizen?

To become a Canadian citizen you must:

• Be 18 years of age or older
• Be a permanent resident of Canada
• Have lived in Canada for at least three of the four years before applying
• Be able to communicate in either English or French

- Know about Canada, and
- Know about the rights and responsibilities of citizenship

You cannot become a Canadian citizen if you:

- Are under a government or judicial order to leave Canada
- Are now charged with an indictable criminal offence
- Were convicted of an indictable offence in the past three years
- Are in prison, on parole or on probation
- Are being investigated for or convicted of war crimes
- Had Canadian citizenship revoked in the last five years

Except for those whose parents were diplomatic employees of another country, children born in Canada are automatically Canadian citizens. Children born in other countries to a Canadian parent have a right to citizenship.

Since 1977, Canadians have been permitted to hold dual citizenship (that is, citizenship in another country).

As a Canadian citizen, you are entitled to many rights and freedoms, including the right to vote in all elections, hold a Canadian passport, and run for public office.

Parents can apply for Canadian citizenship for their children as soon as the child is a permanent resident as long as one parent is a Canadian citizen or is applying to be a citizen. If you meet the basic requirements and are aged 18 to 59, you will be scheduled for a citizenship test to make sure you have a basic understanding of Canada and one of its official languages. (Children under age 18 and people 60 years and older are not required to write the test.)

Citizenship and Immigration Canada will notify you to set a date and time for your test. The test asks simple questions about the responsibilities and privileges of citizenship, the government, the political system, history, geography, people, industry, and voting procedures in Canada. All the information you need to know is available on the Web at www.cic.gc.ca.

If you meet all the requirements to become a citizen, you will receive a notice telling you where and when your citizenship ceremony will take place. At the ceremony you will take the oath of citizenship and receive your certificate of citizenship. The whole process takes about 10-12 months. You will then be entitled to enjoy all of the rights and privileges of Canadian citizenship.

8. What is the "Family Class" of immigration application?

Family class immigrants are people who are sponsored by a close relative who is already a citizen or permanent resident of Canada. Family class applications receive the highest priority and qualifying applicants are usually exempt from the tougher selection criteria applied to skilled worker immigrants.

The sponsoring relatives must promise to look after the care and shelter of the immigrant and the immigrant's dependants for a period of 3 to 10 years, depending on their age and relationship. Applications are evaluated on the relative's ability to look after the immigrants and on the immigrant's ability to successfully settle in Canada.

Sponsors must show that they are willing and able to provide financial help and support. Sponsors must fill out a financial evaluation that shows all their income, debt, and financial obligations. Other family members who are in Canada may want to help support the family class immigrants. This is called co-sponsorship.

The length of sponsorship time is determined by these circumstances:

- If you are sponsoring your spouse, common-law partner, or conjugal partner (conjugal for at least one year), you must provide financial support for three years from the date that person became a permanent resident
- If you are sponsoring the dependant child (less than 22 years of age) of you or your spouse, common law partner, or conjugal partner, you must provide financial support for 10 years from the date that person became a permanent resident or until the child turns 22 years of age, whichever comes first
- If you are sponsoring the dependant child (22 years of age or older) of you or your spouse, common law partner, or conjugal partner, you must provide financial support for three years from the date that person became a permanent resident; or
- If you are sponsoring any other person not mentioned above, you must provide financial support for 10 years from the date that person became a permanent resident,

Canadian citizens and permanent residents over the age of 18 can sponsor an immigration application for their close relatives and the relative's dependants. The definition of a close relative includes:

- Spouses, common-law partners, or conjugal partners 16 years of age or older

- Parents and grandparents
- Dependent children, including adopted children
- Children under 18 years of age whom you intend to adopt
- Children under guardianship
- Brothers, sisters, nephews, nieces, or grandchildren who are orphans, under the age of 18 and not married or in a common-law relationship, or
- If you do not have an aunt, uncle, or family member from the list above who you could sponsor (or if your aunt, uncle, or family member from the list above is already a Canadian citizen, a Native person, or permanent resident), you can sponsor one other relative of any age

The age for dependent children is up to 22 years old. Also, sponsored spouses, common-law partners, conjugal partners, and dependent children will not be refused on the grounds that they represent an excessive medical demand.

One of the objectives of Canada's immigration program is to reunite families. The government may allow you to sponsor one other relative if you do not have any of the close relatives mentioned above, and you do not have any relatives who are Canadian citizens or permanent residents.

Sponsors must sign an undertaking with the Government of Canada. An undertaking is an important promise to the government and the immigrant that the sponsor will provide for the care and shelter of the immigrant and the immigrant's dependants for up to 10 years. Immigrants in the family class will not be eligible for welfare or other public assistance in Canada.

The family class immigrant and the sponsor must also sign a sponsorship agreement. A sponsorship agreement is a promise that the immigrant will make every reasonable effort to provide for his or her own needs and for the needs of any dependants. These promises and obligations cannot be changed or cancelled, even if circumstances change.

Family class applicants and their dependants must undergo a security check and a medical exam by a designated physician. The medical exam can now be done "up-front" before the application, which will help speed the approval process.

An immigration officer may also interview them. Sponsors must pay a processing fee for every applicant aged 19 and older, and a smaller fee for every applicant under the age of 19. This fee is non-refundable, even if the application is rejected.

Applications to sponsor a spouse or a child will generally take eight months to one year to be processed. Applications to sponsor parents or grandparents will generally take between one and three years to be processed. These time estimates vary greatly depending on the country of origin.

Immigrants must prove that they are related to their sponsor. Documents such as birth or marriage certificates, voter registration or military records, and family or personal records or photographs can be used to establish this relation. You can obtain assistance with your family class application from an immigration lawyer or from a Citizenship and Immigration Canada office.

9. Can I work temporarily in Canada?

If you are not a Canadian citizen or a permanent resident, you are not automatically entitled to work in Canada. To work in Canada, foreign workers must obtain a document called an *Employment Authorization* from a Canada Employment Centre or they must be covered under the North American Free Trade Agreement (NAFTA).

An Employment Authorization gives workers permission to work at a specific job for a specific period for a specific employer. There is a small fee for an Employment Authorization and it usually takes one month for an application to be reviewed and approved.

There are two steps to apply for an Employment Authorization. First, your employer must contact a Canada Employment Centre and provide details about the job. The employer must show the Canada Employment Centre that it made a reasonable effort to hire or train a Canadian, but a qualified worker was not available or could not be trained in time.

The Canada Employment Centre will also want to see that the conditions of the position are attractive to Canadian workers, and that allowing a foreign worker to take the job will benefit Canada or the company. This process is called a "Job Confirmation" (formerly known as a "Validation of a Job Offer"). However, confirmations are not required for highly trained professionals such as computer programmers. An immigration lawyer can tell you if a confirmation is needed in your specific circumstances.

The second step in the Employment Authorization process is the approval of the employee. A Canadian visa office will contact the employee, who may be asked to attend an interview or send information by mail. The employee may also be asked to have a medical exam by a designated physician, which the employee will have to pay for. If the employee qualifies and has all the necessary documents, then he or she will receive an Employment Authorization.

Note that it is illegal for an employer to hire someone who does not have an Employment Authorization. Moreover, a work permit will generally only be issued when the use of a foreign worker will not adversely affect employment opportunities for Canadians or permanent residents of Canada.

The spouse and children of a work permit holder can accompany a foreign worker to Canada, but they are not allowed to work in Canada without obtaining their own work permits. Dependants of a work permit holder are permitted to attend school in Canada but are required to first obtain a study permit from Immigration Canada.

Finally, visitors and refugees are generally not allowed to work while they are in Canada. If a visitor finds a job while in Canada, he or she will have to apply for an Employment Authorization at a Canadian government office outside the country. For assistance in applying to work in Canada, contact an immigration lawyer.

10. How is doing business in Canada different under NAFTA?

The *North American Free Trade Act* (NAFTA) has made it faster and easier for many business people to gain temporary entry to Canada for business purposes. Special rules apply to business workers under NAFTA. U.S. or Mexican citizens who want to enter Canada to trade goods, provide services or participate in investment activities may be eligible for entry to Canada under NAFTA.

Businesspersons will be asked to show proof of their citizenship, and they must qualify in one of four categories of businesspersons (discussed in more detail below):

- Business visitors
- Professionals
- Intra-company transferees
- Traders and investors

Once an applicant has qualified for entry into Canada, that person will be given a document called an *Employment Authorization*.

■ Business visitors

Business visitors are people who plan to engage in business activities. They have no intention to enter the Canadian labour market. Business visitors will be asked to provide evidence that they will engage in international business activity.

■ Professionals

Professionals are people who plan to engage in a business activity at a professional level in a designated profession. A list of designated professions is available from Canada Immigration Centres or Canadian visa offices. Professionals must be qualified to work in their occupation, and they must have pre-arranged employment with a Canadian organization. There is no limit on how long a professional may remain in Canada, as long as they have a valid *Employment Authorization*.

■ Intra-company transferees

Intra-company transferees are people who are employed by an organization, and who plan to provide managerial, executive, or specialized services to the organization. Intra-company transferees may not stay in Canada for more than seven years as a manager or executive, or for more than five years as a specialized employee.

Business visitors, professionals, and intra-company transferees can apply to enter the country at a Canadian border or airport.

■ Traders and investors

Special rules apply to traders and investors. Applicants in this category must obtain a visa application from a Canadian embassy, consulate, or Immigration office, and provide details about their proposed activities. Applications are not accepted at Canadian ports of entry. In addition to submitting the completed application to a Canadian embassy or consulate, applicants may be asked to attend an interview. Once entry requirements are met, there is no time limit on how long traders and investors can remain in Canada.

Business people who are covered under NAFTA must still meet the general immigration requirements that govern entry to Canada. For example, people with certain medical conditions or criminal records may not be allowed to enter.

If you need to extend your stay in Canada, you can apply for an extension of your Employment Authorization at any time up to one month before your Employment Authorization expires.

American or Mexican businesspersons who plan to enter Canada temporarily under NAFTA can obtain more information from an immigration lawyer or from a Canada Immigration Centre.

11. Has NAFTA made it easier for Canadian citizens to do business abroad?

The *North American Free Trade Act* has made it easier for Canadian business people to gain temporary entry to the United States or Mexico for business purposes. Canadian citizens who want to trade goods, provide services, or participate in investment activities may enter the United States or Mexico under special NAFTA immigration rules.

Business people must satisfy the entrance requirements in one of four categories. The categories are business visitors, intra-company transferees, professionals, and traders or investors (see the previous question). Business people must also satisfy the general health and security requirements. A Canadian citizen who applies for admission to the United States as a businessperson does not need a visa. Business visitors, professionals, and intra-company transferees can apply to enter the United States or Mexico at a port of entry.

Canadian businesspersons who plan to enter the United States or Mexico under NAFTA can obtain more information from an immigration lawyer or from a Canada Immigration Centre.

12. My company has transferred me to Canada. Am I exempt from getting a work permit?

Some workers may be granted a work permit without obtaining a "Confirmation" of the job offer from the federal government. Intra-company transferees are included and are generally defined as senior managers and specialized knowledge workers.

The law states this may include anyone "in senior executive and managerial categories carrying a letter from a company carrying on business in Canada, which identifies the holder as an employee of a branch, subsidiary, affiliate, or parent of that company located outside of Canada and who seeks to enter Canada to work at a senior executive or managerial level for a temporary period at a permanent and continuing establishment of that company in Canada."

A specialized knowledge worker must be able to demonstrate special knowledge of a company's services or products, its international markets, or processes and procedures. Applicants must have worked for at least one of the previous three years in a similar position for the company that plans to transfer them to Canada.

Spouses or common-law partners of skilled workers coming to Canada as temporary foreign workers must get a work permit in their own name, but are generally able to work in Canada without requiring a job confirmation by the government.

13. What is the Point System and why is it important to business immigrants?

The system that is used to decide whether a skilled worker or business class immigrant qualifies to come to Canada is called the Point System. For the different sub-categories of independent immigrants, there may be different minimum point requirements.

Points are awarded for your level of education, occupational training, amount of work experience, occupation, age, and knowledge of French or English. Points are also awarded for having a relative in Canada or for having arranged employment. Additional points are based on government immigration targets, which are adjusted annually. Points are also awarded based on the visa officer's assessment of your ability to successfully settle in Canada. Even if you have the required total number of points, your application may be refused if there have been no points awarded for your occupation or work experience.

Most applicants who have the required number of points can enter Canada as independent immigrants after they pass a medical exam and a security check. People who immigrate through the Business Immigration Program are evaluated differently.

If you do not have the minimum number of points for the category you apply in, your immigration application will be rejected. If your application is rejected, you can re-apply after you have taken appropriate steps to earn more points. You can obtain additional information about the point system from an Immigration Canada office or from your lawyer.

14. What is the "Skilled Worker Class" of immigration application?

The skilled worker or "independent" class has the skills, education, work experience, language ability, and other qualities needed in the Canadian market.

An application for permanent resident status as a skilled worker is generally assessed on six factors in the government's "Point System" and a successful applicant must achieve a minimum of 67 points out of 100, as well as meet other immigration requirements (see the Point System in the previous question).

Applicants in the skilled worker class must have at least one year's worth of paid, full-time work experience. The experience must be in the category of Skill Type 0, or Skill Level A or B on the Canadian National Occupation Classification (NOC). And that experience must have been established in the last 10 years.

The NOC has five bands:

- Skill Type 0 – Management Occupations
- Skill Level A, which is primarily comprised of professional occupations
- Skill Level B, which consists of technical, skilled trades, and para-professional occupations
- Skill Level C, which comprises occupations that primarily consist of intermediate-level, clerical, or supportive functions
- Skill Level D, which consists of elemental sales or service and primary labourer occupations

Only experience in Skill Type 0 or Skill Levels A and B are considered relevant for applicants in the Skilled Worker Class.

The intent of these regulations is to allow individual provinces to support the immigration of people who have expressed interest in settling in their province and who will be able to contribute to the economic development and prosperity of that province.

15. How can other business people immigrate to Canada?

Entrepreneurs, investors, and self-employed immigrants form what is known as the Business Class of application. Again, the "Point System" is applied to each sub-category of the class to determine eligibility.

■ Entrepreneur

An "entrepreneur" is anyone with business experience managing, controlling, and owning a qualifying business with a net worth of at least C\$300,000. Any applicant under the entrepreneur program must have the intention and ability to control at least one-third (33-1/3 percent or greater of the equity) of a qualifying Canadian business.

Within three years of becoming a permanent resident, the entrepreneur must also provide active and ongoing management of the Canadian business and create at least one new full-time job for a Canadian citizen or permanent resident.

Entrepreneurs are chosen based on their personal qualities and not on their business proposal. Applicants must submit a brief outline of the business and a general operating plan with their application.

■ Investor

An "investor" must have managed, operated, controlled, directed, or owned a financially successful business and accumulated a minimum net worth of C$800,000. All investors, regardless of the province or territory where the capital is invested, are required to make an investment of C$400,000 over five years with Citizenship and Immigration Canada Headquarters in Ottawa before the immigrant visa is issued.

The investment is later allocated to Canadian provinces or territories for job creation and economic development. The full amount of the investment is repaid to the investor after five years and fully guaranteed by the participating provinces and territories. The program operates differently at this time in Québec.

■ Self-employed persons

The third category of business immigrants is self-employed persons. A "self-employed" applicant is someone who "intends and has the ability to establish a business in Canada that will create employment for that person."

Self-employed persons must establish or purchase a business in Canada that will keep them employed and the business must contribute significantly to Canada's economic, cultural or athletic life. The applicant may also buy and manage a farm in Canada. Self-employed applicants must have relevant experience. The applicant's skills, business ability, financial assets, and past will be assessed.

Self-employed persons should be self-supporting based on a particular talent or skill. They must present documentation that proves their ability to support themselves and their dependants. Helpful documents could include a record of prior earnings or a history of success and achievement in their field. The application must include a brief outline of the business and a general operating plan.

The self-employed category is a flexible category that accepts many kinds of ventures, but doctors, nurses, lawyers, and dentists should be aware that it is difficult for applicants in these professions to demonstrate they would contribute significantly to the economy. In fact, these professions are not listed on the Occupational List, so you should consider an alternative or complementary occupation. See an immigration lawyer to help you select an appropriate alternative occupation if this applies to you.

■ Application Process

The application process is the same for all three categories. Information and application kits are available at Business Immigrant Co-ordination Centres or from a Canadian visa office. The application package should include your résumé, a statement of financial resources, and an indication of the type of business you plan to buy or start. You and your dependants must also undergo a security check and a medical exam by a designated physician.

The application will be reviewed and you will likely be asked to attend an interview in your home country. At the interview you and your dependants will be asked questions about your job, work experience, education, reasons for emigrating, health, financial situation, and past difficulty with the law. Your answers will help the immigration officer assess your personal suitability, occupational expertise, professional qualifications, and overall ability to settle successfully in Canada.

Note that all business class immigrants must now apply at one of nine Business Immigration Centres located outside Canada at the Canadian Embassy, Canadian High Commission or Canadian Consulate in Beijing, Berlin, Buffalo, Damascus, Hong Kong, London, Paris, Seoul and Singapore.

16. Who can enter Canada as a refugee?

To stay in Canada as a refugee, you must fit into one of three categories:

- Convention refugees abroad
- Country of asylum
- Source country

People who are recognized as refugees are allowed to stay in Canada and apply for permanent resident status. Eventually, they can become Canadian citizens.

■ Convention Refugees

Convention Refugees are people who are unable or unwilling to return to their home country because they believe they will be persecuted because of their race, religion, nationality, membership in a social group, or political opinion.

Persecution has been defined to include such things as death threats, torture, or imprisonment by the government, guerrillas, or other non-government death squads. People who fear persecution in their home country, from which government or police cannot protect them, may make a claim of convention refugee status. The claim may be initially made by mail or in person at an airport, border, or Canada Immigration Centre. A tribunal called the Immigration and Refugee Board will decide the claim.

It is critically important that you see an immigration lawyer before you fill out the forms that Immigration will give you to complete.

These forms are the most important documents that you will ever complete in relation to your refugee claim. It is critical that you consult an immigration lawyer who can discuss your problems in your home country with you. Any changes made on the forms that you provide to Immigration could cause problems at your hearing and may negatively affect your refugee claim.

▪ Country of Asylum

This class includes people who are outside their country of citizenship or habitual residence. These refugees are personally affected by civil war, armed conflict, or massive violations of human rights. These refugees must be privately sponsored or have adequate financial means to support themselves and their dependants.

▪ Source country

This class includes people who would meet the definition of a Convention Refugee Abroad, but who are still living in their country of citizenship or habitual residence. It also includes people who have been detained or imprisoned and are suffering serious deprivations of the rights of freedom of expression, dissent, or the rights to engage in trade union activity. Only citizens or residents of specific countries are eligible under this class. Members of this class are eligible for government assistance or may be privately sponsored.

17. How do I claim refugee status?

Making a claim for refugee status is a complicated process. Claimants should contact an immigration lawyer or a refugee host organization for assistance. There is no government fee for making a refugee claim and it will generally take between eight months and two years for an application to be processed.

A claim for refugee protection can be made at any Canadian port of entry or border crossing, or at a Canada Immigration Centre in any city. Application forms can be obtained by phone or in person at any Canada

Immigration Centre. Include your dependants and your entire family on your application form, so that their claims could be joined to yours, or so your dependants could be referred to when and if you later sponsor your relatives from your home country.

Once an immigration officer decides that a claimant is eligible for consideration as a refugee, the claim is sent to the Immigration and Refugee Board for a decision on the risk of returning to your home country. The Board will determine whether you are a Convention Refugee or a "person in need of protection." Some people, however, are not automatically eligible to have their claim referred to the Board, including individuals:

- Already recognized as Convention Refugees by another country to which they can be safely returned (under Canadian law people may not be able to claim refugee status if they come to Canada from a country that is considered a safe third country)
- Already determined to be protected persons under the *Immigration and Refugee Protection Act* or its regulations
- Who arrived in Canada, directly or indirectly, from a country other than their country of nationality or former habitual residence
- Who were determined to be inadmissible on grounds of security, human rights violations, serious criminality, or organized crime
- Who had a previous refugee protection claim rejected by the Board
- Who had a previous refugee protection claim determined to be ineligible for referral
- Who had a previous refugee protection claim withdrawn or abandoned

When you first apply for refugee status you will be asked to fill out a questionnaire or to attend an interview with a Senior Immigration Official. The questions will focus on your identity, age, family members, criminal record, your route to Canada, the travel documents you used, and your past activities.

If you are eligible, a hearing will be scheduled to take place in several months. Once your forms are filled in and delivered to the Immigration and Refugee Board, you can request an Application to obtain an Employment Authorization document from a Canada Employment Centre.

At the hearing there are normally one or two members of the Immigration and Refugee Board, and a Refugee Claims Officer. These people are generally knowledgeable about refugee applications and the living conditions in the country from which you have fled persecution. An immigration lawyer will make sure you know what will happen at the Board, and will help you prepare for this important hearing. Board members will ask you questions about your application and why you are unable to return to your home country. Although each application for refugee status is evaluated separately, you and your immediate family members will have your separate claims heard together in one hearing.

You have a right to have a lawyer or other representative with you at the hearing, and this right is important. The lawyer who is with you in that room when they are deciding your refugee case can be of critical importance later if your claim is rejected, and you must file an appeal if this is the case.

You also have a right to have an interpreter at the hearing without cost to you. It is important for you to let your lawyer know if the interpreter is properly interpreting what you have said.

If you have an immigration hearing, you will be sent a Decision, and the Reasons for the Decision. If your claim is accepted, then you have been found to be a *Convention Refugee* and you will be allowed to stay in Canada. If you want to become a permanent resident of Canada you should apply to be landed as a Permanent Resident within 180 days of receiving the written decision about your refugee claim. It is important to apply within this time, or you risk losing your chance to become a permanent resident.

If your claim for refugee status is rejected, you have 30 days to leave Canada on your own. Within 15 days, though, a claimant who wants to appeal the decision must apply to have his or her case heard by a Federal Court. In most cases, a claimant can stay in Canada while the Federal Court is hearing his or her case.

Consult with an immigration lawyer as soon as possible after your claim is rejected so you can get help with the appeal. You can remain in Canada while you wait to find out whether your case will be heard. Many appeals are not granted *leave*, which means the case will not be argued.

There is also a review panel called the Post-Determination Refugee Claimants in Canada unit. This group can review decisions made by the Immigration and Refugee Board, but only 5 percent of the cases reviewed are successful. An immigration lawyer can help you file these applications, and will help you in considering what other options are available.

If you are found not to be a refugee after your appeal, a deportation order will be issued against you. If you do not have the money to buy a ticket to return to your home country, the Government of Canada will provide a ticket for you. If you plan to try to return to Canada in the future and settle here as an immigrant or a refugee, you will have to repay the cost of your ticket.

Applying for refugee status is a very complicated and important process. To make sure that your application is properly prepared and handled, you should contact an immigration lawyer. If you cannot afford a lawyer, you may be eligible for legal aid.

■ Refugee Resettlement

Individuals can also apply at a Canadian Mission abroad for refugee resettlement in Canada. To be successful, the permanent resident visa application for resettlement must be accompanied by either a referral from the United Nations High Commissioner for Refugees, or an undertaking for private sponsorship

Unless accompanied by these documents, the application will be considered incomplete and it will be returned to the applicant. In some circumstances, an application for resettlement may be accepted directly if the applicant's country of residence has been deemed to have direct access to a Canadian Mission abroad. The Canadian government regularly publishes a list of countries with direct access to a Canadian Mission.

18. How is an application for refugee status evaluated?

Each application for refugee status is evaluated separately by the Immigration and Refugee Board. The Board considers many important factors when it decides about a refugee claim. The only issue that the Board can determine is whether you meet the definition of *refugee*. After the consideration of your claim, and a complex set of definitions of *refugee*, the Board evaluates whether there is any place within your country where you would be safe, and also whether the authorities in your home country can protect you.

The factors to be considered when assessing a person's ability to establish eligibility have been redefined recently. The focus is now on social rather than economic factors.

If you have been found to be eligible to make a refugee claim, you will be asked to appear at a hearing with the Immigration and Refugee Board. The main purpose of the hearing is for the Board to hear your explanation of what has happened to you, and what would happen if you were to be returned to your home country. Most important, you must demonstrate a need for protection because you would not be safe in your home country. Keep all documents that describe the conditions in your home country. Some examples of useful documents include newspaper reports, reports from human rights groups, or letters from your friends or family that describe the living conditions.

You have the right to have a lawyer attend the hearing with you. Since this hearing is extremely important, it is strongly recommended that you meet with a lawyer and obtain assistance in filling out the Personal Information Form. The lawyer should attend the hearing with you. If you are unable to afford a lawyer, you may qualify for legal aid.

You also have the right to choose whether the hearing is conducted in English or French, and you have the right to have a qualified interpreter present at the hearing. The interpreter is appointed by the board and there is no charge to you. Tell your lawyer or the board members if there are any problems with the interpretation. Although the hearing is normally private and confidential, with your permission a friend or family member can be an observer to the hearing. In most cases, only you, your lawyer, and the Board members will be at the hearing.

The Immigration Review Board hearing is a very important part of making a refugee claim. Your lawyer can help you prepare for the hearing and assist you to present your case in the best possible way.

19. Can a refugee work in Canada?

Refugees are not allowed to work in Canada unless they obtain an *Employment Authorization* document from Immigration Canada.

After a refugee claimant files an application for refugee status, he or she will be notified by Immigration Canada as to when an application for an Employment Authorization can be made. It usually takes between three and four months from the time that a refugee claimant enters Canada until the time that the claimant will receive an Employment Authorization and be allowed to start working. All refugee claimants must be fingerprinted and photographed before they can apply for an Employment Authorization. The refugee and the refugee's dependants must also have a medical exam by a designated physician, and Immigration Canada must know the results of the exam.

The Employment Authorization is valid until the expiry date on the document or until the Immigration and Refugee Board decides not to accept the claimant's application for refugee status, whichever happens first. The refugee will have to pay a processing fee after he or she receives written notice that the board approved the refugee claim. You can obtain more information about Employment Authorizations from a Canada Employment Centre, an Immigration Canada office, or from your lawyer.

20. What happens after refugee status or resettlement is granted?

If you have received a written decision from the Immigration and Refugee Board that your application for refugee status has been approved, you can then apply for permanent resident status. You must apply for permanent resident status within 180 days of receiving the written confirmation of your refugee status from Immigration Canada, or you may lose the chance to become a permanent resident.

To qualify for permanent resident status, the refugee and the refugee's dependants must be in good health, with no criminal records, and have no criminal charges in Canada or abroad. Applicants must not be security risks, and they must hold valid passports or travel documents.

Information and application packages for permanent resident status are available from any Canada Immigration office. Permanent residents have the right to stay in Canada permanently. They enjoy most of the rights given to Canadian citizens, with some exceptions. Permanent residents cannot vote in some elections, or hold a passport, or run for elected office.

21. How do I appeal an immigration decision?

If Immigration Canada does not accept your immigration application, you may have a right to appeal. This right to appeal will depend on the immigration category you applied to. The main three categories are:

- Refugee claimants
- Family-class immigrants
- Business-class immigrants

■ Refugee claimants

If your claim for refugee status was rejected at the Immigration and Refugee Board hearing, you can then file an application for an appeal with the Federal Court of Canada. Your application must be made within 15 days of receiving the Immigration and Refugee Board's decision. Filing an appeal is a complicated process and you should contact an immigration lawyer for assistance. Do not delay in contacting a lawyer, as time is critically important in these appeals.

If your application for an appeal is accepted, you will be given a new hearing in Federal Court. If your application for an appeal is denied, you will be asked to leave Canada.

You can also file an application for an appeal with the Post-Determination Refugee Claimants in Canada unit. This unit falls within the offices of Citizenship and Immigration, but it also reviews decisions made by the Immigration and Refugee Board. Very few cases that go to this unit are successful. For more information about how to appeal a decision made by Immigration Canada, contact an immigration lawyer or an Immigration Canada office.

■ Family-class sponsors

If your application to be a sponsor in the family class was rejected, you can make an appeal to the Immigration Appeal Division of the Immigration and Refugee Board. Immigration Canada will have sent your relative a refusal notice and you will need a copy of this refusal to file an appeal.

■ Business-class immigrants

If your application to immigrate to Canada as a business-class immigrant was rejected, strictly speaking, you cannot appeal. That said, a lawyer can initiate Judicial Review at the Federal Court. Contact an immigration lawyer to help you understand your rights. You also have the option of re-applying at some later time when you have earned more points (see question 13 in this section). If there is a difference between the number of points that you calculate for your application and the number of points that the immigration officer calculates, then the immigration officer's calculation will be used by Immigration Canada to make a decision about your application.

22. Can immigration authorities arrest or detain people?

Canadian immigration law provides that any person who is not a Canadian citizen can be detained while Immigration decides if he or she can enter Canada. Individuals can be detained both when they are attempting to enter Canada and after they are in Canada.

■ Arrest upon entry

Immigration officers have the right to question everyone who is attempting to enter through a Canadian border. You must answer the immigration officer's questions if you want to enter. Your answers may be written down or entered into their computers. Any information you give can be used in subsequent immigration proceedings. Immigration officers may detain you if they believe that:

- You are not who you say you are
- You are not coming to Canada for the reason you say you are
- You were deported or excluded from Canada in the past, and you are attempting to re-enter without proper written permission from Immigration Canada
- You will not leave Canada as directed
- You will be dangerous to others or to yourself
- You do not meet proper immigration requirements, such as sufficient funds to visit Canada

■ Arrest while in Canada

Even if you pass through the Canadian border, immigration or police officers can arrest you once inside Canada for any number of reasons, including:

- They have reasonable grounds to believe you are a danger to others or yourself
- They believe you will not appear for a legally required examination or inquiry
- To fulfill an order for your removal from Canada
- You are working in Canada without a valid work permit
- You have stayed in Canada after your visitor's visa status has expired
- You entered Canada illegally
- You entered Canada with a false passport
- You were deported or excluded from Canada but came back without written permission of Canada's Minister of Immigration
- You did not notify Immigration of a change of address when you moved
- You did not leave Canada by the date given in your departure notice
- You did not show up for a hearing, interview, or for your removal
- For another reason that your case has come to the attention of an Immigration officer — you are charged with committing a crime, for instance

Immigration officers and the police do not need a warrant to arrest you if an order for your removal has been made or if they suspect you have violated certain provisions of the immigration law and you are not a permanent resident. If you are arrested, the arresting officer must tell you why. The arresting officer can search you, but if an immigration or police officer asks you questions when you are not in an immigration inquiry, you do not have to answer them. That said, you should identify yourself.

If you are arrested while in Canada, you have the right to consult with a lawyer, and the immigration officer who arrests you must inform you of this right. You do not need to answer questions until you have spoken with a lawyer. Nevertheless, it may be a good idea to explain the situation particularly if you are arrested because of a simple misunderstanding.

■ Detention at an immigration inquiry

In rare cases, you could be arrested at an immigration inquiry. All immigration inquiries are followed by detention reviews if needed. An inquiry is a hearing held before an immigration adjudicator to decide whether you can enter or stay in Canada. You have the right to legal counsel at an inquiry. The adjudicator has the power to detain you during your inquiry or when your inquiry ends.

Before you go to an inquiry, it is a good idea to arrange for someone who can post a bond on your behalf if you are detained. This person is known as a guarantor. A guarantor is a person who signs a performance bond or deposits money with Immigration on your behalf.

To be accepted as a guarantor, the person must be a Canadian citizen or permanent resident of Canada. The guarantor must be able to show that, if you break the terms and conditions of the bond, he or she has enough money through property ownership, savings, or employment income to pay for you. If you are detained at an inquiry because Immigration saw you as a danger to the public, having a guarantor will probably not be enough to get you released.

■ Where are people held?

If you are detained by immigration authorities, you will be taken to an Immigration office or police station for questioning. Later, you will be held at an immigration detention centre. If there is no Immigration Centre where you live you will be held in jail. You may also be detained in jail as opposed to an immigration detention centre if immigration authorities believe you are a danger to others or to yourself.

■ How can people get released?

There are two ways that a person can be released from detention: after a review by a Senior Immigration Officer (SIO) or by an adjudicator at a detention review hearing or an inquiry.

Soon after you are arrested or detained, an SIO will be notified. If this officer believes you are not a danger to others or to yourself, and that you will show up for interviews, hearings, or removal, the officer can order your release at any time before your first detention review hearing. This rarely happens, however.

If the SIO does not release you within 48 hours of immigration authorities becoming aware of your detention, you will get a detention review hearing before an adjudicator. This hearing is supposed to take place within 48 hours of your arrest. If you are arrested on a Thursday or Friday, however, your hearing might not take place until Monday, and often there are delays because of lack of resources.

The adjudicator will review your case and the reasons for your detention. A case presenting and review officer will make submissions on behalf of Immigration. You will also have the opportunity to present evidence and make submissions. It is up to you to convince the adjudicator that you should be released.

You will be released if the adjudicator decides that:

- You are who you said you were when you arrived at the airport or border
- There is no reason to believe you will not show up for hearings, interviews, or removal
- You are not a danger to others or to yourself

In most cases, you will need to post cash and a substantial bond and agree to certain conditions to be released.

■ Typical terms and conditions upon release

If a senior officer or an adjudicator decides to release you, you may have to agree to certain terms, such as:

- You must report any change of address to Immigration 48 hours before moving
- You must co-operate in obtaining travel documents needed for your removal
- You must agree to report to an Immigration office regularly
- You must agree to be supervised by a third party

You may also be required to make a security deposit or have a performance bond signed on your behalf. A security deposit is money deposited with Immigration Canada to ensure that you will comply with the terms and conditions of your release. If you break any of the terms or conditions, Immigration will keep the money. With a performance bond, money is not actually deposited with Immigration Canada. Instead, your guarantor signs a bond on your behalf for a certain amount of money. If you break any of the terms or conditions without a good reason, your guarantor will be responsible to pay Immigration the amount set out in the bond.

■ What if you are not released?

If you are not released at this point, another detention review hearing must be held within seven days. If you are not released then, your detention must be reviewed every 30 days after that, until you are either released or removed from Canada. There is no limit on how long you can be detained, although you cannot be held indefinitely. At this point, Immigration should be taking steps with your file to have you removed to your country. If you have co-operated and there is no movement on Immigration's behalf, consult a lawyer.

You have the right to legal counsel at every detention review hearing, but legal aid certificates are not usually provided. You also have the right to a qualified interpreter who is provided by Immigration. In an exceptional case, there may be legal grounds to challenge your detention in court. For legal advice, consult a lawyer.

23. What happens in a deportation?

The Canadian government has the power to deport people who are not lawfully allowed to stay in Canada. Anyone who is deported cannot return to Canada without the written consent of the Minister of Citizenship and Immigration. Different deportation criteria apply to different categories of people. The main classifications are people who have been denied refugee status, permanent residents, and visitors.

To deport anyone, immigration authorities must have your travel documents and some proof that you are from the country that they are deporting you to. There are some people who cannot be removed because their countries will not provide travel documents. It is important to co-operate with the authorities at this time. As frightening as the prospect of being sent home may be, to be able to return to Canada you must comply with the order to report for removal.

■ People who have been denied refugee status

People who have been denied refugee status will be asked to leave Canada when their refugee claim is denied. Claimants must also leave if they withdraw or abandon their claim. An immigration lawyer can help you make an appeal if you are asked to leave. You will be returned to the last country you were in before arriving in Canada. Many refugees came through the United States, so this means they would be returned to the U.S.

■ Permanent residents

Permanent residents can be deported if they committed serious offences before they arrived in Canada or if the government believes they are security risks. Permanent residents can also be deported if they lie on their immigration applications, are convicted of serious offences in Canada, or lose their status as permanent residents. If you have been charged with an offence in Canada or abroad you should contact an immigration lawyer to discuss how the charge will affect your status as a permanent resident. It is important for every permanent resident to get citizenship as soon as possible. Immigration authorities cannot deport a Canadian citizen.

■ Visitors

Visitors may be deported after their authorized period of stay has expired. Visitors may also be required to leave if they do not comply with the terms and conditions of their visit, or if they extend their stay without permission. Visitors who are convicted of a criminal offence may also be deported.

■ Canadian Citizens

In general, Canadian citizens cannot be deported. In some circumstances, citizens may be returned to a foreign country if they are accused or convicted of a specific crime in that country. This is usually referred to as "extradition."

If you have been asked to leave Canada, contact an immigration lawyer for specific advice and assistance. The most important thing to remember is to give that lawyer adequate time to do any possible work on your behalf. If you do not have Legal Aid, it is definitely too late to apply if you already have been ordered to leave Canada. Unfortunately, last minute visits to a lawyer's office can be very expensive because Legal Aid will likely not assist in paying for legal fees.

24. How does a criminal record affect immigration?

A criminal record will negatively affect your ability to immigrate to Canada or remain here. Criminal records will have a different impact depending on whether the individual is a visitor, a refugee, or a permanent resident.

See question 48 in Section V: Crime & Punishment.

SUITABLE CANDIDATE?

An Asian immigrant allegedly attempted to bribe a Canadian immigration official while applying for a visa. The visa officer decided to refuse the application, citing the alleged bribe as a reason the applicant was not a suitable candidate.

Was the visa officer correct?

No. In the 1995 Supreme Court of Canada case of *Chen* v. *Canada (Minister of Employment and Immigration)*, the court held visa officers do not have an unlimited degree of discretion in assessing whether an applicant is a suitable candidate for immigration. The judges said Canada's immigration legislation and regulations already provide criteria for assessing candidates and visa officers cannot add their own.

WHAT IS PERSECUTION?

Mr. Chan applied to enter Canada as a Convention Refugee because of his fear of being forcibly sterilized for violating China's birth control laws allowing only one child per family. He claimed he had the required "well-founded fear of persecution" by reason of his membership in a particular social group (in this case, his family). Because of his second child, some Chinese government officials had pressured Chan into signing a written undertaking to undergo sterilization within three months.

When he fled China, Canada's Immigration and Refugee Board found he was not a Convention Refugee and held that forced sterilization did not constitute a form of persecution

Was the Board correct?

Yes. In Chan v. Canada (Minister of Employment and Immigration), a 4-3 decision of the Supreme Court of Canada in 1995 held that while a person facing forced sterilization is likely a member of a particular social group (women in most cases), a refugee applicant is required to establish to the board's satisfaction that the alleged fear exists in his or her mind.

Normally the claimant's evidence alone will be sufficient, but in this case Mr. Chan's testimony was inconsistent. The court said Mr. Chan also had to offer some proof of the enforcement procedures being used in his particular region of China. For example, he could have offered a supporting witness in a similar circumstance. He offered no such evidence.

Finally, he produced no evidence that forced sterilization is inflicted upon men in his area. The documentary evidence produced by Mr. Chan suggested that penalties for breach of the one-child policy only applied against women. As well, local authorities took no action to enforce his signed consent to sterilization even though more than a year had lapsed and the fine for the breach of birth control laws had still not been paid.

WWW Resources

Citizenship & Immigration Canada	www.cic.gc.ca

Your Health

C anada's health care system is highly regarded around the world, largely owing to its publicly-financed health care insurance system. The legal structure and rules applied to our health care network are a joint responsibility of federal and provincial governments. For that reason, the approach taken to legally related health care issues is similar in many jurisdictions.

Our personal health — both mental and physical — is our most valuable asset and deserves to be vigorously guarded. As we progress from youth to adulthood and on to our senior years, health issues will arise that may involve complex legal questions. Issues of consent, confidentiality, the right to treatment, and even our ability to sue for harm done to our health commonly arise for many of us or our loved ones.

Medicine and law are alike in that both involve jargon, methods, and principles that only a few are privileged to learn and master. With some basic knowledge of your health rights and responsibilities, however, you can talk to both health care practitioners and lawyers about what is best for you.

1.   Who can refuse or give consent to health treatment?

Under the law in most provinces, a patient of 16 years of age or older, who is mentally competent, normally has the sole right to refuse or consent to any health care treatment — even if refusal increases the seriousness of the illness or the possibility of death. In Québec, the age is 14.

Generally, unless it is an emergency situation, a health care professional must always obtain a patient's consent before starting any treatment or procedure.

For anyone under the age of medical consent, a parent's or guardian's consent is usually needed. Nonetheless, if a medical practitioner believes a minor understands the treatment's nature and consequences and it is in his or her best interests, the minor's consent can be enough. If a minor is incapable of giving consent and parents are not available, a legally qualified medical practitioner can also go ahead in an emergency. If parents refuse consent or consent is unattainable, any person may also apply to a court for consent.

In some provinces, those declared mentally incompetent may also refuse treatment if they inform a health practitioner that they intend to apply to a government review body (for example, Ontario's Consent and Capacity Board) for a review of the incapacity finding.

■ Informed consent required

Under the law, a patient can only properly consent to health treatment if he or she has been properly informed in advance. This includes a full explanation of the treatment, the risks associated with the treatment, the risks of not accepting treatment, and information about alternative treatments.

■ The right to ask questions about treatment

If a health care professional does not provide you with information before treatment, you have the right to ask questions to fully understand all your choices and the risks involved. It is usually a good idea to prepare questions before arriving at your appointment. You always have the right to refuse treatment or request a referral for other medical opinions.

■ Waiving legal rights upon consent to treatment

If a health care professional asks you to sign a form acknowledging your consent to treatment, read it carefully so you can make an informed decision. In serious cases, if you are unsure about consenting or if you think you are being asked to waive any rights, you may want to consult a lawyer.

■ Treatment without consent

If a health care professional provides treatment to you without your consent, you can register a complaint by calling his or her professional organization. In serious cases, you may want to consult a lawyer about your right to sue.

■ Withdrawing consent

Your consent or that of a guardian or substitute decision-maker may be withdrawn at any time. The only exceptions are in cases where withdrawal may endanger your life or create serious problems, and when you no longer have the physical or mental capacity to withdraw consent.

2. Can I give someone else the right to make my medical decisions?

It is increasingly common these days for people organizing their personal and estate plans to sign a document allowing another named individual (such as a spouse, parent or adult child) to make medical or health decisions in the event of their physical or mental incapacity.

In most provinces, the person signing this directive must have reached the age of majority (18 or 19 years of age, depending on the province). In all provinces, another person may also apply to a court for permission to have temporary "substitute decision-making" authority. This authority may have to be renewed after a short period (21 days in B.C., for instance).

A substitute decision-maker is typically required to follow your wishes or instructions regarding health care. When your wishes or instructions are not known, the substitute decision-maker must make decisions that are in your best interests or follow known beliefs.

3. Can I be refused admittance to a hospital or health care facility?

Hospitals generally have a right to refuse admittance or care where a person's life is not endangered by the refusal. Normally, a senior member of the hospital's administration must make this decision.

Reasons for a refusal may be that your condition does not require hospital services, the hospital cannot provide the proper services or treatment, or that treatment would be more appropriate at a later time. Some provinces may also allow hospitals to refuse admittance to anyone who is not entitled to provincially funded health care.

If you or someone else has been refused admittance and life was endangered, you may want to discuss the situation with a lawyer experienced in medical malpractice litigation.

4. What types of care are covered by publicly funded health insurance plans?

Canada maintains a universal health care system that provides health care services with money collected from taxes. The provinces administer these health care "insurance" plans, which pay for essential health care services received by any residents holding a valid, government-supplied health card.

Each province can make its own rules on what and who is covered by health insurance. For example, Ontario requires that you must fall into one of the following categories:

- Be a Canadian citizen, permanent resident, landed immigrant, convention refugee, or registered as an Indian under the *Indian Act*
- Have submitted an Application for Permanent Residence or an Application for Landing and have been confirmed by Citizenship and Immigration Canada as having satisfied the medical requirements for landing
- Be a foreign worker who holds a valid work permit or employment authorization which names a Canadian employer situated in Ontario and your prospective occupation and is valid for at least six months
- Be a foreign clergy member who will be providing services to a religious congregation in Ontario for at least six months
- Hold a Temporary Resident Permit or Minister's Permit with a case type 80 (for adoption only), 86, 97, 88, or 89
- Be the spouse, same sex partner, or dependent child (under 19 years of age) of a foreign clergy member or eligible foreign worker who is to be employed in Ontario for a period of at least three consecutive years
- Hold a work permit or employment authorization under the Live-In Caregivers in Canada Program or the Foreign Domestic movement

- Have been issued a work permit or employment authorization under the Caribbean Commonwealth and Mexican Season Agricultural Workers Program administered by the federal department of Citizenship and Immigration

Ontario also has a residency requirement that you must make the province your permanent and principal home, and be in the province for 153 days in any 12-month period.

In Manitoba, as another example, you must:

- Be a Canadian citizen or have a recognized immigrant status
- Have a permanent residence in Manitoba, and
- Reside in Manitoba for six months in a calendar year

Manitoba does not cover tourists, transients, visitors, students (other than Manitoba residents) or students temporarily from other countries or provinces and territories in Canada attending the province's educational institutions.

In Nova Scotia, you must be:

- A Canadian citizen or be legally entitled to remain in Canada
- A permanent resident in Nova Scotia, and
- Resident in Nova Scotia for at least 6 months in a 12-month period.

Like other provinces, people not eligible for insurance coverage include tourists and visitors to the province, students from other provinces, and inmates of federal penitentiaries.

Under the federal *Canada Health Act*, provincial and territorial governments must insure or cover "medically required" services provided by medical practitioners and insure certain hospital services if they are "medically necessary for the purpose of maintaining health, preventing disease or diagnosing or treating an injury, illness, or disability."

Some health care costs are not covered by provincial plans and a patient may be required to pay extra for hospital administrative costs, a missed appointment when a patient cancels, and the cost for having a doctor fill out forms or write letters at the request of patients.

Other common types of treatment not covered or only partially "insured" include dental treatments, physiotherapist sessions, chiropractic care, and cosmetic or plastic surgery.

5.   Is out-of-province health care covered?

Residents of a province holding a valid health card will usually be insured or reimbursed for health services in another province in Canada.

■ Getting coverage

There are two ways "out of province" health care treatment can be covered. First, most physicians in other provinces, excluding Québec, have the ability to bill your provincial plan directly if you present a valid health card when you receive treatment.

Second, if the physician who is treating you will not bill the province directly, you can apply for reimbursement from your province's plan after you pay for the service. If you are required to pay for services up front, contact your provincial health plan first to confirm that the treatment will be covered when you apply for reimbursement.

■ Out of Canada coverage

Anyone travelling outside Canada is usually covered for only a set fee for emergency health services. Emergency services include acute, unexpected conditions, illnesses, diseases, or injuries that require immediate treatment. Outside Canada, it is important to get private health insurance when you travel.

6.   Who can access my health records?

Whenever you receive treatment or services by a health care professional, hospital, clinic, or laboratory, records are kept with your personal information. Normally, the location where the treatment was provided will keep records about the treatment and your provincial Department or Ministry of Health will keep records of every service billed to the health plan.

Under the law, you generally have the right to have any records held by government kept private. You also have the right to access those records.

This right does not necessarily apply to non-governmental entities, such as your doctor or the local hospital. In fact, the records and files kept by doctors and hospitals are their property and you usually have no right to remove them (though, you usually can view your records and request a file be transferred to another physician).

■ When can health records be released to others?

There are circumstances where your health records may be released or accessed by others, even from government offices:

- If you consent to the release
- If there is a court order to release records
- If the government passes a law allowing records to be released

A release without your consent, for example, might happen in communicable disease cases, where releasing individual health records is believed to help safeguard the health of the general population.

■ Health records held by the government

Records held by the government are usually kept by the provincial Ministry of Health. These include your personal information and the details of medical treatment you have received that has been paid for by the government. This includes blood tests, visits to doctors, and hospital care.

You can usually obtain access to your health records from the Ministry of Health by sending a letter to the Freedom of Information and Privacy Commissioner at your Ministry of Health, together with a small administrative fee, payable to the Minister of Finance. In your letter you must state you are making the request under the freedom of information law.

■ Accessing health records held by a doctor, clinic, or hospital

If you want to access your records from a doctor, clinic, or hospital, you will need to ask if there is a procedure for making such a request. You may be required to make a request in writing and pay an administrative fee. If you need to access records for a legal matter, consult a lawyer.

7. What is the law regarding organ donation?

Across Canada, it is generally against the law to sell or buy human tissue. Many provinces, however, give vehicle drivers or anyone over the age of 16 the option of consenting to organ donation when they receive their licence by filling out and signing an organ donation card. There are also organ donation cards distributed by some private health insurance companies. Note that signing an organ donation card does not always guarantee that your organs will be donated upon your death.

In some provinces, family members have the final say whether organs are donated and a doctor will rarely over-ride a decision even if the deceased indicated they wanted their organs donated. Therefore, it is important to discuss the issue with your family so they can understand your intentions.

8.   What are my rights to an abortion in Canada?

Abortion is legal in Canada, but doctors and hospitals are not legally obliged to perform an abortion. One province, Prince Edward Island, does not supply abortion services in its hospitals or clinics, but may reimburse women who go elsewhere for the procedure.

In Ontario, a woman with a valid Health Card can normally access abortion services at either a hospital or a clinic. Generally, there is no cost for an abortion, although in some cases there may be a small administrative fee.

■ Is there a time limit on how late an abortion can happen?

Although access to abortion is not limited by law, hospitals and clinics may establish their own policies and practices that limit when they will provide abortion services. Most abortions are performed within the first 12 weeks of pregnancy. In some cases, physicians may perform abortions up to the 20th week, but rarely beyond 20 weeks unless the woman's health is at risk.

■ Whose consent is required for an abortion?

All health care treatment, including abortion, requires the consent of the patient. Contrary to what some people may think, a woman does not need the consent of her partner to have an abortion.

If you are 16 years or older, you do not require parental consent. If you are under 16 years of age and your doctor believes you are mentally capable of understanding what an abortion is and the consequences of making the decision to have an abortion, you do not require parental consent. If your doctor does not think you understand and appreciate the consequences of having an abortion, then you will need consent from your guardian, parent, or other relative who is an adult.

9.   Can I be forced to provide a blood sample to police?

No. However, under criminal law, a Justice of the Peace has the authority to issue a warrant authorizing a police officer to require a doctor to take samples of blood if you are not physically or mentally able to give consent.

The samples may be used to determine whether a person has been taking alcohol or drugs. Usually, the warrant is issued when a person is suspected of having control of a vehicle, boat, or plane, or has been involved in an accident.

10. Can an HIV or AIDS test be done without my consent and are the results confidential?

There is no law prohibiting HIV or AIDS testing without consent. Some hospitals and even insurance companies "routinely" test for HIV and AIDS without advance notice. If you consent to a "normal" or "routine" blood test, you must ask what is specifically tested. That said, many health-related institutions believe in informed testing and do not support the idea that HIV/AIDS tests are implied or presumed.

Records of HIV or AIDS tests and results are generally treated with the same degree of confidentiality as other personal health information. Health care professionals owe a duty of confidentiality to their patients under the law, subject to the patient's consent or requirements of the law.

The issue of confidentiality becomes most difficult when the protection of third parties is involved. For instance, the Canadian Medical Association advises physicians that disclosure of testing results to a spouse or sexual partner may not be unethical and may be required when physicians are confronted with a patient who is unwilling to inform a person at risk.

Also, Yukon and Prince Edward Island have legislation that requires or permits physicians to disclose confidential information without a patient's consent if doing so is necessary to protect a third party.

11. What is the law regarding admittance to a psychiatric facility?

Generally, there are two ways for someone to end up in a mental health care or psychiatric facility — voluntarily or involuntarily. In each province, there are guidelines governing who can request or order admittance to these facilities, how long individuals may stay or be kept, and the procedures for reviewing findings of mental incompetence.

Typically, individuals are admitted to a psychiatric or mental health facility when they pose a threat to the personal safety of themselves or others.

■ Voluntary Admission

If you are just looking for a "mental break" from the world and its pressures, a mental health hospital does not have to take you as a patient. In most cases, a voluntary patient must be referred to the facility by a physician for assessment.

In B.C., for example, the law states that a person who does not suffer from a mental disease cannot be admitted as a patient to a mental health care facility. In B.C., the law states a female patient must also be accompanied by a relative or female person for admittance.

Admission to a mental health care facility can be refused if its management or doctors believe hospitalization is not urgent or necessary. The facility must give you reasons for the refusal and you may be able to request that the decision be reconsidered by a provincial review body or even the courts.

■ Involuntary Admission

A common form of involuntary admission arises when a court orders a psychiatric assessment of an accused. Typically, these orders cannot be refused by the facility.

A person may also be admitted as a patient involuntarily upon recommendation of a physician. In Ontario, for example, any doctor may make an application for a psychiatric assessment of an individual and the public authorities (police, hospital officials, etc.) are obliged to detain the person. The physician must give that person written notice of the application and cite reasons.

The detention may be for no more than 72 hours. In that time, a different physician must complete a "certificate of involuntary admission" and assess the condition of the patient. Any patient detained involuntarily is entitled to a hearing before the province's Consent and Capacity Board. The patient has a right to retain counsel.

In Québec, a different timeframe is in place. No one in Québec can be confined in a health or social services institution for psychiatric assessment without his or her consent or authorization by law or the court. Two opinions are needed to maintain the detention. A first psychiatric assessment must be performed within 24 hours of admittance and a second assessment must be performed within 96 hours.

■ Issues of consent

Except in emergencies, the consent of a guardian or substitute decision-maker is needed to conduct medical or psychiatric treatment of a patient found to be mentally incompetent. A patient's guardian, lawyer, spouse, adult child, sibling, or nearest relative may also be able to give consent for a medical or psychiatric procedure on any involuntary patient under 16 years of age.

In Ontario, for example, treatment may not be provided to a person found incapable if that person informs health practitioners of his or her intention to apply to the Consent and Capacity Board for a review of the incapacity finding.

12. Are mental health records confidential?

The federal and provincial governments have legislation on access to any personal information, including medical and mental health. In most cases, the government must refuse anyone access to records held in its departments and agencies without the consent of the individual or unless required by law. You can provide access by giving your consent in writing.

13. What laws govern health care professionals?

Many different kinds of practitioners provide health-related services. Some health care professionals are regulated by law in some provinces and some are not. If a patient suffers because of improper treatment, it may be easier to hold a regulated health care professional accountable in court.

■ Regulated health care professionals

Health care professionals who are regulated by the government are required by law to fulfill certain training criteria to receive a licence to practice. It also means they belong to a professional organization, usually called a College or Society, which is responsible for setting standards for the profession.

The College or Society is responsible for taking complaints and disciplining members of the profession who do not live up to professional standards. Regulated health care professionals include doctors, nurses, chiropractors, physiotherapists, midwives, optometrists, and dentists.

■ Other health care practitioners

If a practitioner is not regulated, there may be other laws that govern some aspects of the profession, such as education and training requirements. Practitioners who are not regulated, however, may not be accountable to a professional body, and therefore, may be able to set their own standards.

Unless the situation is serious enough to warrant criminal charges, if a patient has a problem with the treatment provided by an unregulated practitioner, there may not be a governing body where the patient can make a complaint or prevent the person from practising. Unregulated practitioners may be sued in civil court. Because they might not have insurance, however, a patient who sues might not be able to recover any money.

Before accepting health treatment, determine whether the practitioner is regulated by law and whether he or she belongs to a professional organization.

14. Can I sue a caregiver or health care professional for medical malpractice?

When you believe a doctor, nurse, hospital, or anyone in the health care field has recklessly or carelessly endangered your life, you are entering the world of "torts" and, usually, the law of negligence.

A tort is a private lawsuit pursued in a civil court by one individual against another (it's not like a criminal offence or contractual breach). As the plaintiff, there are several elements you must prove if a medical malpractice action is to succeed.

First, you must prove the defendant (e.g. doctor, nurse, or hospital) owed you a duty of care. This is usually established by showing you were a patient and relied on the health care professional.

Then, you must prove the duty was violated. In negligence cases, this is often done by examining the "reasonable" standard of care or customary practices expected in the medical profession. If the health care provider followed the normal procedures for your type of case, it may be very difficult to prove negligence. Nonetheless, there have been cases where health care professionals who followed proper procedures still have been found negligent.

Next, you must prove that you suffered an injury or loss and that the injury was due to the defendant's conduct and not a pre-existing medical condition or your own post-procedure behaviour. For that reason, negligence actions also require proof the damage or injury was foreseeable by the defendant.

Medical malpractice cases are complex and take a long time to resolve. Fortunately, as in all civil court cases, you are not required to prove all these elements beyond a reasonable doubt, as in a criminal trial. In civil courts, you only need to prove that your case is true on a "balance of probabilities."

Your lawyer will also need to be careful about who is sued. For example, the medical equipment or devices used may have been defective and the operating surgeon may not have been at fault. Also, while hospitals are responsible for their own staff, they may not be responsible for outside physicians with hospital privileges.

ROUTINE PROCEDURES?

A man visited his family physician and complained about pain in the stomach. The doctor felt a large mass in his abdomen and diagnosed it as an abdominal aortic aneurysm. The man was rushed to hospital and placed under the care of another doctor, who was told of the family physician's diagnosis.

The emergency room doctor, however, decided to follow hospital procedures and investigate five other possible causes. In the 3 1/2-hours it took to do the tests, the aneurysm burst and the man died.

Was the second doctor negligent?

Yes. In a similar Ontario Court of Appeal case, the court found the doctor was negligent in not immediately pursuing the first diagnosis. Even though he followed routine hospital emergency procedures, he did not meet the standard of care expected.

DUTY TO WARN ... DOCTOR OR MANUFACTURER?

A woman who had breast implant surgery sued the manufacturer of the implant and her surgeon for failing to warn her about the possibility that the implant could rupture from routine activity. The manufacturer said it told the doctor of the dangers and had fulfilled its duty to the end-consumer.

Is the manufacturer obliged to warn about medical dangers?

In a similar 1995 case, the Supreme Court held the standard of care and duty to warn of potential dangers in medical products is extremely high. While the law recognizes the idea that a manufacturer may fulfill the duty to warn consumers by informing a qualified professional who will ultimately deliver the product (a so-called "learned intermediary"), the court said the manufacturer of this medical product could not rely on that principle because its warning was not adequate. Manufacturers of medical products, said the court, can be reasonably expected to make "clear, complete and current informational disclosure to consumers" concerning the risks in using their products.

DISCRIMINATION

Human rights laws attempt to ensure that the dignity and worth of each person are recognized by society, public institutions, and businesses no matter how different the individual is. Every province and the federal government have human rights laws and a commission or tribunal to oversee administration of the legislation. Canada also has the *Canadian Charter of Rights and Freedoms*, which constitutionally enshrines many of the same fundamental human rights.

Human rights laws prohibit discrimination and harassment based on certain characteristics in certain situations. These characteristics are called prohibited grounds and each human rights "code" sets out its own prohibited grounds, which can include:

- Age
- Ancestry
- Citizenship
- Colour
- Criminal record
- Family status
- Gender
- Handicap or disability
- Marital status
- Nationality/Ethnic origin
- Place of origin
- Political belief

617

- Race or creed
- Receipt of public assistance
- Religion or creed
- Sex
- Sexual orientation

Generally, discrimination and harassment can only be dealt with by a provincial or federal human rights commission or, in the case of unionized employees, through the grievance arbitration process. Courts do not have jurisdiction to deal with discrimination or harassment, although courts may award greater damages if such conduct can be proven in connection with another legal wrong.

Provincial human rights acts or codes apply to most cases of discrimination. The federal *Canadian Human Rights Act* applies if a federally governed institution, such as a bank or airline, is involved. The Canadian Constitution's *Charter of Rights* requires all levels of government to pass laws and enforce them without discrimination on certain prohibited grounds.

There are other laws that deal with human rights, as well. For instance, the *Criminal Code* makes it a crime to spread hate propaganda against an identifiable group. It also provides for greater penalties where a crime is motivated by hatred of a particular group. Provincial employment standards legislation also contains provisions prohibiting discrimination based on sex and age.

1. What is discrimination?

To discriminate means to make distinctions. Discrimination in itself is not prohibited by human rights laws. Discrimination is prohibited only based on certain grounds in certain situations.

Discrimination does not have to be intentional for it to be against the law. It is the effect on the individual that matters. Discrimination can also come about when a rule applied equally to everybody has a disproportionate effect on a particular group of individuals due to that group's unique needs. For instance, only hiring employees above a certain height can constitute discrimination on the basis of sex, since women are generally shorter than men.

Harassment is also a form of discrimination. Harassment means that the harasser acts in an annoying or abusive manner that is known, or ought reasonably to be known, to be unwelcome by the other person.

Sexual harassment is a particular type of gender or sex-based discrimination that occurs in employment settings.

There are situations that seem to be discriminatory but are not because human rights laws have provided an exception to the rules. For example, an ethnic social club is allowed to restrict its membership to people from its particular ethnic group. Another example is that employers are entitled to discriminate against employees who do not have a certain attribute, where that attribute is a genuine requirement of the job, such as perfect vision, certain height, or strength.

2. What are the prohibited types of discrimination?

Human rights laws are concerned with preventing and ending harassment and illegal discrimination. Discrimination is illegal when it is based on irrelevant personal characteristics. These characteristics are called prohibited grounds of discrimination.

■ Race, Ancestry, Place of Origin, Colour, Ethnic Origin, and Citizenship

These terms are often used interchangeably to refer to a person's race or origin but each has its own distinct meaning. Examples of illegal discrimination and harassment may include racial remarks or graffiti in the workplace, explicit or covert policies not to hire or promote certain groups, and refusals to rent or do business with certain ethnic groups or communities. Human rights tribunals have also recognized that discrimination based on language, accent, dress, food, or cultural habits may fall within one or more of the above prohibited grounds.

■ Religion or Creed

Discrimination or harassment based on religion, creed, or spiritual belief is also prohibited. The religion or spiritual belief does not necessarily have to be well organized or from the Christian, Jewish, Muslim, or Hindu traditions. Religious discrimination often arises where authorities fail to accommodate a person's religious observance needs or practices, such as wearing religious clothing or abstaining from work on a religious holiday. The law holds that imposing the same rules or laws on everyone may constitute discrimination.

■ Sex or Gender

Sex or gender discrimination and harassment takes many forms including failing to hire or promote women in employment, firing pregnant employees, sexually harassing in the workplace, refusing to allow men or women to engage in activities or professions traditionally dominated by the other sex, refusing to serve a breastfeeding patron, and paying different wages for work of equal value.

■ Age

Discrimination based on age can also be illegal. Age has a special meaning and is generally defined as between 18 and 65. Generally, it is not illegal to discriminate in employment related matters for those older than 65 or younger than 18.

■ Handicap or Disability

Disability or handicap is broadly defined to mean any degree of physical disability, mental retardation, learning disability, mental disorder, or injury associated with workers' compensation, including the perception of such disability. Generally, the disability must be of some permanence to qualify. A minor cold, flu, or headache would not be considered a disability.

Disability complaints may arise in employment where an employer either refuses to hire a disabled person or refuses to accommodate the disabled employee's needs. An employer may be required to accommodate the needs up to the point of undue hardship. Although there is no set formula for determining undue hardship, such hardship usually occurs at the point where the health and safety of workers or the operational requirements of the business are compromised by the accommodation request. Note that "business inconvenience" is not considered a valid reason for refusing to accommodate.

Varying degrees of the duty to accommodate disabled persons are similarly imposed on landlords in the area of accommodation and businesses in the provision of goods, services, and facilities.

■ Sexual orientation

Human rights laws also prohibit discrimination and harassment against gays, lesbians, bisexuals, and transsexuals and in some cases, their partners and children.

Unequal treatment due to HIV and AIDS is generally considered discrimination on the basis of disability, although it may also constitute discrimination on the basis of sexual orientation.

■ Marital and family status

Marital status and family status are also prohibited grounds in many provincial codes. Marital status means the status of being married, single, widowed, divorced, or separated and includes the status of living with a person of the opposite sex in a conjugal relationship outside marriage.

Family status means the status of being in a parent-child relationship.

■ Criminal record or receiving public assistance

In some cases, having a criminal record or receiving public assistance, such as family benefits, can also be considered prohibited grounds of discrimination.

■ Perceived characteristics

Sometimes, the perception of these characteristics is just as important as the reality. Accordingly, human rights laws may be applicable to those situations where someone is discriminated against or harassed simply because he or she is perceived to be of a certain race, disability, and so on.

There may also be situations where the discrimination and harassment is not specifically related to a prohibited ground, for example, race, but it is so closely identified with it, such as by a person's accent, that human rights laws are applicable. It may also be that the discrimination is experienced on different and multiple levels. For example, a disabled woman of colour may be discriminated against on the basis of race, disability, and sex. It is important therefore not to dismiss a human rights concern just because it does not fit squarely within one of the listed grounds of discrimination.

3. Where do human rights violations usually occur?

Human rights laws generally apply to the following five areas of activity or circumstance:

- Employment
- Accommodation or housing
- Services, goods, and facilities
- Contracts
- Membership in trade unions, vocational or occupational associations

■ Employment

Employment is interpreted very broadly in human rights cases. Employment includes casual, part-time, seasonal, and contract employment and extends to probationary and volunteer situations. There need not be a written employment agreement for an employment relationship to exist. In fact, a complaint can be filed before employment has begun if there is a reason to believe that employment was denied because of illegal discrimination.

Complaints can be filed while employment is ongoing or after it ends so long as the complaint is filed within the timeframe required by law. Complainants are required to mitigate their damages, meaning that they must use all reasonable efforts to reduce their losses by looking for other employment.

In most workplaces, the employee has a choice between filing a human rights complaint and suing an employer for wrongful dismissal in court. The main difference between these two choices is that a court cannot order an employer to reinstate an employee who has been terminated. Generally, a court can only award monetary damages for wrongful dismissal, whereas a human rights tribunal can order broad remedies including reinstatement with back wages in appropriate circumstances.

Although all workplaces are equally governed by human rights laws, unionized employees may have alternatives to filing a complaint. Under labour laws, union workers may file a grievance against their employer under the non-discrimination provisions of the collective agreement between their union and employer. If unionized employees wish to complain of discrimination by their union, they may file an unfair representation complaint at the provincial or federal labour board.

A lawyer familiar with employment law, labour law, and human rights laws can advise you about the options of suing in court, filing a grievance, bringing a complaint to a labour board, or filing a complaint with a human rights commission and which would be best in your circumstances.

■ Accommodation or housing

The second area where human rights laws apply is accommodation. Every person has the right to be free from discrimination and harassment with respect to accommodation, including discrimination based on receipt of public assistance, such as welfare or family benefits. Accommodation complaints may involve the conduct of a landlord, the landlord's agents, occupants of the same premises, or others associated with the building. The discrimination or harassment may be directed at the occupant or the occupant's guests. Typical accommodation problems involve the refusal to rent premises to members of a particular ethnic group, unequal enforcement of rules and harassment of tenants from certain ethnic or cultural backgrounds. Although many legal problems may arise during accommodation such as rent increases and failure to repair, human rights laws do not apply unless a prohibited ground of discrimination is involved.

■ Services, goods, and facilities

The third area is in the provision of goods, services, and facilities. Discrimination and harassment in the provision of goods, services, and facilities is prohibited. Public authorities, community organizations, and private businesses are not free to do business with whomever they please if the reasons are discriminatory. Shops, restaurants, hospitals, schools, insurance companies, hotels, government programs, and other public and private providers of goods and services must serve members of the community equally. Exceptions to this rule are allowed for religious, charitable, and social organizations in certain situations.

■ Contracts

Contracts are the fourth area where human rights apply. If a term of an oral or written contract amounts to discrimination or harassment on a prohibited ground, that term is illegal and unenforceable. Even if a contract is voluntarily entered into or signed, if it contains a provision that is discriminatory, the provision is unenforceable.

■ Membership in trade unions or vocational or occupational associations

Last, refusal to provide membership or equal treatment within a trade union or vocational or occupational association is illegal if the refusal is related to a prohibited ground.

4. What can I do about discrimination or harassment at work?

If you are being illegally discriminated against or harassed at work, and you believe you can confront the person responsible, then you should do so. Immediately bring the problem to the attention of that individual, and tell the person in a polite but firm manner that his or her conduct is not acceptable.

■ Keep written records

Make a written note of your attempts to bring the conduct to an end and the person's response. As well, keep a written record of the incidents of discrimination and harassment as they happen. This may become very useful if you have to prove your version of the events at a later time. You should record what happened, when it happened, where it happened, who was involved, whether others witnessed the same conduct, and what you and others did in response to this conduct.

Generally, you should first take advantage of internal complaint mechanisms such as internal discrimination and harassment dispute procedures or grievance arbitration mechanisms in unionized settings. In many organizations, there are supervisors, managers, or human resources staff who are responsible for dealing with such situations. In unionized settings, union officials may be able to help. If such attempts are not possible or are unsuccessful, you may wish to bring the conduct to the attention of your local human rights commission or tribunal or a lawyer.

■ Time limits for filing a complaint

You should be aware that both provincial and the federal Human Rights Commissions have time limits for filing a complaint. For example, the Ontario Human Rights Commission may refuse to deal with a complaint that is based on facts older than six months before the date of filing. The Canadian Human Rights Commission's time limit is one year. Be aware that contacting a commission is not considered the same as filing a complaint, which involves signing the formal complaint document. Beyond these time limits, the commissions may, in their discretion, refuse to deal with complaints if the reasons for delay are unreasonable or if the delay was caused in bad faith.

If you are unsure about how to proceed, promptly speak to a public service officer at your local human rights commission.

5. How does the human rights commission process work?

Filing a human rights complaint with a human rights commission begins a legal process in which the person filing and the person or organizations complained about all have legal rights. The person who files the complaint is a *complainant* and the person or organization complained about is the *respondent*. If you are a complainant, your goal is to have your situation reach the hearing stage.

Commission staff accept and process complaints and undertake investigations. They usually have broad investigative powers to obtain documents and records. They determine if a complaint is valid or invalid. It will either be dismissed or sent forward in the adjudication process. Depending on the province it could be sent for mediation or to a hearing by one or more commission members sitting as a panel, tribunal, or board of inquiry which functions much like a court.

The panel hears evidence from the parties to the complaint and reaches factual and legal conclusions about whether discrimination or harassment has occurred and orders an appropriate remedy.

Only a small percentage of cases in Canada ever make it to the hearing stage, mostly because some parties agree to settle their complaint along the way or the commission refuses to deal with some complaints for various reasons. Sometimes the refusal is because of a delay, sometimes because the commission does not believe that the evidence warrants proceeding to the hearing stage, and sometimes because it lacks the jurisdiction to pursue the matter.

The federal and some provincial human rights commissions have been criticized for their backlogs and delays in dealing with complaints. The length of time required to deal with a complaint depends on the nature of the complaint and where it is in the commission process.

Some complaints that require investigation still take several years between the date of filing and the date on which the commission makes a final decision on whether to refer the complaint to a hearing or inquiry. The hearing may additionally take several weeks to several months between the time it is appointed and the time when it releases a decision.

Recent initiatives such as mediation appear to have improved the situation at some commissions. Mediation is a process that involves the complainant and respondent agreeing to meet on a voluntary basis to determine if they can settle their dispute. Mediation may result in the parties settling their dispute on terms that they can both agree to without a formal legal decision as to who was right or wrong. Usually, the details of what takes place in mediation remain confidential, and if mediation is unsuccessful the details cannot be used in further legal proceedings.

6. What remedies are available for human rights violations?

If discrimination or harassment is proven, the commissions have broad powers to order parties to do whatever is necessary to ensure that the law is complied with. The purpose of human rights remedies is not to punish the wrongdoer but to put complainants into the position that they would otherwise have been in if the discrimination had not occurred. Monetary and non-monetary remedies are usually available. For example, commissions could order an offender to pay damages or they could order things like reinstatement if a person was removed from a position of employment.

If the commission determines that there are multiple instances of discrimination or harassment, multiple awards of general damages can be ordered. Lawyers' fees are not recoverable at a hearing, but they may be taken into account if the parties reach a settlement among themselves. Examples of non-monetary remedies include job reinstatement, adoption of non-discrimination plans by the respondent, apologies, and staff training.

7.   What role does a lawyer play?

Hiring a lawyer for the purpose of filing or responding to a human rights complaint is not required. That said, because the legal procedures involved are complicated, a lawyer can assist in filing or responding to a human rights complaint and negotiating legally enforceable settlements. If the matter proceeds to investigation, a lawyer can make sure that investigative staff and the commissioners carry out their roles appropriately.

If you hire a lawyer, you will be responsible to pay the lawyer's fee. If you do not hire a lawyer, the commission staff will draft a complaint and investigate for free. Be aware that the commission is not acting on behalf of the complainant or the respondent up to the time the commission decides whether there is enough evidence to warrant a hearing. If a hearing is ordered, the commission, usually through an appointed lawyer, acts on behalf of the public interest. In most cases, the commission's public interest overlaps with a complainant's private interest.

Depending on the extent that the commission's lawyer acts on behalf of the complainant's interests as well, the complainant may or may not require his or her own lawyer at the hearing. Respondents, however, are advised to retain a lawyer to defend their position at the hearing.

Job Requirements Too Strict?

An Ontario man who applied for a job as a fire-fighter was accepted subject to passing a medical exam. Later, it was discovered he had a heart condition and a fire department medical examiner refused to pass him despite the man's own medical experts who said it was a benign condition that would not impact his ability to do the job. The man later obtained a fire-fighting job in a nearby city and complained to the Ontario Human Rights Commission.

Was the fire department allowed to discriminate based on job requirements?

The human rights commission heard conflicting testimony about the impact that the medical condition would have on the man's ability to fight fires. It accepted the man's medical evidence that the risk of stroke was less than 0.2 percent. The commission found that the risk was "minuscule," "insignificant," and "irrelevant" and ordered the department to hire the man within 75 days, pay him the difference in salary, including overtime and pension loss, and reimburse him for travel expenses incurred going to the other job.

Is The Customer Always Right?

A British Columbia cab company developed policy guidelines for transporting blind persons with guide dogs. The policy said drivers must accept passengers with a guide animal unless they had a doctor's note on file indicating they could not transport animals because of an allergy or medical condition. The cab company indicated that blind people could advise dispatchers that they had a guide dog and an appropriate driver would be sent. A blind woman who was denied a pick up because she had a guide dog complained she was being discriminated against because of a disability and that drivers should only be exempt in the case of severe allergies. She also objected to the request that she had to identify the presence of a guide dog before calling a cab, arguing it singled out her disability.

Was there discrimination?

The B.C. Human Rights Commission found the taxi company was required to accommodate persons with guide dogs, but it also had a duty not to discriminate against employees who have disabilities, such as allergies. The commission found the requirement that such employees have a note from their doctor was reasonable. It was unreasonable to expect the cab company to refuse to hire people with allergies. The commission found the complainant wasn't required to reveal the presence of a guide dog, but could not expect to be accommodated if she did not provide the information to the dispatcher. It dismissed the complaint.

Drunk And Discriminated?

A Nova Scotia man who drank on the job and then later checked himself into a mental hospital after his wife left him and took all his possessions complained that he was discriminated against when his employer fired him.

Was there discrimination?

The Nova Scotia commission found that the man was suffering from a mental disability at the time he was fired and the employer was aware of that fact. It ordered the employer to pay the complainant three month's wages and an additional $2,000 in general damages.

No Credit? No Job? No Home?

An Ontario man complained that a landlord had discriminated against him on the basis of citizenship and place of origin because he was rejected for rental accommodation after failing to meet the minimum income, work history and credit history criteria. The man had recently moved to Canada with his family from Bangladesh. His wife had a job and he was looking for work. The couple did not have any credit cards, which were not common in Bangladesh, but he did have $25,000 in savings.

Was there discrimination?

The Ontario commission found that the landlord's tenant criteria amounted to discrimination. It ordered the landlord to pay the man $5,000 and stop rejecting newcomers for rent because they have no credit, employment, or rental history in Canada or if they fail to meet minimum job tenure or income criteria.

A Poisoned Work Environment?

A young woman in the midst of a divorce and custody dispute was desperate for a job and took employment with the respondents. She argued the respondents commented on the size of her breasts, her menstrual cycle, and touched her in a sexual manner. She said she was forced to work in a "poisoned" or inhospitable environment and was fired after contacting the commission to assert her human rights. Her employer denied any sexual harassment or touching and claimed the "sexual banter" was consensual. They cited poor job performance as the reason for her dismissal.

Was there discrimination?

The commission found that the complainant's rights had been violated and she was subject to sexual harassment and a poisoned work environment. It further found she was dismissed in part because of efforts to exert her rights. The commission ordered that one of the respondents attend a gender-based discrimination program and pay $8,470 in damages, plus interest.

Human Rights Commissions and information

Canadian Human Rights Commission	www.chrc-ccdp.ca
British Columbia Human Rights Tribunal	www.bchrt.bc.ca
Alberta Human Rights and Citizenship Commission	www.albertahumanrights.ab.ca
Saskatchewan Human Rights Commission	www.gov.sk.ca/shrc
Manitoba Human Rights Commission	www.gov.mb.ca/hrc
Ontario Human Rights Commission	www.ohrc.on.ca
Québec: Commission des droits de la personne et des droits de la	www.cdpdj.qc.ca
New Brunswick Human Rights Commission	www.gnb.ca
Nova Scotia Human Rights Commission	www.gov.ns.ca/humanrights
Prince Edward Island Human Rights Commission	www.gov.pe.ca/humanrights
Newfoundland and Labrador Human Rights Commission	www.gov.nf.ca/hrc
Yukon Human Rights Commission	www.yhrc.yk.ca

WILLS & ESTATE PLANNING

It is estimated that fewer than 50 percent of Canadians have a will. Every adult who owns property should have a will, especially if they have children. A will performs several important functions. First, it lets you leave instructions for how you want your property to be divided and distributed when you die. This can include everything from land, bank accounts, and investments, to all your personal possessions. Second, it lets you name a person who will wrap up all your personal affairs and who will carry out the instructions you left in your will. If you have children under the age of 18, a will also gives you the opportunity to name a guardian and state your wishes as to who will look after your children if you die. A will can also be an important part of estate planning to minimize your tax burden when giving your property away.

1.   What if I die without a will?

If you die without a will, your property will be divided according to the laws of the province in which you live. A set procedure will divide property according to family relationship. Even if you want your property divided according to provincial law, you should still have a will because it will reduce delays and expenses involved in wrapping up your affairs. See question 21 in this section for other details.

2.   What are the requirements for a valid will?

For a will to be valid, a few important requirements must be met. First, a will must be in writing, signed, and dated. If any of it is typed or not in the handwriting of the person making the will, it must be signed in front of two witnesses and the witnesses must also sign. A videotaped will is not valid. Second, you must be 18 years of age or older and mentally competent to make a will. Generally, a person is mentally competent if they can understand the purpose and effects of making a will. This can be an important question if the person making the will is elderly. A person under the age of 18 can only make a will if he or she is married or if that person is in the Canadian armed forces.

Your will is a very important document. It is also inexpensive to have professionally prepared. Most lawyers charge from $150 to $300 for a simple will. If you do not have a will, consult a lawyer to ensure that your wishes will be followed without complications or unnecessary expense.

3. Are there different types of wills?

There are two main types of wills, attested wills and holograph wills. Both types perform the same function by allowing you to name people who will receive your property when you die, and name a personal representative to make sure your wishes are carried out. The main difference between the two types of wills is how they are written and what things have to be done to make them legal.

▪ Attested Wills

An attested will is the most common. Attested means it is signed by witnesses. Every will that is not completely hand-written by the person making the will must be attested to be valid. Most attested wills are typed or prepared on a computer, or are made on pre-printed fill-in-the-blank forms. An attested will must be signed by the person making the will in front of two witnesses, and the witnesses must also sign their names at the bottom of the will. You and the two witnesses should also write your initials on each page of the will. After signing the will, the witnesses sign a written statement called an affidavit. In this statement, the witnesses must swear that they saw you sign the will and they have no reason to believe you were not capable of making the will. It is important to choose witnesses who are not receiving a gift in the will. They should also not be spouses of anyone receiving a gift in your will. If they are, they may have problems receiving their gifts.

▪ Holograph Wills

A holograph will is less formal than an attested will. The main requirements of a holograph will are that it must be entirely hand-written by the person making it, and it must be signed and dated. Unlike an attested will, it does not require witnesses or affidavits, and can be prepared personally by the person making the will. Although this appears to be the simplest option for preparing a will, it is not a good idea for most people. These wills may not be valid if they are unclear or missing important legal details.

If you want to prepare a will yourself, you can purchase fill-in-the-blank will forms at bookstores and stationary stores. These are attested wills because parts are typewritten and they must be signed by two witnesses.

Wills are extremely important documents. If you want to make sure your will is legal and clearly expresses your wishes, consult a lawyer.

4. What are the formal requirements for a will?

The purpose of a will is to make sure your property and finances can be wrapped up in an orderly way when you die. Most wills have the same general structure. Depending on your situation, however, some parts of a will may or may not be needed. If your situation is complicated, you will need a lot of extra parts to ensure your will is complete and legal.

A will does not have to be on a special form. It just needs to be a written document of some kind. Although it can be hand-written, most wills are professionally prepared and typed.

■ Your name and personal details

Most wills follow a basic structure. First, a will begins by naming the person who is making the will. If you are a man, you are called the testator. If you are a woman, you are called the testatrix. Your name may be followed by your name at birth, married names, and nicknames. Many wills also state your occupation.

■ Statement revoking any wills you wrote in the past

The second part of a typical will is a statement that revokes all prior wills. This cancels any wills you wrote in the past so you will not have two conflicting wills.

■ Statement naming your executor

Next, a will names a personal representative. A personal representative is also commonly called an executor. This is the person who will carry out your wishes. Anyone who is over the age of 18 and mentally competent can be your personal representative. The responsibilities of a personal representative include arranging your burial, proving that the will is legal, collecting information from family members, making a list of all the things you own, calculating all the money you owed to people, and giving out gifts to the people set out in the will. People who will receive gifts under your will are called beneficiaries.

■ List your property and who will receive it

After you have named your personal representative, you can begin to write the main part of your will. This is where you name the different people or organizations that will receive the things you own when you die. You should also name a second person for each gift in your will. This second person is called an alternate beneficiary and receives the gift if the main beneficiary dies before you.

■ Residue clause

Finally, a will should have what is called a residue clause. This is a statement near the end of the will that names a person or organization as the beneficiary of anything not listed in your will or left over after all debts have been paid and all other gifts distributed.

■ Date and sign the will, and have it witnessed

The will should be dated and signed at the bottom. If the will is typed, then two witnesses must also sign at the bottom and initial each page. They will also need to sign a sworn statement, called an affidavit, that confirms that you signed the will in front of them. If you handwrite your entire will from beginning to end, then no witnesses are needed.

Every will should reflect the individual needs and wishes of the person making it. You should consult a lawyer to prepare a will that suits your particular situation.

5. What are the rights of spouses and dependants?

Although the main purpose of a will is to allow people to decide who gets their property when they die, the law establishes restrictions to protect the rights of spouses and dependants.

■ Rights of spouses

Matrimonial law protects the rights of spouses and also affects how property is divided. When a person dies, a surviving spouse has a choice. The spouse can choose to inherit whatever you left him or her in your will or the spouse can choose to receive what is called an equalization payment. An equalization payment means that a calculation is made of what each spouse owns and what his or her debts are as of the date the one spouse died. The spouse with the greater property value total then pays the other spouse half the difference. For example, if the total for the husband was $100,000 and the total for the wife was $60,000, then the difference between them is $40,000. If the husband died, the wife would be entitled to half of that difference, which is $20,000, even if she was not given anything in the will. By choosing an equalization payment instead of an inheritance under the provisions of the will, the will is not cancelled, but gifts to other people will be reduced as a result of the payment.

Special rules apply to several different types of property when calculating the property of each spouse, and the calculation is usually complicated. Equalization payments are normally calculated by a lawyer.

■ Rights of dependants

The second type of person who may have rights to part of an estate, even if not included in a will, is a dependant. Each province has some type of succession law and family law act that lists certain people who you might have to provide for if they are determined to be dependants. These include your spouse, former spouse, common-law spouse, parent, grand-parent, child, grandchild, brother, and sister.

6.   Who is a dependant?

To be a dependant, a person has to show that they were receiving finan-cial support from you or that they had a legal right to receive financial support from you before you died. A dependant may have to prove this in court. If the court decides that the person is a dependant and that person can show a need for financial support, then the court may order that a certain amount of money be paid to them out of the estate.

If you think that you may be entitled to more from an estate than the amount provided for in a will, or if you need to determine the rights of others when preparing your will, consult with a lawyer.

7.   Can I appoint a guardian for my minor children in my will?

You have a legal right to declare in your will that one or more people should have custody of your minor children after your death and also be guardians of their property (inherited money, land, etc.). It is important to note, however, that having custody of your children ("guardian of the person") and having authority over their property ("guardian of proper-ty") are two different rights that are not automatically granted to whomever you name in your will.

A parent, for example, is automatically the "guardian of the person" of his or her minor child, but is not automatically the child's "guardian of property." A parent only receives that authority on behalf of his or her child from a statute or law, a court order or a legally valid document such as a will.

In naming a "guardian of the person," you are appointing someone to have custody of your minor children. This person has the rights and responsibilities of a parent. For example, the person with custody can decide where the child should live, what school the child should go to, and what medical treatment the child should receive.

There are three restrictions on your ability to appoint a person to have custody of your children. First, you must be the only person entitled to custody of your children. If someone else with legal custody of your children survives your death, such as the children's other parent, then the person you appoint would not acquire custody. If both you and the other custodial parent die at the same time, then only a person whom both of you had appointed would acquire custody.

Second, the person you appoint to have custody of your children must consent to the appointment. Third, the custody appointment in your will only lasts for 90 days after the will takes effect. That means the person whom you have appointed to have custody of your children must apply to a court within that period for permanent custody of your children.

Upon application to the court, a judge will choose a person to have permanent custody of your children based on what the court considers to be in their best interests. The court will consider many factors, including the wishes of the children and their relationship with the person applying for custody and with other family members. If there is a surviving non-custodial parent of the children, the court will normally award custody to the parent. If there is no surviving parent, the court will normally follow your wishes as set out in your will on the basis that you, as custodial parent, were the person in the best position to determine the best interests of your children.

8. Can I appoint a guardian for my minor children's property?

Provincial law provides you with the right to appoint one or more persons in your will to be the guardians of your children's property. A person with guardianship of a child's property has charge of and is responsible for the care and management of the property of the child. For example, the guardian may invest the child's money and may decide how it should be used for the benefit of the child.

The main restriction on your ability to appoint someone to be the guardian of your children's property is that you must be the guardian of your children's property at the time of your death. You should note that you are not automatically the legal guardian of your children's property; you must actually apply to a court to be so appointed.

In addition, a guardianship appointment is subject to the same three restrictions as a custody appointment: you must be the only person entitled to guardianship, the person you appoint must consent to act as guardian, and the appointment is only effective for 90 days. The person whom you have appointed to be the guardian of your children's property must apply to a court within that period for permanent guardianship. Again, the court will choose a guardian based on the best interests of your children, but will show a preference for a surviving parent, if any, and if none, for the person named as guardian in your will.

9. What is an executor?

An executor, sometimes referred to as a "personal representative," "estate trustee with a will," or "liquidator," is someone you select to carry out the wishes in your will. In addition to making sure your property goes to the people you have chosen, your personal representative is responsible for performing a number of duties to ensure your personal affairs are wrapped up in an orderly manner following your death. You can appoint more than one personal representative and you can also name an alternate personal representative, who would step in if your personal representative was unable to act.

10. Who can be an executor or personal representative?

Generally, you can select anyone provided he or she is at least 18 years old and able to understand what is expected. If you select someone who is under 18 or not able to understand the role of an executor, the law will appoint a different person. Above all, you should choose someone you trust and you should talk to them about being your executor or personal representative before deciding to appoint them in your will.

11. What are the duties of an executor or personal representative?

Your personal representative or executor must perform a number of duties when you die. Although these duties may vary depending on your particular situation, your personal representative generally assists with funeral arrangements, finds out where your bank accounts are, makes a list of all the things you own and all your debts, cancels all your credit cards, files your final income tax returns, and distributes property to your beneficiaries. It is important to prepare a complete list of debts because all debts must be paid before gifts are paid out to beneficiaries. Gifts to beneficiaries may be reduced by the amount needed to pay the debts. To make sure all debts are paid, personal representatives often run a small ad in the local newspaper asking any creditors to come forward.

12. How is an executor compensated?

An executor is reimbursed by your estate for most of his or her expenses. An executor is also paid a fee for acting as your executor, which is generally 5 percent of the value of your estate.

If you have been named an executor or personal representative, consult with a lawyer about your specific responsibilities. You could be sued if you do not carry out your duties properly.

13. What does it mean to "probate" an estate?

In some cases, your executor or personal representative must probate the will, which means to prove in court that the will meets all legal requirements. Whether a will needs to be taken to court and probated depends on the specific circumstances of that will. If the estate is small and not complicated, then a regular copy of the will may be sufficient to wrap up the affairs of the person who died. If the estate is large and complicated, or if people are challenging the will, then it will be necessary to probate the will to prove it is valid and to establish the authority of the personal representative. For example, if you have a large number of investments, the bank may want to see a probated copy of the will so it knows that the personal representative has the power to deal with your money.

14. Can I prepare my own will?

Your will is a formal document that has to follow certain rules to be legal. Even though you may think you can easily prepare your own will, it will often be missing certain technical legal requirements. Without all the legal requirements, you will not have a legal will and without a legal will, it could become expensive and time-consuming for your family to sort out your personal affairs when you die.

Although it is possible to prepare your own will without the assistance of a lawyer, it is important to seek at least some legal advice to ensure your will is complete and legally binding. There are also certain groups of people who should always seek legal advice when making a will.

Legal advice is critical if you are about to be married or separated, if you have a large estate, if you have assets in other countries, if you have a mental disease, or if you are very elderly.

15. When does a will take effect and can it be changed?

Your will takes effect upon your death and can generally be changed or revoked at any time while you are still alive.

16. Can I sell property mentioned in my will?

Because your will takes effect only upon your death, you are free to sell your property whenever you like and without the consent or permission of the person who is supposed to receive that property under your will. Selling property mentioned in your will does not cancel your will. It just means that your beneficiary does not receive that piece of property. Everything else in your will remains valid.

17. How do I make changes to my will?

If you want to make some minor changes to your will, you can do so without writing an entirely new one. You do, however, need to write a formal document. You should not simply scratch out certain parts of your will and write in your changes. This is usually not legal.

A formal change to your will is called a codicil. A codicil is a document that cancels certain parts of your will or adds new parts to it. It should refer to your will, and say specifically what is being changed. It needs to be prepared in the same way that a will is prepared. If your codicil is typed, it needs to be signed by you and two witnesses. The two witnesses must both be present when you sign. They do not have to be the same two people who witnessed your original will. If you write the entire codicil by hand, then you merely need to sign it yourself without any witnesses. All codicils should be dated.

Although there is no limit on the number of codicils you can have, if you find you have made a lot of changes, you should write a new will. This will avoid confusion caused by having several different documents.

18. How do I cancel my will?

You can also revoke your will completely. Revoking a will means to cancel it. If you want to cancel your will and not replace it with anything right away, you can make a codicil that states you are cancelling your will, or you can physically destroy your will by tearing it up.

If you die without making a new will, your property will be distributed as if you had died without one. If you want to cancel your will and replace it with another, you can do this by writing a new will because most include a clause near the beginning stating that all earlier wills are cancelled.

If you wish to make a change to your will or cancel your will, consult a lawyer for more information and assistance.

19. What happens if I acquire new things after a will is written?

If your will contains a residue clause, you do not need to write a new will every time you acquire a new piece of property. A residue clause is a statement near the end of your will that names a person who will receive anything left over from your estate once all the specific gifts have been made. It acts as a general safety net to make sure nothing is left out of your will. It also includes anything you acquire after you write your will.

So, for example, even though you may not have a specific clause in your will that deals with your new car, it will be given to the person who is the beneficiary of the residue of your estate. If you do not have a residue clause in your will, consult a lawyer about adding one.

20. How does marriage or divorce affect a will?

Your will is usually rendered invalid once you re-marry (unless you put your ex-spouse in your will in contemplation of your new marriage). To show that the will was made with the marriage in mind, it must contain a statement that makes reference to your upcoming marriage and the name of your spouse.

A will is not automatically revoked, however, when you divorce, separate, or dissolve a civil union.

In Québec, if you are living common law or in a civil union, it is important to know that Québec's Civil *Code* does not recognize common-law spouses in estate distributions if there is no valid will. So, having a will in a common-law relationship in Québec is vital.

21. How is property distributed without a will?

The following is a brief overview of how your property will be divided and distributed if you die without a will. If you have a spouse, but no children, your spouse inherits everything. This only applies to legally married spouses. Common law spouses do not automatically receive anything if you die without a will.

If you have a spouse and children then the estate is divvied up differently, depending on which province you live in.

In B.C., Alberta, Saskatchewan, Manitoba, Ontario, Nova Scotia, Northwest Territories, and Nunavut, spouses are first entitled to a preferential share of the estate before it is divided among heirs. The amount varies widely, from $40,000 in Alberta to the first $200,000 in Ontario.

This rule does not hold in Québec, New Brunswick, Newfoundland and Labrador, Prince Edward Island, and the Yukon.

If you have a spouse and one child, then in most instances they will split the balance equally. If you have more than one child, then the spouse inherits one-third and each child receives one-third of the balance. In Manitoba, however, the spouse inherits everything. As well, Québec provides that the spouse inherits one-third of the estate and the child two-thirds.

Generally, if you have children, but no spouse, then the children each inherit an equal portion of your estate. If you have no spouse and no children, your parents inherit your entire estate. If you have no spouse, no children, and no parents, your brothers and sisters divide your estate. If you also have no brothers and sisters, then your nieces and nephews each inherit an equal portion of your estate. If you have no nieces and nephews, then any other next of kin inherit an equal portion of your estate. If you have no living next of kin, then generally your estate goes to the government.

22. Can a will be challenged or changed by others?

If you are not provided for in the will of a family member or a close friend, you may want to consider challenging the validity of the will. While there may be a good reason you were left out, there may also be other possibilities.

There are several ways to challenge a will. In some circumstances, it may be appropriate to claim that the will maker did not know and understand the nature and effect of the gifts made under the will. Where the will represents a dramatic change, you may want to look at the circumstances surrounding the signing of the will. A person's will may not be valid if it was signed under pressure from a family member or other person.

If you think you have been unfairly excluded from a will, consult with a lawyer to determine whether you have legal grounds to challenge the will. If you do, your lawyer can help you start the necessary court proceedings.

23. What is a "joint tenancy"?

If you own property with another person as joint tenants, then on your death, the surviving joint owner acquires your interest in the property automatically by a process called right of survivorship. This means your interest in the property will pass outside your estate to the joint owner of the property, not through your estate to the beneficiaries named in your will.

Co-owners of property can either be joint tenants or tenants in common. Joint tenants have identical proportions and duration of interest in a piece of property, along with identical rights of possession. Joint tenants are treated as a single owner for legal purposes. Tenants in common, on the other hand, may have different proportions or shares of the property as well as different duration of interest. If two people own property as tenants in common and one dies, the deceased person's interest in the property will not pass to the other tenant in common by right of survivorship, but will fall into the estate of the deceased tenant in common and be distributed according to his or her will or according to the laws of intestacy (dying without a valid will).

24. What are the advantages and disadvantages of joint tenancy?

In joint tenancies, the automatic transfer of property created by the right of survivorship can be very advantageous. Because the property does not fall into the deceased joint tenant's estate, no probate should be required to change the registration of title and the property will not be subject to probate fees or the claims of creditors.

Note that transferring property to yourself and another person in joint tenancy can also create significant problems. Creating a joint tenancy is the same as making an immediate gift, in that you have given up part of the value of and control over the property. The jointly held property may become subject to the claims of the spouse or creditors of the other joint tenant and cannot be disposed of without the consent of the other joint tenant.

There may also be income tax consequences at the time of the transfer and afterward. Unless the property is your principal residence or the other joint tenant is your spouse, any increase in value in the property from the date you acquired it to the date of the transfer will be immediately taxable to you. After the transfer, the joint owners will each be entitled to an equal part of any income earned from the property and any increase in value of the property.

Normally, each joint owner will be liable for an equal part of the tax on this income and any increase in the value of the properties. In some circumstances, however, you may be taxed on the income and increase in value even though these benefits are received by the other joint owner.

Finally, on the death of the first joint tenant, the estate of the first joint tenant, not the surviving joint tenant, will have to pay tax on any increase in value of the property, other than a principal residence.

25. How do I create a joint tenancy?

A person may convey property to you and one or more other people as joint tenants. Alternatively, you may convey your own property to yourself and another person to create a joint tenancy. The important point is that a joint tenancy must be intentionally created by the same document and with very precise language. The law creates a presumption in favour of tenancies in common unless the document's language explicitly creates a joint tenancy.

26. How do I end a joint tenancy?

You may eliminate the right of survivorship by ending the joint tenancy before your death through a process called severance. Severance means that the joint tenants disrupt the unity of their interests in the property through mutual agreement or unilateral action so they become tenants in common instead of joint tenants.

Severance may also occur by operation of law. If a matrimonial home is owned in joint tenancy by one spouse with a person who is not the other spouse, then matrimonial law provides that the joint tenancy is severed on the death of the owner spouse. If all joint tenants die simultaneously, then the property will be dealt with as if the joint tenants had been tenants in common.

27. Can I transfer assets outside my will?

You may designate beneficiaries to receive certain financial assets such as life insurance proceeds, RRSPs, or pension plan benefits. These assets may be claimed by and paid directly to the designated beneficiary upon your death. The assets are not administered by the executors you name in your will and they are unaffected by the directions in your will regarding the distribution of your estate. In other words, these assets are transferred outside your estate.

28. How can I designate a beneficiary?

Beneficiaries may generally be designated right on the insurance policy contract or financial plan document at the time you take out the insurance or open the plan or at a later time. If you intend to designate one adult beneficiary, then the simplest way to do so is to complete the beneficiary designation form provided by the insurance company or financial institution and to file it with the company or institution.

Alternatively, you may make a beneficiary designation in your will. In this case, you must identify, either generally or specifically, the life insurance policy, RRSP, or other plan under which you are designating the beneficiary. Your will only affects policies and plans that are in existence at the time you make your will. Therefore, if you acquire any new insurance policies or financial plans after you have signed your will, you must prepare a new will or a codicil to designate beneficiaries for those policies or plans. It is a good idea to send a copy of any beneficiary designation in your will to the insurance company or financial institution affected by it.

You may wish to designate two or more beneficiaries to receive equal or unequal shares of the proceeds of your insurance policy, RRSP, or other plan, or you may wish to designate an alternate beneficiary in case the first one dies before you. If you wish to designate a child under the age of 18 as your beneficiary, then it is essential that you name another person to act as trustee of the proceeds for the child.

If there is more than one conflicting beneficiary designation in existence at your death, the one signed most recently will prevail.

29. What are the advantages of designating a beneficiary?

Insurance proceeds flow to your designated beneficiary free of tax. Insurance proceeds paid to a designated beneficiary are also statutorily protected from any claims by your creditors. In addition, because they pass outside your estate, insurance proceeds paid to a designated beneficiary are not included in the value of your estate for the purpose of calculating probate fees. If the beneficiary designation is contained in your will, it is important to confirm with a lawyer that it is properly worded to achieve these results.

Proceeds from other financial assets and plans, on the other hand, may be subject to tax on your death even though they are paid directly to your designated beneficiary. For example, unless you leave your RRSP or RRIF to your spouse, the entire value of the RRSP or RRIF will be included in your taxable income in the year you die, and your executors will have to satisfy the tax liability out of your estate because those assets have passed outside your estate to your designated beneficiary. In addition, creditors of your estate may be able to trace proceeds of financial assets, other than insurance, into the hands of the beneficiary to whom they are paid.

If you have not designated any beneficiary at all, or if your designated beneficiary dies before you and you have not designated an alternate, then the proceeds of the insurance policy, RRSP, or other plan will normally be paid into and dealt with as part of your estate. This means the proceeds will be subject to claims of creditors and any probate fees like any other asset of your estate.

Not So Simple Division

Ralph, who lives in Ontario, dies in a car accident, leaving his wife, Sally, and one child, Brian, and an estate worth $500,000 after his debts were paid. He died without a will

How will his estate be divided?

In Ontario, Sally is entitled to the first $200,000 of the estate, leaving a balance of $300,000. She is then entitled to one-half of the balance for a total of $350,000. Sally and Brian will then each receive $75,000.

How Far Down The Line?

Anne lived in Alberta. She died tragically in a fire, leaving an estate of $200,000, but no will. She had no children and her husband and parents and sister predeceased her, but her brother and her sister's son, a nephew, are still alive.

Who will inherit her estate?

The brother will inherit half the estate and the nephew is entitled to the portion that his mother would have received under the laws of intestacy.

DEALING WITH LEFTOVERS

Martha wrote her will in 1999. She designated that certain relatives would receive specific assets. Her cousin Bob was left her rare coins and automobiles, while her sister was left a cottage property in a prosperous cottage region. She provided that the residue of her estate would go to her favourite charity, the local humane society. Later, Martha bought a condominium and died in 2003.

What happens to the condo?

The property becomes part of the estate that will go to the charity.

WHERE PROPERTY & ESTATE LAW MEET

Brothers Sam and Rob bought a cottage as joint tenants. Sam later died and left everything to his parents.

Are the parents entitled to the cottage?

No. Sam's interest in the cottage ceased to exist on his death and title went to his brother, Rob. If they held the cottage as tenants in common, his share would have become part of his estate.

IS IT VALID?

Jack sat down at his computer and typed out his last will and testament, printed it, and simply placed the document in his safe deposit box.

Is the will valid?

No. The document needed to be signed by Jack and independent witnesses. Or, he could have written a will in his own handwriting and signed it. This is known as a holograph will.

Probate Fees Across Canada:
As of March 21, 2005

Jurisdiction	Fee Schedule
Alberta	For estates valued at: • Up to $10,000: $25 • $10,001 to $24,999: $100 • $25,000 to $124,999: $200 • $125,000 to $249,999: $300 • $250,000 and over: $400
British Columbia	For estates valued at: • Up to $10,000: $0 • $10,001 to $25,000: $200 • $25,001 to $124,999: $200 • $6 for every $1,000 or part of $1,000 for the value over $25,000 but not more than $50,000 • Plus $14 for every $1,000 or part of $1,000 exceeding $50,000
Manitoba	• $50 for the first $10,000, plus $6 for every $1,000 thereafter
New Brunswick	• $5 for each $1,000
Newfoundland and Labrador	• $85 for the first $1,000 • $500 per $1,000 • Plus $50 for the Order
Northwest Territories and Nunavut	• Calculated on the value of all property, real and personal, within the Northwest Territories, after deducting all debts and liabilities against that property: • $10,000 or under: $25 • $10,001 to $25,000: $100 • $25,001 to $125,000: $200 • $125,001 to $250,000: $300 • Over $250,000: $400
Nova Scotia	For estates valued at: • Up to $10,000: $70 • $10,001 to $25,000: $176 • $25,001 to $50,000: $293 • $50,001 to $100,000: $820 • $100,001 and over: $820, plus $13.85 for each additional $1,000 of fraction thereof in excess of $100,000

Jurisdiction	Fee Schedule
Ontario	• $5 on each $1,000 for the first $50,000 and $15 per $1,000 thereafter
Prince Edward Island	For estates valued at: • Up to $10,000: $50 • $10,001 to $25,000: $100 • $25,001 to $50,000: $200 • $50,001 to $100,000: $400 • $400 plus $4 for each $1,000 or fraction thereof in excess of $100,000 • Also a 02% closing fee
Quebec	• $65 for non-notarial "English form" will • $0 for notarial will
Saskatchewan	• $7 on each $1,000
Yukon	• No fee for a Grant of Letters Probate and Administration if estate does not exceed $25,000 in value • For estates exceeding $25,000 in value: $140

Powers of Attorney

1. What is a power of attorney for personal care?

A power of attorney is a written document in which you give someone the power to make decisions about your personal care should you become unable to make these decisions yourself.

A power of attorney for personal care can include authority over your health care, medical treatment, diet, housing, clothing, hygiene, and safety. Although the person you give this power to is called your attorney, it does not mean he or she is your lawyer. Your attorney, in this context, is usually your spouse, a relative, or a close friend.

2. What are the benefits of a power of attorney for personal care?

The main purpose of a power of attorney for personal care is to give you control and peace of mind. It lets you appoint someone you trust to make decisions on your behalf and it ensures that your health will be in the hands of someone you have personally chosen. It also gives you a chance to determine the kind of care you may or may not want. For example, you may want to specifically request a certain kind of medical treatment over another. In this way, a power of attorney for personal care is often similar to a living will.

A living will is a document that expresses whether and how you want to be kept alive by medical machines if there is little hope of your recovery. In it, a person will generally indicate at what point he or she would like medical treatments discontinued. Though a living will can be in any written form, it often forms part of a power of attorney for personal care.

3. Who can be appointed as an attorney for personal care?

There are certain rules about who can give a power of attorney for personal care, and who can be appointed as an attorney.

To give a power of attorney for personal care, you must be 16 years of age or older. You must also understand whether your attorney truly cares about your well-being and what authority you are giving that person. The attorney you appoint must also be 16 or older, mentally competent, and not someone who is being paid to provide you with health care, residential, social, training, or support services. If a person is being paid to provide you with any of these services, that person can only be your attorney if he or she is also your spouse, common law spouse, same-sex partner, or relative.

Above all, you should select someone you know well and trust to follow your instructions or wishes. Before you make your decision, ask that person if he or she is willing to be your attorney. Also, talk about your wishes and that person's responsibilities. You can appoint more than one attorney, and you can also name an alternate to step in if the main attorney is unable to act for any reason.

4. What are the requirements for a valid power of attorney for personal care?

To be legal, a power of attorney needs to be set out in writing and signed by you and two witnesses. The two witnesses must both be present when you sign. People who the law does not allow to be witnesses include the attorney you are appointing, the attorney's spouse or partner, your own spouse or partner, your child, or any person under the age of 18.

Drafting a power of attorney involves a number of technical legal details. It can also cause many problems if it is not done correctly. Always consult a lawyer to prepare a power of attorney for personal care.

5. When does a power of attorney for personal care take effect?

A power of attorney for personal care only takes effect if you become mentally incapable of making some or all of your personal care decisions. A power of attorney can generally be revoked at any time up to that point.

Most often, the person you appointed as your attorney is the one who decides when you become incapable of making personal care decisions. If you want someone else to be responsible for that decision, you can name another in your power of attorney documents. For example, you may want a formal assessment by a medical professional to confirm your incapacity. You could name a particular medical professional, or you could just make a general request that your incapacity be confirmed. In this case, the person who assesses you is called a capacity assessor.

6. Can you revoke a power of attorney for personal care?

Generally, a power of attorney lasts until your death, although you can revoke a power of attorney at any time when you are mentally competent. Revoking a power of attorney means that it is cancelled and no longer effective.

There is no special form to complete to revoke a power of attorney, but you must revoke the power of attorney in writing and sign it in front of two witnesses. Both witnesses must be present when you sign. The witnesses must also sign. They do not need to be the same witnesses who signed the original power of attorney. There are restrictions, however, on who can be a witness to the cancellation of your power of attorney. The following people cannot be witnesses: your attorney, the spouse or partner of your attorney, your own spouse or partner, your child, anyone under the age of 18, or anyone who has been appointed as your guardian. Your power of attorney will not be cancelled if the revocation is not properly witnessed.

Give a copy of the revocation to anyone who was aware of the previous power of attorney. This way, everyone will know that it has been cancelled. Consult a lawyer to revoke your power of attorney.

7.   What happens if I don't have a power of attorney for personal care?

A power of attorney for personal care is a written document in which you give someone the power to make decisions about your personal care if you become unable to make these decisions yourself.

If you become mentally incapable and you do not have a power of attorney for personal care, your family has automatic authority to make certain personal care decisions on your behalf. Also, a relative or friend can apply to the court to become your guardian.

8.   Can my family make personal care decisions for me?

If you do not have a signed power of attorney for personal care designating a specific person as your representative and decision maker, in many provinces, a "substitute decision maker" law helps decide who has most right to take that role.

In order of priority, assuming there is no named attorney for personal care, substitute decision makers include: 1) a guardian appointed by the court, 2) your spouse, 3) your children, 4) your parents, 5) your brothers or sisters, and 6) other relatives. If there is more than one person in the group (more than one child or sibling) and they disagree about treatment, a representative of the government's Public Guardian and Trustee office has the right to make the decision and break the deadlock.

Generally, your immediate family members (spouse, children, parents, etc.) will be permitted by health care professionals to make certain personal care decisions for you, which often means they do not need to apply to the court for permission. For example, your family will be asked to make decisions about your medical treatment, decisions about personal assistance services such as bathing, and decisions about whether to admit you to a long-term care facility.

The highest priority always goes to your legal representative, as declared in a power of attorney for personal care or by court order. For example, any member of your family could become your legal representative by applying to your province's Public Guardian Office or Consent and Capacity Board. That family member would then have priority over other family members and would be asked first when decisions need to be made.

As a final resort, the Office of the Public Guardian and Trustee can make personal care decisions on your behalf.

9. Who can apply to the court to be my guardian for personal care?

If you become mentally incapable of making personal care decisions and you do not have a power of attorney for personal care, any relative or friend can apply to the court to become your guardian of the person, provided that person is at least 18 years old and is not being paid to provide you with health care, residential, social, training, or support services. If that person is being paid to provide you with any of these services, he or she can only apply if that person is your spouse, partner or relative. Your guardian is responsible for making all of your personal care decisions. Your guardian must keep in touch with you, and explain to you the kinds of decisions that are being made. Your guardian also has a responsibility to make decisions in a way that is consistent with how you would have made them yourself.

If you do not create a power of attorney for personal care or other health care directive, there will be immediate uncertainty in your family as to who you want to act as your representative. In many provinces, a "substitute decision maker" law comes into effect that helps decide who has most right to take that role. In order of priority, assuming there is no named attorney for personal care, substitute decision makers include: 1) a guardian appointed by the court, 2) your spouse, 3) your children, 4) your parents, 5) your brothers or sisters, and 6) other relatives. If there is more than one person in the group (more than one child or sibling) and they disagree about treatment, a representative of the government's Public Guardian and Trustee office has the right to make the decision and break the deadlock.

If you would like your health and personal care to be handled in a certain way, consult with a lawyer about making a power of attorney for personal care.

10. What is a power of attorney for property?

A power of attorney for property is a written document in which you give someone the power to make decisions about your property and finances if you become unable to make these decisions yourself. For example, your attorney for property could be responsible for taking care of your banking matters, managing your investments, running your business, buying and selling real estate on your behalf, or paying your monthly bills. The only thing you could not appoint an attorney to do is to write your will. Although the person you give this power to is called your attorney, it does not mean that person is your lawyer. Most often, your attorney is your spouse, a relative, or a close friend.

11. What can your attorney for property do?

The kinds of things your attorney can do depends entirely on how much power you hand over. You could give a general power of attorney for property that covers all your property and financial affairs. Or, you could give a more specific power of attorney for property that allows the attorney to handle only some of your affairs. For example, you could even limit the power of attorney to a single real estate transaction while you are out of the country.

You must clearly outline what you are allowing your attorney to do and when. For example, often people wish to prepare a power of attorney in case they become unable to take care of certain things as they get older. If you only want your power of attorney to take effect at some point in the future or upon a specific occurrence, then you must clearly state this.

12. How long does your power of attorney for property last?

If you do not limit your power of attorney in any way, then it continues to have effect until your death. In fact, you may often hear a power of attorney being called a continuing power of attorney for property. This means that the power of attorney continues to have effect even if you become mentally incompetent. If you have an old power of attorney, check with a lawyer to determine if the document still applies should you become mentally incompetent.

13. Who can give a power of attorney for property?

There are certain rules about who can give a power of attorney for property and who can be appointed. To give a power of attorney for property, you must be 18 or older and you must be aware of the property you own and its general value. You must also understand what it means to appoint an attorney and know what authority you are giving your attorney and you must understand the possibility that the attorney could misuse the power you are giving that person. Your attorney must be someone who is 18 or older and mentally competent.

Although it may be best to select someone who has some knowledge of financial matters, above all you should select someone you know well and trust. You can appoint more than one attorney and you can also name an alternate attorney who would step in if the main attorney is unable to act for some reason. If you are uncomfortable selecting a family member or friend as your attorney, you may also want to consider selecting a trust company to be your attorney for financial matters. Often people choose trust companies because they are professional and impartial.

14. What are the requirements for a valid power of attorney for property?

To be legal, a power of attorney needs to be set out in writing, and signed by you and two witnesses. The two witnesses must both be present when you sign. People who the law does not allow to be witnesses include: the attorney you are appointing, the attorney's spouse or partner, your own spouse or partner, your child, or any person under the age of 18.

Drafting a power of attorney for property involves a number of technical legal details. It can also cause many problems if it is not done correctly. Always consult a lawyer if you want to make a power of attorney for property.

15. When does a power of attorney for property take effect?

A power of attorney for property takes effect as soon as it is signed and witnessed.

If you do not want your power of attorney for property to take effect immediately, you must specifically state in the power of attorney when it will take effect. For example, if you want the power of attorney to come into effect only if you become mentally incompetent, you must say so in the power of attorney document.

16. Can I revoke a power of attorney for property?

Generally, a power of attorney lasts until your death, although you can revoke it at any time when you are mentally competent. By revoking a power of attorney, it means that it is cancelled and no longer effective. Although there is no special form that must be completed to revoke a power of attorney, the cancellation must be written and signed in front of two witnesses who are both present when you sign. The two witnesses must then also sign.

Although the witnesses do not need to be the same witnesses who signed the original power of attorney, under the law your witnesses cannot be your attorney, the spouse or partner of your attorney, your own spouse or partner, your child, or anyone under the age of 18. Your power of attorney will not be legally cancelled if the revocation is not properly witnessed. Give a copy of the revocation to anyone who was aware of the previous power of attorney. This way, these people will know it has been cancelled.

17. What happens if I do not have a power of attorney for property?

Many people incorrectly believe that if they are unable to make decisions about their property or financial matters, their immediate family can do it for them. Unlike personal or health care decisions, the law does not permit family members to have automatic rights over the management of a mentally or physically incapable person.

For any financial decisions, legal authority is needed. This can be declared by naming someone in a continuing power of attorney for property. If you become unable to make decisions about your property or finances and you do not have a power of attorney for property, someone must apply to a court for permission to be your representative or a guardian must be appointed by either the provincial Office of the Public Guardian and Trustee or by the court.

18. Can a guardian for property be appointed for me?

A guardian for property may be appointed if you become hospitalized because of an illness or an accident. For example, if you are in a car accident and you become unconscious, someone will need to look after your property and financial affairs while you are in the hospital.

First, you need to be formally declared mentally incapable of handling your affairs. This can usually be done by a psychiatrist in the hospital where you are. But if the hospital does not have a psychiatrist, then a request must be made for a capacity assessor to do the formal assessment.

Once an assessment finds you mentally incompetent, a Certificate of Incapacity will be issued. The Public Guardian and Trustee will then become your guardian first. As the guardian, it will first seek out any family member who can replace it as your guardian. Provided there are no disagreements among family members as to who should be the replacement guardian, the Public Guardian and Trustee will hand over guardianship immediately. That person will then have guardianship while you are mentally incompetent.

A guardian for property may also be appointed if you are not hospitalized, but someone thinks you are incapable of handling your property and financial affairs. For example, an adult child may believe that her aging parent is forgetting to pay the monthly bills.

First, a mental assessment of the person must be done. This mental assessment cannot be done unless the person consents to the assessment. Unless there is a court order, no one can force the person to undergo an assessment. If the person agrees, and the assessment results indicate that the person is mentally incompetent, the person's consent is still needed before a guardian can be appointed.

If the person consents to having a guardian for property, then the Public Guardian and Trustee will become the guardian first. The person's family can then apply to the Public Guardian and Trustee to replace it as the incapable person's guardian. Provided that the family agrees on who should be guardian, the Public Guardian and Trustee will hand over guardianship immediately to that person.

If the person does not agree to a mental assessment or does not consent to having a guardian, then the only other option is to make an application to the court. An application for guardianship can only be made by people 18 years of age or older. People who are paid to provide health care, residential, social, training, or support services to an incapable person generally cannot apply, unless they are also the person's spouse, partner, relative, guardian, or attorney for property or personal care. The court will decide whether the person is mentally incapable and will name a guardian if necessary. In certain circumstances, a trust company may be a good choice for a guardian of property. Applying to court can be very expensive and complicated. You should consult with a lawyer before making an application.

A guardian may also be appointed for a person who is a patient in a psychiatric hospital. Once the person is found to be mentally incompetent, the Public Guardian and Trustee will become the guardian first. Any family member can then apply to replace the trustee as the legal guardian.

If you are applying to become a guardian, you should consult a lawyer for more information. Also, if someone is applying to be your guardian, and you do not agree, consult a lawyer or visit a legal clinic for more information.

19. What is a living will?

A living will is a document or can form a part of a document that allows you to leave instructions about your future medical treatment. In particular, it lets you decide whether you want to be kept alive by medical machines if your recovery is unlikely. Even though it is called a will, it is not part of a regular will. Instead, it is usually written as part of a power of attorney for personal care. Although a living will is a legal document, if someone in your family has strong objections to your wishes for medical treatment to be discontinued, your wishes may not actually be carried out. A living will is not binding, but it can be very helpful to give direction to your family members.

If you would like to leave certain instructions for your health or medical care, consult with a lawyer about making a power of attorney for personal care.

HOW POWERFUL IS A POWER OF ATTORNEY?

Elaine went to her lawyer and had him make out a power of attorney for property, naming her sister, Beth as her attorney. Elaine later suffered a stroke and was left incapacitated. She was being kept alive by medical devices, which she told her sister was something she never wanted to happen.

Can Beth use the power of attorney to direct the doctors to turn off the machines?

No. A power of attorney for property covers only issues related to Elaine's property. She needed a power of attorney for personal care.

INDEX